Transportation Geography

McGRAW-HILL SERIES IN GEOGRAPHY

Edward J. Taaffe and John W. Webb, *Consulting Editors*

Broek and Webb A Geography of Mankind
Carlson Africa's Lands and Nations
Cressey Asia's Lands and Peoples
Cressey Land of the 500 Million: A Geography of China
Demko, Rose, and Schnell Population Geography: A Reader
Detwyler Man's Impact on Environment
Eliot Hurst Transportation Geography: Comments and Readings
Fryer Emerging Southeast Asia: A Study in Growth and Stagnation
Fryer World Economic Development
Kolars and Nystuen Geography: The Study of Location, Culture, and Environment
Lanegran and Palm An Invitation to Geography
Mather Climatology: Fundamentals and Applications
Murphy The American City: An Urban Geography
Pounds Europe and the Soviet Union
Pounds Political Geography
Raisz General Cartography
Raisz Principles of Cartography
Starkey and Robinson The Anglo-American Realm
Thoman and Corbin The Geography of Economic Activity
Trewartha An Introduction to Climate
Trewartha, Robinson, and Hammond Fundamentals of Physical Geography
Trewartha, Robinson, and Hammond Elements of Geography: Physical and Cultural
Trewartha, Robinson, and Hammond Physical Elements of Geography (A republication of Part I of the above)
Van Riper Man's Physical World
Watts Principles of Biogeography: An Introduction to the Functional Mechanisms of Ecosystems
Yeates An Introduction to Quantitative Analysis in Human Geography

TRANSPORTATION GEOGRAPHY

Comments and Readings

edited by
Michael E. Eliot Hurst
Simon Fraser University
Burnaby, British Columbia
Canada

McGraw-Hill Book Company

New York
St. Louis
San Francisco
Düsseldorf
Johannesburg
Kuala Lumpur
London
Mexico
Montreal
New Delhi
Panama
Rio de Janeiro
Singapore
Sydney
Toronto

Transportation Geography: Comments and Readings

2 3 4 5 6 7 8 9 0 KPKP 7 9 8 7 6 5 4

This book was set in Times Roman and Vega by Black Dot, Inc. The editors were Janis Yates and Helen Greenberg; the designer was Merrill Haber; and the production supervisor was Leroy A. Young. The printer and binder was Kingsport Press, Inc.

Library of Congress Cataloging in Publication Data

Eliot Hurst, Michael E
Transportation geography.

(McGraw-Hill series in geography)
Includes bibliographies.
1. Transportation—Addresses, essays, lectures.
2. Geography, Commercial—Addresses, essays, lectures.
I. Title
HE323.H87 380.5'08 73-8630
ISBN 0-07-019190-5

To Nicholas and the future generations of communicators

Contents

List of Contributors

R. T. Aangeenbrug
University of Kansas

R. F. Abler
Pennsylvania State University

R. E. Alcaly
Columbia University

S. H. Beaver
University of Keele

P. W. Brooks

R. Borgstrom
California State University, Northridge

C. H. Cooley

K. R. Cox
The Ohio State University

M. E. Eliot Hurst
Simon Fraser University

W. L. Garrison
University of Pittsburgh

H. L. Gauthier
The Ohio State University

P. R. Gould
Pennsylvania State University

D. G. Janelle
University of Western Ontario

J. B. Kenyon
University of Georgia

C. C. Kissling
University of Canterbury

J. F. Kolars
University of Michigan

H. J. Malin
University of Michigan

D. F. Marble
Northwestern University

B. V. Martin
Alan M. Voorhees and Associates Ltd., London

R. L. Morrill
University of Washington

J. M. Munro
Simon Fraser University

P. J. Rimmer
Australian National University

P. J. Schwind
University of Hawaii

R. H. T. Smith
Monash University

W. R. Stanley
University of South Carolina

E. J. Taaffe
The Ohio State University

G. Törnqvist
University of Lund

E. L. Ullman
University of Washington

C. B. Warden

J. W. Watson
University of Edinburgh

Preface

Movement, communication, and travel are integral parts of our everyday lives. In geography, many argue, such concepts are basic to the different landscape patterns and senses of place which we study. It is surprising, therefore, that very few accounts of transportation geography exist in the English language and that still relatively few departments of geography in North America include this subdiscipline as a regular part of their curriculum.

Having carried out graduate research in transportation geography and been faced with teaching such a course at a new university in 1966, I searched for instructional materials. Despite the strong traditions in European geography, and its obvious practical applicability to the North American situation, I had to assemble new materials for my class. To put this book in perspective, I began it simply because there was no suitable alternative.

At first I considered assembling a collection of readings for my own students as a stopgap measure until a textbook arrived. On reflection, I saw no reason why the readings should be merely a stopgap; a set of readings and comments can stand or fall by themselves. Thus the long and tortuous path from my selection to the final text began.

The general framework for the readings was provided by the reports issued by Northwestern University in the early 1960s; the book's division into networks, flows, nodes, and interrelationships comes from the breakdown used in those reports. Since a wide range of literature was available from neighboring disciplines, I had to make a choice in order to end up with a book short enough to be published. I chose, for example, to exclude articles on rates and costs and to limit the contribution of economists to two articles. Following from that, since I found courses in transportation economics readily available to students in geography, I emphasized the works of geographers themselves, with all the strengths and weaknesses that this approach entails. It should be borne in mind, however, that the transportation system is as firmly entrenched in an economic milieu as it is in cultural, political, and geographic milieus. In choosing this framework and these constraints, I found the writings to vary in complexity. In particular, some may wish to omit the section on modal systems, to cover it first, since it contains straightforward descriptive material, rather than the more complex conceptual material treated in the other parts. However, complexity or other considerations aside, I personally felt that the discussion of modes most naturally follows the consideration of networks and flows.

The problems of final selection were equally great; matters of space, cost, and sometimes the inability to contact all parties involved caused the initial selection to be pared to an absolutely minimal core of articles and comments. At the same time, to compensate for omissions, my interstitial commentary has grown somewhat. However, this commentary is by no means complete, and readers are, therefore, urged to expand their knowledge by referring to the bibliographies supplied at the end of each part. In this way, the reader will find it easy to do further research on topics that interest him.

It should also be remembered that this book was conceived in 1966–1967; since then, transportation geography has been accepted and taught in North America, and other texts have been written or are in gestation. The focus of this book has changed during the past seven years from what is new in transportation geography to what is now accepted as the core of the subdiscipline. As the final part of the book suggests, we are now at a point when we can begin to explore new areas and concerns. This last part, therefore, represents books still very much in the future.

I must gratefully acknowledge the help given by the many authors and publishers without whose cooperation this book could not have been compiled. I also appreciate the comments of E. J. Taaffe, consulting editor of the McGraw-Hill Series in Geography and of several anonymous reviewers, as well as the encouragement of Janis Yates and the typing skills of Barbara Shankland. Not least, I must thank the many undergraduates at Simon Fraser who suffered through the book's birth pangs, and who offered many constructive comments. The final responsibilities for error and omission lie, of course, with the compiler and commentator. To those whose articles were excised as time went along, I can only suggest they visit the *new* McGraw-Hill headquarters in New York, where they will find their articles enshrined in a corporate highrise.

Michael E. Eliot Hurst

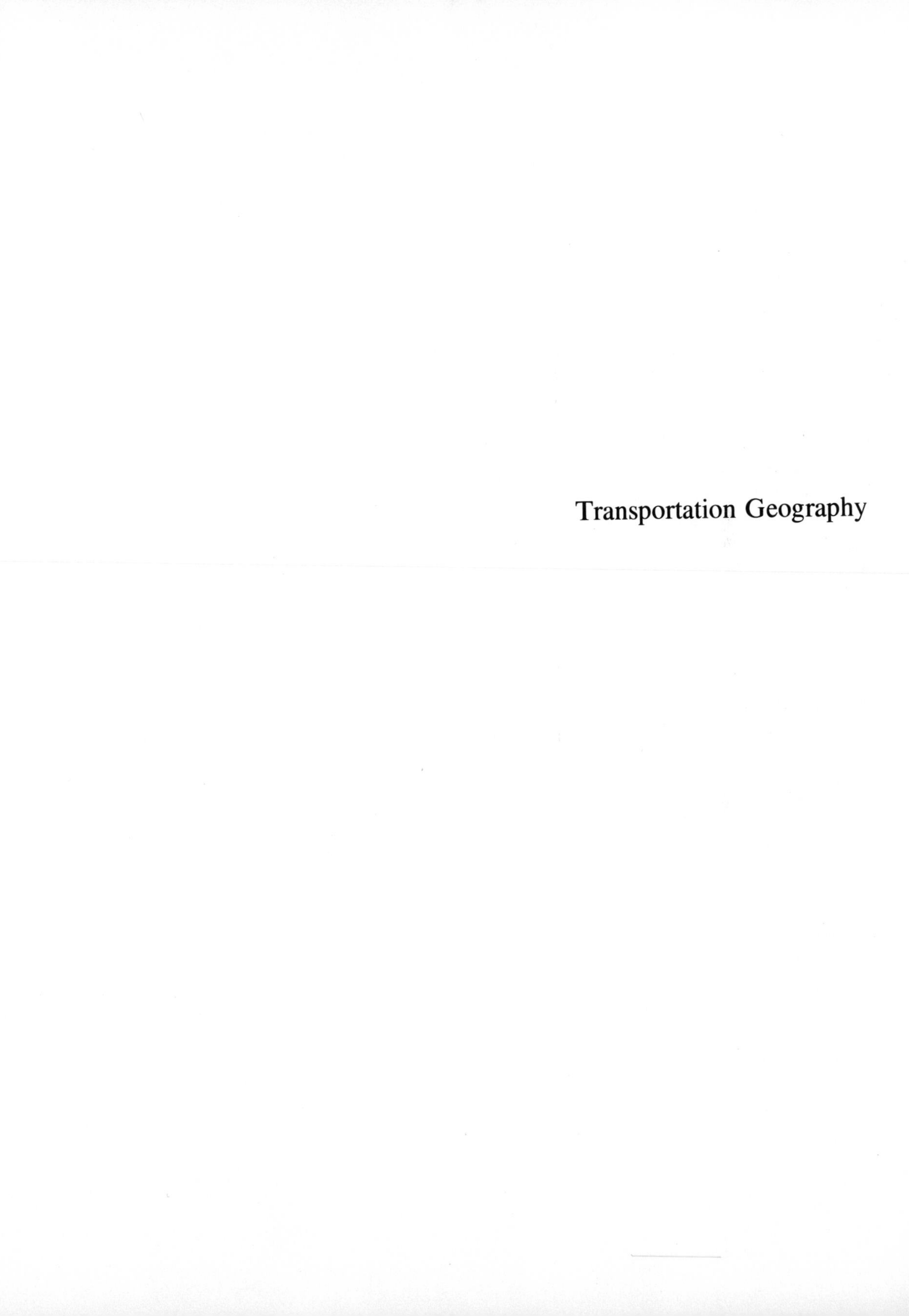

Transportation Geography

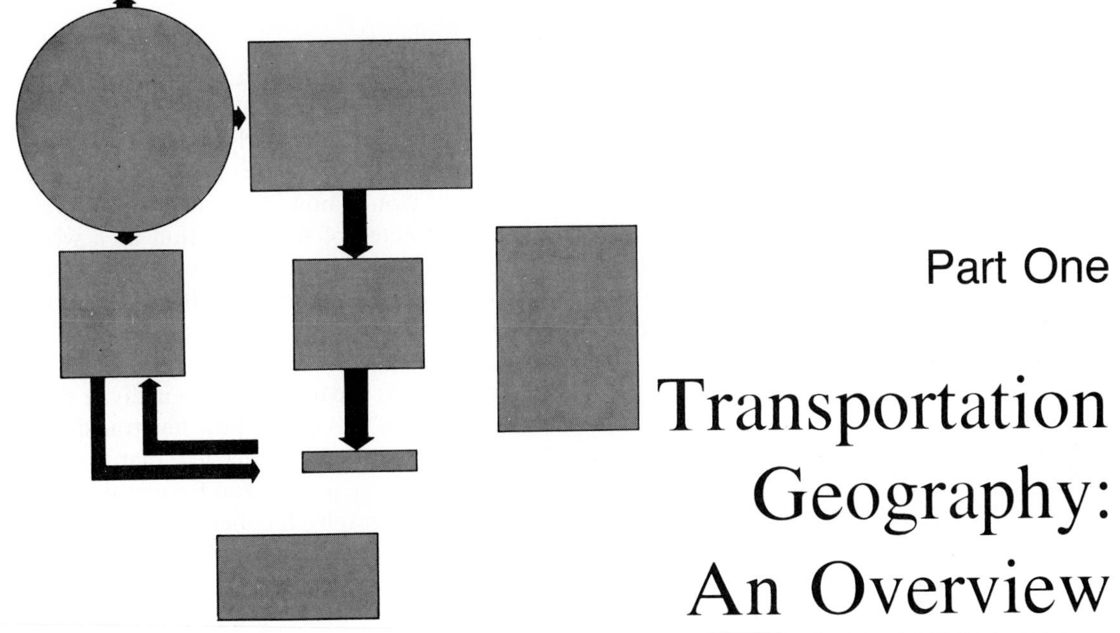

Part One

Transportation Geography: An Overview

Selection 1

The Geographic Study of Transportation, Its Definition, Growth, and Scope

M. E. Eliot Hurst

"Transportation is a measure of the relations between areas and is therefore an essential part of geography," and so began Ullman's review of the field of transportation geography in 1954.[1] Although during the past decades there have been enormous changes in the field, mainly in the use of quantitative methods and other new techniques, that basic dictum still

This is an adaptation in part of two papers read in 1972 at the Association of American Geographers' annual meeting, Kansas City, and at the IGU Symposium Ca. 21, York University, Toronto. Subsequently published in *Economic Geography*, vol. 49, no. 2, 1973, pp. 163–180, and in W. P. Adams and F. M. Helleiner (eds.), *International Geography 1972*, Toronto: Toronto University Press, vol. 2, pp. 1195–1197, respectively.

stands. The relations and connections between areas are frequently reflected in the character of transportation facilities and in the flow of traffic, involving such basic geographical concepts as *spatial interaction* and *areal association*. The overcoming of distance is so basic to geography that spatial differentiation cannot develop without movement. This concern with all spatial interactions, movements, and connections has been summed up by French geographers in the word *circulation*.*

Circulation and its study is maintained by some geographers, like Ullman (Selection 3) and Crowe,[2] to provide a deeper insight into the meaning of areal differences, providing a key for measuring the likenesses and differences among places on the earth. These two saw movement as an indicator of the degree of connection between areas on the earth's surface, and as underlying all patterns of interchange. This idea is still retained today, although in a more refined way, in the geometric and absolute spatial concepts of Bunge or Nystuen,[3] in Berry's use of factor analysis to relate spatial structures and commodity flows,[4] and in Haggett's attempts to erect an "integrated regional system" around movement, networks, nodes, hierarchies and surfaces (Fig. 1-1).[5] This should not, however, be taken as a *carte blanche* to think of transportation as merely a network of conduits through which inanimate objects stochastically flow, nor as simply a matrix of origins and destinations representing particular points of input and output. As long ago as 1894 we were warned by C. H. Cooley that ". . . there can be no adequate theory of transportation which has regard only to some one aspect of its social functions, as the economic aspect. That is not the only aspect, nor can we only truly say that it is more important than the others. All are coordinate, equally indispensable to social progress." An early plea for the comprehensive treatment of transportation via what we would now call *systems analysis!* "The character of transportation as a whole and in detail, at any particular time and throughout its history, is altogether determined by its interrelations with physical and social forces and conditions. To understand transportation means simply to analyze these interrelations."† And yet how few transportation geographers have heeded that warning in the last 80 years. All too frequently transportation geography has become a treatment of conduits and units (albeit increasingly treated more rigorously), as if the reality of our everyday world were in a sociopolitical vacuum.

Transportation geographers have not been alone in ignoring these realities, for equally geography has existed to some degree in an intellectual vacuum. Descriptive geography located and described but did not generally attempt to explain why something was where it was; it had its roots in the desire to amass information about the newly revealed environments of Darwin's world. It described that which was most visible, and to the transport geographer those were transport modes, layouts and trade flows. Where it attempted to explain the occurrence of phenomena and their interrelationships, it tended to rely on physical determinism or simple economic rationalizations. There was little concern with change, uncertainty, or the socioeconomic fabric of society.

Quantitative and predictive geography has its roots in the more recent past, although the legacy of particularism and description persist. The recent changes in the other social sciences, notably their use of quantitative methods, aided in turn by the growth of com-

*The word *circulation*, used by French geographers, has no exact English equivalent, but it represents very well our concern with all spatial interactions and connections, whether they be flows of goods, people, money, credit, ideas, or innovations.

†Selection 2, below, p. 15.

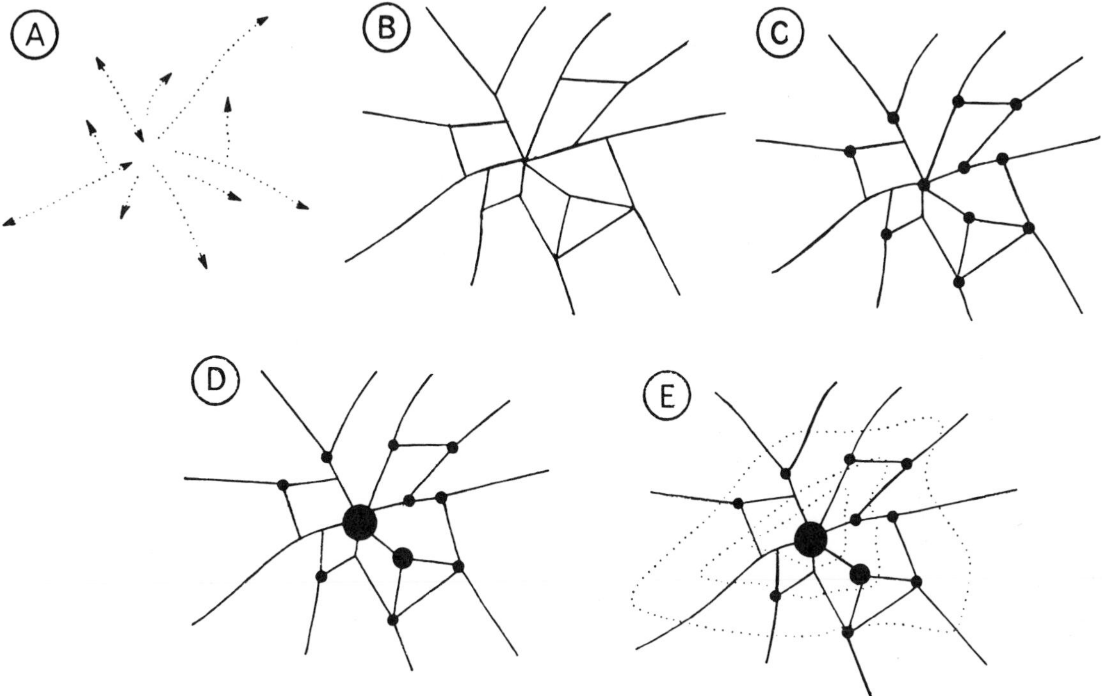

Fig. 1-1 Stages in the analysis of an integrated regional system. A = movements; B = networks; C = nodes; D = hierarchies; E = surfaces. (*Source: Haggett, 1965, p. 18*)

puter sciences, has affected geography. The increasing prestige of these other social sciences, and their use of models and statistical techniques in an attempt to manage human behavior, have encouraged geographers to adopt something of their methodology and their concern with prediction. The concern with precision, measurement and normative situations, shown by this second approach, has led to the adoption of a wide range of statistical tools and models from regression analysis through linear programming to graph theory. This newer rigorous framework for geography (including transportation geography) has provided us with some extremely useful tools, which the simple gathering of facts alone could not do.

These developments within geography have not occurred without criticism. The concern with statistical "explanation" has led to some absolutist approaches and the strait jacket of a Grand Theory (to borrow C. Wright Mills' phrase). There have been accusations of geographers lifting theories and models from other disciplines with little concern for their real explanatory value or even applicability within the geographic domain; that economic geographers do not know enough economics to handle economic explanations and that they do not know where economic explanation is no longer totally applicable and cultural explanation begins; that many quantitative studies display shallow empiricism and irrelevant theorizing; and that in making mathematical rigor their ultimate goal, they forget that mathematics is basically conceptual rather than computational. Hand in hand with this quantitative orientation has grown a doctrinal emphasis on the value of the scientific method in the social sciences, probably best illustrated by the earlier unidimensional and "closed" view of Harvey,[6] even though Luckermann had previously warned all geographers of the pitfalls of such a stance.[7]

More recently a newer trend has been growing in geography, including transportation studies, which focuses attention on man himself—the human condition, man's behavior—and on the societal framework. As Buttimer has pointed out, behaviorists, existentialists, and others now openly question whether the scientific method can continue to serve a useful function by just measuring and explaining the objective façade and mechanical linkages of social reality.[8] Geographers should not be content with merely outlining the "objective" dimensions of economic and social patterns in space, the bare networks and nodes of the transportation geographer. To increase our understanding of the landscape, we need also to incorporate "subjective" dimensions of decision making, political frameworks, and governmental legislation. This concern for the human dimension is evident in two guest editorials in the journal *Economic Geography* by Vance and Parsons, who pleaded for us to be free of subservience to any single doctrinal solution and for us to look at man as a fallible human being subject to a wide range of political and cultural constraints.[9] In this sense neither the stockpiling of facts about transport networks nor excessive attention to optimal solutions or abstract spatial analyses will help us to explain or understand transportation within a societal setting.

THE DEVELOPMENT OF TRANSPORTATION GEOGRAPHY

Literature in transportation geography roughly parallels the sequence noted above. Until the 1950s most work came from European rather than North American geographers. This early work revealed a difference in approach between the two sets of geographers, although they both fall under the general rubric of "description." Whereas those few in North America who were concerned with transport dealt mainly with route classification, descriptive mapping of route location, and mapping flows, European geographers concentrated on modes of transportation and the commodities carried. Capot-Rey,[10] Otremba,[11] Morgan,[12] and Seally[13] represent various facets of this latter approach; Ullman,[14] Jefferson,[15] and the Ullman-Meyer review illustrate the former. This general approach toward transportation as merely an explication of strategic routes and sites of logistical support was restated more recently by Smith—". . . the ultimate aim in geographical studies of transportation is the description and explanation of this phenomenon as a feature of the earth's surface."[16] This general view led Thomas to remark that North American work was out of balance compared to that in Europe; he asked ". . . should not both peanuts and pilgrims be considered in a study of transportation?"[17] Despite the changes described below, this lack of a cultural (and I would add societal) input still holds today.

In counterplay to these developments of the early 1950s, one North American researcher, Edward Ullman, did attempt to establish a broad base for a theoretical approach to transportation although it was by no means universally accepted.‡ He laid out a three-factor typology to explain movement or interaction between two areas—*complementarity,* in the cultural/economic sense of a demand in one area that the other area can supply; *intervening opportunity,* which can inhibit interaction

‡Selection 3 is an earlier version of the more widely known article.

between the two areas because the demand can be more easily met by a third area; and *transferability,* which involves substituting one demand for another when the frictional effects of the distance between the two areas lessens the likelihood of interaction.[18]

By the end of the decade more noticeable and important changes occurred, with the initiative shifting to North America and the quantitative stream of geography, including the introduction to transport of location theory and spatial analysis, regional science, and varied techniques such as that of linear programming. Garrison, who was largely responsible for drawing the attention of the geographic world to the newly developing interdisciplinary location analysis field, provided a stimulus to new studies of flow data that were rooted in the economic landscape.[19] In addition, along with a group of workers at the University of Washington, Garrison pursued another new area for geographers, the study of the impact of highway change.[20] These latter group studies were some of the first to recognize the wider impact of transportation, but the sociopolitical environment of the decision making that led up to the planning of new highways and their impact on that sociopolitical milieu were assumed as constant.

Much of this work was linked to the general location theory cluster of the contemporary spatial analyses, but of particular importance was the introduction to the English-speaking world of Christaller's earlier work on central place theory, and its modification to intracity as well as intercity linkages carried out by Berry and Garrison.[21] Again some attempt, albeit superficial, to review the interdependence of transport with the economy (very narrowly defined) was made about the same time by Berry.[22] Alongside the work of the Garrison-Berry group was yet another innovation, the use of the so-called gravity model. This model was a fundamental part of Ullman's earlier approach to transportation, but later in the 1950s it became widely used in planning and regional science and became for a while the centerpin of urban transportation studies.[23]

Without doubt a very useful but simplistic device, the gravity model was overapplied and subsequently came under considerable criticism and review.[24] Its enthusiastic overuse illustrates very well an inherent defect in geographical work, whereby a simplistic device, whose structure may parallel certain real conditions, is therefore assumed to equal reality and be truly explanatory. Its use has now declined, although its basic conception is used in a wide variety of situations up to the present day.[25] These broad areas of research marked a distinct break with the work reviewed at the beginning of this selection—that is, the reliance for the first time on rigorous analytic methods from mathematics and statistics. The use of these new techniques (for geography) was to be intensified in the 1960s, when they became the hallmark of a new approach in geography, the so-called quantitative revolution.

If the 1950s represented a period of considerable change in the development of transportation geography from a somewhat amorphous descriptive study to a field of much experimentation and innovation in new techniques, the 1960s marked a period of consolidation and the rise of a distinctive North American approach. A crucial role in this consolidation was played by the Transportation Center at Northwestern University, whose work spans the two decades mentioned here. The research work at the Center pioneered such approaches as network analysis utilizing graph theory; the determination of the spatial structure of demand for transportation; the application of probability concepts to route development, and in part to travel behavior; and the application of a broad systems framework to transportation studies.[26] There has been a considerable spinoff from the Center's work, and the basic framework of Parts One, Two, Three and Four of this book is grounded in the research carried out by the Center over a period of 20 years. Network analysis, treating the characteristics of networks by structure, accessibility, circuitry, and flow, has spawned considerable theoretical work, as well as some empirical studies, including work with obvious application outside transportation proper.[27]

Because of the holistic nature of the systems approach, interest was partly oriented to the wider "cultural" or *operational milieu*§ in which transportation has to be considered.[28] The early application of what we can call "behavioral concepts" was grounded in behaviorism, so that many of the studies were mechanistic. However, Marble and Nystuen[29] laid out a theoretical basis for some of the work, which has been extended by Rushton and others to a central place framework[30] and to empirical studies of travel behavior in urban areas as some of the weaknesses of existing metropolitan transportation studies have become obvious.[31] This latter research area is being intensified in the early 1970s and may well mark a major reorientation for the coming decades.[32] There is no doubt that the general plea for relevance to be heard in the discipline today is reflected in studies of political decision making, group conflict, psychological hazard, corporate power and lobbying, as well as individual orientation in the travel decision, as they become overt in urban and nonurban travel patterns.[33]

Although I have picked out strands of development in the area of transportation geography, this is somewhat misleading to the extent that it implies one or several concerted efforts; in fact efforts, although they may fall under such rubrics as "descriptive approach" or "quantitative," have been very dispersed. In addition to the work areas cited above, other areas of study include transport in developing areas,[34] spatial processes and flows,[35] continued study of individual modes in both Europe and North America,[36] historical studies,[37] and many descriptive accounts on subregional, regional, and national scales.[38]

This dispersion is also reflected in the fact that transportation geography still lacks a unified theory that integrates the principles enunciated in this wide range of studies from network analysis, on the one hand, to the development of narrow-gauge railroads, on the other. Although a considerable amount of the research in transportation geography makes use of analytic techniques, the search still continues for meaningful generalizations and principles to incorporate into a unified theory. In one sense, of course, such a search may well be irrelevant and misleading. Although it is always convenient (and academically respectable) to order one's concepts in a neat epistemological framework, such a search should not divert us from increased understanding of the interdependent role transport plays in our society. At the same time, I should add that such a theory of transport would provide a unifying link both inside and outside of geography, and might well pinpoint interrelationships which we presently overlook.

§By *operational milieu* is meant the milieu which is interposed between the decision maker and the objective reality of the environment. The milieu consists of interrelated elements such as a values-system, cultural factors, the economic system, etc. In behavioral terms this milieu includes the decision making leading to transportation networks, and their ultimate use in movement terms.

A FUNCTIONAL APPROACH

This lack of success in finding a grand theory or paradigm for transport studies, and the disparate range of work carried on, should not deter us from laying out a tentative framework. In order to lay the groundwork for transportation geography, Parts One to Four of this book will fall within the umbrella of a "functional" or systems approach. For various reasons pointed out in Part Five (pp. 285ff.) we will ultimately have to go beyond that, but for the moment the approach used by the Transportation Center at Northwestern University will suffice to provide the foundation or basic building blocks.||

If we could imagine that we were faced with studying transportation in a particular area of the earth's surface, how would we go about unraveling the developmental sequence and the relationships of transport with other elements in the landscape? We might begin by assessing the characteristics of the area, which might have some influence on *circulation:* the general economic development of the area; the spatial location of socioeconomic activities; the technology available; relative cost structures; the interests, perceptions and preferences of decision-making (including political and military decisions) groups; and the outlook for the future as perceived by the latter group. In addition to these six broad areas of examination, we could look at the historical pattern development in the area and the physical environment involved. This is not an exhaustive list, of course, and there are other influential factors—e.g., the position of regions in relation to international air routes might affect the development of air transportation.

This list is essentially a *functional* one in that it emphasizes the area's development in terms of some function of the area's characteristics. It is also *systematic* in that we imply that transport structure or circulation is to be understood in terms of relationships to other elements in a general system. A bold statement of functional and systematic relationships, such as this one, is too general to give much information about the substantive character of transportation. To do this in order to better understand transport's role in our selected area, the concept of a transport system would have to be disaggregated into its component subsystems, though by their nature they are not independent elements. For example, the layout of routeways (transport network) is dependent upon the volume of movement (the flow) to some extent, and vice versa; both, of course, are functionally dependent on the geographic characteristics of the areas outlined above.

If the concept of *circulation* is disaggregated, the following elements or components of the transport system in our imaginary area could be identified and studied:

1 As an *inventory* (a stock of road route miles, number of vehicles, etc.)

2 As a *network* (the geometric structure of the route system)

3 As *flows* (what movement occurs, and how intensively)

4 As *modal systems* (what type of transport occurs)

5 As the *interrelationships* of the four elements or subsystems noted above.

In total this scheme is represented in Fig. 1-2, where additional elements not considered by this functional approach are also included.# Box 2 of Fig. 1-2 contains points 1, 2 and 4; box 5 includes point 3; and box 1 represents the general idea of movement or circulation. The total figure represents point 5, the inter-

||The most complete functional and systems approach to transportation is to be found in the reports of the Northwestern University Transportation Center's Transportation Geography Study, Task 1V021701A04701, Contract DA 44-177-TC-685, U.S. Army Transportation Command. The thirteen-part report, carried out from 1960 to 1965, a brilliant pioneering transportation analysis, is not generally available, but the final part, by W. L. Garrison and D. F. Marble, "A Prolegomenon to the Forecasting of Transportation Development," June 1965, is available from the Northwestern University Center as a research report, part of which is reproduced as Selection 5.

#For a fuller description of this "model" see Part Five, pp. 285ff.

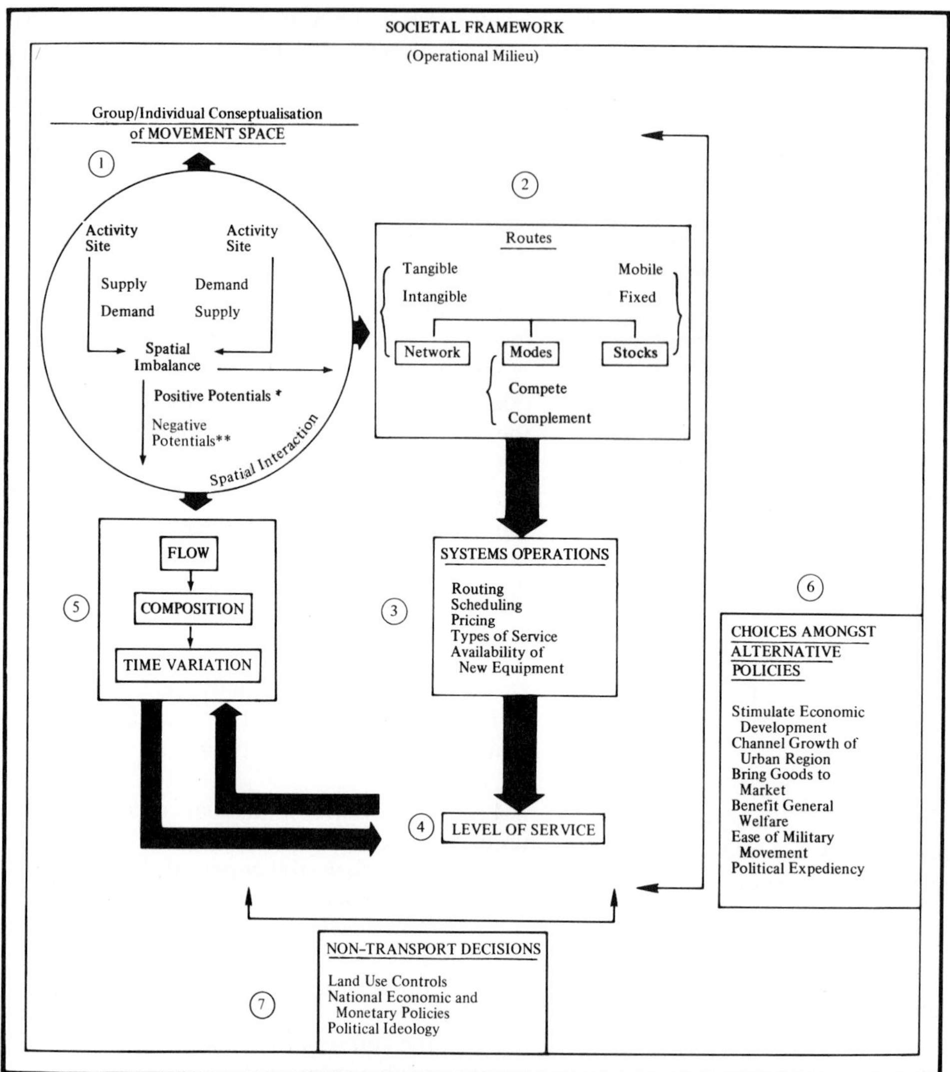

Fig. 1-2 The transport system. Positive potentials* refer to complementarity, intervening opportunity, cultural affinity, etc. Negative potentials** refer to distance, costs, transferability, political barriers, etc.

dependencies. All we need add for the moment is that boxes 3 and 4 represent an operational or management component, and boxes 6 and 7 represent the societal or political context. The emphasis in the next four parts of the book, however, are boxes 2 and 5, and to some extent, box 1.

We should now analyze those five factors a little more closely:

Inventory

The stocks or inventory of basic transport equipment can either be classified as (1) mobile (cars, buses, trucks, railroad equipment) or (2) fixed facilities (miles of railroad or roadway). The quantities of these transport stocks can be understood to varying degrees in terms of a functional relationship between them and variables such as income and population. Generally the distribution of these stocks is most closely related to income, population, and the size of the area. Relatively few studies outside of the Transportation Center's unpublished work have taken this approach, partly because of the lack of data, but there is no doubt from the results obtained from those studies which were carried out[39] that there is a clear relationship between this measure of transport "supply" and the "demand" of the operational milieu within which the subsystem is contained. Because of the lack of published material, this area of analysis is not directly covered in the book, but Selections 8 and 22 use the matter of stocks or inventory as part of a wider approach.

Networks

The layout, geometry, or pattern of the transport system, or the location of routes, falls under the rubric of "networks." It also includes analysis of the location of intersections, nodes, and terminals; the density and length of routes; the accessibility of individual points on a network to other points; and the distances traveled in order to reach every point on a network. These notions are related to factors conditioning the development of transport.

Work on this subsystem has been more substantial than the former; much of the historical research in transportation geography has concerned attempts to determine reasons for route location.[40] On the analytic side most attention has been paid to whole systems or networks rather than single routes, extending the analysis from principles of route location to theories of network growth.[41] The selections in Part Two of the book illustrate this approach.

Flows

This refers simply to the movement of people, commodities, and messages; flows are the very activity of transportation. Because many different types of flow can be identified, a standardized method of measurement is difficult to attain. Flows can be analyzed by the application of transport flow models, such as the gravity model,[42] intervening opportunity,[43] and transportation (linear programming) models[44] in a temporal or regional framework. A serious limit to such studies has been the lack of flow data—for example, the kinds of records kept by the trucking industry tend to mitigate against detailed analysis[45]—though a number of studies on a theoretical level can be found outside of geography.[46] Part Three of the book examines the kinds of approaches that can be taken in this disaggregation.

Modes

Traditionally one of the main approaches to transport has been via an examination of the various types or means of movement, in order to identify their particular technical characteristics, their cost structure, their historical evolution, and their regional growth patterns. Each mode of transport, for reasons that will become evident later, plays a different, though sometimes overlapping, role in the supply of transportation. Thus railroads seem best suited to long-haul transportation of heavy commodities, which are often of small value per unit of carload traffic. On the other hand, air transport specializes in speed, long-haul, and high-value goods needing rapid delivery. There is overlap or competition between the modes, and technical change is tending to increase that overlap and competition. Part Four reproduces a few samples of the work carried out in this area. However, the emphasis in North America over the last 15 years on three approaches—network flows, network location, and network interdependence with the economy—especially with the stress on particular analytical techniques, has meant that studies of modes have tended to be pushed into the background.[47] However, as a vital part of the transportation subsystem, with unique carrying/spatial characteristics, this neglect is unwarranted. Elsewhere such studies continue at a fairly high rate.

Interrelationships

This differs from the previous four factors in that it does not attempt to codify structures or functions, but rather to look at the relationships among transport systems and the relationships with the whole socioeconomic system. Studies in this area attempt to develop a set of principles of transport interdependence with the socioeconomy which might illustrate how a change in modal or accessibility patterns influences the sites and development of economic activities in a broad regional or urban framework. At one level there are relationships between, say, highway and railroad networks. In some areas highways are supplementary to the railroad networks; in others the highway both supplements and complements, and in still others it competes with the railroad network. These network relations are evidenced by a combination of stock conditions, characteristics of flows, network structure, and other use characteristics. On another level, viewing transportation interdependence with the larger milieu of which it is part requires the use of various mixes of transport in the economic growth of a region or within the linkages and structure of an urban hierarchy and intercity relationships, or in intraurban functioning.[48] Some of these approaches are examined in Parts Five and Six.

Such an approach to studying transportation, represented either by this list of factors or the boxes in Fig. 1-2 in our selected region on the earth's surface, would hopefully allow us to *describe, understand,* and even *explain* circulation as the infrastructure of the geographic landscape. That circulation will be limited, directed, and channeled by a composite conglomeratic transport system. But any change in that system changes the social and economic "environment" within which the system operates, and vice versa. The replacement, for example, of a primitive route system by a more satisfactory railroad system in a developing country may affect the pattern of development profoundly. Places advantageously located on the new railroad system may grow at rates different from those located on the system of routes and tracks, and many nodes on this latter system may actually decline in size. This is comparable to the changes identified in Christaller's central place model[49] or Losch's location model.[50] When, for example, roads were first paved on a widespread basis in North America (the 1920s and 1930s), relative positions of hamlets and rural market towns shifted, as did patterns of trade and other factors relating to transport development and use.[51] The development of such geographic landscapes is inherently shaped by the processes, growth, and development of patterns of circulation.

The interrelationships of such a close union are obviously difficult to identify, one of the reasons why no satisfactory unified theory of transportation with clearly enunciated general principles has yet appeared. Yet obviously each of the basic behavior or activity sectors which the geographer examines are implicitly concerned with movement of some kind. Agricultural location theory prescribes output shipments from farm to market and the movement of fertilizers, machinery, and other material inputs from the market to the farm. The theoretical sequence of land uses is both a determinant of where marketing inputs will be shipped and a reflection of the mounting costs of these same inputs with increased distance from the market or source. Likewise industrial location theory imposes certain patterns on the transport of fuels, raw and semifinished materials as inputs from source to factory site, and in the shipment of output from factory to wholesaler, retailer, householder, or other production unit. Central place theory, or its modifications, similarly define the movement of consumers from place of residence to tertiary outlet. Studies of regional growth, settlement patterns, cultural groups, and decision making all contain elements of circulation—money, people, ideas, innovations, values, etc. And so we come a full circle, to the opening sentences of this selection, which identified transportation as playing a crucial role in any analysis and understanding of man and his milieus.

GOING FURTHER

This collection of readings, in the way it is organized, reflects to some degree the approach to transportation geography outlined in the preceding subsections, particularly Parts One, Two, Three and Four. Parts Five and Six are reflected in the remaining boxes of Fig. 1-2. Thus, where Part Two is concerned with networks, Part Three with flows, and Part Four with a selection of modal systems, Part Five is concerned with the interrelationships studied in the earlier parts but goes beyond their mechanistic approach to the broader societal and political frameworks, including a relatively neglected area for transport geographers, communications systems and the circulation of ideas. Finally Part Six examines circulation patterns from a different perspective; rather than taking a theoretical approach, these selections examine the role of transportation in the economic growth and development of a region and look at some of the causes of that perennial problem of urban living, intracity movement.

The remaining essays in the first part, or overview, reflect some alternative ways of approaching transportation, albeit they all reflect the same concern with finding a comprehensive approach to the topic of *circulation.*

It was C. H. Cooley's words of warning that we reprinted earlier: ". . . there can be no adequate theory of transportation which has only regard to some one aspect . . . [such as] . . . the economic aspect . . . [all aspects] . . . are coordinate, equally indispensable to social progress." The selection of his work presented in this collection, is literally that . . . an edited selection. The original paper runs to some 40,000 words, about one half the length of this book. But it remains unique; no paper on the theory of transportation has equaled or surpassed it since. This is not to belittle the other two contributions, however, which are also classics in their own right. The essay by E. L. Ullman, although less well known than later revisions, sets out his distinctive approach to transportation alluded to here. In explaining interaction between two areas, Ullman uses the three factors of complementarity, intervening opportunity, and transferability. Although this simplistic conception is now open to criticism, since it involves a deterministic framework where movement is always to the nearest area, outside influences are minimized, and behavior is considered thoroughly rational, it still remains as a useful teaching or heuristic device. Finally in this part is a selection by J. Wreford Watson who sees the concept of "distance" as an indicator of the correlation between phenomena and as underlying the factor of spatial relations. Distance in this usage underlies all geography, not least the study of transportation.

NOTES

1 E. L. Ullman with the assistance of H. M. Mayer, "Transportation Geography" in *American Geography: Inventory and Prospect,* P. E. James and C. L. Jones (eds.), Syracuse: Syracuse University Press, 1954, p. 311.

2 P. R. Crowe, "On Progress in Geography," *The Scottish Geographical Magazine,* vol. 54,

no. 1, 1938, pp. 1–19. In addition to Ullman's article reprinted here, see his "The Role of Transportation and the Bases for Interaction" in W. L. Thomas (ed.), *Man's Role in Changing the Face of the Earth,* Chicago: Chicago University Press, 1956, pp. 862–880.

3 W. Bunge, *Theoretical Geography,* 2d. ed., Lund: C. W. K. Gleerup, 1966; see especially chs. 5, 7 and 8; J. D. Nystuen, "Identification of Some Fundamental Spatial Concepts," *Papers of the Michigan Academy of Science, Arts and Letters,* vol. XLVIII, 1963, pp. 373–384.

4 B. J. L. Berry, *Essays on Commodity Flows and the Spatial Structure of the Indian Economy,* Chicago: University of Chicago, Department of Geography, Research Paper no. 111, 1966.

5 P. Haggett, *Locational Analysis in Human Geography,* New York: St. Martin's Press, 1966. See also his *Geography: A Modern Synthesis,* New York: Harper & Row, 1972, where this viewpoint is developed to encompass the entire geographical approach *per se.*

6 D. Harvey, *Explanation in Geography,* London: Edward Arnold, 1969.

7 F. Luckermann, "Toward a More Geographic Economic Geography," *Professional Geographer,* vol. X, 1958, pp. 2–10; and "On Explanation, Model, and Description," *Professional Geographer,* vol. XI, no. 1, 1960, pp. 1–2.

8 A. Buttimer, "Social Space in Interdisciplinary Perspective," *Geographical Review,* vol. 59, 1969, pp. 416–426.

9 J. J. Parsons, "Toward a More Humane Geography," guest editorial, *Economic Geography,* vol. 45, no. 3, 1969, p. i.

J. E. Vance, "Moral Rectitude Among Economic Geographers," guest editorial, *Economic Geography,* vol. 45, no. 4, 1969, p. i.

10 R. Capot-Rey, *Geographie de la circulation sur les continents,* Paris, 1946.

11 E. Otremba, *Allgemeine Geographie des Welthandels und des Weltuerkehrs,* Stuttgart: W. Keller and Co., 1957.

12 F. W. Morgan, *Ports and Harbours,* 2d. ed., London: Hutchinson University Library, 1958.

13 K. R. Seally, *The Geography of Air Transport,* London: Hutchinson University Library, 1957.

14 E. L. Ullman, *American Commodity Flow: A Geographical Interpretation of Rail and Water Traffic Based on Principles of Spatial Interchange,* Seattle: University of Washington Press, 1957. Earlier works of Ullman's which are also of interest include: *Mobile: Industrial Seaport and Trade Center,* Chicago: University of Chicago, 1943; "The Railroad Pattern of the United States," *Geographical Review,* vol. 39, 1949, pp. 242–256; "Mapping the World's Ocean Trade: A Research Proposal," *Professional Geographer,* vol. 1, no. 2, 1949, pp. 19–22; and *United States Railroads Classified According to Capacity and Relative Importance* (map), New York, 1951.

15 M. Jefferson, "The Civilising Rails," *Economic Geography,* vol. 4, 1928, pp. 217–231; two papers of H. M. Mayer are of interest in this connection too—"Localisation of Railway Facilities in Metropolitan Centers as Typified by Chicago," *Journal of Land and Public Utility Economics,* 1944, pp. 299–325; and "The Railway Terminal Problem of Central Chicago," *Economic Geography,* vol. 21, 1945, pp. 62–76.

16 R. H. T. Smith, "Toward a Measure of Complementarity," *Economic Geography,* vol. 40, 1964, pp. 1–8.

17 B. Thomas, "Methods and Objectives in Transportation Geography," *Professional Geographer,* vol. 8, no. 4, 1956, pp. 2–5.

18 E. L. Ullman, "The Role of Transportation and the Bases for Interaction" in W. L. Thomas (ed.), *Man's Role in Changing the Face of the Earth,* University of Chicago Press, 1956, pp. 862–880. The earlier paper is "Geography as spatial interaction" in *Interregional Linkages* (*Proceedings* of the Western Committee on Regional Economic Analysis of the Social Science Research Council), D. Revzan and E. S. Englebert (eds.), Berkeley, 1954, pp. 1–12.

19 W. L. Garrison, "Spatial Structure of the Economy," Parts I, II, and III, *Annals* of the Association of American Geographers, vols. 49 and 50, 1959 and 1960, pp. 232–239, pp. 471–482, pp. 357–373. See also an earlier paper, "Estimates of the Parameters of Spatial Interaction,"

Papers and Proceedings, Regional Science Association, vol. 2, 1956, pp. 280–288.

20 W. L. Garrison and M. Marts, *Influence of Highway Improvements on Urban Land: A Brief Summary,* Seattle: University of Washington, Departments of Geography and Civil Engineering, 1958; W. L. Garrison, B. J. L. Berry, D. F. Marble, J. D. Nystuen, and R. Morrill, *Studies of Highway Development and Geographic Change,* Seattle: University of Washington Press, 1959.

21 B. J. L. Berry and W. L. Garrison, "Recent Developments of Central Place Theory," *Papers and Proceedings,* Regional Science Association, vol. 4, 1958, pp. 107–120.

22 B. J. L. Berry, "Recent Studies Concerning the Role of Transportation in the Space Economy," *Annals* of the Association of American Geographers, vol. 49, 1959, pp. 328–342.

23 G. A. P. Carrothers, "An Historical Review of the Gravity and Potential Concepts of Human Interaction," *Journal of the American Institute of Planners,* vol. 22, 1956, pp. 94–102; W. Isard, *Methods of Regional Analysis,* Cambridge, Mass: MIT Press, 1960, pp. 493–568.

24 See, for example, F. Luckermann and P. W. Porter, "Gravity and Potential Models in Economic Geography," *Annals* of the Association of American Geographers, vol. 50, 1960, pp. 493–504; D. L. Huff, "Ecological Characteristics of Consumer Behaviour," *Papers and Proceedings,* Regional Science Association, vol. 7, 1961, pp. 19–28; G. Olsson, *Distance and Human Interaction: A Review and Bibliography,* Philadelphia: Regional Science Research Institute, 1965.

25 See, for example, R. L. Creighton, *Urban Transportation Planning,* Urbana: University of Illinois Press, 1970, chaps. 3 and 11; or R. I. Wolfe, "The Inertia Model," *Journal of Leisure Research,* vol. 4, 1972, pp. 73–76.

26 Two noteworthy published reports from this study are K. J. Kansky, *Structure of Transportation Networks,* University of Chicago, Department of Geography, Research Paper No. 84, 1963; E. D. Perle, *The Demand for Transportation: Regional and Commodity Studies in the U.S.,* University of Chicago, Department of Geography, Research Paper No. 95, 1964. The bulk of the reports remain unpublished, though they are on file at the library, Transportation Center, Northwestern University.

27 P. Haggett, 1966 (*op cit.*), pp. 70–71 and 237–240; P. Haggett, "Network Models in Geography" in R. J. Chorley and P. Haggett (eds.), *Models in Geography,* London: Methuen, 1967, chap. 15; and P. Haggett and R. J. Chorley, *Network Analysis in Geography,* London: Edward Arnold, 1969. This latest effort relates network models in both human and physical geography.

28 M. E. Eliot Hurst, *A Geography of Economic Behaviour,* North Scituate, Mass.: Duxbury Press, 1972.

29 D. F. Marble, "A Theoretical Exploration of Individual Travel Behaviour" and J. D. Nystuen, "A Theory and Simulation of Intraurban Travel," both in W. L. Garrison and D. F. Marble (eds.), *Quantitative Geography,* Part 1, Evanston: Northwestern University, 1967, pp. 33–53 and 54–83.

30 For example, G. Rushton, R. G. Golledge, and W. A. V. Clark, "Formulation and Test of a Normative Model for the Spatial Allocation of Grocery Expenditures by a Dispersed Population," *Annals* of the Association of American Geographers, vol. 57, 1967, pp. 389–400.

31 M. E. Eliot Hurst, "The Structure of Movement and Household Travel Behaviour," *Urban Studies,* vol. 6, no. 1, 1969, pp. 70–82; see also F. Stuart Chapin and H. C. Hightower, "Household Activity Patterns and Land Use," *Journal, American Institute of Planners,* August 1965, pp. 222–231; F. E. Horton and D. R. Reynolds, *Urban Environmental Perception and Individual Travel Behaviour,* Special Publication No. 2, Department of Geography, University of Iowa, 1970; and F. E. Horton and D. R. Reynolds, "Action Space Differentials in Cities," in *Perspectives in Geography, Vol. 1, Models of Spatial Variation,* H. McConnell and D. W. Yaseen (eds.), 1971, pp. 83–104.

32 A special symposium, entitled "Social Perspectives in Transportation Geography," was held at the A.A.G. annual meeting in 1972; papers included J. Wolpert and A. J. Humphrey, "The Equity of Highway Concessions"; H. L. Gauthier. "The Appalachian Highway Development Program: Development for Whom?"; and G. J. Fielding, "Attitudes to Urban Freeways," now published in a special number of *Economic Geography,* vol. 49, no. 2, 1973.

33 G. J. Fielding, "Locating Urban Freeways: A Method for Resolving Conflict," in *Geographic Studies of Urban Transportation and Network Analysis,* F. E. Horton (ed.), Northwestern University, Studies in Geography, No. 16, pp. 76–101; J. Wolpert, "The Transition to Interdependence in Location Decisions," paper presented at the A.A.G. annual meeting, 1968.

34 E. Taaffe, R. Morrill, and P. Gould, "Transport Expansion in Underdeveloped Countries: A Comparative Analysis," *Geographical Review,* vol. 53, 1963, pp. 503–529; A. M. O'Connor, *Railways and Development in Uganda: A Study in Economic Geography,* Nairobi: Oxford University Press, 1966; D. Marble, "Some Cultural and Social Aspects of Transport Impact in Underdeveloped Areas," in F. Pitts (ed.), *Urban Systems and Economic Development,* Eugene: University of Oregon, School of Business Administration, 1962, pp. 39–43; R. H. T. Smith and A. M. Hay, "A Theory of the Spatial Structure of Internal Trade in Underdeveloped Countries," *Geographical Analysis,* vol. 1, no. 2, 1969, pp. 121–136.

35 P. Haggett, *op cit.,* 1966; B. J. L. Berry (1966) *op cit.,* E. Von Boventer, "Towards a United Theory of Spatial Economic Structure," *Papers and Proceedings,* Regional Science Association, vol. 10, 1963, pp. 163–187.

36 W. R. Siddall, "Railroad Gauges and Spatial Interaction," *Geographical Review,* vol. 59, 1969, pp. 29–57; D. K. Fleming, "The Independent Transport Carrier in Ocean Tramp Trades," *Economic Geography,* vol. 44, 1968, pp. 21–36; G. Manners, "The Pipeline Revolution," *Geography,* vol. 47, 1962, pp. 154–163, and many others.

37 D. W. Meinig, "A Comparative Historical Geography of Two Rail Nets: Columbia Basin and Southern Australia," *Annals* of the Association of American Geographers, vol. 52, 1962, pp. 394–413; or F. H. Thomas, *The Denver and Rio Grande Western Railroad: a Geographic Analysis,* Northwestern University Press, 1960.

38 These range from B. Thomas, *Trade Routes of Algeria and the Sahara,* Berkeley: University of California Press, 1957; P. R. Gould, *The Development of the Transportation Pattern in Ghana,* Evanston: Department of Geography, Northwestern University, Studies in Geography No. 5 and J. H. Appleton, *The Geography of Communications in Great Britain,* London: Oxford University Press, 1962; to J. Bird, "Road and Rail in the Central Massif of France," *Annals* of the Association of American Geographers, vol. 44, 1954, pp. 1–14; R. P. Momsen, *Routes Over the Serra Do Mar,* Muncie, Ind.: Ball State University, 1965; D. E. Snyder, "Commercial Passenger Linkages and the Metropolitan Modality of Montevideo," *Economic Geography,* vol. 38, 1962, pp. 95–112; D. A. Smith, "Interaction within a Fragmented State: The Example of Hawaii," *Economic Geography,* vol. 39, 1963, pp. 234–244; J. Garrison, "Barstow, California: A Transportation Focus in a Desert Environment," *Economic Geography,* vol. 29, 1953, pp. 159–167.

39 See W. L. Garrison and D. F. Marble, "Comparisons of Transportation Stocks," in *A Prolegomenon to the Forecasting of Transportation Development,* Research Report Transportation Center, Northwestern University, 1965, pp. 21–36.

40 See, for example, Meinig, *op cit.*

41 Haggett, *op cit.,* 1966, 1967, and 1972; also revealed in the Transportation Center reports.

42 M. Schneider, "Gravity Models and Trip Distribution Theory," *Papers and Proceedings,* Regional Science Association, vol. 5, 1959, pp. 51–56; and see a recent attempt at application in R. Earickson, *The Spatial Behaviour of Hospital Patients,* Chicago: University of Chicago, Department of Geography, Research Paper 124, 1970, pp. 65–69.

43 B. Harris, "A Note on the Probability of Interaction at a Distance," *Journal of Regional Science,* vol. 5, no. 2, 1964, pp. 31–35.

44 P. Rimmer, "The Transportation Method of Linear Programming with a New Zealand Example," *New Zealand Geographer,* vol. 24, 1968, pp. 90–99; R. Morrill, "The Movement of Persons and the Transportation Problem," in *Quantitative Geography,* Part 1, W. L. Garrison and D. F. Marble (eds.), Northwestern University, Department of Geography, 1967; K. R. Cox, "The Application of Linear Programming to Geographic Problems," *Tijds. Voor Economische en Soc. Geografie*, November–December, 1965, vol. 56, pp. 228–236; and Garrison (1959), *op cit.*, Part 2.

45 See *Highway Research Board*, Special Report 120, 1971, which deals with urban commodity flows and the problems of both obtaining and analyzing data on trucking, mail services, etc. Also two earlier studies are worth mentioning: J. D. Fellman, *Truck Transportation Patterns of Chicago*, Department of Geography Research Paper, University of Chicago, 1950; and M. Helvig, *Chicago's External Truck Movements*, Department of Geography Research Paper, University of Chicago, 1964.

46 See, for example, W. D. Ashton, *The Theory of Traffic Flow*, London: Methuen, 1966.

47 In J. O. Wheeler's review of work in transportation geography, "An Overview of Research in Transportation Geography," *East Lakes Geographer*, vol. 7, 1971, pp. 3–12, the three research foci are identified as ". . . (1) networks: their location, structure, and evolution; (2) flows on networks; and (3) the significance and impact of network and flows on the space economy" (p. 8), while modes receive virtually no mention.

48 H. Gauthier, "Transportation and the Growth of the Sao Paulo Economy," *Journal of Regional Science*, vol. 8, no. 1, 1968, pp. 77–94; R. Taaffe, "Transportation and Regional Specialisation: The Example of Soviet Central Asia," *Annals* of the Association of American Geographers, vol. 52, 1962, pp. 80–98.

49 W. Christaller, *Central Places in Southern Germany*, trans. by C. W. Bashin, Englewood Cliffs, N.J.: Prentice-Hall, 1966.

50 A. Losch, *The Economics of Location*, trans. by W. H. Woglom, New Haven: Yale University Press, 1954.

51 P. Haggett, 1966, *op cit.*, pp. 82–85.

Selection 2

The Theory of Transportation

C. H. Cooley

The character of transportation as a whole and in detail, at any particular time and throughout its history, is altogether determined by its interrelations with physical and social forces and conditions. To understand transportation means simply to analyze these interrelations.

1. MECHANICAL AND GEOMETRICAL NOTIONS

We think of transportation as a movement of things—masses of any sort—from one place to another. Anything answering this description comes under the idea in its most general form. If we add to this a conception underlying all action directed to an end, namely, that its excellence consists in accomplishing the end with the least possible expenditure of time and force, we have the most general basis possible for the judgment of transportation from a mechanical standpoint. From this standpoint, transportation is best which accomplishes the movement of things with the least force and in the shortest time. Speed, then, is one fundamental test, while economy

Reprinted with permission from the publications of the *American Economic Association*, vol. IX, no. 3, May 1894. Edited by M. E. Eliot Hurst.

of force, translated in the light of actual conditions, means cheapness. Speed and cheapness never cease in the most complex development of transportation to be the simplest test of its efficiency.

We can gain some notion of these mechanical *and* geometrical properties if we look at a simple model. Our model area might be a physically uniform farming area. We could then ask ourselves—what form would the road system take that connected the farms in such an area? In building roads there is of course always a tendency to take the shortest route. But the literal and absolute application of this principle would require the building of roads from every point to every other; in other words the turning into roads of the whole surface of the earth, with enormous labor and the complete destruction of farms. It is clear that some sort of a compromise must be made between the principle that calls for directness and the principle that calls for economy of labor and space. In effect what happens is that a hierarchy of route systems arises. A group of neighboring farms is served by a common route, feeding into a common route serving several such neighborhood groups. Several such common routes would in turn coalesce into a major artery leading to the principal market centers of our model area.* Such hypothetical conditions do not exist since mountains and other physical features break up the physical homogeneity of our model, but the railroad system of the period in the Mississippi Valley approximates this *radial* pattern. It can also be found in the older part of cities like Boston, or in many European cities.

By contrast to this hierarchical radial pattern, frequently a rectilinear pattern is found. While the former is the most convenient from the point of view of transportation, the latter

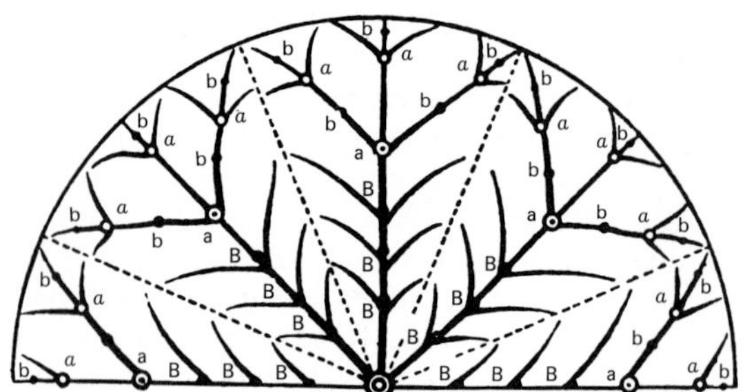

Fig. 2-1.

is the most convenient from the point of view of architecture, building, and the surveying of land. This gridiron pattern is common in North American cities, and in the more recently settled agricultural areas of the West, where the surveyor frequently proceeded or traveled alongside the settler.

The cause for this variety in arrangement, this difference between old and new as to the degree in which the geometrical requirements of transportation are met, is not far to seek. Where growth is gradual and arrangement unpremeditated, where paths gradually become roads and roads after a long course of time develop into city streets, where, in other words, the city is laid out without regard to the requirements of building and convenient allotment, the natural arrangement prevails. On the other hand, when the arrangement is planned beforehand the rectangular arrangement is chosen as the more convenient. The city of Washington offers an excellent example of the deliberate and scientific reconciliation of the two ideas. To a plan generally rectangular is added a system of diagonal avenues having their principal point of convergence at the national Capitol.

Besides such geometric properties we must also consider mechanical factors. This is not to unduly stress the factor of "friction" of movement, but the degree of ease of movement, whether over land or through water or a pipeline, is important. Some routeways of necessity are faced with physical obstacles—

**Editor's note:* This is illustrated in Fig. 2-1. Essentially, Cooley is drawing at this point on the earlier work (1850) of the German geographer J. G. Kohl.

great distances or mountain ranges; others are made easier by the existence of inland waterways or oceans. From this relationship comes the close relationship between the study of transportation and that of physical geography.

One cannot hope to understand transportation without at the same time understanding the geographical facts that condition it. And as these physical facts are permanent, relatively at least to the social facts which the study of transportation must also embrace, a theory of their influence forms the groundwork of the theory of transportation.

The immediate object of transportation with reference to the physical features of the earth's surface is to overcome natural obstacles by making use of their natural advantages. The division into land and water movement is a fundamental one in the study of transportation.†

As transportation has adapted itself to physical obstacles, or in some cases altered the latter, there has been a steady advance in the mechanical abilities of the various modes—speed, economy, miniminization of physical obstacles. To detail all of these would be to write the technical history of transportation. It suffices, however, to point out that every change in the construction of routeways, from the primitive track through the jungle to the most elaborate of modern systems of railway construction, has its definite relation to physical conditions and arises out of the interaction between these conditions and the need for various sorts of transportation. So with the different motive forces and all the techniques of their use, from the direct application of human strength, which characterizes the beginnings both of land and water transport, to the steam engine which unites them again in their latest attainment; and so with all that relates to vehicles.

†*Editor's note:* This distinction is pursued in Part Four of this book and therefore will not be discussed further at this point.

A fact characteristic of all this development is that progress in one sort of transportation depends in some measure upon that in others; that there is a general interdependence. The construction of wheels was well known in antiquity, but they did not come into general use for land transportation until modern times, and then only in certain countries; the use of wheels had to await better roads. So in railways, the roads are fitted to the vehicle, the vehicle to the roads, and both to the motive power. No one of these can develop independently. Different kinds of land transportation depend upon one another; the traffic of city streets and country roads could not be maintained without railroads, nor railroads without it. In a less but very marked degree, land and water transport are mutually dependent. Steamship conveyance would probably have amounted to little without the contemporary development of railroads, and railroad conveyance certainly could not be what it is without steamships.

2. TRANSPORTATION AND ORGANIZED SOCIETY

The need for the movement of things and persons underlies every sort of social organization, every institution whatever. It is equally necessary to that economic organization which supplies society with food and other material goods, and to those psychical organizations, the church, education, research and the like, which, though ideal in their aims, require material instruments. The transfer of books, of scientific instruments and, above all, of men charged with many different social functions, is as necessary to society in its way as the transfer of raw materials. There can be no adequate theory of transportation which has regard only to some one aspect of its social function, as the economic aspect. That is not the only aspect, nor can one truly say that it is more important than the others.

All are coordinate, equally indispensable to social progress.

Precisely because transportation underlies social development it is in turn determined by that development. It is a tool of the economic, the political, the military organizations, and the character of the tool varies with their needs. A constant factor in the development of transportation is the natural obstacles, the frictional factors it has to overcome and the natural forces it employs; but even these in their practical bearings are relative to social development. The art of scientific sailing converts a contrary wind from an obstacle into an assisting force. When men discover how to utilize coal through steam and the steam engine, it is as if there were a new and ample creation of natural power. The natural forces were always there, but they exist for man only as they are discovered and used by art. The mechanical arts, again, do not advance in an accidental manner, but are intimately associated with economic and political conditions as well as with the progress of physical science. We have the railroad not only because of the ingenuity of men like Stephenson, but because the great economic need of the time was back of that ingenuity urging it on. The chief characteristic of the economic revolution begun in the latter part of the previous century was industrial concentration and specialization. These could not go far without better means of land movement, and the canals first and then the railroads supplied that means. The railroad is bound up with the other changes of the period, in part a cause, in part an effect.

Transportation, in a social sense, aids the physical organization of society. Without movement and connectivity the constituent parts of a society could not be unified or interdependent; specialization of activity would be impossible. To link up those parts, to emphasize those relationships, *communication* occurs. *Communication* is here used in the widest sense of the communication of ideas and goods between places spatially and temporally separated. These are the threads that hold society together; upon them all unity depends. Using this wide definition of communication we can categorize movement as:

1 *The mechanism of material communication*
   a *Place communication*—transportation, *per se*
   b *Time communication*—storage, etc.
2 *The mechanism of psychical communication*
   a *Place communication*—speech, physical gestures, newspapers, mail, telegraph, etc.
   b *Time communication*—the printed/written word as a document of cultural continuance; the spoken myth, etc.

However imperfect this categorization may be, it does spell out the role of transportation in organized society. But it must also be remembered that the role of communications will vary between societies. To some societies efficiency in the physical and mechanical sense dealt with in the first subsection may be sufficient; to others security and military factors may be of prime importance; to industrial societies maximum individual accessibility may be the moving force. To fully understand transportation then, one needs to know its relationship to military, political, economic and cultural institutions; this would be a twofold inquiry—*first,* to understand the arrangements within particular modes of transportation, and *secondly,* to relate those to society at large.

a. Military Institutions

Military considerations have influenced transportation arrangements from earliest times to the present day; they have led through time to the improvement of accessibility, such as, for example, through the building of the Roman roadway system. The Roman routes system extended over the length and breadth of their empire, from Britain to the Far East. The more important roads were well constructed and paved with stone. They were distinctly military in character, intended mainly for the passage of men and supplies to the military camps and forts, and were located accordingly. Whatever trade took place over them was secondary, and they never would have been built for such trading. This remarkable system of Roman roads was basically to ensure military access.

The swift transfer of armies and supplies to possible seats of war and the rapid communication of information and commands are the chief requirements of military transportation. Swiftness and security from interruption by the seasons are much more important than economy or capacity to carry any great bulk of commodities. Military roads in early history are commonly distinguished by a solid and expensive style of construction and by a directness that takes very little account of minor natural obstacles. That this last was the case with the Roman roads has often been remarked. They proceed for the most part in a right line over hills and other obstructions that might have been avoided by a little deviation. This peculiarity is probably to be explained partly by the greater importance given to speed than to economy of labor in the minds of the projectors of the road, and partly by the fact that military roads are usually constructed by a despotic central power situated far from the spot where the work is done. Enterprises carried on at arm's length in this way by a power having no detailed knowledge of or interest in local circumstances must always tend to take on a certain arbitrary uniformity. Plans are drawn at the center of administration based on a general knowledge of localities, and carried out to the letter by subordinates who have no authority to deviate from them.

As society changes and priorities change, those earlier military influences go on playing a role. The Roman roads in Europe survived in part the breaking up of the Empire and the setting up of new national boundaries. In many areas they had precisely the same influence upon transportation and settlement as a river or other natural highway, and their influence can still be traced on the landscape patterns. Thus the geography of Europe today retains important traces left by the military transportation of Rome.

The development of other modes of transportation, like railroads, has not necessarily changed this state of affairs. Some railroad systems certainly were developed largely to open up new industrial trading patterns, though the construction of the first line to the American Pacific coast was hastened by military considerations. In France, Germany, and Russia, many of the early railroad lines, in contrast, were heavily influenced by military requirement. The choice of routes upon military grounds may result in quite a different arrangement of lines from that which would best answer economic needs. Both must, to be sure, overcome the same obstacles in the same way, so that on the technical side they are likely to be nearly or quite the same. But it is clear, without discussing the matter in detail, that the location of those lines which will best serve trade is likely to be different from the location of those whose chief aim is rapid movement with a view to strategical operations at possible seats of war.‡

b. Political Organization

Political institutions can influence transportation at several levels—at the microlevel in the way a railroad company or a freight forwarding company is organized, from the president

‡*Editor's note:* The role of the military in the development of the U.S. "defense" highway or interstate freeway system comes to mind here.

down to the foreman; at another level, merchants' and carriers' associations may influence the imposition of tolls and levies, may lobby to increase their share of the transportation market, and may try to influence the amount of investment in the infrastructure in general; at still other levels of the local, regional, and national governments, political considerations may govern the particular investment of funds, the levying of extra charges, the negotiation of treaties, and the administration of political boundaries. In some societies, the state at its highest level assumes all responsibilities for transportation. Transportation may have a character almost exclusively political, particularly if one adds in direct or indirect influences from the economic sphere of society.

Among the more obvious political influences is the role of political boundaries. Customs duties, laws discriminating in any way against foreign traders, restrictions on immigration and travel, and the like all have a notable action in limiting movement and determining its character. But within states, political influences are strong too. I know of no time or country, when economic transportation existed at all, in which it was not in an important degree a concern of the coercive, governing, organization of society—the political state, large or small, general or local. From the time of the earliest movements of the land trade to the present day, roads, bridges, harbors, and often the vehicles and other instruments of carriage have been a public concern. At one time it was the local authority—lord, city, monastery, etc.—that controlled and exploited it; sometimes a commercial federation like the Hanseatic League; at other times the central government itself. The policy of *laissez faire,* of turning over transportation to individual initiative and control, has never entirely prevailed. The public regulation of railroads, highways, and shipping has a considerable history in both the United States and Western Europe. This role is frequently overlooked since the Industrial Revolution stressed the economic role of transportation, as is evidenced by its main study within the discipline of economics. In the United States, although it is true that the private enterprise system has played a strong role in the development and maintenance of the transportation system, and for a long period played a dominant role,§ public regulation does occur, albeit negative in character (i.e., largely prescribing what private enterprise shall not do).

We touch here upon that aspect of the matter which is of most importance at the present day, the question, that is, of what part the political state should take in relation to economic transportation. The problem here is that of the apportionment of functions between the state, or the coercive form of association, on the one hand, and individuals or private and voluntary associations, on the other. It is purely a problem of expediency and the proper basis for a solution must be found in a careful analysis of the various social functions of transportation to which we will return at the end of this selection.

c. Cultural Institutions

There is no doubt that just as military and political influences have affected transportation development since earliest times, so have cultural factors. The balance of these latter factors has changed through time, however. Earlier religious institutions played a vital role in the state and economy, varying from the organization of fairs and markets, the building of bridges and other links, to the levying of tolls and the encouragement of pilgrimages and often trade. Certainly their role in com-

§*Editor's note:* I have only changed the tense here. Since Cooley wrote this, public control has increased, even in the United States, and it is tempting to change this passage. However, I leave it largely as he intended it.

munications was vital—in the medieval period books and other documents were largely entrusted to monasteries, universities, and other religious institutions.

Today the communication of ideas has a more widespread base, and most of the economic influence of the church has been superseded by individuals and the state apparatus. The former, communications, is however still strongly influenced by the general cultural attributes of a society. Newspapers, books, letters, telephones, as well as face-to-face contacts are an important purveyor of personal communication, but science, education, literature, and art, through learned societies, universities, books, bibliographies, exhibition, all contribute to the communication of ideas. If one rightly considers the enormous intricacy and importance of these psychical processes of society, this social thinking, perceiving, feeling and deciding in all its unspeakable multiplicity, he may well conclude that its adequate analysis and interpretation is the most complex and difficult problem ever offered to science.

However, transportation as such, and communication as such, do have their own characteristics which tend to separate them as objects of study. That movement of physical masses which is the essential thing in transportation either does not take place at all in the communication of thought, or if it does it is merely incidental and not of the essence of the thing. Transportation is physical, communication psychical. The latter belongs to a distinct branch of study, immeasurable importance and complexity, namely, social psychology. It cannot profitably be dissociated from that field of inquiry which embraces language as an instrument of social organization and all the material agencies that language employs.

I think, then, that a separation can advantageously be made between the theory of transportation and the theory of communication,‖ notwithstanding that they use, in part, the same vehicles, have a common aim in the overcoming of space, and exert in many ways an analogous influence upon social development. A study of communication from the point of view of place relations may be undertaken in connection with the study of transportation; but such a study cannot penetrate more than skin-deep into the social meaning of communication. In transportation place relations and the overcoming of obstacles in space are everything. In communication place relations, as such, are of diminishing importance, and since the introduction of the telegraph it may almost be said that there are no place relations. Space—distance—as an obstacle to communication has so nearly been overcome that it is hardly worth considering. In the transportation of material goods and of persons such a result is inconceivable, and in this field the "annihilation of space" must remain a figure of speech. Although the conquest of physical obstacles to movement is a principal feature of the development of transportation, yet it is clear that this conquest is only relative. It cannot be said, on the whole, that territorial relations were ever more important in the exchange of goods than now. Efficient transportation greatly modifies and extends them, making them world-wide instead of local, but has no tendency to diminish their general significance.

d. Economic Organization

The study of the economic basis of transportation covers two aspects, that of the economic structure existing within transportation itself and that of the relation of transportation

‖*Editor's note:* Some transportation geographers would not agree here. Ronald Abler shows in fact (in Selection 19) that although there are differences in one sense, there are more similarities. The psychological basis of urban transportation is also underlined in Selection 29.

to the economic organization of society at large. The former subject, as well as the latter, is one of very great importance, including as it does the private or internal aspect of all the problems of transportation—such questions, for example, as that of the theory of railroad rates regarded as a means of getting the greatest possible private revenue. In practice, however, it will be convenient to treat the two together, taking chiefly the public standpoint but referring to the private where it seems important to do so. We come, then, to the relation of transportation to economic society.

It is true of course that all forms of social organization have some economic basis. Organizations devoted primarily to other ends, like the family, state, and school, need material commodities, and thus have, secondarily, an economic organization of some kind. There are also societal forms that are primarily economic—the division of labor and mechanisms of production and exchange for instance. All forms of social organization require economic nourishment.

We strike the keynote of this matter when we say that the study of economic transportation is equivalent to the study of economy in its place relations. Transportation is a mechanism for moving things and persons from one place to another, and so far as economic phenomena are related to this movement they are related to transportation. Whatever is connected with territorial conditions, with the surface of the earth considered as an area, is connected with transportation, which is a mechanism conformed to these conditions.

The whole matter, then, of the distribution of population, wealth and industries over the face of the earth is in one of its aspects a matter of transportation. We have before us such great questions as that of the territorial division of labor, general and local, the concentration of population in cities, the location of cities, and the relation of territorial conditions to prices, markets, competition and other phases of economic exchange. These are, to be sure, questions of transportation in only one of their many aspects; but that one is important, perhaps as important as any.

Population Distribution and the Rise of Cities

Without transportation mankind would necessarily be pretty evenly distributed over the surface of the earth, the main irregularities being those due to differences in the fertility of the soil. The earth is the only primary source of food, and man must stay where the food is produced unless he can have it brought to him. The existence of the smallest village involves the movement of commodities to and from it, the beginnings of social transportation. Any efficient organization of industry is quite inconceivable without the concentration of men and other industrial forces in cities and other foci of industrial activity. Economy of force and concentration are inseparable. All kinds of industry except agriculture are distinctly and directly centralizing in their tendency. Nor is agriculture a real exception, since efficient agriculture means specialized agriculture, and specialization implies centers of collection and distribution. Transportation is the instrument of all social organization in place. Only to the degree that transportation is reliable and efficient can this segregation of man, his crops, and his industrial products take place. However, just as transportation can free man in respect to place relations and produce specialization and concentration, so can it cause decentralization and dispersion. Thus the growth of cities is an example to some degree of the concentrative force, while the abilities of urban transportation can be used to disperse urban living.

The development of transportation and of the territorial division of labor proceeds side by side. Neither can be said to go before the other, since they are mutually dependent. The only source of local or international trade in ancient or modern time is international or local specialization in production—something is produced in one place which is lacking in another. In the presence of an active demand for these distance commodities they tend to move from the place where they are produced to the place requiring them; transportation is set up. On the other hand the transportation resulting from these forces is by no means a mere passive effect but becomes in turn a very active cause of counterchanges. It enormously stimulates and greatly modifies that specialization to which it owes its origin. Under the spur of transportation existing differences in production are increased and new ones are introduced that could not well have been maintained previously. Amid the complication of causes and effects, of reiterated interaction, from which economic life as a whole results, transportation, determined in great measure by permanent natural conditions, has its firm position as one of the fundamental and comparatively independent causes. There is no first cause: this one is as early as any.

On account of its peculiar relation to place-specialization in industry, transportation increases more rapidly than production. As the efficiency of productive processes is multiplied by the division of labor, the bulk of goods carried is increased not only proportionately but far more than proportionately. A greater share of the whole product must be conveyed from one place to another. Thus in a less economically complex society, where half of what is consumed is produced at home, the other half only will require transportation. If owing to greater territorial division of labor nine-tenths of what is consumed comes from abroad, transportation must increase in the same ratio, independently of that general increase of production which goes on, of course, at the same time. Conveyance, then, is an industry that must ever grow much more rapidly than industries in general. One puts the matter forcibly if not accurately when he says that transportation increases as the square of production.

There seem to be two underlying reasons for the territorial division of labor suggested in our discussion to this point. Place specialization in industry is necessary, first, because of the economy inherent in the principle of the division of labor; second, because of the existence of local facilities for production. These causes, though everywhere in operation—sometimes in harmony, sometimes at variance—are in theory quite distinct. If the surface of the earth could be conceived as perfectly uniform, offering nowhere peculiar natural encouragement to the development of particular kinds of production, men would yet find their advantage in local specialization because specialization saves force. On the other hand, even though there were no economy in the territorial division of labor as such, yet the face of the earth being diversified as it is, territorial division would result from that diversity. Even in the first case men would aggregate in towns, cities and factories; even in the second they would produce wheat in one place, cattle in another and metals in a third.

The ramifications for transportation are obvious. It was noted earlier that if the landscape were physically homogeneous, transportation tends to take on a complex radial form, the primary roads converging to central points which are themselves connected by secondary roads with other and more important centers. In its operation this tendency is closely associated with the principle of local division of labor, and the two acting together bring about that primary separation into town and country everywhere observed. The tendency of society to divide into town and country comes from the economy of division of labor; the size and location of towns is determined largely by transportation. The blacksmith, the miller, the carpenter, etc., are required in every agricultural community; convenience of access to them and other craftsmen calls for the formation of a village at a point easily reached by converging roads. The question whether this division and concentration of labor shall be carried so far as the building of large towns depends upon the facilities of movement to and from the center.

If those facilities permit we have, situated near the center of a group of country villages, a large town connected with them by converging highways. The country villages themselves, instead of being simply centers where the farmers and craftsmen meet and exchange products, now become the starting point and end of longer movements between the villages and the town. They become centers of collection for such commodities as are produced in the neighborhood and of distribution for such as are brought in from abroad. The division of labor in them is increased by the addition of a class that occupies itself with buying, selling and storing the goods that go abroad or come thence. The formation of the large town is due to precisely the same forces as the formation of the village; the higher division of labor requires factories and other forms of concentrated production which call together a large population and must be located with reference to the conditions of transportation. And these large towns are again connected with great cities whose existence is due to the same general causes.

In the larger town we see another sort of local division of labor introduced in the specialization of the various parts of the city. The separation between city and suburbs, between the portions assigned to residence and to business, is an example. It is this that chiefly determines the character of local passenger movement by street and rapid transit. Here also we see at work the general principle that the degree of specialization is determined by the efficiency of transportation. Only as the machinery of this local movement is developed can we have that separation between the place of living and the place of working that permits certain parts of cities to be devoted wholly to industry, others to homes, yet others to wholesaling or retailing. Only restaurants, retail provision and drug shops, and other places where small and frequent purchases must be made are without this segregation.#

The larger the city the greater the part played in it by those industries that are concerned with movement. At an important center we have radial movements in and out—centrifugal and centripetal—of a very complex character. There is, to begin with, the local or primary movement of commodities to and from the country in the immediate vicinity. This is of the same sort as that about a country village. Next is the other local movement peculiar to the large centers of population and exchange. To accomplish this we have for commodities a countless multitude of trucks; for persons, transit vehicles, bicycles and the like. Even the movement up and down becomes here so important that we cannot well omit freight and passenger elevators from the list of means of transportation. All of these devices, of course, have their numerous *personnel* and their important and costly mechanism—tracks, overhead and underground structures, wires, cables, power plants and service facilities. Together they make, as any one may see, an industry that takes up a great part of the labor and wealth of the city.

Not only the local movement, but the longer movement connecting the city with other towns and cities, requires its own complex machinery. The terminal structure of railroads for the accommodation of passengers and freight, offices, storage warehouses, hotels, grain elevators, docks and the like are an

#Editor's note: As a precursor of central place theory and its modification and application to internal city structures, these ideas are quite remarkable.

important and conspicuous part of city structure on the material side and the people connected with them are equally important on the personal side. All industries concerned with the collection of commodities and persons in the city for shipment away from it, in the distribution of commodities and persons coming in from without, or in the transfer and storage of what is passing through the city, are a part of the machinery of this secondary or distant movement. Nor should it be forgotten that the whole mechanism of commercial exchange —wholesale and retail shops and stores, banks and other instruments of trade—is in one sense a part of the means for the movement of commodities and persons.

All those forms of place-specialization that have been described can be conceived to exist in a country without natural diversity of surface. They would grow up out of the economy resulting from the division of labor even were they not, as in fact, stimulated and modified by a difference in the natural capabilities of places. It grows more complex when we add all the differences of physique—variations in resource availability, fertility of soil, in the case of transportation. If we add these factors to what we have already laid out in a model situation we may summarize the relationships of transportation to population distribution and city location as:

1 Non-economic causes, as military and political, have a notable influence, especially in the earlier history of societies.

2 Of economic causes the most general is pressure toward greater division of labor: the efficient use of natural forces is inseparable from the concentration of population and wealth. This cause acts independently of particular places and has of itself alone no action in fixing location.

Two influences chiefly determine the location of cities: local facilities for production and local relations to transportation. The former of these acts mostly through the coarser and primary manufacturing industries. The finer manufactures seek the most convenient centers of distribution, that is, of transportation.

Transportation, itself guided in its course chiefly by the physical diversity of the earth's surface, is the main cause of the location of cities in an industrial society. The mode of its action is that *population and wealth tend to collect at a break in transportation;* the reason being in the first place the necessity for the material and symbolic machinery of transfer at breaks, and in the second the tendency of other economic activities to collect where that machinery exists.

Markets, Prices, and Competition Transportation in the measure of its efficiency is concerned with overcoming the economic costs imposed by time and place. Transportation, in the sense of free movement extends the scope of agriculture, labor, capital, etc. By just overcoming the friction of distance, transportation can extend effective demand. Where crude means of conveyance prevent the movement of goods the demand of the people of a single place is limited in its working to the close vicinity of that place, while the needs of other places are not felt as a demand. Facility of movement, by extending the scope of demand, tends also, other things equal, to make it uniform and to give it a more varied character. It becomes more uniform, because not so much affected by accidental local changes.

Supply tends to become more uniform in different times and places. This is very obvious in the provision of basic foodstuffs. The great famines of former times are now almost unknown because of the ease with which a local scarcity can be remedied by importation. Though the interdependence of nations as to these necessaries is increased, it has also become generalized; thus, while the dependence of a Western European industrial nation upon the rest of the world for grain is greater than ever before, it is less than ever a dependence upon any particular grain-growing country. The supply may come from North America or say Australia.

Quick transportation diminishes the need for holding large stocks of goods. With improved means of transportation, dealers are far less compelled than formerly to anticipate the demands of their customers a long time ahead. In many lines of trade the stock held is hardly more than samples. This is particularly the case in the wholesale trade, where goods are commonly shipped from the factories after the order is taken. The factories, in turn, adopt the same plan with raw materials; they hold as little as they can and prefer to buy only for immediate needs.

The outcome of this is that the whole economic process is greatly hastened. The holding of a stock involves the lengthening of the time between production and consumption. Under present methods that time is almost completely reduced. If other things were held equal, efficient transportation would tend to diminish the need for capital in production and exchange.

We see the same facts from a somewhat different point of view when we look at markets. A market is the area over which competition extends, and though it has no sharp boundaries it is clearly determined by facility of transportation and communication. The means of quick movement enable things distributed over a wide area to be offered simultaneously in one place; or they enable things collected in one place to be offered simultaneously in many places. This is competition on its material side. Communication is the symbolic or physical mechanism and permits the competitive bidding that must accompany the transactions of the market. If the retail dealers over a circle of a hundred miles' radius are connected by telephone with the wholesale dealers of a single large city, and can have their purchases sent thence in two or three hours, the competition is almost as perfect as among the dealers of a single place. As the distance becomes greater, the time of movement longer, and communication more difficult, competition becomes imperfect; but in the case of durable and staple commodities it has some action over whole countries, continents, or even the world.

The normal effect of more efficient transportation upon prices is to make them lower and to lessen the variations of the prices of any particular commodity in different times or places. After what has already been said these effects need little further discussion. The cost of movement enters into the price of all that has to be moved; and for this reason alone, without regarding more indirect results, prices fall with less costly movement. A tendency to equality of price at different times and places follows from the action upon supply and demand already spoken of. It may be added that the substitution of one commodity for another that serves a similar purpose, such as the using of corn or rye meal when wheat flow is expensive, is facilitated by cheap and rapid transportation.

When approaching these economic factors *rent* also becomes of importance. Rent is closely connected with transportation because it is a matter of areas and distances, of place relations. Earlier I said that the study of the economic relations of transportation was nearly equivalent to the study of society in its place relations; and this notion holds true at the present point.

Rent would exist as a result of transportation alone, were there no differences in the fertility of soils. That is to say, varying productivity, a fundamental conception of the Ricardian theory, is not indispensable to the existence of rent. Nor is it necessary that the supply of land be limited. In the case of an unlimited area of uniform soil rent would exist, and its law would be as follows:

Rent arises from differences in the cost of getting commodities to market, and is measured by the difference between this cost in any given case and that in the case of the most remote land which it pays to cultivate.

There is of course nothing new in this proposition, but it emphasizes the fact, perhaps imperfectly realized, that the conditions of movement are an independent cause of rent, coordinate with fertility and the margin of cultivation.

Transportation is, accordingly, an element entering into all rent, and changes in transportation change rents. It is the tendency of progressing facility of movement, other things remaining equal, to lower rents by diminishing the differences in the cost of reaching markets. A familiar example is the fall of agricultural rents in England, due to that development of steamships and railroads which gave American wheat fields access to English markets. Something of the same sort has also taken place between the eastern and western parts of the United States. Agricultural rents in many parts of the east went down and farms in fact were abandoned, because the cheapening of railway movement decreased the advantage of their situation.

This principle is also applicable to ground rents in cities. Increased accessibility (for example by improved rapid transit) tends to diminish ground rents by distributing city population and business over a wider area. This is particularly true for housing, where a cheap and efficient means of urban transportation increases access to and from the workplace, and so increases the number of potential dwelling places and reduces the rent per unit area as the supply of land increases in proportion to the demand. Actually the amount of land increases as the square of the radius from the central city; particularly where the speed of transit is improved, large areas of suburban living at relatively low ground rents can be opened up. Precisely the same relationship exists if instead of speed one talks about say halving the costs, and instead of dwelling places one substitutes "area for profitable cultivation." The relationship between transportation and rent can be restated as:

In so far as rents depend directly upon facilitity of access to a given center (whether facility be measured in time or in cost), they vary near the center inversely as the square of the efficiency of transportation (that is inversely as the square of speed, directly as the square of cost). The area of the rent-yielding circle, on the other hand, varies directly as the square of the efficiency of transportation.

Finally we must turn to the matter of *rates*. We have so far assumed constant charges, with little differentiation between the modes of transportation. Rates as a whole should be such as to afford a reasonable return to investment, and though they are adjustable should not be reduced below the minimum representing the immediate costs of movement. Thus there should be no discrimination among people or places, even where competition might do this, since it places people and places at considerable disadvantages.** Rates on any particular commodity, not among the

***Editor's note:* Again Cooley has a long section on rates, which arose out of his concern for public regulation. We must remember that he wrote during the period of cutthroat competition and many unfair practices; this was the stage of concentration in nineteenth-century capitalism where many large corporations were formed. In fact, historically, although many railroad companies did not willingly submit themselves to public regulation, U.S. federal legislation in 1887 led to the establishment of the ICC (Interstate Commerce Commission). In addition Cooley's concern may reflect the fact that despite the ICC, U.S. Attorney General Olney was able to write to a railroad president "The Commission [ICC] . . . is, or can be made of great use to the railroads. It satisfies the popular clamor for a government supervision of railroads, at the same time that supervision is almost nominal. Further, the older such a commission gets to be, the more inclined it will be found to take the business and railroad point of view."

raw products of immovable natural agents are to be proportional to distance, except that for short distances a minimum may be sufficient to cover the immediate expense of handling the freight. The classification of commodities, other than raw products, is to be such as to make rates as nearly as possible proportional to value.

The application of any rating policy would disturb existing conditions of competition, and the question of just how much this disturbance ought to be admitted as a reason against changes otherwise desirable is a practical inquiry of considerable importance. The merchants of a given city may have been enabled by actual rates to compete in markets from which they would be shut out were rates what they should be; or industries may have been established in places where they could no longer maintain themselves. In answer to such objections, however, it is pertinent to inquire whether an unsettled and planless state of things is not continually working wrongs of this character, and whether anything looking toward a rational and permanent adjustment is not preferable to chaos. . . .

3. CONCLUSION††

In considering all these factors, whether they be military, religious, political, or economic, we finish with the idea of transportation as a highly organic activity and a distinct social function. Transportation is not agriculture, nor manufacture, nor trade; it is something having a distinct character of its own, quite apart from these. To overstress its economic functions, although they are vital components of both the transportation system and the landscape it serves, loses sight of the fact that it is one of several fundamental social processes. Transportation is an agency by which every part of society is brought into relation with every other, and interdependence, specialization, organization made possible. To treat transportation as an industry does not do justice to such interrelationship.

Not only does transportation hold this unique position as the physical basis and instrument of social organization, it also politically, like the nation state does at another level, holds society together. A good example of this role is that of the Roman road—such a road is, in its simplest view, merely a long strip of ground devoted to a public end. But we can build upon that—the public end is social consolidation through military power; it is an instrument of unification; it is continuous and laid out upon a definite plan; it is a total thing; any one part of it is meaningless outside of the context in which it was constructed. If a mile is impassable there might be no road at all. And to get the most good of it, it must be used by uniform methods, by vehicles particularly suited to it. A uniform route system, part of a larger social milieu, opening up access, changing place relationships, is the first stage of the organic character of transportation. It is followed by uniformity of vehicles and methods as we pass from Roman road to say railroad systems. The continuous strip of ground remains, but upon it is developed elaborate mechanical structures and elaborate organizational factors—as such accessibility improves, place relationships are extended yet further. The widest unity, the most advantageous and economical organization, can now be planned according to a comprehensive plan and unified instruments and methods—the common end being the efficient performance of the social function of transportation. From the organic character of transportation *per se* we have moved logically

††*Editor's note:* Cooley's final chapter is in essence not a conclusion to his "theory" of transportation but rather a continuation of his plea for planning and regulation in transportation. I have therefore heavily edited his remarks, hopefully in the spirit of the rest of his long essay.

to an organic character in the means of carrying it on.

Such is the crucial role of transportation in the future of our society. Our societal landscapes are as they are because of the availability of physical and psychical transportation and communication. Transportation being a fundamental and general process, influencing and influenced by our political, cultural, military and economic organization, pertains to society as a whole rather than to any particular part of it. To consider just the industrial aspects of transportation neglects these societal ramifications. But just as transportation is so important to the running of societies as we know them, so it cannot be left to a purely *laissez faire* situation; it must have a high degree of organization, to be carried on with general aims, by uniform instruments and uniform methods.

Selection 3

Geography as Spatial Interaction

E. L. Ullman

Perhaps the essential intellectual contribution of human geography can be summarized by the concepts of site and situation. Site refers to local, underlying areal conditions and leads to defining geography as the study of the "relations between men and the environment." Situation refers to the effects of one area, or rather phenomena in one area, on another area. It should logically focus on the connections between areas and leads to such terms as "circulation" and "regional interdependence," or to specific aspects such as "diffusion" or "centralization."

This situational concept is defined here as "spatial interaction," and is intended as a more positive and dynamic concept than either situation, relations, or even circulation. In a sense it provides a "motor" for situation concepts.

Site thus might be conceived of as a *vertical* relationship—type of soil correlated with type of agriculture on top of the soil—and situation a *horizontal* relationship—effect of market in one place on type of agriculture in some other area.

As early as 1889 Sir Halford Mackinder noted the same dualism as follows: "The chief distinction in political geography seems to be founded on the facts that man travels and man settles."[1]

An example of alternate interpretation based on site and situation is provided by the age-old puzzle of assigning reasons for the growth of particular civilizations in particular places. Thus Toynbee in his challenge and response theory uses a site concept with a new twist—the challenging effect of a relatively poor environment. Pierre Gourou, the Belgian geographer, asks whether substitution of the effects of an unfavorable environment for a favorable one represents an advance over previous environmental determinism. He poses as an alternate possibility a situation concept—the rise of civilizations and contrasting ideas was facilitated, as in parts of Europe.[2] Without going into the merits of

Interregional Linkages, ed. by D. Revzan and E. S. Englebert, Berkeley: University of California, 1954, pp. 1–12. This article also appears in E. L. Ullman's *Geography as Spatial Interaction: Studies in Regional Development Cities, and Transportation*, University of Washington Press, 1973. Reprinted by permission of the author and editors.

either explanation, undoubtedly site, situation and other factors are all involved in any total understanding.

In practice the two concepts, site or relation of man to environment, and situation or spatial interaction, are intermingled in application, as Mackinder implied, and probably represent extremes on a continuum. It is important, however, to recognize the two, if for no other reason than that the first concept has received the greatest attention and the second has tended to be ignored. The late recognition and acceptance by geographers of the concept of a functional or nodal region is an illustration.[3]

If the vertical or site type of study has preoccupied most geographical work, this does not mean it is either the more important or more distinctly geographical. Thus Hartshorne approves Hettner's conclusion: "No phenomenon on the earth surface may be considered for itself; it is understandable only through the apprehension of its location with reference to other places on the earth."[4]

Others have explicitly argued for the concept in recent years, although using different terms. In 1932 Whitaker published an eloquent brief paper on regional interdependence.[5] He applied the concept quite properly to both physical and human geography. Because of limitations of space this [work] will deal only with human geography.

In 1949 Platt presented to the A.A.G. a lively argument for the concept and an example, subsequently published, based on Tierra del Fuego.[6] He also noted, optimistically, that geography had already gone beyond the concepts and practices emphasized by Hartshorne's pre-war publication, "The Nature of Geography," which he said should be regarded as a milestone, not a tombstone. Platt also adds quite properly a historical, dynamic dimension to his functional treatment.

Perhaps the strongest plea for a dynamic or kinetic approach, however, was in a paper by P. R. Crowe entitled, "On Progress in Geography" in the *Scottish Geographical Magazine* for 1938.[7] Crowe severely and properly, I believe, criticized geography for not getting very far with a morphological, descriptive approach and suggested that a more fruitful study would be to concentrate on currents and men and things moving rather than on static description of facilities and areas.[8]

In view of the at least implicit recognition given the concept it is surprising how little work has been done with it. Hartshorne notes this and suggests that perhaps the reason why relative location, as he calls it, is largely ignored is because it is inconvenient in a regional treatment constantly to leave a region and more out of it.[9] One answer to this obviously is to focus on the interaction. This alone provides a good excuse for this [work].

The few works which do stress the interaction concept (except for Platt's regional example), unfortunately, give us few clues for making it operational—for measuring interaction, classifying the types, and attempting to erect a theory or system of explanation. This [work] will suggest a system, based on previous examination of new quantitative measures of commodity and other flows. The complexities inherent in the many and different types of interaction will also be noted along with some errors in previous particularistic explanations based on erroneous single factor analysis.

THE BASES FOR INTERACTION

1. Complementarity

It has been asserted that circulation or interaction is a result of areal differentiation; to a degree this is true but mere differentiation does not produce interchange. Numerous different areas in the world have no connections with each other.

In order to have interaction between two areas there must be demand in one and a supply in the other. Thus an automobile industry in one area would use the tires produced in another but not the buggy whips produced in still another. Specific complementarity is required before interchange takes place. Complementarity is thus the first factor in an interaction system, because it makes possible the establishment of transport routes.

So important is complementarity that relatively low-value bulk products move all over the world, utilizing, it is true, relatively cheap water transport for most of the haul. Some cheap products in the distant interior of continents, however, also move long distances. Thus when the steel mills were built in Chicago they required coking coal and reached out as far as West Virginia to get suitable supplies, in spite of the fact that the distance was more than 500 miles by land transport and the coal was relatively low value.

Complementarity is a function both of natural and cultural areal differentiation and of areal differentiation based simply on the operation of economies of scale.[10] One larger plant may be so much more economical than several smaller ones that it can afford to import raw materials and ship finished products great distances, and thus interaction may take place between two apparently similar regions, such as shipment of specialized logging equipment from Washington to forest areas of the south. In this case the similarity in other respects of the two regions provides the market and encourages the interaction. This, however, is insufficient to affect significantly many total interactions because specialized products dominate the total trade of many regions. Thus total shipments from Washington to southern states are low because of the dominance of forest products in each. (Fig. 3-1).

Another example of similarity producing complementarity is provided by the overseas Chinese who furnish a significant market for the mother country's export handicrafts and other products.[11] The same occurs with Italians and other transplanted nationals. Perhaps one could generalize and say that similar cultures but different natural environments tend to promote interchange.

2. Intervening Opportunity

Complementarity, however, generates interchange between two areas only if no intervening, complementary source of supply is available. Thus few forest products moved from the Pacific Northwest to the markets of the interior northeast 60 years ago, primarily because the Great Lakes area provided an intervening course. Florida attracts more amenity migrants from the Northeast than does more distant California. Many fewer people probably go from New Haven to Philadelphia than would be the case if there were no New York City in between as an intervening opportunity. This, presumably, is a manifestation of Stouffer's law of intervening opportunity,[12] a fundamental determinant of spatial interaction, and the second factor proposed for a system of explanation.

Under certain circumstances intervening opportunity might ultimately help to create interaction between distant complementary areas by providing a nearby complementary source which would make construction of transport routes profitable and thus pay for part of the cost of constructing a route to the more distant source. On a small scale this process is followed in building logging railroads; the line is extended bit by bit as timber is cut nearer the mill and ultimately trains are run long distances between mill and supply as the nearby supplies are exhausted. If the line had to be constructed the long distance initially, it might never have been built. On a larger and more complex scale this is what happens in transcontinental railroads—every effort is made to develop way business, and as this business develops it contributes to some

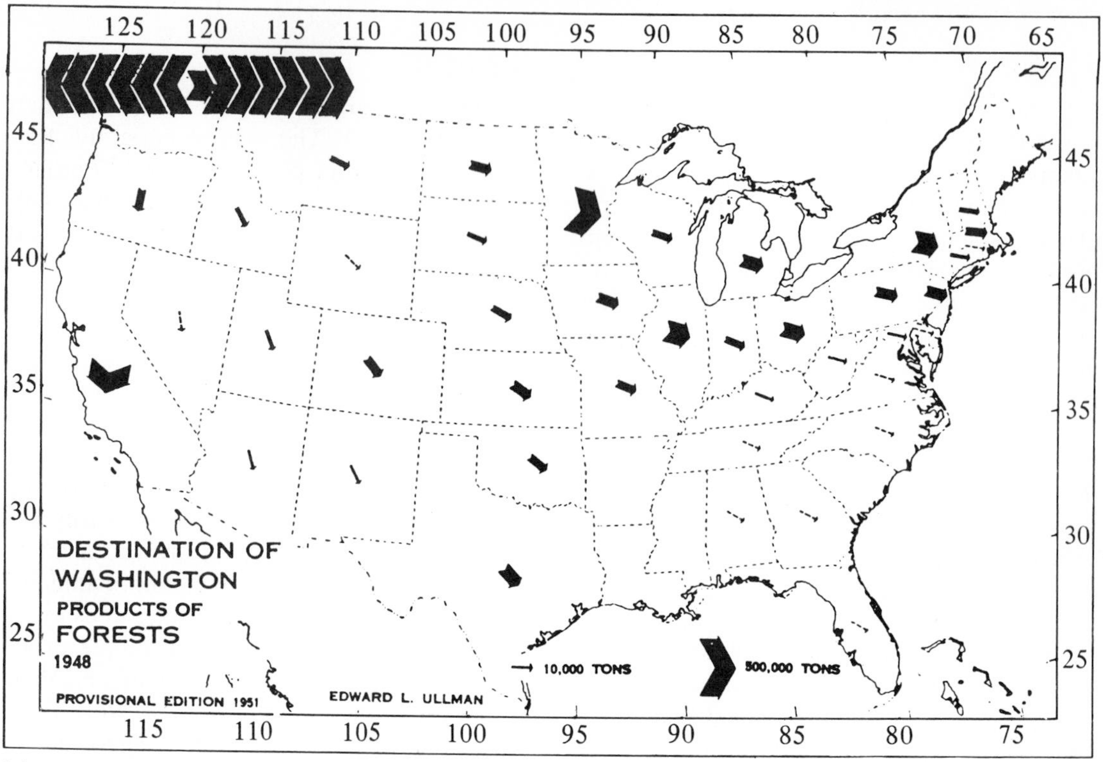
125
120
115
110
105
100
95
90
85
80
75
70
65
45
40
35
30
25
DESTINATION OF
WASHINGTON
PRODUCTS OF
FORESTS
1948
PROVISIONAL EDITION 1951
EDWARD L. ULLMAN
10,000 TONS
500,000 TONS

(a)

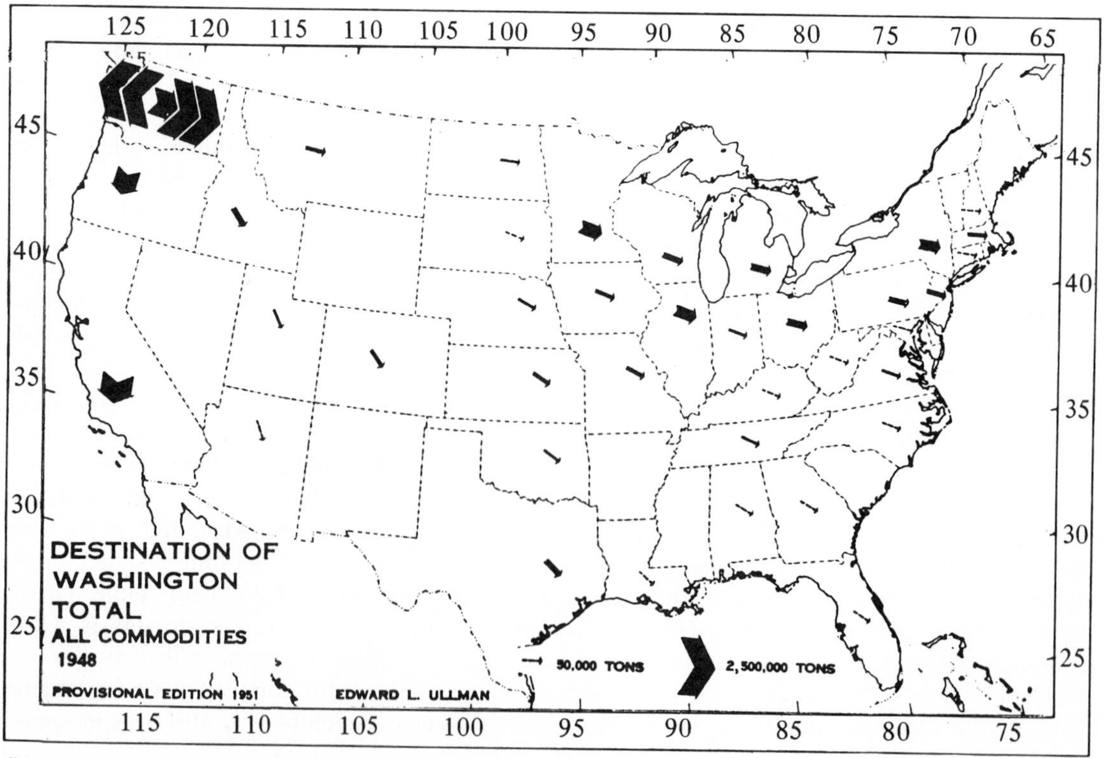
125
120
115
110
105
100
95
90
85
80
75
70
65
45
40
35
30
25
DESTINATION OF
WASHINGTON
TOTAL
ALL COMMODITIES
1948
PROVISIONAL EDITION 1951
EDWARD L. ULLMAN
50,000 TONS
2,500,000 TONS

(b)

of the fixed costs for long distance interchange.

3. Distance

A final factor required in an interaction system is distance, measured in real terms of time and cost.* If the distance between market and supply were too great and too costly to overcome, interaction would not take place in spite of perfect complementarity and lack of intervening opportunity. Thus alternate goods would be substituted where possible; bricks would be used instead of wood, etc.

Thus we might consider [that] the factor of *intervening opportunity* results in a *substitution of areas* and the factor of *distance* results in a *substitution of products.*

It is a mistake, therefore, to assume that all places, even giant commercial centers, are linked equally with other producing areas and centers of the world. Distance and intervening opportunity drastically trim down the relative quantity of such dramatic, long-distance relationships which international trade enthusiasts like to emphasize. Great Britain and the United States provide two contrasting examples. To reach enough complementary sources Britain must trade with the world. The United States, on the other hand, can reach sufficiently complementary areas merely by trading within its own borders to account for the overwhelming bulk of its trade, with much of the remainder coming from Canada and the nearby Caribbean.

Fig. 3-1 ***a.*** Destination, by state, of forest products shipped by rail from Washington, 1948. Width of arrows is proportionate to volume. Arrows within Washington represent intrastate movements. (Tons are short tons of 2,000 pounds.)

b. Destination, by state, of total commodities shipped by rail from Washington, 1948. Note scale of arrows is one-fifth that on Fig. 3-1*a*. (Tons are short tons of 2,000 pounds.)

**Editor's note:* Ullman later used the term *transferability* rather than distance (see p. 5).

To sum up: a system explaining material interaction can be based on three factors: 1) *complementarity*—a function or areal differentiation promoting spatial interaction; 2) *intervening complementarity* (or "opportunities") between two regions or places; 3) *distance,* measured in real terms including cost and time of transport and effect of improvement in facilities.

The system proposed applies primarily to interaction based on physical movement, principally of goods, but also to a large extent for people. It does not apply to spread of ideas or most other types of communication, except as they accompany the flow of goods or people, which admittedly is often the case. Intervening opportunity, for example, would seem to facilitate rather than check the spread of ideas. Similarity of two regions also probably would facilitate the spread of ideas more than difference or complementarity, although the latter would be important for some cases.

An empirical formula often employed to describe many types of interaction is a gravity model which states that interaction between two places is directly proportionate to the product of the populations or some other measures of volume of two places and inversely proportionate to the distance (or distance to some exponent) apart of the two areas. This measure if often written P_1P_2/d (population place[13] times population place[2] divided by d, the distance apart of the two places).

This model, however, is useless in describing many interactions because it assumes perfect or near perfect complementarity, a condition which seldom obtains for physical flows. Some form of the model apparently does come close to describing many interchanges, even for goods in a few cases, but apparently primarily for many more or less universal, undifferentiated types of flow such as migration of some people or telephone calls between cities. It has been developed by Zipf, Stewart, Dodd, and others.[13]

The three-factor system of complementarity, intervening opportunity and distance, however, I believe, will cover any case of material interaction of goods or people. The system should be kept in mind by investigators lest they be led astray by assigning exclusive weight to only one of the factors in attempting to explain past interactions or in predicting potential interaction when underlying conditions change.

TRAFFIC vs. FACILITIES AS GENERATORS OF INTERCHANGE

Examples of erroneous single-factor explanations are numerous. One type concerns the relative role of traffic vs. facilities as promoters of interchange. Thus New York City was the largest port in the United States before the Erie Canal was built, as Albion has shown,[14] and its size, plus some settlement in the West made feasible construction of the Erie Canal just as the opening of the Canal had the effect later of drastically cutting real distance and thus enormously facilitating interchange and the growth of New York. Likewise, the great voyages of discovery were made in large part to tap the growing traffic between the Orient and Europe. Between these two centers were no significant intervening opportunities, although some were discovered as the routes were developed.

A more detailed example is provided by the opening of the St. Gothard Pass across the Swiss Alps in the 13th century.[15] According to an earlier, ingenious interpretation by the German historian Aloya Schulte, in 1900, it was the invention and construction of a suspension, chain bridge along the vertical walls of the Gorges of Schoellenen that opened up this best of all passes and produced a flood of traffic through Switzerland. Thus it was not William Tell who founded the independence of Switzerland but an unknown blacksmith who built the chain bridge which opened Switzerland to the currents of freedom from the south and the trade to support many people. Twenty-five years later careful research by scholars changed this interpretation indicating: 1) that before the hanging bridge was built, the precipitous gorge was actually by-passed without too great difficulty by taking a longer route through Oberalp; 2) hanging bridges of the type noted were in reality common in the Alps by the 13th century; 3) the key bridge was not really the one indicated but rather another farther down, which was built of stone masonry by an unknown mason, requiring much more effort and capital than a mere suspension bridge, and, finally 4) (and most important) this key bridge and the rest of the route was not built until traffic was sufficient to pay for it! The traffic was generated by increased activity in the complementary regions of Flanders and the upper Po Valley, between which were few intervening complementary sources. Thus one must conclude that traffic was equally, if not more, instrumental in creating the route than was provision of the route.

A still different type of erroneous single-factor analysis concerns the role of certain features of the natural environment in promoting or retarding interchange. Mountain ranges, for example, are commonly thought of as barriers to interchange but in many cases their barrier quality may be more than compensated for by the differentiation or complementarity which they produce. Thus climate, in many instances, differs on two sides of a mountain range; this difference may create interchange. More directly the mountains themselves may be so different as to generate interaction, as in the case of transhumance—the moving of animals from lowland winter pastures to mountain summer pastures. Even more important in the modern world is the production of minerals in mountains associated with folding, faulting, uncovering of subsurface deposits by stream erosion, or other factors. The central Appalachians thus provide enormous quantities of coal producing the largest single commodity flow in America. The Colorado Rockies, because of minerals, at one time had a denser network of rail lines than neighboring plains areas, in spite of formidable difficulties of penetration.

POTENTIAL NEW INTERACTION

An example of the second reason for using the system, to predict or understand potential new interaction under changed conditions, is provided by Portland, Maine, and Canada. At the end of the 19th century Portland was known as the winter outlet for Canada because it was the nearest ice-free port. The Grand-Trunk Railroad built a line to the city and extensive docks. Canadian wheat was shipped out in quantity. Then Canada decided to keep the wheat flows within its borders and diverted the trade to the more distant ice-free ocean ports of St. Johns and Halifax in the Maritime Provinces of Canada. Portland declined. Recently two changes have occurred: During World War II a pipeline for gasoline was constructed from Portland to Montreal to save long tanker trips through submarine infested waters and to insure a year-around supply. This gave Portland a shot in the arm and resulted in construction of large tank farms.

The second change can be illustrated by a story. In the summer of 1950, on a Sunday night, I stood on the international border between Derby Line, Vermont, and Rock Island, Quebec, and marveled at the constant stream of cars returning to Canada. I asked the customs inspector the reason, and he replied, "Ninety per cent of the cars are bound for Quebec City and are coming from Old Orchard Beach, Maine." Old Orchard Beach is near Portland and is the nearest ocean port. The Dominion government in this case could hardly force tourists to drive a whole extra day to reach the Maritimes. Thus: (1) Portland's potential complementarity reasserted itself; (2) no intervening opportunity (ocean beach) occurs between Portland and Quebec, and (3) the distance is short enough so that it can be driven in a long weekend trip. Presumably if the distance were much greater residents of Quebec would confine their swimming to the bath tub and use sun lamps. Needless to say, the underlying change permitting both interactions was the invention and development of the automobile, and, in conjunction with the tourist movement, increased leisure and higher standard of living, both fundamental trends, especially in Anglo-America!

A similar example, but one in the nature of a prediction, is the reasonable expectation by Professor Folke Kristensson, of the Stockholm School of Economics, that as living standards rise in Sweden, Swedish diet will change, as the American diet has, and more year-around fresh fruits and vegetables will be consumed. This will result in increased interaction between Sweden and the nearest complementary sources—Italy, Southern France, North Africa, etc., just as occurred between the northeastern United States, Florida and California, a fundamental feature today of the American interaction pattern.

In fact, it is difficult to conceive of any changes, technical, political, social, or economic, which do not have some effect on interaction patterns.

FURTHER CHARACTERISTICS, CONDITIONS AND EFFECTS OF INTERACTION

Once the decision is made to focus on interaction a host of topics and subconcepts present themselves for analysis. Space allows only sample treatment of the following: 1) two characteristics of interaction, direction and length of haul; 2) some conditioning factors, especially type of commodity and political sovereignty; and 3) the effect of increased interaction on areal differentiation.

Direction

Movement along a route is generally unbalanced, a probable result of complementarity because it is unlikely that each of two regions will have exactly what the other wants in like quantity. However, strong forces work to promote a balance for two reasons: (1) to make transportation of many goods and persons more economical by using facilities fully, and (2) to pay for the import.

The second factor may be taken care of by return flows of different types—capital movements, tourist or immigrant remittances, triangular or multilateral trade, gradual shift of population, etc.

The first type, to balance movement in order to make transportation cheaper, often results in establishing low return haul or "ballast" rates. The classical example of this was the export of coal from England to counterbalance imports of bulky raw materials. The coal shipments reached such great proportions that they actually unbalanced the trade in the other direction in the early 20th century.

In other cases a return load may not be obtainable, but compensation is provided in other ways. Many U.S. transcontinental railroads, for example, have rebuilt their lines so that their ruling grades eastbound, the direction of heavy flows representing heavy western raw materials moving to the eastern market, are less than the ruling grades westbound, the light direction.

In ocean shipping, and even land transport, much triangular (or multiangular!) trade is carried on in order to obtain full loads.

In many areas, however, even this is not feasible as in the Olympic Peninsula of Washington where heavy raw materials are shipped out by rail and ship and finished products are brought in by truck. This produces high transport costs per mile.

For many media of interaction the problem does not arise. Pipelines run even better on one-way flows, part of the reason for the low cost of this form of transportation, which already covers more route miles than railroads in the United States, and one of the reasons why industries and population do not move to oil as much as to coal. Communication facilities (radio, telephone, telegraph) work in similar fashion. In fact radio and television provide spectacular examples of overwhelmingly greater cheapness for one-way flow, as witness the few transmitters and the numerous receivers. Nor should it be forgotten that large volume in one direction can itself produce low rates. Coal is an example; tankers, outside of a very few trades, also apparently find it unprofitable either to alter their construction to carry other cargo or to move to other wharves in order to obtain return hauls.

Length of Haul and Break of Bulk

It is a general rule that the longer the haul the less the cost per mile. Thus the effect of distance is not directly proportional to increases. Distant areas characteristically are blanketed in freight rates, the nearer distant point having the same rate as the more distant one. Thus steamship rates from the United States generally are the same to any port in the Havre–Hamburg range. Related to this is the high cost of breaking bulk—unloading or loading, and terminal charges. For both these reasons end points along a flow line, either at raw material or market or at one raw material when two are used, are favored locations for processing, as Hoover and others have noted.[16] This is probably an underlying factor in the higher freight rates on iron ore and coal combined, which the steel industry in the Valley district around Youngstown pays over Cleveland or Pittsburgh, sources, or break of bulk points, for iron ore and coal respectively.[17]

The lower cost per mile of long hauls applies to all forms of transport, but particularly to ocean trade where terminal costs are high. Nevertheless slight increases in distance on long hauls may be reflected in subsequent development. Thus Liverpool and west of England ports concentrate on the Atlantic trade and Eastern ports on the North Sea and Baltic trades.

Under certain special conditions the underlying influence of short distance increases on long hauls is given free play to operate. During World War II American troops were billeted in the west of England; as a result U.S. troops had to take the right flank in the invasion of Europe in order to avoid entangling U.S. supply lines with the British. The final result of the U.S. armies moving across Europe on the right flank, according to Lieut. Gen. Sir Frederick Morgan, was the establishment of the U.S. zone in Germany in the South and the British zone in the North.[18] Thus is seen in operation a peculiar (or "parallel") long distance effect of position but one in accord with logical reasons, once the conditions prevailing are known. Somewhat similar parallel corridors are provided by U.S. transcontinental rail routes which connect Seattle with St. Paul or Los Angeles with Kansas City.

Effect of Type Commodity on Movement

It appears reasonable that low value goods would tend to move shorter distances than high value commodities. To a large degree this is true; thus gold is mined in the mountains of Central New Guinea and flown out; bricks, sand and gravel are rarely shipped long distances. Low value commodities are also charged lower rates per mile to encourage their shipment presumably because they cannot bear the higher costs.[19] Many exceptions exist to this rule, however. If no alternate sources (intervening opportunities) of supply for necessities exist they may move relatively long distances even over land as witness some historic salt trades or even the flow of Pocahontas coal as far east as New England, south to Georgia and west to North Dakota. Furthermore, low value goods that can be handled in bulk can be loaded and unloaded far more cheaply than higher value packaged goods, and thus take advantage of water transportation. Any commodity, to use the Maritime Commission terms, that can be "scooped, dumped, poured, pumped, blown or sucked" has great mobility in many areas. Oil also is piped overland across half of America. And finally, as is well known, transport costs over the oceans are relatively so low that many ores or grain can move around the world by water. Still other types of flows are differentially affected by barriers. High tension lines and natural gas pipelines, for example, can convey energy across mountains relatively easily and cheaply.

Political Sovereignty as a Conditioning Factor

Few influences have been greater in distorting spatial interaction than political control of areas and the consequent channeling of trade and interaction. This is so well known as to need little amplification. However, to drive home the point two extreme examples may be noted: (1) the enormous reach of the Russian Empire in the 19th century following the fur trade across Siberia to Alaska and even down the Pacific Coast as far south as California; (2) the control by Spain of America from California on the North to Argentina on the South from the 17th to the early 19th centuries. Trade with Buenos Aires was allowed only via routes running across the Atlantic from Spain to Panama and then south along the length of the Andes. No wonder that the British found it profitable to smuggle directly into Buenos Aires from the sea!

In both these cases the interaction evolved step by step in a sort of domino fashion until a literally non-viable arrangement was produced, which could not be economically maintained.

Two Other Conditioning Circumstances

Examples of two other conditioning circumstances which time precludes treating are:

1 Temporal characteristics, particular war conditions which will produce quite different interactions from peacetime, as use of air power indicates.

2 Types of milieu within which interaction occurs: intraurban areas with heavy passenger flows, and extraurban areas with heavy commodity flows; ocean realms in which some cultures possess sea skills as in Greece, England or Polynesia and continental realms where some cultures exhibited great overland mobility as the Mongols or Kazaks did for horsemen but not for goods.

Effects of Increased Interaction on Areal Differentiation

A feature of the modern commercial world is the enormously increased flow of goods and peoples facilitated by revolutionary improvements in transportation and communication. The great trade routes of the past were mere trickles compared to today's volume movements.

It is often asserted that this increased transportation and trade has accentuated areal differentiation by allowing areas to specialize on what they can do best. To a great degree this is true, but the more significant effect has been to change the *scale* of areal differentiation. Cheap transportation enables large areas such as the corn belt or wheat belts to specialize; thus they are more sharply differentiated from their neighbors, but within these areas there is less differentiation. On a small scale therefore increased interaction has often tended to produce greater uniformity. This contrasts with conditions prior to modern transportation as shown by von Thunen's famous model of the *Isolierte Staat* with concentric rings of different land uses around a city arising in response to cost of transportation to market. Now transport costs are relatively so low in accessible areas that other characteristics of production and rent paying ability are generally more controlling than transport costs.

A second common notion is that the transportation pattern and rate structure produce an artificial geography which presumably prevents the best sort of areal specialization. To a degree this may be true, but I suggest that a more correct generalization may be that freight rates and provision of transportation tend to accentuate and perpetuate initial areal differentiation. Freight rates in the United States are generally made on a commodity basis; low rates are granted on volume movements which specialization tends to provide. Thus new areas or small producers may find it difficult to compete initially. John Alexander found that the fertile cash grain area of Central Illinois had low rates per mile to principal markets for its main product, corn, but high rates on cattle, whereas rates in the less fertile cattle producing area of Western Illinois were reversed—low on cattle and high on corn.[20] The rate structure thus tended to accentuate and perpetuate areal specialization based on natural conditions.

CONCLUSION

Site and situation concepts and their extension to cover the relation of man to environment and to spatial interaction furnish in broad fashion perhaps the main basis for geographical theory.

This [work] has attempted to provide the beginnings of a system explaining the basis of spatial interaction, a system based on complementarity, intervening opportunity and distance. Perhaps route might be a fourth factor, although it is largely subsumed under distance. Additional generalizations and hypotheses covering important subsystems or topics have also been attempted. These hypotheses, in large part, have grown out of consideration of many new quantitative data, principally mapping of traffic flow and origins and destinations, which space has prevented presenting or discussing in detail. Undoubtedly many of the generalizations can be refined and some may be superseded by others. Still other new ones await discovery and development.

Other disciplines also are increasingly concerning themselves with interaction, although different labels may be attached to it. In economics the term linkages is used, and appears to be a topic of growing interest, especially among regional economists. In international relations, in the field of political science, study of interaction patterns has been called "one of the two basic ways to describe and explain international politics," the other being a decision making approach.[21] In history and other fields the diffusion of ideas and their effects has been treated often, and is considered a major unifying thesis by some.[22]

In sociology interaction is extensively investigated although often defined somewhat more narrowly and specifically than [here]. Some sociologists even define sociology as the study of social interaction; by the same token geography might be defined as spatial interaction.

The purpose of this [work], therefore, has been to try to make explicit that which has only been implicit in most geographical writing. The concept, like everything else, is not new. Focusing research on interaction may well provide a fruitful avenue of advance for many disciplines.

NOTES

1 H. J. Mackinder, "The Physical Basis of Political Geography," *Scottish Geography Magazine,* Vol. 6, 1890, pp. 78–84.

2 Pierre Gourou, "Civilisations et Malchance Geographique," *Annales, Economies, Societes, Civilisations,* October–December 1949, pp. 445–50.

3 Cf. G. W. S. Robinson, "The Geographical Region: Form and Function," *Scottish Geographical Magazine,* Vol. 69, 1953, pp. 49–58, or D. S. Whittlesey, "The Regional Concept and the Regional Method" in *American Geography: Inventory and Prospect,* Syracuse: Syracuse University Press, 1954, pp. 36–44.

4 Richard Hartshorne, *The Nature of Geography,* Lancaster, 1939, p. 283.

5 J. R. Whitaker, "Regional Interdependence," *Journal of Geography,* Vol. 31, 1932, pp. 164–65.

6 R. S. Platt, "Reconnaissance in Dynamic Regional Geography: Tierra del Fuego," *Revista Geografica* (Rio de Janeiro), Vols. V–VIII, 1949, pp. 3–22.

7 P. R. Crowe, "On Progress in Geography," *Scottish Geographical Magazine,* Vol. 54, 1938, pp. 1–19.

8 Elsewhere in the world appreciation of features of the concept is found. Cf. Aldo Sestine, "L'Organizzazione Umana dello Spazio Terrestre," *Revista Geografica Italiana,* LIX, 1952, pp. 73–92.

9 Richard Hartshorne, *op. cit.*

10 Cf. Bertil Ohlin, *Interregional and International Trade,* Cambridge, Mass.: Harvard University Press, 1933.

11 Theodore Herman, *An Analysis of China's Export Handicraft Industries to 1930,* Ph.D. thesis in geography, University of Washington, Seattle, 1954.

12 S. Stouffer, "Intervening Opportunities: A Theory Relating Mobility to Distances," *American Sociological Review,* Vol. 15, 1940, pp. 845–67. (This theory was applied to intracity migration, but the concept, with appropriate modification of detail, is applicable to other interactions, I believe.)

13 Cf. G. K. Zipf, *Human Behavior and the Principle of Least Effort,* Reading, Mass.: Addison-Wesley, 1949; J. Q. Stewart, "Empirical Mathematical Rules Concerning the Distribution and Equilibrium of Population," *Geographical Review,* Vol. 37, 1947, pp. 461–85; S. C. Dodd,

"The Interactance Hypotheses: A Gravity Model Fitting Physical Masses and Human Behavior," *American Sociological Review,* Vol. 15, 1950, pp. 245–56; Joseph A. Cavanaugh, "Formulation. Analysis and Testing of the Interactance Hypotheses." *American Sociological Review,* Vol. 15, 1950, pp. 763–66; and other writings by the same and other authors. It should be noted that interaction in sociology is defined more narrowly than its use [here].

14 R. Albion, *Rise of New York Port,* New York, 1939.

15 Chas. Gilliard, "L'Ouverture du Gothard," *Annales d'Historie Economique et Sociale,* Vol. 1, 1929, pp. 177–82.

16 E. M. Hoover, *The Location of Economic Activity,* New York: McGraw-Hill, 1946.

17 Cf. Allan Rodgers, "The Iron and Steel Industry of the Mahoning and Shenango Valleys," *Economic Geography,* Vol. 28, 1952, pp. 331–42.

18 Sir Frederick Morgan, *Overture to Overload,* Doubleday, Garden City, N.Y., 1950, pp. 113–14 and 247–50.

19 Cf. E. F. Penrose, "The Place of Transport in Economic and Political Geography," *Transport and Communications Review,* Vol. 5, 1952, pp. 1–8.

20 John W. Alexander, "Freight Rates as a Geographic Factor in Illinois," *Economic Geography,* Vol. 20, 1944, pp. 25–30.

21 Karl W. Deutsch, *Political Community at the International Level: Problems of Definition and Measurement* (Foreign Policy Analysis Series No. 2), Princeton University, September 1953. Introduction by Richard C. Snyder.

22 Cf. Gilbert Highet, *The Migration of Ideas,* Oxford University Press, New York, 1954.

Selection 4

Geography—A Discipline in Distance

J. W. Watson

THE IMPORTANCE OF DISTANCE

Distance, as a measurable phenomenon, is basic to the study of geography. When a geographer observes a fact and locates it as part of the earth's scene, he expresses that location as a distance from the prime meridian and the equator. If his observations record other locations, as they probably will, (most phenomena occurring in groups), he will trace out a distribution having breadth, length and depth. His distribution map, then, becomes a measure of the distances reached by objects in their attempt to make or keep a place for themselves on the globe. May this not be the important thing about measuring distance? For the distances reached are an indication of the extent to which objects have adapted themselves to, or dominated, their environment. To me, this has always been a most stimulating fact about geography: its emphasis on distance is an emphasis on *extent.* It provides a record of the extent to which forces, whether inanimate or animate, have shaped the earth and, in doing so, have shaped themselves.

I feel that the idea of geographical extent should be particularly linked with historical period; in fact, that the basis of temporal periodicity could be, and perhaps should be,

Scottish Geographical Magazine, vol. 71, no. 1, 1955, pp. 1–13. Reprinted by permission of the author and editors.

spatial extent. The connection is a fruitful one, wherever it has been tested. In historical geology, for example, many periods are defined by the maximum extent reached by a certain formation. In glaciography we are all familiar with the terms Günz, Mindel, Riss and Würm which describe the maximum extent of the four chief phases of Quaternary ice in Europe. To measure periods by extent has proved universally acceptable in this case.

If with ice, why not with other factors; with even immaterial factors, such as religion? Not a few geographers, notably Griffith Taylor, have used this method in the cultural field with striking results. I suggest that the historians might find it increasingly meaningful. Indeed, they are doing so; for that is one of the outstanding features, if I am not mistaken, of Latourette's recent *History of Christianity*. There he seems to feel that the geographical reach of an idea has frequently been so important as to indicate the main stages in its development and *become normative to its historic description;* certainly he appeals to geography as a measure of the varying success of the Christian Church.

Perhaps one could even go so far as to suggest that the very quality of that faith grew in stature as it grew in extent. There was something significant in the very act of reaching out itself. Geography proved, experientially, what in essence was recognized to be a universal faith. If this conclusion is a valid one, then the use of geographical expansion could well become normative for establishing the great periods of cultural progress. History would become the growth needed to make geography, or, if one preferred it, geography would be the scope required to make history.

THE USE OF DISTANCE

When distance is treated as the extent to which objects adapt themselves to, or dominate, their environment, then it offers valuable clues to their relationship with the environment, a relationship that leads geography on from description to explanation. It is when the geographer plots his description in terms of distance that he has a yardstick to use for explanation. But till then, he is very much in the dark, and is in danger of making false correlations.

To be more specific, let us take the study of the arctic—a characteristic type of country at the polar extremities of the world, made up of a stunted vegetation of lichens and mosses, on permanently frozen soils, where even the summers are cool. Plotting this type of country, the geographer finds several interesting distributions, such as that it extends far further from the poles in the northern hemisphere than it does in the south; in our hemisphere it extends further south on the east side of the continent than it does on the west; its furthest extent is around the shores of Hudson Bay, in Canada.

The large grouping of land masses in the northern hemisphere, and the onset of northeast winds and currents, moving from polar regions, were early recognized as responsible for the major disparities. However, the reach of the arctic to as far south as Akimiski Island, in James Bay, that is, to about 55°N, long went without adequate explanation. It seemed an anomaly, especially when men assumed that Hudson Bay, to the north of this, contained open water even in winter. The anomaly was so great that eventually observations were checked more thoroughly, when it was found that the Bay was, in truth, frozen; the explanation which the facts alone warranted.[1] Here was a case, then, where the explanations led to better geography.

Usually it is better geography which leads to the explanations. Part of our difficulty in trying to make geography a science is that we have unduly limited ourselves in what we consider to be geography, and therefore have come short of really satisfying conclusions. Perhaps this is because most of us have only the time to examine one aspect, and consequently do not appreciate the other sides of our subject. But the plotting of geographical distance leads almost inevitably to correlating it with *all* aspects of distance, and thus a most helpful side of geography is developed. Griffith Taylor has referred to geography as the "correlative" science. For, in its study of the physical and human environment, it learns from and, indeed, comprises part of other disciplines, particularly as it emphasises distances and distributions. To plot these and understand them it is led to explore the other sciences for the distance and bounds with which they are concerned. Since many of these, like astronomy, geology, climatology, pedology and plant ecology, have similar methods, they strengthen the scientific tradition in geography. They have kept geography within physical, determinable limits, and given the subject its interest in the physical environment in all its totality, which is one of its chief glories.

However, that should not restrict geographical research to the physical effects of the environment, or, rather, to the effects of the physical environment. Important though these may be, and they are, they are not enough to explain all the phenomena. Other and greater distances open up. Physical factors may explain the distribution of an area like the arctic sufficiently well, because it is related primarily to other physical, or natural, phenomena, such as the reach of polar air masses, polar ocean currents, etc. The distance to which the arctic has extended is due almost solely to physical factors.

If we had to explain the distances reached by the desert, however, we would come upon a very different story. The deserts are more complex. They can be related to human factors to a much greater extent. The desert scene has reached further than the strictly desert climate. It has extended to where ignorant agriculturists and improvident pastoralists have destroyed the plant and animal life holding back the desert;[2] it has become involved in the human race, in economics, in sociology, in politics, in history. Wasteful economies or systems of social organization have let in the waste, and so enlarged the bounds of the desert. Man has been the deciding factor, not nature.

There are many other cases where man has tipped the natural balance. In another instance, that of the struggle between bog and forest in the Scottish Highlands, I have indicated that man's intervention accounted for the expansion of the one against the other in a not uncertain way, particularly where commercial sheep farming replaced the old economy.[3]

As we learn to measure distance better, therefore, as we try to separate out the distances to which *man* has pushed out a boundary, and add it to the distance which *nature* can account for, we shall provide a better explanation of the facts.

THE HUMAN FACTOR IN DISTANCE

The concentration on man-made distributions in geography must surely be regarded as one of the main advances in the subject during the last half century. It has come to complement the study of natural distributions, and thus alleviated any tendency to overstress sheer physical distance, or, I should say, the physical factor in distance. It has taught us to see distance in human terms, especially in economic terms, as a measure of the success or failure of this or that economy. Distance is not related to land mass, so much as to land-man ratios; it is not set against climate, so much as against the climate of ideas.

May I go back to Canada again for an example vastly different from that of the arctic. It concerns itself with the distribution of the Niagara fruit belt, a small but not unimportant region of southern Ontario. Having expanded the maximum distance which temperature and topography would allow, it is now shrinking in size, its margins are retreating and it is threatened with probable extinction. We can imagine that an observer at a hundred years' remove, looking back on its disappearance, might be inclined to think that the climate had turned cooler. Peach cultivation is insecure where the July temperature falls below an average of 70°, or where winter minima are less than −15° F. It would only take a fall of two degrees to plunge the Niagara climate below these critical limits and thus endanger the peach-growing economy.

Our postulated observer would be puzzled to find, however, that the climate had warmed up, if anything, and not grown cooler. That is the present trend.[4] He might have wondered, then, how the orchards had dwindled and died out; that is, unless he had been observant enough to read the climate of the mind. Then he would have seen that, over a generation or two, the fruit farmers had struggled, not against isotherms, but against urbanization, and against the urban mentality which subordinated all uses of land to the business or convenience, the profit or pleasure of the Niagara cities. As I have indicated elsewhere, "Many orchard growers have given up farming and sold out to urban interests in Hamilton or St. Catharines because they have got the idea that the complete invasion of the fruit belt is inevitable. Once a substantial number think that way, then the whole climate of opinion may alter, and we may say goodbye to the fruit belt with as much finality as if a new glacial age were advancing on us."[5]

Many geographers have shown how and to what extent climate has affected the distribution of plant and animal life, together with that of man and his works; I have yet to discover a systematic treatment of what the mental climate has done along these lines. Yet I am convinced that the mental climate is, in many cases, as important, if not more so, than the physical one, leading to the destruction of certain plants or animals and the preservation of others, over quite large areas, chiefly for reasons of human taste. Until we get maps of isothoughts, if I may be allowed to coin the word, as well as isotherms, that is, maps of the bounds of certain types of thinking, we cannot explain the distributions of plants and animals. Too often agricultural belts are taken to be matters of temperature rather than temperament; yet if temperament were to be studied geographically, it could be shown to have much to do with the taste for, and therefore the distribution of, certain crops and animals.

For example, the widespread use of reindeer in northern Europe and Asia led people to conclude that they would be as widely used in North America, if introduced. But the temperament of the Canadian Eskimos is against herding, as many observers have noticed, and so only an insignificant number of reindeer have been bred and domiciled in the Canadian arctic.

As geographers explore the avenues of what man has done, they see him introduce factors of distance, or even types of distance, that have less and less to do with physical causes, and more and more to do with economic and social ones. Consequently, geographers have been led from the physical to the social sciences.

THE SIGNIFICANCE OF COST DISTANCE

For instance, in studying roads and railways they have had to qualify "geographical" distances by "cost" distances. As communications became more important in human affairs and, indeed, took on a vital rôle, cost distance came to exert a preponderant influence in human geography, particularly in the distribution of economics and social and political systems. The much reduced cost of contacting the riches of the East by sea, instead of by overland caravan routes, helped in a substantial way to reorientate Europe to the Atlantic. In fact, cost would probably have instigated, in any event, what the Turks are usually credited with having done, namely, started the westward course of Empire among Europe's more aggressive nations. Even had the Turks not cut the caravan route to the East, cost would have done so, once the seaways of the world came into full competition with the landways.

I think it would be a fascinating exercise to trace the effects of cost distance upon the rise and expansion, growth or fall of nations, or at any rate of nations as geographical entities. However, I must admit to being less familiar with these larger fields than with the field of the city. Here it was shown, thirty years ago, that the economic competition for space was one of the chief causes, if not the principal one, of the location, function and form of the city. It should be added that the idea was American, and applies mainly to America. It has yet to be worked out for the cities of the Old World, although it is possibly true enough of our great commercial and industrial settlements.

The argument is, in brief, that the city grew up at, or at least centered itself in, the cost center of its region. It maintained itself by maintaining that center as the point of lowest cost access to the highest profit area, in terms of the particular raw materials, markets, skills and services at its command. It thus came to create a spatial pattern which was the reflection of its economic order. Burgess suggested that that was essentially a zonal pattern, the zones of urban development coinciding with zones of increasing or decreasing cost.

The nucleus of every city was the point for which there was greatest competition, it being the point of lowest cost access to all the varied demands of the region. It was by no means the geographical center, either of the city itself, or of the region. Factors other than mere geographical distance came into play. The geographical center, the point of easiest linear access to the city and region, might be displaced by political boundaries, by the system of land survey, by the vagaries of land speculation, and by other unique factors, each of which could raise its cost and so lower its value as an economic center.

Thus, the centering of cities and the development of urban zones were essentially economic. This is an important point in the Burgess theory of urban growth, especially so, if interpreted in terms of cost distance. The theory has been generally ignored or criticized by geographers because it never seemed to accord with the azonal, irregular pattern typical of most settlements. Usually the actual, geographical form is anything but zonal. It may assume a stellar form, or be quite unique. In a city which I long studied, Hamilton, Ontario, a most irregular pattern obtained. In the east the working-class residential area stretched out further from the city center than one of the best residential areas in the south. On the face of it, this was anything but the concentric arrangement of zones postulated by Burgess. However, close observation showed that the working-class district, nearly two miles to the east, was much less costly to reach, particularly during the days of city expansion, than the first-class area, about half a mile away. The latter district was along the slope of a steep escarpment beyond the city trams and was therefore almost exclusively the purlieu of those who could afford a carriage and pair. Even after [street cars] entered the district, most people used their own conveyances; and in any case, by then, the area had become a high cost region to live in for other reasons—land was dear to buy, houses were heavily taxed, and so on. Thus, a person living at "X" in the first-class district was actually thrice as remote from the city center as another living at "Y" in the working-class zone, though twice as near in terms of geographical distance. Consequently, X lived in the outermost cost zone, and in this respect, was like residents of commuter suburbs on the edge of the country. (See Fig. 4-1.)

Of course, it might be argued, in this case, that cost distance was but a reflection of the topography: it went back to physical geography. The areas of highest cost lay along the slope of the escarpment, which was the area of least access. This is true enough. However, the significant thing is not the slope itself, but the amount of work needed to climb the slope, or, more important still, the work entailed in maintaining oneself, one's house, garden, car, one's share of road, sewage etc., upon this slope.

Cost distance is much more than a matter of slope. In fact, it is a good deal closer to a people's psychology of slope than to slope itself. For some reason a slope with a commanding view is sought for, indeed, fiercely competed for, in a Canadian city. From what I have observed of Rio de Janeiro, where some of the worst slums are up on the hills, this is not the attitude of all people. But since it is the ruling attitude in Hamilton, it has its cost.

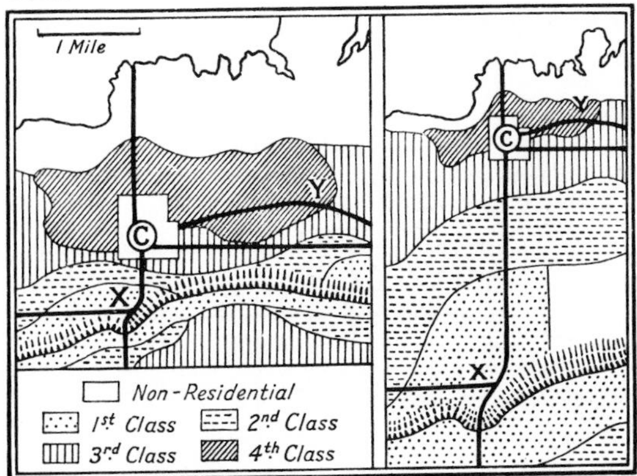

Fig. 4-1 A comparison of physical and cost distance and shape, Hamilton, Ont. The physical elongation of the city is east-west; the cost elongation, north-south.

To go back to our example, if we assumed that the steepening of the slope lengthened the distance in, i.e., increased the work of, reaching the homes on the escarpment by two or even three times, compared with those on the plain below, we still would not have explained why the costs of lots were six to seven times higher, or taxes were nine to ten times as great! Economic and social factors have increased the cost of living on the escarpment *out of all proportion to the physical distances involved.* They have thus created something new, a new environment, a new geography: cost geography.

Geographers have become so familiar with the physical shapes of cities, or countries, that they have often found it difficult to appreciate the *cost shape*. Yet the cost shape may be the *real* shape of a place in terms of daily living, or at least of many of the most important living considerations. Chauncey Harris has made a beginning of his study of the economic proportions of the United States, and has drawn a series of maps showing the size of each state as a measure of its economy. The economic size is something very different from the actual one.[6] But the states must vary equally as much in cost *shape*. Thus, thanks to the dominance of east-west routes in North America, most states must be much narrower along their east-west axis in terms of cost distance, than along their north-south one, whatever the actual distance may be.

An aspect of cost distance is *time* distance. Generally low wage earners cannot afford the time to be far distant from their place of work, as compared with professional and business men. This is a main factor in distinguishing the rooming-class zone from the commuter zone. But in the commuter zone, there may be fierce competition between places on the basis of time distance. In this connection, a recent study of time and distance around Edinburgh . . . showed that some sites were much closer in time to the city than neighbouring ones and that, in certain cases, towns or villages physically nearer to Edinburgh were nevertheless more remote on a time-distance basis than their competitors.[7] Obviously, then, isochronous belts have little to do with geographical equidistance, but create distributions of their own, which are the really valid ones in explaining the distribution of the commuter population.

Perhaps that is enough to indicate that the geographer's measurement of distance, and that his study of resultant distributions, must be qualified by the cost factor, wherever man is concerned. In many circumstances his distributions are much more likely to result from cost considerations than anything else.

THE SIGNIFICANCE OF SOCIAL DISTANCE

However, he should realize that just as there are economic distances which have little to do with physical ones, so there are social distances which have little to do with economic ones. There *are* anomalies in the cost-zonation of cities which are difficult to explain except by social barriers. Thus, whereas by all the laws of economics, residential areas near to an expanding urban center, should give way to commercial uses of land, or at least to a transition zone where residential and commercial uses interpenetrate each other, purely social forces may arise resisting such a change, and compelling change to go in other directions. Social barriers of this kind may be immense. And they may be very real: just as real in fact as the barriers of cost, or as physical divides. Indeed, in most highly developed regions, human watersheds are just as significant to a geographer's distributions, channeling the flow of ideas, interests, associations, customs and activities now to one side of them and now to the other, as natural watersheds. I have said in another connection, that geographers should concern themselves with the social Himalayas of the world as much as with the physical ones.

Let me refer again to Hamilton, if I may. A study was initiated there . . . of "work force" in relation to "work place." In one case the workers of a certain textile plant, placed towards the west of the city, were found to live mainly in its central or eastern parts. (See Fig. 4-2*a*.) The plant was divided from the west end of the city by a fairly deep and wide ravine, which was taken to be reason enough for the very asymmetric distribution of the work force. However, a bridge had been built across this ravine more than thirty years ago, and it was *physically* as convenient to live

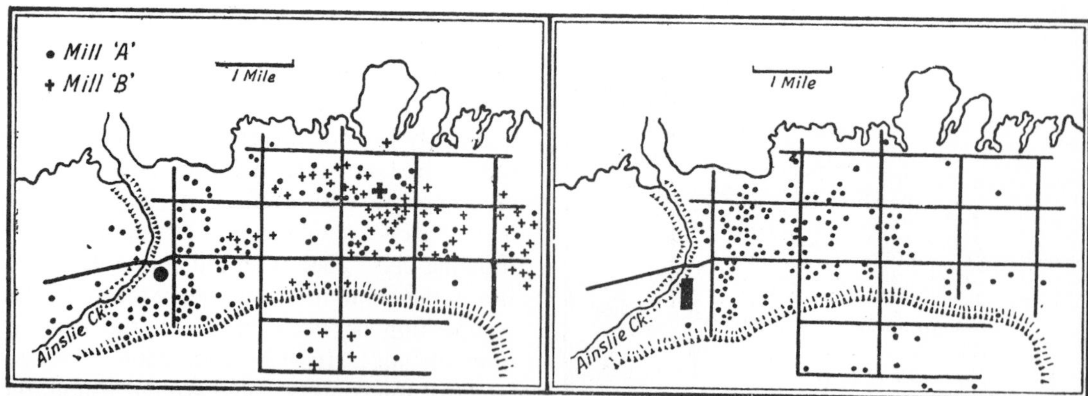

Figs. 4-2*a*, 4-2*b* Work-place and work-folk in Hamilton, Ont. Note how the workers of Mill A, Fig. 4-2*a*, and of the Frid-Chatham industrial area, Fig. 4-2*b*, live in the main well to the east of their place of work. This is due to social geography rather than to the supposed barrier of Ainslie Creek.

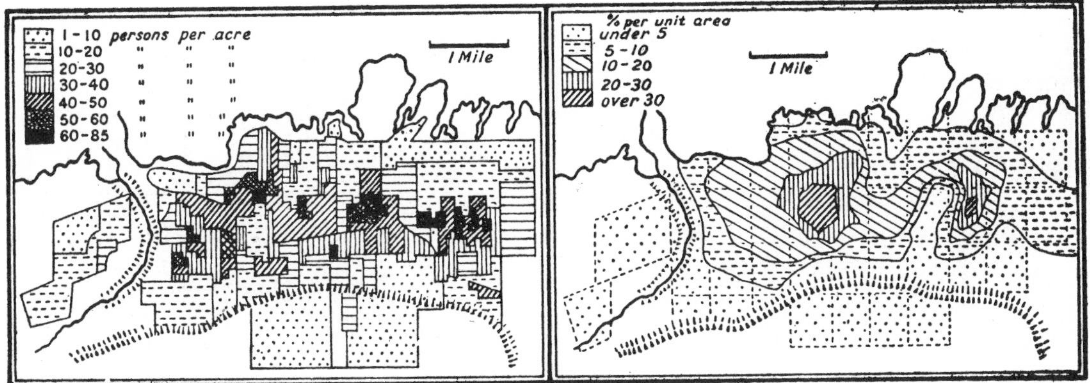

Figs. 4-3*a*, 4-3*b* Population densities and social hazards in Hamilton, Ont. The chief densities and hazards are to be found in transitional areas around the center and eastern subcenter of the city. Note how free the west and south are of population pressure and social disintegration. Major social hazards used in plotting the map were marital discord, child neglect, juvenile delinquency, theft, drunkenness.

west of it as east of it. In the last thirty years a good number of workers might have been expected to have located in the west, yet they had not done so. The *cost factor* was thus called upon to explain the situation. There was no [street car] west of the bridge in the early days of the city's westward expansion, and this may have made it costly for workers to have lived in the west. But the [street car] soon went in and it is now as cheap to reach the plant from the west as from the east. Indeed, it can be reached at half the cost in *time*. Nevertheless, few workers have taken up residence in the west.

More recently a whole new industrial area has grown up within the bottom of the ravine. (See Fig. 4-2*b*.) It is physically as convenient and financially as cheap for people to reach the bottomlands from the western edge of the ravine as from the eastern, yet virtually no workers, employed at these plants, come from the western bank. They have preferred living in the east of the city, although, as I have shown elsewhere, that is overcrowded and, in many parts, socially unstable.[8] (See Figs. 4-3*a* and 4-3*b*.)

It is only when we invoke the factor of social distance that we can explain this otherwise extraordinary distribution of the work force. For the fact is, the western district was opened up by, and is now composed almost entirely of, business and professional men; it consists of Canadian-born residents, most of whom are of British extraction; it contains the university, and most of its families send their children to college; many of them patronize private schools; they are expected to support charities on a substantial scale, and in many other ways, to take a lead in community affairs (Figs. 4-4*a*, 4-4*b*). They are socially remote from the workers in the nearby factories who are, for the most part, unskilled or only semi-skilled personnel, who include a substantial number of foreign-born residents, mostly of Continental European extraction, and who are far from a position to support charities. On the contrary, their position tempts them to be interested in fraternities, co-operatives and credit unions. (See Figs. 4-5*a*, 4-5*b*.) *These* are the facts, not the ravine, which account for the peculiar distribution of the work force.

All this will indicate, no doubt, that there is still room for research on the geographical effects of social distance. This is the force that in so many cases has the decisive and last say

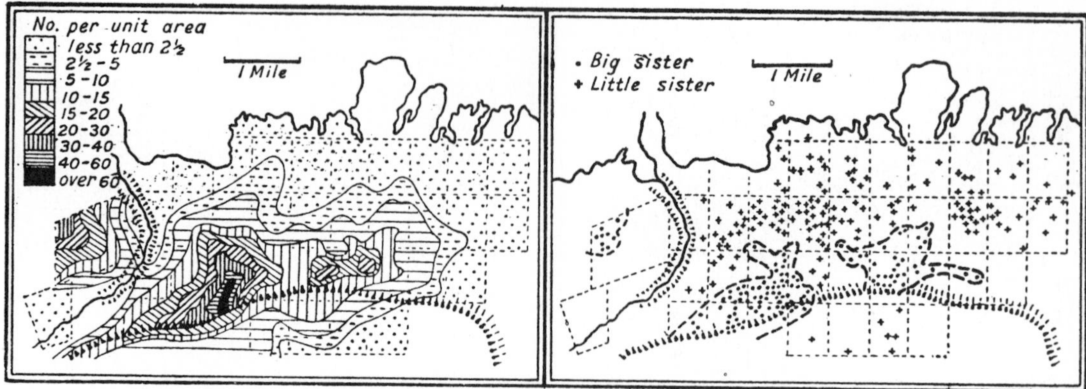

Figs. 4-4*a*, 4-4*b* The people of the western and southern suburbs of Hamilton, Ont., are the chief supporters of private school and university, and take a lead in charities. Fig. 4-4*a* shows the number of people per unit area (4 city blocks square) sending children to private schools and college. Fig. 4-4*b* shows the distribution of Big Sisters, women of means who sponsor and look after Little Sisters, girl delinquents.

in the geographical distributions in which we are most interested; in the distributions of frontiers, cultures, settlements, trade, industry, and population.

Sir Arthur Keith once implied as much in his study of race where he suggested that the early differentiation of racial stock was due, not so much to mountains and climate, as to strong in-group attachments, amounting in many cases to a sense of social superiority, that raised well-nigh impassable barriers to racial admixture.[9] One compares this with the work of Grafton Elliot Smith in which he postulated the movement of ice caps, and also the oscillating effects of mountain ridges, as the separating agents.[10] But it is possible that

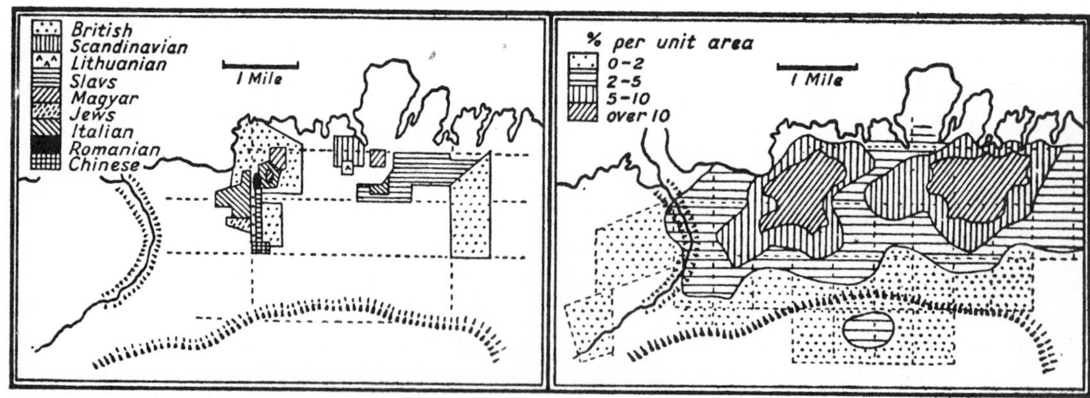

Figs. 4-5*a*, 4-5*b* The northern-central and eastern parts of Hamilton, Ont., close to the commercial and industrial regions of the city, are crowded with immigrants. Ethnic societies, working-class fraternal associations, co-operative and credit unions are principal social organizations. Fig. 4-5*a* shows the distribution of the chief foreign-born elements in Hamilton's population; 4-5*b* the percentage of the total population per unit area (4 city blocks square) interested in co-operatives.

he got the racial cart before the psychological horse. It may well have been the powerful effect of social distance that first separated races from each other and *made them retreat to, or stay within, the shelter of ice-rimmed basins*. This is something still unsettled and therefore worthwhile investigating: where, and to what extent, and in what ways has social distance created the principal distributions between races, between economics, between nations, between cities and between neighborhoods? At all levels of investigation the question needs to be asked, and the answers mapped, systematized, and explained.

SUMMARY

To sum up, then: in attempting to describe the earth as it is, the geographer sees two great categories of scenes; those which result largely, if not altogether, from physical forces; and those which derive from human activities, particularly from economic functions and social behavior. Beginning to measure the earth in terms of geographical distances, he is led on to the consideration of economic and social ones. In doing so he becomes more aware of the total number of factors at play in creating his spatial patterns and he is able to give a better, more comprehensive, explanation of the facts. Also, in doing so, he assumes his classic rôle of linking the physical sciences with the social sciences in what is truly a science of the earth. And finally, in doing so, he realizes again how, and how much, geography has become the measure of man, measuring the reach of his success or the degree of his failure as man has struggled to extend his ideas, his ways, his numbers and his control over the world around him.

To my way of thinking this is what makes geography worthy of inclusion in the circle of higher learning. By its very nature, it impinges upon, and gathers from, so many modes of thought. Thus it is all but bound to assist a person in gaining a fuller and sounder view of the earth and man.

I say "by its very nature" because, as this [work] will have indicated, geography cannot stop at anything short of the whole of man in relation to all the earth. It is impossible to stop, for example, at the description of the physical environment, because physical distances make us most aware of their own shortcomings, and lead beyond the mere mathematics of latitude and longitude, or the geology of rocks and relief, the physics of the atmosphere, the chemistry of soil and the biology of plants and animals to those vast and shining vistas of man's intervention, endeavor and will. Here the geographer views the full impact of the human economy as it has stripped off forests, ploughed up grassland, laid waste the green and lovely earth or made the desert blossom as the rose. Emblazoned on almost every hill, and stamped into almost every valley, is the sign that man has made, and is constantly making, his own geography. And so the geographer must go on to those ultimate distances, traced out in history and expressed in society, where the people, in their hamlets, cities, and nations, through their customs, idiosyncrasies, and aspirations, indeed in all the manifestations of their being, change and master the earth, to make of it but the imprint of their own purposes and soul. Geographical distances are, in the last resort, the distances of the human spirit itself.

Seen in this way geography might be said to have increasing value in a world that all too often and all too much has lost the world view: in a world that will not admit the full distance to which the world reality itself is carrying us. Everyone knows that the social forces at work in the world, and the world economy, are such as to draw us, willy-nilly, into ever closer relationships. Yet at the same time people do not prepare themselves, or what is perhaps more important, see to it that the schools and universities prepare their children, to try to understand and appraise this new world order.

If geography can help, as I believe it can, in integrating and coordinating facts learned from the whole range of scholarship, and if in doing so, it can assist us to see the world as it really is, and to see the world in its entirety, then I believe it will have earned for itself a rightful place among the highest disciplines of the mind.

NOTES

1 Hare, F. K., and Montgomery, M. Ice, Open Water and Winter Climate in the Eastern Arctic of N. America. Pt. 1. *Arctic,* 1949, Vol. 2(*2*): 78–89. Montgomery, M. Does the Bay Freeze? *The Beaver,* June 1951, No. 282:12–15.

2 Musset, M. Les Resources Végétales du Sahara. *Annales de Géographie,* 1933, No. 240: 651–55.

3 Watson, J. W. Forest or Bog: Man the Deciding Factor. A Study of the Vegetation of the Districts of Lorn, Mid-Argyll, Knapdale and Kintyre in Argyllshire. *S.G.M.,* 1939, 55(3): 148–161.

4 Ahlmann, H. W. *Glacier Variations and Climatic Fluctuations.* New York: American Geographical Society, 1953. Pp. 1–51.

5 Watson, J. W. Basic Problems of Regional Planning in Canada. *Community Planning Review,* 1954: 488–92.

6 Harris, C. D. *A Manufacturing View of the United States,* University of Chicago, Dept. of Geography publication, 1954.

7 Macgregor, D. R., Daily Travel: A Study in Time and Distance around Edinburgh, *S.G.M.,* 1953, 69(*3*): 117–127.

8 Watson, J. W., Hamilton and its Environs. *Canadian Geographical Journal,* May 1945.

9 Keith, A., *Ethnos, or the Problem of Race considered from a New Point of View.* London: Routledge, 1931.

10 Smith, G. E. *Human History.* London: Jonathan Cape Ltd., 1930.

FURTHER READINGS TO PART ONE

At the time of publication there are only two general texts on transportation in English.

J. E. Becht, *A Geography of Transportation and Business Logistics,* Dubuque, Iowa: Wm. C. Brown, 1970.

E. J. Taaffe and H. L. Gauthier, Jr., *Geography of Transportation,* Englewood Cliffs, N.J.: Prentice-Hall, 1973.

Both are paperbacks, the former not particularly satisfactory from any standpoint; the latter follows the Northwestern tradition and is an excellent text to read in conjunction with Parts One to Five of this book. Those who want an alternative to the Northwestern approach, and who can read French, German, or Russian; can turn to:

R. Capot-Rey, *Geographie de la circulation sur les continents,* Paris: Gallimard, 1946.

R. Clozier, *Geographie de la circulation,* Paris: Genin, 1963.

J. Labasse, *L'organisation de l'espace: Elements de geographie volontaire,* Paris: Hermann, 1966, especially chapter 3, pp. 119–176.

I. V. Nikolsky, *Geografia Transporta,* Moscow: State Publications in Geography, 1960.

E. Ottremba, *Allgemeine Geographie des Welthandels und des Weltver-*

kehrs, Stuttgart: Franckh'sche Verlagshandlung, W. Keller and Co., 1957.

Reading fundamental to the role of transportation in the landscape will be found in:

W. Bunge, *Theoretical Geography,* Lund Studies in Geography, (2d. ed.), Series C, No. 1, C. W. K. Gleerup, Ltd., Lund, 1966, especially chapters 5, 8 and 9.

P. R. Crowe, "On Progress in Geography," *Scottish Geographical Magazine,* vol. 54, 1938, pp. 1–19.

B. B. Gorizontov and S. S. Tsenin, "Problems in the Geography of Economic-transport Links of the World Socialist System," *Soviet Geography,* vol. 6, no. 1, 1965, pp. 25–29.

E. F. Penrose, "The Place of Transport in Economic and Political Geography," *Transport and Communications Review,* vol. 5, 1952, pp. 1–8.

E. J. Taaffe, "The Transportation Network and the Changing American Landscape," in S. B. Cohen (ed.), *Problems and Trends in American Geography,* New York: Basic Books, 1967, chap. 2, pp. 15–25.

Of a rather different order, but very apposite to these general considerations are:

W. L. Garrison, B. J. L. Berry, D. F. Marble, J. D. Nystuen, and R. L. Morrill, *Studies of Highway Development and Geographic Change,* Seattle: University of Washington Press, 1959.

J. Mercier, "La revolution des transports et les transports," *Revue Economique,* vol. 4, 1960, pp. 609–35.

E. L. Ullman, "The Role of Transportation and the Basis for Interaction" in W. L. Thomas (ed.), *Man's Role in Changing the Face of the Earth,* Chicago: University of Chicago Press, 1956, pp. 862–880.

R. I. Wolfe, *Transportation and Politics,* Princeton, N.J.: Van Nostrand, 1963.

The Northwestern approach is set out in:

W. L. Garrison and D. F. Marble, *A Prolegomenon to the Forecasting of Transportation Development,* Research Report, Transportation Center, Northwestern University, 1965.

To gain some idea of the diversity of the transportation concept in contemporary American society, the following set of readings will be very useful:

M. T. Farris and P. T. McElhiney, *Modern Transportation: Selected Readings,* Boston: Houghton Mifflin, 1967.

Reviews of the state of the "art" in the last twenty years can be explored through:

B. J. L. Berry, "Recent Studies Concerning the Role of Transportation in the Space Economy," *Annals* of the Association of American Geographers, vol. 49, 1959, pp. 328–342.

P. O. Muller, "Recent Developments in the Spatial Analysis of Transportation," *The Pennsylvania Geographer,* vol. IX, no. 4, December 1971, pp. 14–17.

E. J. Taaffe, "Some Recent Books in Transportation," *Annals* of the Association of American Geographers, vol. 47, 1957, pp. 100–103.

B. Thomas, "Methods and Objectives in Transportation Geography," *Professional Geographer,* vol. 8, 1956, pp. 2–5.

E. L. Ullman and H. M. Mayer, "Transportation Geography" in P. E. James and C. L. Jones (eds.), *American Geography: Inventory and Prospect,* Syracuse, N.Y.: Syracuse University Press, 1954, chap. 13, pp. 310–332.

J. E. Wheeler, "An Overview of Research in Transportation Geography," *East Lakes Geographer,* vol. 7, December 1971, pp. 3–12.

In addition, there are a number of bibliographic sources which are useful when dealing with topics in transportation geography, including:

W. R. Black and F. E. Horton, "A Bibliography of Selected Research on Networks and Urban Transportation Relevant to Current Transportation Geography Research," Northwestern University, Department of Geography, Research Report No. 28, 1969.

Northwestern University, *Sources of Information on Transportation,* Evanston, Ill.: Transportation Center/Northwestern University Press, 1964.

W. R. Siddall, "Transportation Geography: A Bibliography" (3d ed.), Manhattan, Kan.: Kansas State University Library, Bibliography Series No. 1, 1969.

R. I. Wolfe and B. Hickok, "An Annotated Bibliography of the Geography of Transportation," Berkeley, Calif.: Institute of Transportation and Traffic Engineering, University of California, Information Circular No. 29, 1961.

Serials, with regular or irregular publication:

Institute of Transportation and Traffic Engineering, University of California, Berkeley, *Library References* (irregular).

Transportation Center Library, Northwestern University, *Current Literature in Traffic and Transportation* (monthly).

Other more specialized sources exist, some of which are noted in later sections.

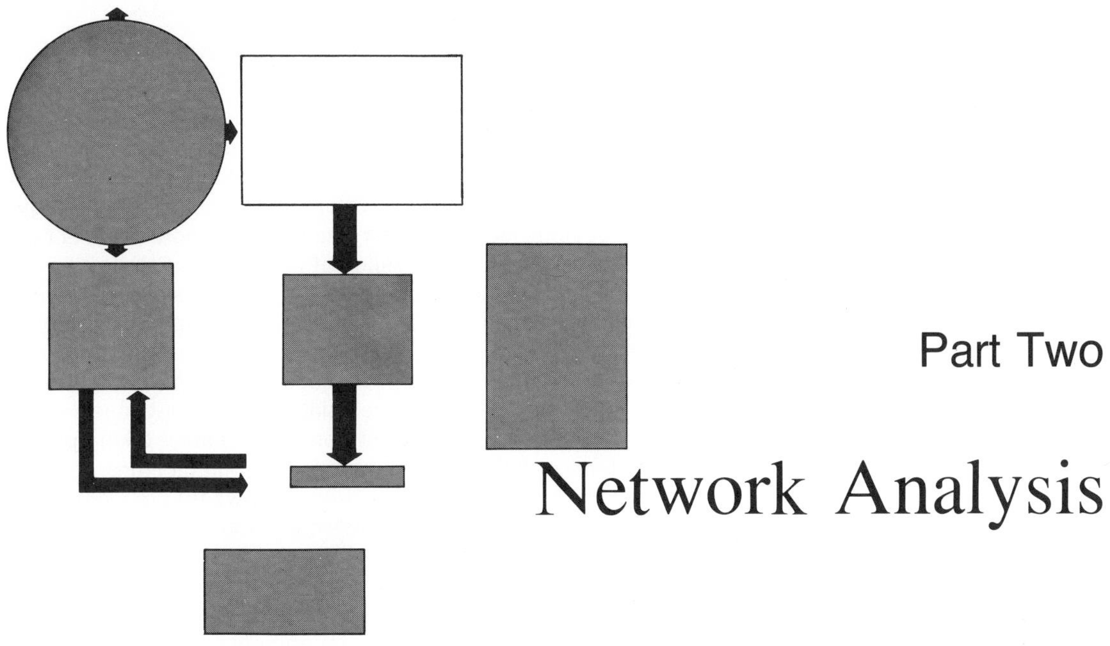

Part Two

Network Analysis

INTRODUCTION

Referring back to Fig. 1-2 (p. 8), if we assume that we now have some knowledge of movement as such taking place, based on what the four selections of Part One have indicated, we can now turn our attention to the components of boxes 2 and 5—stocks, networks, flows, and modes.

Part One has set the stage; movement takes place between points of demand and supply, desire and fulfillment. Briefly we can move on to a consideration of the stocks needed to fulfill that demand and supply. One might list aggregate measures of the transportation of a region or country, as say:

Number of automobiles	Cost of transportation
Miles of road	Number of workers
Miles of railroad	Fuel used in transportation
Ton miles hauled	Number of trucks
Number of railroad cars	Transportation industry profits

And this list is also somewhat less than all-inclusive.* If we reflect back to the

*This account is taken from W. L. Garrison and D. Marble, *A Prolegomenon to the Forecasting of Transportation Development*, Research Report, Transportation Center, Northwestern University, 1965, pp. 21–36. See also the first section of suggested further readings at the conclusion of this part.

list of factors presented earlier (p. 7), we could posit a relationship between the two—i.e., the amount of transportation stocks is related to such factors as the general level of economic development, available technology, cost structures, and societal decisions. As Taaffe et al. show in Selection 22, the amount of one transport stock, miles of highway, in Ghana and Nigeria is related to two basic factors—population and area—with varying relationships to other factors, such as the economic development of a particular region within the two countries, as well as to certain physical factors like swamps and escarpments.† For our purposes, however, we will also take this stock inventory as a given, since relatively little published work exists. We can assume therefore that in addition to movement taking place, a given area has a stock or inventory of fixed and mobile facilities, relative to societal, political, and economic factors, which allows that movement to occur. Given this, then, what sorts of network systems do these facilities pass through? What are the characteristics of route location, the location of intersections and terminals, density and length of routes, accessibility or connectivity of the network? The answers to these questions must convey some notion of the spatial or geometrical arrangement of routes, intersections, and nodes on the earth's surface.

Much attention has been given in geographic and economic literature to the indirect implications of network structure, particularly through the concept of *accessibility.*‡ The theories of location commonly used in these disciplines contain implicit and explicit notions of varying accessibility and relative location, ranging from Von Thunen's model to Christaller's central places in a hierarchy of service areas. Most of these usages depend on measures like physical distance, cost, and time, which, though valuable for cer-

†These factors are also dealt with in more detail in M. E. Eliot Hurst, *A Geography of Economic Behaviour,* North Scituate, Mass.: Duxbury Press, 1972, chap. 13, pp. 267–270.

‡See especially W. Isard, *Location and Space Economy,* Cambridge, Mass.: MIT Press, 1956, chap. 2.

Schematic Representation of Transport Systems

FUNCTION	Nature: **Imaginary**	Nature: **Object**	
Intangible	Radio Television	Telephone cable systems	Messages/ information transported
Tangible	Airlines Steamer route	Railway Highway	Goods/people transported
	Network has no virtual existence, independent of transport	Network exists independently of unit of transport	

Source: From an idea by B. Turnbull

tain analyses, do not allow us to compare and evaluate one regional network with another modal network in that same region or another one. Another associated problem is the variability of the networks themselves, which makes comparisons very difficult. The table on page 54, "Schematic Representation of Transport Systems," illustrates the double dichotomy of function and nature, in which networks appear as either "object" or "imaginary," tangible or intangible. What is needed is some method by which we can analyze the common characteristics of all these modal networks. In fact, methods have now appeared which allow us to make general assessments of transport systems regardless of the model type or region. Such assessments deal with the geometrical properties of transport networks.

No matter what type of system is studied (the range of the table), common geometrical properties can be analyzed, such as (1) origins or nodes, (2) routes or links, and (3) destinations or nodes, (or more simply, nodes and routes [diagram on page 56]). Networks are structures designed to tie together nodes via routes, whether they be flows of people, goods, money, information, or anything else that is moved from one place to another. A transport network is then "a set of geographic locations interconnected in a system by a number of routes."§ The geometric structure of a transport network is the *topological* pattern formed by those elements, the nodes and the routes.‖

This work on the geometric properties of networks has two main thrusts: (1) to ascertain what measures will describe the structure of the transport networks and (2) to ascertain how these measures are related to the characteristics of the area in which the transport networks are situated. Arising from these two main research areas have been attempts to simulate networks—that is, given some information about the nature and development of an area, can the network(s) be replicated?#

In order to describe, analyze, compare, and replicate network systems, a method of accurate and consistent measurement is needed. To this end, networks have been approximated by the use of *graph theory,* a branch of topology.** Such graphs allow us to look at entire transport networks, and their parts, in terms of the whole. More specifically, graph theoretic methods have been used to translate observed relationships of networks into numerical and symbolic forms. Thus, as in part *b* of the diagram on page 56 a graph may be said to consist of *edges* representing routes and *vertices* representing nodes, airports, break of bulk points, etc. The manner in which a number of edges and vertices are interconnected may be measured by

§K. Kansky, *Structure of Transportation Networks,* Chicago: University of Chicago, Department of Geography, Research Paper No. 84, 1963, p. 1.

‖By *topological* we mean that locations (nodes) are reckoned in terms of their position on the geometric net, not by their actual locations. In part *b* of the figure on page 56, places are indicated in terms of their position on the networks, not, as in part *a*, in terms of their location on the topographic map.

#There are many difficulties in such a process, but attempts have been made to replicate networks by, for example, Kansky, *op cit.,* pp. 122–147, and by R. L. Morrill, "Migration and the Growth of Urban Settlement," *Lund Studies in Geography, Series B, Human Geography,* No. 26, 1965, pp. 130–170.

**An excellent elementary introduction to graph theory is 0. Ore, *Graphs and their Uses,* New York: Random House Library Editions, 1964.

(a)

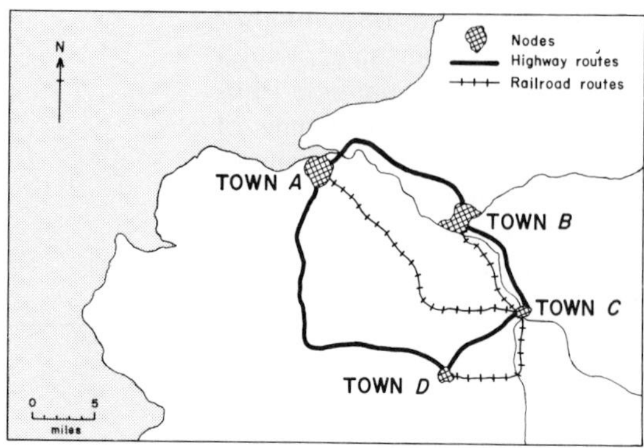

(b)

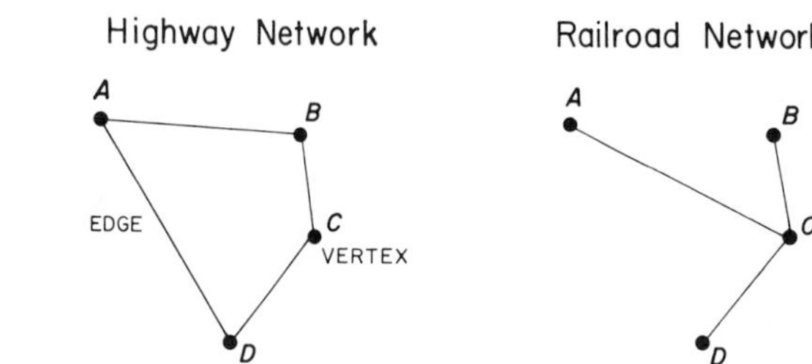

Elemental graphic properties of a network: (a) in *situ,* (b) graphic form. Both indicate the existence of nodes or vertices, and routes or edges.

several indices developed within graph theory. These succinct though perhaps unfamiliar ways of measuring network relationships, such as the *cyclomatic number* and *alpha* and *gamma indices,* are described in Selection 5. These indices measure and reflect the topological attributes of a network. That is, they reveal and translate into uniform and consistent measures the geometric structure of a network so that these attributes may be described, compared with other networks, and, as in the latter part of Selection 5, related to regional characteristics such as level of economic development, size, or shape. Such studies of network structures vary in the amount of information they contain. At a minimum, edges and vertices are related by relatively simple indices (the selections in Part Two), but more complex analyses may include information on angles, lengths, or capacities of routes. Selection 12 in Part Three is an example of a more complex analysis using both networks and flow data (in weighted graphs) to determine interregional relationships.

Garrison and Marble's work (Selection 5) serves both as an introduction to the unfamiliar way of treating network systems and as an example of how these indices can be related to areal or "environmental" characteristics. Although they conclude somewhat pessimistically, the selections that follow and the Further Readings indicate that these methods indeed have great potential.

Garrison's earlier work (Selection 6) examines one aspect of network geometry—the analysis of the position of particular places on a route system. Using now a more refined measure of accessibility (the Shimbel-Katz index), he was able to analyze the relative accessibility of forty-five places in the Southeastern part of the United States which were linked by the newly developed Interstate Highway System. The nodes or vertices were defined in part by their population size and in part by their position on the network. Although some of the results are predictable by visual examination (e.g., the location of low-accessibility places), the Shimbel-Katz index reveals a more unexpected pattern of high-accessibility places.

Kissling (Selection 7) carries these measures further, including that of "accessibility." He relates the importance of network links to physical characteristics such as gradients, curves, and passing opportunities, extending the unweighted links dealt with by Garrison and Marble. The practical application of such graph weightings is shown by its indication of where highway improvements would have their greatest impact, and by the ability to calculate "least cost" routeways in networks between all pairs of vertices. Obviously there is a need for more sophisticated measures of the spatial separation of nodes, and Kissling's method applied here to Nova Scotia could be duplicated in other regional situations.

These three selections represent only a tiny cross section of this new method of analysis. Its scope and breadth can be judged by the Further Readings, particularly by Haggett and Chorley's book, which shows not only its application to transport but also to other networks in physical geography.††

In the final selection (8), Kolars and Malin show that network analysis is not necessarily achieved by graph theory alone. Here they examine the network structure of Turkish railroads using a rather different technique, that of the *gravity model.* It is placed at the end of Part Two partly because it is an alternative technique for network analysis and partly as a link to Part Three, where the gravity model will be reintroduced.

††An earlier example is M. J. Woldenberg and B. J. L. Berry, "Rivers and Central Places: Analagous Systems?" *Journal of Regional Science,* vol. 7, no. 2, 1967, pp. 129–139. An interesting application to another branch of geography is shown by F. R. Pitts, "A Graph Theoretic Approach to Historical Geography," *Professional Geographer,* vol. 17, no. 5, 1965, pp. 15–20.

Selection 5

Graph Theoretic Concepts

W. L. Garrison and D. F. Marble

Networks possess many different structural properties. At the most simple level of conceptualization, a network may be thought of as composed of points and lines. At higher levels of complexity, the notions of distance, capacity, angles between lines, and so on, may be introduced. It is possible also to consider networks at different levels of aggregation, either by (1) using measures of the characteristics of entire networks or (2) using measures of relationships among links (or nodes) on the network. There is another alternative of course. It is to study individual links (or nodes) without reference to other links (or nodes) on the system. The latter is not a viable alternate at the level of generalization at which the present research takes place.

Fig. 5-1 shows the internal airline routes of Guatemala, and Fig. 5-2 shows the internal airline routes of Honduras. The maps are minimal in the sense that they show only the existence (or non-existence) of routes, and the location of terminals. The maps also show the lengths of routes, of course, but map information on length of route is somewhat difficult to interpret. Length of route in combination with information on amount hauled over the route provides a metric of the tie between two places on the network. Information is not available on simple maps, such as the sample map, to indicate amount of traffic, so length of route does not show the strength of ties between places. Also, it is widely known that cost of transportation is a nonlinear function of distance. Put another way, the cost of moving the first mile on a trip between two points is not the same as the cost of moving the second mile. It is generally much more costly to move the first mile than it is to move each succeeding mile. Still a further observation might be made regarding the distance measure. In the case of air transportation, the distance between two points may be variable; it depends upon the choice of route by the pilot. In the case of North Atlantic routes, for instance, flight path distances may vary greatly from day to day. For similar reasons the time required to travel between two points is a variable, and the cost of moving between two points is a variable. The interpretation of distance on a map, then, would seem to require transforming the distance onto some sort of a linear scale. The transformation would depend upon whether or not distance is given a cost interpretation, and it might require regarding the distance as a variable and recording its mean and variance.

The more elementary consideration of the existence or non-existence of terminals and the existence or non-existence of routes seems somewhat easier to interpret than the questions of route length. Albeit, terminals may vary in facilities as may routes. For the moment, attention will be given to questions of the layout of transportation networks viewed in the simplest manner—the existence of terminals and the existence or non-existence of routes.

Surely any analysts would agree that the sample networks (Figs. 5-1 and 5-2) differ in layout. It is equally clear that different analysts would have difficulty communicating just what they meant by statements that the systems differ. These statements reveal one

A Prolegomenon to the Forecasting of Transportation Development, Research Report, Transportation Center, Northwestern University, 1965, pp. 40–68 and 89–96. Reprinted by permission of the authors and the Transportation Center.

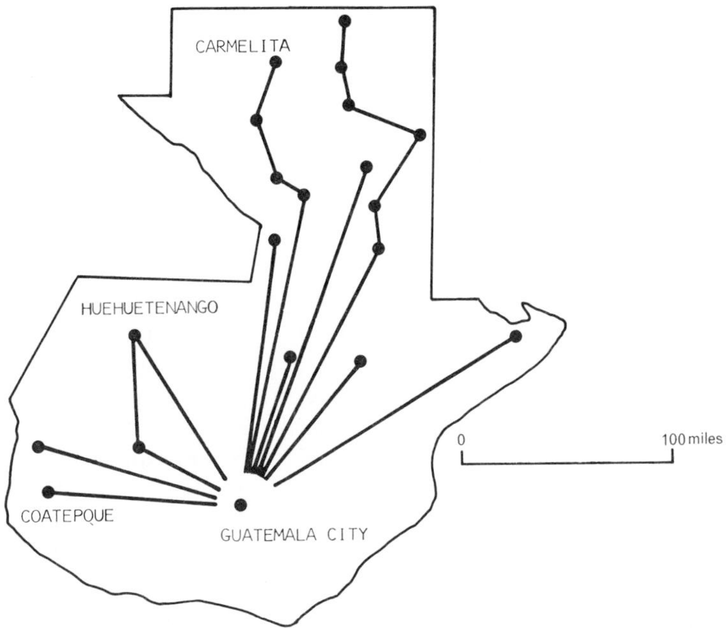

Fig. 5-1 Internal airline routes of Guatemala.

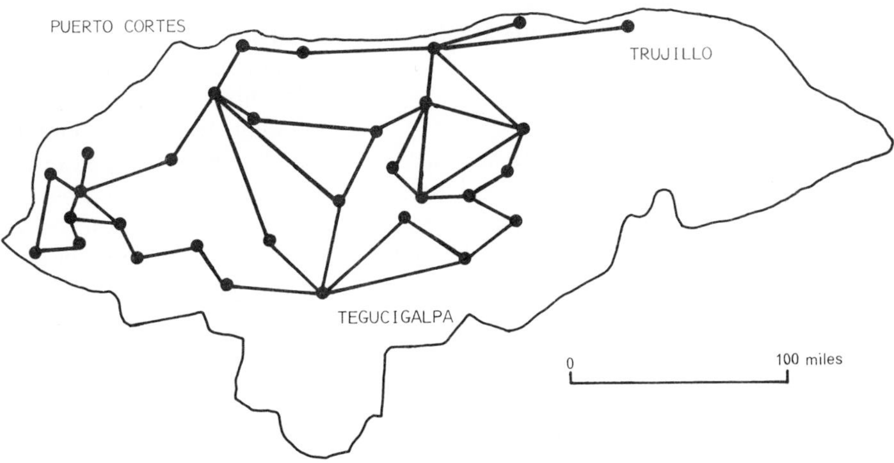

Fig. 5-2 Internal airline routes of Honduras.

of the central problems in this research: that is, the establishment of meaningful ways to codify structures of transportation networks. The remainder of this [work] details the work which was undertaken in this general area.

GRAPH THEORETIC CONCEPTS

The purpose of this section is to provide a brief introduction to some of the graph-theoretic concepts which will be utilized in the subsequent empirical studies. The reader who has some acquaintance with this topic, derived perhaps from a study of Berge,[1] Ore,[2] or Seshu and Reed,[3] may wish to proceed directly to the material dealing with the substantive investigations of network structure.

Primitive Notions

Basically, a linear graph is a collection, or set, of line segments and points. The line segments are commonly known as *edges,* while the points which form the other basic element of the graph are normally known as *vertices.* The two primitive concepts, edges and vertices, are combined to form what is called a linear graph. Collections or sets of this nature may be either finite or infinite depending upon the number of elements that they contain. In the following discussion only finite graphs will be considered.

Classification

Graphs may be broken down into several different classes. One of the most basic breakdowns is that of *non-oriented* and *oriented graphs* (see Fig. 5-3). In non-oriented graphs, the only operational concept is that of *incidence:* the notion that the end points of one or more edges may coincide with a vertex (that is, the edges are incident upon that vertex). The oriented, or directed, graph on the other hand also recognizes a sense of *direction* of the edges. In this case it is recognized that an edge is incident upon two vertices and also that a sense of direction is implied from one vertex to the other. So far, operations have been discussed in terms of a very simple set of concepts. Measurement has dealt only with binary relations such as existence or non-existence, and incidence or non-incidence, with no introduction of notions of metrization. It is possible to introduce into the system certain metrics so that a specific numerical value is associated with each edge and/or vertex. For instance, distances between urban centers on a transport network might be associated with the edges of the graph of that network. Each edge in the graph would then have associated with it a specific numerical value, or weight, and the resulting graph would be a weighted graph, or net. (See the discussion by Hohn, Seshu, and Aufenkamp.[4]) In an even more complex case, it would be possible to assign weights to the nodes or vertices of the graph, as well as the edges. When this is done, the system's configuration more closely resembles that of a stochastic process (see Bartlett[5]), rather than a linear graph.

A third important classification deals with mapping the graph onto the plane. A graph which can be mapped onto a plane, such that no two edges have a point in common that is not a vertex, is known as a *planar graph.* Graphs which cannot be so mapped are known as *non-planar graphs.* This distinction is important in the study of transportation networks due to the problem of involuntary intersections, that is, intersections created by the physical crossing of two or more routes connecting nodes in the system. In general, planar graphs correspond to those systems which may be constructed without creating involuntary intersections. Empirical examination of

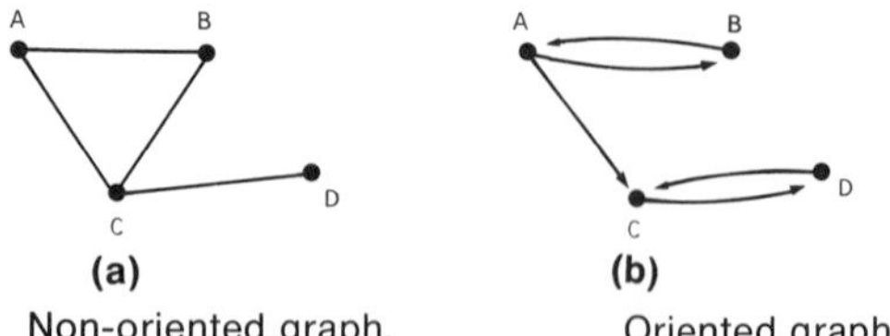

(a) Non-oriented graph. **(b)** Oriented graph.

Fig. 5-3

transportation systems indicates that surface routes, rail and highway, tend to have the characteristics of planar graphs, while airline routes appear more like non-planar graphs.

If the transportation network is regarded as a graph, it becomes useful to develop certain summary indices which relate to the structure of the network. Some information has been lost in passing from the actual system to its graph or matrix representation, and further loss becomes necessary in order to assist in information handling. The problem here is similar to one encountered in most forms of statistics where data has been gathered in the form of a frequency distribution. In order to obtain a readily comprehensible summary index of the distribution, and in order to be able to distinguish between different distributions, certain summary measures such as mean, variance, etc., have been developed. The problem at hand in the present case is to compile a set of analogous measures pertaining to the structure of the graph.

Isomorphisms

It is easy to see that a given graph may be structured in several different ways, for example, relabelling the nodes and edges. In such a case it would be useful to have some precise way of recognizing that the graphs are really identical even though they may be arranged differently and that their vertices and edges may bear different labels. This situation represents what is known mathematically as an *isomorphism*. Two graphs, say G and G*, can be said to be isomorphic if there is a one-to-one correspondence between the vertices of G and G*, which preserves the incidence relationships. (See Fig. 5-4.)

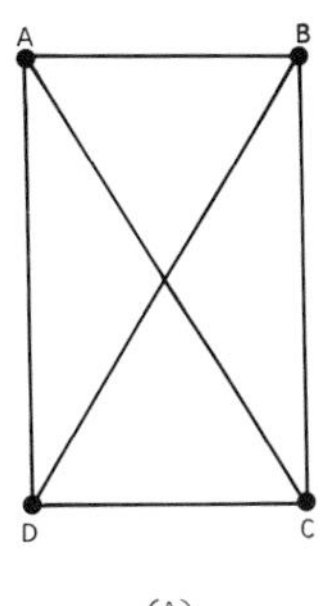

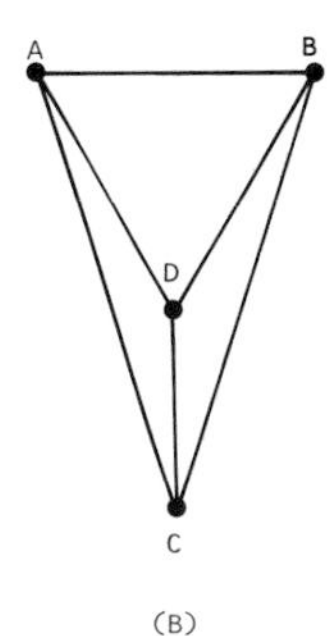

Fig. 5-4 Two isomorphic graphs.

Connectivity

It is possible to count the number of edges that are incident at a particular vertex, and this number is known as the *degree* of the vertex. A *path* is a collection of vertices and a subset of their incident edges such that the degree of each internal vertex is two and the degree of each terminal vertex is one. A *circuit* is a closed path where all vertices are of degree two.

Now, using these concepts, the very important notion of connectivity may be introduced. A graph G is said to be *connected* if there exists a path between any pair of vertices in the graph. Thus, from an intuitive standpoint, we may feel that a graph is connected if it is in "one piece." Suppose the graph is not connected; then this means that there are pairs of points or vertices in the system which cannot be joined in a path. The graph is then *unconnected* and it is intuitively obvious that it must consist of a number of "connected pieces." These "pieces" of the larger graph are subgraphs and are known as *maximally connected* subgraphs. The number of these maximal connected subgraphs in any finite graph, G, is denoted by p and, as a consequence, $p = 1$ for a graph G if, and only if, G is connected. This count of the number of maximal connected subgraphs present represents one of the simplest descriptions of the structure of a graph and provides an index that remains invariant under all isomorphic transformations. The technical name for this index is the *zeroth Betti number.*

Trees and Fundamental Circuits

One notion commonly encountered in graph theory is that of a *tree.* A tree is defined as a connected subgraph of a connected graph which contains all the vertices of the graph but which does not contain any circuits. A given finite graph is a tree if, and only if, there exists exactly one path between any two vertices of the graph. It can be shown that if a tree contains v vertices, it contains $v - 1$ edges. For instance, in a transport system the smallest number of routes that will completely connect five urban places is four. Conversely, it can be shown that the maximum number of routes between n points is $n(n - 1)/2$; that is, ten transport routes would be required to connect completely a system containing five urban places. (See Fig. 5-5.)

Fundamental Circuits

For a given graph and a given tree defined on the graph, elements of the graph may be divided into two classes, *branches* and *cords*. Branches are those elements which are contained in the tree whereas cords are elements that are not in the tree and are therefore in its complement (or *co-tree*). It also may be shown that a connected graph consisting of v vertices and e edges contains $v - 1$ branches and $e - v + 1$ cords. If one cord should be added to a tree, a graph is obtained that is no longer a tree. The cord and the path in the tree between the vertices of the cord constitutes a circuit. This is, however, a unique circuit and the only circuit of the resulting graph.

The *fundamental circuits* of a connected graph G for a tree T are the $e - v + 1$ circuits consisting of each cord and its unique tree path. In a more general sense, this number is given by $\mu = e - v + p$, where v is the number of vertices, e the number of edges, and p the number of maximal connected subgraphs. The index μ is invariant under isomorphic transformations and is known as *nullity, cyclomatic number*, or *first Betti number*.

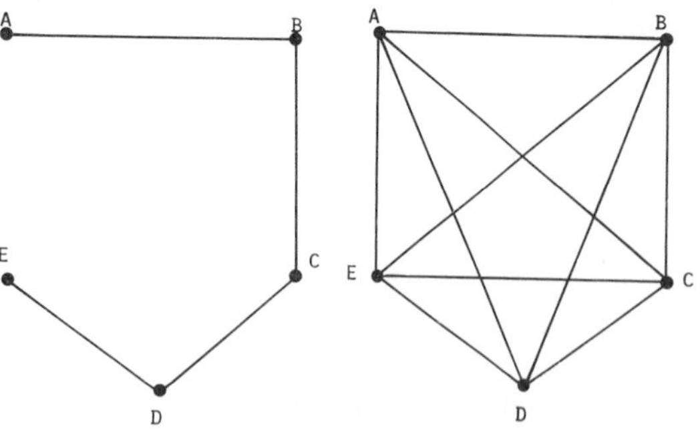

Fig. 5-5a Minimal network (tree). *V*-5; *E*-4.

Fig. 5-5b Completely connected network. *V*-5; *E*-10.

Matrix Representation

It has been observed that the most fundamental characteristic of a graph is the relationship between the edges and the vertices. The graph is completely specified as soon as it is known which edges are incident upon which vertices. Such a specification can be made through a simple diagram, such as has been used in the preceding discussion, or even more compactly by means of a matrix.

The matrix representation which has proven most useful in many types of network analysis is known as the *connection matrix*. In a graph with v vertices, the connection matrix is a $v \times v$ matrix where each row and each column correspond to a specific vertex in the graph. The elements of the matrix are zero or one depending upon the existence or non-existence of an edge directly connecting the two vertices. That is, $c_{ij} = 1$ if there is an edge which is incident at one end upon vertex i and at the other upon vertex j. The element $c_{ij} = 0$ if no such direct connection exists. The elements upon the principal diagonal, the c_{ii}, which represent internal or self linkages are usually defined as either all zeros or all ones, depending upon the structure of the problem being investigated. (See Fig. 5-6.)

In a system that is not completely connected, there will be many places between which no direct link will exist. However, it is quite possible that these places may be reached by moving through one or more intermediate vertices, that is, via some indirect route. Given the connection matrix, it is pos-

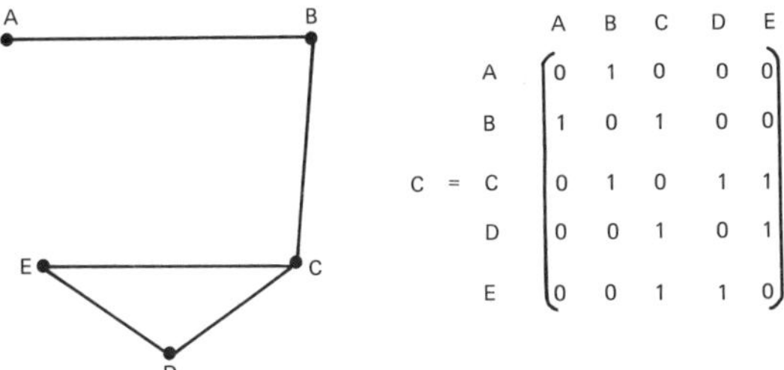

Fig. 5-6 A graph and its connection matrix.

sible to determine how many indirect routes of any given length connect any two vertices in the system. For instance, if it is desired to know the number of two-link routes that exist between two vertices in the system, say i and j, we may do so by finding the square of the original connection matrix. The *ij-th* element of the matrix C^2 is then interpreted as the number of two-link routes connecting vertex i and vertex j. (See Fig. 5-7.) A similar procedure is followed for routes with greater numbers of links. C^5, for instance, will indicate how many five-link routes exist between each vertex and every other vertex. The entries in these cells, however, contain an unknown number of redundant paths since many paths have been counted which contain edges with a multiplicity greater than one. However, it is possible to calculate the number on non-redundant paths (that is, those containing only edges of multiplicity one) of any given length by means of a relatively complex mathematical manipulation. (See the work by Ross and Harary.[6])

We may imagine two vertices in the system which are quite "remote" from each other. That is, there are no direct links between them, no two-stage, no three-stage, no four-stage, etc., links. In this case, the corresponding element of successive powers of the connection matrix will remain at zero. Eventually, the entry in this cell will change from zero to some non-zero number if the graph is connected. If the two vertices are the "most remote" on the system, it can be seen that the matrix will now contain no zeros. The power to which the original connection matrix has been raised to obtain this situation is known as the *solution time* of the network, or the *diameter* of the system. Put another way, the diameter or solution time of the system may be found by listing the number of links in the shortest path between each pair of nodes and selecting the largest of these numbers.

THE DEVELOPMENT OF STRUCTURAL INDICES

If the transportation network is viewed as a graph, it becomes useful to develop certain summary indices which relate to the structure of the network. A certain amount of information has been lost in passing from the actual system to its graph or matrix representation, and further loss becomes necessary in order to assist in information handling. The problem here is similar to one encountered in most forms of statistics where data has been gathered in the form of a frequency distribution. In order to obtain a readily comprehensible summary index of the distribution, and in order to be able to distinguish between different distributions, certain summary measures such as mean, variance, etc., have been developed. The problem at hand in the present case is to compile a set of similar measures pertaining to the structure of the graph.

The Betti Numbers

In the study of the theory of linear graphs, mathematicians have developed certain in-

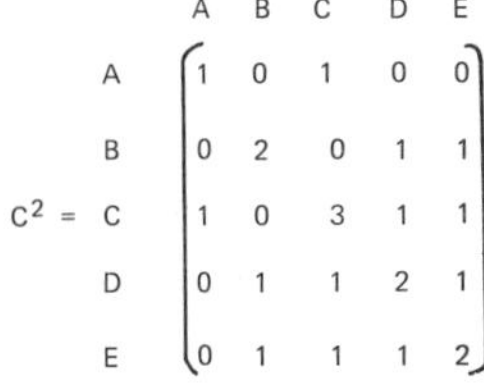

Fig. 5-7 Square of the matrix C.

dices which are regarded as invariant; that is, their values are not changed by ismorphic transformations of the graph. Perhaps the easiest to comprehend of these are the 0th Betti numbers, which is a count of the number of disconnected parts of the network, and the 1st Betti number, or cyclomatic number, as it is commonly known, which presents a somewhat more sophisticated index pertaining to network structure. If one cord is added to a tree, a graph is obtained with a unique single circuit known as a fundamental circuit. If this operation of cord addition is repeated for a graph with v vertices, there are $e - v + 1$ circuits consisting of each cord and its unique tree path. In a more general fashion, if the graph is not connected, it consists of maximal connected subgraphs. A tree can be defined for each subgraph and a set of these trees is called a *forest* of G. It follows that there are $v - p$ elements in the forest and $e - v + p$ elements not in the forest. This number is μ, the cyclomatic number, and it is a count of the number of fundamental circuits existing in the graph. In one sense, the cyclomatic number may be considered to be a measure of redundancy in the system. Since it was noted that a tree provides one, and only one, path between any pair of points, it can be seen that additional paths provided by circuits are redundant and that the total number of circuits present in the graph may be considered as a crude measure of the redundancy of the system. As may be seen from the structure of this index, any tree or disconnected graph has a cyclomatic number of 0, whereas as the graph moves closer and closer to the completely connected state, the cyclomatic number increases. (See Fig. 5-8.) Applying this notion to the structure of transportation networks, it might be hypothesized that the magnitude of the cyclomatic number which characterizes a nation's transportation system would bear a direct relationship to the level of social and economic development of the nation.

The Alpha and Gamma Indices

While the cyclomatic number does provide an index of network structure that is invariant under isomorphic transformations, it does not provide a readily intelligible measure of structure since it is bounded below by zero and bounded above only by some number which is a function of the number of nodes in the system. Ideally, it would be desirable to transform this index in such a manner that has common upper and lower bounds for all networks. Two additional measures are suggested which have this property, and which also remain invariant under isomorphic transformations. They will be defined as the *alpha* and *gamma* indices.

The gamma index for a planar network with e edges and v vertices is defined as $\propto = e/3(v - 2)$. This is the ratio of the observed number of edges, e, to the maximum number of edges *in a planar graph*. Obviously, this index would have a slightly different structure where non-planar graphs were under consideration (for example, airline routes). In any network, the maximum number of direct connections is strictly a function of the number of nodes present. For a given network, as the number of edges in the system decreases, the gamma index will approach one as an upper limit. It appears to be most convenient to express this index as a percentage and it is therefore multiplied by 100, giving it a range from 0 to 100, and it is then interpreted as percent connected.

The alpha index is somewhat similar, consisting of the ratio of the observed number of fundamental circuits to the maximum number of fundamental circuits which may exist in the system. The observed number of fundamental circuits is, of course, the cyclomatic number. Whereas the maximum number of fundamental circuits is equal to the number of edges present in a completely connected planar graph minus the number of edges contained in the complete tree. Therefore, for a

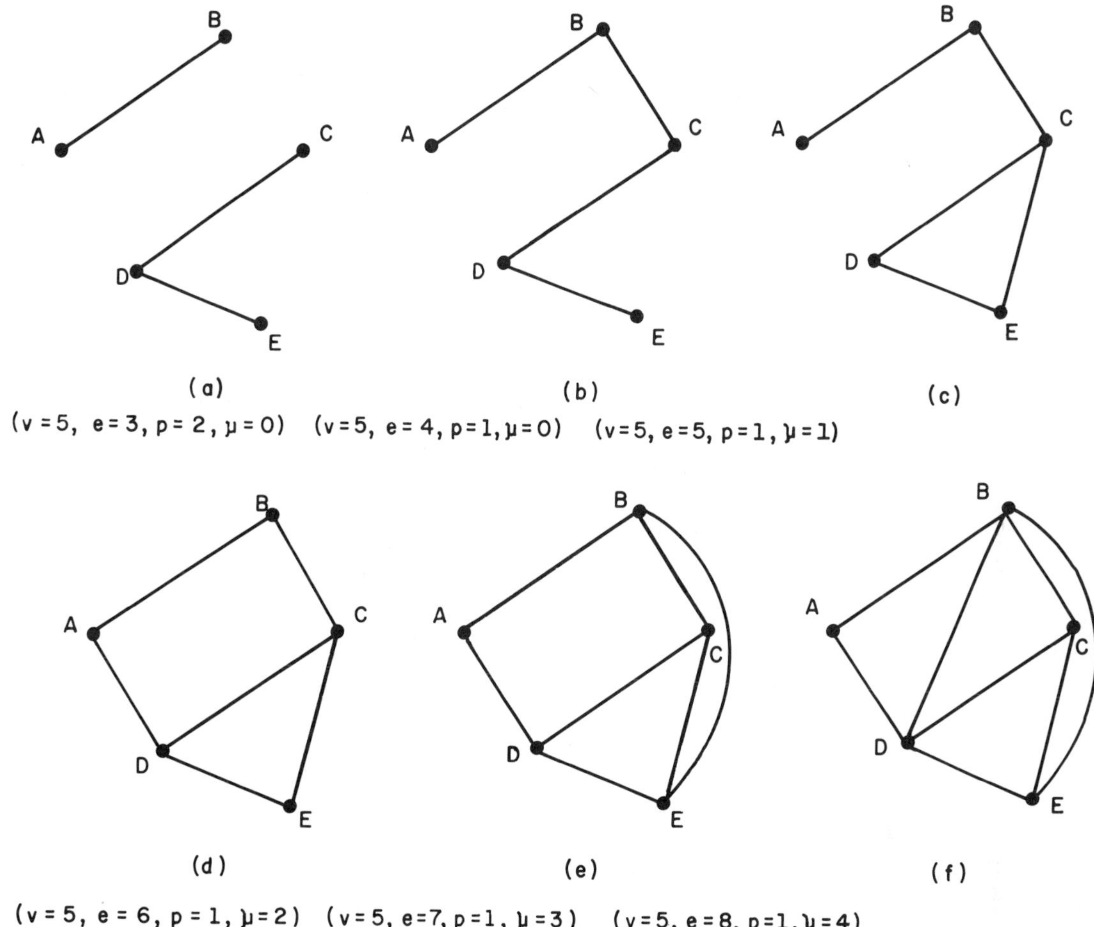

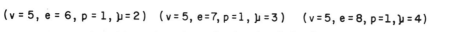

Fig. 5-8 The relation of the cyclomatic number to network structure.

planar graph, the alpha index will have the form $\propto = \mu/2v - 5$. This index is also multiplied by 100 to give it a range from 0 to 100 and an interpretation as percent redundant.

The two indices provide two percentage measures of the structure of a network. The alpha index may be interpreted as a percent redundant with a tree having zero redundancy and a maximally connected network having 100 percent redundancy. The gamma index, on the other hand, may be interpreted as a percent connected with a completely unconnected system having a zero value and a completely connected system having a value of 100 percent.

The indices which have been suggested here are far from exhaustive and, in their present form, are far from adequate. Perhaps their major deficiency, together with that incurred in the general use of graph-theoretic models, is the lack of a precise statement pertaining to the angular structure of the network. The work by Beckman[7] has shown how important this item is in the analysis of transportation systems. However the incorporation of such a measure would be extremely difficult, and it would appear wise to first evaluate the empirical performance of the proposed indices.

INTERNATION COMPARISONS OF INDICES OF NETWORK STRUCTURE

The previous sections have discussed how the structure of transportation networks may be viewed from a rather simple mathematical point of view and have presented a number of network measures. The measures represent succinct, though perhaps unfamiliar, ways to summarize the structure of transportation networks. The present section reports the use of regression studies of these measures to answer the question "Can the structures of transportation systems be related to the features of the areas within which they are located?" In addition to the measures developed [elsewhere], certain other measures developed for other aspects of the research were used in the regression studies. This [work] presents, in turn, the measurements used in the regression analyses, the computations made, and the results of the computations.

Inputs: The Independent Variables

The characteristics of areas containing transportation networks were represented by independent or explanatory variables. These variables fall into two categories—characteristics of areas that are functions of (1) the level and nature of economic, social, and resource development, and (2) the physical makeup of the area. The former may be described as development variables and the latter as physical variables.

Development Variables

There is widespread agreement that transportation development is closely correlated with the level of national development. In the preceding section, certain indices were developed to measure the structure of transportation development. Before the relation between the level of national development and these transportation measures can be investigated, measures must be established for the notion of "national development." Much work has been done on the notion of development, and the problem of measurement has been solved elsewhere to a degree sufficient for the current needs of this research. The ensuing discussion takes advantage of a detailed statistical analysis of the development measurement question by Brian J. L. Berry.[8]

Statistics are available for many nations treating such matters as the value of foreign trade, value of imports, development of energy resources, population density, and newspaper circulation. Berry found some 43 such measures for some 95 nations. Any one of these might serve as an index of development in an approximate fashion. The notion is tempting that if one measure is a useful one, two or more indices should be better. However, an inspection of the set of statistics will reveal quickly that various measures are redundant on each other. Berry's contribution was the combining of these statistics in a manner that established the basic factors that underlie variations of the statistics. These results were obtained from a direct factor analysis of a table showing the ranks of 95 countries on the 43 available statistical measures. Nations were ranked from 1 to 95. The nation with a score of 1 would be that nation with the highest value. The nation with the score of 95 was that nation with the lowest value.

Berry's work revealed that four basic factors underlie variations in measures of degrees of development. These factors were: technological level, demographic level, income and external relations level, and size level. Nearly all of the variability that occurred in the 43 statistics could be attributed to the first two of the factors. The remaining two factors were relatively unimportant. Technological level takes account of various measures that may be made on the degree of urbanization, industrialization, transportation, trade, income, and the like. Demographic level reflects largely birth and death rates, population densities, population per unit of cultivated land, and similar measures.

In summary, development may be measured by synthesizing certain available statistics. The study of these statistics has revealed that the development of a nation may be measured on two scales: a technological scale and a demographic scale. Also, it was noted that although these scales were derived from a rather complex set of operations on a large number of statistics, it is possible to assign values appropriate to individual areas using simple information and a relatively simple technique. Thus, a relatively simple set of information will yield measures of development interpretable in terms of a large set of statistical indices.

Physical Variables

The nature of the transportation network may depend upon the physical properties of the area it traverses. Three physical properties of areas were measured—size, shape, and relief.

Information on the size of areas is available in a number of places. The data used here were taken from tables in the *Encyclopaedia Britannica* and rounded by two decimal points. For example, Tunisia was reported as 48,332 square miles in size. This was recorded as 483 for purposes of this study.

Shape was measured on maps. The longest axis across each nation was determined by inspection and a perpendicular constructed across the nation at the midpoint of the longest axis. The measure of shape was obtained by dividing the airline distance along the longest axis by the airline distance along the perpendicular. It might be noted that this is not a completely satisfactory measure of shape. A nation shaped like a rectangle may have the same measure of shape as a nation shaped like an ellipse if the ratio is the same for the two areas. It might also be noted that this measure of shape is a pure number and, so far as the measure is concerned, is independent of size.

As is true of shape, there is no entirely satisfactory measure of the relief of areas. The measure used here was constructed in an *ad hoc* manner and proved to be suitable to the study. Three lines were drawn at random across each area of study, and the airline length of each line was measured. The distance along each route was also measured along the surface using profiles in the *Times Atlas*. These surface routes, of course, were greater than or equal to the airline distances. The airline route was taken to be 100 percent and the surface route a percentage larger than 100 percent. For each country, the "percent larger" sums were added and divided by three, and the resulting value was used to express the relief of the area of study.

The Data

Transportation networks within 25 nations were selected for analysis and values of the 5 independent variables described above were computed for each nation. Table 5-1 presents the list of nations studied and the values of the independent variables. Preliminary investigation of the sizes of areas and the characteristics of their transportation systems revealed existence of nonlinear relationships. Before computations were made, the raw data on size were converted into natural logarithms. Table 5-2 displays the associations among the independent variables in terms of the correlation coefficients between variables taken two at a time.

Table 5-1 Observed Values of Independent Variables

	Techno-logical develop-ment*	Demo-graphic level*	Size†	Shape	Relief
1. Tunisia	351	32	4.683	2.677	5.51
2. Ceylon	323	14	4.403	2.510	3.54
3. Ghana	355	15	4.962	2.506	2.83
4. Bolivia	370	18	5.672	2.135	20.00
5. Iraq	344	25	5.234	2.376	2.21
6. Nigeria	394	0	5.530	2.164	3.60
7. Sudan	410	6	5.985	2.093	4.48
8. Thailand	400	9	5.297	2.245	5.41
9. France	125	38	5.327	1.468	12.04
10. Mexico	222	19	5.881	2.422	20.96
11. Yugoslavia	241	16	4.994	2.553	23.25
12. Sweden	154	55	5.239	2.872	8.34
13. Poland	182	25	5.080	2.155	3.15
14. Czechoslovakia	159	38	4.693	2.706	13.93
15. Hungary	221	29	4.555	2.521	5.94
16. Bulgaria	279	47	4.631	2.438	12.97
17. Finland	202	46	5.114	2.780	0.35
18. Angola	438	28	5.682	1.809	1.42
19. Algeria	323	26	5.963	1.230	1.52
20. Cuba	256	37	4.645	2.979	12.78
21. Rumania	258	23	4.962	2.135	25.01
22. Malaya	256	17	4.705	2.159	19.51
23. Iran	372	12	5.803	2.422	8.50
24. Turkey	283	8	5.481	2.692	19.45
25. Chile	239	24	5.456	3.100	66.80

*From Berry (Reference 8), Table 8-1, cols. 1 and 2, "Second Values." Twenty was added to each "Demographic Level" entry.

†Natural log of computed value.

The Dependent Variables

The rationale underlying this study is that transportation structure is dependent upon the characteristics of the area containing the network. The characteristics of areas have been summarized in terms of the independent variables just discussed. The dependent variables to be discussed now are those measures of transportation that are pertinent to the notion of transportation structure. These measures fall into two categories: (1) the measures based on graph-theoretic considerations and (2) measures based on certain other work.

Graph-Theoretic Measures

Six measures of a graph-theoretic type were made on transportation networks in each of the 25 nations selected for study. These were:

1 The number of vertices, nodes, or places.

2 The number of edges, links, or routes. A variety of sources were used for the vertex and edge measurements. Sources included *World Railways*[9] and maps published in various issues of the journal *Road International.* Definitions of vertices, and thus of edges, were partly topological and partly based on certain information contained on the maps.

Any intersection of routes was defined a vertex. Also, any place on the network deemed significant by the person who drafted the map was taken to be a vertex. End points were always treated as vertices.

3 *Alpha index.* This is the cyclomatic number (see item 5 below), divided by the maximum possible number of complete circuits, or $/(2v - 5)$.

4 *Gamma index.* This is the number of observed edges divided by the maximum possible number of edges in a planar graph with the observed number of vertices, or $e/3(v - 2)$.

5 *Cyclomatic number.* This is the measure of the number of circuits in the transportation system, or the number of links in the system excess to the number required to tie the vertices together in a minimal way. $\mu = e - (v - 1)$.

6 *Diameter.* This is a measure of the "span" of the transportation systems. It is the minimum number of links that must be traversed in order to move between the two points that are the greatest distance apart on the network.

Other Dependent Variables

The above are six measure of some of the structural characteristics of transportation networks. These were supplemented by an additional measure that was adopted after extensive empirical measurements of transportation networks (Kansky[10]). Measurements of the lengths of edges in miles proved practicable, and preliminary correlations indicated that such measures were significantly related to variables such as technological development. Consequently, measures were made in the nations under study of the average length of edges. Two measures were made, one for highways and one for railroads.

The Data

On the basis of preliminary graphic analysis, it was decided to transform many of the dependent variables to their natural logarithms. These transformations are listed below:

1 Vertices, transformed to the natural logarithm of the observed number.

2 Edges, transformed to the natural logarithm of the observed number.

3 Cyclomatic number, one added to the observed value and the result transformed to its natural logarithm.

4 Average highway edge length, transformed to the natural logarithm of the observed value.

5 Average railroad edge length, transformed to the natural logarithm of the natural logarithm of the observed value.

The purpose of these transformations was to assume linearities in the regression analyses. *No attempt is made to indicate the presence of these transformations in various tables that follow in this selection.*

Table 5-4 indicates the relationships between the dependent and independent variables taken two at a time. It may be noted, for

Table 5-2 Correlation Matrix, Independent Variables

Technological development	Demographic level	Size	Shape	Relief
1				
–.61	1			
.35	–.40	1		
–.24	.21	–.43	1	
–.27	–.04	.05	.36	1

Table 5-3 Observed Values of the Dependent Variables

Nation	No. of nodes	No. of edges	Alpha index	Gamma index	Cyclomatic number(+1)*	Diameter	Average edge length (hwy)†	Average edge length (rail)†
1. Tunisia	3.970	4.043	5.00	37.30	1.792	19	0.218	0.150
2. Ceylon	3.466	3.434	0.00	34.40	0.000	14	0.162	0.275
3. Ghana	3.714	3.714	1.30	35.00	0.693	15	0.215	0.237
4. Bolivia	4.060	4.078	1.80	35.11	1.099	31	0.190	0.291
5. Iraq	3.496	3.496	1.63	35.48	0.693	21	0.185	0.259
6. Nigeria	3.989	4.159	10.70	41.00	2.398	14	0.227	0.362
7. Sudan	3.296	3.296	2.04	36.00	0.693	13	0.232	0.356
8. Thailand	3.989	4.007	1.94	35.25	1.099	24	0.219	0.300
9. France	6.433	6.733	17.67	45.16	5.389	43	0.149	0.214
10. Mexico	5.236	5.371	7.54	38.50	3.332	43	0.223	0.284
11. Yugoslavia	5.553	5.727	9.78	39.90	3.912	35	0.180	0.151
12. Sweden	5.771	6.094	19.30	46.20	4.812	41	0.222	0.185
13. Poland	5.226	5.529	18.25	45.60	4.205	21	0.148	0.186
14. Czechoslovakia	5.553	5.802	14.14	43.00	4.290	41	0.130	0.170
15. Hungary	5.645	5.916	15.68	44.00	4.477	31	0.133	0.074
16. Bulgaria	4.454	4.554	6.00	37.70	2.303	17	0.155	0.139
17. Finland	5.118	5.170	3.00	35.60	2.303	36	0.131	0.181
18. Angola	4.248	4.344	5.90	37.70	2.079	8	0.275	0.319
19. Algeria	4.220	4.407	11.40	41.40	2.708	18	0.243	0.226
20. Cuba	4.511	4.682	10.20	40.40	2.890	24	0.178	0.168
21. Rumania	5.493	5.645	8.50	39.10	3.714	27	0.156	0.160
22. Malaya	3.951	3.931	0.00	34.00	0.000	21	0.186	0.233
23. Iran	3.689	3.611	0.00	32.45	0.000	—	0.237	0.351
24. Turkey	4.727	4.718	0.45	33.60	0.693	—	0.159	0.271
25. Chile	5.004	5.050	3.75	35.30	2.485	—	0.202	0.086

*Natural log.
†Natural log of natural log.

example, that there is a correlation of −.86 between the natural logarithm of the number of vertices and the index of technological development. This indicates, as would be expected, that the more developed the area, the greater the number of nodes or vertices on the transportation system. It may also be noted that the more developed the country, the shorter is the average edge length.

The Computations

Eight regression analyses were made. In each analysis the value of a dependent variable was assigned to the independent variables to the extent that variations in the data indicated that assignments were warranted. This section contains a discussion of the regression model used, the steps in computation, and the outputs from the regressions. It will be noted in this section that these computations were very good in the sense that much of the variability in individual estimates of error and correlation was recomputed. These computations were continued in this incremental fashion until all 5 of the regression coefficients were determined. Since there were 5 of the regression coefficients for each of the 10 regressions, some 50 regressions were actually run. It is most convenient, however, to speak of 10 regressions in all. The preliminary 4 regressions of each of the dependent variables are of greatest interest in regard to the estimates of error to be discussed below.

Outputs

The outputs from the calculations fall into two categories: (1) the regression coefficients, and (2) various estimates of error or reliability of the regressions. The regression coefficients are given in Table 5-5; these are numerical values of the *b*'s in the linear regression equation given above. For the first regression, for instance, we have:

$$y = 6.30 - .008x_1 - .006x_2 = .201x_3 - .267x_4 - .007x_5 =$$

or: number of vertices on network = 6.30 − .008 index of technological development − .006 index of demographic level + .201 size measure − .267 shape measure − .007 relief measure + error of the estimate

and similar equations may be written for the 9 remaining regressions.

Several different measures were made of the reliability of the regressions. Table 5-6 presents a measure of how well the regressions work. The coefficients of determination, sometimes termed the power of the model, are numerically the squares of the multiple correlation coefficients, and they may be interpreted as the percent of the variability in the dependent variable associated with variation in the independent variables. The first entry indicates that some 73 percent of nation-to-nation variation in the number of vertices may be associated with the level of technological development, and the right-hand entry of the first column indicates that some 77 percent of the variability from nation-to-nation in number of vertices may be associated with the five independent variables taken altogether.

A number of other outputs from the regression bear on the "goodness" of the regressions. The 22 to 25 nations used in this study may be viewed as a sample from a larger set of nations, though it might be somewhat difficult to decide on the number of nations in the world. The United Nations' *Statistical Yearbooks* list approximately 260 political divisions, but about 100 of these are subdivisions of larger units. Ginsburg[11] found it practicable to consider about 140 countries. Thus, the computations made here might be re-

Table 5-4 Summary: Simple Coefficients of Correlation Between the Dependent and Independent Variables

	Technological development	Demographic level	Size	Shape	Relief
1. Vertices	−.86	.53	−.15	.08	.30
2. Edges	−.85	.55	−.16	.05	.26
3. Alpha index	−.64	.50	−.12	−.14	−.09
4. Gamma index	−.61	.49	−.14	−.18	−.15
5. Cyclomatic number	−.73	.56	−.13	−.04	.11
6. Diameter	−.79	.44	−.02	.24	.49
7. Average edge length (highway)	.67	−.34	.64	−.27	−.10
8. Average edge length (rail)	.66	−.62	.61	−.40	−.40

Table 5-5 Summary: Regression Coefficients of the Eight Regressions

	Technological development	Demographic level	Size	Shape	Relief	Constant term
1. Vertices	−.008	−.006	.201	−.267	−.007	6.30
2. Edges	−.009	−.007	.213	−.335	−.006	6.74
3. Alpha index	−.049	.068	1.208	−3.306	−.090	22.123
4. Gamma index	−.031	.043	.412	−2.419	−.071	50.543
5. Cyclomatic number	−.012	.027	.354	−.799	.001	5.278
6. Diameter	−.0918	.012	10.101	7.447	.347	−21.565
7. Average edge length (highway)	.0003	.0007	.0423	.0027	.0002	−.1424
8. Average edge length (rail)	.0001	−.0023	.0802	.0138	−.0025	−.1757

garded as a sample from approximately 140 areas. Still a broader view might be adopted. The 140 areas might be regarded as displaying patterns from a larger universe of transportation network structures that might have developed, given the conditions that control network development. This set of possible patterns might be very large or even unlimited in number. Reasoning this way, the sample might be regarded as one from an extremely large universe of possible transportation network structures. Table 5-7 presents the variance ratios for the regressions. In connection with the coefficients of determination of the regressions (Table 5-6), it was mentioned that these may be regarded as the amount of variation in the dependent variable associated with variations in the independent variables. The variance ratios permit significance tests of the increments in the variation explained by the regressions as individual regression coefficients are added. It may be seen that the reduction in the variance associated with technological development is extremely significant and that other reductions in variance are significant on occasion.

The regression equations may be viewed as forecasting devices. Observations on the independent variables may be entered into the equations and estimates of transportation structure derived. A change in some character of an area, such as level of technological development, may be postulated and new values of transportation structure estimated. Persons using regression equations of this sort for estimating purposes should proceed with caution, of course. For one thing, estimates that extend beyond the range of variability in the original data should be made only with great care. Too, the regressions limit themselves to measures of structure and do not display exactly how a change will take place on the map. In addition to the preceding points, the behavior of errors of estimation is critical where estimates are made. For this reason, a number of measures bearing on errors of estimation were obtained in the course of the regression calculations.

Table 5-8 presents the standard errors of estimate for the eight regressions. In discussing the regression equation earlier in this section, mention was made of the error term that must be introduced into the equation in order to correct the computed structure value to the actual observed value. The standard error of the estimate is a measure of the distribution of these error terms (their means are zeros). For the first regression, for example, about 66 percent of the computed values from the regressions lie within plus or minus one standard error or plus or minus .457 of the observed values; 95 percent lie within plus or minus two standard deviations, or plus or minus .950.

Results

It might be wise to repeat certain comments made earlier on the structure of this study before going on to a summary of the results of the regressions, because the results of the regressions must be judged within the overall structure of the study. Earlier the question was asked, "Can the structures of transportation systems be related to the features of the areas within which they are located?" In terms of certain measures of structure and certain ways of measuring the "characteristics of the features of the areas," the answer to this question is a definite yes. But beyond this it is desired to answer this question in the affirmative so far as the actual networks or maps of the transportation systems of areas are concerned. That is, the ultimate answer to the question requires generating the actual transportation network, given the characteristics of the area that contains the network. The first step in obtaining the ultimate answer to this question is that of generating the characteristics of network structure, so our ability to answer the question with a yes in the case of the characteristics of the network is an essential part of the objective of the overall objective of the research.

Simplicity and preciseness may always be taken to be desirable attributes of models. It might be noted again that the regression equations used in this study have these attributes. Measurement requirements for calculating values of the dependent variables are not at all demanding. Computation of size, shape, and relief are simple and straightforward. While development of the technological development and demographic level scales required a great deal of statistical work, values on these scales may be estimated from very simple information. The values of the independent variables are also very simple to measure, although they too depend upon certain mathematical considerations.

As was mentioned before, the fit of the regression model to the data may be regarded as quite good. This is a relative matter, of course. Also, it was noted that the residuals or errors were such that introduction of new

Table 5-6 Summary of Coefficients of Determination of the Eight Regressions

	Technological development	Demographic level	Size	Shape	Relief
1. Vertices	.73	.73	.76	.77	.77
2. Edges	.73	.73	.75	.76	.77
3. Alpha index	.42	.44	.46	.54	.57
4. Gamma index	.37	.40	.41	.52	.56
5. Cyclomatic number	.54	.56	.59	.62	.62
6. Diameter	.62	.62	.67	.75	.80
7. Average edge length (highway)	.45	.46	.66	.67	.67
8. Average edge length (rail)	.43	.51	.63	.65	.77

Table 5-7 Variance Ratios with 1 and *m-j* Degrees of Freedom

j equal / Variable	Technological development 1	Demographic level 2	Size 3	Shape 4	Relief 5	*m* No. of observations
1. Vertices	63.31*	.01	2.32	.48	.76	25
2. Edges	61.27*	.07	2.23	.90	.39	25
3. Alpha index	16.43	.75	.83	3.53	1.18	25
4. Gamma index	13.73*	.83	.45	4.44†	1.67	25
5. Cyclomatic number	26.62*	1.03	1.51	1.84	.00	25
6. Diameter	32.33*	.15	3.73	4.30†	4.21	22
7. Average edge length (highway)	18.69*	.33	13.08*	.14	.14	25
8. Average edge length (rail)	17.30*	3.45	7.38*	.61	10.26*	25

*Significant at the 1% level.
†Significant at the 5% level.

data into the regressions and limited projections may be made with confidence.

It was remarked earlier that these regressions are but one stage of an effort to reproduce actual transportation networks from data on the characteristics of areas. The question of the overall pertinence of the regressions will be left open until that portion of the research is discussed. However, it is possible to make certain summary remarks on the relationships within the regressions and those remarks will be made here. Tables given earlier in this discussion give the units within which the data were measured, the regression coefficients, and the variance ratios.

The regression coefficients are subject to certain general interpretations. The table showing variance ratios (Table 5-7) permits identification of those regression coefficients associated with the stronger relations between independent and dependent variables. It may be seen from this table that technological development is always a major determinate of structure, with other of the independent variables important only in certain cases. Referring to the technological development column of regression coefficients in the summary of regression coefficients (Table 5-6), it may be seen that for the first six regressions the more developed the country (and smaller the measure of technological development) the higher the value of the dependent variable. Just the reverse is true for the last two regressions. The more highly developed the country, the smaller the average edge length and the smaller the structure index. The demographic measure is of little importance, and size is of importance only in the case of the last four measures. The greater the size, the greater the average edge length and structure index, this being more true for highways than for railroads. The shape measure is significant in relation to diameter and the gamma index, while relief has its greatest effect on the edge length for railroads.

The above statements are a mixture of observations based on the magnitudes of the regression coefficients and their relative significance in the variance ratio tests. Additional findings may be made by writing out the in-

Table 5-8 Standard Errors of Estimate*

Variable	Standard error of estimate
1. Vertices	.457
2. Edges	.514
3. Alpha index	4.617
4. Gamma index	3.033
5. Cyclomatic number	1.127
6. Diameter	5.488
7. Average edge length (highway)	.026
8. Average edge length (rail)	.043

*Unbiased.

dividual regression equations and studying their sensitivity to variations in the independent variables.

The structural indices used in this study are, with the exception of average edge length, all basically derived from information about the number of nodes and edges in the graph. Some redundancy might well be expected, and a casual examination of the regression coefficients for, say, the alpha and gamma indices (see Table 5-5) reveals a very similar pattern of response to variations in the level of the independent variables.

Computation of the simple intercorrelations between the dependent variables in the various regressions reveals that the redundancy is quite high in almost all cases; for example, the simple correlation between the alpha and gamma indices for 22 nations is 0.998 (see Table 5-9). Analysis of these interdependencies by means of principal components analysis (with varimax rotation to "simple structure") reveals that the six indices may be collapsed into three factors (see Table 5-10). The first two of these factors accounted for nearly 98 percent of the observed communality. The first, and by far the most important, expressed network complexity as a function of the number of nodes, the number of edges, and the cyclomatic number; the second factor combines the alpha and gamma indices into a measure of network completeness, while the third factor, which may be interpreted as a size measure, related the number of nodes, the number of edges, and the diameter of the network.

This information about redundancy would appear to indicate that the eight regressions could be replaced by, say, three regressions with very little loss of information.

This section has reported the measurements used, computation, and results from eight regression studies. These regression studies established relationships between certain measurements of transportation network structure and measurements of the characteristics of the areas within which these networks lie. It was found that measures of network structure could be related rather closely to the characteristics of the areas containing the networks and that the technological development was the more important factor conditioning the character of transportation systems.

Table 5-9 Correlation Matrix—Dependent Variables*

No. of nodes	No. of edges	Alpha index	Gamma index	Cyclomatic number	Diameter
1					
.98	1				
.73	.75	1			
.71	.74	.99	1		
.96	.97	.70	.79	1	
.75	.70	.48	.46	.65	1

*Based upon first 22 observations.

Table 5-10 Rotated Factor Loadings of the Graph-theoretic Structure Indices

Variable	Factor 1	2	3
1. Nodes	0.638	0.388	0.660
2. Edges	0.687	0.419	0.576
3. Alpha index	0.294	0.911	0.286
4. Gamma index	0.313	0.919	0.237
5. Cyclomatic number	0.724	0.492	0.461
6. Diameter	0.283	0.208	0.740
Percent of communality*	85.6	12.0	2.4

*Over all factors.

THE STRUCTURE OF LOCAL SERVICE AIRLINE ROUTES

Figs. 5-1 and 5-2 displayed the route structure of local service airlines in Guatemala and Honduras. It was pointed out that these systems appeared to be in some way basically different, since the system in Guatemala seemed to focus upon Guatemala City, whereas the Honduran network appeared to have no such overall focal point. Table 5-11 displays various indices pertaining to network structure for these two nations. It seems that while the Honduran network is larger in size and displays a higher average number of connections per node, it is less directly connected than the Guatemalan network, but on the other hand displays a higher percentage of redundant routes. These indices provide some information about the basic network structure in the two countries; but they do not provide information on the marked visual differences in structure.

In a previous technical report,[12] this line of analysis was pursued further and two nations were selected (Argentina and Venezuela) and the connection matrices corresponding to their local service airline networks were subjected to principal components analysis. The results of this analysis appeared to indicate the existence of the following structural characteristics:

1 An overall field effect centered upon the primate city (Caracas or Buenos Aires).

2 Major regionalization effects which broke out large distinctive portions of the network.

3 Minor regionalization effects which isolated specific structural details within the major regions.

The factors which were isolated accounted for some 38 percent of the observed variation, and it was noted that in no case were "neighborhood effects" (the notions that points are most likely to be linked to their near neighbors) or the existence of long strings or chains pointed out.

Subsequent analysis has thrown considerable doubt upon these earlier conclusions, and it now appears that principal components analysis, when combined with varimax rotation to simple structure, will only isolate small clusters of nodes which display similar patterns of *direct* linkages. This can be demonstrated through a reexamination of the Venezuelan local air service network. The network examined here (circa 1963) differs from the one originally examined (circa 1961) but not in a significant fashion. Some of the results of the principal components analysis are shown in Table 5-12. Twelve significant factors, accounting for 87.2 percent of the variance, were extracted through the application of principal components analysis with varimax rotation to simple structure. The first factor,

Table 5-11 Guatemala and Honduras: Indices of Local Service Airline Route Structure

	Guatemala	Honduras
1. Nodes	20.0	32.0
2. Routes	20.0	45.0
3. Mean number of Connections/node	2.0	2.8
4. Cyclomatic number	1.0	14.0
5. Gamma index*	10.5	9.1
6. Alpha index*	0.6	3.0

*Nonplanar basis.

Table 5-12 Rotated Factor Loadings—Connection Matrix, Venezuelan Air Routes, 1963

	Factor*				
Variable	1	2	3	4	5
1. Caracas	−0.177	0.086	0.005	0.146	0.240
2. Las Piedras	0.132	0.015	0.013	0.019	0.078
3. Maracaibo	0.743	−0.053	0.069	0.070	0.003
4. Coro	−0.176	0.327	0.166	0.191	−0.165
5. Porto Cabello	−0.073	0.803	0.044	0.047	0.049
6. Barquismeto	0.023	0.341	0.035	0.030	0.049
7. Valera	0.094	−0.170	0.112	0.104	−0.130
8. Sta. Barbera	0.909	−0.052	0.096	0.098	−0.080
9. Casigua	0.894	0.031	0.077	0.082	−0.062
10. Merida	0.047	−0.163	0.117	0.113	−0.127
11. Barinas	0.087	0.243	−0.119	−0.588	0.227
12. San Antonio	0.726	−0.144	0.111	0.109	−0.109
13. St. Domingo	−0.151	−0.193	0.145	−0.416	−0.133
14. Guasdualito	−0.147	−0.153	0.150	−0.836	−0.134
15. Palmarito	−0.078	−0.001	0.074	−0.909	−0.061
16. San Fernando	−0.019	0.062	−0.955	0.001	0.085
17. Caicara	−0.093	−0.065	−0.810	0.097	−0.086
18. Puerto Paez	−0.093	−0.065	−0.810	0.097	−0.086
19. Puerto Avacucho	−0.103	−0.075	−0.950	0.111	−0.103
20. Valle de la Pascua	−0.026	0.053	−0.002	0.009	0.040
21. Anaco	−0.080	−0.037	0.074	0.095	0.048
22. Barcelona	−0.108	−0.053	0.098	0.113	0.827
23. Cumana	−0.030	0.050	0.008	0.012	0.967
24. Porlamer	−0.141	−0.113	0.141	0.154	0.765
25. Guiria	−0.096	−0.062	0.094	0.095	−0.033
26. Pedernales	−0.084	−0.062	0.086	0.090	−0.068
27. Maturin	−0.070	0.018	0.058	0.057	0.250
28. Tucupita	−0.088	−0.057	0.090	0.093	−0.075
29. San Tome	−0.186	−0.207	0.201	0.233	0.236
30. Cuidad Bolivar	−0.151	−0.122	0.158	0.168	−0.056
31. Puerto Ordaz	−0.097	−0.047	0.093	0.093	−0.073
32. El Dorado	−0.086	−0.045	0.085	0.084	−0.067
33. Canaima	−0.056	−0.011	0.054	0.051	−0.059
34. Icabaru	−0.106	−0.068	0.105	0.109	−0.087
35. Santa Elena	−0.084	−0.052	0.085	0.087	−0.064
36. San Felipe	−0.149	0.875	0.140	0.149	−0.133
37. Carupano	−0.149	−0.071	0.140	0.108	0.214
38. Elorza	−0.094	−0.073	0.105	−0.867	−0.089
Percent of communality over all variables	13.6	11.4	10.9	9.9	7.7

*Only the first five out of twelve significant factors are shown here.

Table 5-13 Subnet Connections and Loadings

Node	16	17	18	19	Loading on factor three*
16	—	×	×	×	−0.955
17	×	—		×	−0.810
18	×		—	×	−0.810
19	×	×	×	—	−0.950

Note: All other connections are identical except that node 16 is also linked to Caracas.

accounting for 13.6 percent of the variance, isolated a group of five nodes apparently centering on Maracaibo; the second factor (11.4 percent), a group of four nodes lying between Caracas and Maracaibo; the third factor (10.9 percent), an isolated group of four nodes south of Caracas, etc. The first seven of these minor regions are disjoint, but factors 8 and 9 identify clusters of nodes which overlap slightly with previously identified groups.

Factor 3 provides a fairly clear-cut case in point. Nodes 17 and 18 have identical patterns of direct connection to and from the network; nodes 16 and 19 are nearly identical, and each is quite similar to 17 and 18 (see *columns* in Table 5-13). No other nodes in the system have a similar pattern of direct connections. The four nodes in question all load heavily upon factor 3, and no other node or group of nodes does so. The analysis is evidently heavily biased by the (relatively) large number of zero elements in the connection matrix.

It would appear that this problem might be avoided, at least in part, if a denser matrix were the subject for analysis. For a given network a matrix, P, with zeros only along the main diagonal may be generated by setting P_{ij} equal to the minimum number of edges passed over in going from node i to node j. P is commonly referred to as the "shortest path matrix."

The shortest path matrix for the Venezuelan network was developed[13] and was subjected to the same form of analysis as the connection matrix. The rotated factor loadings are displayed in Table 5-14. Here, five significant factors explaining some 92 percent of the variance were isolated (versus 12 factors and 87 percent in the previous case). This analysis classifies nodes upon the basis of similarity in their profiles of accessibility from the system. Again the factors break out groups of nodes, but this time the groups are larger and they tend to correspond somewhat more closely to the visual impression we receive of network structure. Factor 1 isolates a major group of nodes centered on the Caracas-Maracaibo axis and identifies this as a major structural component of the network. Factor 2 points out a cluster of nodes in the SE which are tributary to Maturin; factors 3 and 4 break out smaller, isolated clusters lying south and southwest of Caracas; while factor 5 isolates a small region in the northeast lying between Maturin and Caracas; this latter region shows a small degree of overlap with the group of nodes isolated by factor 2.

The restructuring of the basic data matrix appears to have eliminated some of the problems encountered in the earlier analysis, but the results noted here should not be classed as more than a tentative structure until the problem has been more fully investigated.

CONCLUDING REMARKS

The material discussed in this [work] has dealt with theoretical and empirical investigations of what has been termed the internal structure, or layout, of transport networks. The problem was one that had received only cursory attention in the past and the present investigations, while illuminating certain points, have failed to provide an entirely satisfactory set of results. Part of the problem appears to lie in the line of attack which was chosen; the graph theoretic model of network structure has proved to be strong in some areas, but disappointingly weak in others. . . .

Table 5-14 Rotated Factor Loadings—Shortest Path Matrix, Venezuelan Air Routes, 1963

Variable	Factor 1	2	3	4	5
1. Caracas	0.692	−0.157	0.294	−0.511	−0.374
2. Las Piedras	0.859	−0.027	0.155	−0.333	−0.221
3. Maracaibo	0.940	0.032	0.086	−0.224	−0.161
4. Coro	0.809	0.027	0.107	−0.313	−0.146
5. Porto Cabello	0.676	−0.075	0.220	−0.468	−0.267
6. Barquismeto	0.859	−0.031	0.165	−0.349	−0.216
7. Valera	0.931	0.047	0.070	−0.198	−0.111
8. Sta. Barbera	0.941	0.093	0.015	−0.127	−0.099
9. Casigua	0.943	0.136	−0.038	−0.049	−0.046
10. Merida	0.944	0.072	0.036	−0.146	−0.103
11. Barinas	0.452	0.047	0.776	−0.340	−0.191
12. San Antonio	0.955	0.090	0.017	−0.125	−0.094
13. St. Domingo	−0.010	0.330	0.923	0.007	0.084
14. Guasdualito	0.046	0.292	0.946	−0.035	0.055
15. Palmarito	0.187	0.208	0.938	−0.142	−0.025
16. San Fernando	0.455	0.001	0.127	−0.841	−0.218
17. Caicara	0.352	0.059	0.061	−0.888	−0.157
18. Puerto Paez	0.352	0.059	0.061	−0.888	−0.157
19. Puerto Ayacucho	0.326	0.077	0.043	−0.909	−0.140
20. Valle de la Pascua	0.628	−0.188	0.292	−0.497	−0.345
21. Anaco	0.606	−0.220	0.288	−0.486	−0.343
22. Barcelona	0.384	−0.338	0.090	−0.302	−0.766
23. Cumana	0.507	−0.004	0.179	−0.387	−0.687
24. Porlamar	0.229	−0.151	−0.009	−0.182	−0.918
25. Guiria	0.119	−0.477	−0.100	−0.083	−0.800
26. Pedernales	0.193	−0.635	−0.021	−0.146	−0.618
27. Maturin	0.250	−0.669	−0.018	−0.191	−0.642
28. Tucupita	0.160	−0.679	−0.030	−0.121	−0.588
29. San Tome	0.338	−0.366	0.110	−0.302	−0.672
30. Cuidad Bolivar	−0.023	−0.900	−0.193	−0.015	−0.354
31. Puerto Ordaz	0.051	−0.830	−0.124	−0.051	−0.466
32. El Dorado	−0.163	−0.893	−0.314	0.085	−0.161
33. Canaima	−0.063	−0.885	−0.189	0.019	−0.316
34. Icabaru	−0.244	−0.835	−0.384	0.144	−0.040
35. Santa Elena	−0.281	−0.787	−0.417	0.170	0.017
36. San Felipe	0.623	−0.037	0.182	−0.436	−0.225
37. Carupano	0.086	−0.381	−0.128	−0.062	−0.883
38. Elorza	0.077	0.268	0.945	−0.059	0.038
Percent of communality over all factors	46.6	27.3	9.3	5.4	3.4

While much of the investigative effort devoted to this topic has not been as productive as was originally hoped, the work was nevertheless provided a number of invaluable guidelines for future explorations of this topic.

REFERENCES

1 C. Berge, *The Theory of Graphs and Its Applications.* New York: John Wiley and Sons, 1962.

2 O. Ore, *Graphs and Their Uses.* New York: Random House, 1963.

3 S. Seshu and M. B. Reed, *Linear Graphs and Electrical Networks.* Reading: Addison-Wesley, 1961.

4 F. E. Hohn, S. Seshu, and D. D. Aufenkamp, "The Theory of Nets," *Transactions of the Institute of Radio Engineers.* EC-VI, 1957, pp. 154–61.

5 M. S. Bartlett, *An Introduction to Stochastic Processes.* Cambridge, England: Cambridge University Press, 1955.

6 Ian C. Ross and Frank Harary, "On the Determination of Redundancies in Sociometric Chains," *Psychometrika,* XVII, 1952, pp. 195–208.

7 M. Beekmann, "A Continuous Model of Transportation," *Econometrica* XX, 1952, pp. 643–60.

8 B. J. L. Berry, "Basic Patterns of Economic Development," in N. S. Ginsburg (ed.) *Atlas of Economic Development.* Chicago: University of Chicago Press, 1961.

9 Henry Sampson (ed.), *World Railways.* London: Sampson Low's Ltd., 1960.

10 K. J. Kansky, *International and Interregional Comparative Studies.* Submitted under Contract DA 44-177-TC-685, U.S. Army Transportation Research Command, Fort Eustis, Virginia, 1962.

11 N. S. Ginsburg, *Atlas of Economic Development.* Chicago: University of Chicago Press, 1962.

12 W. L. Garrison and D. F. Marble, *Approaches to the Development of a Forecasting Capability for National and Regional Transportation Systems.* Submitted under Contract DA 44-177-TC-685, U.S. Army Transportation Research Command, Fort Eustis, Virginia, 1962.

13 D. F. Marble, *NODAC—A Computer Program for the Computation of Two Simple Node Accessibility Measures in Networks.* Technical Report No. 10, Earth Sciences Computer Study (NONR 1228-33, NR 389-135), Northwestern University, 1965.

Selection 6

Connectivity of the Interstate Highway System

W. L. Garrison

A recent informal survey of two thousand motorists disclosed that less than two percent knew what the National System of Interstate and Defense Highways or the Interstate Highway System was. Undoubtedly, this proportion does not apply to the readers of this [work]. But readers may not be familiar with certain of the needs for research regarding the Interstate System, so a general discussion precedes presentation of the problem treated [here]. The problem treated is introduced in the paragraph below. This is followed by the general discussion which gives some characteristics of the Interstate System and the relevance of the research problem. Analyses of the problem and evaluation of results follow.

Everyone knows that the success of an activity is conditioned by its relative location, among other things. The Interstate Highway System is inducing changes in the relative location of urban centers and, thus, the success of activities within these centers. Locations of cities relative to each other are changing, city tributary areas are shifting, and the relative location of sites within cities is changing. General notions stressing locations relative to markets and/or raw materials and in association with compatible activities are available in the literature. However, present concepts of transportation systems are not at this level of generality. Present concepts relate to particular places—such as the head of navigation and break of bulk places—and lack the generality of notions from location theory. Thus, they are of little value for the problem of transportation-induced shifts in relative location. What concepts are appropriate? In this [work] the Interstate System is treated as a graph and the usefulness of concepts from the theory of graphs is examined. Examination of the graph yields several measures which may be thought of as indices of connectiveness, status indices, accessibility indices, or indices of relative location. The [work] is elementary, both in its use of graph theory and in the analysis of the Interstate System. It reports the results of a pilot study from which it is hoped that more incisive studies will be developed.

The paragraph above is incorrect in one respect. There are certain concepts of transportation systems in the programming literature which are at a high level of generality. The ordinary transportation problem of linear programming is a case in point.* The transportation problem may be approached from the theory of graphs, of course. The search [here] is for a level of approximation which is more elementary than those approximations using programming formats, but which is useful for the consideration of location problems.

THE INTERSTATE SYSTEM

The Interstate System comprises 41,000 miles of high-speed, low transportation cost, limited-access facilities linking many of the major cities of the nation (Fig. 6-1). The concept of the Interstate System dates back a number of years prior to implementation in 1956.[1] Pre-

Papers of the Regional Science Association, vol. 6, 1960, pp. 121–137. Reprinted by permission of the author and editor.

**Editor's note:* Linear programming is introduced in Part Three on pages 145–159.

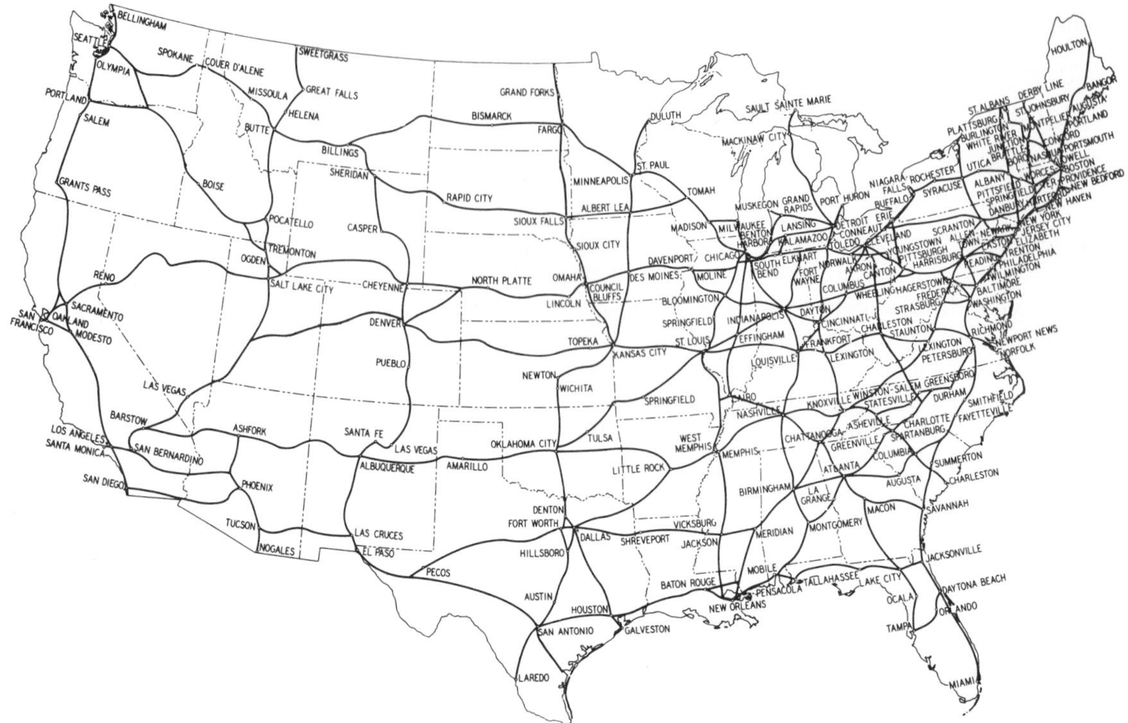

Fig. 6-1 The National System of Interstate Highways, 1957, comprising 41,000 miles of expressway facilities.

vious federal highway policy has resulted in the federal aid primary system of about a quarter of a million miles, the federal aid secondary system (the farm to market system), and certain national parks and forest roads. The result of this previous policy is a relatively fine-scale network linking urban centers of all classes with each other, and linking urban centers with their tributary areas. The Interstate System is more gross in scale—in a sense it lies on top of previous highway systems and it emphasizes linkages within and between major cities.

Perhaps two things may be gleaned from this brief statement. First, the Interstate System may be thought of as a large city or metropolitan system of highways since it provides links between (and within) metropolitan areas. This represents a marked shift in federal policy because previous highway policy might be characterized as catering to rural areas and small urban centers. Another notion is that the Interstate System may be thought of as a new highway network. In many ways it is more comparable to networks of airline and railroad routes than present highway networks.

Magnitude of Changes Induced

How far-reaching will be the location shifts following construction of the Interstate Highway System? The writer is inclined to the view that these changes will be as significant as those induced by other major technological changes in transportation systems—railroad developments or paving of rural roads. Many do not share this strong an opinion and some discussion of points of view is appropriate.

It may be argued that the situation is very

different today from what it was when other transportation networks, say railroads, were developed. The railroads opened up large areas to distant markets, especially in the western United States. Consequently, many new industries were developed which produced directly from resources and exported products long distances. Extensive wheat farming is an example of an industry developed in this way. Also, railroads enabled centralization of many manufacturing and service activities from small local establishments to giant national centers. The iron and steel industry serves as an example of this type of change. Production which was previously highly decentralized gave way to competition from large centers of production. The key to these changes was a marked reduction in unit transportation cost with the introduction of the railroad. With reduced unit transportation cost new resources could be brought into the economy and new efficiencies of large-scale production could be realized.

The Interstate Highway System is also markedly reducing unit transportation cost. This is especially true of the portions of the Interstate System within urban centers, where congestion costs are high.[2] It is here that one might look first for changes induced by the Interstate System. What new resources will be brought into the economy? Most striking, perhaps, is the possibility for upgrading to urban land uses resources formerly used for typically rural land uses. Production of amenities from residential sites and recreational amenities are two cases in point. What activities will be centralized from local to larger scale? Perhaps governmental activities in urban centers will be among those most subject to change. Wholesale activities of all types, newspapers, and department stores might be other activities which will change their structure greatly. The Interstate Highway System will induce changes, but most of the changes will relate to different activities and resources than railroad-induced changes.

The tendency to over-simplify previous experience and use it to evaluate the future (which we have been guilty of doing in the paragraphs above) makes it especially difficult to envision the reshaping of the economy that will follow from the continued development of highways. One forgets, for example, that the pattern of railroad routes developed over a long period of time, and during that time many changes went on rather gradually. First, railroads were built in competition with inland waterways and coastal routes. It was probably very difficult to see widespread changes that these original beginnings foretold. At that time, as even now, cost comparisons between transportation media must have presented great difficulties. How difficult it must have been to visualize which of our industries would find great economies of centralization with the availability of railroad transportation. Many probably pointed out that production of buffalo hides hardly warranted building railroads through the arid West. To what extent are we guilty of the same kind of thinking about highways today?

There is some indication of changes that follow highway construction. It is well-known that marked changes in rural life were brought about by paving of rural highways.[3] It is now necessary to predict marked changes in urban areas which will follow current developments of highways.

Other Conditions

Highways alone are not enough to induce change, of course, just as railroads alone could not remake the face of America. The success of railroads depended upon markets for the products they hauled. Industrialization of Europe and the growth and development of the United States were necessary conditions for the great changes brought about by railroads. Certain conditions are necessary if changes are to be induced by the Interstate System. Continued urbanization and increasing demands for more leisure time at home, amenities, and services are conditions especially pertinent to the changes that will be induced by the Interstate System. Also, governmental conditions, such as the existence of FHA and transportation taxation policy, are important considerations in evaluating highway impact.

Some Research Questions

Decisions on the location of the System and its capacity largely have been made.[4] The Interstate System is limited to 41,000 miles and the general orientation of these routes is fixed. Decisions about capacity decisions have been made. That is, certain operational methods for forecasting traffic are used to determine traffic demands and capacity is installed to meet these demands. However, much research on allocation of facilities is needed, in spite of the fact that many of the major decisions have been made. Methods of making capacity decisions on the Interstate System could be improved. Need for investment in highway facilities seems unlimited and many decisions bearing on location and capacity of facilities similar to those made for the Interstate System will be made in the future.

Certain problems of financing the Interstate System have been recognized. The U.S. Bureau of Public Roads is currently undertaking a highway cost allocation study designed to deal with these problems at the federal level.[5] Surely this study will not provide all the answers at the federal level, and there is need for work on state and local problems of financing. Also, questions of charges to properly allocate traffic among the several kinds of carriers arise when highway financing is reconsidered, as well as from pressures of problems arising in other sectors of the transportation industry.[6]

The Relative Location Problem

Answering any one of the questions mentioned above requires some ability to speak intelligently about the influence of the Interstate System on activities. Answering questions of location and capacity obviously requires insights into effects on traffic by location shifts induced by the facility. Resolving questions of tax equity, financing, and the like requires ability to make intelligent estimates of location shifts. Thus, relative location is at the heart of these problems. The strategic position of some areas will be enhanced while that of others will be diminished when the highway improvements are made. Questions of how much change and where these changes will take place are inseparable.[7]

THE HIGHWAY SYSTEM AS A GRAPH

Notions from graph theory may be useful in evaluating the relative location problem. In the language of graph theory the Interstate Highway System is an ordinary graph with 325 edges terminating at 218 vertices. For convenience in this discussion, edges will be termed *routes,* vertices will be termed *places,* and the graph will be termed *highway system* or *network.* An example of a network is given by Fig. 6-2. Places are marked P_1, P_2, etc., and routes, $L(12)$, $L(23)$, etc. Properties which characterize ordinary graphs and, thus, transportation systems treated as ordinary graphs are:[8]

1 A network has a finite number of places.

2 Each route is a set consisting of two places.

3 Each route joins two different places.

4 At the most, only one route may join a pair of places.

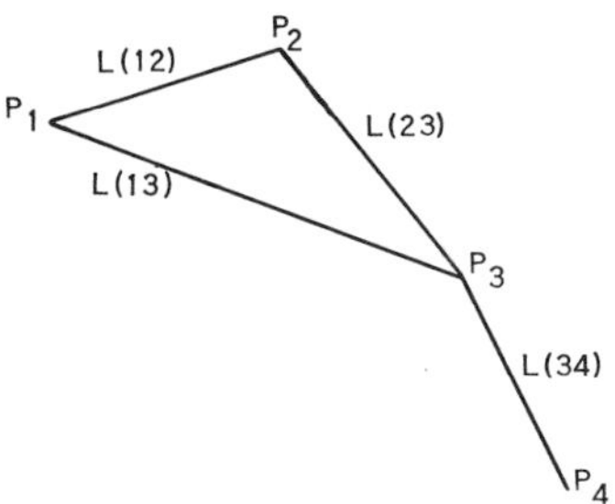

Fig. 6-2.

5 No distinctions are made between the "initial" and the "terminal" places of routes; in other words, routes are two-way.

Identification of Places

It was necessary to adopt operational definitions of a place on the Interstate Highway System. All Standard Metropolitan Areas were recognized as places, provided they were on the System. 143 SMA's are on the System, 23 are not. Each intersection of three or more routes on the System was recognized as a place, regardless of whether or not it was occupied by an urban center which met the size criteria. Also, all ends of routes were recognized as places, e.g., Sweetgrass, Montana. The definition of place was, then, partly topological and partly based on urban size criteria.

These definitions identify a *planar graph*—the intersection of any two routes on the graph is a place on the network. It was decided to use the topological definition of places because these ends of routes and, especially, intersections have locational assets; they are able to ship and receive from several directions. It is worth noting that many intersections on other transportation systems have not developed to the degree that the location at an intersection might seem to warrant. Complicating factors of tariff structures might have contributed to this. In the highway case there is an effect due to presence of demand on a highway which may be important in giving intersections an impetus for development. Heavy streams of traffic create demands for food, lodging and other goods and services, and these are not supplied by the facility itself. There are no dining rooms, staterooms, or swimming pools on the highway as there are on ships.

Consideration of intersections as major places introduces interesting problems which need to be investigated further. As the transportation network is filled-in in an underdeveloped area, for example, intersections on the transportation system are created. These have the effect of introducing new places with strategic locations in the economy and shifting the relative location of places already developed (Fig. 6-3).

Measures of Connectivity

Definitions:

A *path* is a collection of routes P_1P_2, P_2P_3, . . . , P_nP_m, where all *places* are different from each other.

The *length* of a path is the number of routes in it.

The *distance* between two places is the length of the shortest path (or any one of the shortest paths) joining them.

A number of measures have been suggested or may be directly inferred from the concepts of graph theory for measuring the relative cohesiveness of a network or the relative position of places on the network. One such con-

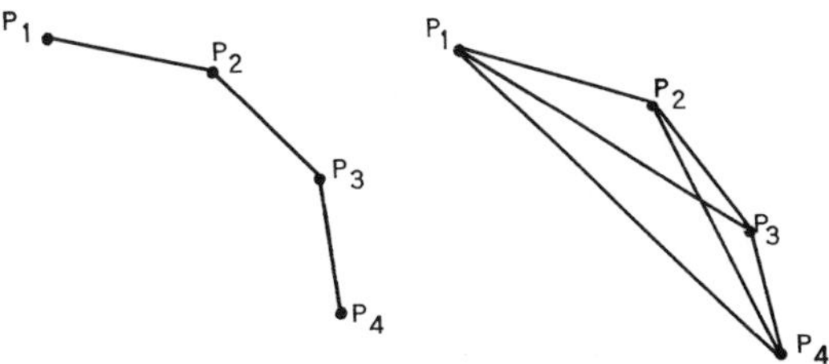

Fig. 6-3 A: Undeveloped area; B: developed area.

cept is the *associated number* of a place. This number is the maximum of the distances from this place to all other places. In Fig. 6-2, the associated number of P_1 is 2; of P_3, 1. The *central place* of a network is that place whose associate number is a minimum. P_3 is the central place of Fig. 6-2. The maximum associated number indicates another characteristic of a network, the *diameter*.

Also, it is known that if there are m places in a network then the maximum possible number of routes, L^*, in the network is

$$L^* = \left[\frac{m(m-1)}{2}\right].$$

Prihar has suggested that the *degree of connectivity* of a network for which the number of places is known can be expressed:[9]

$$\text{maximum connectivity} = L^*/\left[\frac{m(m-1)}{2}\right] = 1$$

$$\text{minimum connectivity} = L^*/(m-1)$$

$$\text{degree of connectivity} = L^*/\text{observed number of routes.}$$

As Prihar suggests, these notions might be very useful in designing networks with several types of cost in mind. If unit over-the-road cost is relatively low and investment cost of facilities high, then the network might take the form of A in Fig. 6-3. If the reverse is true—investment cost low and over-the-road cost high—the network might take the form of B in Fig. 6-3.

Shimbel has suggested a measure of the *dispersion*, $D(X)$, of a network X, namely:[10]

$$D(X) = \sum_{i=1}^{n} \sum_{j=1}^{n} \text{distance } (ij).$$

He has also suggested a measure of the *accessibility* of the network to the ith place:

$$A(iX) = \sum_{j=1}^{n} \text{distance } (ij) \qquad i = 1, \ldots, n.$$

Also,

$$\sum_{i=1}^{n} (iX) = D(X)$$

An ordinary network corresponds to a matrix $X = \{x_{ij}\}$ when:

$x_{ij} = 1$ if, and only if, a route exists between i and j

$x_{ij} = 0$ otherwise.

The matrix corresponding to A of Fig. 6-3 is:

$$X = \begin{matrix} 0 & 1 & 0 & 0 \\ 1 & 0 & 1 & 0 \\ 0 & 1 & 0 & 1 \\ 0 & 0 & 1 & 0 \end{matrix}$$

and the matrix corresponding to B is:

$$X = \begin{matrix} 0 & 1 & 1 & 1 \\ 1 & 0 & 1 & 1 \\ 1 & 1 & 0 & 1 \\ 1 & 1 & 1 & 0 \end{matrix}$$

Examination of the matrix corresponding to a network suggests methods of studying connectiveness. A glance at the ith row or column of the matrix indicates the number of routes associated with the ith place. Examination of the powers of the matrix is also useful. The matrix X^n contains elements indicating the number of ways the ith place may be reached from the jth in n steps. For example, the entry $x_{ij} = C$ indicates that there are C possible ways in the network for place j to be reached from place i in n steps. The sum over the jth column would indicate all the ways available in n steps for place j to be reached from other places. A general notion of connectivity may be obtained from the matrix T where $T = X + X^2 + X^3 + \ldots + X^n$. Shimbel has termed the matrix X^n the *solution matrix*, in the case where powering of the matrix is carried until there are no elements having the value zero. n is the *solution time* of the system. Elements of this matrix show the numbers of ways to reach place j from place i in the n steps. Elements of the matrix T display this information for all routes and a summation across the columns or down the rows of T will produce a vector of numbers indicating what we might call the *accessibility* of each place on the system.

All of the above properties of a graph and associated matrices X^i and T may be proved by reference to definitions of matrix algebra. Consider, for example, the summation

$$x^{(2)}_{ik} = \sum_{j=1}^{n} c_{ij}c_{jk}.$$

The only terms which contribute to this summation are those where $c_{ij} = c_{jk} = 1$. When this is the case, there is a two length path between i and k via j.[11] By definition $x^{(2)}_{ij}$ is the element in the ith row and k^{th} column of the matrix x^2.

ANALYSES

The regional subsystem formed by the Interstate System in a portion of the Southeast United States was selected for exploratory study. This subsystem is shown on the accompanying map (Fig. 6-4). The subsystem has 45 places and 64 routes. This particular subsystem was selected arbitrarily. The small size of the subsystem made computations relatively simple.

There are at least five types of analysis, not all of which have been made here, which might be applied to this subsystem, namely:

1 Analysis of the connection of the subsystem to the larger highway system.

2 Analysis of the subsystem as a whole.

3 Analysis of the position of particular places on the subsystem.

4 Analysis of details of the subsystem within each urban center or place. A comparison of the within-city connections of the Interstate System will reveal marked differences from city to city.[12] One would expect, then, within-city differences from city to city resulting from the construction of the system.

5 Comparative analysis of different transportation graphs. These might be undertaken at any one of the four levels of analysis suggested above.

THE REGIONAL SUBSYSTEM

The following statements may be made about the regional subsystem:

1 Its connectivity is

$$L^* = \frac{45(45-1)}{2} = 1{,}980$$

$$\text{connectivity} = \frac{L^*}{L} = \frac{1{,}980}{64} = 30.94$$

2 The diameter of the network is 12.

3 The central places of the network are at Atlanta, Columbia, Spartanburg, D, Macon, Savannah, Ashville and Greenville.

4 The dispersion of the graph is

$$D(X) = \sum_{i=1}^{n} \sum_{j=1}^{n} \text{distance } (ij) = 9{,}292.$$

Evaluation of Places on the Subsystem

It was noted earlier that there were a number of ways the position of a single place on the system might be evaluated. Examples of evaluation of accessibility or status of places follow.

1 The associated number is one indication of how accessible places are to the network. Associated numbers were computed by deter-

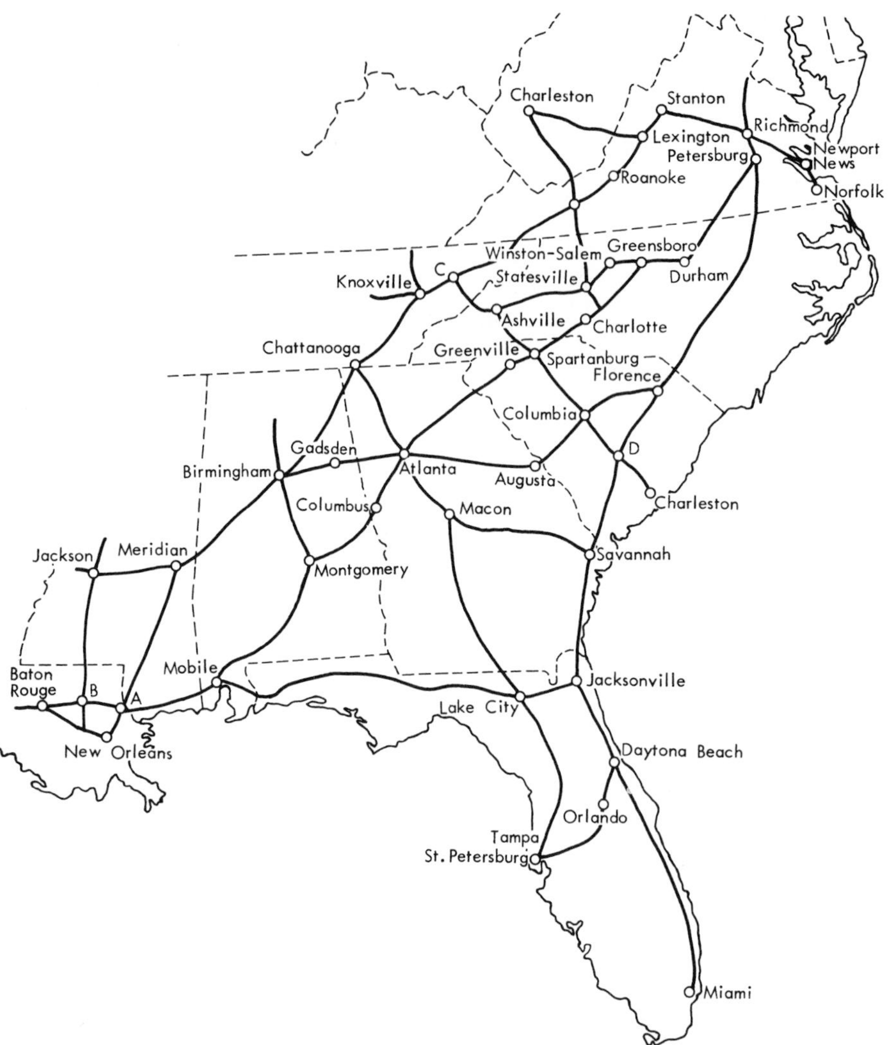

Fig. 6-4 A portion of the Interstate Highway System.

mining the longest distance for each place. The result is given in Table 6-1. It must be remembered that distance by definition is the shortest path between two places.

2 The accessibility index, $A(iX)$, for places on the system is also given in Table 6-1. This may be thought of as the accessibility of places to the network.

3 An alternate method of measuring accessibility has been made following the method suggested by Shimbel and Katz.[13] The operational definition of the method is as follows:

Let X be the n by n matrix corresponding to the subsystem.

$$T = sX + s^2X^2 + s^3X^3 + \ldots + s^rX^r + \ldots$$

s is a scalar, $0 < s \leqslant 1$, measuring the effectiveness of a one-route connection, s^2 is the

Table 6-1 Some Measures of Connectiveness

Place	Associated Number	A(i,X)		Shimbel-Katz Accessibility	
		number	rank	number	rank
Atlanta	7	146	1½	1.88	1
Birmingham	8	173	10	1.37	2
Petersburg	9	189	16½	1.34	3
Columbia	7	157	3	1.35	4
Spartanburg	7	160	4½	1.31	5
A	10	213	24½	1.29	6
Statesville	9	214	26	1.24	7
D	7	168	8	1.22	8
Lake City	8	181	12	1.22	9
B	11	251	38	1.17	10
E	9	218	29½	1.16	11
Macon	7	160	4½	1.16	12
Florence	8	173	10	1.12	13
Mobile	9	213	24½	1.05	14
Meridian	9	199	22	1.01	15
Savannah	7	146	1½	1.01	16
Chattanooga	8	173	10	.99	17
Montgomery	9	196	20	.99	18
New Orleans	11	252	39	.96	19
Charlotte	8	189	16½	.96	20
Ashville	7	183	13½	.95	21
Jacksonville	8	188	15	.95	22
C	8	193	18½	.92	23
Stanton	11	257	40½	.90	24
Augusta	6	165	7	.86	25
Greenville	7	162	6	.86	26
Greensboro	9	215	27	.82	27
Lexington	11	257	40½	.80	28
Columbus	8	183	13½	.80	29
Daytona Beach	9	233	32	.72	30
Gadsen	9	198	21	.70	31
Durham	10	221	31	.68	32
Jackson	10	237	34	.67	33
Baton Rouge	12	293	44	.66	34
Winston-Salem	10	235	33	.65	35
Charleston	10	244	36½	.63	36½
Roanoke	10	244	36½	.63	36½
Knoxville	8	193	18½	.62	38
Newport News	11	259	42	.62	39
Tampa - St. Petersburg	9	217	28	.59	40
Norfolk	12	302	45	.55	41
Orlando	9	243	35	.52	42
Richmond	10	218	29½	.39	43
Charleston	8	212	23	.36	44
Miami	10	269	43	.27	45

effectiveness of a path with two routes, s^r is the effectiveness of an r length path. Using this measure, accessibility of the ith place, a_i, is

$$a_i = \sum_{j=1}^{n} t_{ij} \qquad i = 1, \ldots, n.$$

The relation

$$T + I = (I - sX)^{-1} = I + sX + s^2X^2 + s^3X^3 + \ldots$$

may be used to find T, provided s is selected in a proper manner.

The scalar used was .3 so each one-route path has the weight .3. Two-route paths have the weight $.3 \times .3 = .09$. Three-route paths have the weight $.3^3$. Results of this analysis are presented in Table 6-1.

Comparative Analysis

One regional subsystem might be compared with the subsystem in another region; a regional subsystem might be compared with subsystems of other transportation systems in the same or other regions; and a regional subgraph might be compared with some theoretical construct. A theoretical comparison has been made with a concept of a hierarchical arrangement of urban centers. Hierarchical notions flow from the work of Christaller and Lösch. Briefly, it is argued that there is a system of cities ranging from hamlets through villages, towns, regional capitals, and national capitals, and perhaps even international capitals.[14] The relative accessibility or status of each place might reflect a hierarchical ordering. This notion was tested using the data from the Shimbel-Katz analysis and applying the nearest neighbor statistic. The results are shown in Table 6-2. Although there is a slight tendency for grouping, it is not significant. Consequently the hypothesis that no grouping or hierarchy occurs cannot be rejected. This is by no means a test of whether or not an

Table 6-2 Nearest Neighbor Analysis of Places on the Interstate System[a]

	Nearest Neighbors		
	First	Second	Third
Observed Reflexive Points	34	21	12
Expected Reflexive Points	30	20	13

[a] *The difference between the observed and expected distributions is not significant. The nearest neighbor analysis is based on P. J. Clark, "Grouping in Spatial Distributions,"* SCIENCE, *123 (1956), pp. 373-4.*

hierarchical system of cities exists in the southeast. It is a test of whether or not the connectiveness of the highway system so far as individual places is concerned indicates a hierarchy.

There are a number of ways transportation systems may be compared. The operational question that is most difficult to answer is that of recognizing the systems to be compared. A crude comparison of the Interstate System with the railroad network of the study area has been made by comparing the number of rays or routes at each place.[15] Only a partial analysis was made, using the data in Table 6-3. These results are quite interesting. For one thing, there are almost twice as many rays on the railroad system as there are on the Interstate System. The expected number of rays on the Interstate System (based on the distribution of rays on the railroad system) is quite like the observed number. However, Atlanta would seem to be better served by the Interstate System than by the railroad network and New Orleans and Montgomery less well served. This leads to the tentative observation that in spite of the fact of the relatively sprawling character of the Interstate System, certain central places on the network are emphasized more than are central places on the railroad network. The reverse is also true. This is an interesting conclusion, but it is relatively specious at this state of the investigation.

ACCOMPLISHMENTS

In this [work] we have done no more than introduce the problem of the analysis of transportation networks and suggested some descriptive approaches via modern graph theory. Whether the approaches have merit remains an open question. There are two things in their favor, however. One is the relative simplicity of graph theory; another is the ability to look at the System as a whole or to look at individual parts of it in terms of the whole. There are alternate approaches that have the latter merit, but their application to problems of the scope of the Interstate System would require tremendous effort.[16]

At least two major inadequacies of the approach should be mentioned. For one, graph concepts are in no way normative. Whether or not some arrangement is good or bad, whether or not links should be added to system, and like decision-making questions require empirical statements outside of the usual content of graph theory. Just what sort of relationships need to be specified and how they may be introduced is a subject for study. Also, the user of this method must make rather arbitrary decisions regarding the content of the graph. In the case of the Interstate System, the content of the graph is pretty much by definition. Even this is questionable, since there are routes constructed, under construction, or planned which are very similar in character to the Interstate System, but not integral parts of it. Evaluation of the railroad system in comparison to the Interstate System also required definition of a graph. Problems of definition, and perhaps a host of others, will become clearer as work continues.

Table 6-3 Comparison of Selected Cities

City	Railroad Routes	Interstate Routes	
		Expected[a]	Observed
Atlanta	9	4.8	6
Birmingham	9	4.8	5
Petersburg	5	2.7	3
Columbia	9	4.8	4
Spartanburg	6	3.2	4
Statesville	4	2.2	3
Lake City	5	2.7	4
Macon	6	3.2	3
Florence	5	2.7	3
Mobile	6	3.2	3
Meridian	6	3.2	3
Savannah	7	3.8	3
Chattanooga	6	3.2	4
Montgomery	8	4.3	3
New Orleans	8	4.3	3
Charlotte	7	3.8	3
Total	106	56.9	57

[a] *Number expected if Interstate Routes were distributed in the same manner as railroad routes. The difference between the observed and expected distributions is not significant.*

NOTES

1 See U.S., Congress, House, *Interregional Highways,* 78th Cong., 2nd Sess., House Document 379; _____, *Highway Needs of the National Defense,* 81st Cong., 1st Sess., House Document 249; and "Federal Air Highway Act of 1956," U.S. 70 *Statutes at Large* 374 (1956).

2 Exact saving from freeway use is difficult to estimate. Including the value of time saved, passenger car savings are approximately 2 cents per vehicle mile and truck savings about 10 cents. See American Association of State Highway Officials, *Road User Benefit for Highway Improvement,* Washington, D.C.; City of Los Angeles, Street and Parkway Design Division, *A Study of Freeway System Benefits,* 1954; and Hyman Joseph, "Automobile Operating Costs," *Cats Research News,* 3 (November 13, 1959), pp. 9ff.

3 See, for example, Jean Labatut and Wheaton Lane (eds.), *Highways in Our National Life, a Symposium,* Princeton Univ. Press, 1950.

4 See references given in footnote 1.

5 The study is discussed in *Third Progress Report of the Highway Cost Allocation Study,* 86th Cong., 1st Sess., House Document 91.

6 This problem has been discussed widely in the literature, e.g., *Highway Investment and Financing,* Bulletin 222, Highway Research Board (NAS-NRC, Publication 682), Washington, D.C., 1959.

7 These notions are elaborated in W. L. Garrison, B. J. L. Berry, D. F. Marble, Richard Morrill and J. Nystuen, *Studies of Highway Development and Geographic Change,* Seattle: Univ. of Washington Press, 1959.

8 For bibliographies and expository discussions of graph theory see Dorwin Cartwright, "The Potential Contribution of Graph Theory to Organization Theory," chapter in *Modern Organization Theory,* Mason Haire, ed., New York: Wiley, 1959; Frank Harary, "Graph Theoretic Methods in the Management Sciences," *Management Science,* 5 (1959), pp. 387–403; and Frank Harary and Robert Z. Norman, *Graph Theory as a Mathematical Model in Social Science,* Univ. of Michigan, Institute for Social Research, 1953. Basic references are Denis König, *Theorie der Endlichen und Unendlichen Graphen,* New York: Chelsea Publishing Company, 1950 and Claude Berge, *Theorie des Graphes et ses Applications,* Paris: Dunod, 1958. Berge's chapters 8, 13, 14 and 20 are of special interest.

9 Z. Prihar, "Topological Properties of Telecommunication Networks," *Proceedings,* Institute of Radio Engineers, 44 (1956), pp. 929–933.

10 Alfonso Shimbel, "Structural Parameters of Communication Networks," *Bull. Math. Biophysics,* 15 (1953), pp. 501–507.

11 This method counts paths from j to j, e.g., in 4 steps one might follow the path P_1 P_2, P_2 P_3, P_3 P_2, P_2 P_1. In certain cases, this may not be desired.

12 Maps of the urban configurations of the Interstate System are in U.S. Dept. of Commerce, Bureau of Public Roads, *General Location of National System of Interstate Highways,* September 1955.

13 Shimbel, op. cit., and W. Katz, "A New Status Index Derived from Sociometric Analysis," *Psychometrika,* 18 (1953), pp. 39–43.

14 There is a notion of hierarchy in graph theory, but it is not used here.

15 The count of railroad rays was made using Edward L. Ullman's *U.S. Railroads, Classified According to Capacity and Relative Importance* (Map), New York: Simmons-Boardman Publishing Company, 1950.

16 It might be useful, for example, to merge information on mathematical programming with information on highway networks as is done for electrical networks in Jack Bonnell Dennis' *Mathematical Programming and Electrical Networks,* Technology Press of M.I.T. and Wiley, 1957.

Selection 7

Linkage Importance in a Regional Highway Network

C. C. Kissling

A highway network provides defined channels of movement for the physical flows of goods and people between places. There is little need to stress here the importance of movement in everyday life. Interaction between people and places requires access, and access is only possible if there are connecting links. One may consider a highway network as a system of points and lines as in a graph, the points being the urban centers or road junctions and the lines the individual highway links via which inter-nodal interaction takes place.

Network structure, that is, its layout and the characteristics of its elements, conditions

Canadian Geographer, vol. XIII, no. 2, 1969, pp. 113–129. Reprinted by permission of the author and editor.

how accessible points will be to each other. In any network there will be routeways composed of one or more links which provide the best access between pairs of points whether "best" be defined as the least distance, time or cost path. Some links in a network may contribute more to inter-nodal accessibility than others and on this basis may be compared and assigned an important rating. There are distinct ways by which a network link may be included in a particular routeway sequence. For instance, a link may be the only one connecting different subsections of a network, thus insuring that all routeways between the subsections take in the link. Even when alternative links exist between network subsections, it is possible, because of location, for one link to be favored over all others when the alternative would produce highly circuitous routeways. The relative location of a link in the network can greatly influence the number of times it appears in inter-nodal routeway sequences.

Quite often, within a given network structure, a series of closely parallel links will yield routeways between pairs of points which deviate minimally in value from one another. In such situations a number of routeways may "bend" to include one or two links which offer better value than others close by. The properties on the links themselves rather than their relative location influences the frequency with which they appear in inter-nodal routeway sequences. Where a link provides virtually the only connection and must be included in a number of routeways, its removal from the network would cause, most probably, considerable divergence in routeway patterns. Accessibility levels would become worse. On the other hand, removal of a frequently used link which is closely paralled by others is less likely to cause such divergence or to worsen accessibility levels to the same extent. One may accordingly assess relative linkage importance in terms of their impact upon inter-nodal accessibility levels.

To evaluate linkage importance in this manner one must first express quantitatively the concept of accessibility. Finite measurement of accessibility is only possible between specified objects that are linked by a bounded connecting system. Not all objects have need of access to each other. Any measurement would therefore be meaningless unless interaction is a possibility via some connecting system. The linkage system itself defines the boundary conditions and spatial situation wherein finite measurement can take place.

On a regional highway network the objects between which accessibility might be considered may include the populated urban nodes considered as points, and the sections of highway considered as lines. Simple geometric distance along the highway channel may be taken to represent the disutility associated with the space intervening between two points on the network. Though commonly encountered in the literature, this parameter has serious shortcomings.[1] All intervening spaces of similar dimension are considered to yield equal impediment to interaction regardless of direction or method of transport. Reality refutes such a gross assumption.

Non-Euclidean time distances may be substituted in an attempt to make allowance for movement by different transport media over variable terrain conditions. It is feasible for an indirect routeway between two points to be a faster one than the shortest path. While perhaps more realistic for some forms of interaction, this measure too can seem meaningless for communications media where time taken may be virtually identical over a considerable range of distance. Monetary costs of operation may better represent the disutility of intervening space in such a situation.

Indeed, the routeways between pairs of points which in turn minimize these functions may vary considerably in time and space as may the method of transport. If one substitutes perceived values for the actual distance time or cost parameters, then a whole set of additional measures of accessibility can be considered which recognize that perfect information is seldom found in reality. Clearly no one measurement parameter meets all situations and for a particular study a choice must be made to fit the desired objective.

In this [work] attention is focused upon the 1966 regional highway network linking the urban populations equal or greater than 5,000 inhabitants within the province of Nova Scotia. (See Fig. 7-1.) The named nodes in the schematic representation of the highway network in Fig. 7-1 are the populated urban agglomerations, in some cases representing an amalgamation of a series of nearly contiguous towns: for instance, Glace Bay is included in Sydney, Dartmouth in Halifax, and Stellarton in New Glasgow. Accessibility within this system is measured in terms of the costs incurred in place to place trucking operations. These costs include both operating "over the road" expenses and time costs.

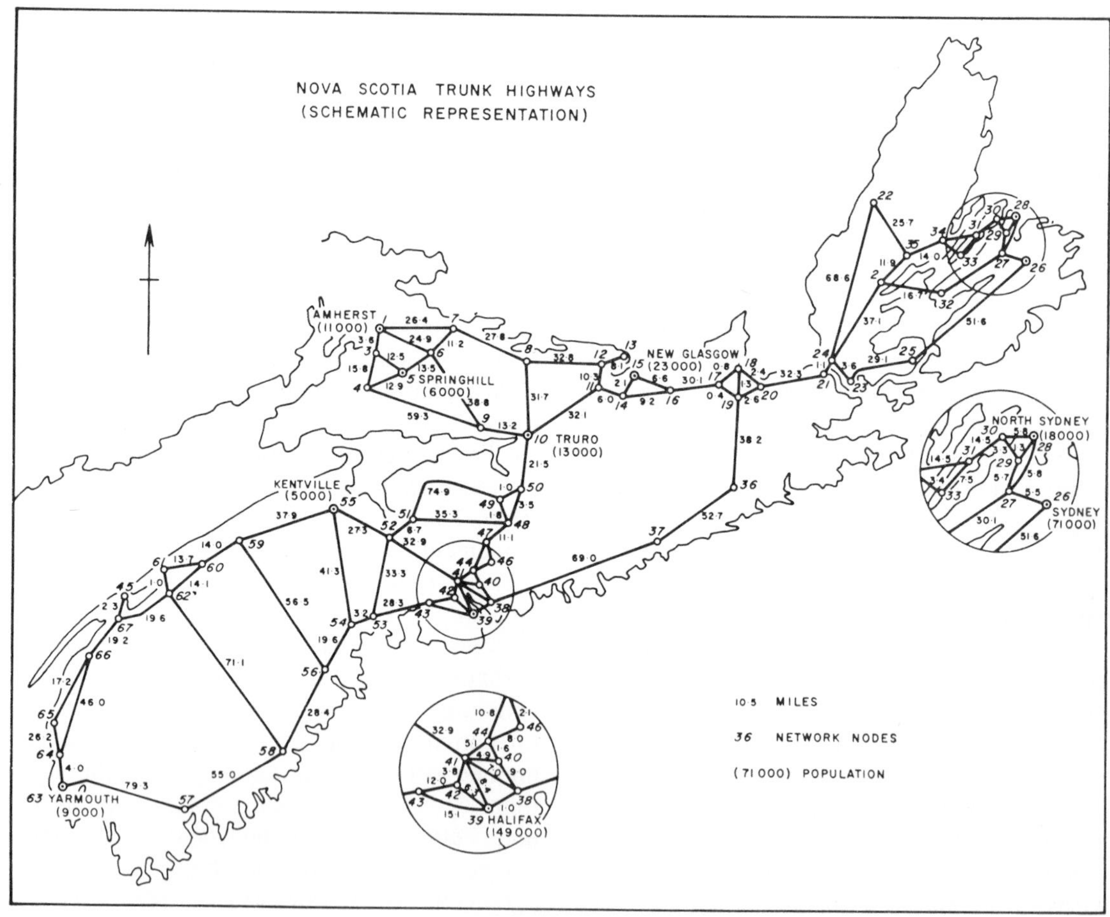

Fig. 7-1.

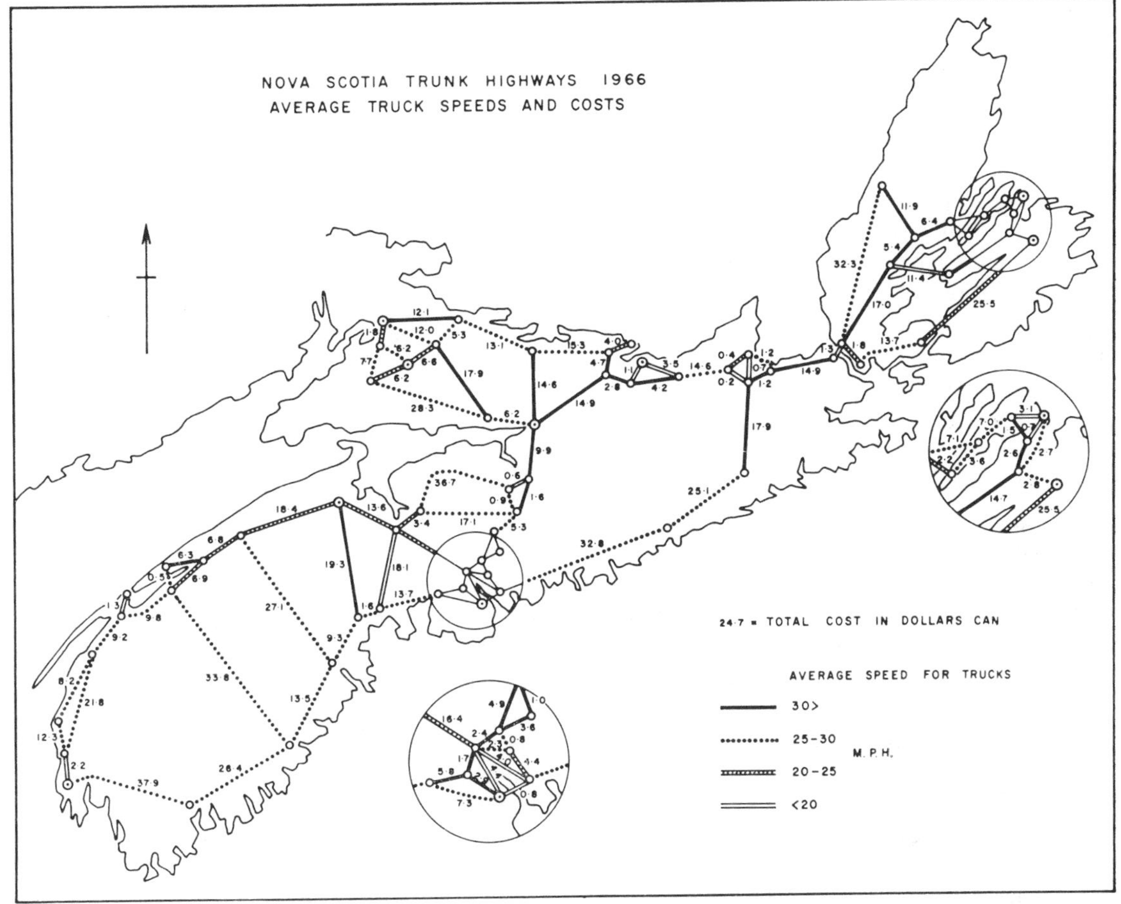

Fig. 7-2.

Expected average costs for operating a typical 30,000-pound gross loaded weight truck on each link in the Nova Scotia highway network were calculated from an analysis of the physical properties of the highways, annual average daily traffic statistics, and the extent of legally controlled speed zones. A detailed highway inventory was compiled, largely from fieldwork, which recorded for each link in the system such parameters as pavement condition and age, number of feet of "critical" gradient,[2] percentage of overtaking opportunity, and the number of speed-reducing curves, structures, and road junctions. The impact of these physical features on truck speed and operating costs has received considerable attention.[3] Average total cost figures and average speeds for each link as depicted in Fig. 7-2 were derived from the highways information in accordance with the relationships described in reference three, actual methods having been discussed elsewhere.[4]

One type of accessibility measure that may be calculated from the analysis of link costs on a network like this has been suggested by

Shimbel.[5] It refers to the accessibility of a vertex i to a network N, symbolically

$$A(iN) = \sum_{j=1}^{n} d(i, j),$$

where A is the accessibility measure, n the number of vertices (nodes or points) in the matrix N, and d the value associated with the minimum path from i to j. It is in fact the summation of the value of routeways connecting a place to all others in the network. In practice this summation may be restricted to specific vertices in the network, for instance the population nodes and not other highway junctions. Table 7-1, columns A and B, details this type of accessibility measure for the province of Nova Scotia.

Following Burton, one may assess the relative importance of a highway link in terms of its contribution to nodal accessibility.[6] The amount of change in accessibility levels, as measured using the Shimbel type of index, caused by the alteration to link layout or value may be taken as a quantitative expression of the relative importance of individual links in the system. A strong drawback to the practical implementation of this method for assessing linkage importance is that the least cost routeways between all pairs of points in the network must be calculated over again for each link in the system. For a large network this becomes prohibitive even with the application of an efficient computerized algorithm for solving minimum routeways. For the Nova Scotia example, ninety-nine runs of the algorithm, detailed later, taking in excess of sixteen hours computing time on an IBM 360/44 machine would have been required to produce a rating for each link.

An alternative method of assessing linkage importance in a network, still in terms of nodal accessibility levels, requires that the minimum-value routeways between all pairs of network nodes be calculated once only. A particular link may appear in more than one routeway sequence connecting all nodes in the network to each other. The number of appearances of a link in such routeways may be taken as an expression of its relative importance. These paths are those which yield the best possible Shimbel type accessibility measures. Furthermore, an additional advantage of this method of assessing linkage importance is that a different type of nodal accessibility can also be derived. This refers to the accessibility of a node in the network to the routeways of the network. A particular node in the network, may because of cen-

Table 7-1 Nodal Accessibility Indices for Nova Scotia

Network place name node	Access Ratings*			
	A	B	C	D
1 Amherst	52.9	6.5	11	13
5 Springhill	51.1	6.3	5	9
10 Truro	34.6	4.7	108	155
15 New Glasgow area	36.9	5.2	6	39
26 Sydney/Glace Bay	66.8	9.1	8	127
28 North Sydney	68.7	9.3	6	111
39 Halifax/Dartmouth	40.2	5.9	11	105
55 Kentville	45.9	6.6	100	35
63 Yarmouth	84.4	11.8	9	7

*A Access to all network nodes in 00's of dollars. B Access to named nodes in 00's of dollars. C Access to all inter-nodal routeways (unweighted). D Access to inter-nodal (named) routeways (weighted). The smaller the figures the better the access ratings on measures A and B; the poorer on measures C and D.

tral location, evidence a relatively good Shimbel type of accessibility measure yet be by-passed by all but a few network routeways. (Compare columns A and C in Table 7-1 for New Glasgow.) Those routeways which do reach a node in this situation are likely to be the ones which either originate or terminate there. In other words a place may lie adjacent but not athwart the main lines of interaction. By summing the number of appearances in routeways of all links incident upon a given node, one may obtain a measure of the relative accessibility of that node to the routeways of the network. Measures of this type for the urban places in Nova Scotia are listed in Column C, Table 7-1.

In practice all routeways need not be treated as equally significant. Those connecting small places quite remote from each other are unlikely to generate the same volume of interaction as routeways connecting large places in close proximity. A particular link may appear in routeways of varying import. Each appearance may be weighted in some manner to take this into account. For instance, application of a simple gravity model may enable one to differentiate between routeways in terms of potential interaction over them. If one assumes potential interaction to be directly proportional to the product of the populations found at either extremity of the routeway linking them, and inversely proportional to the cost of traversing the routeway, one can readily derive an index of routeway importance (see Table 7-2). If each link appearance is scaled according to the routeway in which it appears, then its over-all importance to nodal accessibility and network interaction may be assessed. Linkage importance in Nova Scotia based upon both unweighted and weighted routeways, the latter confined to routeways between named population centres, are depicted graphically in Figs. 7-3 and 7-4.

Table 7-2 Routeway Costs and Routeway Importance Ratings Between Selected Places in Nova Scotia***

		Upper Triangle: Routeway Importance Rating								
Nodes†	Place and Population (thousands)††	Nodes 1	5	10	15	26	28	39	55	63
1	Amherst (11)		.825	.396	.515	.623	.153	2.557	.067	.064
5	Springhill (6)	80		.254	.618	.340	.084	1.523	.039	.036
10	Truro (13)	361	307		1.059	.971	.855	7.776	.143	.098
15	New Glasgow area (23)	491	489	188		3.003	.587	8.918	.179	.577
26	Sydney/Glace Bay (71)	1254	1252	951	767		40.622	8.614	.253	.298
28	North Sydney area (18)	1295	1293	992	808	55		2.467	.062	.074
39	Halifax/Dartmouth (149)	641	587	280	468	1231	1272		7.911	1.478
55	Kentville (5)	816	762	455	643	1406	1447	344		.061
63	Yarmouth (9)	1553	1499	1192	1380	2143	2184	1081	737	

Lower Triangle: Costs via Least-Cost Route (last place decimal)

*Routeway costs are extracted from the relevant portions of Table 7-3.

**Formula for Routeway Importance: $P_i \times P_j / C$, where P_i = population of place i in thousands, P_j = population of place j in thousands, C = truck costs between i and j.

†Node numbers refer to those in Figure 7-1.

††Population figures are taken from Census reports.

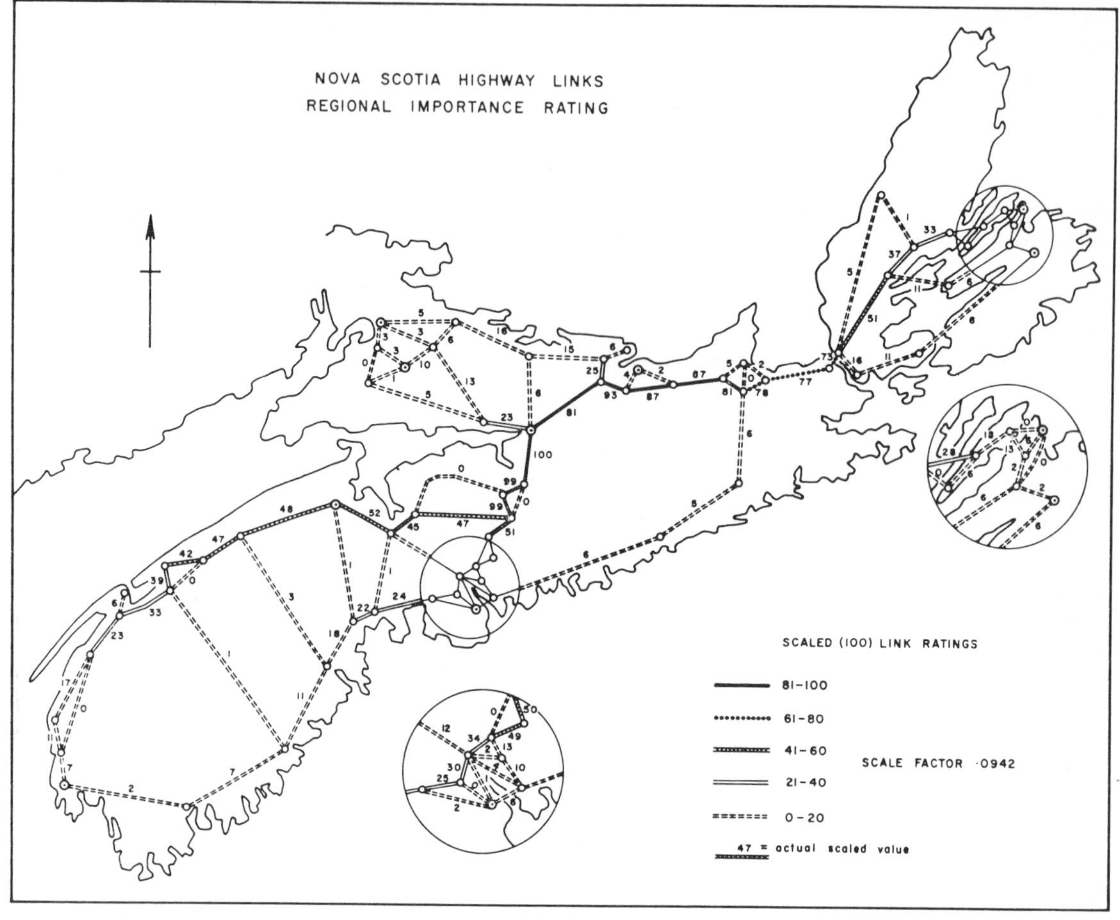

Fig. 7-3.

It must be kept in mind that the presentation of linkage importance in Fig. 7-3 assumes all routeways and all nodes to be equally important in the region. By comparison, Fig. 7-4 emphasizes those links which are the most important in the least-cost routeways between the principal population centers, these routeways being weighted according to the potential interaction index (see Table 7-2).

Derivation of the routeway nodal sequences via the least-cost path is obtained in the manner detailed later. . . . An example of a portion of the computer output from the programmed solution to the Nova Scotia network is given in Table 7-3, the full listings for the sixty-seven nodes being available upon request to the author. Table 7-3 lists the value associated with the least-cost routeway between pairs of nodes and the nodal sequence by which this was obtained. For instance, the value of the routeway between node 50 and node 43 is given in row 50 column 43 as 213 or $21.30 as the parameter chosen is dollars and the last digit is decimal. To find the relevant routeway nodal sequence, scan along row 50 to column 43 and note the figure given in parenthesis.

This number signifies the next but last node traversed on the route from node 50 to node 43. Still scanning along row 50 this time to the column corresponding to the number just found (42) the next node in the sequence will be found in parentheses (41). This process is continued till a zero entry is encountered which signals the next node is the start node, in this case 50. The full routeway sequence for this example is thus read of in reverse order, 43, 42, 41, 44, 46, 47, 48, 49, 50, which may be checked by inspection of Figs. 7-1 and 7-2.

Before turning to a discussion of individual linkage importance ratings in Nova Scotia, it may be advantageous to detail the algorithm used which calculated the least-cost routeways. As this is technical, the reader may wish to pass it over. Fortran IV programs developed by the author designed for use with or without direct access storage depending upon machine configuration and core storage, are available upon request.

The method used is based upon a technique outlined by Shimbel.[7] A structure matrix S may be defined such that any element s_{ij}

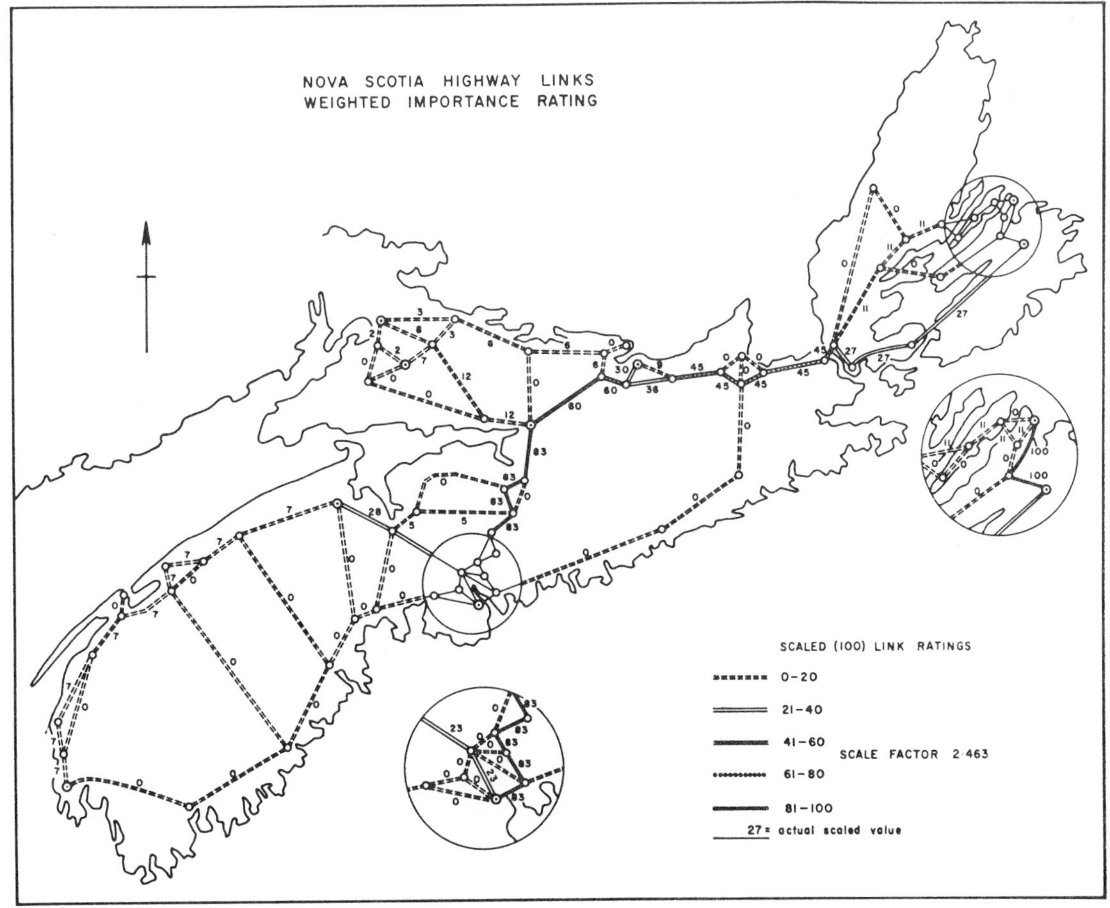

Fig. 7-4.

Table 7-3 Nova Scotia Trucking Inter-nodal Routeway Costs and Routing Sequence Matrix

Row	41	42	43	44	45	46	47	48	49	50
1	598 (44)	615 (41)	673 (42)	574 (46)	1247 (67)	538 (47)	528 (48)	475 (49)	466 (50)	460 (10)
2	948 (44)	965 (41)	1023 (42)	924 (46)	1597 (67)	888 (47)	878 (48)	825 (49)	816 (50)	810 (10)
3	606 (44)	623 (41)	681 (42)	582 (46)	1255 (67)	546 (47)	536 (48)	483 (49)	474 (50)	468 (10)
4	582 (44)	599 (41)	657 (42)	558 (46)	1231 (67)	522 (47)	512 (48)	459 (49)	450 (50)	444 (10)
5	544 (44)	561 (41)	619 (42)	520 (46)	1193 (67)	484 (47)	474 (48)	421 (49)	412 (50)	406 (10)
6	478 (44)	495 (41)	553 (42)	454 (46)	1127 (67)	418 (47)	408 (48)	355 (49)	346 (50)	340 (10)
7	514 (44)	531 (41)	589 (42)	490 (46)	1163 (67)	454 (47)	444 (48)	391 (49)	382 (50)	376 (10)
8	383 (44)	400 (41)	458 (42)	359 (46)	1032 (67)	323 (47)	313 (48)	260 (49)	251 (50)	245 (10)
9	299 (44)	316 (41)	374 (42)	275 (46)	948 (67)	239 (47)	229 (48)	176 (49)	167 (50)	161 (10)
10	237 (44)	254 (41)	312 (42)	213 (46)	886 (67)	177 (47)	167 (48)	114 (49)	105 (50)	99 (0)
11	386 (44)	403 (41)	461 (42)	362 (46)	1035 (67)	326 (47)	316 (48)	263 (49)	254 (50)	248 (10)
12	433 (44)	450 (41)	508 (42)	409 (46)	1082 (67)	373 (47)	363 (48)	310 (49)	301 (50)	295 (10)
13	473 (44)	490 (41)	548 (42)	449 (46)	1122 (67)	413 (47)	403 (48)	350 (49)	341 (50)	335 (10)
14	414 (44)	431 (41)	489 (42)	390 (46)	1063 (67)	354 (47)	344 (48)	291 (49)	282 (50)	276 (10)
15	425 (44)	442 (41)	500 (42)	401 (46)	1074 (67)	365 (47)	355 (48)	302 (49)	293 (50)	287 (10)
16	456 (44)	473 (41)	531 (42)	432 (46)	1105 (67)	396 (47)	386 (48)	333 (49)	324 (50)	318 (10)
17	602 (44)	619 (41)	677 (42)	578 (46)	1251 (67)	542 (47)	532 (48)	479 (49)	470 (50)	464 (10)
18	606 (44)	623 (41)	681 (42)	582 (46)	1255 (67)	546 (47)	536 (48)	483 (49)	474 (50)	468 (10)
19	604 (44)	621 (41)	679 (42)	580 (46)	1253 (67)	544 (47)	534 (48)	481 (49)	472 (50)	466 (10)
20	616 (44)	633 (41)	691 (42)	592 (46)	1265 (67)	556 (47)	546 (48)	493 (49)	484 (50)	478 (10)
21	765 (44)	782 (41)	840 (42)	741 (46)	1414 (67)	705 (47)	695 (48)	642 (49)	633 (50)	627 (10)
22	1101 (44)	1118 (41)	1176 (42)	1077 (46)	1750 (67)	1041 (47)	1031 (48)	978 (49)	969 (50)	963 (10)
23	796 (44)	813 (41)	871 (42)	772 (46)	1445 (67)	736 (47)	726 (48)	673 (49)	664 (50)	658 (10)
24	778 (44)	795 (41)	853 (42)	754 (46)	1427 (67)	718 (47)	708 (48)	655 (49)	646 (50)	640 (10)
25	933 (44)	950 (41)	1008 (42)	909 (46)	1582 (67)	873 (47)	863 (48)	810 (49)	801 (50)	795 (10)
26	1188 (44)	1205 (41)	1263 (42)	1164 (46)	1837 (67)	1128 (47)	1118 (48)	1065 (49)	1056 (50)	1050 (10)
27	1209 (44)	1226 (41)	1284 (42)	1185 (46)	1858 (67)	1149 (47)	1139 (48)	1086 (49)	1077 (50)	1071 (10)
28	1229 (44)	1246 (41)	1304 (42)	1205 (46)	1878 (67)	1169 (47)	1159 (48)	1106 (49)	1097 (50)	1091 (10)
29	1222 (44)	1239 (41)	1297 (42)	1198 (46)	1871 (67)	1162 (47)	1152 (48)	1099 (49)	1090 (50)	1084 (10)
30	1207 (44)	1224 (41)	1282 (42)	1183 (46)	1856 (67)	1147 (47)	1137 (48)	1084 (49)	1075 (50)	1069 (10)
31	1137 (44)	1154 (41)	1212 (42)	1113 (46)	1786 (67)	1077 (47)	1067 (48)	1014 (49)	1005 (50)	999 (10)
32	1062 (44)	1079 (41)	1137 (42)	1038 (46)	1711 (67)	1002 (47)	992 (48)	939 (49)	930 (50)	924 (10)
33	1173 (44)	1190 (41)	1248 (42)	1149 (46)	1822 (67)	1113 (47)	1103 (48)	1050 (49)	1041 (50)	1035 (10)

34	1066 (44)	1083 (41)	1141 (42)	1042 (46)	1715 (67)	1006 (47)	996 (48)	943 (49)	934 (50)	928 (10)
35	1002 (44)	1019 (41)	1077 (42)	978 (46)	1651 (67)	942 (47)	932 (48)	879 (49)	870 (50)	864 (10)
36	618 (38)	615 (39)	659 (39)	637 (40)	1349 (67)	673 (44)	683 (46)	659 (49)	650 (50)	644 (10)
37	367 (38)	364 (39)	408 (39)	386 (40)	1098 (67)	422 (44)	432 (46)	485 (47)	494 (48)	500 (49)
38	40 (0)	37 (39)	81 (39)	59 (40)	771 (67)	95 (44)	105 (46)	158 (47)	167 (48)	173 (49)
39	44 (0)	29 (0)	73 (0)	67 (40)	775 (67)	103 (44)	113 (46)	166 (47)	175 (48)	181 (49)
40	23 (0)	40 (41)	98 (42)	8 (0)	754 (67)	44 (44)	54 (46)	107 (47)	116 (48)	122 (49)
41	0 (0)	17 (0)	75 (42)	24 (0)	731 (67)	60 (44)	70 (46)	123 (47)	132 (48)	138 (49)
42	17 (0)	0 (0)	58 (0)	41 (41)	748 (67)	77 (44)	87 (46)	140 (47)	149 (48)	155 (49)
43	75 (42)	58 (0)	0 (0)	99 (41)	764 (67)	135 (44)	145 (46)	198 (47)	207 (48)	213 (49)
44	24 (0)	41 (41)	99 (42)	0 (0)	755 (67)	36 (0)	46 (46)	99 (47)	108 (48)	114 (49)
45	731 (52)	748 (41)	764 (53)	755 (41)	0 (0)	791 (44)	801 (46)	772 (51)	781 (48)	787 (49)
46	60 (44)	77 (41)	135 (42)	36 (0)	791 (67)	0 (0)	10 (0)	63 (47)	72 (48)	78 (49)
47	70 (44)	87 (41)	145 (42)	46 (46)	801 (67)	10 (0)	0 (0)	53 (0)	62 (48)	68 (49)
48	123 (44)	140 (41)	198 (42)	99 (46)	772 (67)	63 (47)	53 (0)	0 (0)	9 (0)	15 (49)
49	132 (44)	149 (41)	207 (42)	108 (46)	781 (67)	72 (47)	62 (48)	9 (0)	0 (0)	6 (0)
50	138 (44)	155 (41)	213 (42)	114 (46)	787 (67)	78 (47)	68 (48)	15 (49)	6 (0)	0 (0)
51	198 (52)	215 (41)	273 (42)	222 (41)	601 (67)	234 (47)	224 (48)	171 (0)	180 (48)	186 (49)
52	164 (0)	181 (41)	239 (42)	188 (41)	567 (67)	224 (44)	234 (46)	205 (51)	214 (48)	220 (49)
53	212 (42)	195 (43)	137 (0)	236 (41)	627 (67)	272 (44)	282 (46)	335 (47)	344 (48)	350 (49)
54	228 (42)	211 (43)	153 (53)	252 (41)	611 (67)	288 (44)	298 (46)	351 (47)	360 (48)	366 (49)
55	300 (52)	317 (41)	346 (53)	324 (41)	431 (67)	360 (44)	370 (46)	341 (51)	350 (48)	356 (49)
56	321 (42)	304 (43)	246 (53)	345 (41)	518 (67)	381 (44)	391 (46)	444 (47)	453 (48)	459 (49)
57	720 (42)	703 (43)	645 (53)	744 (41)	711 (67)	780 (44)	790 (46)	843 (47)	852 (48)	858 (49)
58	456 (42)	439 (43)	381 (53)	480 (41)	449 (67)	516 (44)	526 (46)	579 (47)	588 (48)	594 (49)
59	484 (52)	501 (41)	517 (53)	508 (41)	247 (67)	544 (44)	554 (46)	525 (51)	534 (48)	540 (49)
60	552 (52)	569 (41)	585 (53)	576 (41)	179 (67)	612 (44)	622 (46)	593 (51)	602 (48)	608 (49)
61	615 (52)	632 (41)	648 (53)	639 (41)	116 (67)	675 (44)	685 (46)	656 (51)	665 (48)	671 (49)
62	620 (52)	637 (41)	653 (53)	644 (41)	111 (67)	680 (44)	690 (46)	661 (51)	670 (48)	676 (49)
63	1037 (52)	1054 (41)	1024 (53)	1061 (41)	332 (67)	1097 (44)	1107 (46)	1078 (51)	1087 (48)	1093 (49)
64	1015 (52)	1032 (41)	1046 (53)	1039 (41)	310 (67)	1075 (44)	1085 (46)	1056 (51)	1065 (48)	1071 (49)
65	892 (52)	909 (41)	925 (53)	916 (41)	187 (67)	952 (44)	962 (46)	933 (51)	942 (48)	948 (49)
66	810 (52)	827 (41)	843 (53)	834 (41)	105 (67)	870 (44)	880 (46)	851 (51)	860 (48)	866 (49)
67	718 (52)	735 (41)	751 (53)	742 (41)	13 (0)	778 (44)	788 (46)	759 (51)	768 (48)	774 (49)
SUMS	37876	38685	41322	37461	66579	36969	36839	35195	35114	35072

N.B. Last cost figure decimal.

represents the value attached to a single link between a pair of nodes i and j. In our example these are the link cost parameters. Where no direct link exists, s_{ij} will equal infinity but for practical computational purposes this may be a sufficiently high value such that other combinations of links will yield a lesser value. Any finite network can be represented by a matrix of order n, where n is the number of vertices included in the network.

A second matrix D, the dispersion matrix, also of order n, may be derived from the structure matrix S, such that any d_{ij} lists the total value associated with the minimum value routeway through the network between any pair of nodes i and j. The determination of matrix D from matrix S is through an iterative process. Matrix $D^{(1)}$ is a matrix which equals the structure matrix S. An element of matrix $D^{(2)}$ may be defined as:

$$(1) \quad d^{(2)}_{ij} = \min_k(d^{(1)}_{ik} + d^{(1)}_{kj}), k = 1, 2, \ldots, N$$

where $d^{(2)}$ is the minimum value which it is possible to incur in moving from a vertex i to a vertex j by either a one- or a two-link path. Generalizing relation (1), matrix $D^{(n)} = (d^{(n)}_{ij})$ such that the elements represent the least value traverse between each i and j in the network from among all possible paths and their associated values consisting of from one to n links where:

$$(2) \quad d^{(n)}_{ij} = \min a, b, \ldots, n-1\ d^{(1)}_{ia} + d^{(1)}_{ab} + d^{(1)} \ldots (n-1)), a, b, \ldots, n-1 = 1, 2, \ldots, N$$

The minimum value for each element $d^{(n)}_{ij}$ will be determined from all possible link combinations of $n - 1$ links. The maximum number of links has an upper limit of $n - 1$ since for any network of n vertices, the maximum number of vertices which may be traversed for a minimum path will be $n - 1$. Relation (2) may be modified to either of the following:

$$(3) \quad d^{(m+1)}_{ij} = \min_k d^{(1)}_{ik} + d^{(m)}_{kj}), k = 1, 2, \ldots, N$$

$$(4) \quad d^{(m+1)}_{ij} = \min_k(d^{(m)}_{ik} + d^{(1)}_{kj}), k = 1, 2, \ldots, N$$

where m is the number of iterations. Successive iterations are undertaken until the best solution is obtained. This occurs when $D^{(m)} = D^{(m+1)}$ since further iterations cannot bring about lesser values than those already obtained.

Reduction in the number of matrices needed in computation can be realized from the following modification:

$$(5) \quad d^{(2m)}_{ij} = \min_k(d^{(m)}_{ik} + d^{(m)}_{kj}), k = 1, 2, \ldots, N$$

A minimum is reached when either $D^{(2m)} = d^{(m)}$ or where $2m = N + 1$, convergence taking place twice as quickly. Pandit has indicated a further modification to speed up the iterative process.[8] As each element in the D matrix become smaller in a given iteration, it is immediately replaced in the matrix and is subsequently used as that same iteration continues.

$$(6) \quad S = D \text{ then } d^{(1)}_{ij} = \min{}_k(d_{ik} + d_{kj}), k = 1, 2, \ldots, N$$

$D^{(1)}$ becomes the required dispersion matrix listing the total transportation costs associated with the minimum path routeway between each pair of nodes i and j in the network after the necessary number of iterations.

Besides considering link costs, one may also include node costs as long as these costs are additive. When node costs are considered, the following applies: $D^{(1)} = (d^{(1)}_{ij})$ is the smaller of the two expressions:

$$(7)\quad d^{(1)}_{ij} = (\min_k d_{ik} + d_{kj} + b_k),\ k = i, j),\quad k = 1, 2, \ldots, N$$

$$\text{or}\quad = (\min_k (d_{ik} + d_{kj}),\ k = i, j)$$

The value b represents the node value.

A routing matrix R may be determined from the original structure matrix S and the dispersion matrix D. The new matrix $R = (r_{ij})$, $ij = 1, 2, \ldots, N$ is a matrix in which the elements r_{ij} are numbered addresses for the node last traversed in moving from i to j along the optimum path.

$r_{ij} = k$ where k is that k for which

$$(8)\quad (s_{kj} + d_{ik} + b_k) = d_{ij},\ k = 1, 2, \ldots, N \quad \text{but } k \neq i, j$$

If no such k exists, then $r_{ij} = 0$ indicating no further intermediate nodes and hence only the last link to traverse.

Links may be directed by specifying the actual s_{ij} value in the structure matrix but setting s_{ji} to the impossibly high value which will ensure no routeways include the link s_{ji} but might include s_{ij}.

Referring again to Figs. 7-3 and 7-4 portraying linkage importance based upon the least-cost routeways calculated as described above, it is obvious that some links are more important in the system than others. Top ranking is accorded links 10–50, 49–50, and 48–49 in Fig. 7-3 when unweighted routeways between all nodes are considered. If the latter two of these links were removed from the network, little change in routing patterns could be expected, nor would over-all costs rise very significantly. This is because an alternative link 48–50, only slightly more costly to traverse, can be substituted for them both. Generally speaking, most links around the Truro area are very important as the majority of routeways pass through this central vicinity. Other important links are situated along the highway (Trans-Canada) leading to Cape Breton Island. All least-cost routeways between Halifax and places in Cape Breton Island by-pass the coastal route north from Halifax in favor of the better road conditions via Truro. Again, the Annapolis Valley appears significantly more important as a routeway focus than does the south coast highway between Halifax and Yarmouth.

The same three links south of Truro retain their high importance rating in Fig. 7-4, but because of the close proximity of the North Sydney area and Sydney/Glace Bay urban populations, the connecting links 26–27 and 27–28 switch from the lowest to highest category of importance. As could be expected, the sheer size of Metropolitan Halifax influences the rating of links in that vicinity especially along the Halifax-Truro axis. There are only two centers with populations of 5,000 or more in the southern section of Nova Scotia, namely Kentville, which barely qualifies, and Yarmouth at the southern extremity. Hence routeways connecting these places rank low (Table 7-3) and so linkage importance ratings are similarly smaller. This is probably a false picture as the Annapolis Valley is quite densely populated with numerous small towns, but only Kentville is larger than the 5,000 mark.

Least-cost trucking routes do not necessarily follow the most recent link additions or improvements in the network even though these may be modern, high speed, and smooth surfaced. For instance, the Bi-Centennial Drive–airport highway from Halifax definitely provides the quickest routeway in that direction particularly for cars. From the point of view of over-all time and operating costs, the former highway still appears more favorable for trucking. Should time costs be rated as worth more than three dollars per hour, then the faster routeway (39–42–41–44–46–47) would become more important.

Average speeds on the links in the Nova Scotia highway network detailed in Fig. 7-2 may seem low. If one adds the values shown on the links in Figure 5 to those of Fig. 7-2, then the maximum average speed keeping within the legal speed restrictions is obtained. Even these may appear low by comparison with other regions but it must be remembered that small settlements are numerous in Nova Scotia especially along the coastal highways. Each of these is protected by speed-restricted zones. The magnitude of average speed reductions below the legal maximum for each link, as detailed in Fig. 7-5, further emphasizes the factors common in Nova Scotia which contribute to the higher costs of trucking and the lower over-all speeds. The proportion of the listed speed reductions in Fig. 7-5 attributable to various causes is portrayed in Fig. 7-6. Prominent are the poor overtaking conditions produced by winding, undulating roads, the considerable extent of critical gradients, and the prevalence of obstructions such as narrow bridges. Besides reducing average speeds considerably for trucks, these features add to operating and time costs.

Comparisons between linkage importance ratings and the characteristics of individual links can be very illuminating. Link 16–17 ranks quite high in both Figures 7-3 and 7-4, yet the average speed over this sec-

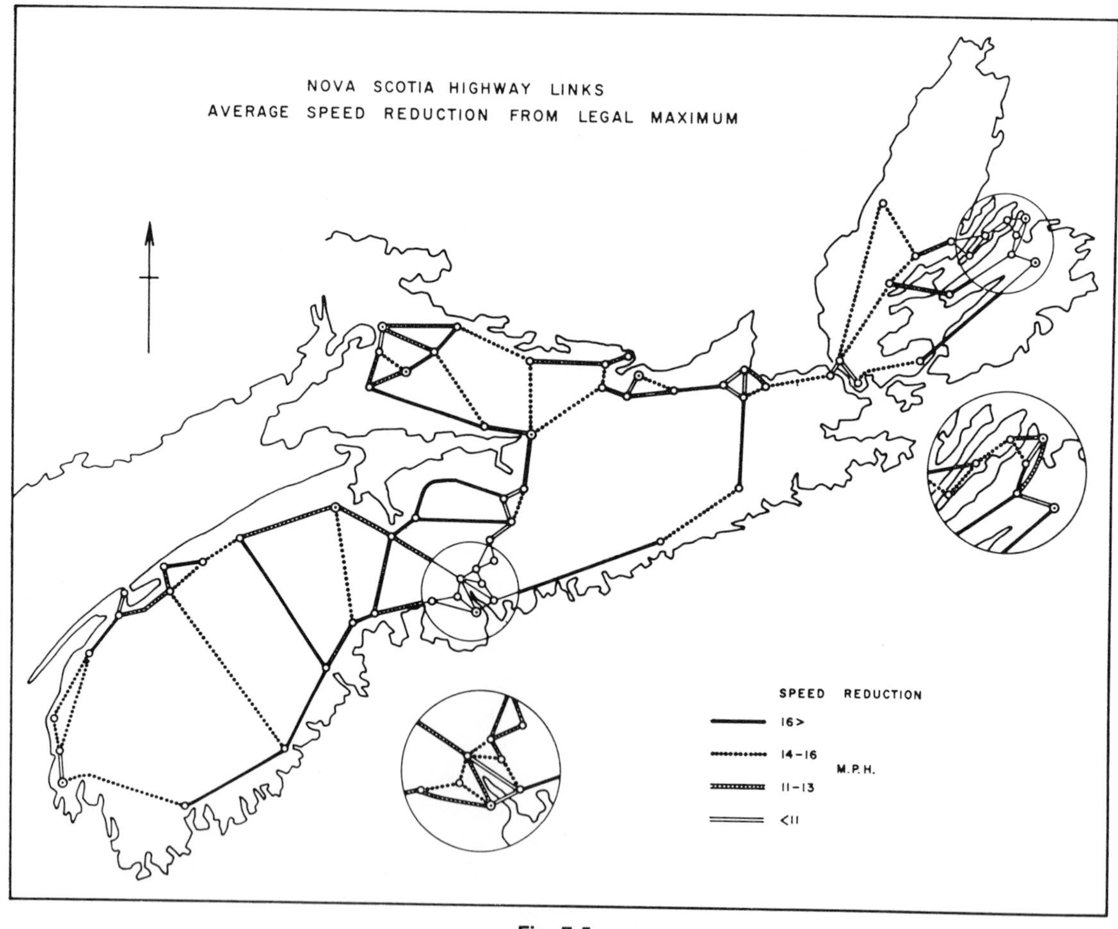

Fig. 7-5.

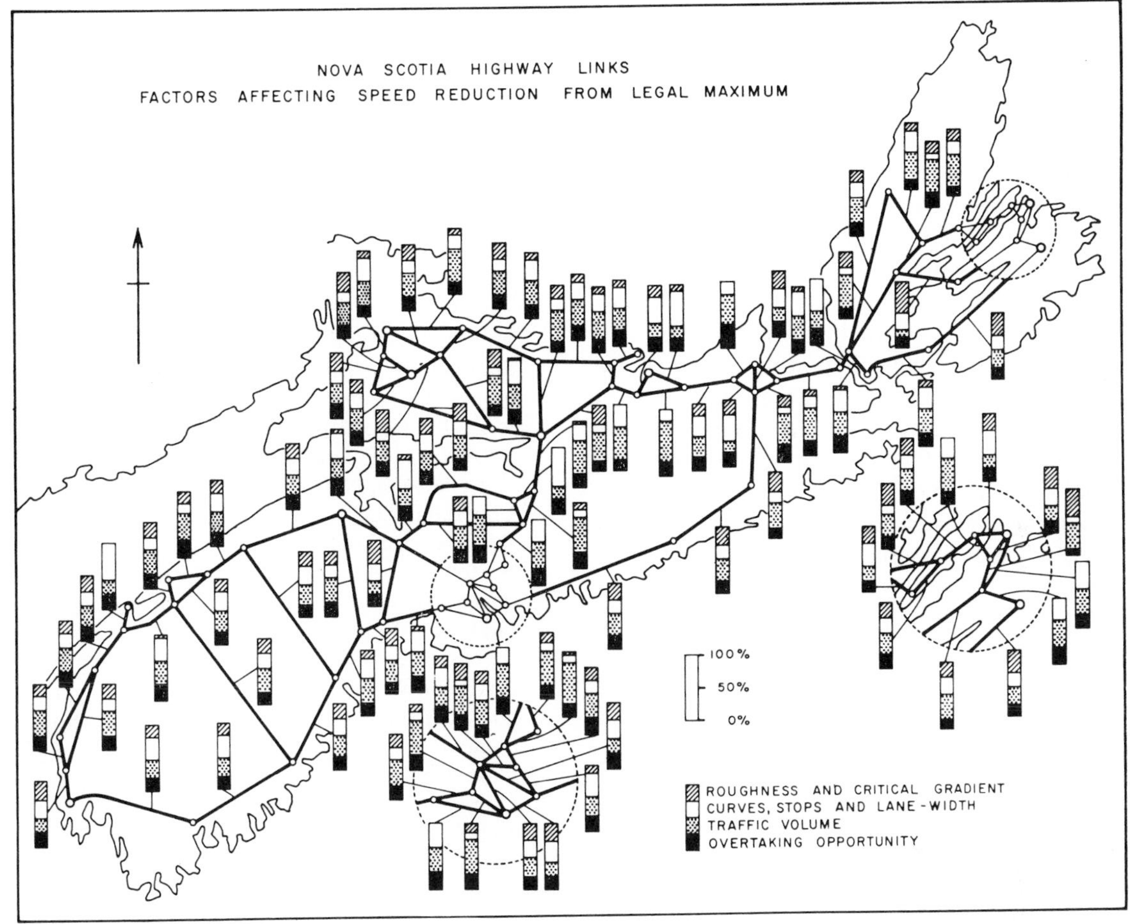

Fig. 7-6.

tion of highway is only 25.8 miles per hour for trucks. It is apparent that an excessive number of speed-reducing curves are responsible, and these mean both increases in wear and tear and severe reduction of overtaking opportunities on a much-travelled highway (Fig. 7-6). Improvements to this link, already in hand when the survey was made, can be expected greatly to enhance regional accessibility levels.

Along the Annapolis Valley average speeds are low with relatively high reductions from legal maximums and from the presence of frequent small towns with their speed zones. Much of this reduction in speed is attributable to surface roughness and traffic volume at the lower end, and to curves, stops for narrow bridges and road junctions, and narrow lane widths elsewhere. Overtaking opportunities are poor throughout. Highway improvements along this populated valley would greatly benefit trucking operations.

Trucking between Amherst near the provincial border, and New Glasgow or places further north would favor the coastal highway from a least-cost point of view, as the Trans-Canada Highway route (1–6–9–10–11) contains many sections with critical gradients. However, many trucking operations require movements to include all major urban centers. In this case the routeway via Truro may be favored, pointing up the utility of improving its features.

From the simple examples given, it is abundantly clear that there is considerable merit in analyzing the least-cost routeways of a regional highway network. These routeways define how accessible places are to each other, and highway linkage importance can be evaluated in terms of accessibility. When linkage importance ratings are seen in relationship to actual link characteristics one may gauge the impact of any improvements. The structure of the network, that is its geometry and link properties, all condition nodal accessibility levels. Accessibility is closely related to levels of urban economic activity.[9] Analysis of network structure is thus likely to reveal probable growth points in the system and, more particularly, to pinpoint existing bottlenecks or areas where improvements would yield greatest benefit to the region, or to a particular place. The approach outlined [here] could equally well be applied to other geographic areas or to different transport systems.

REFERENCES

1. Olsson, G., "Distance and Human Interaction: Review and Bibliography," *Reg. Sci. Res. Inst. Bibl. Ser. no. 2* (1965).
2. For a discussion of "critical" gradients see Can. Good Roads Assoc., *Manual of Geometric Design Standards for Canadian Roads and Streets* (1963).
3. Nat. Acad. of Sci.-Nat. Res. Coun., "Line-Haul Trucking Costs in Relation to Vehicle Gross Weights," *Highway Res. Bd.*, Bull. no. 301 (1961). Amer. Assoc. of State Highway Officials, *Road User Benefit Analyses for Highway Improvements* (1960).
4. Kissling, C. C., "Transportation Networks, Accessibility and Urban Functions," unpubl. PH.D. diss., McGill University (1966).
5. Shimbel, A., "Structural Parameters of Communication Networks," *Bull. of Math. Biophys.* 15 (1953), 501–7. See also Kansky, K. J., "Structure of Transport Networks: Relationships between Network Geometry and Regional Characteristics," *Univ. Chic. Dept. of Geogr.*, Res. Paper no. 84 (1963).
6. Burton, I., "Accessibility in Northern Ontario: An Application of Graph Theory to Regional Highway Network," portion of an unpubl. rept. for the Ont. Dept. Highways. See also Garrison, W., and Marble, D. F., *A Prolegomenon to the Forecasting of Transportation Development*, Final Rep. on Task DA 44-177-TC-685 U.S. Army Aviation Mats. (1965).
7. Shimbel, A., "Structure in Communication Nets," *Proc. of the Symp. on Information Networks*, Polytech. Inst. Brooklyn (1954).
8. Pandit, S., "The Shortest-Route Problem—An Addendum," *Oper. Res.*, 9, no. 1 (1961).
9. Kissling, C. C., "Accessibility and Urban Economic Activity Structure," *Proc. Fifth New Zealand Geogr. Conf.*, Auckland, 1967, N. Z. Geogr. Soc., Conf. Ser. no. 5 (1968), 143–52.

As a useful revision of these rather unfamiliar techniques, let us repeat again the basic conceptions of linear graph theory used:

A transportation system may be considered as a series of nodes or points (urban centers or junctions) and a series of routes or lines connecting them. Transferred to graph theory a linear graph is a collection of line segments (edges) and points (vertices).

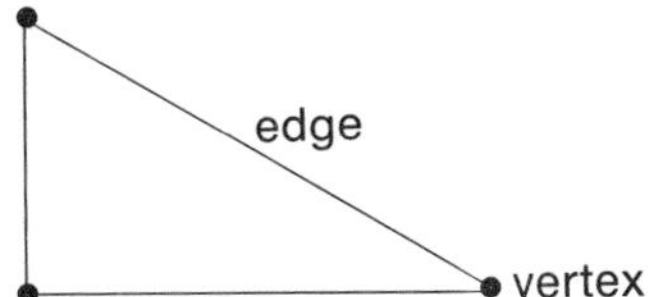

For the purposes of quantitative analysis, certain methods have been developed to describe in mathematical terms the nature of different transport networks.

Three such methods are:

1 *Cyclomatic number* (or first order Betti number or μ)
It has been shown, for example, that low levels of socioeconomic development are reflected in low μ values.
The index may be written as

$$\mu = e - v + p$$

Where μ = the observed number of circuits in the network

v = no. of vertices
e = no. of edges
p = no. of subgraphs

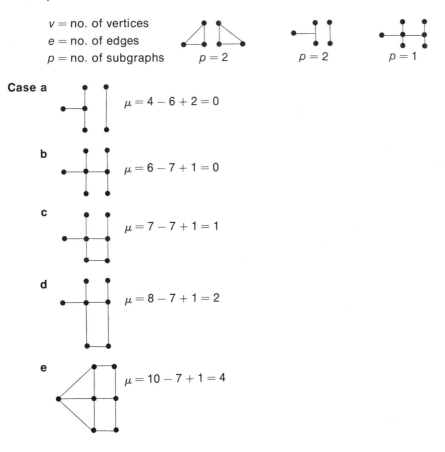

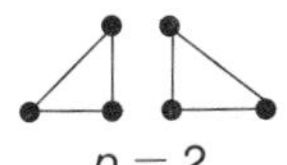

$p = 2$ $\qquad$ $p = 2$ $\qquad$ $p = 1$

Case a

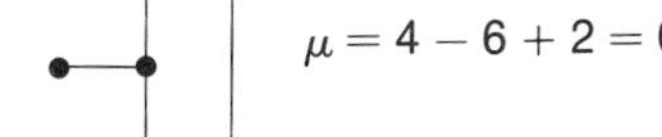

$\mu = 4 - 6 + 2 = 0$

b $\mu = 6 - 7 + 1 = 0$

c $\mu = 7 - 7 + 1 = 1$

d $\mu = 8 - 7 + 1 = 2$

e

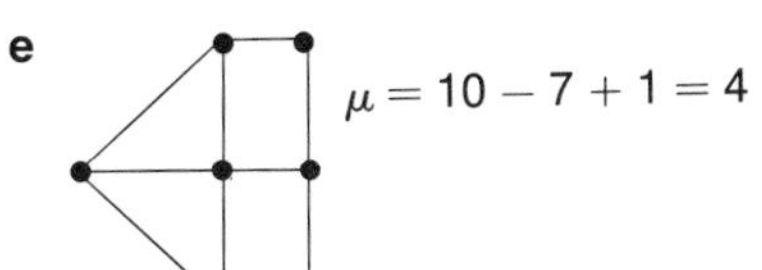

$\mu = 10 - 7 + 1 = 4$

That is, in less developed areas discontinuous trees and graphs are common (case *a*), and in more developed areas highly connected graphs are common (case *e*), with correspondingly high values for μ.

One difficulty which arises is that the upper level of the cyclomatic number depends on the structure of the networks.

Ideally we should be able to transform this index in such a way that it will have common upper and lower bounds for all networks. Two other indices will do this, the *alpha* and *gamma* indices.

2 *Gamma index*

The index represents the ratio of the observed number of edges (*e*) to the maximum possible number of edges.

The relationships may be written:

$$\gamma = \frac{e}{3(v-2)}$$

Case a

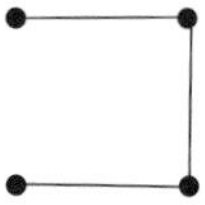

$$\gamma = \frac{3}{3(4-2)} = .30$$

b

$$\gamma = \frac{4}{3(4-2)} = .666$$

c

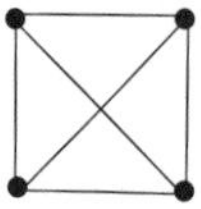

$$\gamma = \frac{6}{3(4-2)} = 1.0$$

That is, as the number of edges increases, the γ index approaches 1.0, and as it decreases it approaches 0.

If the index is $\times$ 100, the network may be expressed as $\times$ percent connected.

3 *Alpha index*

The index represents the ratio of the observed number of fundamental circuits to the maximum number of fundamental circuits which may exist in the system.

The index may be written:

$\alpha = \dfrac{\mu}{(2v-5)}$ and may also be expressed as a percent value.

From **1**:

$\alpha = \dfrac{e - v + p}{2v - 5}$ the result indicates the redundancy of the network.

Case a

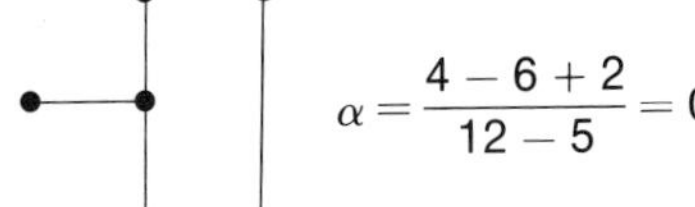

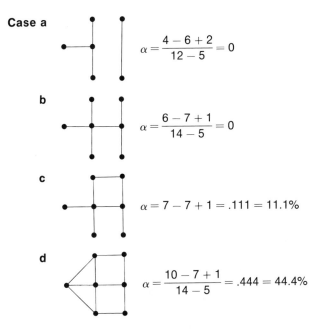

$$\alpha = \frac{4 - 6 + 2}{12 - 5} = 0$$

b

$$\alpha = \frac{6 - 7 + 1}{14 - 5} = 0$$

c

$$\alpha = 7 - 7 + 1 = .111 = 11.1\%$$

d

$$\alpha = \frac{10 - 7 + 1}{14 - 5} = .444 = 44.4\%$$

That is, the greater the connectivity of the system, the greater the redundancy value (case *d*) symbolic of the more developed nations.

As an exercise, it might be useful to practice calculating the following indices for the three networks (figure, page 110):

1 Calculate the indices indicated for the three networks

	a	b	c
a Number of nodes	____	____	____
b Number of routes	____	____	____
c Mean number of links/mode	____	____	____
d Cyclomatic number	____	____	____
e Gamma index γ	____	____	____
f Alpha index α	____	____	____

2 Compare the three networks in terms of these indices.

In addition to the techniques and analytical tools of graph theory, it is possible to look at the network structure of an area, via the gravity model, albeit in a less sophisticated way. In fact, in the following selection the authors also introduce the concept of a stock inventory—a measure of the extent and amount of railroads in Turkey, and the idea of flows, how much

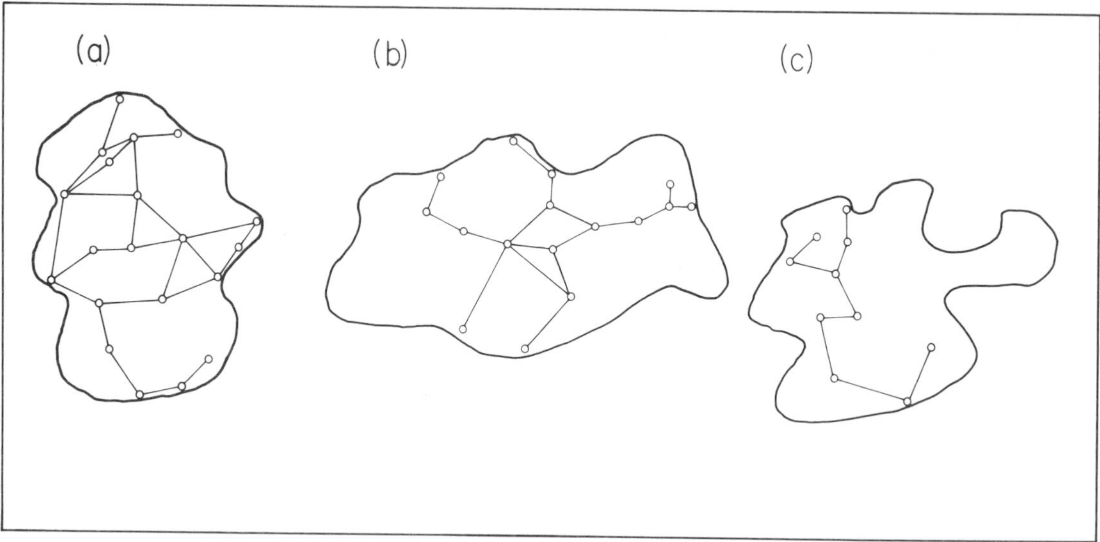

moves where, which we will be concerned with in Part Three. Before turning to this selection, we should, however, be clear as to what the gravity model is and is not.

The gravity model is based on the Newtonian law of universal gravitation, which states that two bodies attract each other in direct proportion to their masses and in inverse proportion to their distance apart. This simple formulation, a number of researchers have noted, can be applied to geography, where the interaction between two regions can be estimated by multiplying together the "mass" of two regions and dividing the product by some function of the distance separating them. We can show this relationship as:

$$Iij = f\left(\frac{PiPj}{dij}\right)$$

where: Iij = the number of interactions between region i and region j
F = an empirical constant
P = some measure of the size or mass of the interacting pair of regions (often measured as the population of the region)
dij = the distance between the region i and region j

If we assume that two cities of 10,000 people each are 100 miles apart, with $F = 1$,* then the interaction would be 1,000 units; at only 10 miles apart the interaction would rise to 10,000 units; at 1,000 miles apart it would fall to 100 units.

The situation described here is analogous to that of *gravitational energy* in Newtonian terms. Frequently a variation of this, equivalent to Newtonian

*Values for the constant are in fact estimated empirically by studying situations in which interactions (I) as well as population (M) and distance (d) values are known.

gravitational force, is used. This could be stated as the force drawing two masses together which is directly proportional to their sum and inversely proportional to the *square* of their distance apart. In equation form this becomes:

$$Iij = F\frac{PiPj}{d^2ij}$$

Both forms have been used,† but this latter analogy to *force,* which fits geographical situations most realistically, is most apt in transportation geography. Swedish geographers, particularly in studies of migration, have conducted a large number of studies which show that spatial interaction decreases with distance; for example, a flow at 20 miles is likely to be only one quarter of that at 10 miles. Their empirical results showed values from −0.4 to as high as −3.3, with a mean of −1.94, or for our purposes, −2.0. This we could write as $I = fD^{-2}$ or $I = f\frac{1}{D^2}$.

†A third analogy to Newtonian *potential energy* is also used. This represents the energy existing in one mass with respect to another:

$iVj = \frac{GPj}{dij}$ where iVj is the potential energy at P, in respect to Pj.

Selection 8

Population and Accessibility: An Analysis of Turkish Railroads

J. Kolars and H. J. Malin

From the bright traceries of Mark Jefferson's "Civilizing Rails" to the patterns of road diffusion described by Taaffe, Morrill, and Gould, there has been continuing interest in the role that transportation plays in the development of nations.[1] If the efficiency of transportation networks currently being created or expanded throughout the developing world is to be maximized in terms of limited capital and future needs, knowledge of how existing networks have grown is essential.

The purpose of this study is to describe a new method for simulating transportation networks in terms of population distributions and major topographic barriers. An example of such a simulation is presented for railroads in Turkey. Ordered comparisons between the real and simulated Turkish networks offer further insight into general transportation theory as well as relating specifically to problems of accessibility in Turkey.

POPULATION AND ACCESSIBILITY

In their analysis of the growth of transportation in Nigeria and Ghana, Taaffe, Morrill,

Geographical Review, vol. 60, 1970, pp. 229–246. Reprinted by permission of the authors and editor.

and Gould point out a strong positive correlation between population and area and the density of the road system in those countries.* They also suggest that "the location of a reporting unit with respect to other distributions may have considerable bearing on its road mileage. For example, a unit with a low population density located between two large cities would tend to have more road mileage than one with the same density and area surrounded by units of correspondingly low densities."[2] In a recent discussion of spatial flow, William Warntz has pointed out that "major transportation arteries in the United States occur on major ridge lines as defined on the potential of population surface."[3] This observation supports our ideas and has suggested a further means of analyzing transportation networks.

New cartographic techniques perfected at the University of Michigan and described below have made it possible to examine further conditions underlying the growth and location of transportation networks.[4] The resulting predictive[5] simulation of the Turkish railroad network, which is based on an aggregate measure of population and the additional factor of major topographic barriers, shows a close correlation with the existing rail network. The simulation also helps to verify the hypothesis that the location of railroads in Turkey reflects relative situational advantages with respect to major population concentrations as well as general population distributions.

Although the influence of a country's highway system on the patterning of its railroad network is undeniable, in the Turkish case the highway variable was excluded from the analysis for strong empirical reasons. In 1939–1940, 93 percent of the Turkish railroad system as it existed in 1965 was complete, while the nation's highway system represented only 26 percent of that existing in 1965.[6] Moreover, thirty years ago the all-weather roads were largely restricted to Thrace, to the Istanbul-Izmir route paralleling the straits and shore of the Aegean, and to a road between Trabzon and the Iranian border. "The vast rural Anatolian area, in particular the plain east of Ankara, was largely neglected."[7] At that time railroads provided most of the country's interregional land transportation, and for the most part they had developed free of the influence of highways. Thus the history of transportation in Turkey fortuitously simplifies the analysis presented here. Today an expanding all-weather highway network competes strongly with the railroads. Given the time and the facilities, a further analysis incorporating both types of transportation systems could be conducted, but such dual considerations fall safely outside the primary purpose of the present discussion.

*See selection 22.

A NEW POPULATION MAP OF TURKEY

Two major reasons for the existence of transportation networks are often predicated: routes exist as links between urban foci, and they are built to connect administrative or manufacturing centers and ports to their hinterlands. In developing economies where one of the most important resources is agricultural products, a corollary of the latter raison d'être may be the linking of urban centers to the rural farm population. This was implied by Mark Jefferson when he chose to outline his rail networks with bands of white that depicted a territory twenty miles in width.[8] In other words, not only must a transportation route such as a railroad penetrate territory, but it must be accessible to the area through which it passes. Thus populations dependent on traditional methods of transportation (in developing countries often ox carts or their equivalents) may still remain beyond the effective reach of modern, more efficient, carriers.

However, Jefferson's measure of ten miles

on either side of a railroad may have been unnecessarily narrow. In Turkey, long before the advent of rail transportation, caravansaries were placed one day's journey apart, or approximately twenty-five miles. The authors have observed that villages on routes leading away from Konya in central Turkey seem to be spaced at approximately the same distance. Therefore this distance has been selected as a computational measure in the present analysis. Assuming that railroads are accessible to the population and to the agricultural produce within twenty-five miles of the line, and that stops will be made wherever potential need dictates, certain inferences can be drawn concerning the relationship between transportation routes (in this case, railroads) and the distribution of population, urban and rural, throughout a developing country with a large agricultural sector.

In order to consider the effect of the distribution of population near, but not on, a given transportation route, a population map of Turkey was compiled using 1960 census data that summed the population within twenty-five miles of every point. This was done by assuming (for ease of computation) that the population of each of the 636 counties (*kaza*) was located at the county seat (*kaza merkezi*). County populations and latitude and longitude for each county seat were recorded; subsequently a grid with intersects at every one-half degree of latitude and longitude (for example, 35°00′N, 37°00′E; 35°00′N, 37°30′E; 35°30′N, 37°00′E) was superposed on the population map and the population within a radius of twenty-five miles of each intersect was summed and recorded. An isopleth map of the resulting summed populations was then prepared (Fig. 8-1).[9] This map shows a population surface in some ways similar to Warntz's population-potential surfaces, but

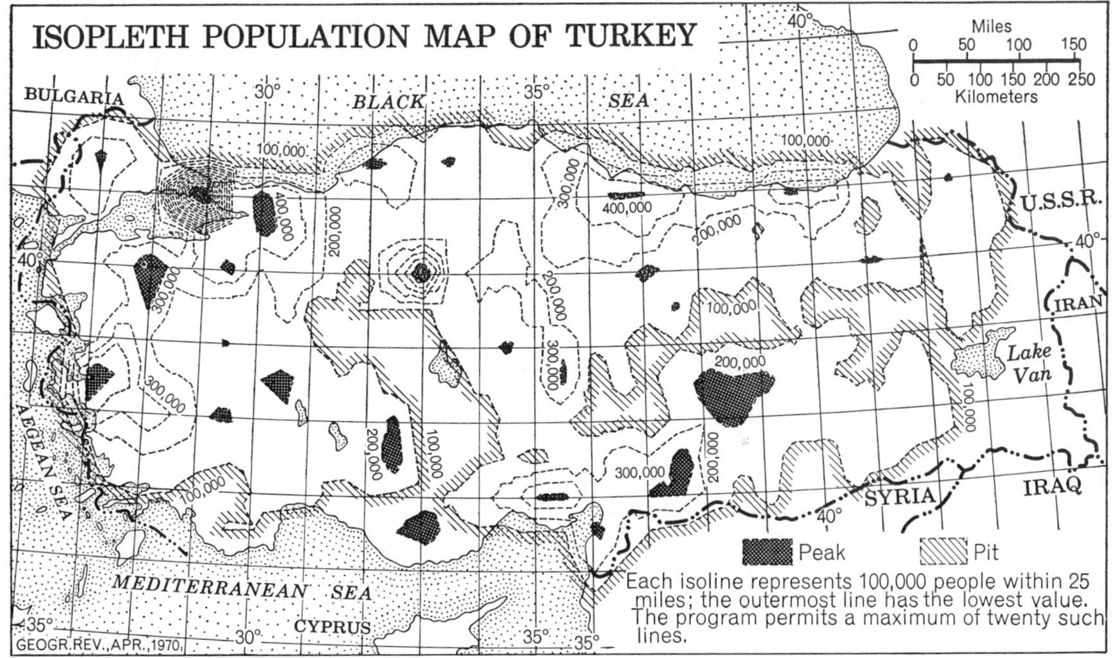

Fig. 8-1.

it differs from them in that no distance-decay function was included in the computation. The nature of the surface can be seen in Fig. 8-2.

The new population map of Turkey reveals a series of high peaks (major cities), plateaus (well-populated rural areas), and pits (where population is least dense). Superposition of an outline map of the political boundaries of the country on the population map revealed many interesting features. For example, along much of the Black Sea coast of Turkey a ship sailing within twenty-five miles of the shore will be within range of at least 100,000 people at any given point, but another ship sailing along the southern Mediterranean shore will be paralleling a relatively sparsely settled area. Surprisingly, although low population densities might be expected in the extreme southeast, an "embayment" of similarly sparse population penetrates nearly to Ankara in the central part of the country (Fig. 8-1). Further inspection reveals lower peaks of population scattered throughout the country and pits, both small and large. Ridge lines reminiscent of those on Warntz's maps connect peaks. Low points on these ridges are similar to his "passes," and high points between pits resemble his "pales."[10]

The peaks of population represent either cities, which are the major sources of capital and entrepreneurial energy capable of generating rail lines, or densely settled rural areas capable of agricultural production. Rail lines might then be assumed to connect higher order peaks to those of lower value in some logical fashion. Since ridge lines between peaks show the locus of points having the largest rural populations within a day's journey by traditional transport methods, they should represent "optimum" routes that give access to the maximum number of farmers and farms. Pits or depressions would be avoided wherever possible. Using these as-

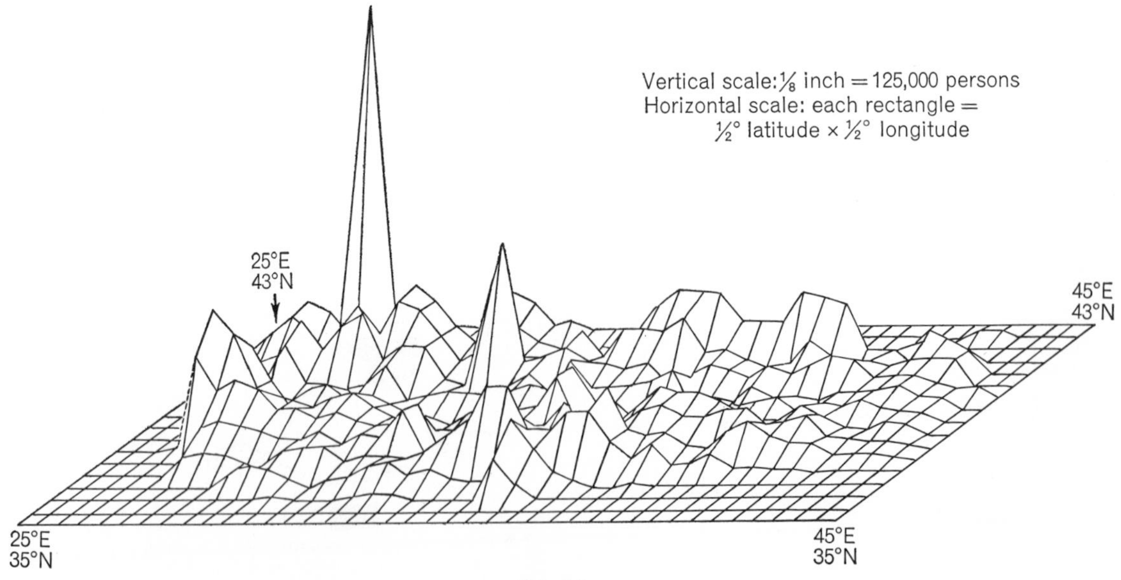

Fig. 8-2.

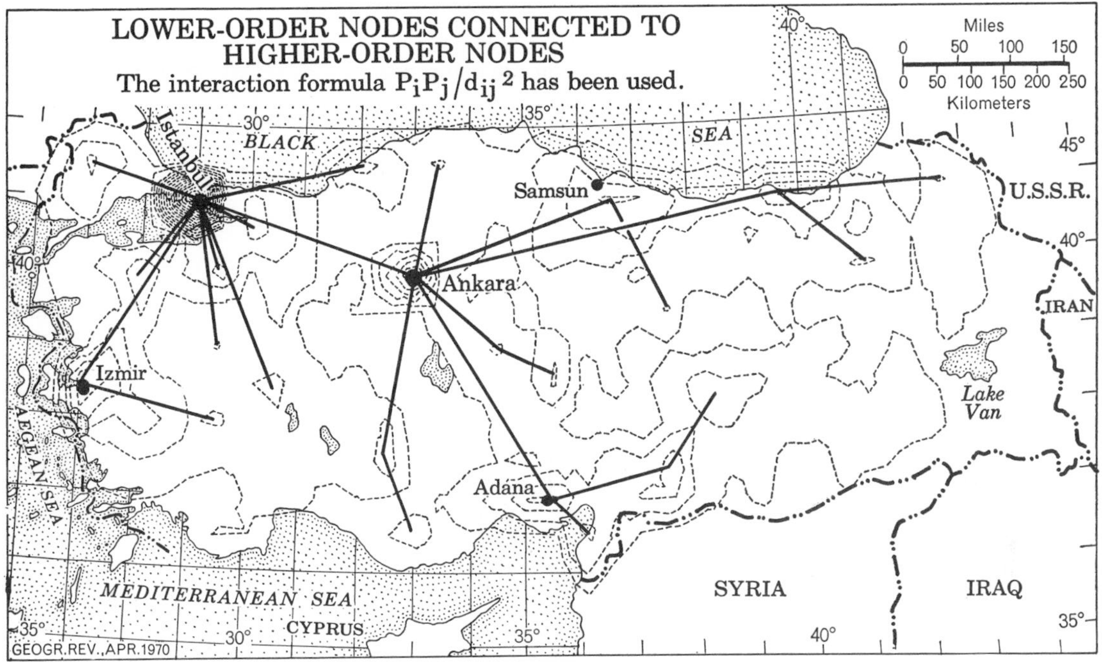

Fig. 8-3.

sumptions and additional ones described later, a rail network was simulated for Turkey. The comparison of the simulated pattern with the existing rail network shows a high degree of correlation; it also reveals a logically consistent set of unpredicted but existing lines and a similar set of predicted but non-existent routes.

THE SIMULATION OF THE RAIL NETWORK

To obtain the results described, a series of steps were followed in the simulation, each step represented by a map. Initially, all peaks were joined by straight-line segments. This was done by computing the interaction potential between all peaks, using the formula: $I = P_iP_j/d^2_{ij}$, where I represents a measure of interaction between city i and city j; P_i equals the population of city i; P_j the population of city j; and d_{ij} the distance between the two cities. The lowest-order peak was first connected to the one other higher order peak with which it shared the greatest value for I. This was repeated for all peaks in ascending order. The resulting interaction network is shown on Fig. 8-3.

The second stage in the simulation was to observe what might be described as a "rule of parsimony" for route lengths. That is, wherever a higher order peak was linked to several lower order peaks by nearly parallel routes, the routes were combined for greater efficiency (Fig. 8-4). It was then reasoned that dead-end routes would be inefficient in actual practice; therefore all end points were connected to their nearest neighbors, regardless of size or interaction value. This produced a network with a western cycle, an eastern cycle, and two centrally located cycles that met at the Ankara population peak (Fig. 8-5). The disadvantage of this network was that it

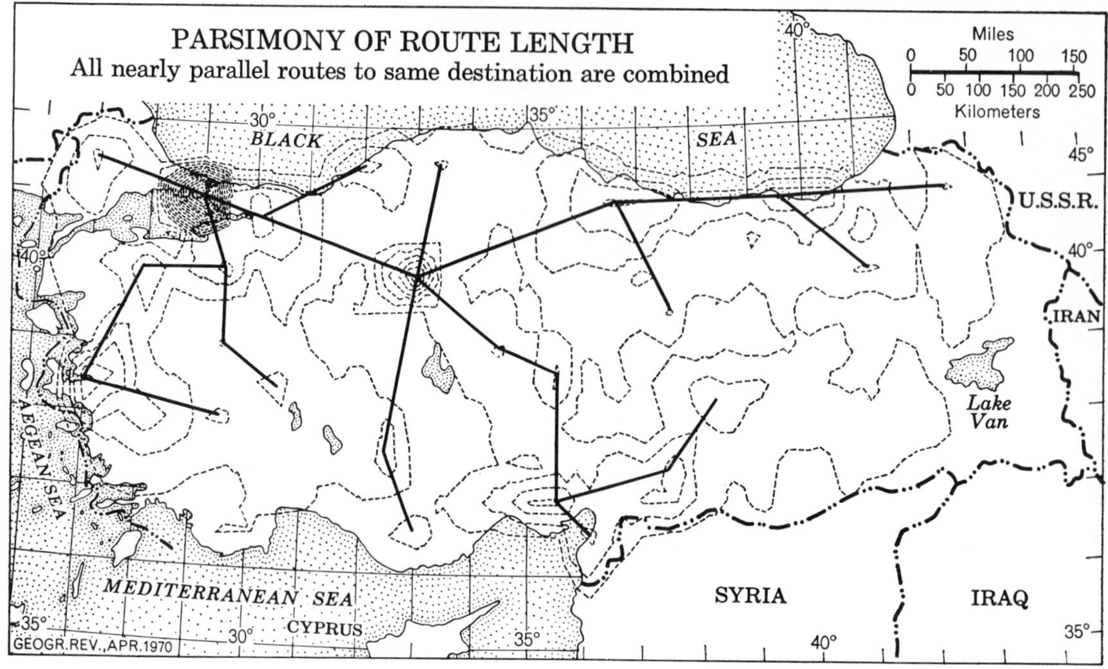

Fig. 8-4.

could be sundered into two or three isolated parts by the cutting of one line segment in the east and another in the west. Similarly, arbitrary removal of any of several nodes, located at peaks of different orders, would also isolate parts of the network. For example, removal of the line between Istanbul and Izmit–Adapazarĭ would divide the whole network into two isolated parts. The same thing would occur with the removal of the Izmit–Adapazarĭ or Istanbul peaks or nodes. This difficulty was overcome by adding two route segments or links (Fig. 8-5). The inclusion of these segments resulted in a redundant network that assures noncentral circulation. In other words, the completed network shown in Fig. 8-5 allows alternate routes to all places. No place or set of places can be isolated by cutting a single line segment or by removing a single node.

The resulting straight line network served as the basis for the final simulation, which was accomplished by curving all the lines to follow intervening ridge crests between population peaks. One final variable was introduced by including on the map major impenetrable mountain chains, with such natural passes as the Cilician Gates, and the coastal boundaries of the country (Fig. 8-6). Typical of the changes that came about from the introduction of these barriers was the necessity to bend the feeder rail line leading to Iskenderun around the gulf of the same name. Fig. 8-7 superposes the existing and simulated route networks. Three additional maps were then prepared for the sake of clarity in discussing the comparison of the two networks (Figs. 8-8 to 8-10).

In order to make systematic comparisons, the real and simulated route segments that lie within one-fourth degree of one another are shown by thin lines on Fig. 8-8. Since this represents the largest possible deviation owing to the cartographic technique employed in aggregating the population, lack of fit between simulated and real routes within these narrow limits has a high probability of reflecting slight variations in the distribution of population rather than unknown causal factors. The other lines show the reciprocal parts of both real and simulated routes that occur more than one-fourth degree away from their counterparts. Since the reciprocal lines fulfill identical functions (connecting the same origins and destinations), they have also been included on Fig. 8-8, though historical and topographical factors that were not included in the simulation may account for lack of a more exact fit. For example, terrain conditions at a larger scale than those used in the simulation would often indicate the greater feasibility of building a real rail line in some area with intermediate rather than maximum local populations. This condition is illustrated by the Konya–Cilician Gates segment (Fig. 8-7). The simulated route is pulled south to serve the Ermenak peak, though in reality the incredibly rough terrain of the Göksu Valley was avoided by a more northerly route across the flat, somber Anatolian steppe. Fig. 8-9 shows those parts of the simulated network for which no equivalents occur in reality,[11] and Fig. 8-10 displays the locations of lines constructed and now in operation that were not predicted by the simulation. The percentages of all categories of real and simulated lines are summarized in Table 8-1.

EVALUATION OF THE MAPS

An analysis of the degree of correspondence between the existing Turkish rail network and the simulated one shows that the present study substantiates the conclusions of Taaffe, Morrill, and Gould—namely, that the initial

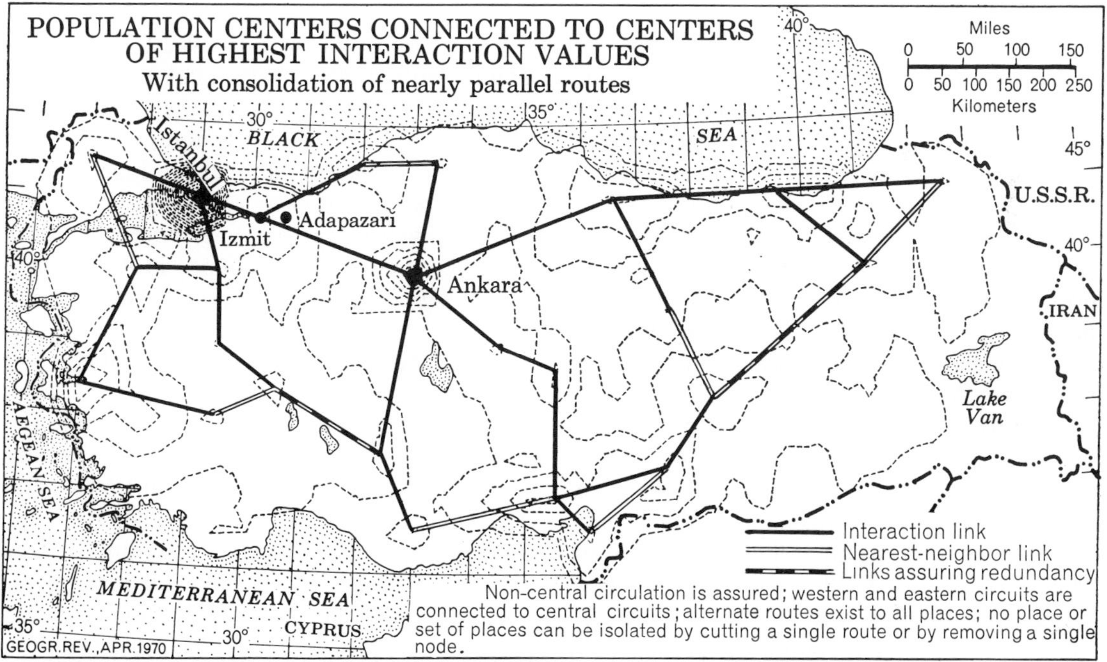

Fig. 8-5.

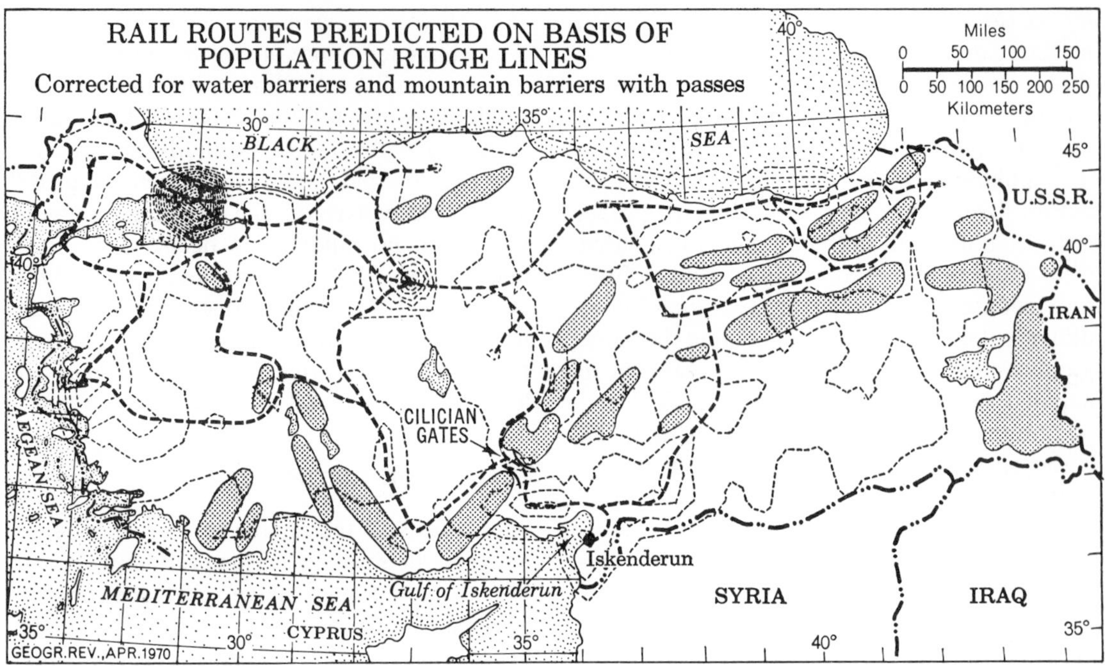

Fig. 8-6.

impetus for rail growth is provided by "(1) the desire to connect an administrative center on the seacoast with an interior area for political and military control; (2) the desire to reach areas of mineral exploitation; (3) the desire to reach areas of potential agricultural export production."[12] However, the Turkish example does not assign the same order of importance to these causes as that given for the network growth patterns in Ghana and Nigeria. Furthermore, the classification scheme of Taaffe, Morrill, and Gould must be expanded to include a category of track that occurs in Turkey but is not present in the African examples. In Turkey, rail lines were also constructed for exogenous political purposes; that is, connecting links with or from rail systems in neighboring countries and transnational routes with origins and destinations outside national boundaries are also important. Although extranational rivalries are important in the Turkish case, just as "extra-African rivalries" are in the West African example, Turkey was never a colony. Thus the desire to cross Turkey in the push to the Orient and to link its rail system with rail networks in adjacent politically independent states motivated investment during the period of intensive railroad building. Foreign powers considered economic influence in Asia Minor more significant than direct administrative control.

In Turkey agricultural exploitation and Ottoman administrative control provided the dominant motivation for initial penetration of the interior. Of the total track laid in Turkey before the demise of the Ottoman Empire and the beginning of the First Turkish Republic (1923), apparently no penetration lines for the express purpose of transporting mineral resources were constructed, although 2,485 miles of railroads were then in operation.[13] Today, the relative significance of mineral resources as a reason for operation reflects the greater concern for economic development. Still, the length of track attributable to mineral exploitation is at best 1378 miles, as compared with 5,009 miles of rail line currently in operation. Table 8-2 gives historical and route-length data pertinent to rail growth from the inception of the first line in 1860 until the present. Examination of the data shown by this table indicates that network growth was a function of both "a continuous process of spatial diffusion and an irregular or sporadic process influenced by many specific economic, social, or political forces,"[14] but that priorities relating to construction were largely as outlined above.

RAIL LINES PRESENT AND PREDICTED

The history of Turkish railroad development does much to explain the patterns shown on Fig. 8-8. With the exception of a general lack of lines to exploit mineral resources, network growth has proceeded in a manner commensurate with the general rules of Taaffe, Morrill, and Gould given above. Initial penetration routes originated at the ports of Izmir, Istanbul, and Adana. That the first penetration of the interior should have occurred from Izmir rather than from the capital and most populous city, Istanbul, long a trade center possessing a magnificent roadstead, is something of an anomaly. However, the lack of social ties between the urban-centered Ottoman elite and rural Anatolian society resulted in little popular demand to connect these two populations. Heavy reliance on sea transport, in addition to the general preindustrial aspect of Turkey in this era, with little necessity for the bulk movement of raw materials to nonexistent urban-centered industrial complexes or the return flow of manufactured goods to the hinterland, left only agriculture and administration as motivating factors for rail construction. Moreover, since the Smyrna figs and

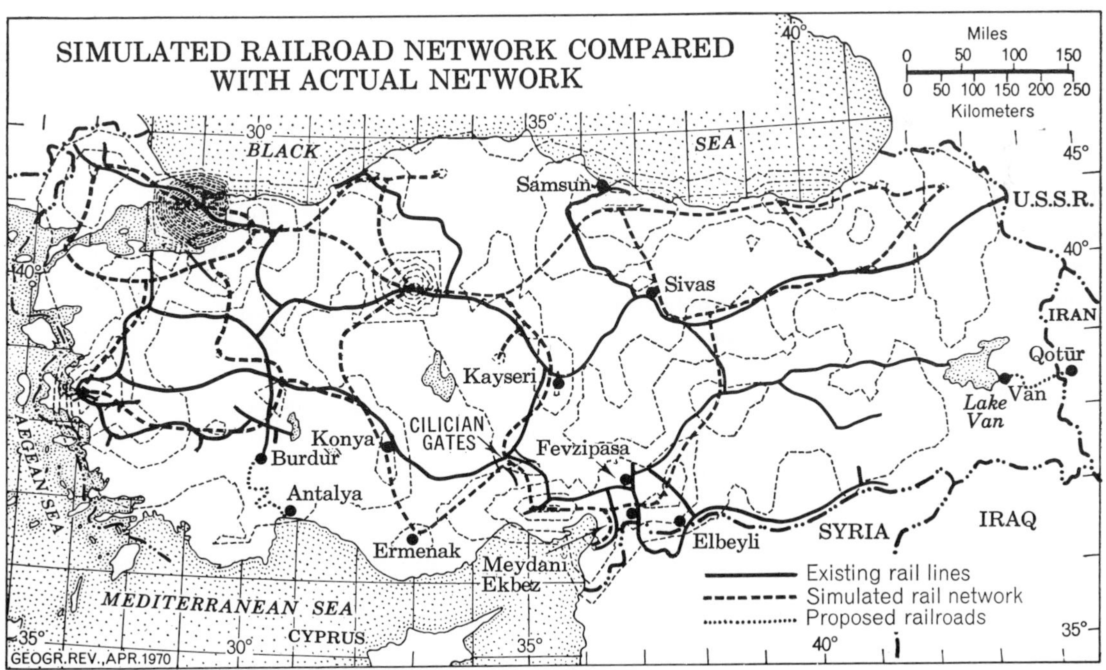

Fig. 8-7.

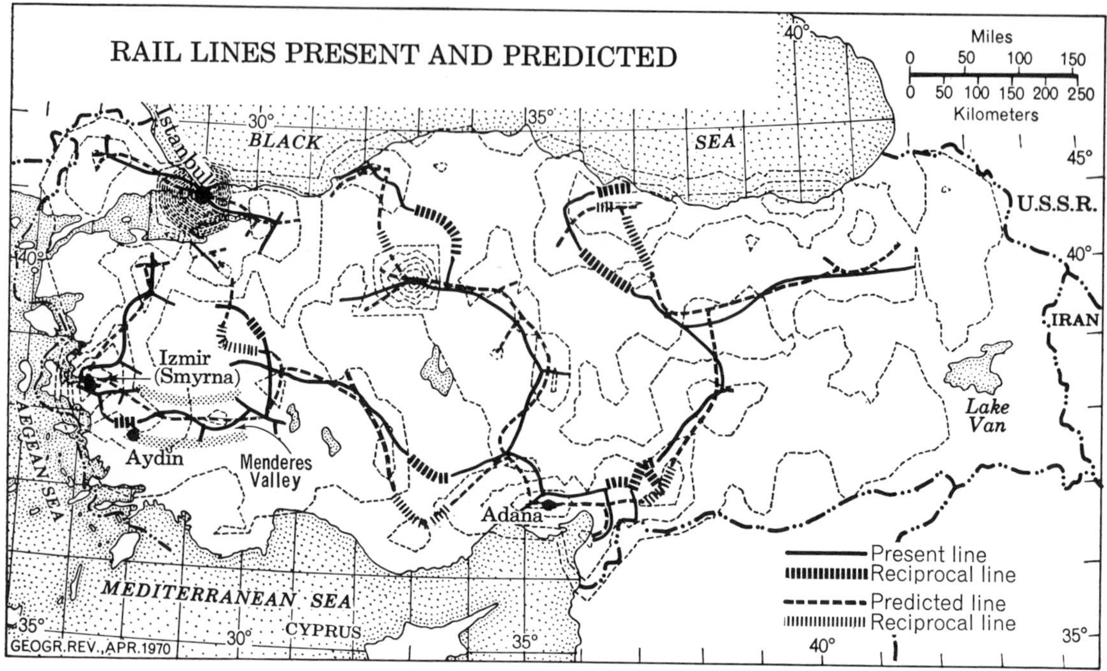

Fig. 8-8.

Sultana raisins consumed by the English to titivate fog-dulled appetites were produced in the Menderes Valley, the foreign search for agricultural produce centered farther south along the Aegean shore.

For instance, an examination of reports to the British government reveals that on the link between Smyrna and Aidin (Izmir–Aydĭn) the transport of passengers was of less than prime importance. Much of the lobbying done in Britain to obtain necessary financial backing and Crown approval was predicated on revenues earned from the transport of foodstuffs.[15] The road journey from Smyrna to Aidin required four to five days of rugged travel; damage to produce from loading and offloading camels and from spoilage because of the delay between harvest and market was the general rule.[16] Proponents of the new line insisted that it would decrease these losses substantially by cutting transport time to three hours,[17] an estimate that later proved to be accurate.

The high proportion of the total network shown on Fig. 8-8 is indicative of the degree of correlation that exists between rail line location and population densities. A possible criticism might be that the simulation is based on the 1960 distribution of population, though railroad construction began almost a century before. However, with the exception of recent rapid growth of cities, the relative distribution

Table 8-1 The Degree of Correspondence Between Real and Simulated Rail Lines

	% of model network	% of real network
Present and predicted (within 1/4°)	69.5	58.5
Present and predicted (reciprocal beyond 1/4°)	7.3	8.6
Total present and predicted	76.8	67.1
Present but not predicted		32.9
Predicted but not present	23.2	
Total	100.0	100.0

of population in Turkey has remained essentially the same during the period in question, though in absolute numbers it has increased many times. It should be remembered, too, that large-scale migration to the cities began only after World War II, and by then most of the existing rail system had been completed. The early growth of Ankara soon after the founding of the republic is the only significant exception.

RAIL LINES PREDICTED BUT NOT PRESENT

Fig. 8-9 shows rail links predicted on the basis of population but not actually present. A striking omission is apparent along the northern

Table 8-2 History of Railway Construction in Turkey, 1860–1964

LINK	DATE	LENGTH (*In miles*)	MOTIVATION[a]	LINK	DATE	LENGTH (*In miles*)	MOTIVATION[a]
Under Ottoman Empire				*Under Ottoman Empire*			
Kizilçullu-Buca	1860	1.2	I	Konya-Yenice	1918	214.9	I, II, IV
Izmir-Aydin	1866	80.7	II, I	Fevzipaşa-Nusaybin	1918	258.3[b]	I, IV
Gaziemir-Seydiköy	1866	.9	I, II	Mardin-Derbesiye	1918	18.6	I, II
Izmir-Turgutlu	1866	57.8	I, II	Toprakkale-Fevzipaşa	1918	39.1	I, II, IV
Istanbul-Izmit	1873	56.5	I, IV				
Turgutlu-Alaşehir	1875	47.2	I, II	*Under Turkish Republic*			
Ayd˘n-Kuyucak	1881	35.4	II, I	Ilica-Balya	1926	18.0	III
Kuyucak-Sarayköy	1882	27.3	II, I	Samsun-Çarşamba	1926	23.6	II, I
Ţorbali-Tire	1883	29.8	II, I	Ankara-Kayseri	1927	236.0	I, II
Ödemiş-Çatal	1884	15.5	I, II	Kayseri-Sivas	1930	137.9	I, II
Mersin-Adana	1886	42.2	II, I, IV	Balikesir-Alayunt	1932	163.3	III
Istanbul-Edirne	1888	197.7	I, IV	Sivas-Samsun	1932	249.6	I, II
Kirklareli-mainline	1888	28.3	I, II	Kayseri-Kardeşgediği	1933	116.1	I, II
Sarayköy-Dinar	1889	90.0	II, I	Elâziğ-mainline	1934	14.9	I, III
Denizli-mainline	1889	5.8	II, I	Fevzipaşa-Diyarbakir	1935	313.0	I, III
Söke-mainline	1889	13.7	II, I	Afyon-Karakuyu	1936	70.8	I, II
Çivril-mainline	1889	19.3	II, I	Burdur-mainline	1936	14.9	I, II
Manisa-Soma	1890	57.4	II, I	Isparta-mainline	1936	8.7	I, II
Izmit-Adapazari	1890	30.4	I, II, IV	Sivas-Çetinkaya	1936	69.6	I, II
Adapazari-Ankara	1892	271.4	I, II, IV	Irmak-Hisarönü-	1937	257.7	III, I, II
Mudanya-Bursa	1892	25.5	II, I	Zonguldak			
Eskişehir-Alayunt	1894	41.6	I, II, IV	Malatya-Çetinkaya	1937	86.9	I, II
Alayunt-Afyon	1895	58.4	I, II, IV	Çetinkaya-Erzurum	1939	270.8	I, III, IV[c]
Afyon-Konya	1896	169.2	I, II, IV	Diyarbak˘r-Kurtulan	1944	98.7	I, III
Russia-Kars-	1899	76.4	I, IV	Tunçbilek-mainline	1944	7.5	III
Sarikamis				Maraş-mainline	1948	17.4	II, I
Alaşehir-Afyon	1900	157.2	II, I	Ereğli-Armutcuk	1953	8.1	III
Eğridir-Dinar	1912	58.6	I, II	Narli-Gaziantep	1953	52.2	I, II
Soma-Bandirma	1912	113.6	I, II	Gaziantep-Barak	1960	62.7	I
Iskenderun-mainline	1913	36.8	I, II	Kütahya-Seydiömer	1962	18.0	III
Sarikamiş-Erzurum	1916	108.1	I, IV	Eläziğ-Tatvan	1964[d]	208.0	I, III

Sources: "Railways of Turkey Map Series," 1939; "Turkey" (2 vols.; *Great Britain, Naval Intelligence Division, Geographical Handbook Series, B. R. 705A,* 1943), Vol. 2, pp. 239–363; "La politique ferroviare en Turquie" (Ankara, 1941), pp. 8, 10, 11, 13–16, 23, 24, 26–29, 31–33, 35–38, and 40–42; *Türkiye Istatistik Yilliği, 1964–65 annuaire statistique de la Turquie* (Ankara, 1965), p. 622; *The Levant Trade Review,* Vol. 17, 1929, pp. 361, 364, 365, and 366; Bernard Lewis: The Emergence of Modern Turkey (London, New York, and Tor to, 1961), pp. 94 and 180–181; Richard D. Robinson: The First Turkish Republic: A Case Study in National Development (Cambridge, Mass., 1963), pp. 297–301.

[a] Motivation for construction as interpreted by the writers: I, administrative (that is, political-military); II, agricultural exploitation; III, resource exploitation (other than agriculture); IV, exogenous political origin.

[b] Indicated mileage excludes track now in Syria.

[c] Only part of this link is of exogenous political origin.

[d] Parts of the link were in operation as early as 1946.

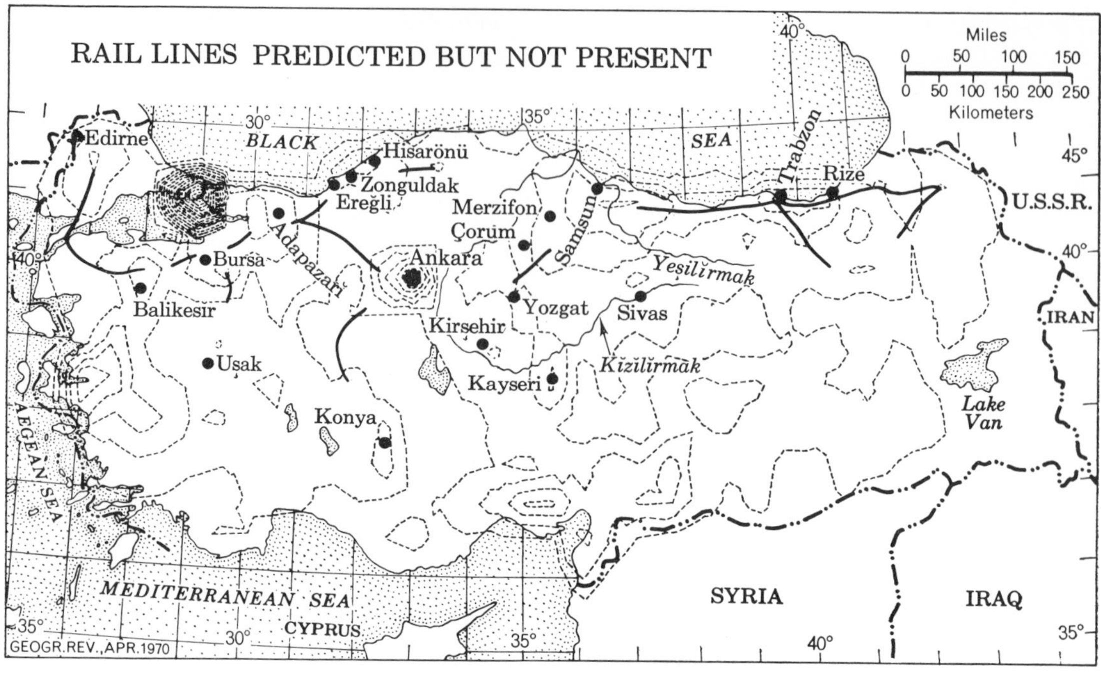

Fig. 8-9.

coast of Turkey from Samsun to Trabzon and Rize. However, the high volume of sea trade along this coast indicates that cabotage successfully obviates the need for rail construction.[18] If this alone were insufficient to preclude construction, the mountainous coastal terrain would lead to prohibitive engineering problems; cost per mile for such a line would be extremely high. Typical of this is the estimated expense of the uncompleted eighteen-mile link proposed between the steel complex at Ereğli and the Zonguldak–Ankara line to the east. A cost of more than $800,000 a mile was considered too high, and the route was vetoed.[19] It may also be noted in passing that the absence of both railroads and well-developed cabotage along the south coast reflects that region's lack of population as well as its rugged terrain.

A second major anomaly occurs with the absence of a real rail line following the route simulated when the population centers of Edirne, Balǐkesir, Bursa, and Adapazarǐ are connected via population ridge lines. In addition to a large volume of coastal shipping within the Sea of Marmara—an efficient substitute for a coastal railway—a marine barrier, the Dardanelles, intersects the projected route between European and Asiatic Turkey. Today's engineering technology could conceivably solve the problem of bridging the strait, albeit by the expenditure of large amounts of capital. But the substitutability of sea lanes, the priorities assigned to the construction of penetration lines into the Asian hinterland, and the overall lack of industrial and technological capacity during the first two decades of the Republic probably all worked against the construction of such a line.

The absence of the Ankara–Konya link is

less easily explained. Here terrain problems are minimal, since the greater part of the intervening area is a flat, nearly featureless plain. The sparsity of population in the region as indicated by the "embayment" shown on the population density map offers an explanation most consistent with this analysis. Economic, agricultural, and population factors are apparently insufficient to justify construction of this line.

The lack of a direct Ankara–Samsun link constitutes another major anomaly, but the Ankara–Kayseri–Sivas–Samsun line (Fig. 8-7) is an obvious substitute. Although no serious topographic barriers exist between Ankara and Samsun, the valleys of the Kĭzĭlĭrmak and the Yeşilĭrmak from Kayseri to Sivas and in the vicinity of Amasya offer suitable alternate routes. On the other hand, the lack of rail service through the relatively densely populated area that includes the cities of Çorum, Yozgat, and Merzifon is a curious omission. Whether a correlation exists between the absence of this line and an administrative antipathy during the early days of the First Republic toward the area because of the bloody Çapanoğlu anti-Kemalist revolt in the summer of 1920 is a question of history left unanswered.

RAIL LINES PRESENT BUT NOT PREDICTED

Fig. 8-10 shows the locations of lines constructed and now in operation that were not predicted by the simulation. In the west the Manisa–Uşak segment and the anomalous short feeder lines are in all likelihood the result of a long history of foreign penetration for commercial purposes. The presence of these additional lines suggests a multiplier effect,

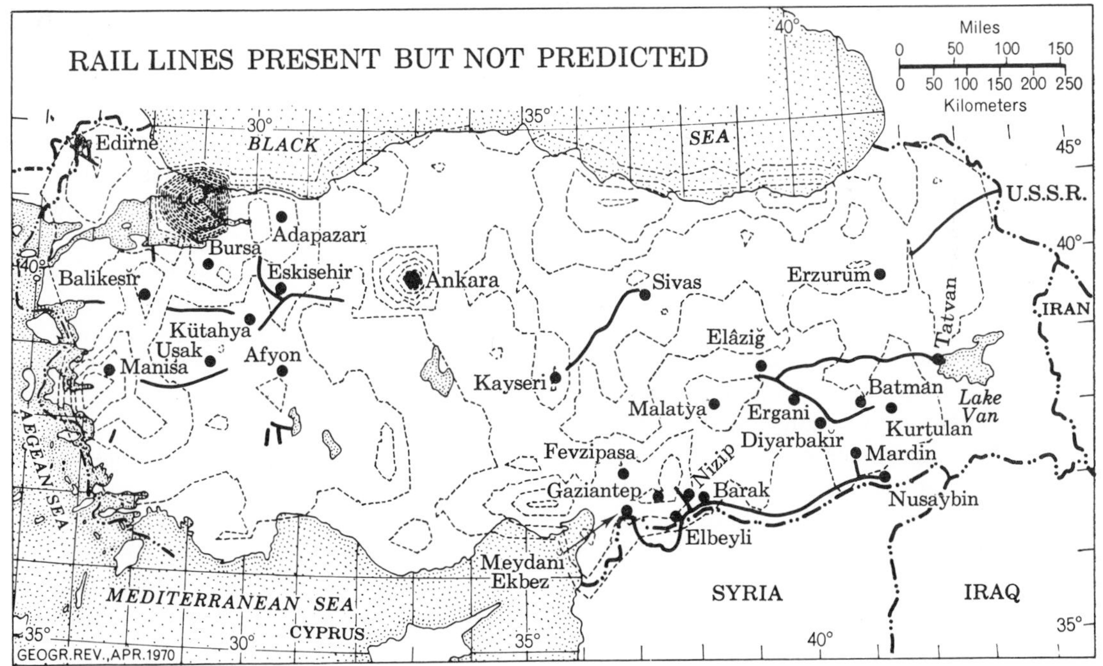

Fig. 8-10.

through which network densities may increase at a more than arithmetical ratio once minimum criteria of population size and agricultural commercialization are satisfied. The Balikesir–Kütahya line was constructed to give better access to chrome and lead mines nearby.

Another set of routes that exist today but were not anticipated in terms of population distribution extends from Malatya to Elâzîğ and from Elâzîğ via Diyarbakîr to Kurtulan. Motivation for this construction is the large copper deposit near the town of Ergani. The route, among the last to be completed (1944), also serves oil fields near Batman and several chrome deposits to the north. It is one of the more important mineral-access lines and has been named the "copper route" by the Turks.

The section of track from the Greek border to Edirne, the route that links Adapazarî to Afyon with an eastward extension toward Ankara, and the long easterly route between Fevzipaşa and Nusaybin[20] with a feeder line to Mardin were not predicted because the simulation treated Turkey as a closed system. If populations external to the country had been considered, these segments, which constitute essential parts of the Berlin to Baghdad Railroad,[21] might have appeared in the simulation. In much the same way, the line between the Russian border and the city of Erzurum can be considered a penetration route from the exterior, since it was constructed by the Russians for political and military purposes and was later inherited by the Turks. The importance of extranational connections is shown again by the route from Elâzîğ, which crosses Lake Van by train ferry to the city of Van and may eventually reach the Iranian border near Qoţūr (Fig. 8-7). This route has neither minerals nor population as incentives for its operation. Access to a critical eastern area in order to insure political hegemony and the desire to reach Iran explain its construction.

ASSESSMENT OF THE METHOD

In addition to supporting current theory concerning the growth of transportation networks, this study identifies exogenous political and military conditions as important additional factors. Transit and access facilities may assume as much importance as the mechanisms of direct administrative control in the development of rail systems in strategic areas. Thus simulations and models that treat the transportation networks of nations as closed systems may show greater variance from reality than those that include larger areas. This was demonstrated when the lack of fit between real and simulated rail networks was analyzed for the Turkish case. In addition to those parts of the simulated and real networks that showed a high degree of correlation, other sets of rails were discovered that either are present in reality and unpredicted or are predicted in the simulation but absent from the real world. Once identified, such sets could be explained with relative ease. The advantage of the analytical method presented here is that it allows the subdividing and ordering of complex spatial systems into subsets that are more easily understood. Within these subsets anomalies are illuminated, which help to pinpoint research questions on which time and effort might be spent most profitably.

From the planners' point of view, such an analysis can provide valuable insight. Preliminary feasibility studies might utilize this method to identify regions in need of additional transportation and areas in which anticipated routes have minimum utility. For example, many maps of Turkey show a projected rail line that crosses the Taurus Mountains from Burdur to Antalya on the Mediterranean coast (Fig. 8-7). But if the conclusions of this study are correct, construction of that line cannot be justified on the basis of population distribution. The fact that new, improved port facilities are being built just west of Antalya, plus the fact that good all-weather highways already lead from the city to both the north and the east, reinforces this conclusion. On the other hand, a direct Ankra–Samsun route via Corum and Merzifon might be worth considering.

Certainly the creation of an extensive all-weather highway system in the last twenty years has reduced the necessity for further railroad construction, and the partial substitutability of highways for rail lines complicates any attempt to delimit desirable new rail routes. However, even if trains must give way to trucks, the method of analysis described here should offer insights into the efficacy of the developing Turkish highway network. By the same token, the application of the method to other parts of the world where rail line construction holds high priority in development planning should assist in the allocation of limited transportation resources.

NOTES

1 For a summary of such research see Peter Haggett and Richard J. Chorley: *Network Analysis in Geography* (London, 1969), especially Chapter 5.

2 Edward J. Taaffe, Richard L. Morrill, and Peter R. Gould: Transport Expansion in Underdeveloped Countries: A Comparative Analysis, *Geogr. Rev.,* Vol. 53, 1963, pp. 503–529; reference on pp. 521–524.

3 William Warntz: The Topology of a Socioeconomic Terrain and Spatial Flows, *Papers of the Regional Sci. Assn.,* Vol. 17, 1966, pp. 47–61; reference on p. 61.

4 The writers are indebted to Waldo Tobler for the advice and computer programs that he provided during this research and to Donald Kolberg for the original program on which subsequent efforts were based (Some Novel Population Maps [unpublished M. A. thesis, Dept. of Geography, Univ. of Michigan, Ann Arbor, 1965]). They are also grateful to Kent Overby for his compilation and preparation of the original data for computer use.

5 More specifically the term "postdictive" should be used, since results of such simulation can only be checked against existing situations. However, "predictive" will be used in this account, because of its more familiar and felicitous construction.

6 The percentages are based on data given in: Z. Y. Hershlag: *Turkey: The Challenge of Growth* (Leiden, 1968), pp. 366 (Table 54) and 232. If only "exploited" lines are considered, the 1939 railroad percentage still remains at 84 percent of the 1965 total.

7 Z. Y. Hershlag: *Turkey: An Economy in Transition* (The Hague, 1958), p. 304.

8 Mark Jefferson: The Civilizing Rails, *Econ. Geogr.,* Vol. 4, 1928, pp. 217–231.

9 All work beyond the initial data collection and key punching was performed by the IBM 7090 computer and a Calcomp plotter.

10 Warntz, *op. cit.,* pp. 47–61.

11 In this discussion the term "route" corresponds to the designation "path" used in graph theory.

12 Taaffe, Morrill, and Gould, *op. cit.,* p. 506.

13 All route lengths were derived from Table 8-2.

14 Taaffe, Morrill, and Gould, *op. cit.,* p. 503.

15 Sir Edward Fitzgerald Law: Report by Major Law on Railways in Asiatic Turkey (presented to both Houses of Parliament by Command of Her Majesty [British Parliamentary Paper], 1896), pp. 10–12. See also Sir M. Stephenson: Railways in Turkey (n.p., 1859), pp. 3–8.

16 Stephenson, *op. cit.,* p. 8.

17 Stephenson, *op. cit.,* p. 5.

18 For a graphic representation see Ali Tanoğlu, Sirri Erinç, and Erol Tumertekin: *Türkiye Atlasĭ* (Istanbul, 1961), Plate 85; and *Türkiye Istatistik Yĭllĭğĭ 1964–65,* Türk Cumhuriyeti Devlet Istatistik Enstitüsü, Yayin No. 510, pp. 598–620 (Tables 514–515).

19 Malcolm D. Rivkin: *Area Development for National Growth: The Turkish Precedent* (New York, 1965), pp. 176–177.

20 The original line leading from Fevzipaşa southward and eastward now enters Syrian territory at Meydanckbez and returns to Turkish soil at Elbeyli (Fig. 8-7). A subsequent lateral link via Gaziantep, Nizip, and Karkamiş completed an eastward link entirely within Turkey (Fig. 8-10).

21 For a discussion of this particular undertaking see Edward Mead Earle: *Turkey, the Great Powers, and the Bagdad Railway* (New York, 1923). It should be noted that the part of the Berlin to Baghdad Railway within Asia Minor consisted of two sections: the Anatolian system, which extended from Istanbul to Konya, and the Baghdad Railway, which continued east from Konya.

FURTHER READINGS TO PART TWO

Although the work on inventories is scattered, the following may be of use. Begin with:

W. L. Garrison and D. F. Marble, "Comparisons of Transportation Stocks" in *A Prolegomenon to the Forecasting of Transportation Development*, Research Report, Transportation Center, Northwestern University, 1965, pp. 21–36.

One of the original reports, if you can get hold of it, is:

Y. Barzel, Y. Grunfeld, R. L. Morrill, and E. J. Taaffe, *Transportation Geography Research*. Submitted under Contract DA 44-177-TC-574, U.S. Army Transportation Research Command, Fort Eustis, Virginia, 1960.

Some elements of this are covered in the contributory work of Peter Gould. See:

P. R. Gould, "The Development of the Transportation Pattern in Ghana, *Studies in Geography*, No. 5, Northwestern University, 1960.

If you want to work this out on your own, some of the factors of development that can be used are outlined by:

B. J. L. Berry, "An Inductive Approach to the Regionalisation of Economic Development" in N. S. Ginsburg (ed.), *Essays on Geography and Economic Development*, Chicago: Research Paper No. 62, Chicago: University of Chicago, 1960.

B. J. L. Berry, "Basic Patterns of Economic Development" in N. S. Ginsburg (ed.), *Atlas of Economic Development*, Chicago: University of Chicago Press, 1961.

Part Six (*a*) tackles the role of transportation in a developing region or nation, but see also:

R. J. Harrison Church, "Geographic Factors in the Development of Transport in Africa," *Transport and Communications Review*, vol. 2, no. 3, 1949, pp. 3–11.

R. W. Fogel, "A Quantitative Approach to the Study of Railroads in American Economic Growth," *Journal of Economic History*, vol. 22, 1962, pp. 163–97.

G. Fromm, *Transport Investment and Economic Development*, Washington, D.C.: The Brookings Institution, 1965.

H. Hunter, *Soviet Transportation Experience*, Washington, D.C.: The Brookings Institution, 1967.

S. Lebergatt, "United States Transport Advance and Externalities," *Journal of Economic History*, vol. 26, 1966, pp. 437–65.

Backup empirical studies will be found in, among others:

R. Ajo, "An Analysis of Automobile Frequences in a Human Geographic Continuum," *Lund Studies in Geography, Series B,* no. 15, 1955.

P. Costas and G. Magahima, "Studies of Present Transportation Patterns: Air Transport," *Ekistics,* vol. 22, 1966, pp. 32–35.

E. Perle, *The Demand for Transportation*, Research Paper No. 95, Chicago: University of Chicago, 1964.

Regional transportation descriptions which contain data on inventories or stocks include:

J. H. Appleton, *The Geography of Communications in Great Britain,* London: Oxford University Press, 1962.

J. E. Becht, *A Geography of Transportation and Business Logistics,* Dubuque, Iowa: Wm. C. Brown Co., 1970.

P. Camu, E. P. Weeks, and Z. W. Semetz, *Economic Geography of Canada,* New York: St. Martin's Press, 1964, especially chap. 9.

A. M. O'Connor, *Railways and Development in Uganda—A Study in Economic Geography,* Nairobi: Oxford University Press, 1966.

In addition, of course, see the transportation census of individual nations and the yearbooks of such organizations as the United Nations.

Turning to networks, simple expositions of this approach will be found in:

R. Abler, J. S. Adams, and P. Gould, "Movement Geometry," "Analysis of Networks and Flows," and "Network Design and Network Performance" in *Spatial Organization,* Englewood Cliffs, N. J.: Prentice-Hall, 1971, chap. 8, pp. 238–288.

P. Haggett, "Networks," "Nodes," and "Hierarchies" in *Locational Analysis in Geography,* London: Edward Arnold, 1965, chap. 3–5.

P. Haggett, "Network Models in Geography" in R. J. Chorley and P. Haggett (eds.), *Models in Geography,* London: Methuen, 1967, chap. 15.

The most complete account to date of the graph theory approach to networks in geography will be found in:

P. Haggett and R. J. Chorley, *Network Analysis in Geography,* London: Edward Arnold, 1969. (This contains an extensive bibliography, pp. 319–335.

A somewhat contrary view of this aspect of transportation geography will be found in my review of the above book in the *Canadian Geographer,* 1971, vol. 15, pp. 150–152.

The Northwestern University approach to network analysis is represented by:

K. Kansky, *The Structure of Transportation Networks,* Department of Geography Research Paper No. 84, Chicago: University of Chicago, 1963.

A selection of papers on the subject include:

W. R. Black, "Growth of the Railway Network of Maine: A Multivariate Approach," Discussion Paper No. 5, University of Iowa, Department of Geography, 1967.

I. Burton and P. Atkinson, *Accessibility in Northern Ontario: An Application of Graph Theory to a Regional Network,* Ontario Department of Highways, 1963.

W. L. Garrison and D. F. Marble, "Factor Analytic Study of the Connectivity of a Transportation Network," *Regional Science Association, Papers and Proceedings,* vol. 12, 1964, pp. 231–38.

H. L. Gauthier, "Transportation and the Growth of São Paulo Economy," *Journal of Regional Science,* vol. 8, 1968, pp. 77–94.

P. Haggett, "On the Extension of the Horton Combinatorial Algorithm to Regional Highway Networks," *Journal of Regional Science,* vol. 7, pp. 281–290.

R. Lachene, "Networks and the Location of Economic Activities," *Regional Science Association, Papers and Proceedings,* vol. 14, 1965, pp. 183–196.

J. D. Nystuen and M. Dacey, "A Graph Theory Interpretation of Nodal Regions," *Papers and Proceedings* of the Regional Science Association, vol. 7, 1961, pp. 29–42. Reprinted in B. J. L. Berry and D. F. Marble (eds.), *Spatial Analysis,* Englewood Cliffs, N. J.: Prentice-Hall, 1968, pp. 407–418.

C. Werner, "The Law of Refraction in Transportation Geography: Its Multivariate Extension," *Canadian Geographer,* vol. 12, 1968, pp. 28–40.

C. Werner, "Networks of Minimum Length," *Canadian Geographer,* vol. 13, 1969, pp. 47–69.

C. Werner, "Two Models for Horton's Law of Stream Numbers," *The Canadian Geographer,* vol. 16, 1972, pp. 50–68.

C. Werner et al., "Research Seminar in Theoretical Transportation Geography," *Studies in Geography,* no. 16, 1968, pp. 128–70.

As a first approach to the gravity model, try Abler, Adams, and Gould, *op cit.,* pp. 221–233.

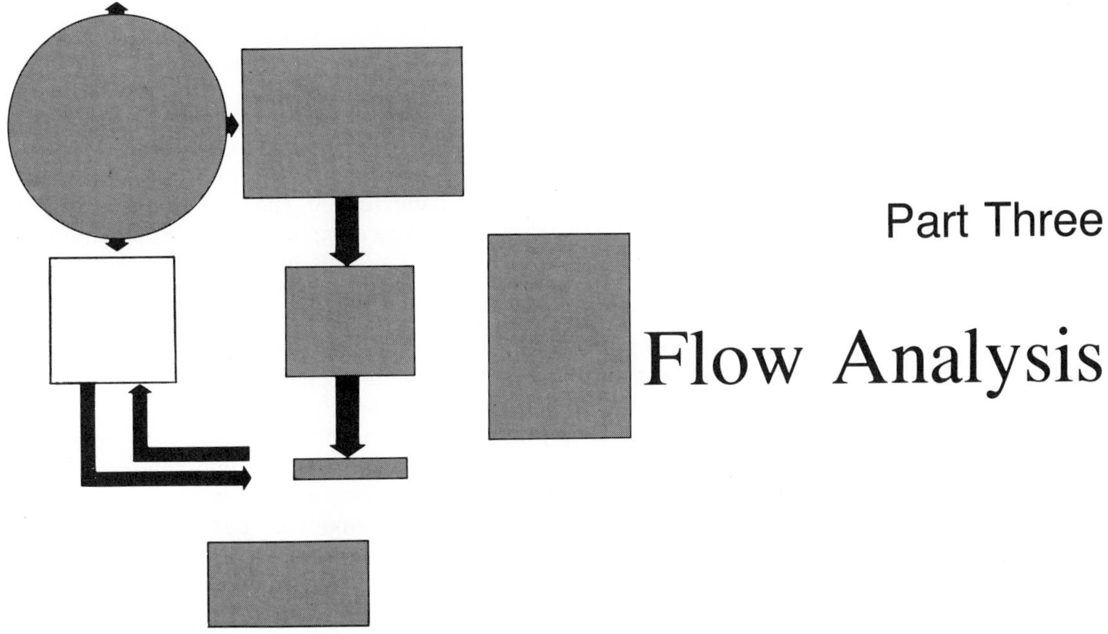

Part Three

Flow Analysis

INTRODUCTION

So far as we have built up this framework: spatial interaction is a given, as are regional/national variations in physical stocks, such that a set of route systems with particular geometric properties (networks) varies over space. We are now in a position to examine how much moves where—in other words, the flow, the very activity of transportation.

Many flow studies center on the movement of goods or commodities. One obvious approach is to look at the flow of commodities to competing ports, which leads to the demarcation of port hinterlands (see also Selection 14). Another approach, largely pursued by economists, considers the broader interregional or international patterns of commodity flows. Still other geographers use advanced techniques such as linear programming to forecast or project such flow patterns (Selection 10). At a more general level, efforts have been made to clarify the complexities of individual regional economic structures. The classic description of an intranation commodity flow is an examination of flows in the United States by E. L. Ullman, who posed the question, What is the pattern of spatial connections in the American economy?* Ullman believed, as we saw in Selection 3, that he had found a logical response to geography and distance, from which he postulated his three-factor typology of spatial interaction: *complementarity, intervening opportunity,* and *transferability.*

As a result of this work, geographers and allied researchers have postulated a relationship between the network structure examined in Part Two and the flow of goods or movement of people over that network. Selection 12 pursues this flow-network relationship further. The relationship is thought to be due in part to the fact that providing a communications system modifies relationships between a set of locations. Thus in channeling the volume, direction, and intensity of movement, the network is in turn influenced by the volume of the flow it conducts. The relationship between certain graph theoretic measures and the corresponding areal characteristics is "based on the intuitive assumption that the structure of a transportation network is a reflection of the network's traffic flow pattern."†

By *flow* is meant simply the volume and direction of the movement of goods, people, and messages. Thus flows, and the interaction that they involve, are the chief objects of many geographical investigations, from the diffusion of innovations to the movement of consumers. Although movement is often a continuous phenomenon, it is nearly always treated as static and discrete. Taking the existence of routes and stocks as given, we are now concerned with accounting for the volume of traffic that flows over different routes or through different nodes. Selection 9, by R. H. T. Smith, reviews the major concepts and methods in commodity flow analysis. The models used to explain or represent movement flow, or exchange, have employed six principal techniques:

In *regional input-output techniques,* flows of various kinds are examined simultaneously for their effects upon the activities of an area.‡

The technique of *linear programming* is frequently used in regional and other flow models. This is an extension of Alfred Weber's *least cost–cost minimization approach,*§ which allows simultaneous consideration of several alternatives. Flows are looked on as part of a maximization technique applied within the restrictive framework of a particular situation. We will return to this technique in Selection 10.

The more general approach represented by *diffusion models* is concerned with the spread or flow of a variety of phenomena: new ideas and techniques, disease, cultural traits, and many others.‖

Another technique, *analysis of transactions,* is used to examine flows of

**American Commodity Flow,* Seattle: University of Washington Press, 1957.

†K. J. Kansky, *Structure of Transport Networks,* Chicago: University of Chicago, Department of Geography, Research Paper No. 84, 1963, p. 26.

‡For a more detailed review see W. Isard, *Methods of Regional Analysis,* Cambridge, Mass.: MIT Press, 1960, chap. 5.

§A. Weber, *Theory of the Location of Industries* (trans. by C. J. Friedrich), 1929. See any standard economic geography text for explanation, e.g., M. E. Eliot Hurst, *A Geography of Economic Behaviour,* Duxbury Press, 1972, chapter 9.

‖See, for example, L. A. Brown and E. G. Moore, "Diffusion Research in Geography: A Perspective" in *Progress in Geography,* vol. 1, 1969, pp. 119–157.

money, mail, telephone calls, and similar phenomena. Smith examines this in Selection 9 and refers to several basic studies, including those of Savage and Deutsch, and Spiegelglas.#

The use of *traffic flow models,* based on empirical studies of road capacities, speed of vehicles, width of road, existence of junctions, and so on, is virtually confined to traffic engineering.**

Finally, mention has already been made of *gravity models,* based on an analogy with classical Newtonian physics, and to which we will return in Selection 11.

But first, let us follow R. H. T. Smith through his review of the objectives of research in commodity flows. He goes beyond the six basic categories mentioned here, and although he deals with some difficult techniques, an understanding of the scope of research in this area is necessary before we look at three particular methods in more detail.

#I. R. Savage and K. Deutsch, "A Statistical Model of the Gross Analysis of Transaction Flows," *Econometrica,* vol. 28, 1960, pp. 551–572; S. Spiegelglas, "Some Aspects of State to State Commodity Flows in the United States," *Journal of Regional Science,* vol. 2, 1960, pp. 71–80.

**See, for example, F. A. Haight, *Mathematical Theories of Traffic Flow,* New York: Academic Press, 1963, or any traffic engineering textbook.

Selection 9

Concepts and Methods in Commodity Flow Analysis

R. H. T. Smith

Commodity flow studies have been justly criticized for their conceptual poverty (36, p. 1). Indeed, until the mid-fifties when some of Ohlin's (60) propositions about interregional trade were reformulated by Ullman (93, 94) into a verbal model of the bases for spatial interaction, the few geographers interested in commodity flows seemed to be preoccupied with the graphical presentation of statistics of traffic flow (16, 99). Studies that simply annotate flow maps and diagrams (themselves generalized and therefore less accurate versions of the basic numerical data) have not ceased (83, 86, 91), but during the last decade there has been an increasing awareness of the need for concept and method in commodity flow studies (13, 35). It is with these concepts and methods that this [work] will be concerned.

[We] will commence with the identification of some of the spatial questions that are asked about commodity flows. Then, the methods (especially those of a quantitative nature) which have been used to examine these questions will be briefly reviewed. [We are] thus more concerned with commodity flows as "objects of research" than as "instruments of research" (55, p. 30, 42), and

Economic Geography, vol. 46, supplement, 1970, pp. 404–416. Reprinted by permission of the author and editor.

such wider issues as "geography as spatial interaction" (95), or regional economic analysis (42, p. 144), will not be considered.

CONCEPTUAL ISSUES

A commodity flow data matrix can be visualized with rows as origins and columns as destinations. Usually the m origins and destinations are point locations (urban centers, transport terminals, or transport junctions [83, 91]). However, sometimes they are aggregated to n regions, where $n < m$ (26, 37). The sum of the i origins (or destinations) in the n sub-aggregates is equal to m; thus,

$$\Sigma_i n = m$$

In the extreme case, where all m origins and destinations are grouped together, $n = 1$; an input-output study of a regional or a national economy might be regarded as an example of such a study (53).

Another way in which this matrix has been modified involves reduction of either the origins or destinations to a smaller number, or to one location only. Thus, studies of port hinterlands (11, 65) focus on a column of the matrix; while foreland analyses (11, 74) are concerned with a row vector. The usual rail or road commodity flow studies use all or some sub-set of the rows and columns (30, 34, 83, 93). A number of essentially different approaches to the flow matrix can thus be recognized, depending on the level of aggregation: m to m, n to m, m to n, and n to n. When $n = 1$ in the n to m and m to n situations, port foreland and hinterland studies are defined.

There are three characteristics of interest in this matrix, in addition to the number and location of the m or n origins and destinations; they are volume of movements, distance moved, and routes and connections. These three characteristics provide the framework for this review. . . . In connection with the first, it could be argued that studies of transportation networks (27, 44) are implicit commodity flow analyses, inasmuch as transport networks exist to facilitate commodity and passenger flows. However, the [work] is concerned mainly with those studies in which both route connections and the quantity shipped (actual, potential, or predicted) are the focus of attention. These are called *shipment volume* studies, and will be discussed in the first section. . . .

It is useful to consider *distance* and *routes* in the context of Table 9-1, in which progression down the rows of the table (i to f to l to s) coincides with greater detail. In an interregional trade study (row i) the volume of movement between the n origins and destinations is known, but precise distance and route characteristics usually are not.[1] When commodity flows between m nodes (usually towns, row f, Table 9-1) are considered, *routes* and *distances* are known. In some cases, flows may move over routes which do not coincide with the most direct, or minimum distance connection. This raises the issue of the *efficiency of commodity flows*. The most common efficiency criterion in commodity

Table 9-1 Components of Commodity Flows

Row	Flows or connections	Terminals or nodes
i	interregional flow	producing and consuming areas
f	inter-nodal flow	urban centers, or other transport terminals
l	inter-nodal links	shippers or traders at terminals
s	inter-nodal strands	consignments between traders (shipments and receipts)

Source: (36, p. 2; 78, pp. 121–22).

flow analyses is the minimization of transport costs in the distribution of a commodity from m origins to m or n destinations, or *vice versa*. Distance has been used as a surrogate for transport costs (40, 46).

It is worth noting from Table 9-1 that f, the intern-nodal flow, comprises the i exchanges between the l inter-nodal links (shippers or traders). Further, an inter-nodal link consists of k strands, or individual consignments from one trader to another such that

$$\Sigma_k s = l$$

and

$$\Sigma_j l = f.$$

Thus

$$\Sigma_m f = l$$

and

$$s \geq l \geq f \geq i$$

Smith and Hay (78) suggest that these strands have systematically related size and length characteristics, depending on the stage of the internal trading process (bulking or distribution) at which they are observed. In-shipments to a bulking station usually are small and short, out-shipments large and long. The reverse holds for distributing stations. Note that this contrasts sharply with the general distance decay proposition (4, p. 191; 43); as distance increases, shipment volume falls off. The contradiction is more apparent than real, however, as strands are components of the larger flow.

The routes over which commodity flows take place have a third, *structural* characteristic which reflects the tendency for sets of origins, or destinations, or origins and destinations (dyads) to have similar commodity movement characteristics. Thus, a number of spatially concentrated, or dispersed, origins may ship to a small number of destinations, and *vice versa;* and dyads may be similarly aligned, revealing significant regional connections.

The remainder of this [work] will consist of a review of the methods which have been employed in the analysis of volume of shipments, efficiency of flows, and structure of flows.

VOLUME OF SHIPMENTS

A common objective in many commodity flow studies is to make diagnostic statements about the magnitude of flows. [Such statements, usually taking the form of "more than" or "less than" might be expected under certain conditions.] The observed flows are arrayed against "predicted" flows over the given routes, and inferences are drawn about the relative magnitude of the actual flows. The subject of this section will be the methods that have been used to predict these "yardstick" flows.

At the simplest level, a variety of ratios and indices has been employed in the study of the volume of shipments. Isard (42, pp. 123–26) noted the utility of the location quotient as a starting point, and it is essentially this notion at the department, regional, and national level for a number of industry sectors that Boudeville (6) employed in his study of regional trade in France. This technique (as well as other ratios) was used by Chojnicki (17, pp. 219–24) in an attempt to characterize Poland's economic regions as "importers" or "exporters," and by Britton (10, pp. 110–11) in describing the traffic characteristics of ports.

Commodity flows through ports have been scrutinized by the relative shift technique (72, 73) where traffic volumes at time $t + 1$ are projected on the basis of the time t share; absolute gains may still constitute a relative loss. A similar approach to inter-voivodship rail flows was used by Morawski (56). Other ratios and indices include: the traffic-capture ratio, the ratio of actual traffic originated at a center or along a route to the total available traffic in the hinterlands (90, 91); a ratio of tons from a given origin to tons from all origins (11); and various ratios between terminating, originating, and bridge traffic over certain segments of a transport network (97, 98). All of these techniques are essentially descriptive, but their utility as points of departure can be considerable.

Transaction flow analysis can yield a more sensitive diagnostic assessment of the actual flow (8, 21, 22, 31, 75, 77, 84, 85). This technique was developed by political scientists, especially Deutsch, in an attempt to quantify information flows and their effects on intra- and international communication. An index is calculated as follows:

$$RA_{ij} = \frac{A_{ij} - E_{ij}}{E_{ij}}$$

where RA_{ij} = relative acceptance from origin i to destination j;

A_{ij} = actual transaction (flow) from origin i to destination j;

E_{ij} = expected transaction (flow) from i to j.

The calculation of expected flows is based on an assumption of origin-destination independence which holds that the flow from i to j reflects the total flows to j (8, p. 882). Thus, in the matrix, if the sum of column 2 was 10 percent of the sum of all column totals, this model would argue that origins 1, 2, 3 . . . , m should ship 10 percent of their respective row totals to destination 2. Certain problems arise with intra-destination shipments, but the model can be modified to take account of this (25, pp. 42–5; 31, 75). A more serious issue concerns the interpretation of the size of the relative acceptance measures, and their departure (+ or –) from zero: how large must an index be to indicate salience (77, 79)?

Simple linear correlation[2] and regression analysis has been used frequently in the analysis of commodity flows, especially in situations involving one origin and many destinations (or *vice versa*). Thus, Brookfield (12, pp. 83–5) correlated coal receipts at English ports and population within a certain distance of the hinterland, but his results were disappointing. Golledge (30, pp. 61–2) obtained strong relationships between town population and total rail receipts and inwards tons from Newcastle, for a set of New South Wales towns. Comparable results have been obtained by Gould for rail shipments from Takoradi, Ghana (33, 34, pp. 96–9), and by Smith (81, 82, 83) for rail shipments from Sydney and Melbourne to railway centers in southern New South Wales. Population is not always an adequate surrogate for demand, however, and the correlation coefficients obtained by Onakomaiya and Smith (63) for shipments of all imported goods, and various subcategories of imports from port cities to inland towns in Nigeria were uniformly low.

The role of distance in predicting commodity flows has also been given considerable attention. In a series of three market studies in Ghana, Gould (34, pp. 157–58) observed a systematic decline in the volume of goods moving as distance increased; the b-value in the regression equations (i.e., the distance exponents) varied inversely with the proportion of the total shipments carried by mechanized transport.[3] Smith (83, pp. 123–30) established a similar relationship between receipts per capita from two major origins at a set of southern New South Wales towns and distance from these origins; this analysis was directed towards market area boundary definition.

The surprising thing about the analyses of the volume of shipments described above is that the two variables in isolation, population and distance, perform as well as they do. Shipment volume between two points is a simultaneous function of both demand and distance considerations (93, pp. 20–7), so that formulations involving both of these variables should be more powerful in identifying those flows that are greater than or less than expected. The gravity and potential notions of human interaction provide an appropriate model in this regard. An extensive review will not be attempted save to note that this model has been used much more frequently in consumer behavior and migration studies than in analyses of commodity flow. The extensive use of gravity notions in geography has prompted some criticism (50), and Pred (68, p. 19) asserted . . . that ". . . the thinking on spatial interaction has reached an impasse because of its apparently unbreakable contract with the concept of gravitation." The following remarks will be confined to the identification of a few of the examples of the uses to which gravity and potential notions have been put in flow analyses.

In his study of Durban's hinterland, Shaffer did not explicitly draw on the gravity model, but his model for predicting traffic from (or to) a port to (or from) inland stations clearly resembles a multiple regression form of the gravity model (76, p. 228). Britton's study of Bristol's market for manufactured goods (9) incorporated a number of extensively modified forms of the gravity model. In the initial model of rail interaction, population, number of manufacturing workers, and retail sales turnover were entered as the "mass" variables, along with distance; however, only distance and population were significant in the explanation of rail interaction, yielding the following equation (9, p. 181):

$$RL_c = 477.6\ \mathrm{P}^{0.6}\ \mathrm{D}^{-1.5}$$

where RL_c = volume of rail interaction

P = population

D = distance

He modified this model by adding a dummy variable for location of destination (9, p. 185), and by attempting to control for multicollinearity in the mass variables, but its essential gravity base remains. Similar equations were developed for road traffic (9, pp. 185–6), and then the road and rail models were further modified by the addition of a rail residual factor to the road model, and *vice versa* (9, p. 188). Britton's is one of the more comprehensive studies of commodity flows constructed from the conceptual base of the gravity model, although analyses by Starkie (88) and Helvig (39) of truck traffic, and by Reed of Indian rail flows (71, pp. 145–71) should not be overlooked in this regard.

Much of Britton's discussion is couched in terms of the bases of movement: complementarity, intervening opportunity, and transferability (93, pp. 20–7). The problem of measuring specific complementarity was considered by Smith who noted that "The mere movement of goods from states A and B to area Z illustrates the existence of complementary trade relationships. However, such movements do not indicate whether there is 'more' or 'less' complementarity between A and Z than between B and Z" (80, pp. 1–2). Using the ICC Rail Carload Waybill Statistics of state-to-state agricultural shipments, the measure involved: first, the prediction of a state's agricultural shipments to New England using a gravity model expression (P_i = rail surplus in origin state i, P_j = New England's population; D_{ij} = airline distance in miles between state centroids, $n = 1$); second, regression of actual rail shipments weighted by the proportion of imports to New England that each shipment represents (Y) on this predicted amount (X); and finally, division of the actual unweighted shipments by the estimates (Y_c) from this simple linear regression equation. The resulting values were interpreted as indices of complementarity.

The gravity and potential model expression was modified by Reed by substituting an intervening opportunity and a competition variable in place of distance (71, pp. 172–79). Although this did not provide a markedly better prediction of Indian rail flows, some of the models that Reed subsequently suggested appeared promising. These incorporated notions of demand (outflows) and supply (inflows) space potentials (3, p. 158).[4] For outflows, Reed (71, p. 182) notes that "... outflows from the study area to the rest of India should be directly related to demand at *i*, the contribution of the study area to supply at *k* (competitive effect), and to the market potential at *k* (redistribution effect) and inversely related to the distance study area to *k*." The improvement in the explanation of volume flows was, however, disappointingly small (71, p. 195).

There have been a number of attempts to formulate a multivariate model to explain patterns of flows. Reference has already been made to the work of Reed (71) and Berry (3), both of whom drew on Linnemann's econometric model of international trade flows (49) in the development of their models; see also Prais (67, pp. 570–73). Linnemann's model to predict the dollar value of trade flows between pairs of countries took the following form (49, pp. 147–50):

$$X_{ij} = b_0 Y_i^{b_1} N_i^{-b_2} Y_j^{b_3} N_j^{-b_4} D_{ij}^{-b_5} P_{ij}^{b_6} C_{ij}^{b_7}$$

where X_{ij} = trade flow between i and j ($US million);

Y_i, Y_j = gross national products of i and j;

N_i, N_j = population of i and j;

D_{ij} = distance between i and j;

P_{ij} = preferential trade factor;

C_{ij} = commodity composition variable.

The important role of the distance and "mass" variables should not be overlooked, although the negative exponents for population of i and j (in addition to the expected negative power for distance) are surprising. In a more recent paper, Yeates (100) proposed a "geograpic" model of international trade:

$$\log X_{ij} = \log b_0 + b_1 \log PC_j + b_2 \log NI_j - b_3 \log D_{ij} + b_4 EEC_j + b_5 EFTA_j + b_6 DA_j + b_7 SA_j + b_8 Comm_j + e$$

Where X_{ij} = trade between i and j;

PC_j = per capita income of j;

NI_j = national income of j;

D_{ij} = distance between i and j;

and EEC_j, $EFTA_j$, DA_j, SA_j, and $Comm_j$ are essentially preferential trade variables indicating on a (1,0) attribute scale whether j belongs to these trade blocks (DA = dollar area, SA = sterling area, and $Comm$ = Communist).

The similarity in intent and structure of the model to Linnemann's earlier formulation should be noted; see also Yeates (101).

Two other multivariate approaches deserve mention in this context; the first (61) is a study of rail and truck unloads of fresh fruit and vegetables at fifteen United States cities, which was concerned with some of the same influences on commodity flows as was Reed's study (71). Of eight independent variables selected to explain the proportion of truck unloads at each city, only three (distance [–], number of refrigerated trucks [+], and a mode preference variable [+]) were significant. An attempt was made to account for location of the city and its supply states by using analysis of covariance (61). Finally, Onakomaiya and Smith (63) developed a seven variable multiple linear regression equation to explain rail shipments of imports from Lagos and Port Harcourt to 22 inland towns in Nigeria. The predictor variables were export earnings at inland stations, population, distance from Lagos, distance from Port Harcourt, percentage employment in non-agricultural occupations, location of station (northern savanna, southern forest), and the presence or absence of a railroad-operated road feeder service. Export earnings ("mass") and distance from Lagos ("friction") accounted for approximately 78 percent of the variation in import receipts. Of the remaining five variables only two (population and road feeder service) accounted for more than 1 percent.

A final method for studying shipment volumes involves elementary matrix manipulation. Where the matrix of flows is of order $n(n > 1)$, and when intraregional flows are known, this matrix, N, can be manipulated to yield information on the strength of regional interconnections. Thus, the matrix of coefficients, X, which converts D (a diagonal matrix representing a situation in which only *intraregional* trade occurs) to N can be regarded as the opportunity cost of intraregional self-sufficiency:

$$D.X = N$$

therefore $X = N.D^{-1}$

Such an approach was described by Smith (77), but data deficiencies prevented its use on a table of Nigerian interregional money flows associated with flows of locally-produced goods.

The majority of techniques that establish "yardstick" flows involve considerations of demand (complementarity) and distance (friction). A few methods predict on the basis of an hypothesized even share at all destinations, on national compared with regional shares (location quotients), on the traffic volumes at earlier time periods (shift techniques), or finally on the total amount received by each destination (transaction flows). In correlation-regression and gravity-potential methods of predicting volume flows, the level of explanation from distance (friction) and population (attractive mass) is high. They appear to be the only two variables with any general applicability, and most others seem to be peculiar to a given situation.

EFFICIENCY OF FLOWS

This area of research is concerned with descriptive and normative characteristics of the routing of commodity flow patterns. Transport networks only rarely link a set of nodes by the shortest distance, and almost any movement over a given route involves a certain amount of distance inefficiency (see Madeyski [51] on "coefficients of prolongation"). A number of essentially descriptive techniques have been used to describe the distance or length-of-haul attributes of commodity flows: Clark (18, pp. 20–7) constructed density polygons and cumulative frequency curves to illustrate the relationship between state-to-state rail shipments and distance. Vasilevskiy (96, pp. 40–6) attempted to account for "irrational" hauls in his system of indices to express the relationship between length of haul and the geographic division of labor.

The formal technique most useful in the study of the efficiency of a commodity flow pattern is the linear programming transportation model. Efficiency usually implies the minimization of distance, or transportation costs, subject to certain constraints. The efficiency criterion, or objective function, can however involve the maximization of some quantity, such as the flow over a given route or through a specified terminal. Modifications of the linear programming format can be made to allow for stockpiling at origins and/or destinations for untenable routes, and for various other conditions specific to a given situation. Comparison with the actual distribution of commodities can pinpoint specific small or large flows over certain routes, while the value of the objective function compared with the actual transport cost bill gives a composite measure of the efficiency of the flow pattern.

There are numerous examples of the application of this methodology (5, pp. 6–11). The movement of coal, a bulky transport-intensive commodity, in England and the United States has been examined by Land (46) and Henderson (40). Using miles as the measure of transport cost, both established that the existing distribution patterns were approximately 10 percent more expensive than those prescribed by the transportation model. Goldman (29) and Casetti (15) have used this model to assess a classic location problem in the steel industry. Other items include an expository article by Cox (19), and studies of Indian wheat movements by Dickason and Wheeler (24), of Indian cement flows by Gosh (32), and of wool movements in eastern Australia by Dent (20).

Morrill and Garrison (57) were concerned with a somewhat different problem: they projected trade patterns in wheat and flour in a five-region system of the U.S. using a spatial price equilibrium model. This model views trade as an outcome of relative location (and, therefore, transportation costs) and regional differences in demand (and supply) characteristics. Their analysis is indicative of the power of this technique to account for such eventualities as drought and population changes (57, p. 124) on the projected trade levels.

Linear programming can be used in at least two other contexts in flow analysis. The first of these is exemplified by Gauthier's work on flows and networks in Brazil (28). He was concerned, not with actual flows (for which data were, as in so many cases, unavailable), but with predicting least-cost flows in a capacitated network. This study represents an admirable fusion of the concepts and methods of graph theory and network analysis (5, pp. 4–24) and linear programming. Gauthier shows that the various highway sub-networks are not mutually exclusive sets, and that the implications of highway improvement for traffic flows must be considered in a context wider than the two centers immediately affected by these improvements.

Inter-sectoral relations within an economy may be identified via input-output analysis (53), and Leontief's work in this regard is well known, e.g., (47), (48). Input-output analysis has also been applied at the sub-national level (45, 54). When an economy is divided both sectorally and areally, interregional input-output analysis enables one to identify inter-industry linkages between areas (42).[5] Such an analysis was performed by Dhar *et al.* (23) for India for three regions and eighteen sectors. In a sense this sort of analysis is essentially predictive, because by varying the regional final demand values, industry output levels and the resulting interregional commodity flows can be forecasted. Such forecasts, however, frequently involve restrictive assumptions, such as stable trading relationships and constant production functions. Mention should also be made of Moses's study (58), in which he used linear programming to compute an optimal trade pattern for regional manufacturing, thus adding a normative dimension to the predictive analysis.

The methodology most useful in assessing the efficiency of commodity flow patterns draws on iterative mathematical allocation procedures. The transportation model of linear programming has been used frequently in this regard, sometimes to establish the least-cost flow pattern with which to compare actual flows, other times to predict volume flows under varying conditions of supply and demand. Linear programming can lend considerable analytical and predictive power to some of the techniques of network analysis, and to interregional input-output analysis.

STRUCTURE OF FLOWS

The analysis of the structure of commodity flows involves the identification of generic locational characteristics of groups of origins, or of groups of destinations, or of groups of origins and destinations (dyads). This type of analysis rests on the proposition that these clusters are not readily apparent from inspection of a pattern of commodity flow such as the flow matrix. Most of the methods used in this endeavor to date involve multivariate inferential statistics, although in some instances, dominance-dependence patterns of points of origin and destination have been derived from elementary manipulations of a flow matrix.

One such method is described by Nystuen and Dacey (59), and was applied to telephone traffic in Washington. An "independent" city is one that records its largest flow to a smaller city; a "subordinate" city is one for which the largest flow is to a larger city. "Small" and "large" can be defined in a number of ways, including commodity receipts (column total), shipments (row total), or the sum of the two (column plus row total). Nystuen and Dacey develop some of the graph theoretic notions associated with the "adjacency matrix," which is the matrix summarizing in binary form the pattern of dominance and dependence. Hay and Smith (37) employed this method to demonstrate the existence of strong north-south inter-town links in pre-civil war Nigeria on the basis of payments for rail shipments of locally produced goods. Peters (66) also investigated the use of dominance-dependence notions, and cohesion indices, using freight revenues recorded in the ICC Rail Carload Waybill Statistics; he was much less concerned with graph theory interpretations than were Nystuen and Dacey.

A somewhat different approach to the structure of flow patterns was adopted by Boxer (7). He sought to develop generalizations about the structure of shipping into and out of the port of Hong Kong. Approximately 600 shipping movements were randomly sampled, and 37 characteristics identified (35 were in binary form). The 37 × 37 correlation matrix pointed up a number of structural attributes of Hong Kong's overseas shipping; the data matrix did not, however, contain information on the actual flows.

Perhaps the most promising approach to this problem involves the extraction of redundancies in the $m \times m$ correlation matrix of commodity flows using factor analysis. In R-mode analysis, the (column) correlation matrix is factored, yielding groups of destinations (factor loadings) similar in terms of the manner in which their needs are assembled (3, p. 148). The factor scores identify those origins important in shipping to each group. Q-mode analysis results in essentially the same information for origins.

Berry's analysis of Indian commodity flows between 36 trade blocs follows this methodology, and the achievements are best summarized by him (3, p. 155):

> The factoring process is essentially taxonomic when applied directly to commodity flow matrices. It explores similarities in flow patterns, groups origins and destinations into functional regions on the basis of these similarities, and reveals the basic anatomy of the flows . . . the process does not reveal directly the distance-decay functions explored by Gould or Smith. Nor does it yield a predictive model of flows in the manner of Linnemann.

McConnell (52, pp. 89–93) applied this

methodology in an attempt to determine whether the countries of the Middle East were complementary or competitive.

The notion of a parsimonious flow matrix is further employed by Berry in his general field theory of spatial structure and spatial behavior (1, 2, 4). This theory contemplates a system that consists of places, attributes of places, and interactions between places, all seen through time (4, pp. 190–1). Factoring the $n \times a$ attribute matrix yields s structural dimensions, and an $n \times s$ structure matrix can be created. Similarly, various forms of interaction, including commodity flows of different kinds, can be used to build an $(n^2 - n)\ x\ y$ interaction matrix, where the $(n^2 - n)$ dyads are treated as individual observations. This matrix can be reduced to an $(n^2 - n)\ x\ b$ behavior matrix, again by factor analysis. Canonical correlation analysis provides the means of observing the similarity between places and groups of places in terms of their scores on the structural and behavioral dimensions (4, pp. 192–255).

Of the three approaches to commodity flow analysis, concern with structure is the most recent. In some ways it shows considerable promise, especially in the direction of incorporating concepts of flow structure and behavior into generalizations about urban and regional locational theory.

SUMMARY

This review . . . has argued that there are three central concerns in commodity flow analysis: 1) the diagnosis as "more than" or "less than" expected for volume flows over individual routes; 2) the efficiency of a given flow pattern; and 3) the structure of commodity flow patterns. Researchers in these areas have availed themselves of a wide range of descriptive indices and statistics, simple and multivariate inferential statistics, and activity analysis techniques. Regression formulations of the gravity and potential model have provided the major diagnostic tool in the study of volume shipments. Further, population (and occasionally other mass variables) and distance are always the most powerful explainers of variation in the volume of shipments. The efficiency of flow patterns is usually defined as the degree to which a given distribution network conforms to the least-transport-cost, or minimum distance, pattern. The transportation model of linear programming is most useful in this regard. Structure (or groupings of origins and/or destinations) in a flow pattern can be detected by R- and Q-mode factor analysis. Some tentative steps have been taken towards the incorporation of these parsimonious dimensions into a general field theory of spatial structure and spatial behavior.

NOTES

1 Topological distances reflecting various degrees of contiguity could be used. In analyses of the ICC Rail Carload Waybill Statistics, a number of authors have used straight-line distances between state centroids (61, 80). This condition severely limits the kind of spatial analyses that can be conducted.

2 Spiegelglas (87, pp. 73–4) used rank order correlation analysis to examine the relationship between the average of population, value added, and personal income ranks for 48 U.S. states, and the ranks of the sum total of rail exports and imports expressed in tons and ton-miles.

3 Parakhonskiy *et al.* (64) developed a method for deriving distance exponents which is based on the expression:

$$VD^x = K$$

where V = volume or number
x = distance exponent

D = distance

K = a constant

4 Implicit volume flow studies using potential models and concepts have also been carried out by Pred (69) and Ray (70).

5 The conceptual structure, but not the methodology, has been employed by Britton (9) and Steed (89).

LITERATURE CITED

1 Berry, B. J. L. "Interdependency of Spatial Structure and Spatial Behavior: A General Field Theory Formulation, *Papers and Proceedings, Regional Science Association,* 21 (1968), pp. 205–27.

2 Berry, B. J. L. "A Synthesis of Formal and Functional Regions Using a General Field Theory of Spatial Behavior," *Spatial Analysis —A Reader in Statistical Geography.* Edited by B. J. L. Berry and D. F. Marble. Englewood Cliffs: Prentice-Hall, 1968, pp. 419–28.

3 Berry, B. J. L., *et al.* "Commodity Flow Patterns," *Essays on Commodity Flows and the Spatial Structure of the Indian Economy.* Edited by B. J. L. Berry *et al.* Chicago: University of Chicago Department of Geography Research Paper No. 111, 1966. pp. 5–188.

4 Berry, B. J. L. "Interdependency of Flows and Spatial Structure: A General Field Theory Formulation," *Essays on Commodity Flows and the Spatial Structure of the Indian Economy.* Edited by B. J. L. Berry *et al.* Chicago: University of Chicago Department of Geography Research Paper No. 111, 1966. pp. 189–255.

5 Black, W. R., and F. E. Horton. *A Bibliography of Selected Research on Networks and Urban Transportation Relevant to Current Transportation Geography Research.* Research Report No. 28, Department of Geography, Northwestern University.

6 Boudeville, J. R. "An Operational Model of Regional Trade in France," *Papers and Proceedings, Regional Science Association,* 7 (1961), pp. 177–91.

7 Boxer, B. *Ocean Shipping in the Evolution of Hong Kong.* Chicago: University of Chicago Department of Geography Research Paper No. 72, 1961.

8 Brams, S. J. "Transaction Flows in the International System," *American Political Science Review,* 60 (1960).

9 Britton, J. N. H. *Regional Analysis and Economic Geography: A Case Study of Manufacturing in the Bristol Region.* London: Bell, 1967.

10 Britton, J. N. H. "The External Relations of Seaports: Some New Considerations," *Tijdschrift Voor Economische en Sociale Geografie,* 56 (1965), pp. 109–12.

11 Britton, J. N. H. *The Ports of Victoria.* Melbourne: Melbourne University Press, 1964.

12 Brookfield, H. C. "A Study in the Economic Geography of the Pre-War Coastwise Coal Trade," *Transactions and Papers, Institute of British Geographers,* No. 19 (1953), pp. 81–94.

13 Bunge, W. L. *Theoretical Geography.* Lund: Lund Studies in Geography, Ser. C, General and Mathematical Geography, No. 1 (1966).

14 Carrothers, G. A. P. "An Historical Review of the Gravity and Potential Concepts of Human Interaction," *Journal of the American Institute of Planners* (Spring, 1956), pp. 94–102.

15 Casetti, E. "Optimal Location of Steel Mills Serving the Quebec and Southern Ontario Steel Market," *Canadian Geographer,* 10 (1966), pp. 27–39.

16 Chapman, A. S. *The Functional Pattern of Freight Traffic in Turkey.* Ann Arbor: University Microfilms, 1954.

17 Chojnicki, Z. "The Structure of Economic Regions in Poland Analyzed by Commodity Flows," *Geographia Polonica,* 1 (1961), pp. 213–30.

18 Clark, J. W. *"Commodity Flow Interconnections Within the U.S. as Reflected in the Carload Waybill Analyses of the ICC, 1949–50."* Unpublished Ph.D. dissertation, University of West Virginia, 1954.

19 Cox, K. R. "The Application of Linear Pro-

gramming to Geographic Problems," *Tijdschrift Voor Economische en Sociale Geografie,* 56 (1965), pp. 228–36.

20 Dent, W. "Optimal Wool Flows for Minimization of Transport Costs," *Australian Journal of Agricultural Economics,* 19 (1966), pp. 142–57.

21 Deutsch, K. "Transaction Flows as Indicators of Political Cohesion," *The Integration of Political Communities.* Edited by P. E. Jacob and J. V. Toscana. New York: J. B. Lippincott Co., 1964.

22 Deutsch, K. *Nationalism and Social Communication.* 2nd ed. Boston: MIT Press, 1962.

23 Dhar, R., R. Venning, and B. J. L. Berry. "Interregional Intersectoral Relations of the Indian Economy," *Essays on Commodity Flows and the Spatial Structure of the Indian Economy.* Edited by B. J. L. Berry *et al.* Chicago: University of Chicago Department of Geography Research Paper No. 111, 1966. pp. 257–334.

24 Dickason, D. G., and J. O. Wheeler. "An Application of Linear Programming: The Case of Indian Wheat Transportation," *National Geographical Journal of India,* 13 (1967), pp. 125–40.

25 Foltz, W. J. *From French West Africa to the Mali Federation.* New Haven: Yale University Press, 1965.

26 Ganguli, B. M. "Significance of Interregional Trade Balance with Special Reference to India," *Papers on National Income and Allied Topics. Vol. II.* Edited by V. K. R. V. Rao *et al.* London: Asia Publishing House, 1963. pp. 95–104.

27 Garrison, W. L. and D. F. Marble. *A Prolegomenon to the Forecasting of Transportation Development—Final Report.* Fort Eustis, Va.: USAAVLABS Technical Report No. 65–35, August, 1965.

28 Gauthier, H. L. "Least Cost Flows in a Capacitated Network: A Brazilian Example," *Geographic Studies of Urban Transportation and Network Analysis.* Edited by F. Horton. Evanston: Northwestern University Studies in Geography No. 16 (1968), pp. 102–27.

29 Goldman, T. A. "Efficient Transportation and Industrial Location," *Papers and Proceedings, Regional Science Association,* 4 (1958), pp. 91–106.

30 Golledge, R. G. "A Geographical Analysis of Newcastle's Rail Freight Traffic," *Economic Geography,* 39 (1963), pp. 60–73.

31 Goodman, L. A. "Statistical Methods for the Preliminary Analysis of Transaction Flows," *Econometrica,* 31 (1963), pp. 197–208.

32 Gosh, A. *Efficiency in Location and Interregional Flows.* Amsterdam: North Holland Publishing Co., 1965.

33 Gould, P. R., and R. H. T. Smith. "Method in Commodity Flow Studies," *Australian Geographer,* 8 (1962), pp. 73–7.

34 Gould, P. R. *The Development of the Transportation Pattern in Ghana.* Evanston: Northwestern University Studies in Geography No. 5, 1960.

35 Haggett, P. *Locational Analysis in Human Geography.* London: Arnold, 1965.

36 Hay, A. M. "Components of Movement in Transport Geography," Paper read to the Institute of British Geographers, January, 1969.

37 Hay, A. M., and R. H. T. Smith. *Interregional Trade and Money Flows in Nigeria, 1964.* Ibadan: Oxford University Press for the Nigerian Institute of Social and Economic Research, 1971.

38 Heady, E. O., and W. Candler. *Linear Programming Methods.* Ames: Iowa State University Press, 1958.

39 Helvig, M. *Chicago's External Truck Movements: Spatial Interactions Between the Chicago Area and its Hinterland.* Chicago: University of Chicago Department of Geography Research Paper No. 90, 1964.

40 Henderson, J. *Efficiency in the Coal Industry.* Cambridge: Harvard University Press, 1958.

41 Ikle, F. C. "Sociological Relationship of Traffic to Population and Distance," *Traffic Quarterly,* 8 (1954), pp. 123–36.

42 Isard, W. *Methods of Regional Analysis: An Introduction to Regional Science.* New York: Technology Press of MIT and Wiley, 1960.

43 Isard, W. *Location and Space-Economy*. New York: Technology Press of MIT and Wiley, 1956.

44 Kansky, K. J. *Structure of Transportation Networks*. Chicago: University of Chicago Department of Geography Research Paper No. 84, 1963.

45 Karaska, G. J. "Interindustry Relations in the Philadelphia Economy," *East Lakes Geographer*, 2 (1966), pp. 80–96.

46 Land, A. H. "An Application of Linear Programming to the Transport of Coking Coal," *Journal of the Royal Statistical Society*, Ser. A (General), 120 (1957), pp. 308–19.

47 Leontief, W. W. "The Structure of Development," *Scientific American*, 214 (1963).

48 Leontief, W. W. "Input-Output Economics," *Scientific American*, 202 (1951).

49 Linnemann, H. *An Econometric Study of International Trade Flows*. Amsterdam: North Holland Publishing Co., 1966.

50 Lukermann, F., and P. W. Porter. "Gravity and Potential Models in Economic Geography," *Annals of the Association of American Geographers*, 50 (1960), pp. 493–504.

51 Madeyski, M. "Transportation Network in Poland, 1960–61," *Przeglad Komunikacyjny*, 11 (1962), pp. 410–17.

52 Mc Connell, J. E. "The Middle East: Competitive or Complementary?" *Tijdschrift Voor Economische en Sociale Geografie*, 58 (1967), pp. 82–93.

53 Miernyk, W. H. *The Elements of Input-Output Analysis*. New York: Random House, 1965.

54 Moore, F. T., and J. W. Petersen. "Regional Analysis: An Interindustry Model of Utah," *The Review of Economics and Statistics*, 37 (1955).

55 Morawski, W. "Balances of Interregional Commodity Flows in Poland: A Value Approach." *Papers and Proceedings, Regional Science Association*. 20 (1967), pp. 29–41.

56 Morawski, W. "Research on the Dynamics of the Interregional Commodity Flows," *Geographia Polonica*, 11 (1967), pp. 129–41.

57 Morrill, R. L., and W. L. Garrison. "Projections of Interregional Patterns of Trade in Wheat and Flour," *Economic Geography*, 36 (1960), pp. 116–26.

58 Moses, L. "A General Equilibrium Model of Production, Interregional Trade, and Location of Industry," *The Review of Economics and Statistics*, 42 (1960), pp. 373–97.

59 Nystuen, J. D., and M. F. Dacey. "A Graph Theory Interpretation of Nodal Regions," *Papers and Proceedings, Regional Science Association*, 7 (1961), pp. 29–42.

60 Ohlin, B. *Interregional and International Trade*, Vol. 39: *Harvard Economic Studies*. Cambridge: Harvard University Press, 1933.

61 Olson, J. M. *The Spatial Utilization of Transportation Modes in Fruit and Vegetable Movements, 1961*. Unpublished M.S. thesis in Geography, University of Wisconsin, 1968.

62 Olsson, G. *Distance and Human Interaction, A Review and Bibliography*. Philadelphia: Regional Science Research Institute, Bibliography Series No. 2, 1965.

63 Onakomaiya, S. O., and R. H. T. Smith. "The Rail Distribution of Imported Goods in Nigeria, 1964," *Nigerian Geographical Journal*, 1972.

64 Parakhonskiy, B. M., O. A. Kibalchich, and F. P. Kravets. *Voprosy Ekonomiki i Perspektivnogo Planirovaniya Passazhirskikih Perevozok*. Moscow: Akademizdat, 1963.

65 Patton, D. J. "General Cargo Hinterlands of New York, Philadelphia, Baltimore and New Orleans," *Annals of the Association of American Geographers*, 48 (1958), pp. 536–55.

66 Peters, W. S. "Measures of Regional Interchange." *Papers and Proceedings, Regional Science Association*, 11 (1963), pp. 285–94.

67 Prais, S. J. "Econometric Research in International Trade: A Review," *Kyklos*, 15 (1962), pp. 560–79.

68 Pred, A. *Behavior and Location, Part I*. Lund: Lund Studies in Geography, Ser. B. Human Geography, No. 27 (1967).

69 Pred. A. "Toward a Typology of Manufacturing Flows," *Geographical Review*, 54 (1964), pp. 65–84.

70 Ray, D. M. *Market Potential and Economic Shadow: A Quantitative Analysis of Industrial*

Location in Southern Ontario. Chicago: University of Chicago Department of Geography Research Paper No. 101, 1965.

71 Reed, W. E. *Areal Interaction in India: Commodity Flows of the Bengal-Bihar Industrial Area*. Chicago: University of Chicago Department of Geography Research Paper No. 110, 1967.

72 Rimmer, P. J. "Recent Changes in the Status of Seaports in the New Zealand Coastal Trade," *Economic Geography,* 43 (1967), pp. 231–43.

73 Rimmer, P. J. "Patterns and Portents: A Study of the Changes in the Status of New Zealand Ports in the Country's Overseas Trade," *Proceedings, Fourth New Zealand Geography Conference* (1965), pp. 137–44.

74 Rodgers, A. L. "The Port of Genova: External and Internal Relations," *Annals of the Association of American Geographers,* 48 (1958), pp. 319–51.

75 Savage, I. R., and K. Deutsch. "A Statistical Model of the Gross Analysis of Transaction Flows," *Econometrica,* 28 (1960), pp. 551–72.

76 Shaffer, N. M. *The Competitive Position of the Port of Durban,* Evanston: Northwestern University Studies in Geography No. 8, 1965.

77 Smith, R. H. T. "Interregional Trade as a Component of National Unity," *Proceedings of the 21st IGU Conference, 1968*. Edited by S. P. Chatterjee, Calcutta: National Committee for Geography, 1970.

78 Smith, R. H. T., and A. M. Hay. "A Theory of the Spatial Structure of Internal Trade in Underdeveloped Countries," *Geographical Analysis,* 1 (1969), pp. 121–36.

79 Smith, R. H. T. "Interregional Trade in Nigeria: A Constraint on National Unity?" Council for Intersocietal Studies and Program of African Studies, Northwestern University, *Proceedings of the Conference: Problems of Integration and Disintegration in Nigeria*. Evanston, March, 1967, pp. 75–100. (Mimeographed.)

80 Smith, R. H. T. "Toward a Measure of Complementarity," *Economic Geography,* 40 (1964), pp. 1–8.

81 Smith, R. H. T. "Transport Competition in Australian Border Areas: The Example of Southern New South Wales," *Economic Geography,* 39 (1963), pp. 1–13.

82 Smith, R. H. T. "Railway Commodity Movements Between New South Wales and Victoria—The 1960 Pre-Standardization Situation," *Australian Geographer,* 9 (1963), pp. 88–96.

83 Smith, R. H. T. *Commodity Movements in Southern New South Wales*. Canberra: Department of Geography. Australian National University, 1962.

84 Soja, E. W. "Transaction Flows and National Integration," Paper read to the Twentieth Anniversary Conference, Program of African Studies, Northwestern University, Evanston (September, 1968).

85 Soja, E. W. "Communications and Territorial Integration in East Africa: An Introduction to Transaction Flow Analysis," *East Lakes Geographer,* 4 (1968), pp. 39–57.

86 Specht, R. E. *A Functional Analysis of the Green Bay and Western Railroad*. Stevens Point, Wis., 1959.

87 Spiegelglas, S. "Some Aspects of State-to-State Commodity Flows in the United States," *Journal of Regional Science,* 2 (1960), pp. 71–80.

88 Starkie, D. N. M. *Traffic and Industry, a Study of Traffic Generation and Spatial Interaction*. London: London School of Economics and Political Science Geographical Papers No. 3 (1967).

89 Steed, G. P. F. "Commodity Flows and Interindustry Linkages of Northern Ireland's Manufacturing Industries," *Tijdschrift Voor Economische en Sociale Geografie,* 59 (1968), pp. 245–59.

90 Thomas, F. H. "Some Relationships Between a Railroad and its Region," *Tijdschrift Voor Economische en Sociale Geografie,* 53 (1962), pp. 155–61.

91 Thomas, F. H. *The Denver and Rio Grande Western Railroad, A Geographical Analysis*. Evanston: Northwestern University Studies in Geography No. 4, 1960.

92 Tomaszewski, W. "Cartographical Solution of the Linear Programming Transportation Problem," *Proceedings of the First Scandi-*

navian-Polish Regional Science Seminar. Warsaw: Polish Scientific Publishers, 1965, pp. 249–53.

93 Ullman, E. L. *American Commodity Flow.* Seattle: University of Washington Press, 1957.

94 Ullman, E. L. "The Role of Transportation and the Bases for Interaction," *Man's Role in Changing the Face of the Earth.* Edited by W. L. Thomas, Jr. Chicago: University of Chicago Press, 1956.

95 Ullman, E. L. "Geography as Spatial Interaction," *Annals of the Association of American Geographers,* 44 (1954), p. 283.

96 Vasilevskiy, L. I. "Basic Research Problems in the Geography of Capitalist and Underdeveloped Countries," *Soviet Geography: Review and Translation,* 4 (1963), pp. 36–58.

97 Wallace, W. H. "The Bridge Line: A Distinctive Type of Anglo-American Railroad," *Economic Geography,* 41 (1965), pp. 1–38.

98 Wallace, W. H. "Freight Traffic Functions of Anglo-American Railroads," *Annals of the Association of American Geographers,* 53 (1963), pp. 312–31.

99 Wallace, W. H. "Railway Traffic and Agriculture in New Zealand," *Economic Geography,* 34 (1958), pp. 168–84.

100 Yeates, M. H. "A Geographic Model of International Trade," Paper presented for the 21st International Geographical Congress, New Delhi, 1968.

101 Yeates, M. H. "A Note Concerning the Development of a Geographic Model of International Trade," *Geographical Analysis,* 1 (1969), pp. 399–404.

Flow patterns are complex; there are also some complex techniques to try and analyze these patterns. Of the techniques reviewed above, just three will be looked at in more detail. First there is the technique of *linear programming* as illustrated by the so-called transportation problem.

Linear programming rests on the assumption that there is a linear relationship of the form $A + B = C$. Typically, there is a series of *simultaneous equations,* which represent the basic conditions of the problem, and a *linear function,* which represents the objective. The word "programming" merely means that a set program or series of rules is followed in order to solve the equations. Suffice to say here that we are concerned with: (1) *supply centers* with known surpluses, (2) *receiving places* with known demands, and (3) known *connecting routes* and *transportation costs.* The problem is, how are the flows arranged between the nodes? This is a restatement of a problem mentioned earlier. Given the network, stocks, and relation of demands to supplies, what flow pattern results? However, a rider must be added to condition 3, namely, that the flows should follow *least-cost* routes. Thus the linear programming technique, outlined in the following selection by Cox, is a step-by-step measure to allocate the flows from and to known points of demand and supply to the optimal least-cost routes. Cox approaches this analysis by sketching the background to its use, and then takes us through successive stages in the calculation of a simple example. I suggest that you practice this computation by taking another hypothetical example yourself.* Cox concludes with a practical application of the transportation problem to flows of aluminium bar in the United States.

*Two simple examples are suggested as an exercise on pp. 159–160.

Selection 10

The Application of Linear Programming to Geographic Problems

K. R. Cox

If one of the foundations of economics is scarcity of resources, then one of the foundations of economic geography is surely the location of that scarcity of resources. In almost every branch of economic geography, an appreciation of the scarcity of different resources and of their location and their locational effects is integral. Linear programming problems are concerned with the efficient use or allocation of limited resources to meet such economic objectives as the maximization of profit, the maximization of tax revenue, or the minimization of transportation cost. Technically, the statement of such problems depends upon two factors: firstly, the availability of scarce resources and the demand for these scarce resources—these are known as the basic conditions of the problem; and secondly, whether the objective is to maximize or minimize a given economic value—this is known as the objective function of the problem.

Problems of allocating scarce resources have many solutions which will satisfy the basic conditions, but the number of solutions which will satisfy both the basic conditions and the objective function is strictly limited; such solutions are termed optimal solutions. Where a description of the problem can be made using straight line (i.e., linear) relationships, the problem is amenable to solution via linear programming techniques. The complete mathematical statement of a linear programming problem includes a set of simultaneous equations which represent the basic conditions of the problem and a linear function which expresses the objective of the problem. These will be outlined below.

The application of linear programming techniques to geographical problems is not new. Garrison[1] has reviewed applications by economists; Marble[2] has brought together a bibliography, and Garrison and Marble[3] together have presented a linear programming formulation for the planning of highway networks. However, there are no clear expositions of the technique and of applications of the technique for geographers as such.

The purpose of this note therefore, is to introduce readers to the applications of linear programming to geographic problems; emphasis will be laid upon that application of linear programming which is of most relevance to the geography of flow patterns—the transportation problem. We will first set out, verbally and algebraically, the nature of the transportation problem, outline a computational procedure for solving such problems and then proceed to a consideration of its application to geographic problems; one of these problems refers to interstate flows of aluminum bar in the U.S.A.; the second problem is one in applied geography and refers to a possible use of the transportation problem in hinterland delineation. We will conclude with a consideration of limitations.

THE TRANSPORTATION PROBLEM

The basic conditions of the transportation problem as it is most usually framed are that

Tijdschrift voor Economische en Sociale Geografie, vol. 56, November–December 1965, pp. 228–236. Reprinted by permission of the author and editor.

for a given commodity, there are several locationally different sources of supply and several sources of demand, likewise different in their locations. Supplies and demands at different places are known. The objective function of the problem is to minimize the total cost or total distance travelled.

To make the problem more explicit, consider Table 10-1, which presents the format for a sample transportation problem. In Table 10-1 surplus regions are listed in the far left-hand column and deficit regions are listed along the top row. In the last column, a_i represents the amount of the given commodity which is available for export from the ith surplus region. The sum of the a_i represented by $\sum_i a_i$ is the total amount of the commodity which is available for export from all surplus regions. In the last row, b_j represents the amount of the commodity demanded by the jth region. $\sum_j b_j$ is the total amount of the commodity demanded by all the deficit regions. $\sum_i a_i = \sum_j b_j$ signifies that total demand is equal to total supply. In the body of the table, c_{ij} represents the cost of transporting one unit of the commodity from the ith surplus region to the jth deficit region. Where data on transportation cost are not available, the c_{ij} may represent a substitute term such as the total distance separating the ith surplus region from the jth deficit region. Also in the body of the table, the x_{ij} represent the unknowns which are the amounts of the commodity shipped from the ith surplus region to the jth deficit region. The problem may now be set out algebraically as finding a set of x_{ij} (flows) such that:

$$\sum_i \sum_j x_{ij}\, c_{ij} = \text{Minimum} \tag{1}$$

i.e., the product of transportation costs between surplus regions on the one hand and deficit region on the other and the respective flows between the same regions is at a minimum. Where necessary, one may substitute the term "total distances" for "transportation costs".

Table 10-1 The Transportation Problem Tableau Destinations (Deficit Regions)

	$i \backslash j$	1	2	3	.	j	.	m	**Totals**
Origins (Surplus Regions)	1	c_{11}	c_{12}	c_{13}	.	c_{1j}	.	c_{1m}	a_1
	2	c_{21}	c_{22}	c_{23}	.	c_{2j}	.	c_{2m}	a_2
	3	c_{31}	c_{32}	c_{33}	.	.	.	.	a_3
	.	.	.	.	.	.	.	.	.
	i	c_{i1}	c_{i2}	.	.	c_{ij} x_{ij}	.	.	a_i
	.	.	.	.	.	.	.	.	.
	n	c_{n1}	c_{n2}	.	.	.	.	.	z_n
Totals		b_1	b_2	b_3	.	b_j	.	b_m	$\sum_i a_i = \sum_j b_j$

Subject to:

$$\sum_j x_{ij} = a_i;\ i = 1, 2, \ldots n. \tag{2}$$

Thus, the flows of aluminum slab from the ith surplus region to all deficit regions is equal to the surplus of aluminum slab in the ith surplus region.

$$\sum_i x_{ij} = b_j;\ j = 1, 2, \ldots m. \tag{3}$$

And, the total of flows of aluminum slab from all surplus regions to the jth deficit region is equal to the deficit of aluminum slab in the jth deficit region.

$$\sum_i a_i = \sum_j b_j \tag{4}$$

Equation 4 states that total surpluses are equal to total deficits.

$$x_{ij} \geq 0 \text{ for all } i \text{ and all } j. \tag{5}$$

Equation 5 ensures that there will be no negative flows (i.e., flows back from a deficit region to a surplus region).

COMPUTATION OF A SOLUTION

In many linear programming problems, computation of an optimal solution would be so long and tedious that the use of an electronic computer is usual. The transportation problem, apart from its utility to the geographer, has the additional virtue of being relatively easy to solve. Manne[4] presents the simplex method for finding an optimal solution very clearly and concisely, as does Dorfman.[5] Ford and Fulkerson[6] have also presented a very simple algorithm (computational procedure) for the solution of this problem, and the reader is urged to consult the listed references. Ford and Fulkerson consider their method to be much more efficient than the commonly used specialized form of the simplex method, particularly on problems of large dimensions.

Here, it is our intention to present an algorithm for solving the simpler types of transportation problems such as those which would fit the format presented in [the] first section of this [work]. The method to be presented here is the stepping stone method of Charnes and Cooper[7] as modified by Vajda.[8] We will first outline the problem to be solved; this will be followed by a step-by-step description of the computational procedure.

The Problem

Three companies manufacturing auto bodies have their markets in four auto manufacturing plants, each of which produces the same type of automobile. These auto body concerns transport the bodies to the auto manufacturing plants for further fabrication. The total output of the auto body plants is absorbed completely by the total demand of the four auto manufacturing plants. The three auto body plants and the four auto manufacturing plants show random geographical locations relative one to another. The relevant data may be set out in matrix form:

Table 10-2 Deficits

Surpluses	W	X	Y	Z	Row Totals
A	20	40	70	50	400
B	100	60	90	80	1500
C	10	110	30	200	900
Column Totals:	700	600	1000	500	

Rows indicate locations of surpluses of car bodies (A, B, C) and columns indicate locations of deficits of car bodies (W, X, Y, Z) for one day. Row totals and column totals stand for supplies of, and demands for, car bodies respectively. The individual cell entries indicate the transportation cost in shillings between a given surplus location and a given deficit location. These are the constraints of the problem. The problem itself is that the auto body suppliers wish to organize their transportation in such a way as to minimize transportation costs. The objective function of the problem therefore, is to arrive at such a pattern of flow as would satisfy this aim of cost minimization.

The Algorithm

Given n rows and m columns, a basic feasible solution of the problem will contain not more than $n + m - 1$ variables, all with positive values. Hence we can expect our solution to contain no more than six cells occupied by figures.

Such a basic feasible solution may be arrived at quite quickly by the following method:

1. Rank the unit costs of transportation per cell, ranking the cheapest costs 1 and the dearest costs mn. Table 10-3 shows the rank order of the unit transportation costs.

Table 10-3

	W	X	Y	Z
A	2	4	7	5
B	10	6	9	8
C	1	11	3	12

2. Take the cell with the lowest unit transportation costs; this is C−W at the intersection of a row supplying 900 auto bodies and a column demanding 700 auto bodies. Since 700 is the smaller, enter this figure in the cell and adjust the row and column totals accordingly:

Table 10-4

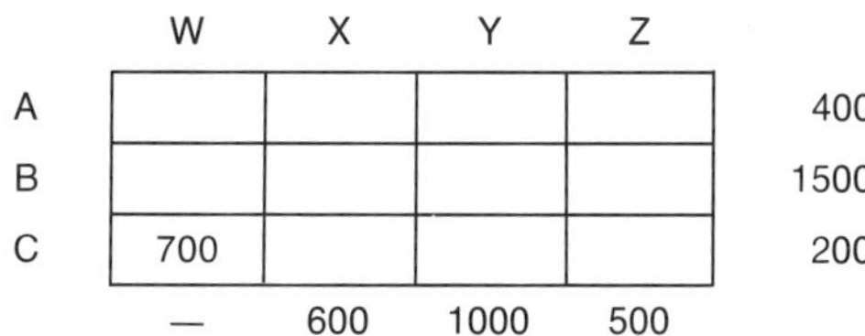

	W	X	Y	Z	
A					400
B					1500
C	700				200
	—	600	1000	500	

3. Operating on this reduced matrix, we now turn to the cell with the second lowest unit transportation costs which is A−W at the intersection of a row now supplying 400 bodies and a column demanding zero auto bodies. Since the demands of this column are exhausted, we turn to the cell with the third lowest unit transportation costs which is C−Y at the intersection of a row supplying 200 auto bodies and a column demanding 1,000 auto bodies. Since 200 is the smaller, enter this figure in the cell and adjust the row and column totals accordingly. Continuing with this iterative procedure, we arrive at a basic feasible solution of the following type:

Table 10-5

	W	X	Y	Z
A		400		
B		200	800	500
C	700		200	

The total transportation cost of this allocational scheme would be 153,000 shillings; as yet, however, we do not know whether this would be the cheapest possible scheme of distribution.

4. In order to test the point as to whether this allocation provides a minimal transportation cost, we must compute fictitious unit costs for every row (g_i) and column (b_j) respectively and compute the fictitious cost for each row-column intersection as a sum of the values for the respective row and column ($g_i + b_j$). These fictitious unit transportation costs will then be compared with the actual unit transportation costs. These costs may be computed on the basis of the values of unit transportation costs for occupied cells in the basic feasible solution; the fictitious costs can then be constructed by making g_1 equal to 0 whereby the others are implicitly fixed on the basis of the actual cell values in the matrix in Table 10-6.

Table 10-6

50	40	70	60	
	40			0
	60	90	80	20
10		30		−40

The fictitious costs of the cells left unoccupied in the basic feasible solution must now be computed, viz.:

Table 10-7

50	40	70	60	
50		70	60	0
70				20
	0		20	−40

5. Comparing the fictitious costs with the true costs, we have three alternatives for each unoccupied cell.

a. If the fictitious unit transportation cost for an unoccupied cell is larger than the true unit transportation cost, then a final solution has not been arrived at and a readjustment is required.

b. If the fictitious cost for an unoccupied cell is equal to the true cost, readjustment is possible but would not lead to any change in the total transportation cost.

c. If the fictitious cost for an unoccupied cell is less than the true cost, readjustment would lead to an increase in the total transportation cost rather than a diminution.

A comparison of true costs with fictitious costs for unoccupied cells shows that in cell A–W the fictitious cost is indeed higher; readjustment is therefore required.

6. Re-adjustments of cell components take place via transfers between cells. The transfers take place according to the following rules:

a. Transfers are made by a circuit that leads from the empty cell by alternating horizontal and vertical steps using only occupied cells.

b. Each individual transfer which is alternately horizontal and vertical is also alternately minus and plus. The first movement away from the empty cell is a minus quantity.

c. The value of the transfer (in terms of auto bodies in this case) is determined by the minimum value in any cell which will be characterized by a minus during the transfer process.

Taking cell A–W we can now trace out a circuit of alternate horizontal and vertical movements a–b–c–d–e as in the matrix in Table 10-8. The minimum value in any minus cell is 400 and hence the transfer takes on the value of 400 auto bodies:

Table 10-8

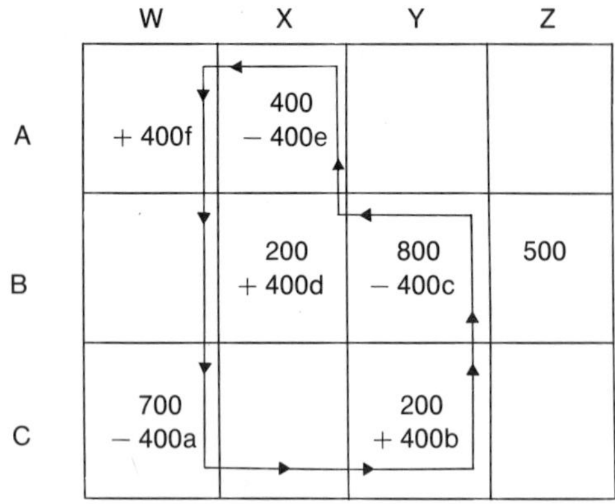

	W	X	Y	Z
A	+ 400f	400 – 400e		
B		200 + 400d	800 – 400c	500
C	700 – 400a		200 + 400b	

Then adjusted solution assumes the form:

Table 10-9

	W	X	Y	Z
A	400			
B		600	400	500
	300		600	

The cost of transportation in such a system of flows is 141,000 shillings as compared with 153.00 shillings for the initial solution.

Returning to our iterative procedure we must now recompute fictitious costs and compare such costs with the true costs in all unoccupied cells.

Table 10-10

20	10	40	30	
	10	40	30	0
70				50
	0		20	– 10

Now, no cell has a fictitious cost which is larger than its true cost and we may conclude that the adjusted solution above is the final solution.

The Dual Solution

The solution to the transportation problem, however, provides us with something more than the minimal transportation cost. The minimal transportation cost is also equal to the answer to a maximization problem for the same array of raw data, i.e., the minimum transportation cost is also equivalent to the maximum total excess of delivered value over the value at the factory. If we regard the transport minimization problem as the primal problem, the opposite maximization problem is known as the dual problem and a solution to it is termed a dual solution. The importance of the dual solution is strengthened further when we note that the dual problem may often be solved more conveniently than the primal solution.

Turning to the final data tableau in the solution to a transportation problem, we find a parallel bonus in the resultant outputs. While the figures in the body of the final shipment plan indicate optimal flows, the final fictitious costs g_i and b_j corresponding to rows and columns respectively, may be interpreted as the value of the product at the surplus location and the value of the product at the deficit location j; we may call these values u_i and v_j respectively. Hence the fictitious costs g_i and b_j in Table 10-10 when interpreted as values u_i and v_j respectively, present us with two sorts of information of critical interest to the economic geographer: (1) the value of u measures the comparative locational advantages of the three auto body plants. One auto body at factory B is therefore, worth 50 shillings more than the product of factory A simply because of proximity to points of consumption. More explicitly, prices f.o.b. at factory B are greater than prices at factory A because A suffers from locational disadvantages and cannot dispose of its output without loss otherwise; (2) the values of v measure the delivered prices that correspond to the most economic allocation of output from the viewpoint of minimum aggregate transportation cost.

The prices that we have obtained in our final tableau (u_i and v_j) are the prices that would result from the uncoordinated efforts of the three car body factories to sell their entire outputs at the maximum possible prices. The transportation problem allows a simultaneous solution of both the flow and value problems.

APPLICATIONS

The use of the transportation problem in analyzing geographical flow patterns should be clear. Given supplies of (e.g.) flour, oil, steel, one can postulate an objective function, such as the minimization of total cost of movement, solve the transportation problem and use the optimal flows derived from the solution as a normative model with which actual flow patterns can be compared.

1. The first example refers to interstate flows of aluminum bar in the U.S.A., based on a 1 percent sample of Waybills taken by the U.S. Interstate Commerce Commission for the year 1960.[9] The actual distribution of surpluses and deficits in the production of aluminum bar is presented in Figure 10-1. From the point of view of optimal solutions, this pattern is especially interesting. As can be seen from the map, surpluses are concentrated in three areas very much separated from each other: the Pacific Northwest, the southwest Gulf coast and New York State. The large deficit in the Midwest, situated between the three surplus regions, presents an interesting problem in the efficient division of a central market between three widely separated and peripheral producing areas. In this particular case, the transportation problem can be used to find optimal interstate flows from states which have surpluses of

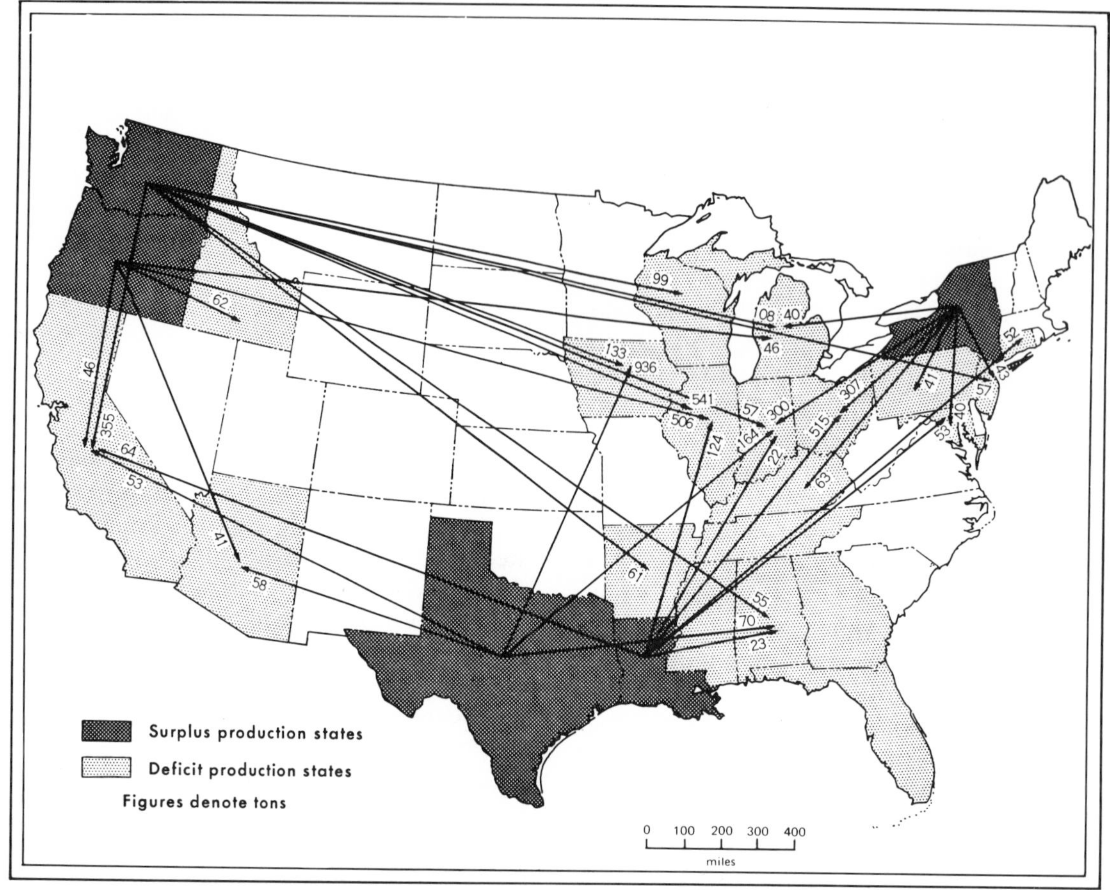

Fig. 10-1.

aluminum bar to states which have deficits of aluminum bar. Data on the surpluses and deficits of this commodity may be obtained but one cannot obtain actual freight rates for all possible combinations of surplus and deficit states; for those states between which there are actual shipments of aluminum bar such freight rate data are available but for those combinations of states which have no actual interchange there are no freight rate data. Our problem must therefore confine itself at least intitially to a minimization of total distances traveled by aluminum bar rather than the minimization of total transportation costs. This relies on the assumption that costs are a linear function of distance, an assumption which we will later have to revise. The actual surpluses and deficits are the basic conditions of the problem (supplies and demands); the objective function of the problem is (in this case) to minimize total distance traveled by interstate movements of aluminum bar. The solution can be rapidly arrived at and the resultant optimal flows may be observed in Fig. 10-2. The optimal flows may be graphically compared with the actual flows in Fig. 10-3. The optimal flow pattern provides us with a normative model of flows with which the actual flow pattern can be compared; this comparison serves as a basis for elaborating a new model in which optimal flows and actual flows are integrated. We may identify three stages in the initial comparison; this initial comparison should be followed by the elaboration of a new model which tries to explain the discrepancies between actual and optimal flow patterns.

Firstly, we must determine whether the optimal flows and the actual flows are statistically different from one another or whether the discrepancies between the two may be accounted for by random sampling error. Chi-square is a statistic which provides us with a measure of the degree to which the divergence between observed values (actual flows) and expected values (optimal flows) is due to random sampling error, resulting from our choice of one particular year from many for a study universe. In this case, the value of chi-square informs us that there is a significant difference at the .99 probability level, which suggests that it is unlikely that the discrepancy could be due to random sampling error.

Second, the computation of a correlation coefficient between actual flows and optimal

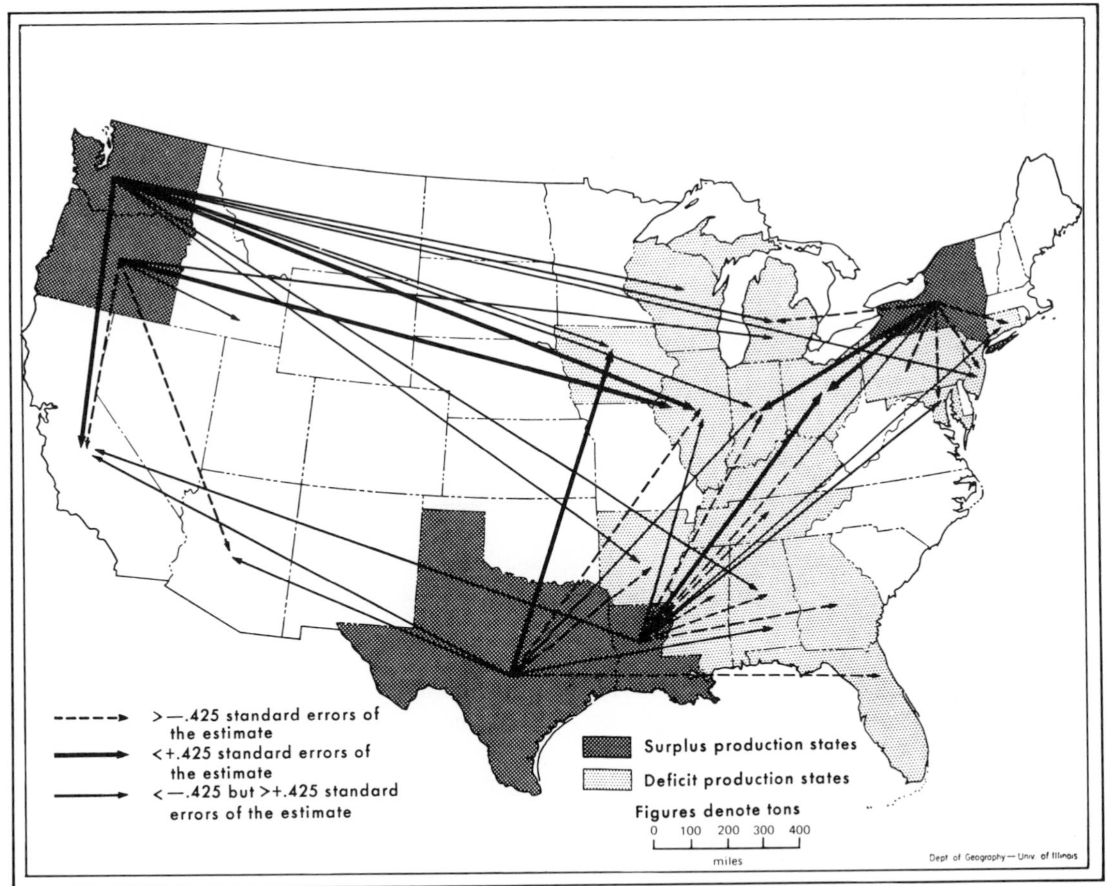

Fig. 10-2.

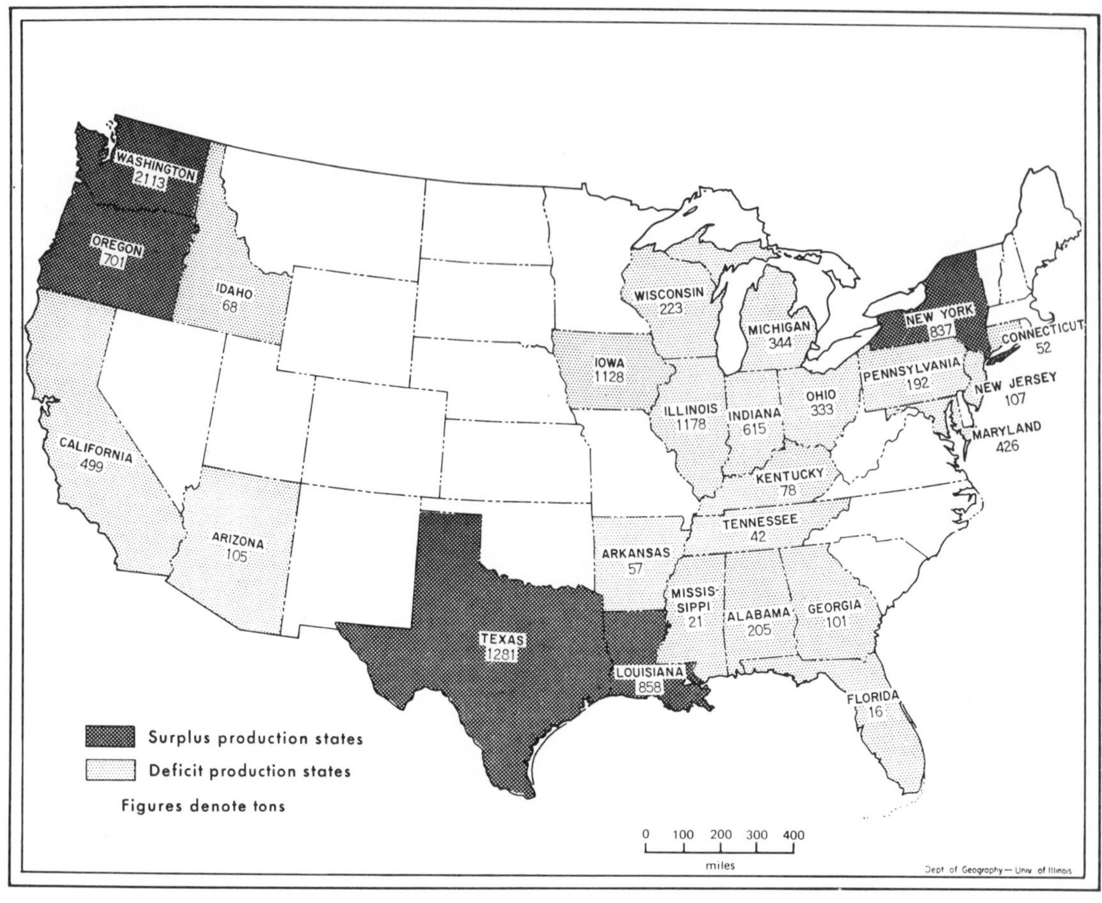

Fig. 10-3.

flows provides us with a measure of the degree to which actual flows adhere to the optimal solution. Bearing in mind that the material which we are studying is a sample from many possible years, we also test the coefficient of correlation for significance. The coefficient of correlation is 0.3732, which indicates that the degree of statistical "explanation" of actual flows afforded by optimal flows is only 13.93 percent. It is significantly different from zero at the 99 percent confidence level.

The coefficient of correlation is an average measure of association for several spatial units; it does not tell us anything about the individual case as compared with the average case. More explicitly, correlation over several spatial units does not tell us whether the dependent and the independent variables are as closely correlated for an individual spatial unit as they are for all spatial units. This problem may be overcome by computing a regression equation and deriving the residuals from regression. The regression equation estimates actual flows on the basis of optimal flows; residuals from regression refer to those flows which are either under-estimated or over-estimated. Under- and over-estimation may, when plotted cartographically, suggest reasons for the magnitude of the correlation coefficient in the form of other variables which thus far have been omitted from the model construction.

Fig. 10-4 shows the distribution of residuals from the regression of actual flows on optimal flows. Thomas[10] has already pointed out that attention to the extreme values on a map of residuals may often suggest new variables which can be incorporated into a regional model; this is so in this case. The map indicates, first, that the higher positive residual values refer to flows between states separated by a comparatively large distance, such as Washington to Illinois, Texas to Iowa and New York to Indiana. Secondly, the lower negative residual values often refer to flows between states separated by comparatively short distances such as Louisiana and Mississippi, Louisiana and Georgia, New York and Connecticut, and Texas and Arkansas. The fusion of this observation with certain ideas from transport economics allows us to hypothesize a new variable which we can include in our model.

It is well known that transportation cost is not a strict linear function of distance. In the case of railway transportation, the cost

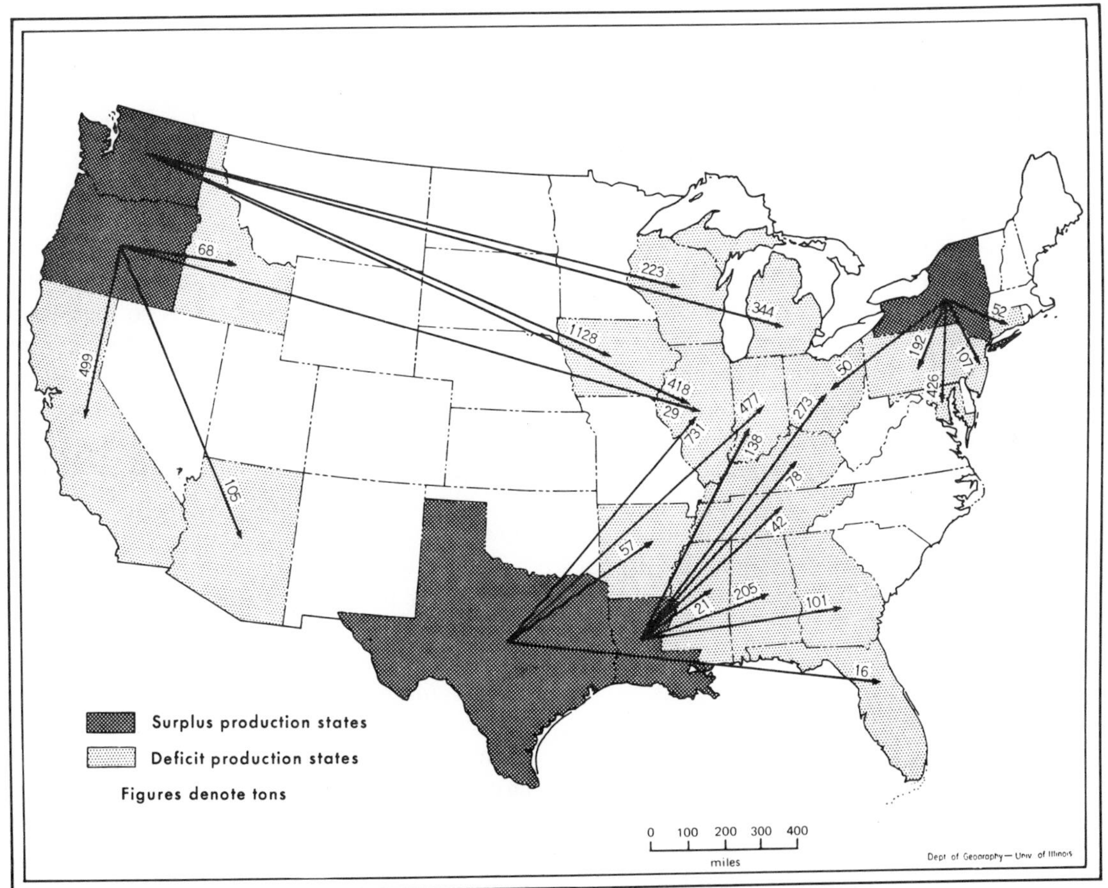

Fig. 10-4.

per ton-mile tends to decrease with increasing distance between origin and destination; this is indicative of a cost curve which is convex upwards and reflects the weight of terminal costs in any assessment of railroad freight charges.[11]

With this in mind it will be appreciated that it may be cheaper per ton-mile to ship aluminum bar from Washington to Illinois than it is per ton-mile to ship aluminum bar from Washington to Idaho. Distance is clearly not the only determinant of transportation costs, and hence we must take into account a measure of the convex transportation cost function in our model. The only available measure is the revenue per ton-mile to the railroad companies. This could not be included in the original objective function of the problem, as figures of revenue per ton-mile are not available for pairs of states between which there is actually no flow of aluminum bar. In order to test the relationship between revenue per ton-mile and the other two variables, revenue per ton-mile had to be approximated for 9 of the 41 pairs of states; for these 9 there were no actual flows and approximations had to be based on distance and the revenue per ton-mile of aluminum slab transported over that distance between other states and this has been incorporated into our analysis as an additional variable.[12]

If we treat this variable as X_3 and actual flows and optimal flows as X_1 and X_2 respectively, we obtain the following matrix of correlation coefficients:

Table 10-11

	X_1	X_2	X_1
X_1	—	.3732	−.2880
X_2		—	.2000
X_3			—

None of these coefficients of correlation are very large but the multiple coefficient of correlation is 0.5255 indicating a degree of statistical "explanation" of 27.62 percent—an improvement of nearly 14 percentage points. Although, the degree of explanation is still not very high, our model presents a basis for further elaboration. New residuals from the regression of actual aluminum flows on optimal flows and revenue per ton-mile present one avenue of approach. The remaining causes of irregularity in the relationship between aluminum flows and the normative pattern might be of a random nature such as the existence of long term agreements between aluminum producer and aluminum consumer or a vertical integration in the corporate structure which would unite both aluminum producer and consumer in one financial unit.

2. Garrison has suggested an example of the way in which the transportation problem format might be used in the solution of a problem in applied geography—the delimitation of service hinterlands.[13] The problem as presented by Garrison is to arrange the tributary areas of urban centres so that, first, the ratio of the population of a service centre to the population of its hinterland is constant for all service centers and their respective hinterlands[14] and second, the sum of the distances separating the inhabitants of hinterland areas from their respective service centers is at a minimum.

Taking our cue from Garrison, let us assume as a purely hypothetical example that a nationalized industry (e.g., electricity generation) catering only for the Scottish market (domestic consumption) and having service offices in Glasgow, Edinburgh, Aberdeen and Dundee wishes to divide up the larger towns of Scotland with 15,000 population or over, in such a way that: (*a*) the ratio of the population of each hinterland to the population of its respective service center is constant; (*b*) the sum total distance from all four service centers to the inhabitants of all the towns serviced is reduced to a minimum. An answer to the first part of the problem may be ensured by setting the populations of the service centers so that (*a*) their sum total population is equivalent to the sum total population of the towns serviced, and (*b*) their new populations have the same rations one to another as their actual populations.[15] The problem can be transformed into a linear programming format by assuming that the service centers are the source of supply (or vice versa) and then solve for an optimal allocation of towns to service centers, using the objective function of minimizing distance traveled. The resultant optimal allocation is presented in Fig. 10-5. As is to be expected in a spatial scheme employing minimum distance as a criterion, the allocation of nearest neighbors to service centers is fairly

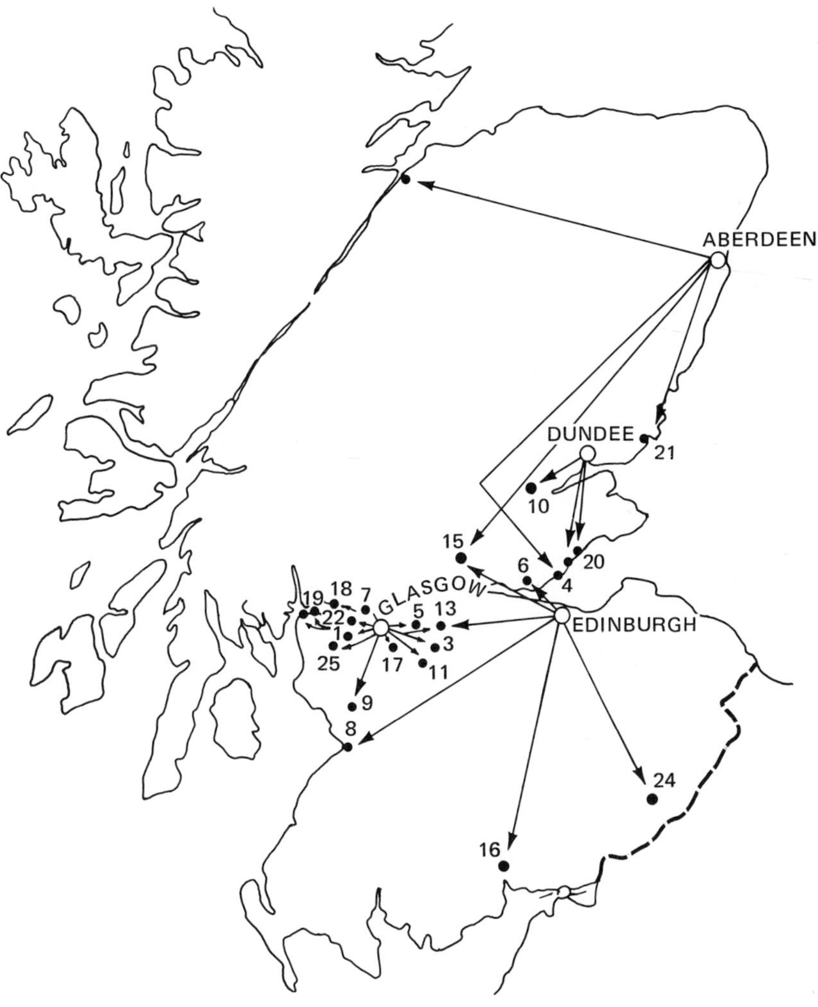

Fig. 10-5.

well adhered to; deviations from this (e.g., the allocation of Arbroath to Aberdeen instead of to Dundee) are referable to the use of hinterlands with populations proportional to those of their respective service centers as a second criterion.

CONCLUSIONS

Such a note as this would be incomplete without a brief assessment of the potential of linear programming in general, and of the transportation problem in particular, as a tool in the formulation and solution of geographic problems.

On the debit side, an initial problem which immediately arises is that of data. The data for many geographic flow patterns are of an extremely fragmentary character; the data for the aluminum bar problem, for example, are derived from a 1 percent sample (although in fairness, it should be noted that Ullman[16] used figures of the same reliability from the same official source, in his book on commodity movements in the U.S.) Gould[17] has recently emphasized the relevance of field-work investigations in providing data for the application of the more sophisticated techniques such as Game Theory. It would be salutary indeed if recent methodological advances in geography only served to emphasize the significance of classical geographic investigation.

Secondly, the transportation problem treats places of supply and demand as points, rather than as areas. This objection is particularly acute in the case where the phenomenon under consideration (e.g., demand for fertilizers) has an eccentric location within the deficit or surplus regions. Linear programming is more appropriate to places of supply and demand which can more legitimately be treated as points (e.g., the Scottish towns). Clearly, the greater the distances between points of supply and demand (and therefore, the greater the costs of transportation), the greater the justification with which areas of surplus and deficit can be treated as points, since the greater the transportation cost between areas of deficit and surplus, the lower the proportional cost of transportation within those areas.

On the credit side, linear programming has a significant contribution to make, not only in pure but also in applied geography. For the latter, optimization has the ability to point up inefficiencies in competing spatial transactions, and to demonstrate alternative, more profitable routings. In pure geography, the transportation problem presents a theoretical framework for the analysis of social and economic flow patterns. Instead of the cartographic representations and brief descriptions so characteristic of current accounts of commodity flow, the solution of the transportation problem provides a theoretical norm with which actual flows can be compared. Actual deviations from the norm of perfect competition can be analyzed (i.e., via regression analysis) as a further step in the study of flow problems and the elaboration of explanatory models. There is, moreover, an increasing awareness of the significance of social and economic movements in geographical evaluation—the regional scientists, for instance, place great emphasis upon what they call "interregional interdependence."[18] Linear programming promises to be an important avenue of approach towards the precise and meaningful analysis of such interdependencies.

NOTES

1 Garrison, W. L., Spatial Structure of the Economy, II, Review Article, *Annals of the Association of American Geographers,* Vol. 49, (December, 1959) p. 471.

2 Marble, D. F., *The Transportation Problem.* Discussion Paper No. 23, Dept. of Geography, University of Washington, September 1, 1959.

3 Garrison, W. L., and D. F. Marble., *Analysis of Highway Networks: A Linear Programming*

Formulation. Highway Research Board, Proceedings of the 37th Annual Meeting. Washington, D.C., 1958.

4 Manne, A. S., *Economic Analysis for Business Decisions*. New York, McGraw-Hill, 1961.

5 Dorfman, R., P. A. Samuelson, and R. M. Solow., *Linear Programming and Economic Analysis*. New York, McGraw-Hill, 1958.

6 Ford, L. R., Jr., and D. R. Fulkerson., Solving the Transportation Problem, *Management Science*, Vol. 3, No. 24, (October, 1956).

7 Charnes, A., and W. W. Cooper. The stepping stone method of explaining Linear Programming Calculations in Transportation problems. *Management Science*, (1958), p. 3–8.

8 Vajda, S., *Readings in Linear Programming*. New York, Wiley, 1958, p. 3–8.

9 Interstate Commerce Commission Bureau of Transport Economics and Statistics, State-to-State Distribution Manufactures and Miscellaneous and Forwarder Traffic (C. L.) Traffic and Revenue—*One Percent Sample of Terminations in the Year 1960*. Washington, D.C., March, 1962, p. 87.

10 Thomas, E. N., *Maps of Residuals from Regression: Their Characteristics and Uses in Geographic Research*. Department of Geography, State University of Iowa, Iowa City, 1960.

11 Hoover, E. M., *The Location of Economic Activity*. New York, McGraw-Hill, 1963, p. 21.

12 Interstate Commerce Commission Bureau of Transport Economics and Statistics, *op. cit.*

13 Garrison, *op. cit.*, Vol. 49, p. 471.

14 Thus if the ratio must be 1 to 4 then possible combinations of service center-hinterland populations might be 25,000 : 100,000; 10,000 : 40,000; and 35,000 : 140,000.

15 Thus if we have three service centers with populations of 10,000, 15,000, and 25,000 while the sum total population of the towns to be served is 100,000, we must first set the sum total population of the service centers to 100,000 and then divide it up in the ratios of 5 to 1, 3 to 1, and 2 to 1 to give us the new assumed populations for each service center respectively i.e., new populations of 20,000, 30,000 and 50,000 respectively.

16 Ullman, E. L., *American Commodity Flow*. Seattle, Washington, University of Washington Press, 1957.

17 Gould, P. R., Man Against his Environment: A Game Theoretic Framework. *Annals of the Association of American Geographers*, Vol. 53, No. 3 (September, 1963).

18 Isard, W., *Methods of Regional Analysis: An Introduction to Regional Science*. M.I.T. Press and John Wiley, 1960.

THE TRANSPORTATION PROBLEM: TWO SUGGESTED EXERCISES

Problem A

A producer of dolomitic limestone for agricultural use has two lime quarries which supply three regional warehouses. Quarry A has a stock of 100 tons of lime and quarry B 200 tons. If the demand from warehouses X, Y, and Z is 90, 60, and 150 tons respectively, and the transport costs (in dollars) are as given, what is the least cost flow pattern?

	Warehouses			
Quarry	X	Y	Z	Supply (tons)
A	30	10	50	100
B	20	40	60	200
Demand (tons)	90	60	150	

Problem B

Three producers of widgets, factories A, B, and C, wish to sell their products to four Gizmo assembly plants, W, X, Y, and Z. With transport costs as given, what are the least cost interactions?

		Gizmo assembly plants				
		W	X	Y	Z	Total widgets produced
Widget producers	A	30	50	90	60	800
	B	110	70	130	80	100
	C	20	120	40	170	200
Total widgets needed		100	200	600	200	

The gravity model which was introduced earlier can be extended in a number of ways. Commonly mass and distance are weighted in some way; mass was earlier equated with population size. However, population numbers per se may conceal significant differences between regions that reflect on the probability of spatial interaction. Walter Isard has argued that just as the weights of different elements are unequal, so should the weights of different people vary; a common weighting is to assess mass as mean per capita income, for example.

Distance can be measured in several ways too. The usual way, again as we saw above, is simply to measure the straight-line distance between the two masses. In the following example of its application to a flow study, distance is equated in some calculations with travel time and travel costs. Other variants, not noted here, are weights which take account of such factors as psychological hazards, numbers of traffic lights, intersections, and type of roads.

Selection 11

Aggregation and Gravity Models: Some Empirical Evidence

R. E. Alcaly

1. INTRODUCTION

The basic formulation of the gravity model that will be considered in this [work] is

$$(1) \quad V_{ij} = K\frac{P_i^{\alpha}P_j^{\beta}}{D_{ij}^{\tau}}$$

where V_{ij} is the volume of travel between cities i and j, P_i and P_j are the populations of cities i and j respectively, D_{ij} is the distance between them, and K, α, β, and τ are parameters to be estimated. Variants of the model have been applied extensively to many other forms of social interaction, particularly intraurban travel.[1] The literature also abounds, however, with commentary on the drawbacks of the model. Isard states:

> A basic obstacle to its [gravity model's] use for projection is the lack of a theory to explain the values or functions which we assign to weights and exponents. Currently, the justification for this gravity model is simply that everything else being equal the interaction between any two populations can be expected to be directly related to their size; and since distance involves friction, inconvenience, and cost, such interaction can be expected to be inversely related to distance.[2]

Other problems of a general nature concern the measurement and definition of the variables and the fact that formula (1) does not include many variables which are relevant to the determination of volumes of social interaction or, in this case, travel volumes.[3]

It may, however, be possible to minimize these shortcomings in the application of such models. This [work] is concerned with the effect of aggregation over modes of travel on the performance of equation (1) in explaining the demand for travel. It has been asserted that (Isard [4; pp. 513–514]):

> When total volume of traffic is disaggregated by type of media, or trip purpose, by type of city or other classification, the peculiarities of each category tend to become more manifest and dominant, and the extent to which the gravity model describes or explains any regular "falling-off" effect (due to distance) tends to decrease.

In particular, the relevance of the distance factor for air travel has been questioned by Richmond (7) and Belmont (2). Their notion was that the relationship between distance and volumes of travel is likely to be different for air travel than for other modes. It seems reasonable to suppose that although the number of trips by all modes is a decreasing function of distance, the proportion of trips taken by air is an increasing function of distance. The net effect is difficult to assess on *a priori* grounds.

The gravity formulation does not include variables which reflect modal peculiarities, but is concerned with far more general factors. Travel by all modes taken together would

Journal of Regional Science, vol. 7, 1967, pp. 61–73. Reprinted by permission of the author and editor.

seem to be more stable and responsive to the variables included in the model and less sensitive to those excluded than would travel by a given mode.[4] Hence, the working hypothesis is that aggregation over modes tends to eliminate some of the peculiar characteristics of travel behavior which manifest themselves in individual modes and thus results in better performances by the gravity model. Section 2 contains a brief description of the data, Section 3 presents the empirical results, and Section 4 is devoted to concluding comments.

2. DATA

The parameters of the model were estimated on the basis of a 1960 cross-section of the California city-pair grid. Sixteen city-pair routes were used and are presented in Table 11-1 together with their distances. The traffic volumes were derived from sundry sources: *CAB Domestic Origin and Destination Survey of Airline Passenger Traffic, 1960;* various railroad companies; Western Greyhound Lines; the California Division of Highways; and *Los Angeles Regional Transportation Study* (LARTS) Survey of 1960. These data were obtained from the U.S. Department of Commerce, Northeast Corridor Transportation Project, through the courtesy of the Stanford Research Institute. The population figures were derived from the U.S. Bureau of the Census, *County and City Data Book,* 1962.

Travel times and travel costs were also used in some of the regressions. These times

Table 11-1 City-pair Routes and Distances

	Distance (miles)		
	Air*	Rail**	Highway***
Bakersfield-Los Angeles	111	169	150
Bakersfield-San Diego	216	297	260
Fresno-Los Angeles	210	277	245
Fresno-San Diego	314	405	365
Los Angeles-Sacramento	360	458	410
Los Angeles-San Diego	109	128	125
Los Angeles-San Francisco	340	470	420
Los Angeles-San Jose	310	423	410
Los Angeles-Santa Barbara	91	103	115
Los Angeles-Stockton	320	409	365
Sacramento-San Diego	467	586	525
Sacramento-San Francisco	77	92	95
Sacramento-San Jose	84	139	130
San Diego-San Francisco	449	598	545
San Diego-San Jose	421	551	525
San Diego-Santa Barbara	194	231	240

Notes: * Terminal to terminal along a great circle.
** Terminal to terminal.
*** Includes average access distance. These data were prepared by J. Goodman, Traffic Research Corporation.

are minimum times and in the case of automobile travel are for off-peak periods. Both times and costs include "access to terminal" portions for air, rail, and bus travel. Costs for these modes refer to coach service. In the case of automobile travel, peak and off-peak automobile costs were available. These data were derived from Joseph and Haikalis (5); various rail, bus, and air schedules; and estimates prepared by J. Goodman, Traffic Research Corporation.

3. EMPIRICAL RESULTS

Taking logarithms of both sides of equation (1) we have the estimated equation

$$\text{(2)}\quad \log V_{ij} = K' + \alpha \log P_i + \beta \log P_j + \gamma \log D_{ij}.$$

In the first instance, equation (2) was estimated separately for air, rail, bus, and automobile travel. These results were then compared with the estimates based on total volume. They are presented in Table 11-2. The standard criteria were used in evaluating the performances of the models. That is, the agreement of the signs and magnitudes of the estimated coefficients with the results expected on the basis of economic theory and *a priori* knowledge, the statistical significance of these coefficients, and the explanatory power (R^2) and significance of the entire relationship were all considered in judging the estimated equations.

Perhaps the most striking aspect of the results presented in Table 11-2 (as well as Tables 11-3, 11-4, 11-5) is the high level of performance of almost all of the estimated equations. The population coefficients are nearly equal in all instances and are close to unity in all equations except those for air and rail travel. One would expect equality since the model assumes, at least implicitly, that the effect of a given volume of population upon the generation of traffic is independent of the population's location. A unitary population elasticity of travel demand implies that, *ceteris paribus*, traffic is proportional to the number of possible pairwise interactions between members of the two populations. The number of possible pairwise interactions is clearly P_iP_j.

The significance of all coefficients except the distance coefficient in the air equation and the constant terms is quite marked throughout. And the small magnitude and insignificance of the distance coefficient in the air equation are consistent with the studies of Richmond (7) and Belmont (2). In addition, the signs and relative magnitudes of the coefficients of the distance variables seem to be quite reasonable. Automobile travel, which involves the greatest input of effort, or disutility, on the part of the traveler and whose convenience relative to other modes is greater the shorter the distance, would be expected to be most responsive to distance. Similarly, distance elasticity of bus and rail travel could be expected to lie somewhere between the air and automobile values. The relative magnitudes of the estimated distance elasticities are consistent with these expectations.

When account is also taken of the explanatory power and significance of the postulated log-linear relationships the aggregate equations seem superior as a group to the individual modal equations. A possible exception is the automobile equation which will be discussed in more detail below. The air relationship has a high level of explanatory power and is quite significant, but suffers from inferior individual coefficient results.

Although, at least at first glance, aggregation seems to improve the results, there are several problems which must be considered. First, there is the question of the appropriate definition of the distance variable when total

Table 11-2 All Modes

Dependent Variable	P_i	P_j	D_{ij}-Air	D_{ij}-Rail	D_{ij}-H'wy	D_{ij}-Avg.	D_{ij}-Wt.Avg.	K'	R^2	F
V_{ij}-Air	2.0899 (5.7374)	2.0175 (5.7974)	−0.3566 (−0.6773)					−46.769 (−5.0986)	.90827**	13.2023
V_{ij}-Rail	2.0987 (5.1144)	1.7485 (4.3431)		−1.2918 (−2.3105)				−38.718 (−3.6925)	.86768***	8.74297
V_{ij}-Bus	0.9003 (4.0400)	0.9958 (4.6450)			−1.2129 (−3.6663)			−9.9196 (−1.7638)	.87035***	8.95096
V_{ij}-Auto	0.9818 (3.5526)	1.0308 (3.8770)			−2.5623 (−6.2454)			−0.3033 (−0.4348 E-01)	.91612**	14.5626
V_{ij}-Total	1.0759 (4.8090)	1.0831 (5.0678)	−2.4599 (−7.6072)					−3.3909 (−0.6019)	.94321*	22.1455
V_{ij}-Total	1.0110 (3.8261)	1.1373 (4.3868)		−2.2531 (−6.2582)				−3.6737 (−0.5441)	.91860**	15.0473
V_{ij}-Total	1.0408 (3.5998)	1.0825 (3.8919)			−2.4548 (−5.7194)			−2.3956 (−0.3283)	.90429**	12.5983
V_{ij}-Total	1.0441 (4.0780)	1.1040 (4.4620)				−2.4178 (−6.5330)		−3.1862 (−0.4914)	.92473**	16.3811
V_{ij}-Total	1.0204 (3.6475)	1.0630 (3.9441)					−2.4825 (−5.8962)	−1.6857 (−0.2378)	.90936**	13.3776

Notes: Numbers in parentheses are t values.

There are 7 degrees of freedom; 3 due the regressions and 4 due the residuals. This is due to the fact that rail volumes were unavailable for eight routes.

*Significant at .01 level of significance.

**Significant at .025 level of significance.

***Significant at .05 level of significance.

Table 11-3 All Modes; Single Population Term, $P_i \cdot P_j$

Dependent Variable	$(P_i \cdot P_j)$	D_{ij}-Air	D_{ij}-Rail	D_{ij}-H'wy	D_{ij}-Avg.	D_{ij}-Wt.Avg.	K''	R^2	F
V_{ij}-Air	2.0434 (6.6076)	−0.3152 (−0.6754)					−46.650 (−5.6006)	.90533*	23.9082
V_{ij}-Rail	1.9021 (4.3124)		−1.2080 (−1.9202)				−38.359 (−3.2367)	.78860***	9.32583
V_{ij}-Bus	0.9596 (4.7834)			−1.2612 (−4.0484)			−10.044 (−1.8633)	.85098**	14.2767
V_{ij}-Auto	1.0122 (4.3702)			−2.5871 (−7.0893)			−0.3671 (−0.5814 E-01)	.91398♯	26.5632
V_{ij}-Total	1.0805 (5.7769)	−2.4640 (−8.7287)					−3.4028 (−0.6754)	.94316♯	41.4852
V_{ij}-Total	1.0819 (4.4185)		−2.2833 (−6.5381)				−3.8030 (−0.5780)	.90335*	23.3673
V_{ij}-Total	1.0667 (4.3569)			−2.4759 (−6.5126)			−2.4501 (−0.3724)	.90267*	23.1867
V_{ij}-Total	1.0805 (4.9019)				−2.4440 (−7.3271)		−3.2667 (−0.5514)	.92137♯	29.2934
V_{ij}-Total	1.0446 (4.4772)					−2.4936 (−6.8255)	−1.7325 (−0.2751)	.91055♯	25.4479

Notes: Numbers in parentheses are t values.
There are 7 degrees of freedom; 3 due the regressions and 4 due the residuals.
♯Significant at .005 level of significance.
*Significant at .01 level of significance.
**Significant at .025 level of significance.
***Significant at .05 level of significance.

volume is the dependent variable. Five measures have been used: air distance, rail distance, highway distance, average distance, and a weighted average of distances where the weights were determined by the ratio of the respective modal volumes to the total volumes on the individual routes. Two factors seem to dictate the use of the weighted average measure. It has a certain *a priori* appeal, and it tends to include a measure of access distance. The latter occurs because only highway distance includes access distance, and highway distance is given greatest weight in the weighted average measure since automobile volumes predominate by wide margins on all routes. Use of the weighted average measure of distance results in an equation which is superior to all the individual modal equations except automobile. This equation, however, does not perform as well as some of the other aggregate equations.

It is interesting to note the great degree of stability of the distance coefficients in the automobile and aggregate equations. The distance elasticity of travel in the aggregate equations tends to reflect the responsiveness of automobile travel to distance. This is a result, of course, of the predominance of automobile travel on all routes. This fact, coupled with the superior level of performance of the automobile equations, leads one to suspect that what is being demonstrated may actually be the applicability of gravity models to automobile travel as opposed to travel by other modes. And, since aggregate travel volumes are dominated by automobile volumes, the aggregate equations perform better as a group than do the individual modal equations.

Second, it was thought that the estimates of the population coefficients might be sensitive to the labeling of the nodes. As illustrated in Table 11-1, several cities appear as both node i and node j in different city-pair routes, e.g., Los Angeles–Sacramento, Sacramento–San

Table 11-4 All Modes Except Rail

Dependent Variable	P_i	P_j	D_{ij}-Air	D_{ij}-H'wy	D_{ij}-Avg.	D_{ij}-Wt.Avg.	K'	R^2	F
V_{ij}-Air	1.3300 (6.0438)	1.4082 (5.3795)	−0.2164 (−0.5100)				−27.326 (−4.5020)	.78750	14.8236
V_{ij}-Bus	0.6190 (6.4540)	0.8323 (7.2796)		−1.0928 (−5.5690)			−3.9171 (−1.4525)	.88301	30.1895
V_{ij}-Auto	1.1524 (7.7080)	1.1141 (6.2519)		−3.0844 (−10.084)			−1.1451 (−0.2724)	.92913	52.4388
V_{ij}-Total	1.1275 (10.386)	1.1211 (8.6814)	−2.7037 (−12.914)				−3.3788 (−1.1284)	.95702	89.0642
V_{ij}-Total	1.0974 (8.4823)	1.1053 (7.1669)		−2.8175 (−10.644)			−1.5398 (−0.4233)	.93868	61.2305
V_{ij}-Total	1.1134 (9.5261)	1.1135 (8.0010)			−2.7690 (−11.912)		−2.4353 (−0.7485)	.95007	76.1200
V_{ij}-Total	1.0898 (8.6472)	1.0901 (7.2525)				−2.8757 (−10.950)	−0.9312 (−0.2613)	.94175	64.6640

Notes: Numbers in parentheses are t values.
There are 15 degrees of freedom; 3 due the regressions and 12 due the residuals.
All the F values are significant at .005 level of significance.

Francisco. Hence, the near equality of the population coefficients might be merely an artifact. All the equations were thus reestimated with a single population term, $P_i \cdot P_j$, substituted for the individual populations. The equation estimated was:

$$(3) \quad \log V_{ij} = K'' + a[\log P_i + \log P_j] + b \log D_{ij}.$$

The results are presented in Table 11-3 and tend to dispel initial fears. In every case the population coefficient lies somewhere between the corresponding pair of population coefficients in Table 11-2. The near equality of the population coefficients seems to be a real, and *a priori* reasonable, result. Furthermore this set of equations seems to confirm the aggregation hypothesis even more strongly than does the group in Table 11-2.

Finally, and probably most importantly, rail volume is not available for eight of the routes. Since this drastically reduces the degrees of freedom the equations were reestimated, omitting rail from consideration. These results are presented in Tables 11-4 and 11-5. The magnitudes of the individual regression coefficients generally remain fairly stable with respect to this change in the sample and continue to be quite reasonable. Two exceptions are the population coefficients of the air and bus equations. In the former case these coefficients assume somewhat more reasonable (closer to unity) values while in the latter instance the opposite appears to be true. Since the equations in Tables 11-4 and 11-5 were estimated on the basis of an expanded sample they would seem to be more accurate representations of the relationships than those presented in Tables 11-2 and 11-3. The equality of population coefficients appears even more pronounced in the former set of equations and there is the expected improvement in the significance of all the coefficients as well as

Table 11-5 All Modes Except Rail; Single Population Term, $P_i \cdot P_j$

Dependent Variable	$(P_i \cdot P_j)$	D_{ij}-Air	D_{ij}-H'wy	D_{ij}-Avg.	D_{ij}-Wt.Avg.	K''	R^2	F
V_{ij}-Air	1.3563 (6.9035)	−0.2278 (−0.5583)				−26.922 (−4.7039)	.78574	23.8370
V_{ij}-Bus	0.6904 (7.0325)		−1.1225 (−5.1904)			−2.8017 (−0.9613)	.84514	35.4747
V_{ij}-Auto	1.1396 (8.5495)		−3.0791 (−10.486)			−1.3451 (−0.3399)	.92882	84.8216
V_{ij}-Total	1.1254 (11.658)	−2.7027 (−13.483)				−3.4122 (−1.2134)	.95701	144.694
V_{ij}-Total	1.1001 (9.5560)		−2.8186 (−11.114)			−1.4988 (−0.4386)	.93866	99.474
V_{ij}-Total	1.1134 (10.711)			−2.7690 (−12.439)		−2.4347 (−0.7968)	.95007	123.695
V_{ij}-Total	1.0899 (9.7208)				−2.8758 (−11.435)	−0.9298 (−0.2778)	.94175	105.079

Notes: Numbers in parentheses are t values.
There are 15 degrees of freedom; 3 due the regressions and 12 due the residuals.
All the F values are significant at .005 level of significance.

Table 11-6 All Modes; Travel Time as Impedance

Dependent Variable	P_i	P_j	T-Air	T-Rail	T-Bus	T-Auto	T-Avg.	K'	R^2	F
V_{ij}-Air	1.9518 (6.7197)	1.8549 (6.2402)	−1.1401 (−1.3230)					−43.3555 (−5.2483)	.92888‡	17.4133
V_{ij}-Rail	2.1399 (4.4110)	1.7125 (3.7555)		−1.4324 (−1.8129)				−43.3792 (−3.4592)	.83041***	6.5290
V_{ij}-Bus	0.9421 (4.7221)	0.9914 (5.2740)			−1.4538 (−4.2957)			−14.4517 (−2.7962)	.89929*	11.9058
V_{ij}-Auto	1.0201 (3.8976)	1.0842 (4.2979)				−2.6694 (−6.6902)		−11.5124 (−1.6624)	.92602*	16.6891
V_{ij}-Total	0.2194 (0.7824)	0.2222 (0.7744)	−4.4250 (−5.3193)					12.1765 (1.5268)	.89121*	10.9222
V_{ij}-Total	1.1340 (2.9341)	1.1102 (3.0561)		−2.6710 (−4.2433)				−12.7512 (−1.2764)	.84034**	7.0178
V_{ij}-Total	1.0834 (3.1529)	1.0459 (3.2306)			−2.7843 (−4.7771)			−10.8441 (−1.2183)	.86900**	8.8448
V_{ij}-Total	1.0775 (3.8946)	1.1337 (4.2515)				−2.5575 (−6.0637)		−13.1350 (−1.7944)	.91382*	14.1381
V_{ij}-Total	1.0587 (3.4306)	1.0428 (3.5596)					−2.8821 (−5.3492)	−10.9648 (−1.3592)	.89227*	11.0433

Notes: Numbers in parentheses are t values.

There are 7 degrees of freedom; 3 due the regressions and 4 due the residuals.

‡Significant at .01 level of significance.

*Significant at .025 level of significance.

**Significant at .05 level of significance.

***Significant at .10 level of significance.

in the significance of all the relationships. When consideration is given, in addition, to the equations' explanatory power, they appear to lend somewhat more dramatic support to the aggregation hypothesis, particularly when the weighted average measure of distance is used. (In this connection, note particularly the large reduction in the R^2 of the air equations in Tables 11-4 and 11-5 from their levels in Tables 11-1 and 11-2.)

Two other sets of equations were estimated, using travel time and travel cost, respectively, as the impedance factor instead of distance. However, in these cases one would expect aggregation to be harmful rather than helpful, since the inclusion of times and/or costs tends to make the equations somewhat more specific to each mode and more like traditional demand equations. The results are listed in Tables 11-6 and 11-7 and tend to bear out this presumption. Aggregation does not seem to improve markedly the models' performance, although it is not entirely clear that it is very harmful either. Perhaps the most striking thing about these equations is their erratic nature and generally inferior level of performance compared to the models which employed distance as the impedance factor.

With time as the impedance factor (Table 11-6), the individual mode and aggregate equations do about equally well on all criteria with the former group of equations having perhaps a slight edge. As was true in the sets of equations with distance impedances, aggregation causes a reduction in the magnitudes of the population coefficients and constant terms of the air and rail equations as well as an increase in the absolute values of the impedance elasticities. The significance of all coefficients except the constant terms also improves. However, in contrast to the other aggregate equations with an air impedance factor, the population coefficients appear to be unreasonably small when air time is used.

The evidence with travel costs as impedance factors (Table 11-7) is even less clear-cut than that with travel times. Unlike the situation with travel times, the aggregate equation with air cost as the impedance factor appears quite reasonable, and the aggregate equation using bus cost has a rather high and significant cost elasticity as well as a surprisingly high R^2. One possible explanation of the latter phenomenon is that bus cost most accurately reflects the total range of travel costs since it lies closest to the middle of their scale, and hence is quite appropriate for use in an aggregate equation. However, when rail is omitted from consideration and the equation reestimated on the basis of the expanded sample, the cost elasticity and R^2 are reduced considerably, the latter to a value of .84403. On the other hand, as was the case with the aggregate equation using average time as impedance, the aggregation equation using average cost does very well on all counts. And the aggregate versions of the other equations seem to perform slightly worse as a group than the individual mode equations. Further investigation of the sets of equations in Tables 11-6 and 11-7 might prove useful in determining more precisely the effects of aggregation in such modified gravity models.

4. CONCLUSION

It would seem to follow from the empirical analysis presented [here] that the crude gravity model as formulated in equation (1) explains travel by all modes better than it explains travel by an individual mode, with the possible exception of automobile travel. These results do not, of course, eliminate some of the basic problems connected with such models which were alluded to earlier. They do, however, offer support for the underlying presumption that such objections are minimized when the model is applied to aggregate data. When the model is altered so as to include times or costs instead of distance as the impedance factor, it more closely resembles the more traditional travel demand

Table 11-7 All Modes; Travel Cost as Impedance

Dependent Variable	P_i	P_j	C-Air	C-Rail	C-Bus	C-Auto	Peak C-Auto	Avg. Auto Cost	C-Avg.	K'	R^2	F
V_{ij}-Air	2.0493 (5.9566)	1.9839 (5.8999)	−0.4549 (−0.6626)							−46.4013 (−5.0752)	.90787*	13.1382
V_{ij}-Rail	1.9958 (4.7351)	1.6638 (3.9866)		−1.3108 (−2.0647)						−40.2232 (−3.5652)	.85045**	7.5824
V_{ij}-Bus	0.9630 (3.8206)	1.0177 (4.3148)			−1.7422 (−3.2846)					−14.6886 (−2.2852)	.84710**	7.3867
V_{ij}-Auto	0.7950 (2.1796)	0.8513 (2.4064)				−2.6329 (−4.3543)				−6.3584 (−0.6489)	.84289**	7.1534
V_{ij}-Auto	0.8411 (2.3413)	0.9066 (2.6041)					−2.8093 (−4.4864)			−7.4513 (−0.7747)	.85049**	7.5850
V_{ij}-Auto	0.8186 (2.2633)	0.8793 (2.5080)						−2.7227 (−4.4245)		−6.9185 (−0.7132)	.84700**	7.3810
V_{ij}-Total	0.8012 (3.4506)	0.8555 (3.7694)	−3.1766 (−6.8561)							−0.8877 (−0.1439)	.93112♯	18.0230
V_{ij}-Total	0.8339 (2.3885)	0.9917 (2.8684)		−2.2973 (−4.3682)						−6.3385 (−0.6782)	.84778**	7.4259
V_{ij}-Total	1.2099 (5.0913)	1.1560 (5.1983)			−3.7068 (−7.4123)					−12.7630 (−2.1061)	.94039♯	21.0349
V_{ij}-Total	0.8587 (2.2828)	0.9085 (2.4901)				−2.5075 (−4.0211)				−8.1368 (−0.8052)	.82580***	6.3206
V_{ij}-Total	0.9029 (2.4330)	0.9613 (2.6730)					−2.6768 (−4.1381)			−9.1830 (−0.9242)	.83367**	6.6831
V_{ij}-Total	0.8813 (2.3606)	0.9352 (2.5841)						−2.5937 (−4.0831)		−8.6729 (−0.8662)	.83004***	6.5114
V_{ij}-Total	0.9008 (3.1781)	0.9689 (3.5120)							−2.9118 (−5.6353)	−5.8920 (−0.7874)	.90174*	12.2362

Notes: Numbers in parentheses are t values.

There are 7 degrees of freedom; 3 due the regressions and 4 due the residuals.

♯Significant at .01 level of significance.

*Significant at .025 level of significance.

**Significant at .05 level of significance.

***Significant at .10 level of significance.

equations. In these instances the effect of aggregation is less certain but appears to be somewhat harmful. It might be expected that this would continue to be the case as additional "demand" variables were included while remaining within the log-linear framework of the model.

NOTES

1 See Carrothers (3) for the historical development of gravity models and an extensive bibliography of their applications.
2 Isard (4; p. 515). This point is also made by Schneider in (8). He states that the cardinal failure of the gravity model is that it is not explanatory and does not really try to be. The gravity model can also be derived from a probability point of view. See Isard (4; pp. 493–498).
3 For example, see Isard (4; pp. 504–512).
4 See Quandt (6; pp. 36–37).

REFERENCES

1 Alcaly, R. E. "The Demand for Air Travel," *Studies in Travel Demand* (Prepared by *Mathematica* for the Department of Commerce under Contract No. C-247-65 (Neg); September 1965).
2 Belmont, Daniel M. "A Study of Airline Interstation Traffic," *Journal of Air Law and Commerce,* 25 (1958), 361–368.
3 Carrothers, Gerald A. P. "An Historical Review of the Gravity and Potential Concepts of Human Interaction," *Journal of the American Institute of Planners,* 22 (1956), 94–102.
4 Isard, Walter *et al. Methods of Regional Analysis.* New York: The Technology Press of M.I.T. and John Wiley and Sons, Inc., 1960.
5 Joseph, Hyman, and George Haikalis. "Economic Evaluation of Traffic Networks; The Los Angeles Metropolitan Peak Hour Driving Study–1960," delivered at the 40th Annual Meeting, Highway Research Board, Washington, D.C., January, 1961.
6 Quandt, R. E. "Some Perspectives on Gravity Models," *Studies in Travel Demand* (prepared by *Mathematica* for the Department of Commerce under Contract No. C-247-65 (Neg.); September 1965).
7 Richmond, Samuel B. "Interspatial Relationships Affecting Air Travel," *Land Economics,* 33 (1957), 65–73.
8 Schneider, Morton. "Gravity Models and Trip Distribution Theory," *Papers and Proceedings, Regional Science Association,* 5 (1959), 51–56.

Flows are *volumetric measures* of spatial interaction. Flow patterns can be analyzed and explained in terms of areal characteristics, the positive or negative factors being supply and demand, on the one hand, and cost and distance (among other factors), on the other. Economic development, regional growth and change, consumer taste preferences, cultural traits, or governmental and military direction can all alter the spatial imbalance that usually must be present to initiate movement. Flow analysis, by any of the methods mentioned, can act as a link between the concept of interaction and the analysis of spatial distribution and relationships. In the final selection in Part Three, H. L. Gauthier links flows and networks; a network is abstracted from the actual roadway system in Brazil, and flows are assigned between centers linked by the network. The calculation involves a development from the primal-dual transportation method noted by Cox, utilizing an out-of-kilter algorithm. Since this is a fairly advanced technique, a reading of the method developed by D. Fulkerson should perhaps precede an in-depth analysis of Gauthier's technique.* Selection 12 also introduces us to the role of transport in a developing area, which will be pursued in more depth in Part Six (*a*).

*L. Ford and D. Fulkerson, *Flows in Networks,* Princeton, N.J.: Princeton University Press, 1962, especially Chapters 1 and 3.

Selection 12

Least Cost Flows in a Capacitated Network: A Brazilian Example

H. L. Gauthier

A. PURPOSE

In the planning of a program of economic development, investments in transportation generally are regarded as safer than investments in directly productive activities. As Hirschman has observed, there is an attraction in investment ventures that are difficult to prove wrong before they are started or are unlikely to become obvious failures.[1] In Brazil, especially in the State of São Paulo, there is some indication that the development planners are following a course of action in which highway construction is a "lead" factor in the development process.

In an earlier study, the author found a high degree of relationship between the development of highway accessibility in one time period and the growth of manufacturing in a subsequent period.[2] The analysis of the highway network was in terms of graph theory, with the network being abstracted to a valued graph in which the connections between centers were weighted according to the cost of transporting a unit of commodity per unit of distance over laterite, gravel-surfaced, and paved highways. Although the type of road construction was a variable in the analysis of nodal accessibility to the network, no attempt was made to introduce a consideration of the capacities of the highways. A logical extension of the analysis would be a consideration of the spatial interaction between nodes in terms of the actual utilization of the highway linkages. Unfortunately, origin-destination data have not been collected for Brazil's federal highways, much less the state of municipal roads. However, it is possible, given line-haul costs and capacities, to estimate the maximum flow at minimal costs between nodes in the network. The resulting theoretical flows are indicative of the potential for spatial interaction.

The purpose of this [work] is to determine the least cost flows in a capacitated network. To accomplish this objective, a network is abstracted as a graph and subjected to a search routine to determine the paths over which flow is probable between two centers. The out-of-kilter algorithm developed by D. Fulkerson is used to determine the maximum flow at minimal cost within the sub-networks delimited by the search routine. These procedures are applied to the São Paulo highway network of 1960, and some policy implications of the results are discussed.

B. LEAST COST FLOWS

Search Procedure

In determining the maximum flow at minimal cost in a network, there is a logical necessity to limit the paths utilized in the solution to the problem. Without such a restriction, computations generally are inefficient and lead to impractical results. Intuitively, it is improbable that flow will occur on all paths between a

Northwestern University Studies in Geography, no. 16, pp. 102–127. Reprinted by permission of the author and editor.

given source and sink. This is especially true when those paths lead through intermediate nodes that are remote to a series of direct paths between the source and sink.

In the process of selecting shipment routes, long circuitous paths are uneconomic and if possible avoided. This does not mean the transport user is an optimizer. He does not select necessarily the least cost route, although his decision is made within a range of choices having definite economic limits imposed by the least cost path.

If $C = (c_1, c_2, \ldots, c_n)$ is a set of costs such that some element of the set applies to each linkage in the network, the problem is to find

$$\min_{X} \quad [\Sigma c_{ij}] \quad x_i \epsilon c \quad x_j \epsilon c$$

where X is a set of nodes forming the endpoints of paths from the source to the sink. Spatially the search is limited to a few paths forming a subset of the network.

Let x_s and x_t be the source and sink nodes respectively. Let the straight line distance between them be d_{ij} and the length of the minimal cost path between them be v_{ij}. Allowing v_{ij} to be the distance from x_s and x_t for intermediate nodes to be included in the subset of the network, the search space is delimited as an ellipse with its foci at x_s and x_t (Fig. 12-1). It is the locus of points for which the sum of the distances from x_s to x_t is equal to v_{ij}. That is,

$$(1) \quad v_1(x, y) + v_2(x, y) = v_{ij}$$

The value v_{ij} equals the major axis, $2a$, of the ellipse and establishes the coordinate points for the minor axis, $2b$. Assigning coordinate point designations to the nodes in the network, the sub-network includes all nodes that satisfy the relationship

$$(2) \quad \frac{x^2}{a^2} + \frac{y^2}{b^2} < 1$$

where

a = the length of the semimajor axis
b = the length of the semiminor axis

The arcs connecting those nodes constitute the path sequence between x_s and x_t.

It is conceivable that an arc linking two nodes in the sub-network may intercept the boundary of the ellipse. To avoid creating a disconnected pair of nodes in the sub-network that are actually an ordered pair in the network, it is advisable to identify the spatial limits of the sub-network in terms of a circuit, the vertices of which are those nodes lying closest to the boundary of the ellipse.

The Out-of-Kilter Algorithm

The out-of-kilter algorithm for minimal cost flow problems generalizes the primal-dual transportation method so it may be initiated with an infeasible dual solution, as well as an infeasible primal solution.[3] The method begins with an arbitrary flow, feasible or not, together with an arbitrary pricing vector and then uses a labeling procedure to adjust an arc of the network that fails to satisfy the

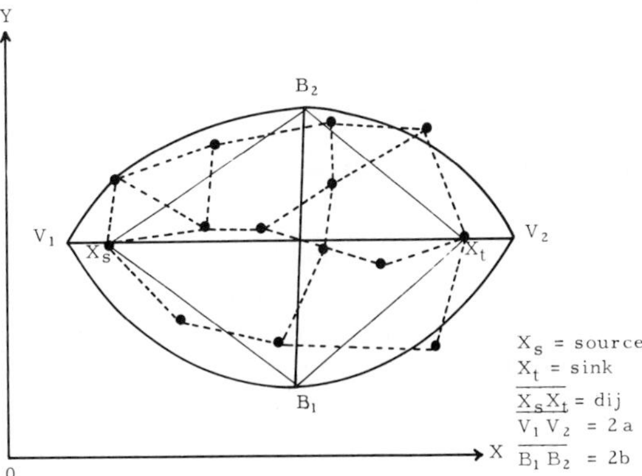

Fig. 12-1 Delimitation of a sub-network.

optimality properties.[4] Dantzig regards the freedom to begin with any flow and pricing vector, rather than starting with particular ones that satisfy certain optimality properties, as the most attractive feature of the method.[5] The algorithm keeps the relative cost factors non-negative while it works toward feasibility, so that when a feasible solution is obtained it will be optimal.

By definition a flow is a non-negative integral vector with components for each arc that satisfy the conservation equation

$$(3) \quad \Sigma_j(x_{ij} - x_{ji}) = 0 \qquad (i, j = 1, \ldots, n)$$

A flow is feasible it if satisfies the relation

$$(4) \quad l_{ij} \leq x_{ij} \leq u_{ij}$$

where

l_{ij} = a lower bound on the amount of flow
u_{ij} = an upper bound on the amount of flow

A feasible flow that minimizes the cost

$$(5) \quad \Sigma_i \Sigma_j \, c_{ij} x_{ij}$$

over all feasible flows is optimal.

Let $\pi = (\pi i)$ be a pricing vector of integers, one component for each node. The optimality properties for the problem are that

$$(6) \quad c_{ij} + \pi_i - \pi_j > 0 \rightarrow x_{ij} = l_{ij}$$

$$(7) \quad c_{ij} + \pi_i - \pi_j < 0 \rightarrow x_{ij} = u_{ij}$$

hold for all arcs ij. That is, if x is a feasible flow and there is a pricing vector π such that (6) and (7) hold, then x is optimal. The notation may be simplified by setting

$$(8) \quad \bar{c}_{ij} = c_{ij} + \pi_i - \pi_j$$

If, for a given flow x and a pricing vector π, an arc ij is in one of the following states:

$$(9) \quad \begin{aligned} &(\alpha) \quad \bar{c}_{ij} > 0,\ x_{ij} = l_{ij} \\ &(\beta) \quad \bar{c}_{ij} = 0,\ l_{ij} \leq x_{ij} \leq u_{ij} \\ &(\gamma) \quad \bar{c}_{ij} < 0,\ x_{ij} = u_{ij} \end{aligned}$$

it is considered in-kilter and the flow is optimal. If an arc is out-of-kilter it is in one of the following states:

$$(10) \quad \begin{aligned} &(\alpha_1) \quad \bar{c}_{ij} > 0,\ x_{ij} < l_{ij} \\ &(\beta_1) \quad \bar{c}_{ij} = 0,\ x_{ij} < l_{ij} \\ &(\gamma_1) \quad \bar{c}_{ij} < 0,\ x_{ij} < l_{ij} \\ &(\alpha_2) \quad \bar{c}_{ij} > 0,\ x_{ij} > l_{ij} \\ &(\beta_2) \quad \bar{c}_{ij} = 0,\ x_{ij} > u_{ij} \\ &(\gamma_2) \quad \bar{c}_{ij} < 0,\ x_{ij} > u_{ij} \end{aligned}$$

To solve the problem it is necessary to get all arcs in-kilter.

For each state that an arc is in, there is a non-negative integer called the kilter number of the arc. An in-kilter arc has a kilter number of zero. Out-of-kilter arcs have positive kilter numbers that measure either the infeasibility of the arc flow or the degree to which the optimality properties (6) and (7) are not satisfied. To get all arcs in-kilter, Fulkerson uses a modified labeling procedure that searches for a flow-augmenting path from one node to another. The search procedure is carried out in such a way that all in-kilter arcs stay in-kilter, whereas the kilter number for any out-ot-kilter arc either decreases or stays the same. Thus, all arc kilter numbers are monotone, non-increasing throughout the computation.

The labeling method terminates in one of two ways, called a breakthrough and a non-breakthrough, respectively: either the sink receives a label, or no more labels can be assigned and the sink has not been labeled. If non-breakthrough results, it is impossible to increase the flow between the source and the sink. If a breakthrough occurs, a path from the origin to the sink can be flow-augmented, the increase in x being determined by the original out-of-kilter state of the arc. By alternative applications of the labeling and flow-augmenting process the kilter numbers are reduced to zero. When all arcs are in-kilter, the flow is feasible and optimal in terms of minimal costs.

THE SÃO PAULO NETWORK

Network as a Graph

The São Paulo highway network of 1960 is abstracted as a graph by regarding urban centers as a set of nodes (X), and the highway routes as a set of arcs (U). The incidence relationship between the two sets (Γ) is given by the pattern of connections existing in 1960. The resulting graph, $N = (X, U) = (X, \Gamma)$, is finite, oriented and connected. Associated with each arc are three non-negative integers: l_{ij} (the arc lower bound), u_{ij} (the arc upper bound), and c_{ij} (the arc cost).

Line Haul Costs

The obtainment of firm estimates of transportation costs in Brazil is a difficult undertaking at best. In large measure this is due to the fact that the trucking industry is characterized by a large number of very small firms. Fleet operations are the exception. In most cases, the driver is the vehicle owner, who seldom is knowledgeable of the accounting procedures necessary to establish actual operating expenses. Consequently, the values, c_{ij}, are based on average operating cost data supplied by the Departmento Estradas de Rodagem do Estado de São Paulo, commonly called DER.

To estimate transfer costs as a function of distance, the procedure commonly employed by Brazilian transportation economists is the one suggested by Pires Ferreira.[6] His procedure is based on the formulation

$$(11)\quad y^2 - D_1{}^2x^2 - 2D_1D_2x - 2k = 0$$

where

y = the total costs

D_1 = the variable costs incurred by a vehicle traveling a distance

D_2 = the fixed overhead charges

$2k$ = initial outlays for equipment and administrative expenses; considered equal to the constant of integration multiplied by 2.

Allowing $C = -D_1{}^2$, $E = -(D_1D_2)$, and $F = 2k$, Equation (9) can be rewritten as

$$(12)\quad y^2 + Cx^2 + Ex + F = 0$$

Thus we have a special case of the general second degree equation

$$(13)\quad Ay^2 + Bxy + Cx^2 + 2Dy + 2Ex + F = 0$$

In the manner of treating a conic section, we can determine the nature of the curve by the discriminant $\Delta = B^2 - 4AC$. When $B = 0$, $A = 1$, and $C = -D_1{}^2$, we have

$$(14)\quad \Delta = -C = D_1{}^2 > 0$$

Therefore, when $\Delta > 0$, equation (11) represents a hyperbola. Applying Pires' formulations to the data on average operating costs, we can derive a set of values that relate transportation costs to length of haul over different road types (Table 12-1).

Arc Capacities

The values l_{ij} are set equal to zero, as there is no reason to assume any given highway will be included in the solution of the maximum flow–minimum cost problem. The values u_{ij} are considered equal to the capacities of the highways. The estimates of capacity are based on the formulations of the DER.[7] The procedure employed is analogous to that developed by the Highway Research Board in the United States.

The maximum number of vehicles of a specified type which can pass over a highway during a twenty-four hour period, with consideration given to only speed, spacing interval, and surface type, constitutes the basic capacity of the road. From this basic capacity is derived an operational capacity with allowances for driver characteristics, essential vehicle maintenance en route, and unforeseen operational developments. Factors for highways characteristics, e.g., condition of road surface, width of motorable surface and shoulders, curves and gradients, are applied to the operational capacity to obtain a practical daily capacity in vehicles per day. Assuming the use of five ton trucks hauling an average three ton load, the practical daily capacity is expressed in short tons per day.

The Via Anghanguera between São Paulo and Campinas, for example, is a four-lane divided highway with an all-weather surfacing of bituminous concrete. The DER estimates the basic capacity, with a 300-foot minimum vehicle spacing, to be 21,100 vehicles per day. Allowing a twenty percent reduction for driver characteristics, essential vehicle maintenance en route, and unforeseen operational developments, the operation capacity is estimated at 16,900 vehicles per day. The operational capacity is adjusted by considering the specific highway characteristics listed in Table 12-2. The result is a daily capacity of 14,544 vehicles for a two-way movement on the Via Anghanguera.

Half this figure represents the capacity for forward movement only. Assuming the use of five-ton trucks hauling an average three-ton load, the practical forward daily capacity is 21,816 short tons per day.

Table 12-1 The Relation of Transport Costs to Length of Haul

	Cr$/Ton		
Distance (klms)	Paved	Gravel	Laterite
0	9.4	9.4	9.4
10	25.9	31.8	40.5
20	37.7	45.3	58.0
30	47.1	56.8	71.3
40	56.0	66.2	82.8
50	64.1	75.1	93.6
60	72.1	83.4	103.5
70	79.8	91.4	111.9
80	87.1	99.3	119.5
90	94.2	107.1	126.6
100	100.9	114.8	132.7

Results

For purposes of analysis, three nodes on the São Paulo highway network are considered alternately as sources and sinks. They are the urban centers of São Paulo, Riberão Prêto, and Bauru. The selection of these nodes is based on their relative importance in the factor analytic dimensions of network accessibility.[8] Of the more than 150 nodes of the 1960 highway network, São Paulo, Riberão Prêto, and Bauru have the highest factor loadings on the principal dimensions of network accessibility. They are major foci for spatially distinctive clusters of nodes with similar structural patterns of direct and attenuated connectivity.

Table 12-2 Adjustment Factors for Highway Capacity

Characteristics	Via Anghanguera	Factor value
Width of motorable surface	42 feet	2.2
Shoulder width	6–12 feet	1.0
Highway alignment	Gradients less than 5 percent and curves not less than 150 ft. radius	0.9
Surface deterioration and maintenance	Surface condition is good and subsoil is moist	1.0
Turning and cross movement	Controlled access	0.85
Operational phasing	Sustained movement	0.50

To delimit the geographic area to those paths most likely used between Riberão Prêto and São Paulo, Bauru and São Paulo, and Bauru and Riberão Prêto, the length of the minimal cost paths v_{ij} between the centers are determined.[9] Between Riberão Prêto and São Paulo the minimal path is 336 kilometers, and consists of the paved federal highways BR 106, from Riberão Prêto to Limerira, and BR 33, from Limeira to São Paulo. Between Bauru and São Paulo, it is 360 kilometers, the distance between the two centers on the paved state highway. The minimal path between Bauru and Riberão Prêto is 210 kilometers, and consists of a gravel road from Bauru to Jau, a bituminous treated road from Jau to São Carlos, and a gravel road from São Carlos to Riberão Prêto (Fig. 12-2). Knowing v_{ij}, the major axes and the minor axes are determined for the ellipses delimiting the three sub-networks (Table 12-3). With Riberão Prêto and Bauru as points of origin in Cartesian Grids, the coordinate positions of other nodes are determined. Nodes are included in the sub-networks if they satisfy Equation 2. Then the boundary of each ellipse is adjusted to identify a sub-network in terms of a circuit (Fig. 12-2). As a result, thirty nodes are included in the Riberão Prêto–São Paulo sub-network, thirty in the Bauru–São Paulo sub-network, and eighteen in the Bauru–Riberão Prêto sub-network. The sets of nodes in the sub-networks are not mutually exclusive (Table 12-4).

Within a sub-network, each arc has associated with it the cost of a unit of flow and the capacity constraints on that flow. Applying the out-of-kilter algorithm, the maximum flow at minimal cost is determined for the capacitated sub-networks (Tables 12-5, 12-6, 12-7). In all three cases there is a feasible flow and the optimality requirements of Equations (6) and (7) are satisfied. Given the existing connections between Riberão Prêto and São Paulo, the maximum flow is 12,140 short tons per day at a cost of Cr$5,577,256. For the Bauru–São Paulo sub-network, the maximum flow is 14,954 short tons at a cost of Cr$6,836,209. For the Bauru–Riberão Prêto sub-network, it is 5,666 short tons at a cost of Cr$2,084,079. On a ton-kilometer basis, the comparable costs are Cr$1.19 t/klm (São Paulo–Bauru), Cr$1.32 t/klm (Riberão Prêto–São Paulo) and Cr$1.50 t/klm (Bauru–Riberão Prêto).

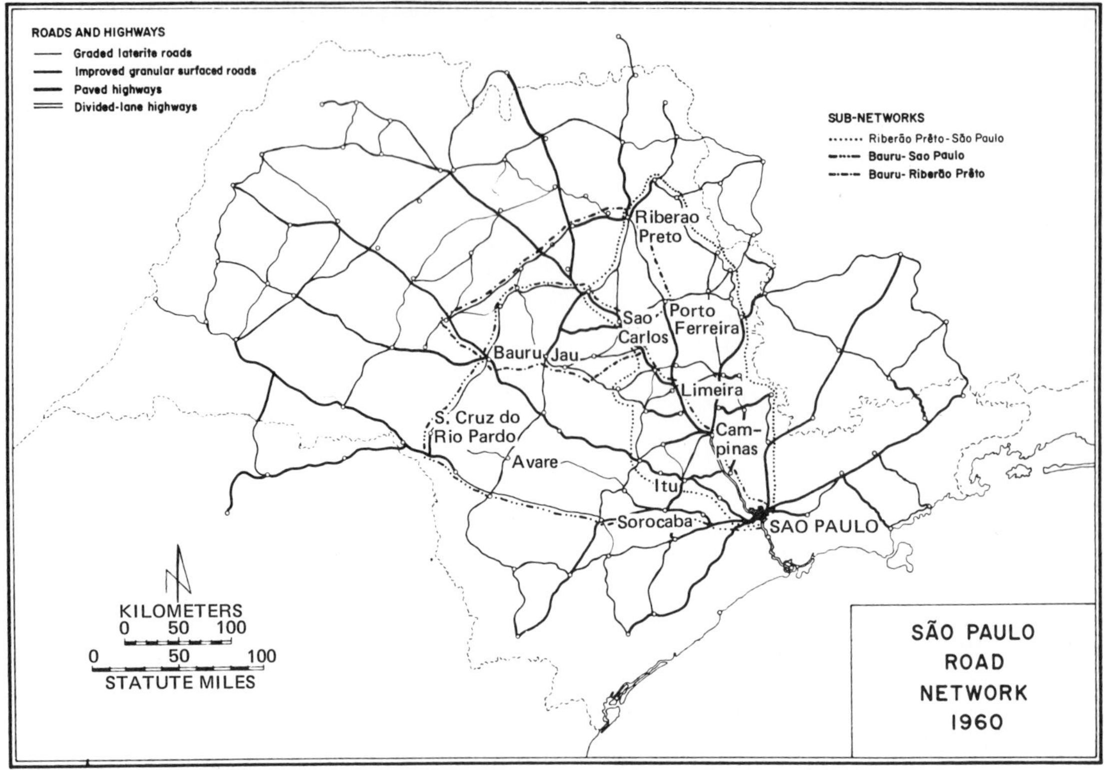

Fig. 12-2.

C. INTERPRETATION

The maximum flows between Riberão Prêto and São Paulo, and between Bauru and São Paulo, are in accord with expectations. Since 1955, highway construction in the State of São Paulo has been characterized by a continual increase in bituminous concrete and bituminous surface-treated highways. The Plano de Ação of the State Government, for the period 1958–62, called for the replacement of many gravel-surfaced arterial roads with paved ones. The objective was to reduce transport costs which are a major component

Table 12-3 Values for the Ellipses

Source	Sink	D_{ij} (klm)	Major axis 2 (klm)	Minor axis 2 (klm)
Riberão Prêto	São Paulo	295	336	191
Bauru	São Paulo	280	360	234
Bauru	Riberão Prêto	180	210	176

Table 12-4 Nodes in the Sub-networks*

Riberão Prêto–São Paulo	Bauru–São Paulo	Bauru–Ribẽrao Prêto
Riberão Prêto	Bauru	Bauru
Batatais	Iacanga	Pirajui
Altinopolis	Ibitinga	Iacanga
Mococa	Jau	Jau
S. José do Rio Pardo	S. Cruz do Rio Pardo	Dois Corregos
Casa Branca	E	D
Vargem Grande	Piraju	Ibitinga
S. João da Boa Vista	Itai	Itapolis
A	Avaré	C
Porto Ferreira	São Manuel	Araraquara
Araraquara	Dois Corregos	Matão
São Carlos	D	Jaboticabal
Rio Claro	Araraquara	B
Araras	São Carlos	São Carlos
Mogi Mirim	B	Porto Ferreira
Itapira	São Pedro	A
Socorro	Rio Claro	Sertãozinho
Amparo	Limeira	Riberão Prêto
Jaquariuna	Piracicaba	
Limeira	Americana	
São Pedro	Campinas	
Piracicaba	Capivari	
Americana	Tiete	
Campinas	Tatui	
Tiete	Itapetininga	
Capivari	Sorocaba	
Jundiaí	Itu	
Bragança Paulista	Jundiaí	
Itu	São Roque	
São Paulo	São Paulo	

*Dummy nodes, indicated by alphabetic characters, are included to maintain a topologically planar network.

in the consumer prices of commodities, and thus a restrictive factor on the rate of economic growth.[10] Much of the new construction, as well as the upgrading of existing roadways, either focused directly on São Paulo or was in the form of extensions to roads which focused on São Paulo. As a consequence, the capital city has been connected with the major regional centers of the State, including Riberão Prêto and Bauru, by high capacity, low cost highways.

With respect to São Padlo's connections to the regional centers there are some bottlenecks that restrict the utilization of the high capacity highways, and they may be forcing the planners to follow a program of induced decision making in setting their priorities. For example, the Via Anghanguera has an existing capacity of about 22,000 short tons per day. Yet the maximum flow between Riberão Prêto and São Paulo, which to a large extent passes over the Via Anghanguera, is only slightly more than 12,000 short tons per day. As evident in Table 12-5, there are bottlenecks in the system that, in several instances, restrict the utilization of this high capacity

Table 12-5 Least Cost Flows in Riberão Prêto – São Paulo Sub-network

Arcs (i, j)	Cost c_{ij} (cruzeiros)	Upper Capacity u_{ij} (short tons)	Lower Capacity l_{ij} (short tons)	Flow* x_{ij} (short tons)
Riberão Prêto-Batatais	51	5498	0	1107
Riberão Prêto-A	74	2306	0	2306
Riberão Prêto-Porto Ferreira	96	8727	0	8727
Batatais-Altinopolis	59	1476	0	1107
Altinopolis-Mococa	95	1107	0	1107
Mococa-S.J. do Rio Pardo	66	536	0	0
Mococa-Casa Branca	64	1230	0	1107
S.J. do Rio Pardo-Casa Branco	54	1093	0	0
S.J. do Rio Pardo-Vargem Grande	63	1230	0	0
Casa Branca-Vargem Grande	48	1661	0	0
Casa Branca-Porto Ferreira	72	1661	0	0
Casa Branca-Mogi Mirim	108	1845	0	1107
Vargem Grande-S.J. da Boa Vista	50	1476	0	0
S.J. da Boa Vista-Mogi Mirim	80	7757	0	0
A-Araraquara	66	2306	0	0
A-São Carlos	72	2306	0	2306
Porto Ferreira-São Carlos	74	1661	0	0
Porto Ferreira-Rio Claro	73	8727	0	8727
Araraquara-São Carlos	53	10774	0	0
São Carlos-Rio Claro	93	9696	0	2306
Araras-Rio Claro	59	803	0	0
Rio Claro-Limeira	38	9696	0	2306
Rio Claro-São Pedro	79	1661	0	0
Rio Claro-Piracicaba	70	1084	0	0
Araras-Mogi Mirim	76	1661	0	1337
Araras-Limeira	42	8727	0	7390
Mogi Mirim-Itapira	36	5498	0	0
Mogi Mirim-Jaquariuna	47	8727	0	2444
Mogi Mirim-Limeira	79	1661	0	0
Itapira-Amparo	80	803	0	0
Amparo-Socorro	70	3665	0	0
Socorro-Bragança Paulista	76	1107	0	0
Amparo-Jundiaí	81	4887	0	0
Jaquariuna-Amparo	48	4887	0	0
Jaquariuna-Campinas	39	8727	0	2444
Limeira-Piracicaba	60	1868	0	0
Limeira-Americana	38	9696	0	9696
São Pedro-Piracicaba	75	2076	0	0
Piracicaba-Americana	47	6109	0	0
Piracicaba-Tiete	68	1661	0	0
Americana-Campinas	53	9696	0	9696
Campinas-Jundiaí	56	21816	0	12140
Campinas-Itu	75	1661	0	0
Capivari-Campinas	65	8727	0	0

Table 12-5 (continued)

Tiete–Capivari	61	1845	0	0
Tiete–Itu	66	8727	0	0
Capivari–Itu	85	1084	0	0
Jundiaí–São Paulo	71	21816	0	12140
Bragança Paulista–São Paulo	94	7757	0	0
Itu–São Paulo	101	8727	0	0

Total flow... 12,140 short tons per day
Total cost... CR$5,577,256

*All kilter numbers are zero.

Node Prices

Node	π	Node	π
Riberão Prêto	0	Itapira	413
Batatais	51	Socorro	472
Altinopolis	110	Amparo	542
Mococa	205	Jaquariuna	424
S. José do Rio Pardo	271	Limeira	343
Casa Branca	269	São Pedro	384
Vargem Grande	317	Piracicaba	375
S. José do Boa Vista	367	Americana	410
Node "A"	140	Campinas	463
Porto Ferreira	228	Capivari	504
Araraquara	206	Tiete	443
São Carlos	212	Jundiaí	519
Araras	301	Bragança Paulista	590
Rio Claro	305	Itu	509
Mogi Mirim	377	São Paulo	590

route and result in flows being forced onto higher cost paths. One major restriction is the connection between Limeira and Campinas which has a capacity of only 9,700 short tons per day. In the maximum flow solution, it is saturated and forces the diversion of flow from Riberão Prêto to São Paulo by way of relatively high cost routes, e.g., the path from Araras to Jaguariuna to Campinas. Although the highway plan of 1958 did not specify an extension of the Via Anghanguera at this time, the present plans of the DER call for the extension of the divided four-lane highway from Campinas to Limeira, and eventually to Riberão Prêto. The result of this decision to eliminate an obvious bottleneck will be a doubling of the maximum flow between Riberão Prêto and São Paulo and an additional reduction in costs (Table 12-8).

The maximum flow in the Bauru–Riberão Prêto sub-network is interesting. Not only is it considerably less than that in the other sub-networks, its costs per ton-kilometer are the highest, even though the distance between the

Table 12-6 Least Cost Flows in Bauru–São Paulo Sub-network

Arcs (i, j)	Cost c_{ij} (cruzeiros)	Upper Capacity u_{ij} (short tons)	Lower Capacity l_{ij} (short tons)	Flow* x_{ij} (short tons)
Bauru–Iacanga	79	1845	0	1845
Bauru–Jau	83	2076	0	2076
Bauru–S. Cruz do Rio Pardo	103	2306	0	2306
Bauru–São Manuel	84	8738	0	8727
Iacanga–Ibitinga	46	1845	0	1845
Ibitinga–Jau	113	957	0	0
Ibitinga–Araraquara	91	1845	0	1845
Jau–São Manuel	71	1537	0	0
Jau–Dois Corregos	58	2076	0	2076
Jau–D	44	6787	0	0
S. Cruz do Rio Pardo–E	35	6787	0	1235
S. Cruz do Rio Pardo–Avaré	127	1071	0	1071
E–Piraju	47	6109	0	1235
Piraju–Itai	68	2076	0	1235
Itai–Itapetininga	143	2076	0	1235
Avaré–Itai	71	1661	0	0
Avaré–São Manuel	83	1845	0	0
Avaré–Tatui	155	1061	0	1071
São Manuel–Teite	118	8727	0	8727
Dois Corregos–B	90	1661	0	1661
Dois Corregos–São Pedro	95	1868	0	415
D–Araraquara	52	6787	0	0
D–São Carlos	81	6787	0	0
Araraquara–São Carlos	53	10774	0	1845
São Carlos–B	51	10774	0	1845
B–Rio Claro	42	9696	0	3506
São Pedro–Rio Claro	79	1661	0	0
São Pedro–Piracicaba	75	2076	0	415
Rio Claro–Limeira	38	9696	0	3506
Rio Claro–Piracicaba	70	1084	0	0
Limeira–Americana	38	9696	0	3506
Piracicaba–Limeira	60	1868	0	0
Piracicaba–Americana	47	6109	0	415
Piracicaba–Tiete	68	1661	0	0
Americana–Campinas	53	9696	0	3921
Campinas–Itu	75	1661	0	0
Campinas–Jundiaí	56	21816	0	3921
Capivari–Campinas	65	8727	0	0
Capivari–Itu	85	1084	0	0
Tiete–Capivari	61	1845	0	0
Tiete–Itu	66	8727	0	8727
Tatui–Tiete	60	1661	0	0
Tatui–Sorocaba	79	2076	0	1071
Itapetininga–Tatui	69	1730	0	0

Table 12-6 (continued)

(i, j)	c_{ij}	u_{ij}	l_{ij}	x_{ij}
Itapetininga-Sorocaba	75	8727	0	1235
Sorocaba-Itu	60	8727	0	0
Sorocaba-São Roque	56	8727	0	2306
Itu-Jundiaí	54	8727	0	0
Itu-São Paulo	101	8727	0	8727
Jundiaí-São Paulo	71	21816	0	3921
São Roque-São Paulo	72	8727	0	2306

Total flow = 14,954 short tons per day
Total cost – CR$6,836,209

*All kilter numbers are zero.

Node prices

Node	π	Node	π
Bauru	0	São Pedro	316
Iacanga	79	Rio Claro	362
Ibitinga	125	Limeira	400
Jau	163	Piracicaba	391
S. Cruz do Rio Pardo	122	Americana	438
Node "E"	157	Campinas	491
Piraju	204	Capivari	512
Itai	272	Tiete	451
Avaré	256	Tatui	411
São Manuel	234	Itapetininga	415
Dois Corregos	221	Sorocaba	490
Node "D"	207	Itu	517
Araraquara	216	Jundiaí	547
São Carlos	269	São Roque	546
Node "B"	320	São Paulo	618

centers is less. Obviously, the construction program under the Plano de Ação has not resulted in the same improvement in transportation between these two regional centers as it has between them and São Paulo. This is somewhat surprising in view of the expressed desire of the State Government to provide infrastructure that will increase the attractiveness of the regional centers as locations for industry, which has tended in the past to concentrate in the São Paulo metropolitan area. It is virtually impossible for this objective to be achieved under a program that provides high capacity, low cost connections between the regional centers and São Paulo, but not between the regional centers themselves. Such a program only increases the attractiveness of the São Paulo metropolitan area as an industrial location, and at the expense of the regional centers.

Increasingly aware of the difficulties involved in establishing the regional centers as secondary targets for the factor movements of labor and capital that have focused on São

Table 12-7 Least Cost Flows in Bauru–Riberão Prêto Sub-network

Arcs (i, j)	Cost c_{ij} (cruzeiros)	Upper Capacity u_{ij} (short tons)	Lower Capacity l_{ij} (short tons)	Flow* x_{ij} (short tons)
Bauru-Pirajui	67	6787	0	1845
Bauru-Iacanga	79	1845	0	1845
Bauru-Jau	83	2076	0	2076
Pirajui-Iacanga	105	1147	0	0
Pirajui-Itabolis	101	1845	0	1845
Iacanga-Ibitinga	46	1845	0	1845
Jau-Dois Corregos	58	2076	0	0
Jau-D	44	6787	0	2076
Jau-Ibitinga	113	957	0	0
Dois Corregos-B	90	1661	0	0
D-Araraquara	52	6787	0	2076
D-São Carlos	81	6787	0	0
Ibitinga-Itapolis	59	820	0	0
Ibitinga-Araraquara	91	1845	0	1845
Itapolis-C	50	1845	0	1845
C-Jaboticabal	63	1845	0	1845
Araraquara-Matão	45	10774	0	1615
Araraquara-A	66	2306	0	2306
Matão-C	47	10774	0	0
Matão-Jaboticabal	57	6109	0	1615
Jaboticabal-Sertãozinho	51	5498	0	3460
B-São Carlos	51	10774	0	0
São Carlos-Porto Ferreira	74	1661	0	0
São Carlos-A	72	6787	0	0
São Carlos-Araraquara	53	10774	0	0
Porto Ferreira-Riberão Prêto	96	8727	0	0
A-Riberão Prêto	74	2306	0	2306
Sertãozinho-Riberão Prêto	38	5498	0	3460

Total flow = 5,766 short tons per day
Total cost – CR$2,084,079

*All kilter numbers are zero.

Node Prices

Node	π
Bauru	0
Pirajui	67
Iacanga	172
Jau	213
Dois Corrego	271
Node "D"	257

Table 12-7 (continued)

Node Prices	
Node	π
Ibitinga	218
Itapolis	277
Node "C"	348
Araraquara	309
Matão	354
Jaboticabal	411
Node "B"	361
São Carlos	338
Porto Ferreira	412
Node "A"	410
Sertãozinho	462
Riberão Prêto	500

Paulo, the State Government is concerned that the spatial interaction between the regional centers be improved. An indication of this concern are two proposals in the present plans of the DER to improve highway connections between Bauru and Riberão Prêto. The gravel road from Bauru to Jau will be paved, increasing its capacity from approximately 2,000 short tons per day to over 6,000. Also, the gravel road from São Carlos to Riberão Prêto will be upgraded by bituminous surfacing, increasing its capacity from 2,500 short tons per day to 5,500. The results of both projects will be to increase the maximum flow between the centers by over forty percent and to reduce substantially the average transportation costs (Table 12-8). Theoretically, these improvements should help create conditions that increase the attractiveness of the two centers as foci for capital investments, given the permissive role of transportation in the process of economic development. How-

Table 12-8 Highway Changes and Their Effect on Least Cost Flows

Sub-network	Flow (short tons)	Cost (cruzeiros)		
		Total	Per unit flow	Per ton-kilometer
I. Riberão Prêto–São Paulo				
A. Present network	12,140	5,577,256	459.41	1.32
B. Addition: four lane divided highway Campinas to Limeira	25,229	11,362,405	450.37	1.29
II. Bauru–São Paulo				
Present network	14,954	6,836,209	457.14	1.19
III. Bauru–Riberão Prêto				
A. Present network	5,766	2,084,079	361.44	1.50
B. Addition: paved highway Bauru to Jau	9,465	3,386,440	357.78	1.42
C. Addition: paved highway São Carlos to Riberão Prêto	9,799	3,356,930	342.58	1.40
IV. São Paulo–Bauru–Riberão Prêto				
A. Present network	25,158	11,653,437	463.21	1.23
B. Addition: paved highways Bauru to Jau and São Carlos to Riberão Prêto	25,158	11,296,907	448.34	1.09

ever, this may prove to be an unwarranted expectation.

As the sub-networks are not mutually exclusive sets, the proposed improvements in highway conditions between Bauru and Riberão Prêto involve arcs contained in the other sub-networks; the Bauru–Jau arc is in the Bauru–São Paulo sub-network and the São Carlos–Riberão Prêto arc is in the Riberão Prêto–São Paulo sub-network. Considering the two sub-networks jointly, with São Paulo being a common source node, we can consider the proposed highway improvements in terms of their effect on flows between São Paulo and the two regional centers.[11] From Table 12-8, it is apparent that the improvements, while they do not increase the flow between São Paulo and the regional centers, do affect the cost of the maximum flow. Indeed, the cost reductions are greater than they are between Bauru and Riberão Prêto. Thus, one consequence of the plan to improve the potential for spatial interaction between the two regional centers will be a greater reduction in the transport barrier between those centers and the growth pole of São Paulo. This should increase the locational advantages of São Paulo relative to the regional centers.

The advantages accruing to São Paulo as a result of highway improvements in the Bauru–Riberão Prêto sub-network do not mean necessarily that the proposed changes should be abandoned. Obviously, other benefits resulting from transportation improvement must be taken into account in determining the advisability of the construction program. However, the results do emphasize the necessity of considering improvements in a transportation linkage in terms of their system-wide impact and not just in terms of the two centers situated at their endpoints. In this regard, the determination of least cost flows in a capacitated network can be most instructive.

NOTES

1 A. O. Hirschman. *The Strategy of Economic Development.* New Haven: Yale University Press, 1958, Chapter 5.

2 H. L. Gauthier. "Transportation and the Growth of the São Paulo Economy." *Journal of Regional Science,* Vol. 8, No. 1, pp. 1–18.

3 L. Ford and D. Fulkerson. *Flows in Networks.* Princeton: Princeton University Press, Chapter 3.

4 For a detailed discussion of the labeling process, see Ford and Fulkerson, *op. cit.,* Chapter 1.

5 George Dantzig. *Linear Programming and Extensions.* Princeton: Princeton University Press, 1963, p. 404.

6 Jurandyr Pires Ferreira. "Teoria Racional das Tarifas." *Revista do DER,* Vol. XXIV, No. 87/88, December, 1963, pp. 45–68.

7 Renato de Sousa Nogueira. "Capacidade de Trafego das Estradas." *Revista do DER,* Vol. XVI, No. 58, March, 1950, pp. 116–122.

8 H. Gauthier. *op. cit.,* pp. 12–13.

9 This is accomplished by a minor modification in the out-of-kilter algorithm. To construct a feasible flow from x_s to x_t of a given value v that minimizes Equation (4), one adds a return flow arc t, s with $l_{ts} = u_{ts} = v$, and $c_{ts} = 0$ to get the problem in a circulation form. When $v = 1$ and for all arcs, other than t, s, $u_{ij} = 1$, $l_{ij} = 0$, and c_{ij} equals the line-haul cost between x_i and x_j, the algorithm yields the minimal spanning tree from x_s to x_t.

10 The Joint Brazil–United States Economic Development Commission. Brazilian Technical Studies, Washington: Institute of Inter-American Affairs, 1955, p. 265.

11 The problem of considering multiple sinks can be simplified by reducing the problem to the case of a single source and sink. See Ford and Fulkerson, *op. cit.,* pp. 15–17.

FURTHER READINGS TO PART THREE

Some general follow-up material on flows will be found in:

P. R. Gould and R. H. T. Smith, "Method in Commodity Flow Studies," *Australian Geographer,* vol. 8, 1962, pp. 73–77.

R. H. T. Smith, "Toward a Measure of Complementarity," *Economic Geography,* vol. 40, 1964, pp. 1–8.

E. L. Ullman, *American Commodity Flow,* Seattle: University of Washington Press, 1957.

Applications to manufacturing flows can begin with:

A. Pred, "Toward a Typology of Manufacturing Flows," *Geographical Review,* vol. 54, 1964, pp. 65–84.

G. P. F. Steed, "Commodity Flows and Interindustry Linkages of Northern Ireland's Manufacturing Industries," *Tijdschrift Voor Economische en sociale Geografie,* vol. 59, 1968, pp. 245–59.

The gravity model is extended in:

W. R. Black, "Substitution and Concentration: An Examination of the Distance Exponent in Gravity Model Commodity Flow Studies," *Discussion Paper,* no. 1, Indiana University, Department of Geography, 1971.

W. R. Black, "Interregional Commodity Flows: Some Experiments with the Gravity Model," *Journal of Regional Science,* vol. 12, no. 1, 1972, pp. 107–118.

and reviewed in:

G. A. P. Carrothers, "An Historical Review of the Gravity and Potential Concepts of Human Interaction," *Journal of the American Institute of Planners,* Spring 1956, pp. 94–102.

The regional analysis of flows can be found in:

J. N. H. Britton, *Regional Analysis and Economic Geography: A Case Study of Manufacturing in the Bristol Region,* London: Bell, 1967.

Z. Chojnicki, "The Structure of Economic Regions in Poland Analyzed by Commodity Flows," *Geographic Polonica,* vol. 1, 1961, pp. 213–230.

A. M. Hay and R. H. T. Smith, *Interregional Trade and Money Flows in Nigeria,* 1964, Ibadan: Oxford University Press, 1971.

R. Olsson, "Commodity Flows and Regional Interdependence," *Papers and Proceedings,* Regional Science Association, vol. 12, 1964, pp. 225–230.

W. S. Peters, "Measures of Regional Interchange," *Papers and Proceedings,* Regional Science Association, vol. 11, 1963, pp. 285–294.

Two further applications of linear programming are:

D. G. Dickason and J. O. Wheeler, "An Application of Linear Programming: The Case of Indian Wheat Transportation," *National Geographical Journal of India,* vol. 13, 1967, pp. 125–140.

R. L. Morrill and W. L. Garrison, "Projections of Interregional Patterns of

Trade in Wheat and Flow," *Economic Geography,* vol. 36, 1960, pp. 116–126.

Transaction flows are explicated in:

K. Deutsch, "Transaction Flows as Indicators of Political Cohesion" in P. E. Jacob and J. V. Toscana (eds.), *The Integration of Political Communities,* New York: Lippincott, 1964.

I. R. Savage and K. Deutsch, "A Statistical Model of the Gross Analysis of Transaction Flows," *Econometrica,* vol. 28, 1960, pp. 551–572.

Two topics mentioned before which should not be forgotten are:

(1) urban commodity flows:

M. Helvig, *Chicago's External Truck Movements: Spatial Interactions Between the Chicago Area and Its Hinterland,* Chicago: University of Chicago, Department of Geography, Research Paper No. 90, 1964.

Highway Reseach Board, *Urban Commodity Flow,* Special Report 120, 1970.

V. Johannessan, "Oslo's Goods Transport Survey," *Traffic Engineering and Control,* vol. 5, no. 11, 1964, pp. 646–648.

R. T. Wood, "Measuring Urban Freight in the Tri-state Region" in *The Urban Movement of Goods,* consultative group on transportation research, O.E.C.D., proceedings of the third Technology Assessment Review, 1970.

(2) Port hinterlands; samples are:

D. J. Patton, "General Cargo Hinterlands of New York, Philadelphia, Baltimore and New Orleans," *Annals* of the Association of American Geographers, vol. 48, 1958, pp. 536–555.

P. J. Rimmer, "Recent Changes in the Status of Seaports in the New Zealand Coastal Trade," *Economic Geography,* vol. 43, 1967, pp. 231–243.

Finally, this section has not dealt with a more holistic approach to flow analysis over time and space, since the studies are very lengthy. Two approaches to this are in part spin-offs from the Northwestern University approach:

B. J. L. Berry *et al., Essays on Commodity Flows and the Spatial Structure of the Indian Economy,* Chicago: University of Chicago, Department of Geography, Research Paper No. 111, 1966.

W. E. Reed, *Areal Interaction in India: Commodity Flows of the Bengal-Bihar Industrial Area,* Chicago: University of Chicago, Department of Geography, Research Paper No. 110, 1967.

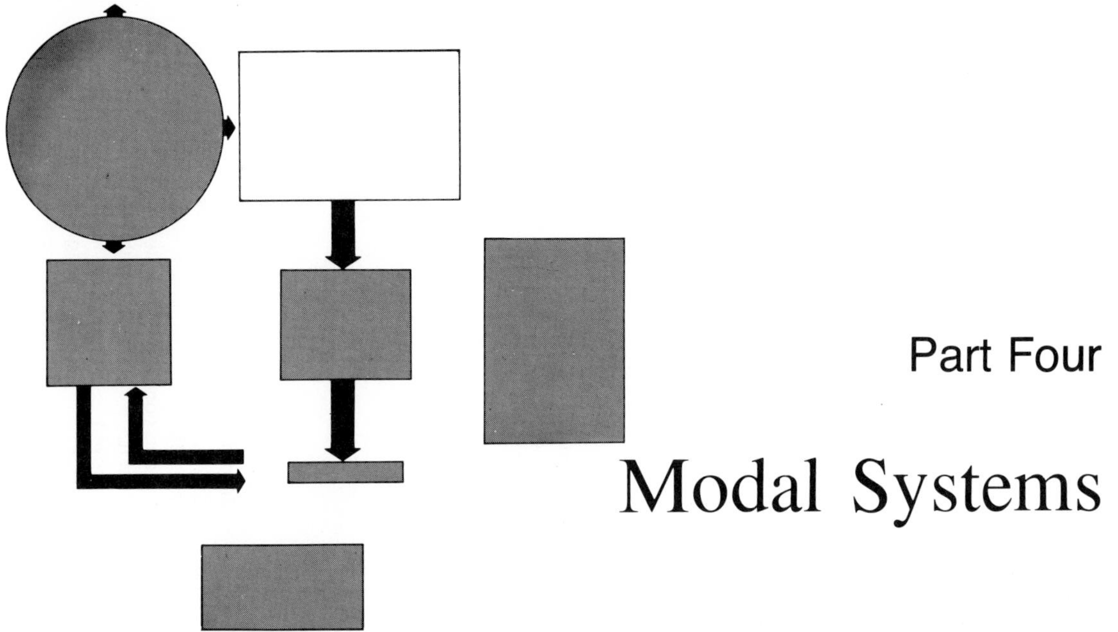

Part Four

Modal Systems

INTRODUCTION

If demand and supply exist, then movement takes place, spatially through a network on whose structure certain stocks or units of transport occur, that movement or intensity of usage being measurable by volume or flow (Part Three). We can now state that these relations and connections between areas are measurable also in terms of different *modes* of transport.

Each mode of transport—air, road, rail, waterway, pipeline—has its own distinctive characteristics, its own spatial relationships, and each plays, though often overlapping, a different role in the supply of transportation. Thus railways seem best suited to long-haul transportation of heavy commodities which are often of small value per unit load; trucking excels in door-to-door, specialized, less-than truckload traffic with emphasis on the shorter haul; air transport specializes in speed and in long-haul, high-value goods requiring quick delivery; inland waterway and ocean shipping have an advantage in hauling bulk goods of low value which can use slow transportation and are amenable to bulk handling and movement; pipelines can transport liquids, semiliquids, or, more recently, solids, in a one-way flow at reasonable speed and in a continuous stream (see table "Modal Systems:

Modal Systems: Comparative Characteristics

Mode	Costs	Unit cost mile (rail = 1.0)	Distance	Rates	Characteristic goods	Distinctions	Drawbacks
Railroad	Capital intensive; Large initial investment (including right of way); Profitability rests on intensity of use: 350,000 to 500,000 tons/mile/year is operational margin; terminal costs high	1.0	Increasing effectiveness with length of haul; large shipments cheaper by long or short haul	Subject to class rates, freight rate territories in-transit rates, etc.	Minerals; unprocessed agricultural products; building materials; chemicals; Passenger traffic minor*	Large volumes of bulk goods in comparatively short time at low costs	Cost and time of assembling units
Waterways	Investment low, especially where natural waterways utilized; terminal and handling costs several times line-haul costs	0.29	Increasing effectiveness with length of haul		Marine: semifinished and finished products; inland: bulk raw goods—coke, coal, oil, grain, sand, gravel, cement; passenger traffic negligible	Low freight rates, slow speed, especially of goods carriage	Slow speed
Motor transport	Fixed costs negligible, operate on small margins—operating costs high; vehicle turnover high	4.5	Short hauls, less costly than rail; wide areal coverage	Rail acts as price leader	Perishable goods, lumber; Passenger traffic important	Light loads, short distances, short time; flexible and convenient; improved service; Minimizes distribution costs	Inadequate capacity for moving heavy volumes, bulk materials; high costs of long hauls; high vehicle operating costs

Air transport	Fixed costs low; investment in stock very high; terminal, takeoff costs high	16.3	Long hauls; economy with distance	Rates set by national and international regulations	Passenger traffic dominant; perishable, lightweight, high-value goods	Speed	Very high costs
Pipelines	Fixed costs high; large economies through diameter of pipe; costs increase almost directly with distance; viscosity adds costs	0.21	Long haul in bulk		Crude oil and petroleum products in large volume; natural gas; some solids	Bulk movement of liquids	Restricted commodity use; regular flow and demand needed; large market

*In Europe, passenger revenues usually exceed freight revenues.

Source: M. M. Eliot Hurst (1972), p. 290.

Comparative Characteristics). There is overlap or competition between the modes, and technical change is increasing this tendency.

When we come to compare these different modes of transport, one of the problems is to find a common denominator. *Ton miles hauled* literally assesses movement in terms of one ton moved one mile; this measurement tends to overemphasize those modes carrying heavy goods and those moving long distances. An alternative procedure is to measure transportation by the revenues generated, which in turn tends to emphasize high-value goods and high-value charges or rates. The table "U.S. Domestic Transportation, Relative Modal Shares" compares these measures for U.S. domestic traffic. These relative shares, of course, have not been constant over time; railways were the dominant mode of transport in the United States in the early twentieth century and even up to 1945 hauled 60 percent of the total U.S. ton mileage. While at present in the United States all modes haul more ton miles in total than they did in 1945, the relative shares have changed, and most of the increase in ton mileage has gone to the new modes of transportation, particularly to trucking.

This modal pattern is an example from a highly developed Western economy; other examples are rather different. Western Europe shows a smaller relative drop in the percentage of ton miles and passenger miles moved by rail and a very limited dependence on air travel. These differences arise from different standards of living, population densities, and differing conceptions of distance. The planned socialist economies, like that of the Soviet Union, place a much stronger emphasis on railroads for both passenger and freight traffic; the Soviet railroad system carries over 70 percent of intercity freight. Japan, another advanced economy but with different developmental characteristics, is also more strongly rail-oriented, carrying over 50 percent of the freight ton miles. Since it has an island situation, water transport between the islands plays an important role, and between 30 and 40 percent of the ton miles of frieght are moved by coastal shipping. Only recently has Japan launched a road building program or the Soviet Union a road or air program.

Like these two examples, countries emerging from peasant/subsistent economies tend to be rail-oriented. India, Pakistan, and China, for instance, depend on rail movements, backed up by inland waterways. But developing

U.S. Domestic Transportation, Relative Modal Shares

	% ton miles	% revenue
Railroad	42.0	42.0
Truck	25.0	40.0
Pipeline	17.0	3.5
Inland water	15.9	1.5
Air	0.1	13.0

Source: Farris and McElhiney (1967), p. 2.

countries with lower population densities rely more heavily on highways, with air routes and pipelines sometimes playing significant roles. In Columbia, for example, 57 percent of freight traffic in 1960 was carried by truck, 17 percent by rail, and 16 percent by inland rivers, and 7 percent by coastal shipping and pipelines, a response to very different spatial and developmental conditions.

RAILROADS

In market-exchange economies, the history of railroad development is in large part a history of efforts to raise enough capital. In other words, this mode is capital intensive. And no wonder: it has to provide not only actual rolling stock but also the right of way, which motor carriers do only indirectly and airlines not at all. The profitability of this investment depends on intensity of use; so, to be economically viable, a railroad requires sufficient traffic moving over a given route to permit economy of scale operations. In Europe the figure is usually 350,000 tons per mile per year to justify a section of railway economically; in North America a figure of about 400,000 tons per mile per year is used to justify the building of a new rail link. These are economic conditions, and usually there may be alternative social justifications. About 37 percent of U.S. railway mileage cannot be justified on the economic grounds noted above, since it carries less than 1,000 tons per mile per day. About 50 percent of the U.S. rail freight traffic is carried on only 10 percent of the network, averaging 39,000 tons per day per mile, mainly in two broad bands of movement: (1) west to east across the industrial belt of the United States and (2) a parallel set from the east Kentucky coalfields to the East and Northeast. Potential traffic may also justify construction, though if large movements were very distant, it might be practical to begin with some other mode.

We assume in North America and Western Europe that when we look at a world map of railways, we have in existence an extensive interacting system of movement. However, there are thirty-nine different railway track gauges in use today, ranging from 1 foot 3 inches to 5 feet 6 inches, and thirteen of these gauges are the principal track gauges in one or more countries. These must be considered as an impediment to movement where a number of different gauges are involved. India has about fifty-two break of gauge points; Australia has three dominant gauge widths. The circumstances that have led to such gauge choices are sometimes bizarre. W. R. Siddal gives this account of one situation: "choice of gauge was sometimes made by a committee . . . and in more than one case the decision of the committee was a compromise . . . in South Africa the first railroad was built to a gauge of 4′8½″, and a later line was built at 2′6″. The government took over the railroads in 1873 and opened the question of a proper gauge, whereupon a Parliamentary Committee compromised on 3′6″!" [p. 43]*

Another factor of importance to railways is distance. Railways become

*"Railroad Gauges and Spatial Interaction," *Geographical Review*, vol. 59, 1969, pp. 29–57.

increasingly efficient with increasing length of haul, as the high costs of terminal operations are spread over a greater number of ton miles. Assuming a five-ton shipment, the operating costs for Nigerian railways are: †

for 10 miles—32 cents per mile
50 miles—8 cents per mile
500 miles—3 cents per mile

For a larger shipment the cost is lower for both long and short hauls. Railways of course do not operate in isolation, and they meet competition in many areas, particularly for heavy volumes of industrial raw materials. As the table "Modal Systems" indicates, the unit cost of movement by pipeline and waterway can be one-fifth to one-third the cost of moving comparable volumes by rail, although comparable figures for road transport would be four to five times more costly, and by air freight about sixteen times as great.

This simple picture of railroad freight rates is disturbed by the fact that rail rates do not have a straight-line relationship to distance but are curvilinear because of the effects of terminal and handling costs which are distributed over greater and greater hauls. Further distortions can be illustrated by the variability of U.S. rail freight rates, which is caused by five factors.

1 The existence of *freight rate territories.* Rates varied until recently among five regions, with the Eastern price set at 100, the Southern at 139, the Western trunk at 147, the Southwestern at 175, and the Mountain Pacific at 191. Since this practice was branded discriminatory (though in fact it reflected the varying regional intensity of traffic), the differentials were eventually eliminated.

2 *Rate-group principle.* Rates are grouped in steps. Nodes along each route are divided into groups, all the points in the same group having the same rate over broad zones, rising in steps at the zone boundaries.

3 *Class rates.* The Interstate Commerce Commission (ICC) authorizes rates applicable to items moving in small quantities; these rates vary for thirty classes. A commodity in class 400 has four times the base rate (100), while the rate for class 13 would be 13 percent of the base rate.

4 *Commodity rates.* These are rates allowed by the ICC for goods moving in large quantities between specific origins and destinations. These are the commonly used rates for the bulk of freight.

5 *In-transit rates.* These are special-privilege rates granted by the ICC which allow goods to travel at an initial raw freight rate, despite intermediate processing. Thus rates are highly complex systems of prices based on both costs and demand.

At one time railways were the predominant long-haulage carrier, but more recently there has been an adjustment to the traffic to which they are most suited, so that they are now carriers of such items as unprocessed agricultural products, building materials, and chemicals. In the United States 55 percent of rail traffic is in the haulage of minerals; 65 percent in Eastern

† Stanford Research Institute, "The Economic Coordination of Transport Development in Nigeria" (1961), p. 91.

Europe consists of fuel, ores, and metals, and 70 percent in the Soviet Union, with the addition of lumber. Conversely there has been a decline in certain types of traffic that formerly moved by rail. Perishable goods are now sent largely by truck, crude petroleum by pipeline, and coal has declined with a shift toward new energy sources. Passenger traffic forms only a small portion of total revenue in North America, and it may have a negative effect. Railways find it difficult to compete for the 9 percent of passengers in the United States who do not travel between nodes by automobile with buses and aircraft.‡ Efforts to compete in the freight area are being carried out with the unitized train, piggyback services, and faster schedules. Unit trains are entire trains devoted to one commodity from one node to another, which can offer rate reductions and speedy service.§ Speed and reliability are important, yet in normal train operations, average speeds can be reduced to 15 to 20 miles per hour because of terminal operations.

Briefly, the advantages of railroads lie in their capacity to carry large volumes of heavy items in comparatively short time at low cost; drawbacks include assembly, and terminal and time costs. The unit train, *pregnant whale, high cube, Big John* and *trilevel rack* are ways of overcoming these difficulties.‖ Railways seem better for long hauls (average haul length is 400 miles in the United States, 75 to 150 miles in Western Europe) than for short hauls.

In the following selection, P. J. Schwind examines one aspect of these changes in railroad operations: the impact on spatial patterns of rail traffic flows of "piggyback" or "trailer-on-flatcar" (TOFC) operations.

‡ One effort to try and counteract this negative role of railroad passengers is the recently constituted quasi-public AMTRAK organization in the United States.

§ The Pennsylvania Railroad can haul coal in unit trains from Clearfield to New Jersey for $2.88 a ton, as against $4.38 by regular freight services.

‖ These are various kinds of large-capacity freight cars. For example, the *pregnant whale* is a supertanker with 30,000-gallon capacity, compared with the regular 8,000-gallon tanker.

Selection 13

The Geography of Railroad Piggyback Operations

P. J. Schwind

Railroad piggyback operations are producing some identifiable effects on the spatial pattern of traffic flows between areas in North America. These effects are due to the particular nature of piggyback operations in comparison to those of regular railroad freight service and intercity highway trucking, all of which are engaged in the line haul movement of goods. Piggyback operations are also affecting patterns of interaction within cities as well as between cities. Occasional manifestations of piggyback operations can be seen in features of the cultural landscape, particularly in urban areas. Piggyback service also brings with it

Traffic Quarterly, vol. 21, 1967, pp. 237–248. Reprinted by permission of the author, editor, and the Eno Foundation.

its own pattern of intangible spatial features such as rate structures and delivery times.

The term "TOFC" refers to the specialized concept of rail-motor carrier coordination involved in placing motor truck trailers on railroad flatcars for the line haul movement, with pickup and delivery of the trailer being performed "on the ground" by truck tractor units. Loading and unloading of standard wheeled trailers is performed by driving the trailers up onto the flatcars by means of a ramp, or by lifting the trailers directly on and off by means of a crane straddling both the track and the adjacent driveway. The more popular expression, "piggyback," is therefore imprecise in that it can denote other transport operations involving a change of transportation medium without transfer of lading, in which "the movement unit of one form of transport is placed upon the movement unit of another form."[1] Other examples of "piggyback" operations would be railroad car or automobile ferries, or the movement of loaded truck trailers across the ocean in ships, although this latter operation is being popularized as "fishyback." [Here] the terms "piggyback" and "TOFC" will be used interchangeably, but only in the stricter sense of the definition of trailer-on-flatcar. Also to be understood under the definition of piggyback are container-on-flatcar (COFC) operations, in which demountable trailer bodies are loaded on flatcars without their wheel carriages, or "bogies."

Several broad hypotheses relating to the geographic implications of piggyback operations may be formulated. First, piggyback route networks (as subsystems of railroad networks) reflect, and contribute to, a general increase in mutual accessibility of major urban centers. If connections (measured by road quality, speed of truck and rail service, etc.) among smaller towns remain unchanged, these smaller settlements may be said to suffer a decline in accessibility, relative to that of large cities. The pattern of the Federal Interstate Highway System, in comparison to the pattern of the previous federal highways, is a clear example of improved connections between metropolitan areas with smaller centers being bypassed. Piggyback routes involve similar changes in accessibility and connectivity within the national rail net.

The second hypothesis follows closely from the first: that piggyback traffic flows tend to be more highly concentrated or channelized over high-capacity trunk routes between major points of traffic generation than is the case for the aggregate of all railroad traffic. Here again, piggyback traffic flow patterns may not be unique, but representative of larger trends: the Interstate Highway System may handle 20 percent of the nation's highway traffic over one percent of the highway route mileage. A third hypothesis is that the spatial pattern of piggyback rates reflects the fact that piggyback operations lie between rail carload and highway truck operations in line haul efficiency per ton/mile of the carrying unit.

The fourth general hypothesis relates to the distribution of goods and the general pattern of land use within urban areas. Like truck operations, piggyback pickup and delivery operations can provide essentially ubiquitous coverage of a metropolitan area, limited only by time/cost distance from the ramp location. This situation tends to free shippers from rail line locations, just as truck operations have done, and requires piggyback ramps in turn to be located with as good access as possible to concentrations of shippers, with the constraint that a piggyback ramp itself must be located on a railroad line. The efficiency and flexibility of piggyback service, relative to railroad car operation, in handling terminal area distribution of small freight shipments should also cause changes in the pattern of rail switching facilities and operations. Such changes would include a decline in car movements to individual industrial plants and warehouses, with abandonment of some private switching tracks; rail movements within cities would become increasingly concentrated on bulk commodity shipments to large industries, and on large-scale car interchange movements. Since piggyback operations are directly competitive with intercity highway trucking, yet make use of local cartage trucking for short haul pickup and delivery, it is to be expected that short-haul truck traffic will increase relative to long-haul intercity truck traffic.

A brief outline of the history and present regulatory and institutional organization of piggyback operations can be found in a previous article by the author.[2] Piggyback traffic has increased very rapidly between 1954 and the present (1966). Its average annual growth rate of 10 to 15 percent contrasts sharply with the net decline in total rail carloadings since 1955. The great excitement in the railroad industry about piggyback operations (along with auto-rack hauling of automobiles and innovations in bulk commodity hauling such as the unit train) is due to this rapid growth rate, and not so much to the percentage of piggyback carloadings to total carloadings (only 3.5 percent in 1965). There is wide variance in the projections of the continued growth rate of piggyback traffic and in the estimates of the eventual place that TOFC operations will assume in the total transportation mix of rail and motor carriage. Perhaps 10 to 15 percent of all intercity freight movement could be handled profitably by piggyback.[3] This percentage would clearly be much higher for the movement of perishable foodstuffs, manufactures, miscellaneous parcel freight, and freight forwarder shipments, commodities particularly suited to piggyback movement in trailerloads.

TOFC ROUTE PATTERNS

Piggyback operations cover a substantial part of the rail trunk line route mileage and reach most of the major cities of the United States. Container-van shipments can also move without break-of-bulk between inland United States points and many foreign points. Fig. 13-1, "Piggyback Routes to and from Chicago," shows only the major conceivable piggyback rail routes from Chicago. This fact should be borne in mind in comparing Fig. 13-1 with maps showing the total national rail and authorized interstate highway networks. Such maps are widely reproduced, for example in the transportation text by Norton.[4] Chicago has direct single-line access, via the eighteen trunk line railroads which reach it, to 662 piggyback ramps or 45 percent of the 1456 piggyback ramps of the 65 railroads originating TOFC traffic. Utilizing connecting railroads, TOFC traffic originating in Chicago can reach virtually every TOFC ramp point in the United States.

If the proportion of all rail routes over which piggyback traffic is operated into certain gateway cities (Chicago, Cincinnati, Kansas City, Minneapolis–St. Paul, Omaha, and St. Louis) is any indication, TOFC traffic may move over as much as 90 percent of United States railroad route mileage. The essential difference between the total rail network and the pattern of piggyback routes is that the rail portion of piggyback routes is almost entirely limited to main lines and some secondary lines, and does not extend over the finer-grained network of short branch lines and spurs. In its predominantly arterial nature, the piggyback route network resembles the Interstate Highway System more than the total rail net.

The ultimate distribution of piggyback traffic to and from a multitude of points is achieved by motor truck. These points include not only all conceivable origins and destinations within the terminal districts of large cities,[5] but also a large number of smaller towns which are reached, in piggyback service, by highway from a neighboring city which

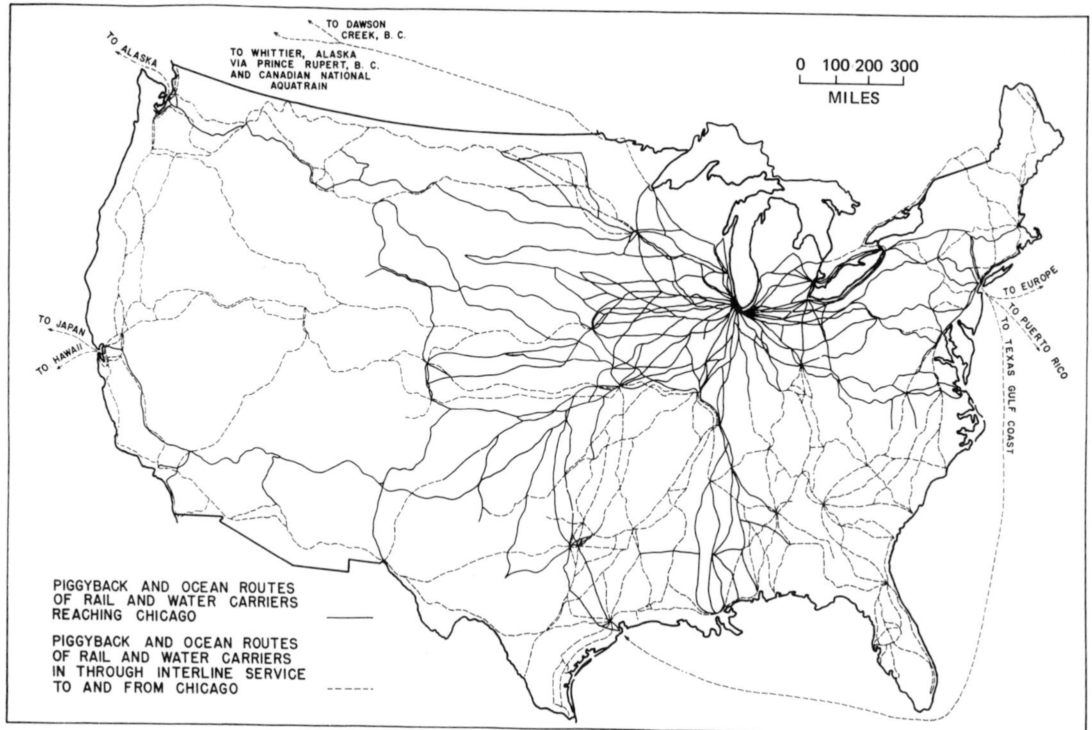

Fig. 13-1 Piggyback routes to and from Chicago.

is a "piggyback railhead" or ramp location. In contrast to the total number of places accessible to piggyback operations by highway service, the number of piggyback ramp points is limited to those locations where volume of traffic warrants the construction and operation of ramp facilities. Such locations are generally metropolitan areas and other larger urban places. Of the 219 Standard Metropolitan Statistical Areas defined in 1963 by the Bureau of the Census, 195 have one or more piggyback ramps, and the remainder (almost all of which are within highly urbanized regions) are easily served by highway from nearby ramp points. Similarly, forty-three of the state capitals within the continental United States have direct piggyback service; none of the remaining five capitals are SMSA's. The overall pattern of piggyback routes and points, then, is one of highly arterial routes with a restricted number of points.

An analysis using several of Kansky's indices of network connectivity[6] suggests, rather inconclusively, that total rail networks have higher degrees of connectivity than piggyback route networks (which are largely subsystems of total rail networks), but that individual piggyback train operations along a path have greater connectivity (or less network friction) than regular rail freight operations along the same path, by necessitating fewer stops for yard handling and train service between major points on line.

An issue not touched upon in the analysis of relative connectivity of transport networks is the nature or quality of the operation which takes place over the networks. The quality of the operations of various modes of transportation bears as directly upon interaction among points and regions as does the physical network pattern. When time-cost and/or money-cost (transferability) of overcoming space is reduced, the potential for interaction—the demand for transportation—is correspondingly increased.[7] The "quality" of a transportation operation, in the sense intended here, is therefore a function primarily of the time-efficiency (speed) of line haul and terminal operations, and likewise of the cost-efficiency of these movements.

Figs. 13-2 and 13-3 are generalized representations, in the format of the rail and truck delivery time maps in the transportation section of the *Atlas of Illinois Resources*,[8] of the point-to-point running times from Chicago of rail freight and piggyback operations. Fig. 13-4 shows the approximate areas to which piggyback operations have faster running times from Chicago than the regular freight train operations. The running times used in the preparation of Fig. 13-2 are taken from various railroad freight schedules and are the fastest available rail times, in hours, from Chicago to each of more than 100 points. The TOFC running times mapped in Fig. 13-3, like the regular freight times in Fig. 13-2, are taken directly from railroad schedules and include no allowance for terminal area operations. Loading and unloading of piggyback trailers on and off flatcars normally take about two hours before and after actual train departure or arrival. Additional time must also be al-

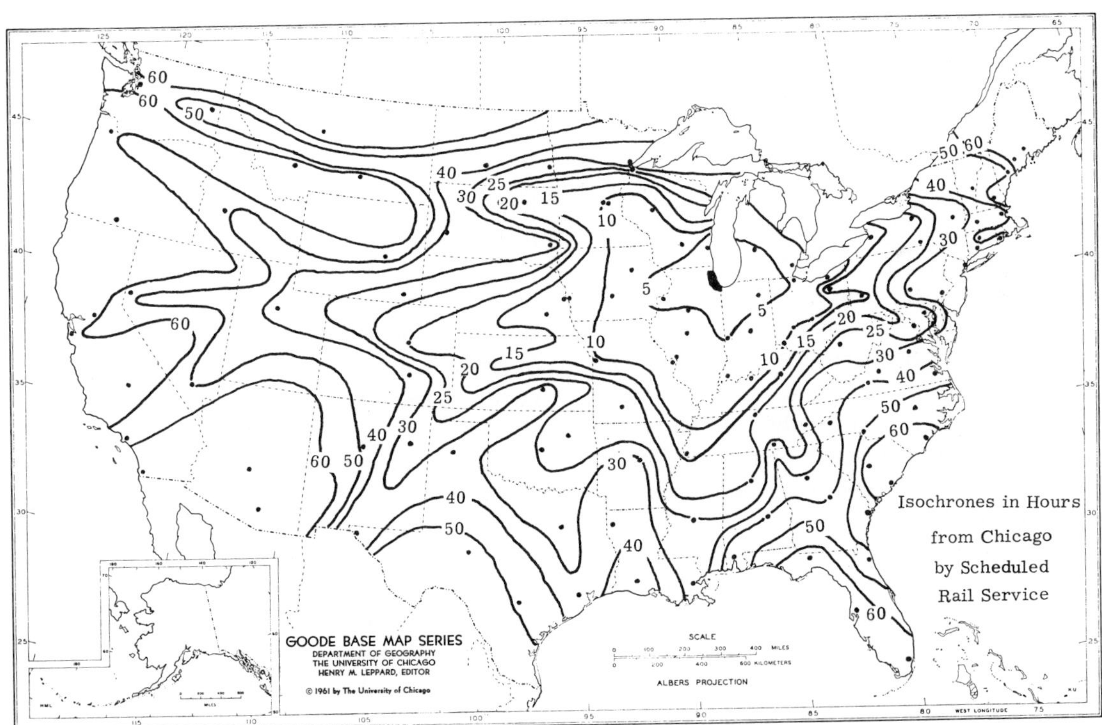

Fig. 13-2 Rail freight running time from Chicago.

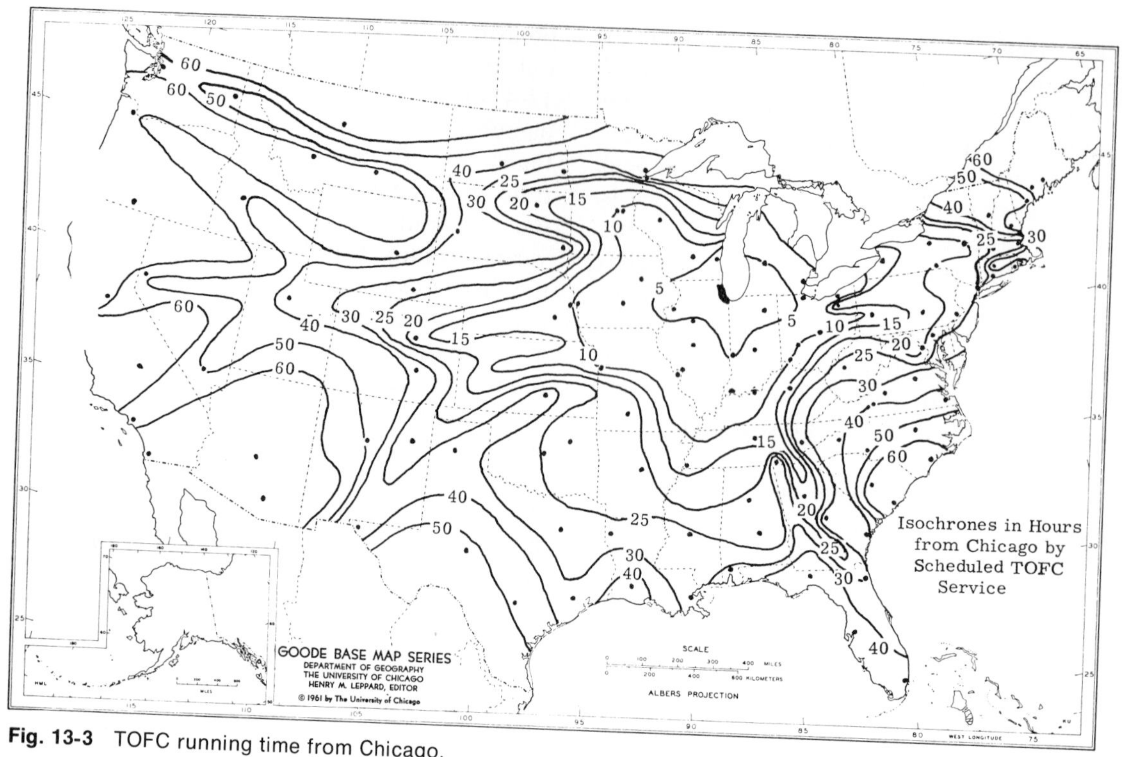

Fig. 13-3 TOFC running time from Chicago.

lowed for the local cartage operation, i.e., pickup and delivery of trailers. On the basis of point-to-point running times, piggyback service is no faster than rail fast-freight service from Chicago to many parts of the United States, as can be seen by comparing isochrones in Figs. 13-2 and 13-3. Identical TOFC and regular fast-freight running times occur when both piggyback and carload traffic are handled in the same trains, as is the case on most railroads. The special high-speed all-TOFC trains of a few railroads result, however, in certain areas of reduced space/time friction, or "TOFC time advantage," from Chicago (Fig. 13-4). The areas of TOFC time advantage are actually a series of disjoint anomalous points produced where the fast all-TOFC trains stop. This pattern, in relation to the bypassed intermediate areas receiving slower service, is difficult to interpolate cartographically.

Each part of the country for which piggyback operations provide faster-than-carload service to or from Chicago is either a region of sizeable markets for Chicago-manufactured goods, a region which produces many goods sold in Chicago, or a region providing large quantities of perishable foodstuffs for the Chicago market. (High-value package freight and perishables are the commodity groups for which high-speed, low-damage piggyback handling is most suitable.) Maps of rail and piggyback running times from Chicago therefore support the notion that piggyback service improves the "quality of connectivity" and reduces "space-time friction" between major urban centers within important production or market regions. Thus we can identify the national piggyback route network as an extensive, rather than intensive, arterial network with a particularly channelized transportation operation in certain sectors of high transportation demand.

TOFC TRAFFIC FLOWS

The predominant traffic pattern of TOFC operations is the haulage of high-value manufactured goods, perishable foods (meat, fresh fruits and vegetables, and frozen foods), and miscellaneous package freight shipments of freight forwarders and shipper associations. Shippers of these commodities demand rapid, damage-free handling of their goods in transit, both during the line haul movement and in terminal area pickup and delivery. The quick service, relatively low rates, flexibility of trailer equipment ownership, and convenience of TOFC pickup and delivery operations are particularly suitable to the "total distribution" transportation requirements of many freight forwarders and consolidators and other large shippers. Information on the spatial pattern and balance of TOFC flows indicates that hauls in TOFC traffic tend to be long, perhaps averaging as much as 1,000–1,500 miles for eastbound movements of meat and perishables and westbound movements of empty refrigerated trailers. These flows move, in the aggregate, with a minimum of circuity and are highly concentrated between a small number of points. In analyzing TOFC traffic data for one railroad, it was discovered that there were

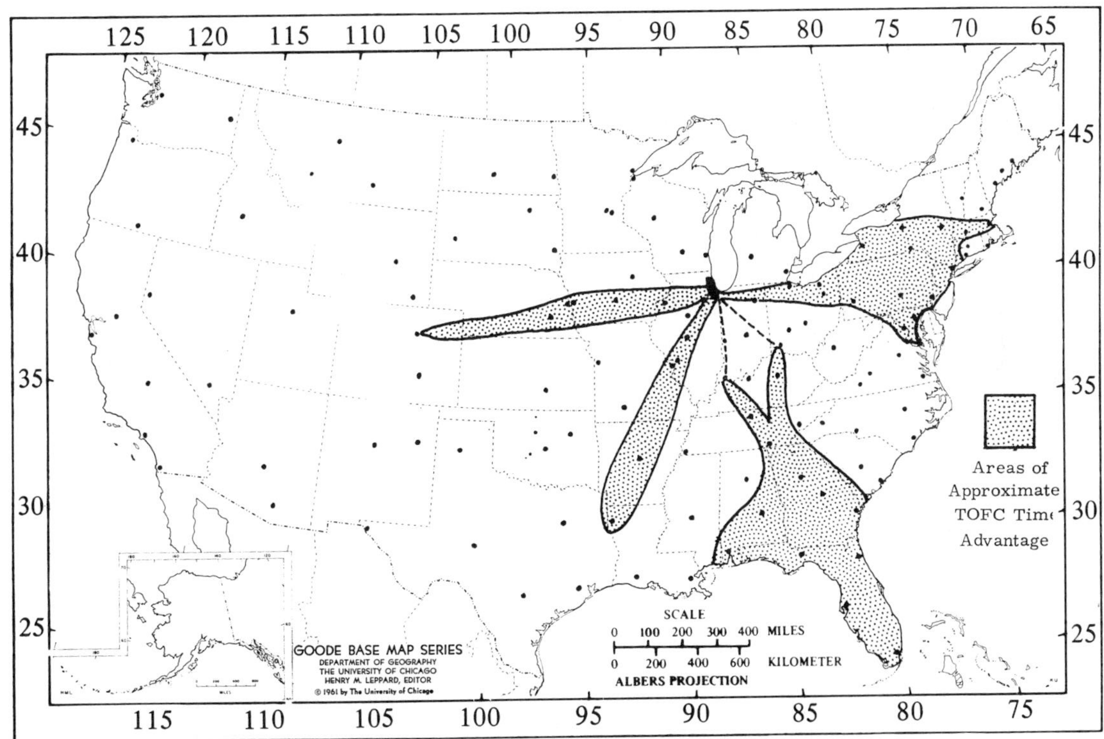

Fig. 13-4 Approximate areas of TOFC time advantage over regular rail freight service from Chicago.

few cases of interaction by TOFC between points less than 300 miles apart, with a slight increase in the ratio of actual to potential traffic over increasing distance (to 1,000 miles). This trend is, however, of little predictive value for national aggregate TOFC traffic patterns.

TOFC COST AND EFFICIENCY FACTORS

Piggyback operations combine some of the cost and service advantages of both carload freight and motor truck operations. Piggyback trailers in trains achieve a much greater line haul economy of operation per trailer than do trailers driven over the highways. The primary reason for the greater line haul economy of piggyback operations is their labor requirement: a train with one hundred or more piggyback trailers requires a train crew of as few as five men, while highway operation would require at least 100 drivers to move the same volume of traffic. Piggyback movements can avoid most of the costly and time-consuming rail terminal operations, providing pickup and delivery service nearly the equal of motor freight service in speed, economy, and flexibility, to both urban locations and points along lightly trafficked railroad branch lines receiving slow, infrequent carload service. Piggyback terminal operations are somewhat less efficient than intercity motor freight operations since pickup and delivery is not an integral movement with the line haul; rather, this service is performed by a common carrier or private local cartage operator. In addition,

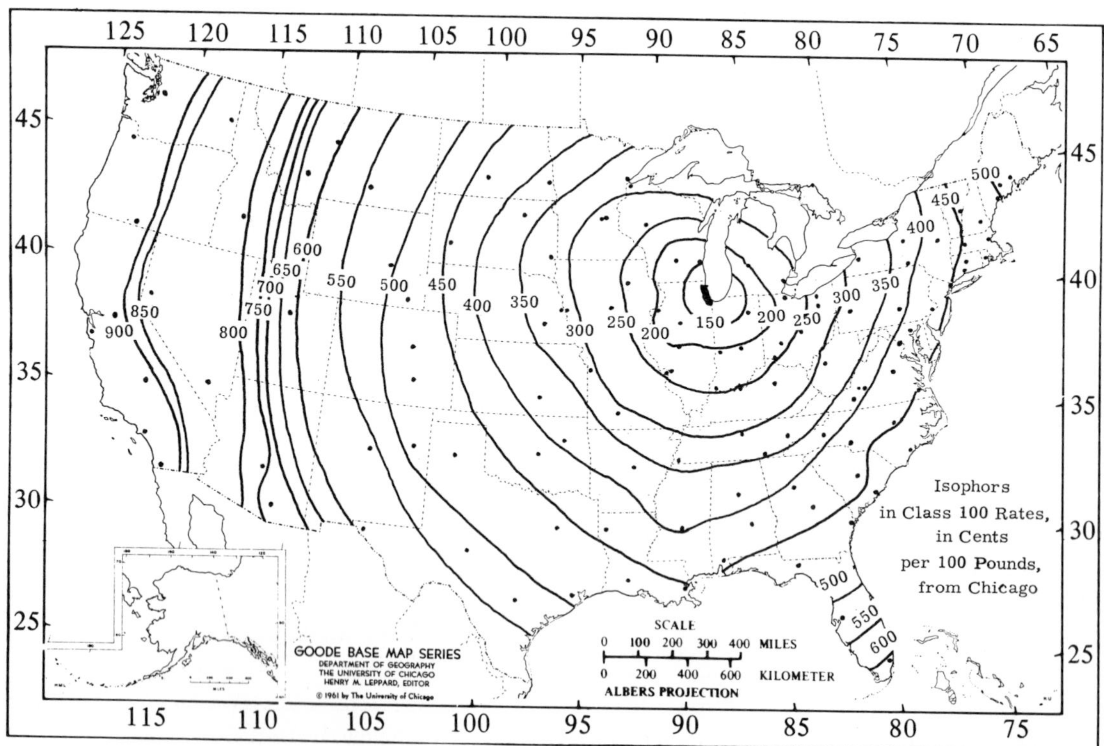

Fig. 13-5 Rail carload rates from Chicago.

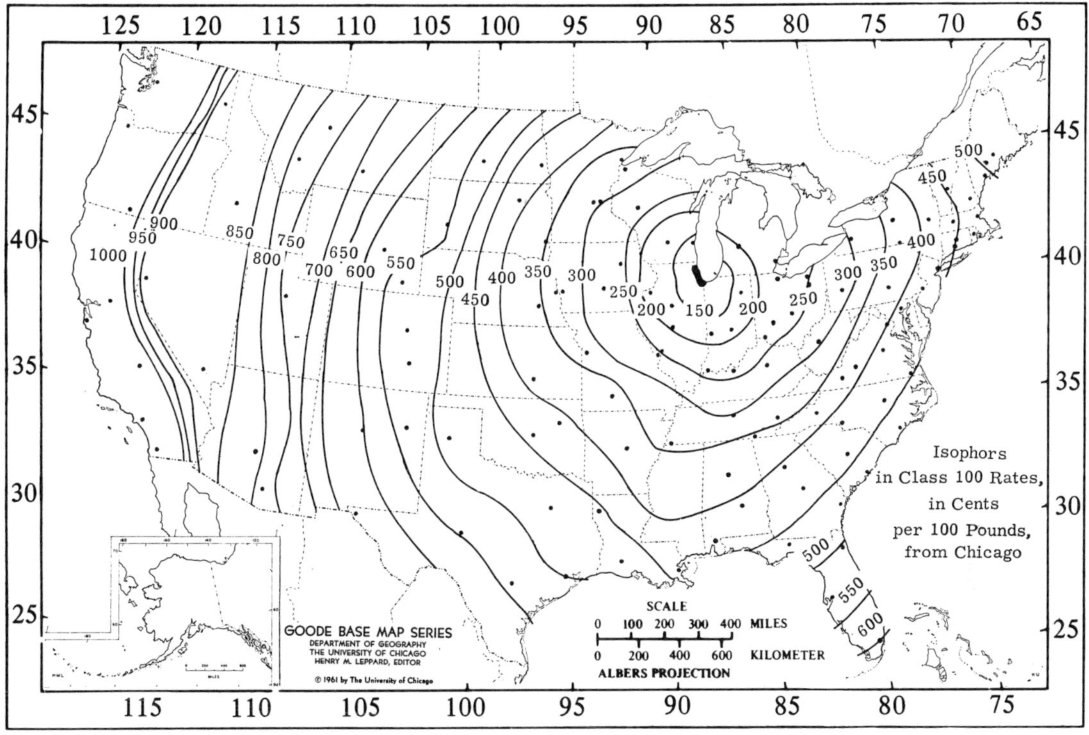

Fig. 13-6 Motor carrier trailerload rates from Chicago.

cost and time delays are incurred in the loading and unloading of trailers on and off flatcars, and by the necessity for the traffic to accumulate for a trainload departing at a fixed time of day.

Although TOFC service on long hauls achieves somewhat greater efficiency in equipment and labor utilization than truck movement, it is not as efficient in the long-haul transport of goods as boxcar movement would be. TOFC equipment wastes payload space and capacity relative to boxcar equipment; has a higher tare (dead weight)-to-payload ratio; and incurs somewhat higher operating costs per train weight to maintain high running speeds. Yet piggyback operations constitute an improvement in efficiency over boxcar movement in the sense that total transfer time from origin to destination is reduced, transfers of lading are reduced, and terminal turnaround time of equipment is reduced. Due to the costs of both TOFC and rail terminal operations, piggyback service becomes advantageous to the shipper only when the line haul economies of rail movement over long distances can be expressed. It is, in fact, questionable whether any form of rail or piggyback freight movement can compete efficiently against trucks for under-300-mile trips.[9]

The spatial structures of rail carload, motor carrier, and TOFC Class 100 rates from Chicago have been mapped (in Figs. 13-5, 13-6, and 13-7) using a very rough version of Alexander's technique of interpolated isophors, where isophors are "constructed as lines connecting the innermost points of equal freight

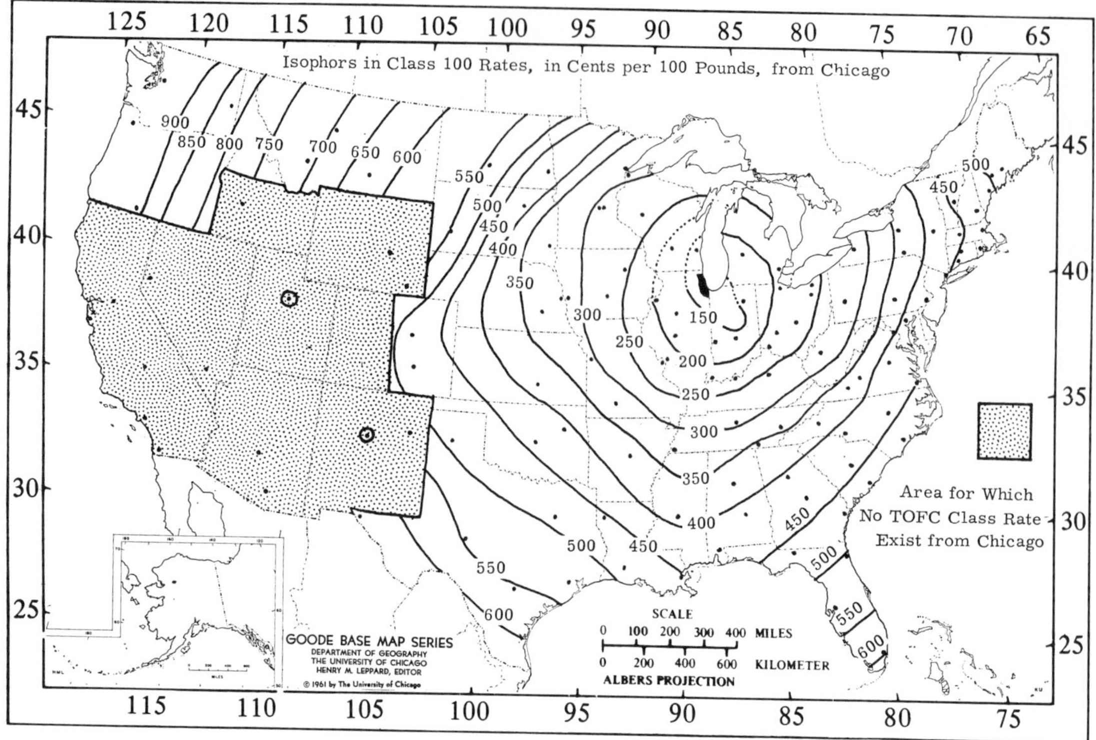

Fig. 13-7 TOFC Plan II trailerload rates from Chicago.

rates."[10] The marked variations of rates with distance and direction, discovered by Alexander *et al.* for Wisconsin, did not show up well in the present series of maps, undoubtedly because of the paucity of points to which rates were determined, and the necessarily great liberties that were taken in interpolating the isophors—of rounded values such as 150, 200, etc.—between points with specific rates. No attempt has been made in the preparation of the rate maps to interpolate isophors to conform to rail lines and highways as transportation arteries. Class 100 rates were chosen for their generality (as opposed to commodity rates), for their relative ease of determination, and because the Class 100 rate to any point is the base 100 on which any other rates (higher or lower) are determined as a percentage of the Class 100 rate.[11] However, it is doubtful whether the class rate structure has any great significance in the spatial organization of economic activity, since in all probability almost the entirety of rail carload freight (proportions are unknown for motor freight and piggyback operations) moves under specific commodity rates, and not class rates.[12]

If class rates reflected cost of service accurately, we might expect to see three concentric zones of rate advantage from Chicago: motor carrier, TOFC, and rail carload, respectively. Instead, TOFC Plan II rates (for which the rail carrier provides complete door-to-door piggyback service) were originally established throughout the country to be at parity with motor carrier rates. Where TOFC rates now are lower, the reason is that motor carrier rate bureaus have sought and obtained rate increases which the railroads have not chosen to duplicate for Plan II piggyback service. Rail carload rates likewise reflect historical regional political pressures and forces of competition more than rigorous cost analysis.[13] Fig. 13-8 shows areas of relative freight rate advantage.

TOFC TERMINALS

Piggyback operations involve particular spatial patterns of traffic and land use within metropolitan terminal areas. The ramps or other unloading facilities do not require the complex arrangement of classification yards, freight houses, and private industrial switch tracks required for the handling of boxcar and less-than-carload-lot terminal movements. Once arrived at the piggyback terminal facility, the trailerloads on the train "sort themselves" by ultimate destination and do not require further rail handling. In this respect, the originating and terminating piggyback trips, as well as many of the interlined movements which are transferred over streets and expressways instead of over the belt and transfer railroads, become part of the aggregate highway traffic pattern of the particular urban area. While the exact costs of rail carload and truck pickup and delivery service

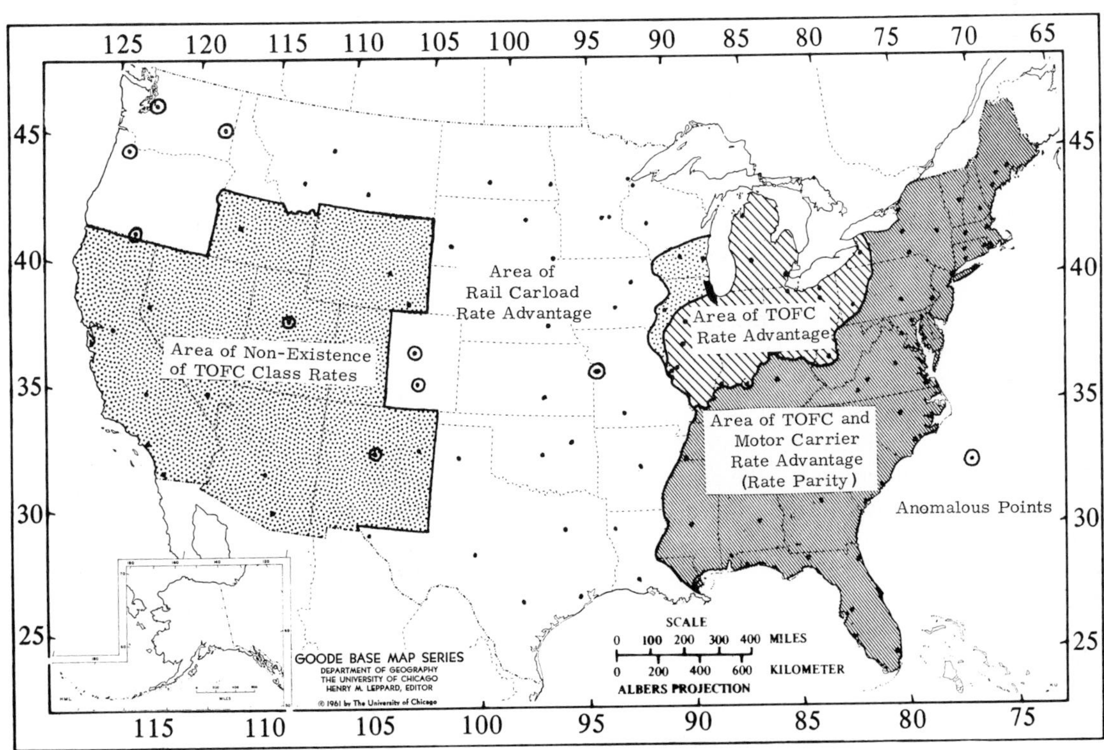

Fig. 13-8 Areas of freight rate advantage.

within cities are not known, it is clear that TOFC service is more efficient than carload service with respect to speed of pickup, delivery, and interchange operations.

Locating a piggyback terminal facility requires decisions regarding the position of the facility in relation to areas of traffic generation, the cost of land at various sites, and accessibility to the railroad's main line with a minimum of delay. Ideally, TOFC terminal facilities should both achieve accessibility to the maximum possible number of shippers at the minimum possible expense for local truck cartage, and minimize the costs incurred for trailer loading and unloading, car switching, and other operating expenses by being large consolidated facilities. The latter goal is, however, not consistent with the goal of minimization of cartage costs, which requires a wide distribution of smaller terminals throughout a metropolitan area. Ultimately a piggyback terminal is railroad-oriented in that it must be built on railroad trackage, usually also on a site with existing yard facilities requiring a minimum of expenditure for ramp construction and yard operations (train makeup, etc.). There is unresolved debate as to whether a central or peripheral location is best for piggyback facilities, in terms of access to traffic and total costs of development and operation of the terminal.

In Chicago, the location of existing railroad yards has probably been the single most important factor in determining the actual locations of TOFC facilities. Compared to the pattern of TOFC terminals within the Chicago metropolitan area, the pattern of truck terminals is much more highly concentrated within the south central industrial sector of the city. The pattern of truck terminals reflects a greater locational flexibility and closer orientation to major areas of truck traffic generation than that of TOFC terminals. A long-range question in urban land use in Chicago and other large cities is to what extent the growth of piggyback operations, and the construction of piggyback terminals, will enable partial abandonment of much of the overbuilt and obsolete railroad plant of transfer yards and industrial switch tracks, with allocation of the land to more productive uses.

NOTES

1 F. H. Mossman and N. Morton, *Principles of Transportation* (New York: Ronald Press, 1957), p. 383.

2 P. J. Schwind, "Railroad Piggyback Operations: A Geographic Problem," *Bulletin of the Illinois Geographical Society,* VIII (December 1965), pp. 28–39.

3 "TOFC: 10 Years of Steady Growth," *Railway Age,* CLV (November 25, 1963), 44, 46.

4 H. S. Norton, *Modern Transportation Economics* (Columbus: Charles E. Merrill Books, Inc., 1963), pp. 30, 47.

5 Terminal districts or zones (for both rail and motor carriers) are those areas around certain cities within which all individual points constitute a single origin or destination, in terms of the structure of freight rates and the certification of common carriers.

6 K. J. Kansky, *Structure of Transportation Networks* (Department of Geography Research Paper No. 84; Chicago: University of Chicago, 1963).

7 E. L. Ullman, "The Role of Transportation and the Bases for Interaction," in W. L. Thomas, Jr. (ed.), *Man's Role in Changing the Face of the Earth* (Chicago: University of Chicago Press, 1956), pp. 867–68.

8 University of Illinois, Department of Geography, *Atlas of Illinois Resources, Section 4: Transportation* (Springfield: State of Illinois, Division of Industrial Planning and Development, 1960), pp. 16, 25.

9 D. P. Morgan, "What Price Piggyback?" *Trains,* XX (May 1960), p. 41.

10 J. W. Alexander *et al.,* "Freight Rates: Selected Aspects of Uniform and Nodal Regions," *Economic Geography,* XXXIV (1958), p. 5.

11 The rate basis for any commodity not taking a specific commodity rate is first determined from the Uniform Freight Classification.

12 "A one-day survey showed only five carloads out of 2,000, or one-fourth of one percent, moved over the Baltimore and Ohio lines on class rates." J. G. Shott, *Progress in Piggyback and Containerization* (Washington, D.C.: Public Affairs Institute, 1961), p. 43.

13 See Alexander *et al., op. cit.*, pp. 2–4.

WATER TRANSPORT

The leading characteristics of water transport are low freight rates, specialization in a few bulk commodities, and low speed; for example, barges on inland waterways move an average of 5 miles per hour. There are great contrasts in the use of this mode; in the United States inland waterways carry about 16 percent of all intercity freight, whereas in Great Britain the usage is minimal. In 1946, in the United States the comparable total was 3.1 percent; an increase has taken place as waterways have become increasingly competitive through technological improvements. Investment is small, compared to that of the railways, if natural waterways are used. Inland waterways tend to carry bulk goods such as oil, grain, or sand.*

The position is slightly different for marine transport, which is free from much of the competition of fast inland modes. Hence marine transport hauls a much larger proportion of semifinished and finished commodities. However, costs are complex, handling charges are high, and the terminal and handling costs can be almost triple those of the voyage proper (*line-haul costs*). Other costs, imposed in part by other media, are incurred in packaging, containerization, and turnaround. Even for railways, terminal costs are usually equal to line-haul costs for a movement of 300 miles; by sea, on the other hand, terminal costs can still be double or triple line-haul costs on a 3,000-mile journey.

The *general costs* of the marine transport system are important too. The system suffers from times of excess capacity alternating with periods of high demand. Capacity responds very slowly to these changes of demand; reductions are slow, since the lifespan of a ship is over 20 years. Voyage costs are fixed largely independently of the cargo carried, and the marginal costs of carrying extra cargo up to the vessel's capacity are small, so that there are often economic pressures in times of excess capacity to accept extra cargo at any price in excess of the handling costs for the marginal cargo. Since in the short run the supply of vessels is inelastic, shortages of shipping are reflected in upward price swings. Marine rate structures are complex, governed by international rate agreements which are essentially restrictive, to hold down competition and keep up prices, as well as including national practices to subsidize construction and cargo preference laws. Marine vessels are undergoing technical changes, particularly to increase

*This is true in North America and Western Europe, but in Bangladesh (Formerly East Pakistan) jute and rice are hauled, and in Nigeria 70 percent of the Niger River traffic downstream consists of ground nuts and palm kernals, and upstream, 20 percent salt and 50 percent cement.

capacity and usage, so that there are now tankers (which, since they are partly automatic, lower handling costs) for liquid sulphur, latex, fruit juices, and liquid gases. Container use is growing too, and the most recent trend has been to build ships specifically designed for containerization.† S. H. Beaver in the following selection stresses the role of the technological environment in changing the "geographical value" of various kinds of ocean shipping.

†G. Beishlag, "The Container Revolution in Ocean Shipping," *The Pennsylvania Geographer*, 1968, pp. 1–5.

Selection 14

Ships and Shipping: The Geographical Consequences of Technological Progress

S. H. Beaver

A few years ago as President of Section E of the British Association, I took as the theme of my address "Technology and Geography."[1] In this present discourse I wish to follow a line which . . . had to be omitted from that address with no more than a passing comment. The theme is the study of changes in the geography of ocean shipping that have resulted from technological changes in the nature and function of ships.

At the risk of some repetition, may I first enunciate my view of what I might call the "whole geographical environment." I do not wish at this moment to enter into controversy over "what is a geographical factor," for the subject has so recently been aired in the pages of *Geography*,[2] but simply to express my conviction that the geographical environment includes not merely the physical environment—geology, soils, the surface configuration of the land and the atmospheric envelope—but also the biological environment—the plant and animal life—and all those man-made aspects of the environment which are often equally important, namely the economic environment, together with the social and political environments, and, above all, the technological environment, which conditions the ability of mankind to make use of the physical environment in which it finds itself. Without all these aspects being taken into consideration our geography is but half-baked and is certainly . . . far too deterministic.

In other words, I would expand Stamp's famous diagram, which had been used in teaching at the London School of Economics . . . and subsequently blossomed out in his *Applied Geography*, so as to include those aspects of the environment for which man himself is responsible[3] (Fig. 14-1).

Geography, Vol. 52, 1967, pp. 133–156. Reprinted by permission of the author and the editor.

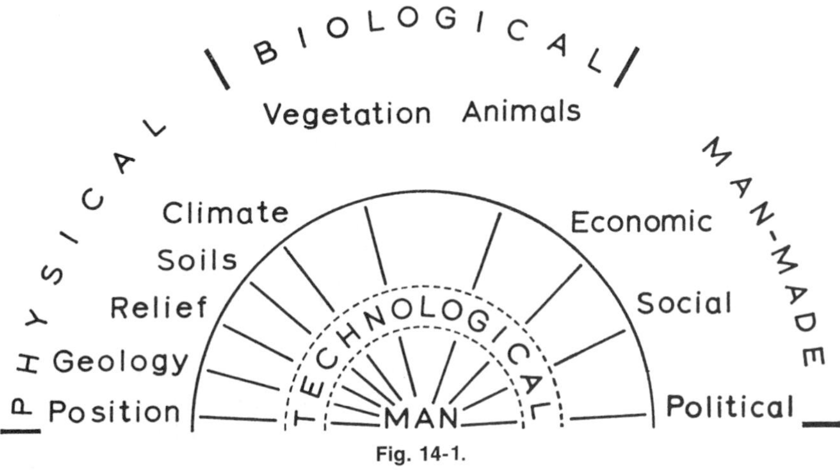

Fig. 14-1.

. . . I would say that all human activity takes place in an environment which has three major aspects; the first of these is the natural environment (including the physical and biological aspects as I have defined these above), and the other two are the main subdivisions of the man-made environment, technological on the one hand and economic, social and political on the other. Each of these three aspects is subject to change—though the first is clearly the most stable—and each will vary in its importance according to the nature of the activity. The technological environment acts as a filter between man and all the other aspects of the total environment, controlling his ability to adapt himself to them and to modify them.

Without more ado let me examine this thesis as it applies to ocean shipping.

The physical environment within which the shipping industry works comprises, first and foremost, the sea—the seas and oceans in their general relationships to the land masses, and in relation to the climatic belts and ocean currents; but the land is also important—the physical form of the coasts and the physical nature of the seaward approaches to ports and harbors. Here, clearly, we have a stable environment, virtually unalterable by man whatever his state of technological advancement. But man is not completely impotent—the arrow on Stamp's diagram does not only point in one direction. The coastline can be modified in detail so as to create ports where the physical environment did not naturally offer a suitable site; and of course two major and far-reaching alterations to the physical environment of shipping were provided by the Suez and Panama canals, creating ocean routes which were hitherto impossible.

The technical environment of shipping includes the techniques of ship construction, methods of propulsion and navigation. Here, for me at least, lies the main fascination of the study of ships and shipping. The economic geography of shipping in the medieval Arab Mediterranean world was very different from that which—stemming largely from the introduction of the Portuguese "caravel" which could sail against the wind—developed after the discovery (or rediscovery, at the end of the fifteenth century) of America and of the Cape route to India. The geography of world shipping in the days of sail was fundamentally different from that which developed after the introduction of steam propulsion. The routes were altered and coal became a most important item of trade, and within the twentieth century a whole series of "revolutions" has affected shipping, resulting from the introduction of oil-fired boilers and of diesel engines, both of which require oil, and not coal, to be carried across the oceans in tankers of ever-increasing size, from the development of refrigeration facilities in ships, from the construction of bulk-cargo carriers of various kinds, and even from the development of radar aids to navigation. Here, in contrast to the physical environment, we have an environment which is never static for very long, particularly in modern times. Indeed it is becoming increasingly difficult to keep abreast of all the changes. Of course, the technological changes do not occur simply and solely as a result of inventions and innovations; they are intimately bound up with the economic environment, which often provides the necessary stimulus.

The economic environment of shipping is essentially conditioned by the laws of supply and demand, natural or as interfered with by governments. It concerns the relationship of producing to consuming areas, the location of sources of food supplies and raw materials, of fuels and of manufactured goods; and it involves too the distribution of the world's population and wealth, which engender passenger as well as freight traffic. Here too is another aspect of the total environment that is capable of much manipulation by man, particularly through tariffs and quotas, and by shipping subsidies of one form or another, quite apart from the changes brought about by differential rates of agricultural and industrial development in various parts of the world, and by changes in nature of the demand for natural products and raw materials.

There is one aspect of the economic environment of shipping that marks it off clearly from other forms of transport such as rail, road or canal. The "highway" is free for all, and no capital charges are involved as in the case of railways; the only charge is for propulsion through a relatively frictionless medium. The same thing, of course, applies to aircraft; and one of the most interesting aspects of the man-made environment of shipping is now the competition that the aircraft has provided, particularly in respect of passenger traffic, and the effects of this competition on certain parts of the shipping industry.

You will readily appreciate that I have here outlined enough material for a whole course of lectures rather than a single discourse, and I must therefore select certain topics only for more detailed treatment. I propose to concentrate on three major aspects of the geographical consequences of technical progress: first, the substitution of oil for coal; secondly, the development of refrigeration; and thirdly, the changes in the nature of international trade that have been in part the cause and in part the result of changes in ship construction and methods of propulsion.

Before doing so, however, it will be instruc-

Table 14-1 Trade with Britain, 1905—Imports
The percentage of countries' exports received by Britain (1962 figures in parentheses)

1905	Country	1962
85	New Zealand	(57)
93	South Africa	(36)
52	Canada	(14)
57	Egypt	(3)
65	Gold Coast	(19)
66	Ceylon	(30)
26	India	(23)
33	U.S.A.	(5)
53	Peru	(10)
36	Argentina	(17)
30	Brazil	(6)
47	Spain	(24)
37	Norway	(18)
36	Sweden	(13)
31	Russia	(4)

Table 14-2 Trade with Britain, 1905—Exports
The percentage of countries' imports supplied by Britain (1962 figures in parentheses)

68	India	(17)
50	New Zealand	(44)
64	South Africa	(23)
74	Nigeria	(36)
72	Gold Coast	(30)
32	Egypt	(7)
34	Argentina	(9)
44	Chile	(8)
43	Peru	(6)
44	Colombia	(6)
32	Uruguay	(8)
24	Canada	(9)

tive to glance back half a century at the British trade pattern and at the mercantile marine that catered for it before the First World War. In 1910, the United Kingdom owned 40 per cent of the world's shipping and carried about half of all the world's ocean traffic. There were few competitors, for of all the other countries of the world only Norway owned a merchant fleet that was greater than the requirements of its own domestic trade. One half of the British mercantile marine consisted of tramp ships, which depended on the export of coal —73 million tons of it in 1913 (plus another 21 million tons supplied as bunkers)—and on the import of bulk freights—grain, ores, fertilisers and timber. The extent to which British exports and imports also dominated the world's ocean shipping but particularly that of the British Empire is shown in Tables 14-1, 14-2 and 14-3.

The development of this world-wide trade had engendered the provision of coaling stations at convenient points in relation to the major shipping routes (Fig. 14-2). Many of these were islands, and some of them were fortified, and of course they also acted as fuelling bases for the British Navy which policed the oceans and kept open the lifelines of the British Empire.

Another technological development, without which the growth of the shipping business in particular would have been impossible, was the submarine telegraph cable. The tramp ship must be ready to carry anything, any time, anywhere, and its operators, in order to direct it to the points at which traffic is offering, must be able to communicate with it rapidly; and in the days before the invention of radio telegraphy this could only be accomplished by cable, when the ship was in port. Between the laying of the first trans-Atlantic cable by the *Great Eastern* in 1866 and the end of the century, a whole network of submarine cables was stretched across the world's oceans—and a map of the British ones (Fig. 14-3) shows clearly the importance of the trade routes that linked the various parts of the Empire—and also the non-Empire sources of Britains' food and raw material supplies—to the Home Country.

The extent to which the pattern of the world's trade has altered during the last half-century may be gauged in part from the second series of figures in the above tables for 1962. The *proportion* of Britain's total trade represented by the Commonwealth countries

Table 14-3 British Trade in 1905
(Percentage of total value; 1962 figures in parentheses)

Exports: Textiles, 40% (6); iron and steel and machinery, 16% (39); coal, 8% (0·8).
Imports: Grain and flour, 13% (5); meat, 10% (7); other food products, 21% (20); textile fibres, 17% (3); manufactured textile and metal goods, 13% (15)
Exports to: British Empire, 30% (30); U.S.A., 11% (8); Europe, 34% (37)
Imports from: British Empire, 23% (31); U.S.A., 21% (11); Europe, 33% (34)

Source (Tables 14-1, 14-2, 14-3): **Bartholomew's Atlas of the World's Commerce,** ***1907, Plates 18–19, and*** **Statesman's Year Book,** ***1965.***

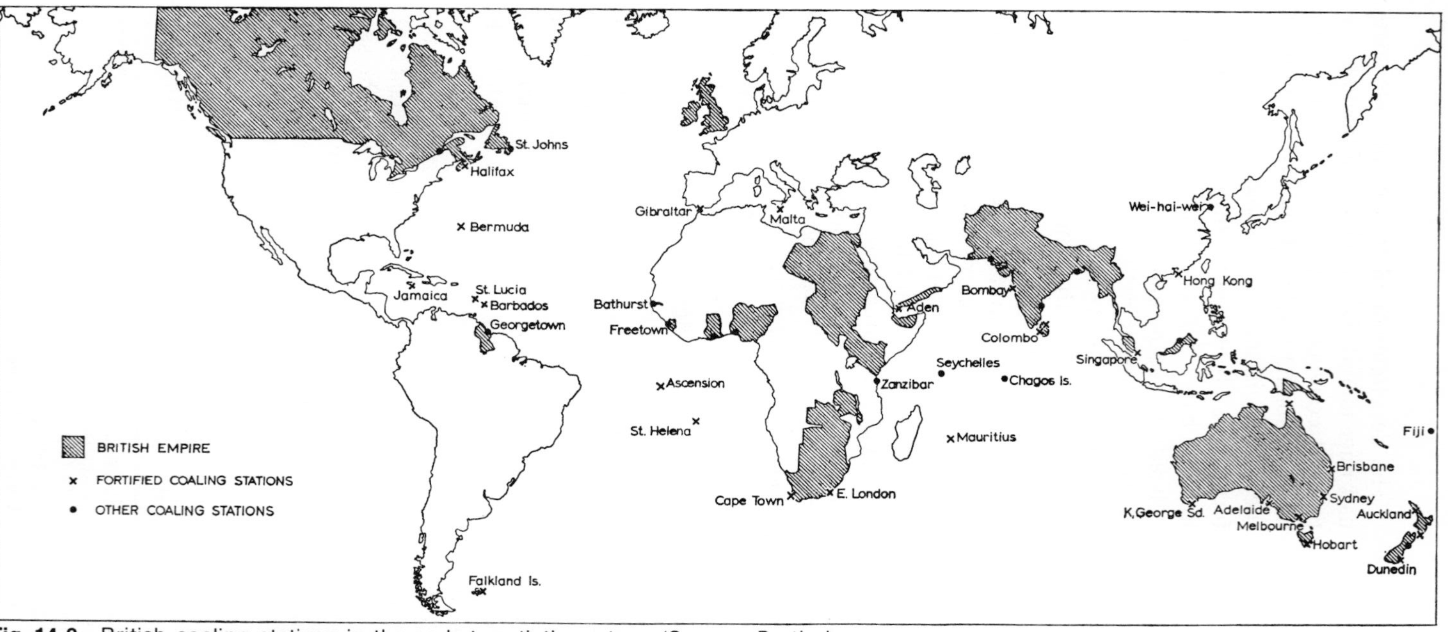

Fig. 14-2 British coaling stations in the early twentieth century. (***Source:*** *Bartholomew's Atlas of the World's Commerce*, London: George Newnes, 1907)

and Europe has changed but little, or has actually risen slightly, but the importance of Britain in the trade of the Commonwealth countries is far less overwhelming than it was in the early years of the century, and has shrunk to much smaller proportions in the case of the South American countries and those of Europe. All of which, and also the fundamental changes in the character of British imports and exports,* implies a great broadening in the world's ocean traffic, with a greater variety of routes and traffics. And it is this that has in part been responsible for, and has in part been created by, the technological changes that form the subject of this address.

THE SEA CARRIAGE OF OIL

Three major technological factors are involved in the development of the sea carriage of petroleum during the last hundred years—developments which have escalated enormously since the Second World War. The first is the development of the automobile in all its various forms, which has provided a large part of the total world demand for petroleum products—a demand which now amounts to some 1,500 million tons a year. The geography of the world's oil resources being what it is, in relation to the major regions of demand, there is no alternative to the long-distance movement of oil by sea. The second factor is the technology of tanker construction, which has undergone a revolution in the last twenty years; the largest ships afloat are now tankers, and the world's tanker fleet now represents one-fifth of the total merchant marine in number of ships, but nearly two-fifths of the total by tonnage. And they all use oil fuel. The third factor, intimately bound up with economic and political considerations as well, is the more recent development of oil refineries at the market end of the sea-lane rather than on the oilfields themselves. This has engendered the large-scale movement of crude oil as opposed to refined products; and combined with the second factor, the increasing size of the tanker, it has considerably modified the geography of the world's shipping routes and ports.

It was in 1859 that the world's petroleum industry was launched by the discovery of oil at Titusville in Pennsylvania. Two years later the first cargo of American oil, in barrels, crossed the Atlantic from the Delaware River to London in the 224-ton sailing brig *Elizabeth Watts*. In 1864, $7\frac{1}{2}$ million gallons were shipped (in barrels) from Philadelphia—but the barrel is uneconomic in its use of cargo space, and in 1869 the 794-ton *Charles* was equipped with iron tanks inside its wooden hull. The solution was obviously the iron-built ship, and two were launched on the Tyne (though curiously enough there appears to be no evidence of their having been used for oil carriage). But it required a courageous decision to install coal-fired boilers in an oil-carrying ship, and it was not until 1884 that the first ship of this kind—the *Gluckauf,* 2307 tons—was launched at Newcastle. This step having been taken, however, progress was fairly rapid and by 1907, for example, the Shell Company and its associate, the Royal Dutch Petroleum Company, had a combined fleet of 38 tankers,[4] and the world's total tanker fleet had reached 250 vessels by 1912, amounting in all to nearly $1\frac{1}{2}$ million gross tons.

It must be remembered that at this time, oil was mainly used for lubrication and illumination. The principal suppliers were the United States, where Pennsylvania produced mainly light oils for illumination and Texas and California heavier oils for lubrication, and Russia,

*Note especially, in Table 14-3, the catastrophic decline in the proportion of the total export trade represented by textiles (and the corresponding reduction in imports of fibers), and the considerable increase in exports of the products of the steel and engineering industries; and note also that petroleum, insignificant in 1905, now represents 12 per cent of the total imports.

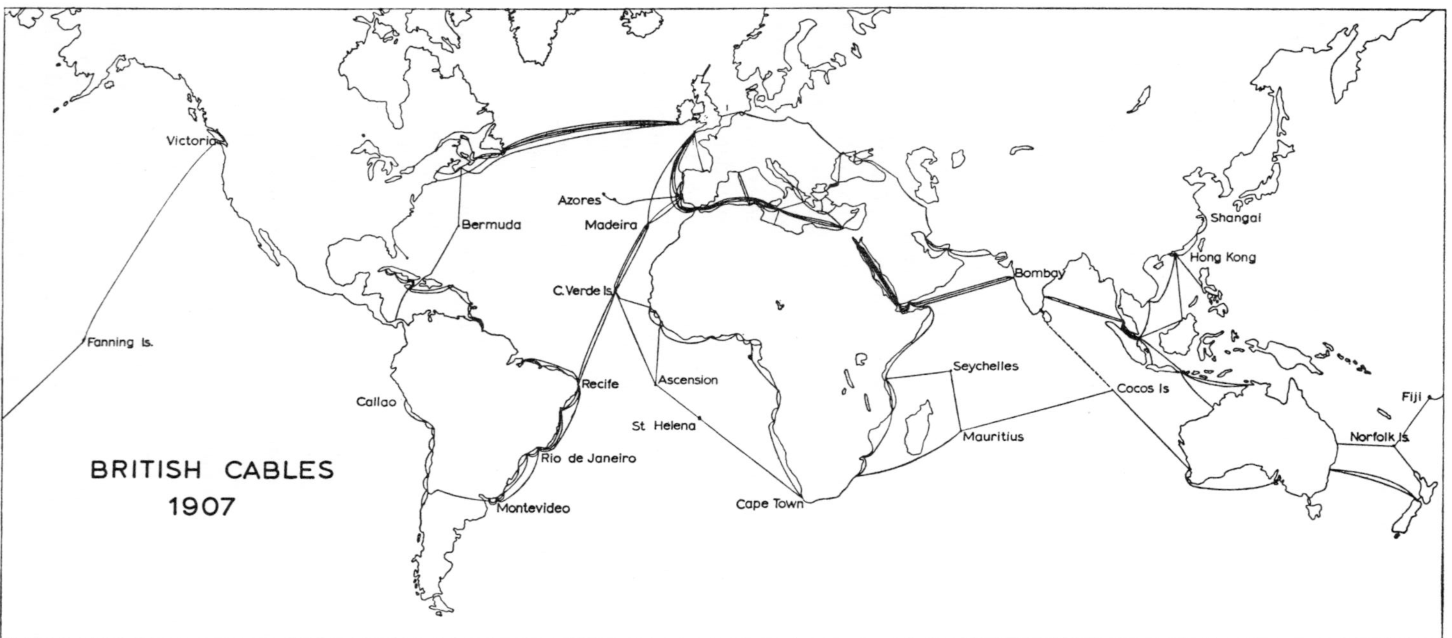

Fig. 14-3 British Cables, 1907. (***Source:*** *Bartholomew's Atlas of the World's Commerce*, London: George Newnes, 1907)

where the Baku fields produced heavy oil (exported via Batoum on the Black Sea); these two countries together provided 90 per cent of the world's output in the early years of this century. The only other producers of importance were Rumania, the Dutch East Indies and Burma.

Without going into further details, suffice it to say that the development of the internal combustion and diesel engines for road vehicles, the use of oil fuel in shipping, the expansion of air transport and the growth of oil-refining industries, mainly in the producing countries, had brought the world oil production to close on 300 million tons in the late thirties—a fourfold expansion since 1918; and the sea traffic in oil was catered for by some 1,600 tankers, totalling about 11 million tons gross and representing 15 per cent of the world's mercantile marine. The standard ocean-going tanker at this time was a vessel of about 10,000–12,000 tons. Most of the world's oil refineries were in the producing areas, and though a fair amount of crude oil was carried, much of the traffic was in refined products, distributed to a great number of ports for which this size of ship—a little larger than the standard "tramp"—was most convenient.

During the war, the United States built over 600 T2-type tankers, of 16,000 tons deadweight. These were the "super-tankers" of the period, and many of them are still afloat, either as built or converted to dry cargo or chemical carriers. After the war, however, things began to develop very rapidly indeed. In the late 1940's, tankers of 24,000 tons deadweight made their appearance (the first British one was launched on the Tyne in 1949); then came more "super-tankers" of 40,000 tons, then the "giant" tankers of 60,000 tons in the late 1950's, then the "mammoths" (perhaps "whales" would be a better term!) of 100,000 tons in the early 1960's, and finally—though the end is not yet in sight—the 209,000-ton *Idemitsu Maru* which made her maiden round trip between Japan and the Persian Gulf in December 1966. Some 300,000-tonners are on order in Japan, and builders are thinking in terms of 500,000 tons or even larger still.

What is behind this extraordinary technical revolution? First and foremost is the great expansion of production and consumption. The world production of crude oil almost doubled between 1938 and 1950, and trebled again between 1950 and 1965, reaching over 1,500 million tons in the latter year. And in 1965 the world's tanker fleet totalled 90 million d.w.t. (about 58 million gross registered tons (g.r.t.), nearly six times the pre-war figure), and oil movement represented one-half of all the world's ocean trade. This enormous increase in output reflects in the main three technological developments in the field of transport, to say nothing of the use of oil as a fuel in industry and for the production of electricity. The first is, of course, the phenomenal increase in the use of motor vehicles, the world output of which rose from about 4 millions in 1938 to 22 millions in 1964; the second is the equally spectacular rise in the world's fleet of military and commercial aircraft; and the third is the almost complete substitution of oil for coal as the fuel used in the propulsion of ships.

Clearly, the geographical consequences of

Table 14-4 Britain's Oil Supplies, 1903–1905

55% from U.S.A.; 37% from Russia; 3% from Rumania
Total: 296 million gallons, of which 84 per cent "illuminating" oil and 16 per cent "lubricating" oil

Source: Bartholomew's Atlas of the World's Commerce, *1907, Plate 152.*

Table 14-5 World Shipping; Coal and Oil Fuel

Fuel	Per cent of total gross tonnage			
	1914	1939	1947	1962
Coal	88·8	44·7	26·2	3
Oil fuel for boilers	2·6	30·6	52·5	50
Oil for diesel engines	0·4	17·4	20·3	47
Sail	8·0	1·8	1·0	0

the figures shown in Table 14-5 are profound. British exports of coal to the coaling stations of yesterday have been reduced to nothing, with important repercussions on tramp shipping, as we shall see later on; some of these places have retained their significance as oiling stations—contributing thus to the maritime traffic in petroleum products—and other new refuelling points have come into existence, as for example in the Canary Islands, which are now the major oiling stations for vessels on the U.K.-Plate run. Sometimes, indeed, they serve as the *only* refuelling point, sufficient oil fuel being taken on at Teneriffe for the voyage either to London and back or to the Plate and back.

A second reason for the tanker revolution is the changed pattern of world trade in oil, with the development of refineries at the receiving end instead of on the oilfields. Before the war, only 20 per cent of the ocean traffic in petroleum was in crude oil; but the position is now completely reversed and at the present time 80 per cent of it is crude. In the growth of refineries at ports in the consuming areas two factors, amongst others, have been of particular importance: (1) the realization, particularly after the seizure of Abadan in 1951, of the risk involved in having refineries located in areas of political instability, and (2) the growth of the petrochemical industries which now accompany many of the great European, Japanese and American refineries, and which provide the essential basis for the expanding output of plastics and man-made fibers, the great new industries of the mid-twentieth century. These petrochemical industries, requiring immense capital resources and highly skilled technicians and scientists, could hardly be attached to the oilfields of the Middle East, for example, where they would have no local market in great industrial areas, and no supporting or ancillary industries. A further point is that if only crude oil is to be carried, the tanker can be vast yet simple, and lacking the refinements and flexibility necessary for the carriage of a variety of refined products. For example, the specific gravity of oil varies from the 0·7 of petroleum spirit to the 0·96 of heavy fuel oil. So a tanker that is designed to carry a full load of spirit cannot carry a full load if any of its cargo is of oils with a specific gravity higher than 0·7.

A third reason is the changed pattern of emphasis in the world's oil production, with the Middle East having replaced the Americas as Europe's main source of supply, and having replaced the East Indies as the main source for Japan. This means a longer journey for the crude oil—6350 miles from the Persian Gulf to the U.K. via the Suez Canal* as against 4,000 miles or so from the Caribbean. And longer journeys demand a reduction in the cost of transport per ton, which can best be effected by increasing the size of the tanker. Moreover, the Suez trouble of 1956 provided the incentive for the construction of large tankers that would use the Cape route to Europe—longer by 14 days and 5000 miles but avoiding the Canal dues.

Size, in the case of tankers, brings economies of construction costs (per ton), and particularly of operational costs. A 100,000-ton tanker requires very few more crew than one of 20,000 tons, and the cost of transporting

**Editor's note:* The closure of the Suez Canal has increased the distances from the Persian Gulf, intensifying this trend.

a ton of oil in such a large vessel is less than half what it is in the smaller ship. Bes estimated that in 1959, if a 16,000-ton tanker represented 100 units of cost per ton-mile, a 100,000-ton vessel would be 38 units.[5] And a 100,000-ton tanker requires a good deal less than five times as much steel and labor in its construction as five 20,000-tonners.

The development of the huge tanker would have been impossible, however, without improved technology—in terms of better structural and plate steel, the use of welding in place of riveting (thus producing a smoother hull which has less frictional resistance to movement through water), and improved naval architecture and methods of construction. The key factors, however, are deadweight capacity, dimension draught, speed and the methods of propulsion. With the last of these, we need not be concerned, for whether it be by diesel engines or steam turbines, the fuel—at least until the perfection of the nuclear ship—would be oil. But dimensions and draught certainly have geographic consequences of far-reaching importance, and as the size of tankers increases the number of ports that can receive them becomes fewer and it becomes impossible to use the Suez and Panama Canals.[6] The Suez Canal can take a vessel of 37-foot draught. This just allows a 45,000-ton tanker to pass through when fully loaded; a 60,000-tonner would have to go through partly loaded, topping up at one of the pipeline terminals in Syria or Tripoli for the final journey to western Europe—or else it would have to go via the Cape. The proposed Suez Canal improvements will increase the draught to 42 feet, allowing tankers of 65,000 tons to pass through fully loaded. The Panama Canal is even more restrictive, and its draught of 34 feet excludes all the large tankers.

The capacity of these huge tankers varies with the temperature and density of the ocean waters in which they sail—and the Plimsoll marks indicate this variability (Fig. 14-4). Thus one of the Esso fleet of 87,000 d.w.t. vessels can carry only 83,725 tons of oil round the Cape during the southern winter, and 86,075 tons at the equinoctial periods. So during the southern winter, with their capacity in these waters reduced, they may restrict their operations to the northern hemisphere, loading at eastern Mediterranean ports only: Banias, Sidon, Tripoli or Marsa el Brega.

The geography of the world's crude oil traffic now shows seven major streams.[7] These are (1) Caribbean to U.S.A. Atlantic coast, (2) Caribbean to U.K. and western Europe,

Table 14-6 Britain's Oil Supplies, 1964

Crude (million tons)		*Refined* (million tons)	
Kuwait	18·0	Europe	7·6
Iraq	11·2	N. & S. America	7·3
Libya	8·9*	Middle East	3·3
South America	6·7	Others	0·4
Iran	3·7	Total	18·6
Nigeria	3·3		
Abu Dhabi	2·4†		
Saudi Arabia	1·8		
Others	3·5		
Total	59·5		

* Began 1962. † Began 1963.

SOURCE: U.K. Chamber of Shipping, *Report, 1965–6*, p. 215.

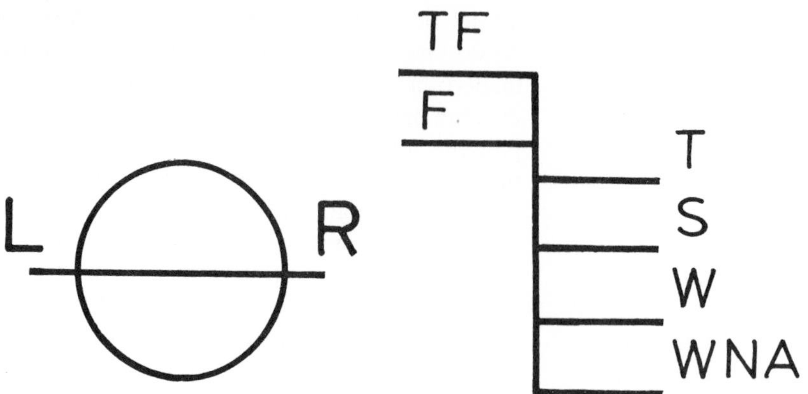

Fig. 14-4 The Plimsoll Line. L.R.: Lloyd's Register; T.F.: Tropical Fresh Water; F.: Fresh Water; T: Tropical; S: Summer; W.: Winter; W.N.A.: Winter North Atlantic.

(3) U.S. Gulf ports to U.S. Atlantic ports, (4) Middle East to U.K. and western Europe, (5) Middle East to Japan, (6) Middle East to U.S.A. Atlantic coast, (7) North Africa to southern and western Europe. In a recent year, 1962,[8] two-thirds of the world's tankers were employed on these major routes—30 per cent between the Middle East and western Europe (including U.K.), 9 per cent on the Middle East–Japan route, 9 per cent between U.S. Gulf and Atlantic ports (a traffic entirely reserved for U.S.-owned tankers), 8 per cent between the Caribbean and western Europe, 6 per cent on the Caribbean–U.S. route and 5 per cent between the Middle East and the United States. For the rest, there are of course the oilfields of southeast Asia and the very considerable short-sea traffic in western European waters, particularly in refined products. The North African traffic has only developed within the last few years.

As for the ports, the arrival of the giant tanker has provoked some very interesting developments. In the Persian Gulf area the terminals have, of course, been built from scratch in hitherto almost unoccupied areas, so the provision of jetties and deep-water facilities has been relatively easy. Mena el Ahmadi, the largest oil terminal in the world, can take tankers of any actual or foreseeable size, and so can Ras Tanura—to take but two examples. But in western Europe the problem has been to adapt existing ports to accommodate ever larger and larger vessels. In Great Britain, the Grangemouth refinery, one of the oldest, can only be served by tankers of up to 20,000 tons—so a 57-mile pipeline was constructed from Finnart, on the fjord of Loch Long, where great water depth is attained only a few yards from the shore. The British Petroleum Company's Llandarcy refinery, near Swansea, was similarly hampered by the 20,000-ton limit of Queen's Dock, Swansea—so a 62-mile pipeline was laid to Milford Haven, where also two other oil companies (Esso and Regent) have established terminals and refineries. But Milford Haven is a ria, not a fjord, and so long jetties are necessary to reach the deep water. Both the terminals there can take two 100,000-ton tankers at once.

Fawley, on Southampton Water, could not take the Esso 80,000-ton tankers, which were therefore obliged to unload part of their cargo at Milford Haven and then proceed to Fawley for final discharge. But a £2 million dredging program in the port approaches solved this problem in 1963. The Isle of Grain and Thames Haven have similar problems with sandbanks and can only be served by 50,000-tonners, drawing 40 feet. The Stanlow refinery alongside the Manchester Ship Canal cannot even take a 20,000-tonner, and so a jetty terminal was built at Tranmere (floating, because of the 30-foot tidal range!) to accommodate two 60,000-ton tankers at once.

On the Continent, Europoort (Rotterdam) has a 52-foot draught oil port to take 100,000-ton tankers, and improvements are currently in progress to increase the draught to 62 feet for 200,000-tonners. Antwerp has recently made provision for 70,000-tonners. Lavera, near Marseilles, has only 37-foot draught, and so new jetties are planned in the Gulf of Fos. And so one could go on multiplying the examples. Perhaps the most striking of all is the development by Gulf Oil at Bantry Bay in southwest Ireland, where a terminal with a water depth of 75 feet, capable of taking 300,000-ton tankers, is in the course of construction.

Japan has had fewer difficulties, and it is perhaps because of this that she has been leading the world in the production of ever more gigantic ships to carry her crude oil from Persian Gulf ports to the homeland.

It would indeed seem in the case of the tanker that the greater the technical progress, the more stringent does the geographical control become, and the fewer the localities which are capable of coping with the results. The giant tanker is most certainly not a way to lessen the influence of the physical environment!

THE SEABORNE TRADE IN LIQUEFIED GASES[9]

This is an entirely post-war development. The first vessels to be adapted for the carriage of liquid gas were rebuilt, from a dry-cargo carrier and a tanker respectively, in 1947, but much of the traffic has only developed in the 1960's, and the world fleet of liquid-gas tankers totalled 95 ships in 1964, of 348,000 g.r.t. —an increase of 80 per cent in two years! Two kinds of product are involved, LPG (liquid petroleum gas)—propane, propylene, the butanes and butylenes—and LNG (liquid natural gas)—methane and ethane in their liquefied state. And two separate geographies result. The traffic in LPG is much more widespread than that in LNG, because it depends on the distribution of various products from oil refineries to a large number of separate destinations. Thus an investigation made in 1964[10] showed that no less than 121 ports in many parts of the world, 56 of them in Europe, received calls from LPG tankers. The most important were Le Havre (including Gonfreville) and Port de Bouc in France, Grangemouth, Immingham and Fawley in England, Rotterdam and Antwerp, the Iberian ports of Lisbon, Barcelona, Cartagena and Valencia, Augusta in Sicily, Teneriffe in the Canary Islands, Trinidad, Maracaibo and Aruba in the Caribbean, and Buenos Aires. In the European–North African area the trade is mostly coastwise, in small tankers of up to 1500 tons. But in the Caribbean–South American area, where distances between, e.g., Venezuela and Brazil, or Venezuela, Trinidad and U.S. east coast ports, are greater, larger tankers are used, of up to 8000 tons. The latest route to be developed (since 1961) is from Kuwait and Saudi Arabia (Ras Tanura) to Japan, a distance of 6,000 miles, and, for this traffic, much larger vessels, of up to 20,000–40,000 tons are employed.

The traffic in natural gas is of a different kind. Natural gas fields in the European–North African area have developed only since 1950, first at Lacq in southern France, then in 1956 in Algeria, in 1959 in northern Netherlands, and in 1963 in the Sahara. It is the

Saharan gas that has brought new ships and a new traffic route into being. From the port of Arzew in western Algeria, two British LNG carriers of 20,000 g.r.t., capable of carrying 12,000 tons of liquefied methane, now make 29 round trips a year each, in 1965 providing Britain (via the Canvey Island terminal) with some 10 per cent of her gas requirement. A similar development via the Libyan port of Marsa el Brega will shortly supply Italy, Spain and France with LNG.

Tankers for liquefied gas transport are much more costly than ordinary oil tankers, for they require strong pressure tanks and special temperature control. Methane, for example, is carried at −258° F (−160° C). And the arrival of this liquefied gas at its destination port poses problems of storage, which are sometimes solved only by the digging of huge underground tanks. The future of this traffic will depend, of course, on developments in gas production in the North Sea area, but for the moment it has produced an interesting new facet of the geography of shipping.

REFRIGERATION

The development of refrigeration in ships was hastened by the increasing shortage of meat in Britain in the mid-nineteenth century—itself a result of the expansion of population—and by the increasing surplus of cattle, sheep and lambs in Australia, New Zealand and southern South America. The first successful transatlantic shipment of fresh meat, packed in salt and ice—carefully insulated, of course—took place from the U.S.A. to Britain in 1874. This kind of arrangement would have been impossible for traffic from the southern hemisphere, but once a successful freezing machine had been devised, with the use of charcoal or such things as slag-wool, sawdust and cow-hair as insulating material, progress was rapid, and between 1877 and 1883, frozen-meat shipments were started from South America to France and England, and from Australia and New Zealand to England.

To this traffic was added the temperature-controlled shipment of West Indian bananas in 1886 and of Australian apples in 1888. From 1899, Lloyd's Register of Shipping took note of refrigerated space in ships, and in 1900 there were 300 such vessels in the world's merchant marine, with 35 million cubic feet of refrigerated cargo space. Progress thereafter was steady but not spectacular.[11] (Table 14-7.)

The largest modern cargo liners may have as much as 600,000 cubic feet of refrigerated space; and 20 per cent of the refrigerated ships in use actually represent 70 per cent of the total capacity.

The technical details of changes in the methods of temperature control need not concern us unduly. From cold-air machines, working on the simple principle of cooling by expansion, through carbon dioxide (CO_2) machines, ammonia (NH_3) compressors to the modern dichlorodifluoromethane (CCl_2F_2) compressors, it is simply a question of greater efficiency of cooling and more precise control over the temperature of the holds. An important geographical factor involved in the whole business of refrigerated ocean transport is the temperature of the sea itself—for whereas in the North Atlantic summer maximum water temperatures are of the order of 65° to 80°F, in the tropics temperatures of 85° or even 90°F may be encountered, and the expense of keeping this heat from seeping through the ship into the holds is correspondingly greater.

In general, the commodities to be carried

Table 14-7

Year	No. of ships	Refrigerated space (million cubic feet)
1917	900	80
1932	1300	130
1957	2500	180

Table 14-8 Refrigerated Space in Shipping, 1959

Country	No. of ships	d.w.t. ('000)	Refrigerated space ('000 cubic feet)	Passengers
U.K.	333	3127	84,991	40,096
U.S.A.	82	705	12,790	11,679
Sweden	107	608	10,275	866
France	95	471	9,840	14,106
Germany	62	222	8,637	658
Norway	109	504	8,280	2,924

will require to be either frozen or merely chilled. For carcass meat and butter, temperatures of 10–15°F are necessary, or perhaps 18–20°F if the voyage is a short one. Fish and poultry demand slightly cooler conditions, under 10°F, and some packaged food stuffs such as fruit and vegetables may also need such low temperatures. Cargoes to be chilled divide themselves into two categories. First are the living organisms such as fruit, which breathe and produce CO_2 and heat; fruit must be under-ripe, and the closest possible control of the temperature and CO_2 content of the refrigerated chambers is necessary. Apples are carried at 31–35°F, oranges at 37–40°F, grapefruit at 45–52°F, and bananas at 53–58°F; vegetables usually at a little above freezing point. Secondly, there is chilled meat. At a temperature of 31°F meat will keep for a limited time only. Formerly the Argentine–U.K. run was sufficiently short to permit beef to be merely chilled and not frozen, whilst the Australian run was too long; but the development of techniques to inject CO_1 into the chambers, so as to maintain the CO_2 content at 10 per cent, has enabled Australian and New Zealand meat to be sent to Britain in a chilled condition instead of being frozen. Other animal products need temperatures in the thirties—bacon 30°F, shell eggs 32°F and cheese 38°F, for example.

Two types of ship, in general, are fitted with refrigerated cargo space, the passenger–cargo liner and the cargo liner. In the first group come such well-known British examples as the Union Castle passenger fleet plying between Southampton and South African ports and the P. & O. liners on the Australian run. In the second group are the many fleets of cargo liners that carry either no passengers at all, or no more than twelve. Perhaps occupying an intermediate position are the Blue Star liners on the Argentine run—mainly meat ships but accommodating up to 100 passengers as well. The relative importance of the first six nations of the world in this business of refrigerated shipping is indicated in the following table, which emphasizes the importance of the refrigerated cargo capacity of the passenger liner fleets of the U.K., U.S.A. and France in particular, and the overwhelming importance of British shipping in this type of trade—which has its origin fundamentally in the geographical disposition of the former British Empire.

Amongst the traffics now served by refrigerated shipping are the Argentine meat trade, the meat and dairy trades of Australia and New Zealand, the fruit exports of South Africa, Australia and New Zealand, Brazil, Israel and California, and the specialized banana traffic of West Africa, Central America and the West Indies—an impressive part of the world's ocean shipping, all due to the invention of the refrigerator.

THE DEVELOPMENT OF THE BULK CARRIER

There are four attributes that characterize a great deal of the world's commodity traffic:

it is bulky, it is non-perishable, it is of low value in relation to its bulk, and it moves across the oceans in large quantities at different times of the year. It was this kind of traffic that gave rise to the typical tramp ship.[12] Tramp shipping really began after the opening of the Suez Canal in 1869, and it expanded continuously until the First World War, carrying coal, ores, grain, timber, sugar, phosphate and other bulk cargoes. The typical tramp ship of a few decades ago was a strong, seaworthy vessel without frills, averaging perhaps 6,000–7,000 gross tons (say 9000 tons deadweight) and working at a speed of 7–10 knots; small enough to get into most of the world's ports, and large enough to carry a paying load—slowly.

The tramp shipping business suffered severely during the depression of the inter-war period, and many governments, including eventually the British,[13] were forced to provide financial assistance. The enormous losses sustained during the Second World War—amounting to 32 million tons (12 million Commonwealth, 10 million allied and neutral and 10 million enemy)—were more than counterbalanced by the launching of 40 million tons of new ships in the United States, including over 2700 "Liberty" ships of 10,000 tons produced by prefabrication methods, and with welded hulls, at yards in New England and California.

After the war, with so many of the "Liberty" and "Victory" ships remaining afloat—either transferred to foreign owners or laid up as the U.S. "mothball" merchant fleet—little new tramp shipping was built, and though there were periods of increased traffic due to the Korean war, American coal shipments to Europe and the Suez crisis, some 25 per cent of the world's tramps were laid up in 1959.[14] The tramp fleet at this time totalled about $23\frac{1}{2}$ million d.w.t. (about 16.7 million g.r.t.), a higher figure than ever before,[15] but it only represented 16 per cent of the world's merchant marine, as against 46 per cent in 1914.

The reasons for the relative and absolute decline of the British tramp traffic and of the conventional tramp ship are not far to seek. There is first the serious decline in the total oceanic movement of coal which was always the staple, particularly of the British tramp. With so much of the bulk imports of grain and other commodities directed towards Britain and western Europe, it was of the utmost importance that assured outwards cargoes of coal were available, for most of the exports from these industrialized areas are not cheap, bulky raw materials or foodstuffs. Secondly, there is the increasing tendency for cargoes to be carried in *liners* running to schedules; this began to be serious during the periods when most of the tramps were out of service and the liners had cargo space available. By 1965, for example, no less than 34 per cent of the total British merchant fleet (by gross tonnage) consisted of cargo liners, which outnumbered tramps by two to one.[16] Associated with this tendency are two other factors: initially, the development of storage facilities, notably for grain, in producing countries, so that immediate shipment of the harvest is no longer necessary and the traffic can be evened out, at rates that may well be lower if the demand is less concentrated; and, further, the desirability in many trades of having smaller but regular shipments of materials carried in liners rather than irregular and less reliable bulk cargoes. Thirdly, there is the tendency towards the shipment of processed rather than raw commodities (linseed oil instead of bags of oil seeds from Argentina, for example), and these may require more specialized accommodation. Somewhat similar in its effect is the technical progress in the manufacture of synthetic materials which has greatly reduced the traffic in raw rubber and in Chilean nitrates.

A fourth clue may be sought in the tendency for vessels to be chartered on a long-term basis for the carriage of certain commodities between certain ports, thus assuring a greater regularity of supply and some freedom from the speculative freight-rate market in which the tramp inevitably works. And a fifth factor is undoubtedly the exaggerated nationalism and protectionism that affects the free market in ocean transport—of which the grossest example is that of the U.S.A., which prohibits all foreign vessels from carrying cargo between any two U.S. ports and stipulates that one-half of all cargoes shipped under foreign aid programs must be in American vessels. Such limitations as these hit the tramp fleets of Norway and Greece in particular, for these countries have little foreign trade of their own to fall back on, in contrast to Britain.

Finally, and perhaps most important of all, there is the development, within the last decade, of the specialized bulk carrier for iron ore and certain other traffics. The tramp is now being challenged, indeed, in what used to be its most assured field of employment, the carriage of bulk cargoes that move in one direction only. The economies of size and speed, which reduce labor costs per ton-mile, and the specialized handling gear that reduces the time spent in port, far outweigh the disadvantage of being in ballast for half the round trip; and indeed bulk carriers are now being built which can carry several different sorts of cargo equally well—say iron ore, grain and even oil.

This is not to say that tramp shipping has been by any means extinguished. The British tramp fleet in 1965 numbered nearly 400 ships with a gross tonnage of 3 millions (apart from vessels engaged solely in coastwise trade); this still represented nearly one-fifth of our total merchant marine.[17] And about 800 of the "Liberty" ships were still afloat in 1965, some of them usefully employed, under various flags, in carrying grain from up-river ports of the Plate, or in the scrap trade, where their slow speed was of no consequence. There is still grain to be carried from Australia, Argentina, the St. Lawrence, northeastern U.S.A. and the Black Sea to Britain and western Europe, or to India and to Japan; some coal still moves from Britain[18] and the Rhine to Mediterranean ports, and from eastern U.S.A. to Europe and to Japan; iron ore is still carried in tramps from Brazil, north and west Africa to the U.S.A. and U.K./European ports, and from India and Malaya to Japan; timber still comes from the Baltic and White Sea areas to western Europe and Britain, and from British Columbia; sugar is still available as a bulk cargo from Mauritius and Queensland, and phosphate from North Africa. And the up-to-date tramp ship of today is a very different vessel from its predecessor of a few decades ago, as Table 14-9 demonstrates.[19]

In the early 1960's some 15 per cent of the world's tramp fleet comprised ships of over 13,000 tons; the average size was 10,700 tons, and the average speed 12 knots.

The tramp, then, is meeting competition

Table 14-9 Typical Tramp Ships

Date	Propulsion	Size (d.w.t.)	Speed (knots)	Fuel consumption (tons per day)	Fuel cost per 1000 ton-miles s.	d.
Pre-1914	Steam (coal)	8400	10	30 (coal)	26	9
1938	Steam (coal)	9250	10½	20 (coal)	17	5
1938	Steam (oil)	9250	10½	13·6 (fuel oil)	13	0
1938	Motor	9200	10	6–7 (diesel oil)	11	2
1954	Motor	11,000	12	12 (oil)	10	4

from the cargo liner and from the bulk carrier. It is the bulk carrier, however, which has introduced a number of new and interesting features into the world's ocean traffic, and it is worth analysing these developments in some detail.[20] The growth of the bulk-carrier fleets is spectacular: it began in about 1955; by 1960 there were 365 bulk carriers afloat, totaling 6.6 million d.w.t., and by 1965 there were 1000, totalling 22 million d.w.t., with another 9.4 million tons on the order books of the shipyards. Four main types of ship have been evolved in response to the physical and economic demands of the traffic: (1) ore-carriers, (2) bulk carriers capable of taking either ore or crude oil, (3) general-purpose bulk carriers of the U.B.S. (Universal Bulk Ship) type, and (4) a larger variety of U.B.S. designed to carry dry bulk cargoes and crude oil (Fig. 14-5). It will, of course, be appreciated that although some of these ships may be strictly confined to one particular route, others, and particularly the U.B.S. in the 20,000–30,000 d.w.t. class, are essentially tramps in that they can enter a variety of traffics and routes and minimize the amount of voyaging in ballast. And the distinction between the four types mentioned is becoming blurred as large ships designed for both liquid and dry cargoes of various types in bulk make their appearance.

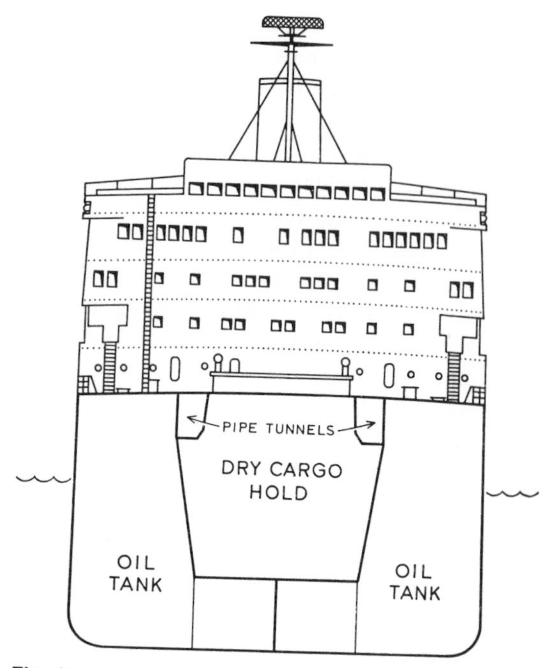

Fig. 14-5 Midship section of a modern bulk carrier. The center holds carry iron ore, with oil at the sides and below. (Adapted from J. Bes, *Bulk Carriers*, p. 19)

The "bulk" in the title of these ships applies as much to the ships themselves as to their cargoes. The average deadweight tonnage in 1965 was about 26,000, but two-thirds of the ore-carriers on the stocks in the same year were of over 50,000 d.w.t. and the largest vessels already in service are 80,000-ton iron-ore-carriers plying from Lourenço Marques to Japan. Since a 35,000-ton bulk carrier will have a draught of about 34 feet it is obvious that the same kind of geographical limitation is likely to operate as in the case of the giant tankers. Indeed, as a generalization it may be said that the larger vessels are restricted to the ore/coal oil business, whilst the grain carriers are generally smaller, below about 28,000 d.w.t. And with a few exceptions, British ports are at a very serious disadvantage in the development of such traffics, because of severe limitations of draught and lock-entrances to dock systems.

The incentive for the development of the large ore-carrier came after the Second World War, as more and more distant ore-sources had to be used by Britain, Europe, the United States and Japan. The Swedish Grängesberg Company had for several decades been exporting iron ore from Luleå and Narvik in special ships, but in 1963 it entered the Liberian ore trade with 65,000-ton carriers plying between Lower Buchanan and Rotterdam. The French Dreyfus Company has a fleet of 32,500 d.w.t. vessels on the West Africa to

Dunkirk run. These are but two examples—apart from the Japanese one quoted above. Clearly the use of such ships depends on the availability of appropriate port facilities at both ends of the line—and there lies the rub. Rotterdam and several Japanese ports can take these big ships, but in Britain, of our normal ore-importing ports with adjacent iron and steel works, only the Tyne can take a 35,000-ton vessel; Glasgow, Newport and Middlesbrough can only take 20,000-tonners (though improvements are in progress at the mouth of the Tees), and Port Talbot, which serves the huge post-war Margam works, can take no more than 10,000 d.w.t. It is obvious that the British iron and steel industry will be increasingly disadvantaged through the inability to make use of the large ore-carriers.[21]

Somewhat similar to the ore-carriers are the vessels built primarily for the United States coal export trade.[22] The Hampton Roads–Japan route involves the passage of the Panama Canal, so 30,000-ton vessels are employed. Incidentally, these ships can load in 1 day and discharge in 6 days—but these figures (what a contrast with the old-fashioned tramp!) are bettered by the 68,000-ton ships plying between Hampton Roads and Rotterdam, where they can discharge this huge cargo in under 3 days! Large ships are also used between Hampton Roads and the Plate; they pick up Brazilian iron ore at Victoria for the return voyage.

The development of the ore- and oil-carrying ship was prompted in some measure by the Labrador iron-ore traffic, which of course shuts down for nearly half the year because of the freezing of the Gulf of St. Lawrence; though in fact the Grängesberg Company had a somewhat similar arrangement from 1959 with outward cargoes of Swedish ore and inward cargoes of oil. The Labrador ships thus carry ore in the summer and oil in the winter—a simple and effective arrangement. Naturally enough, the cubic space within the ship occupied by iron ore is very different from that occupied by oil, and the internal arrangement of the holds is correspondingly different both from that of the ordinary tramp and from that of the oil tanker (Fig. 14-5).

The U.B.S. is essentially an up-to-date tramp, of 20,000–22,000 d.w.t. with a speed of 15 knots, and very carefully designed to facilitate the use of grabs in unloading bulk cargoes and to accommodate bulk goods with varying storage factors (weight per cubic foot, etc.,) without instability.[23] They are single-deck ships with partial 'tween decks on each side divided into watertight compartments for water ballast or dry cargo. Like other bulk carriers (including the latest oil tankers) they have all their engines and accommodation aft.

It is instructive, finally, to look at the flag distribution of these bulk carriers (Fig. 14-6). The inability of so many British ports to cope with ships of this size,[24] and the antiquity of the loading and unloading arrangements so often present—to say nothing of the restrictive practices which militate against the installation of highly mechanized equipment—have resulted in Britain occupying a rather poor third place behind Liberia and Norway. Liberia is, of course, the classic case of the "flag of convenience," and its shipping is largely financed by capital from the United States. Norway has always been in the van of developments in tramp shipping and cargo carrying in general.

I have tried to confine myself to examples of the direct geographical consequences of technological progress. But there are many examples of indirect consequences that work in particular through the medium of economics. Any technological advances in shipbuilding techniques that reduce the cost of building or the cost of operating a ship will be reflected in changed geographical values; advantages will be conferred on certain traffics, on certain flags, perhaps, or on certain ports; and, even allowing for the overall expansion of the

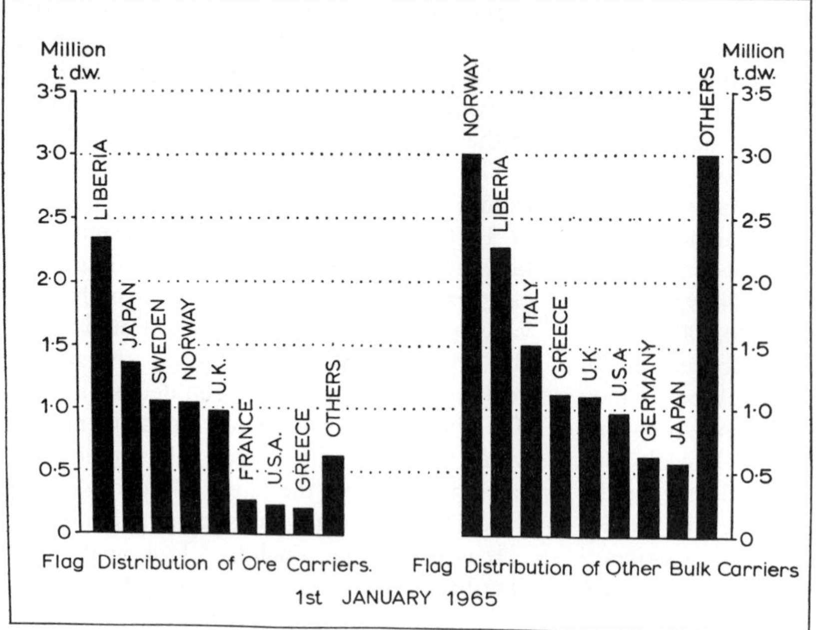

Fig. 14-6 Flag distribution of ore carriers and other bulk carriers, 1965. (Redrawn from J. Bes, *Bulk Carriers*, p. 50)

world's shipping, other parts of the whole shipping and trade system will be correspondingly disadvantaged. And, as I pointed out [elsewhere], it would be foolish to assume that all technological progress necessarily increases man's control over his physical environment; the larger the super-tankers and bulk carriers become, the fewer the routes and ports they can use, and the more restrictive, therefore, becomes the influence of the physical geography of the coastline. Nothing ever stands still in economic geography. In some branches of our subject—geomorphology, for example—though ideas and methods may change, the subject matter at least remains constant, but in economic geography both subject matter and the methodology are constantly on the move. Perhaps that is why there are far more geomorphologists than economic geographers among our students and colleagues!

REFERENCES

1 *Advancement of Science,* Vol. XVIII, 1961, pp. 315–327.

2 M. Simons, "What is a geographical factor?" *Geography,* Vol. 51, 1966, pp. 210–217.

3 L. D. Stamp, *Applied Geography,* Harmondsworth: Penguin Books, 1960. See also "Some neglected aspects of Geography," *Geography,* Vol. 36, 1951, pp. 1–14. Diagram on p. 3.

4 J. Lamb, *Oil Tanker Cargoes,* Charles Griffin & Co. Ltd., 1964.

5 J. Bes, *Tanker Shipping,* Hilversum, 1963. See also Lord Geddes, "The operation of the big tankers," *J. Inst. Transport,* July 1966, pp. 399–408.

6 J. R. Parkinson, *Economics of Ship Building in the U.K.,* Cambridge University Press, 1960, chapter 9. The direct saving of steel in a welded ship (amounting to as much as 12 per cent in a big tanker or liner) may reduce the cost of building by 2 or 3 per cent whilst the increased speed possible in the absence of the thousands of pro-

jecting rivers may be as much as 20 per cent. Thus the overall saving in the cost of building a ship with a certain cargo capacity and for a certain speed may be as much as 10 per cent.

7 P. R. Odell, *An Economic Geography of Oil*, G. Bell & Sons Ltd., 1963, chapter 7.

8 J. Bes, *op. cit.*

9 W. Suhren, *The Seaborne Trade in Liquefied Gases and International Shipping*, Bergen, 1965.

10 *Ibid.*

11 H. R. Howells, "Marine refrigeration," *Inst. of Mechanical Engineers*, 1959.

12 "The tramp . . . is a self-contained unit of transport. It is not attached continuously to any given trade route; it does not conduct its operation in concert with others; its sailings are determined by no fixed plan. The function of the tramp, in short, is to fluctuate from one route to another, according to the shipping requirements of the various trades. Its movements are determined by the law of supply and demand; it goes where its voyage will yield the greatest profit; and it undertakes no obligation beyond that involved in each particular venture." (*Report of the Royal Commission on Shipping Rings*, Vol. I, Cd. 4668, H.M.S.O., 1909, p. 75.)

13 British Shipping (Assistance) Act, 1935. On the inter-war period see S. G. Sturmey, *British Shipping and World Competition*, Athlone Press, 1962, chapter IV.

14 H. Gripaios, *Tramp Shipping*, Thomas Nelson & Sons Ltd., 1959.

15 A. G. Course, *The Deep Sea Tramp*, Hollis & Carter, 1960.

16 Chamber of Shipping of U.K., *Annual Report*, 1965–6.

17 *Ibid.*

18 But British exports declined from 14 million tons in 1953 to 8 million tons in 1963 and under 4 millions in 1965.

19 H. Gripaios, *op. cit.*

20 J. Bes, *Bulk Carriers*, Hilversum, 1965.

21 In 1964, for example, the British Iron and Steel Corporation had 75 ore-carrying ships on long-term charter, but only 5 of these were over 24,000 d.w.t. It is, however, planned to create a tidal basin at Port Talbot, which will take 65,000-tonners.

22 These were preceded in 1956–7 by converted T2 oil tankers—see above, p. 215—which were rebuilt in response to the high level of transatlantic coal rates ruling at that period.

23 Coal requires 45–50 cubic feet per ton, iron ore 15–25 cubic feet, phosphate 30–35 cubic feet, barley 52–55 cubic feet.

24 Only London, Hull and Avonmouth can cope with big U.B.S. tramps, for example.

It should be clear from the foregoing that we cannot ignore the special terminal point for marine transportation: the seaport. James Bird has erected a very simple, but effective, model of the evolution of a seaport, his Anyport model.* Based inductively on a series of investigations of British seaports, the model traces the evolution of the installations of a port. Obviously ports in Britain and elsewhere in the world differ considerably in detail, but most appear to go through the same sequential development since they basically serve very similar ends—the world's shipping fleets. Before describing his model, Bird's *caveat* to the original formulation bears repeating: the purpose of the model is not to display a pattern into which all ports must be forced but to provide a base with which to compare the development of actual ports anywhere in the world. "Each new step in the story of Anyport involves an addition to or a change in the physical layout of the port, helping to build up to the complex pattern of a modern major port."†

The figure on page 228 and the table on page 230 show the eras of

*J. Bird, *The Major Seaports of the United Kingdom*, London: Hutchinson, 1963.
†Ibid., p. 27.

development of Anyport, each step of which is terminated by an alteration or addition to the port layout. Not that the older installations are no longer used; on the contrary, the vestiges of former eras can be recognized alongside those of more recent ones. Anyport is assumed to begin its life at an estuary head with a tidal range greater than 15 feet. The primitive port begins at some point along Anyport's estuary where an easier and therefore busier place for a harbor can be found, perhaps where a tributary enters, causing a slight indentation, with higher ground giving some protection to the site. In Britain such a port could not carry on commerce until it was proclaimed a legal port. The customs house would be sited very close to the original core of the port, where it may remain as a landmark (in North America too), even though most ships would berth some distance away. The port develops linearly along the waterfront until it is limited by some natural feature or perhaps defensive work of the port. Transit sheds may line the quays, with warehouses for longer storage behind. A bridge may separate seagoing vessels from river traffic, and a road probably transverse to the waterfront leads into the port's hinterland.

Eventually the lineal development of the port must outstrip the areal

growth of the town, and when this can be demonstrated, the second era of *marginal quay extension* can be said to have begun. If this extension were to go on indefinitely, the port would be unduly lengthened; customs surveillance, originally based entirely on the custom house, would be made difficult. So the early port engineers strive for additional quayage without increasing the area of the port.

Marginal quay elaboration consists of short jetties or cuts in the riverbanks called hithes, or tidal graving docks, where ships can be overhauled during the terminal turnround. As ships grow larger, the original harbor becomes congested. Whole fleets sheer and range together in the tideway. Engineers have literally to break new ground. In the case of Anyport, the harbor is expanded by the excavation of a dock upon a land-encroaching site of an estuarine floodplain. An alternative solution is to excavate mud flats between tide marks. In both cases, digging of the dock proceeds within an encircling cofferdam, and the quaysides around the hole are built up far above high-water level by the spoil from the excavation. In the early nineteenth century sailing ships were still relatively small, and so dock engineers strove for the maximum quay length possible in a given area. If the water site permits (in Anyport's case, if the river had been wider), peninsular jetties afford a

The six eras of Anyport
Top

I. The *primitive* port is taken as sited where a left-bank tributary has caused an embayment, largely dry at low tides (coarse stipple in the estuary) and upstream of estuarine marshes (fine stipple on the right of the diagram).

II. *Marginal quay extension*, downstream and opposite the above nucleus.

III. *Marginal quay elaboration*, jetties and hithes (cuts in the river bank).

W. Warehouses: quayside buildings, warehouses or transit sheds; semicircular town wall with stronghold where the wall meets the estuary downstream.

Center

I–III. Same as top.

IV. *Dock elaboration* era.

DD. Dry dock associated with later docks; Q, continuing marginal quay extension.

T and W. Transit sheds and warehouses.

Bottom

I–IV. Same as center.

V. *Simple lineal quayage*, over 500m in one line, with 8.5m minimum alongside.

VI. *Specialized quayage,* notable at T-head jetties and at large wharves.

T. Transit sheds, or in the river, jetties serving a continuous frontage of industry. Container berths are usually in the downstream area of ports, in reconstructed areas of docks with simple lineal quayage, or where deep water lies against wide areas of flat land (existing or reclaimed).

The scale has been omitted on purpose from each section of this illustration.

Summary of the Development of a Major Port

Era	Terminated by the epoch of . . .
I Primitive	the overflowing of the port function from the *primitive* nucleus of the port, or the change in location of the dominant port function
II Marginal quay extension	the change from a simple continuous line of quays
III Marginal quay elaboration	the opening of a dock or the expansion of the harbor
IV Dock elaboration	the opening of a dock with simple lineal quayage
V Simple lineal quayage*	the provision of oil berths in deep water
VI Specialized quayage	the occupation of all waterside sites between the port nucleus and the open sea

*Minimum requirements for *simple lineal quayage* have been empirically derived from a study of the development of actual ports. They are as follows: 1,500 feet of quay in one uninterrupted line, and 26 feet minimum depth alongside, with an approach channel having a minimum depth of 26 feet; if the quay is in an impounded dock, the entrance lock should be at least 750 feet long.
Source: Bird, *op cit.*

great length of quay line within a small compass. They can be distinguished from the earlier jetties of marginal quay elaboration by their greater length and width. Even compact, elaborate quayage in docks or jetties has to be provided progressively farther away from the nucleus, and later installations of this fourth era, *dock elaboration,* are tied back to the central distribution area by the railway. Defects of the docks and quays with elaborate outlines become apparent as the largest ships using the port become even longer. The short runs of quays cannot easily be expanded. Engineers begin to design longer quays where the longest and shortest general cargo vessels can berth together if necessary. Such quays eliminate short dead-end spurs for both road and rail transport, and there is no back-to-back quayside working at adjacent berths. If the opening of a dock with elaborate quayage marks the fourth era of development, the opening of a dock with *simple lineal quayage* marks the fifth era; this is a twentieth-century development.

The story of Anyport would end with the provision of simple lineal quayage if all the cargoes received were general cargo packaged goods or goods in small lots in the holds of dry cargo liners. But side by side with the increase of general cargo trade there has grown up a trade in goods specifically destined for waterside depots and factories. Perhaps the first industries to have made a distinctive mark on the waterfront are shipbuilding and ship-repairing, and fishing. But during this century Anyport has found it necessary to provide additional *specialized quayage* for large-scale industry and bulk cargoes. Ships have become in some instances more specialized carriers of cargoes—the bulk carriers. The first important class of such vessels comprised grain clippers, colliers, and oil tankers. Since oil requires distinctive port handling techniques, provision by Anyport of oil berths in deep water may be taken as beginning a sixth era of specialized quayage provided on the grand scale. It must be admitted that conversion of quays from general cargo to specialization on single cargo has gone on since the nineteenth century. Container cargo berths are the latest example of such a trend, and they may even call into recognition a "special" case of specialized quayage—the era of *container quayage.*

Thus Anyport's growth in area has been traced from the port nucleus to the threshold of the open sea. Note, however, that this sixth era is fundamentally different from those preceding it. For the first time the function of the quayage is used as a distinguishing characteristic rather than the layout of the berths. This has two implications: (1) berths from earlier eras could be adapted for new specialized uses; (2) specialized quayage can spread upstream, while earlier developments were predominantly downstream.

Bird also applied his work on British seaports to Australia.‡ There he found that the small tidal range made impounded wet docks unnecessary, but otherwise the model was a useful comparative tool. B. S. Hoyle also used the device in East Africa.§ Again, although no exact fit was found, since none was expected, the device was useful. Hoyle added a preliminary stage to the era of primitive port installations—the *dhow traffic* era, where little or no port facility was needed.

Other approaches to ports are, of course, possible. Ports can be considered as part of the maritime sector of the economy; they can be considered merely as evolving terminal nodes of a country's transport network; or their competitive roles can be assessed in terms of how they subdivide the immediate hinterland of a country. It is this latter approach which J. B. Kenyon takes in the next selection. Here he analyzes the changing positions of selected U.S. ports, the interchange or break of bulk points between two different modes—the land-based mode and the port domestic hinterlands—and the sea-based mode and its trading orientations. He stresses, however, that the relative positions between ports and modes is as much a reflection of the human decisions concerned in financial and organizational decisions as it is a reflection of the structure of the modes and hinterlands.

‡J. Bird, *Seaport Gateways of Australia,* Oxford University Press, 1968.
§B. S. Hoyle, *The Seaports of East Africa,* East African Publishing House, 1967, pp. 26–36.

Selection 15

Elements in Inter-port Competition in the United States

J. B. Kenyon

During the years since World War II there have been significant shifts in the circumstances affecting competition among United States ports for deepwater foreign and domestic trade. Against a background of massive inertia, these have had the effect of promoting a gradual evolution in the roles and relative patterns of the various ocean ports. Thus in spite of considerable year-to-year fluctuations in the volumes handled by ports in general

Economic Geography, vol. 46, no. 1, 1970, pp. 1–24. Reprinted by permission of the author and editor.

and in particular, there emerges a pattern of long-term trends among American ports, shaped by a number of changes in methods of handling and transportation. These are combined, of course, with changes in the overall patterns of origin and destination and commodity composition of oceanborne shipments, both inland and overseas. Leading factors affecting American interport competition for general cargo may be grouped under several headings: economic changes in the various classes of hinterland, the expansion of the St. Lawrence Seaway to competitive dimensions, changes in rail rate territories, railroad mergers, the rise of motor truck inland transportation, containerization of oceangoing freight, differential expansion of port facilities and structural works (infrastructure), differential efforts to facilitate the business and administrative contacts of ocean trade within the port, and finally field solicitation of trade.

The object of this [work] is to analyze the shifting magnitudes and composition of general cargo freight among selected United States ports in terms of the extent and make-up of their domestic hinterlands, their overseas trade orientation, and the economic character of the port metropolis itself, and to review some of the changing conditions and practices that seem to hold special significance to the competitive struggle among American ports. Finally, attention is turned briefly to the availability of developable space at the selected ports for the kind of terminal activity which seems necessary in the near future.

The truism that the future grows out of the past, that the structure of the past affects and shapes prospective growth, is certainly borne out in the case of the deep-sea port, where enormous investment in physical plant, in business activity, and in habits of traders and shippers have molded patterns which change only slowly. The early development of the American economy in the Northeast and the still-dominant trade routes to Western Europe have traditionally favored the growth of ports in the North Atlantic Range, especially New York.

For years the Port of New York has overwhelmingly dominated the transshipment function of goods between land and ocean transportation. Its stature as the Nation's largest urban agglomeration and consuming center and as a focus of routes of transport to the American Midwest—in a sense the industrial heartland of the nation—has attracted a major share of the activities involved in, and associated with, ocean shipping. The marketing, processing, financing, and other services concentrated at that city have historically led to the upward spiral of increased sailings, attracting increased volumes of cargo, which in turn stimulated further increases in facilities and service. With the progressive enlargement of vessels and maritime facilities in the port, advantages accrued from the economies of large scale and led to further concentration of shipping activity in the Port of New York. Though much of such growth resulted from the expansion and diversification of the American economy, some developed also from diversion of trade from other, smaller ports. Thus, the story of port competition for general cargo is primarily the struggle against New York by smaller ports.[1]

Increases in the scale of goods-handling have in general reduced small ports to relicts, except where they serve as nearby outlets for large outbound flows of bulk commodities, or, in a few instances, as important but specialized points of entry for inbound commodities. In general, however, the small ports have declined, especially in their general cargo activity, into quiescence. Only the medium-sized ports in sizable metropolitan centers, with competitive access to large producing and especially consuming regions, seem in a position to challenge the dominance of New

Table 15-1 Waterborne Foreign Trade by U.S. Customs District, 1967

	Boston	*New York*	*Philadelphia*	*Baltimore*	*New Orleans*	*Chicago*
Total						
Value ($mil.)	750.4	12,426.9	1,852.4	1,466.5	3,481.9	709.5
Per cent of U.S.	2.07	34.26	5.11	4.04	9.60	1.96
Weight (mil. lbs,)	19,492.1	118,143.5	98,379.4	45,747.6	82,980.6	23,809.2
Per cent of U.S.	2.19	13.30	11.08	5.15	9.34	2.68
Cents per lb.	3.8	10.5	1.9	3.2	4.2	3.0
Exports						
Value ($mil.)	103.7	5,958.9	496.3	601.5	2,479.9	266.7
Per cent of U.S.	0.55	31.74	2.64	3.20	13.21	1.42
Weight (.000 lbs,)	1,443.8	14,104.7	6,139.1	9,008.0	54,059.0	5,519.8
Per cent of U.S.	0.39	3.76	1.64	2.40	14.40	1.47
Cents per lb.	7.2	42.2	8.1	6.7	4.6	4.8
Imports						
Value ($mil.)	646.7	6,468.0	1,356.1	865.0	1,002.0	442.8
Per cent of U.S.	3.70	36.97	7.75	4.94	5.73	2.53
Weight (.000 lbs.)	18,048.3	104,038.8	92,240.3	36,739.6	28,921.6	18,289.4
Per cent of U.S.	3.52	20.29	17.99	7.16	5.64	3.57
Cents per lb.	3.6	6.2	1.5	2.4	3.5	2.4

Source: U.S. Department of Commerce, *Highlights of U.S. Export and Import Trade.* FT 990/December, 1967.

York. Thus, the focus of this study will be on the situations of five such ports in their efforts to wrest a share of New York's trade, in the light of their regional positions and in terms of emergent goods-handling practices.

The opening of the St. Lawrence Seaway to competitive ocean shipping in 1959 created in large measure a new element of competition for midwestern freight to the established ports of both the Atlantic and Gulf Coasts. Though shipping in the Great Lakes had traditionally been large, it had been composed mainly of bulk goods moving within the Lakes themselves or into the St. Lawrence River for possible transshipment to overseas points. The enlargement of the Seaway has meant an actual and further potential growth primarily in the movement of oceanborne general cargo to and from the Lakes. Thus the Lakes may now be considered a fourth coast of the United States.

The ports selected for analysis, besides New York, are Boston, Philadelphia, Baltimore, New Orleans, and Chicago. Each has a large metropolitan economy and functions as a sizable consuming center; each is a major focus of land transport routes; and each has the benefit of a low rail-rate territory which favors it over other major ports. Yet each differs from the others in its distance from New York, its nearness to the Midwest, its history of port activity, the extent of its infrastructure (both physical and administrative), and the nature and rate of growth of its special hinterland. Furthermore, two of these, New Orleans and Chicago, are on other coasts, and have particular advantages in trade in certain world regions. Since revenue to the port area, measured in the various terms of economic activity, accrues largely from the handling of general (packaged) cargo, in contrast to the typically mechanical handling of bulk cargo, the emphasis of this study will be on general cargo moving in deepwater trade, both domestic and foreign, through the selected ports.

The advent of containerization of freight seems to hold equal if not greater promise in the handling of waterborne than railroad cargo. Though the level of optimism regarding containerization varies among ports, this form of cargo handling is regarded with high expectations by many; indeed to some it represents the wave of the future. The prospects for its expansion depend, of course, on the degree to which a port's general cargo composition is conducive to containerization and the land and facilities available for its handling. Thus it is necessary, even in a general review such as this, to take some cognizance of a port's container potential in order to put the various elements relevant to the strength of its competitive position into some perspective.

THE MAGNITUDE AND COMPOSITION OF CARGO VOLUMES

In order to draw a comparison of the cargo volumes among the ports in question, presentations in terms of both weight and value have been prepared (Table 15-1).[2] Since general cargo is usually of far higher value per pound than bulk cargo, the ratio of value per pound reflects the much greater emphasis on general cargo at New York than at the other ports in question. The fact that bulk cargo is limited in types of commodities suggests that New York is also much more diversified in its operation than the others. Just as great size makes for diversification—or specialization in the nonstandardized—in business and manufacturing, it does also in transportation.

In 1967, imports exceeded exports both in value and tonnage for each port except New Orleans. Whereas imports consist significantly of petroleum products and tropical foodstuffs in the five old ocean ports (excluding Chicago), these commodities are augmented by large quantities of ore at all ports but New York and Boston. Outbound movements consist to a greater degree of manufactured goods, although New Orleans and Chicago boast large outbound grain flows. Beyond this, each port, and especially New York, handles a wide variety of goods.

In spite of the considerable fluctuation of

Table 15-2 Percentage Growth in Waterborne Foreign Trade by Value and Weight Between 1955 and 1965 by U.S. Customs District

Percentage growth	*Boston*	*New York*	*Philadelphia*	*Baltimore*	*New Orleans*	*Chicago*
Value (adjusted)[a]						
Total	22.1	33.1	39.6	33.4	42.4	412.9
Export	8.4	35.6	32.0	7.2	68.2	419.4
Import	24.6	30.7	43.8	70.6	5.5	407.3
Weight						
Total	21.5	40.4	(5.3)	(0.5)	70.5	310.6
Export	6.1	(21.0)	(11.2)	(29.3)	105.9	153.4
Import	23.2	57.4	(4.4)	13.3	13.4	478.2

[a] Dollar values adjusted according to wholesale price index, given in U.S. office of Business Economics, *1967 Business Statistics*, 16th Biennial Edition, 1967, p. 41.

Note: Parentheses around numbers indicate decline.

Source: Derived from U.S. Bureau of the Census, Foreign Trade Division, *United States Waterborne Foreign Trade*. Summary Reports. FT 958, Calendar Years 1955 and 1965.

foreign trade by port from year to year, one sees a picture of general growth among all ports, and especially of Chicago during the recent past, even though dollar figures are corrected for inflation (Table 15-2). The directional orientations of the ports in question seem to be accentuating: import specialization at Boston, Philadelphia, and Baltimore, and export specialization at New Orleans. New York's balance between export and import trade continues. Growth by value may be characterized as moderate at Boston, considerable in New York, Philadelphia, and Baltimore, rapid at New Orleans, and burgeoning at Chicago.

Measured by weight, however, a somewhat different picture emerges. Here one sees absolute declines in volume in export trade at New York, Philadelphia, and Baltimore, and a decline also in import tonnage at Philadelphia. Thus the value growth in the face of tonnage decline can only mean the rapid rise in value of commodities handled, or rather a shift from low-grade to high-grade goods, particularly among exports. The rapid growth of New Orleans and Chicago in exports may also suggest—but not prove—an absolute diversion of traffic away from the large eastern ports. Boston's small size is seen to be accompanied by weak growth in exports, illustrating the long, protracted relative atrophy of Boston's export trade, and its tendency to become mainly a port for the inbound flow of goods to local consumers.

GENERAL CARGO TRAFFIC

Since there is not a widely accepted definition of general cargo with an accompanying list of commodities comprising it, such a definition and list were developed in this study. General cargo is here defined as including those commodities which in 1965 were normally handled in packaged form, in unit volumes, typically by longshoremen, manually or with fork-lift trucks and the like. This is in contrast to the fully mechanized systems typically utilized in handling loose, or bulk, cargo. A list of 56 commodities comprising bulk cargo was developed, and all other commodities are here considered to be general cargo. For purposes of comparability a list of the same commodities was prepared for 1955.[3] Not only are more and more commodities now being handled in bulk form, making such a listing decreasingly accurate from year to year, but different commodities are handled differently in various ports (Table 15-3).

In distinguishing general from bulk cargo, it is evident that the preponderance of tonnage handled at each port is bulk, but that this is least the case in New York. Yet it should be noted that Baltimore and New Orleans handle almost as large a proportion of general cargo as New York, whereas Boston, Philadelphia, and Chicago are more specialized in bulk cargo.

The erratic pattern of tonnage growth between 1955 and 1965 is evident, a decade in which total United States tonnage grew by 25.3 per cent (general cargo 23.7 per cent and bulk cargo 25.5 per cent). Thus the national growth rate was exceeded only by New Orleans—bulk cargo only—and Chicago, by virtue of the opening of the St. Lawrence Seaway. The absolute declines in general cargo tonnages handled by Boston and New York, and the slow growth of Philadelphia, Baltimore, and New Orleans indicate a higher-than-average rate of growth in general cargo elsewhere during those years. However, one must remember that considerable year-to-year fluctuations do occur in shipping figures, and that in 1965 military shipments undoubtedly far exceeded those of 1955. It is clear that New York's position remains dominant in both foreign and coastwise trade, in spite of regional leadership and dynamacy evinced by

Table 15-3 Composition of Deepwater Traffic, by Port, 1965 (.000 Short Tons)

	Boston (Port)	*New York (Port)*	*Philadelphia (Harbor)*	*Baltimore (Harbor)*	*New Orleans (Port)*	*Chicago (Port)*
All Cargo						
Port total	19,855	153,830	47,735	44,267	88,877	45,973
General cargo	1,103	20,106	3,103	5,444	10,900	4,093
Per cent of port total	5.55	13.07	6.31	12.30	12.26	8.90
Bulk cargo	18,752	133,725	44,631	38,823	77,977	41,880
Per cent of port total	94.43	86.92	93.50	87.70	87.73	91.09
Per cent of U.S. by category						
Port total	0.56	12.08	3.75	3.48	6.98	3.61
General cargo	0.68	12.48	1.93	3.38	6.76	2.54
Bulk cargo	1.69	12.03	4.01	3.50	7.01	3.77
Per cent growth, 1965/1955						
Port total	4.2	3.1	(2.4)	(3.4)	88.8	18.0
General cargo	(26.6)	(21.3)	4.9	3.5	9.6	79.1
Bulk cargo	6.9	8.5	(2.8)	(4.3)	110.0	14.2
General Cargo						
Foreign trade	831	11,502	2,389	3,224	5,161	2,067
Imports	719	6,847	1,734	1,470	2,135	1,318
Exports	111	4,655	655	1,754	3,026	749
Coastwise trade (includes Lakewise)	213	4,708	461	1,589	505	437
Receipts	209	2,996	236	480	171	300
Shipments	4	1,713	225	1,110	334	137
Per cent of U.S. by category						
Foreign trade	1.26	17.51	3.64	4.91	7.85	3.15
Imports	2.10	20.02	5.07	4.28	6.24	3.85
Exports	0.35	14.78	2.08	5.57	9.60	2.38
Coastwise trade (includes Lakewise)	0.82	18.00	1.76	6.08	1.93	1.67
Receipts	0.80	11.45	0.90	1.83	0.65	1.15
Shipments	0.02	6.55	0.86	4.24	1.28	0.52

Note: Parentheses around numbers indicate decline.

Source: U.S. Corps of Engineers, *Waterborne Commerce of the United States*. Calendar year 1955, and calendar year 1965, *Waterways and Harbors*, Volume I, *Atlantic Coast*, Volume II, *Gulf Coast, Mississippi River System and Antilles*, Part III, *Great Lakes*, and Part V, *National Summaries*. (U.S. Army Engineer District, Detroit, 1955, and 1965).

both New Orleans and Chicago (Table 15-3). Boston, on the other hand, is shown to be particularly weak, especially in its outbound movement, as a result of a combination of disadvantages, as will be shown below.

Thus the pattern of relative size, composition, and growth is a complex one, further complicated by the noncomparability of available data. Overall figures often mask shifts in commodity composition, as well as shifts in points of origin and destination of shipments.

FOREIGN TRADE PATTERNS

In general, the dominant flow of traffic of each port is across the North Atlantic to Western Europe, in a trade relatively high in value per pound. It is interesting that in all six of the ports studied nearly half of the export trade (by value) is with Western (non-Communist) Europe. The United States as a whole sent 38 per cent of its waterborne exports to Europe in 1967, slightly less than any of these ports, which suggests that each of these is heavily engaged in the competition for such trade. Import trade was less even; New York drew 44 per cent of its imports from Europe, but Chicago registered fully 50 per cent. Though the other Atlantic ports fell somewhat behind New York in the proportion of their inbound trade coming from Western Europe, New Orleans drew only one-fifth of its imports from Europe.

The fact that New Orleans and Chicago lie on different coasts from New York, however, gives them undoubted advantages in nearby foreign areas. Although the Chicago Custom Region's largest foreign trade is with Western Europe, the importance of its trade with Canada is clear (Table 15-4). Likewise, the significance of the New Orleans Region's ties to Latin America are shown. Thus proximity appears to play a role, but a subordinate one, in the pattern of waterborne foreign commerce.[4]

In contrast to relations with Europe, trade with Japan, another highly industrialized area, reveals a rather different pattern. The export component of total port trade with Japan is lowest at New York and Chicago, whereas, to the others, which ship relatively large vol-

Table 15-4 Percentage Distribution of Value of Waterborne Foreign Trade by World Area and U.S. Customs Region, 1967

	U.S. Total	*Atlantic Districts (Incl. Portland, Providence, and Bridgeport)*	*New York Region*	*Baltimore Region (Incl. Norfolk, Philadelphia)*	*New Orleans Region (Incl. Mobile, Baton Rouge)*	*Chicago Region (Incl. Detroit, Milwaukee, and Cleveland)*
Exports						
Total	100.0	100.0	100.0	100.0	100.0	100.0
Western Hemisphere	18.4	8.1	21.5	12.8	17.2	32.4
Canada	2.1	4.2	.....	0.4	0.5	28.7
20 Latin Am. Republics	13.6	3.8	18.7	11.6	14.3	3.5
Central Am. Common Mkt.	1.5	.....	1.8	0.5	2.2	0.3
Western Europe	38.0	44.8	41.6	51.2	45.1	45.9
Asia	32.9	37.7	23.9	25.4	29.4	12.9
Japan	12.8	28.0	6.2	10.2	11.2	5.9
Southern Asia	6.9	2.2	4.2	6.7	10.8	2.4
Australia and Oceania	4.0	6.1	4.6	3.9	2.1	3.1
Africa	5.7	2.1	7.8	5.6	4.6	4.7
Imports						
Total	100.0	100.0	100.0	100.0	100.0	100.0
Western Hemisphere	28.0	36.8	20.6	36.7	49.0	30.2
Canada	4.9	6.3	1.2	5.0	1.4	28.6
20 Latin Am. Republics	18.7	17.2	16.6	28.4	36.8	1.6
Central Am. Common Mkt.	1.6	0.6	1.3	0.4	6.6	.....
Western Europe	35.6	36.4	44.1	33.7	20.2	50.0
Asia	27.9	15.7	27.2	17.7	20.9	16.8
Japan	16.2	9.7	14.1	7.5	10.5	13.0
Southern Asia	2.1	1.2	1.9	1.9	2.8	0.2
Australia and Oceania	3.2	8.0	2.1	4.6	0.9	0.5
Africa	4.5	2.4	4.5	7.0	8.2	2.1

Source: Same as for Table 15-1.

umes of scrap to Japan, this export component is of greater local significance.

It is useful, however, to consider also the implications of commerce measured by weight. In the Atlantic Districts (including the coast of New England), for instance, exports to Japan account for 28 per cent by value, but 75 per cent by weight, illustrating the low grade of such exports (Table 15-4). This situation is repeated in the Baltimore region (including Philadelphia and Norfolk). In New York and New Orleans the balance between the percentage of export to Japan by weight and by value is more nearly even, though in Chicago the small volume of such export is of higher value per pound.

In terms of exports, New Orleans does a greater share of its trade with Japan than does New York, whereas in terms of imports from Japan, New York draws a larger proportion of its trade from Japan than does New Orleans. New Orleans is oriented to a greater degree in its export flows to Latin America, as mentioned, and especially to the lands of the Caribbean (Table 15-4). Although New Orleans is closer than New York to the West Coast of South America, New York is closer to the Atlantic Coast of South America than is New Orleans.[5] Yet distance does not seem to be an overriding criterion in the pattern of trade with various parts of the globe among these ports, except where the advantage is overwhelming.

Thus the trade of Europe, Africa, Latin America, and Asia seems subject to competition by any and all of these ports. Though each may endeavor to consolidate its position in a region closest to it, all look especially to trade with Europe, trade which is not only largest in absolute terms but richest in terms of its high-value, general cargo content. The distribution of this trade among these ports, however, must be sought in terms other than coastal position alone.

HINTERLANDS AND PORT SERVICE AREAS

Every port serves a variety of hinterlands, which differ in their economic makeup, generation of waterborne trade, size, and growth rates. Furthermore, the success of competition among the various ports for such trade differs, and this affects the development of those ports. In this study, several types of hinterland are considered: the low rail-rate hinterland, which is divided into the metropolitan and the outer low-rate areas; and the Eastern Midwest (Fig. 15-1).[6]

The metropolitan hinterland consists of the Standard Consolidated Areas of New York and Chicago and the Standard Metropolitan Statistical Area of each of the other port cities. It is assumed that this whole area is within easy reach of the waterfront and the many activities associated with maritime shipment. The metropolitan hinterland thus includes a functionally integrated urban entity, the back-

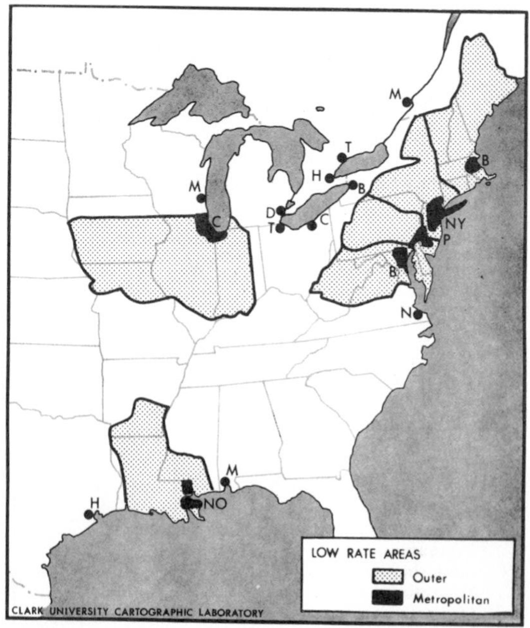

Fig. 15-1 Low rail-rate areas of selected ports.

yard of the port: an area within which the port should dominate overwhelmingly (but not exclusively) in the handling of maritime transport. It is further assumed that the preponderance of general cargo will move between points in the zone and the wharves by truck rather than rail. Patton points out, however, that large shipments may move by rail under carload rates, even for short distances.[7] Waterborne traffic from the metropolitan hinterlands may be regarded as most likely to move across local wharves, although shipments through one port may be generated within the central city of another port.

The low-rate area is construed as that area within which most commodity rates on general cargo are lower to the port in question than to any leading competitor. Beyond these areas, rates are likely to be equalized to adjacent ports, or even to a whole range of ports. Thus these low-rate areas tend to be small, relative to the whole hinterland of the port.

A word at this point, however, on the derivation of these zones. Since rail commodity rates differ among commodities, mainly as a result of historical precedent, there is no one absolute zone of low, or favorable, rates to any port. These zones, therefore, are at best approximate. They are delimited here not from the lengthy research into specific point-to-point rates (which needs to be performed), but rather on the eclectic basis of reliance on the judgment of persons of long experience in dealing with rates to the particular port, and with relevant published works. For instance, in the case of rates to Chicago, Draine provides data on a small sample of general cargo rates, suggestive of the pattern here shown, whereas Schenker points to the equalization of rates on tractors from Springfield or Peoria, Illinois, to Chicago and Milwaukee.[8] Thus any such rate area is a compromise—an area of statistical predominance—and here, at best, approximate.

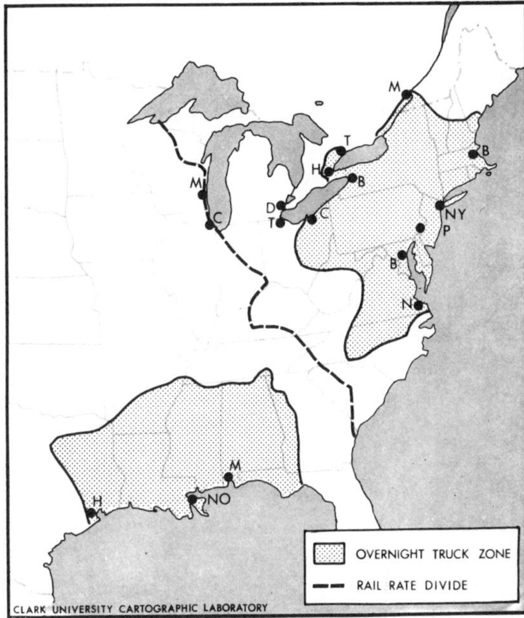

Fig. 15-2 Overnight truck delivery zones and rail rate divide between New York and New Orleans.

Truck Territories

The role of motor carriage in the transport of high-value, manufactured goods has been increasing rapidly since World War II. Although the cost is higher than rail, delivery time, and particularly the reliability of delivery at the appointed time, is better than rail transport. Therefore, any meaningful analysis of port interaction must take account of this form of service. Accordingly, the primary truck hinterlands of the two most dynamic ports on their respective coasts, New York and New Orleans, have been delimited (Fig. 15-2). Not only is motor carriage increasing significantly in the transport of maritime, as well as domestic internal freight, but its rates are less subject to equalization than are those of the railroads.[9] The overnight delivery zone is the area within which motor common carriers will promise next-morning delivery of goods received on the particular week-day. The radius varies to some extent among motor lines, but over-the-road trucks are typically dispatched at the close of the working day and arrive at the destination terminal prior to the beginning of the next working day. Their typical maximum overnight radius averages perhaps 400 miles, but is often extended to major cities and varies with the character and quality of highway connections (Fig. 15-2). The significance of truck transport decreases with distance, so that, beyond the radii shown, the preponderance of maritime freight is undoubtedly carried by rail, supplemented in the case of New Orleans by barge transport. It should be noticed that the overnight trucking radius of New York includes the two largest cities of Canada, which are shown by Patton to provice a significant volume of ocean cargo through New York.[10] Several major motor common carriers operate from New York to Toronto and Montreal respectively.[11]

These zones define theoretical hinterlands of the several ports in which they should either dominate the traffic completely, or at least enjoy an advantage over their competitors. But since success depends to an important degree on scale of operation, it seems clear that the strength of all North Atlantic and Gulf ports will be heavily dependent upon their ability to compete beyond these nearby zones for the trade of the Eastern Midwest.[12]

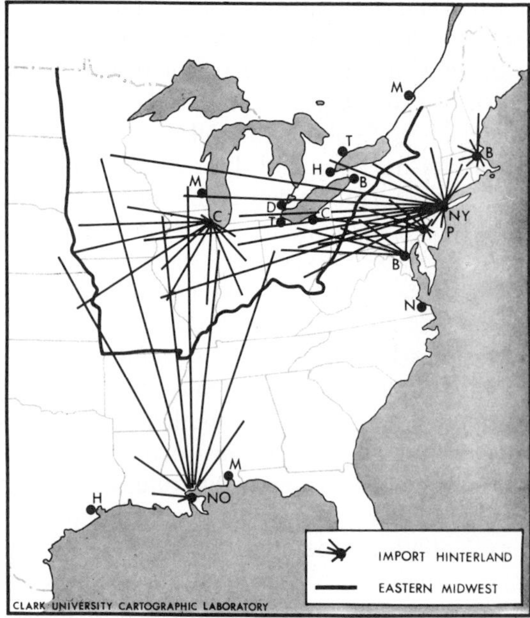

Fig. 15-3 Generalized import hinterland of selected ports. (After Donald J. Patton, Edwin H. Draine, Massachusetts Port Authority, and Delaware River Port Authority)

Thus the Eastern Midwest is a regional construct including the area which generates a substantial portion of United States waterborne trade but is not entirely dominated by any one port. Its trade is the main prize of competition among American ports.

THE MIDWESTERN INDUSTRIAL CORE

The Eastern Midwest is here delimited, east of Louisville, by the limits of the Midwest Equal Rail Rate Area, an area within which carload rail export and import rates are equalized to ports on the North Atlantic Range (Fig. 15-3). The Eastern Midwest is bounded on the west to include those states which are the most heavily industrialized and generate the bulk of waterborne trade. Its boundary crosses the Missouri only to include the metropolitan areas of Kansas City and Omaha.

THE METROPOLITAN HINTERLAND

Statistics on relative size of population, manufacturing industry, and foreign exports generated by manufacturing for the various hinterlands of the selected ports show the dominant size of the New York metropolitan area in bold relief (Table 15-5). Combined with the small increment provided in its outer low-rate area, it gives the Port of New York the largest population and manufacturing industry (measured in value added by manufactures) of any of the ports.

However, in contradistinction, the substantial size of the Chicago metropolitan complex, combined with its large and heavily manufactural outer low-rate area, give that port more potential manufactured exports than New York. Furthermore, the Chicago area evidently generates more manufactured export freight per dollar of value added by manufactures than the New York area does. In fact, New York ranks lowest among the six ports in this regard (Table 15-6). The much smaller economic size of the low-rate hinterlands of Boston, Philadelphia, Baltimore, and especially New Orleans are also evident. The differential size of the overnight truck zones of New York and New Orleans also contrast vividly in the table. Finally the magnitude of the Eastern Midwest—41 per cent of United States manufacturing and 29 per cent of

Table 15-5 Hinterland Characteristics of Selected U.S. Ports

Hinterland	*Per cent of U.S.*			*Per cent growth in value added by manufactures 1963/1954*
	Population, 1960 (U.S. only)	*Value added by manufactures, 1963*	*Origin of manufactured exports, 1963*	
U.S., total	100.00	100.00	100.00	64.1
Boston				
Low-rate area	5.06	5.88	3.71	52.2
Metropolitan	1.45	1.57	1.03	52.8[b]
Outer	3.61	4.31	2.68	51.9
New York				
Low-rate area	10.61	12.69	8.19	46.3
Metropolitan (S.C.A.)	8.23	9.96	3.50[a]	45.9
Outer	2.38	2.74	4.69[a]	47.7
Philadelphia				
Low-rate area	5.08	6.08	4.14	57.7
Metropolitan	2.42	3.14	2.26	49.9
Outer	2.66	2.95	1.88	66.9
Baltimore				
Low-rate area	3.23	2.28	1.47	60.3
Metropolitan	0.96	1.23	0.57	49.5
Outer	2.27	1.05	0.90	75.2
New Orleans				
Low-rate area	2.26	1.19	2.18	58.1
Metropolitan	0.51	0.32	0.34	63.1
Outer	1.75	0.87	1.85	56.4
Chicago				
Low-rate area (S.C.A.)	9.12	12.27	9.17	57.4
Metropolitan	3.79	6.22	3.73	50.0
Outer	5.33	6.06	5.43	65.8
Overnight trucking area				
New York	32.79	38.27	25.75	47.8
New Orleans	9.27	6.77	5.46	86.6
Eastern Midwest	33.28	41.26	28.75	51.8

Sources: U.S. Bureau of the Census. *County and City Data Book: 1967.* A Statistical Abstract Supplement (Washington: Government Printing Office, 1967); *U.S. Census of Manufactures, 1963.* Volume I, *Summary and Subject Statistics;* Volume III, *Area Statistics* (Washington: Government Printing Office, 1966); and *U.S. Census of Manufactures, 1954.* Volume III, *Area Statistics* (Washington: Government Printing Office, 1956).

Note: Metropolitan areas are S.C.A.'s for New York and Chicago; S.M.S.A.'s for other ports.

[a] Data for Somerset and Middlesex Counties, N.J., are included in Outer Low-rate Area and excluded from S.C.A.

[b] 1954 area held constant.

Table 15-6 Selected Indicators of Economic Structure and Growth, for Metropolitan Areas of Ports, 1963

	Boston SMSA	*New York SCA*	*Philadelphia SMSA*	*Baltimore SMSA*	*New Orleans SMSA*	*Chicago SCA*
Per cent of U.S.						
Population, 1960	1.45	8.23	2.42	0.96	0.51	3.79
Wholesale trade sales	2.29	19.03	2.86	0.88	0.74	6.74
Public warehouse space	2.90	16.11	7.09	0.93	0.88	6.73
Origin of manufactured exports	1.03	3.50[b]	2.26	0.57	0.34	3.73
Per cent Growth						
Population, 1960/50	7.5	14.3	18.3	22.9	27.3	21.6
Wholesale sales, 1963/54[a]	35.5	56.5	45.2	45.3	51.6	44.6
Value added by manufactures 1963/54	52.8	45.9	49.9	49.5	63.1	50.0
Ratio Per Capita						
Value added by manufactures ($)	1,161	1,296	1,389	1,364	682	1,757
Wholesale sales ($,000)	3,157	4,622	2,361	1,824	2,927	3,553
Public warehouse space (,000 sq. ft.)	1,445	1,410	2,110	697	1,250	1,280
General cargo, deep water (short tons), 1965	0.43	1.36	0.71	3.15	12.02	0.60
Waterborne foreign trade, 1967 ($)	289	842	427	849	3,839	104
Selected Ratios, 1963						
Wholesale/retail sales	2.06	3.15	1.79	1.39	2.36	2.27
Heaviness Index (Purchases fuel and electric energy per dollar of value added) (c)	1.96	1.56[b]	2.90	3.09	4.02	3.03
Origin of manufactured exports/value added by manufacture	.056	.032[c]	.061	.039	.088	.051

Sources: *County and City Data Book, op. cit.; U.S. Census of Manufactures, 1954, 1963, op. cit.; U.S. Census of Business*, 1963, Vol. IV: *Wholesale Trade, Summary Statistics*, Part II: *Commodity Line Sales, Public Warehousing* (Government Printing Office, Washington, D.C., 1966), and calculations from data given in Tables 15-1,2 and 5 .

[a] Metropolitan areas as of 1963, except Boston, for which 1954 figures on 13 outlying towns are not included.

[b] Does not include Somerset and Middlesex Counties, New Jersey.

[c] Origin of manufactured exports does not include Somerset and Middlesex Counties, New Jersey; thus ratio is slightly low.

United States manufactured exports—is testimony to the significance of competition for this trade.

One of the main factors one would expect to find underlying the growth of port traffic is the economic growth of the port's hinterland. Yet comparison of the growth of differing sectors of waterborne traffic with growth of the metropolitan and outer low-rate areas reveals a complex and equivocal relationship (Tables 15-2, 15-3, and 15-5).

Since the metropolitan area seems the most nearly captive in terms of freight generation, and since it normally accounts for a large share of such waterborne freight, especially of that which is inbound, its growth characteristics are significant. We note that none of the metropolitan or outer low-rate areas grew in manufacturing as fast as the Nation as a whole (Table 15-5). Only in the case of New Orleans did the metropolitan area grow in manufacturing at a rate approximating that of the Nation, while the New York SCA's growth, considering the inflation of the dollar during the interval, may be considered sluggish.

The most meaningful comparison to be made between port traffic and manufactured output is general cargo, since that component of traffic consists in significant part of manufactured products. The relationship between amount and growth of manufacturing appears related, yet weakly so, to the amount and growth of port traffic, even of general cargo. Most manufacturing is destined for domestic consumption; most consumes domestic materials. Much general cargo consists of foodstuffs and other commodities not extensively involved in manufacturing.

Incisive research on this point would need to probe into the commodity mix of waterborne freight through a port. For example, while Baltimore's metropolitan area did not grow spectacularly, its outer low-rate area showed sufficiently strong expansion to raise the overall rate of growth of its low-rate hinterland to the highest level among the case ports. Baltimore's sizable growth in value of imports during the decade 1955–1965 may reflect this manufacturing growth, although the port's absolute decline in exports (by weight) offsets this growth and suggests a shift in the economic structure of the area and of the composition of waterborne traffic. Much of Baltimore's decrease in volume of exports resulted from a severe drop in the volume of corn (and other grains) and in bituminous coal.

In all, we cannot discern a conclusive relationship between change in waterborne traffic and in metropolitan growth in manufacturing from the data developed here, although the strong showing of New Orleans in each category suggests such a general relationship. Even allowing for such a correlation, certainly supported in the literature and by common sense, the disparate trends here suggest that other factors may be of more importance.

Competition for Outlying Territory

The differential growth of the overnight trucking zone of New Orleans over that of New York is, of course, significant, although its importance to New Orleans is diminished by the fact that much of this growth (that which is not within the metropolitan hinterland of New Orleans) is occurring in East Texas; a sizable amount is in the immediate hinterland of Houston.[13] Furthermore, the Port of Baton Rouge vies with New Orleans for deepwater trade. With its new general cargo facility at Port Allen, Baton Rouge may well offer increased competition to New Orleans in the future. Comparison of the trade volume of a port and the economy of its low-rate area suggests that such regional development is only partly responsible for differential growth of the transshipment function of the port. It underscores again the significance of competition for trade generated beyond such captive areas, notably the Midwest.

There have been a number of hinterland studies of American ports—some by academic scholars, most by public agencies—but few have provided comparability from one port to another. Patton contributed one such study in 1955, relating to the origin and destination of rail carload freight moving through selected ports.[14] Although the Bureau of the Census is now moving into the analysis of transportation, we still do not have systematic data on the land movement of maritime freight. The uncertainty inherent in the estimation of hinterlands from secondary data necessitates the considerable degree of generalization used in [here] (Fig. 15-2). The area loosely shown combines data given by Patton and Draine with testimony of port traffic men in each of the port cities, and, in the case of Boston and Philadelphia, consultation of systematic studies prepared for the respective port authorities.

There is little doubt but that, overall, the Port of Boston is reduced to the service of its low-rate area, which is itself deeply penetrated by the Port of New York.[15] Philadelphia and Baltimore vie with New York for the traffic of western Pennsylvania and eastern Ohio, whereas Chicago builds its position in its low-rate area and westward. New York and New Orleans emerge as the giants in this territorial struggle, competing for the entire Eastern Midwest as well as territory to the south and west. Since in port operation success breeds success, the presence of a large and essentially captive nearby hinterland strengthens the port in its competition for disputed trade. The adequacy and caliber of the port's total structure, including not only its physical infrastructure but also its financial and commercial development and its organization, are all fundamental to its competitive struggle.

FUNCTIONAL CHARACTERISTICS OF THE PORT METROPOLISES

Though some elements in the dominance of New York over its competition are revealed in the indicators, elements of relative weakness may also be suggested (Table 15-6). Whereas that port accounts for only about 8 per cent of the Nation's people and about 12 per cent of the waterborne tonnage (Table 15-3), the New York SCA contains over 16 per cent of United States public warehouse space and does almost 20 per cent of all wholesale business. Although ratios among such measures of size are weak gauges of strength, since the composition of the economy and the particular pattern of linkages and of flows within each metropolitan web are distinctive, several are nonetheless calculated as gross indicators of port strength.

Because population size serves only as a rough indicator of overall magnitude of the metropolitan economy, which is not measurable directly in published statistics, selected data are shown on a per capita basis. They show that except for real strength in wholesale trade, the New York area does not rank particularly high. Even in tons of general cargo (1965) per capita (1960), the Port of New York ranks behind Baltimore, and far behind New Orleans. When waterborne cargo (the foreign trade portion) is measured by value, New York still ranks slightly behind Baltimore and far behind New Orleans. This obtains in spite of the preponderance of high-grade freight, such as machinery, which passes through New York.

This suggests, if we may ignore for the moment differences in the industrial mixes of the two metropolitan areas and differences in the composition of cargo passing through the ports (two ambitious assumptions), that New Orleans functions to a greater extent as a point of transshipment as opposed to freight generation. The low level of manufacturing per capita in New Orleans further supports this contention. Chicago is shown clearly in this series as a strong manufacturing and wholesale center, with a small general cargo port function relative to its population size.

A key indicator of the strength of the port in its goods distribution function is the ratio of wholesale to retail trade. Since the volume of retailing may be taken as a general function of the size (modified perhaps by personal affluence, preferences, etc.) of the metropolitan population, and, since a considerable portion of wholesale sales are to retailers (although they are increasingly to manufacturers), this ratio suggests the general extent of wholesaling beyond metropolitan needs and thus the reach of the city into outlying territory. New York's pre-eminence as a wholesale center stands out sharply, as does the weakness of Philadelphia and Baltimore perhaps because of their proximity to larger centers.

But wholesaling involves assembly as well as distribution, and serves both those engaged in domestic and in foreign trade. The assembly of goods, especially for overseas consignment, is particularly facilitated by location in New York, because of that city's immense diversity in manufacturing and inventory as well as its focal position in land transport. There can be little doubt that such diversity and its wholesale organization strengthens New York in the same way as does the port's diversity in overseas contacts and the frequency of its sailings.

Manufacturing Composition

Another indicator of significance to the port function is the general composition of manufacturing industries—the industrial mix (Table 15-6). The degree of heaviness, taken as the ratio of purchased fuel and electricity to value added by manufacture, is calculated for each of the six ports. It is not surprising that New York, with its large concentration of apparel-making and other light industries, ranks lowest, closely followed by Boston. Both these cities are remote from fuel sources, and are characterized by high fuel and power costs. Baltimore, Chicago, and Philadelphia are all closer to major coal supplies, and all are strong in iron and steel producing and fabricating; Philadelphia and Chicago are also strong in petroleum refining. New Orleans' industry is heaviest, reflecting both its low fuel costs (natural gas) and its proximity to a variety of petroleum and chemical deposits. Conversely, it may be regarded as less well represented in the lighter industries.

The degree of heaviness of local industry is relevant to port activity and potential in several ways. Heavy industries are typically involved in the early stages of processing and often consume raw or crude materials, which are usually handled in bulk, often in large quantity. Steel mills or sugar refineries at waterside assure a sizable volume of inbound trade through the port.

The outbound volume, suggested in the ratio of "origin of manufactured exports" to value added by manufacture (also given in Table 15-6), appears directly related to heaviness. In each series, New York ranks lowest and New Orleans highest. This suggests that insofar as locally-generated exports are concerned New York depends more upon its diversity, while New Orleans is supported to a greater extent by its local output of chemicals, stone, clay and glass products, and petroleum products. Locally manufactured products appear more likely to move out through the local port than another port, and are thus to a degree captive, yet there is little assurance that they will generate waterborne trade, or that exporting industries will necessarily be attracted to the port city.

Still, New York managed to maintain its pre-eminence in port activity. Its wholesale trade, already by far the largest among these ports, grew faster than did that of the other ports between 1954 and 1963. But the indicators (Table 15-6) do not reveal the concentration of freight forwarders, shipping agents, and goods-handlers of many types crowded into the few square miles that consitute Manhattan. The long-standing habit of shippers, agents with home offices in New York, and promotional agencies to route goods through that port undoubtedly plays a strong role in its support.

As the port with by far the largest total number of sailings, it is natural that New York offers service to the greatest number of overseas points. The position of New York as last port of call on the North Atlantic Range means it is the topping-out port, and thus tends to handle the cream of ocean-going cargo. Furthermore, as last port of call it offers the earliest arrival at the overseas destination, which further enhances its attractiveness to the shipper. In addition, New York is often the first inbound port of call, since ships typically move down, then back up the North Atlantic Range. All of these are real advantages which help maintain New York's leadership.

Yet New York's relative share of the total United States trade is slipping slowly as a result of a number of factors, some of which have been reviewed. There are also a number of new elements which have meaningful implications for the future of this competition, and which therefore are worth some notice.

NEW ELEMENTS

The expansion of the St. Lawrence Seaway is perhaps the single most important development in the relations among North American ports to appear in this century.[16] At the opening of the Seaway in 1959 every large city on the Great Lakes looked to its potential as a world port. Some, particularly Chicago, Toledo, and Detroit, followed closely by Cleveland, Milwaukee, Buffalo, and others are cutting significantly into the flow of midwestern traffic through tidewater and delta ports. Such impediments as seasonality of the Seaway seem difficult to overcome; such others as deficiencies in channel and harbor dimensions, and traffic congestion in the Welland Canal will undoubtedly be remedied. Moreover, it remains problematical whether the Seaway can become economically self-supporting under the present toll structure and the existing conditions of competition.

The rapid growth of the Port of Chicago, however, bears witness to the impact of the opening of this fourth coast. Although traditionally the ports on the Great Lakes have specialized in the handling of bulk cargo in large volumes, it is to be noted that Chicago's trade in general cargo is now well above that of both Philadelphia and Boston and growing spectacularly. Though it is clear that this growth is over a small base, and therefore quantitatively less impressive, it is also evident that Chicago and the other Great Lakes ports have the considerable natural advantage of proximity by land to Midwestern points, whereas their northerly route to Europe places them closer to that prime market than one might expect.[17] Long-term growth will probably favor the larger among the Great Lakes ports against the smaller, and bring net increase in their overall share of United States waterborne trade at the expense of the Atlantic and Gulf ports.[18] The rate structure of the railroads may undergo further adjustment in the service of these ports from inland points, and further favor this growth.

The preponderance of growth in all of the Great Lakes ports has been in the handling of bulk commodities: ores, coal, and grain. Although this emphasis will no doubt persist, it is likely that growth will occur in the handling of general cargo, as the organization of waterborne commerce becomes better developed in those ports. The growth of general cargo will probably be limited to a select few of the larger ports, located conveniently on the road to Chicago. Competition, especially from Milwaukee and Toledo, will probably limit Chicago's share primarily to Chicago's low-rate hinterland.[19]

Rail Rates and Mergers

In spite of the increasing diversion of land movement of traffic to the motor truck, the railroad remains the major carrier of maritime freight, especially beyond 200 miles. Its rate structure and efforts to solicit freight have had a significant if not dominant effect on the routing of traffic. For many years a rate differential prevailed between the Midwest and North Atlantic ports, such that Baltimore enjoyed a rate differential of 3c. and Philadelphia 2c. per hundredweight below New York. New York and Boston have traditionally been equalized. Under this rate structure, Baltimore drew freight, particularly steel products from central Pennsylvania and western New York, as shown by Patton.[20] Yet one of Patton's major findings is that in spite of these differentials New York outdrew both Philadelphia and Baltimore throughout their whole area of competition, except in their immediate hinterlands. Furthermore, New York today draws some export shipments from the city of Boston.[21] Clearly, factors other than slight rate differentials account for New York's preeminence. In 1962, export rail rates were equalized between points in the Midwest and North Atlantic ports. Though Baltimore and Philadelphia, therefore, have lost an important advantage in bulk cargo rates, they appear to be regaining that advantage in terms of general cargo, especially containerized freight.[22]

Between 1955 and 1965 both Baltimore and Philadelphia lost tonnage. This loss was in the bulk commodities; both gained in general cargo. However, during this same period New York gained bulk tonnage but lost some general cargo. If these figures are valid indicators of trends, they seem to support the contention that bulk cargo is most sensitive to rail rate changes, and that the loss of a rate advantage has hurt Philadelphia and Baltimore. The diversion of general cargo from New York to its more southerly competitors, which such differential growth would suggest, implies that this cargo is more subject to other factors.

Although equalization of rail rates to Gulf ports has long been practiced by the railroads, rates to Gulf ports have not been equalized with rates to Atlantic ports in systematic fashion.[23] The traditionally depressed rail rates of the Mississippi, Ohio, and Missouri Valleys have undoubtedly extended the impact of New Orleans deeper into the Midwest than would have otherwise been the case.

Since the opening of the St. Lawrence Seaway to deep sea shipping, railroads serving Lake ports have begun establishment of reduced rates from inland points to those ports. However, those railroads, such as the New York Central and the Pennsylvania (now the Penn-Central) which serve lake ports as well as Atlantic ports, also find themselves in direct competition with the St. Lawrence Seaway, and will, of course, plan their strategy accordingly. On the other hand, some railroads such as the Illinois Central and the Gulf, Mobile and Ohio serve both Chicago and Gulf ports. Any benefit in rate structure to Chicago will have to be weighed against the adverse effect of possible diversion from what is probably a much longer haul to the Gulf of Mexico. Yet, all of these roads face competition from roads serving other ports, and which are concerned to maximize their traffic to those ports.[24] Thus it is difficult for railroads to withold a rate advantage from one port on the basis that they wish to favor another.

The merger of a growing number of American railroads will further reduce their role in guiding shipments through a particular port, since increasingly they will be serving more than one port. The shorter lines typically serving only one port are being blanketed in major rail mergers, and, therefore, will decline in their hitherto important role of freight solicitation and preferential routing.

The Growth of Motor Truck Carriage

The impact of increasing use of the motor truck is essentially a function of the increase in the generation of waterborne trade, particularly general cargo within the low-rate areas of the ports. This is so, not because of the rail rate structure of these areas but because they lie typically within one or two hundred miles of the port, and are thus within range of telling truck competition. Since motor rates are not usually equalized and tend to bear a more direct relation to distance than do rail rates, their impact is to favor the closest viable port. Though an increasing share of waterborne freight will undoubtedly be carried by truck, it is unlikely that this will have much effect on the relative hinterland territories of the various ports, except perhaps to reduce the reach of one port directly into the central city of another.

Containerization

Perhaps the most important new development in the manner of handling of cargo is containerization. Officials in each of the selected North Atlantic ports regard this as the key to the future, with respect to general cargo. The Port of New York Authority, on the basis of careful study, estimated that by 1975 containerized tonnage will have grown by more than seven million long tons, so that by then almost half of the port's total general cargo will be moving in containers.[25]

Containerization materially increases the efficiency of cargo-handling over the piers, reduces the incidence of damage to goods during transit, and virtually eliminates pilferage. Its use requires large amounts of upland, or landward, space, for storage of containers and access by rail and motor transport vehicles. It involves high capital investment in gantry cranes and other equipment as well as in the containers themselves. Therefore, whereas it affords considerable advantages, it also carries high costs, and is feasible only where large, regular freight flows are involved.

Containers used in ocean shipping are different than those used by the railroads in their piggyback service; ocean containers are much heavier and sturdier. Normally, they are owned by the ship line and often move empty during the backhaul portion of their overland journeys. Therefore, it appears that their use will be greatest to and from inland points relatively close to the port, either in the port city or within a reasonable distance from it, say 200 miles. Empty backhauls of heavy containers from greater distances would become increasingly expensive and would tend to offset the advantages of their use. Therefore, it appears that, should containerization become widespread, it would tend to re-assert the friction of distance in the routing of freight and thus constrict the size of port hinterlands.

Yet, on the other hand, the economies of large scale are powerful, and tend to concentrate container-handling in few rather than many ports, with the expectation of enlarging, rather than shrinking, the area of their hinterlands. Under these ambivalent conditions it is clear that some form of equilibrium will develop—insofar as the underlying geographic and economic conditions remain stable—balancing the benefits and costs of containerization.

It must be recognized that containerization will be appropriate only for a certain array of commodities, now handled as general cargo. It will be most advantageous to domestic overseas points, such as Puerto Rico, Hawaii, or Alaska, where there are no customs to be cleared. Furthermore, the weight of the containers themselves discourages their use in extremely long voyages, such as across the Pacific or into the Indian Ocean. Other factors relating to the potential development of containerization include the level of economic development, the condition of highways to the interior of the overseas territory, the national laws of that country regarding containerized handling of freight, the distance to inland points of origin and destination, and the level of damage and loss of freight at the port.

It is instructive, then, to note the stress being placed by officials in the North Atlantic ports on the future role of the container. They have little doubt that the ports that are best equipped to handle these units will be the future leaders. If containerization of foreign trade should develop strongly, it will probably result in the decentralization of break-bulk points of entry from the seaports to inland major cities as well. At present, if the container is not to be opened until it reaches an inland point, it is the usual practice for the consignee to pay the expenses of a customs official to such point of entry. Thus large inland points of generation of heavy flows of container traffic, which will be able to justify a permanent customs office, would seem to hold an advantage over the smaller city, and thus serve further to concentrate the inland generation of such freight. This effect of the economies of large scale along with such advantages as preferential rail rates to large inland cities would combine to promote the further growth of such places.

New Orleans officials seem much less enthusiastic than their northeastern counterparts about the role of containerization. Perhaps this is because the distance from New Orleans to the Midwest is greater than from the Atlantic ports, perhaps because overseas points served by New Orleans are, to a greater extent, underdeveloped, or perhaps because overseas routes from New Orleans are longer than those from the North Atlantic ports. In other words, containerization ". . . must develop in terms of a favorable geographic position on a given route that affords a minimum sailing time and quick turn-around."[26] Of at least equal importance is the general doubt that longshore labor will accommodate containerization. In any case, its prospects seem less bright to officials in New Orleans.

The Development of New Facilities

It appears that the growth of containerization will have the effect of further concentration of trade in those ports which prepare themselves for it. New York is presently far in the lead and has every intention to remain there. Present programs of construction will provide 37 full containership berths in Newark Bay by 1975, and another 20 at adjacent Elizabeth Port Authority Piers. The two facilities cover more than 1,300 acres.

In addition to the new containership facilities mentioned above, the Port of New York is in the best position to meet future needs of port operation. Its harbor is by far the largest among the selected ports and has additional potentially developable waterfront on Staten Island, and, through dredging and redevelopment, elsewhere in Newark Bay and the lower Hackensack. Equally important, however, is the fact that its port organization is strong and effective. These give New York a commanding advantage, not easily matched by any of the other ports.

Land for new port terminal facilities and other elements of physical infrastructure is limited in the Boston area, although container handling could be accommodated at Castle Island (South Boston) and in East Boston. In general, however, new development at Boston may involve the re-use of earlier terminal facilities, especially along the Mystic and Chelsea Rivers. Provision of adequate space for the necessary storage, rail and truck access, and handling space may be difficult to provide on a large scale.

Like Boston, Philadelphia also has a close-in general cargo waterfront, lacking in upland space for efficient expansion. As in many ports, new development is likely to take place downstream. Although Philadelphia has built new facilities just below the city, it is now looking farther downstream to the area of Chester, Pennsylvania, for new development.

Baltimore appears less cramped than Philadelphia, however, in terms of space for present and future handling of containerized general cargo. At the present time this is handled at the Canton Railroad Piers, the Sea-Land Terminal, and the large Dundalk Marine Terminal on the site of a former small airport. This terminal, second most significant on the Atlantic-Gulf Coast, has nearly 1,500 feet of usable berthing space with ample upland room for storage and handling.

New Orleans has the disadvantage of requiring levees along all waterways, since the city lies ten or more feet below the level of the Mississippi River and in some sections actually below sea level. Locks are required between the Mississippi and canals connecting with the sea, of which the most important is the Innerharbor Navigation Canal. It is along the Gulf Outlet Canal, extending eastward from this canal, however, that new terminal construction will likely take place. The Gulf Outlet Canal, incidentally, is a much more direct route to the sea than the Mississippi; it reduces the distance between New Orleans and the Gulf from 127 to 66 miles.[27] The marshy character of the terrain in which New Orleans is situated renders difficult and expensive the stabilization of extensive land for marine terminal use. But the land is there, and is being developed to meet anticipated needs. New Orleans is fortunate, on the other hand, that the configuration of its harbor initially dictated the construction of quay-type wharves on the Mississippi Levee. This arrangement, combined with the parallel trackage of the terminal railroad (the New Orleans Public Belt Railroad), makes for a relatively efficient waterfront stretching some 20 miles along the river.

Chicago has a particularly difficult problem in finding room for expansion of its port area. Not only is most of the city's lake front held as parkland by the Chicago Park District, but the twelve-mile Calumet River is narrow and circuitous, and crosses one of the busiest traffic corridors of the world: the rail and highway arteries funneling around the south end of Lake Michigan. The present general cargo waterfront is located mainly in Lake Calumet, where growth is severly constricted by adjacent rail and highway lines. In spite of this, it is probable that new port development, especially of container terminals, will take place at Lake Calumet or at the mouth of the Calumet River (at 92nd Street).

CONCLUSION

It is clear that great inertia (or perhaps momentum) characterizes the ports of the United States. Their success is only partly determined by their regional location, the size of their local and nearby economy, and their proximity to overseas trading areas. It is also importantly predicated upon the extent of their commercial, financial, and organizational structure, and especially upon their ability and will to prepare for the future. Although New York, the natural opponent of every other large United States port, is in a region growing less rapidly than some others, especially in terms of heavy industry, it demonstrates the will to retain its lead and great resilience in its ability to meet new situations. Not only does it have all the momentum of large-scale operation in transshipment as well as in wholesale distribution, it has what appears to be ample room for the efficient handling of containerized cargo, for the present and for the near future. It has aggressive public organization addressed both to the development and promotion of the port, and to the abatement of some of the major ills that beset all ports. Its advantages remain strong and its hold tenacious.

Boston and Philadelphia both lack such effective port organization, both suffer from proximity to New York, and both lack large tracts of nearby waterfront, well served by rail transportation, and otherwise suitable for development as containership terminals. Yet though Philadelphia is more strongly oriented to manufacturing, especially heavy manufacturing, Boston remains strong in wholesaling. Both of these functions suggest the continuance and perhaps long-range growth of cargo, especially inbound, which will be resistant to diversion.

Baltimore has a number of advantages, including adequate space for containerized freight-handling, strong port organization, and relative proximity to the Midwest, which new rates on containerized rail traffic seem to be taking into account. These, and the advantage of proximity to bituminous coal fields, whch it shares with Philadelphia over New York and Boston, may portend renewed vigor for the Port of Baltimore.

Of the ports investigated, however, New Orleans and Chicago, safely distant from New York, seem to have the best chances to grow disproportionately. The rearrangement attendant upon the opening of the St. Lawrence Seaway has not yet run its course, and holds considerable, but not unlimited, promise for Chicago. That port is limited, however, by the lack of extensive land needed for container-handling, and, although not specifically investigated here, from the competition of other Lakeside ports.

New Orleans stands to benefit from expansion of its regional economy, and from probable enlargement of trade with northern Latin America and the Pacific, New Orleans balances a strong transshipment function reachir.g deep into the interior with a growing local complex of heavy industry. In terms of water front potential, the city is fortunate in that the form of original water front involved quay-type terminals along the river rather than the finger-type piers, which are generally unable to accommodate the increased speed of modern cargo handling. New Orleans is also fortunate in having large tracts of land available for port expansion, even though some of this is marshy and requires reclamation. And, like New York's, its port organization is strong and aggressive.

It is no accident, therefore, that New Orleans pioneered in the consolidation of port-associated buisness in a single office structure, the International Trade Mart, located appropriately at the foot of Canal, the main street of the city. Nor is it surprising to see New York follow with the construction of the World Trade Center, to be housed in the two tallest buildings in the world.

NOTES

1 For a thorough account of the absolute rise and relative decline of the Port of New York see Benjamin Chinitz: *Freight and the Metropolis* (New York Region Study, Cambridge, Mass., 1960).

2 For discussion of the problems underlying the differentiation and classification of ports by size and type, see R. E. Carter: A Comparative Analysis of United States Ports and Their Traffic Characteristics, *Econ. Geog.*, Vol. 38, 1962, pp. 162–175; F. W. Morgan: *Ports and Harbours, A Functional Classification of Ports* (London 1961), Chap. 4; J. B. Kenyon: Land Use Admixture in the Built-up Urban Waterfront: Extent and Implications, *Econ. Geog.*, Vol. 44, 1968, pp. 152–177; Peter J. Rimmer: The Problem of Comparing and Classifying Ports, *Prof. Geogr.*, Vol. 18, No. 2, 1966, pp. 83–91. See also Donald Patton: Some Recent Literature on Ports, *Annals Assn. of Amer. Geogrs.*, Vol. 47, 1957, pp. 193–196.

3 Although there is no universally accepted breakdown, this list is in general conformity with that produced by the U.S. Bureau of the Census Foreign Trade Office, *Domestic Movements of Selected Commodities in the United States Waterborne Foreign Trade* (Government Printing Office, Washington, 1959).

4 The role of distance in the selection of a port is most pronounced in low-grade (low value

per ton) freight. See F. W. Morgan: "Hinterlands," Chapter 7 in *Ports and Harbours, op. cit.*, pp. 111–131.

5 The distance from Buenos Aires to New York by the shortest track is 5,871 nautical miles; from New Orleans, 6,237. U.S. Naval Oceanographic Office, Distance Between Ports. (U.S. Government Printing Office, Washington, 1964.)

6 The need to balance consideration of the port's foreland, or overseas trade territory, with its hinterland, or landward trade area, was stressed by Guido G. Weigend: Some Elements in the Study of Port Geography, *Geogr. Rev.*, Vol. 48, 1958, pp. 185–200. A penetrating analysis of ports on the basis of hinterland and foreland characteristics is given by John N. H. Britton: The External Relations of Seaports; Some New Considerations, *Tijdschr. voor Econ. en Sciale Geogr.*, Vol. 56, No. 3, May–June, 1965, pp. 109–112. Also, A. J. Sargent: *Seaports and Hinterlands*, London, 1938; and Morgan, *op. cit.*, Chapter 7, "Hinterlands." The notion of the hinterland in non-sea trade terms is developed in Howard L. Green: Hinterland Boundaries of New York City and Boston in Southern New England, *Econ. Geog.*, Vol. 31, 1955, pp. 283–300.

7 Donald J. Patton: General Cargo Hinterlands of New York, Philadelphia, Baltimore, and New Orleans, *Annals Assn. of Amer. Geogrs.*, Vol. 48, 1958, p. 443.

8 Edwin H. Draine: *Import Traffic of Chicago and Its Hinterland* (Research Paper No. 81, Department of Geography, University of Chicago, 1963), esp. Ch. 3, and maps on pp. 26 and 57; Eric Schenker: *The Port of Milwaukee: An Economic Review* (Madison, Wis., University of Wisconsin Press, 1967), p. 65.

9 Export rail carloads of general cargo unloaded at the Port of New York declined steadily from approximately 334,000 in 1946 to 73,000 in 1966. Part of this loss, however, is countered by growth in piggyback (including marine container) traffic. Port of New York Authority, Port of New York's Foreign Trade/1967, New York, 1967, p. 26.

10 Patton, *op. cit.*

11 Port of New York Authority, *Metropolitan Transportation:* 1980, Ch. 18: "Motor Freight and Its Terminal Needs" (Port of New York Authority, New York, 1963), pp. 209–227.

12 A good picture of domestic and coastwise commodity movement, as well as foreign trade (dry cargo and tanker) is given by Edward L. Ullman: *American Commodity Flow* (University of Washington Press, Seattle, 1957).

13 For a view of the dynamic characters of two of New Orleans' gulf competitors see E. J. Foscue: The Ports of Texas and their Hinterlands, *Tijdsch. voor Econ. en Sociale Geogr.*, Vol. 48, No. 1, January, 1957, pp. 1–14; and Edward L. Ullman: *Mobile, Industrial Seaport and Trade Center* (Department of Geography, University of Chicago, 1943).

14 Patton, *op. cit.*

15 For a pre-World War I view of Boston see Edwin J. Clapp: *The Port of Boston*, New Haven, 1916.

16 The growth of traffic on the Seaway is shown vividly in *Traffic Report of the St. Lawrence Seaway*, prepared by the St. Lawrence Seaway Authority and the St. Lawrence Seaway Development Corporation (annual, Queen's Printer, Ottawa).

17 The distance between Bishop Rock and New York is 2,922 nautical miles, and 3759 nautical miles to Chicago by the Strait of Belle Isle, United States Naval Oceanographic Office, *op. cit.* Mayer points out that the all-water route from Chicago to Antwerp is only 189 statute miles longer than the combined rail-water route via New York and New York Central Railroad. Harold M. Mayer: *The Port of Chicago and the St. Lawrence Seaway* (Research Paper No. 49, Department of Geography, University of Chicago, 1957), p. 29.

18 For a more thorough discussion of the potential impact of the Seaway, see Mayer, *ibid.*

19 See especially, Draine, *op. cit.*, Schenker, *op. cit.*, and Mayer, *op. cit.*

20 Patton, *op. cit.*

21 Rowland and MacNeal: *Port of Boston: Waterborne Commerce Market and Development Requirements* (mimeographed, New York, 1964).

22 Edwin Draine in personal correspondence, September 27, 1968.

23 Interstate Commerce Commission, *Docket No. 3718,* Export and Import Rates To and From Southern Ports, Vol. 205 (Government Printing Office, Washington, D.C., 1946), pp. 511–562.

24 Donald Patton finds that although port promotion by the railroads has been significant in the routing of traffic, the efforts of various single-port railroads tend to cancel each other out. (Personal correspondence, November 12, 1968.)

25 *Container Shipping: Full Ahead* (Port of New York Authority, New York, 1967).

26 Draine, correspondence, *op. cit.*

27 U.S. Corps of Engineers, *Waterborne Commerce of the United States, Calendar Year 1965,* Part 2: *Waterways and Harbors, Gulf Coast, Mississippi River System and Antilles* (District Engineer, U.S. Army Corps of Engineers, New Orleans, 1965).

Inland waterways are in direct competition with overland media. Their advantage is cheapness; their disadvantages are slowness, weather conditions, etc. It has been found, however, that water carriers have an advantage over railroads: they bear only a few costs of their routeways. The fully distributed costs of river barge transport are about 0.2 cents/ton mile, five to 10 times smaller than the equivalent rail costs. Thus the economy of water transport for bulk movement of commodities that do not require prompt delivery is sufficient to absorb all terminal and transshipment costs and yet still remain below rail costs. Cost advantages are also related to the quantities carried; a single barge can carry up to 1 million gallons of petroleum, with eight barges in tow, thus exceeding a rail train capacity three or four times. Another illustration of the low costs is the fact that a gallon of crude oil can move 1,700 miles by waterway for *less* than the cost of moving one gallon of gasoline 10 miles from a refinery by truck. However, the full potential of water transport can be achieved only by shipments in very large quantities.

The average length of haul is 532 miles in the United States compared with 464 miles for railroad, 314 for pipelines carrying crude oil, 267 for trucks, and 261 miles for pipelines carrying refined oil. Speeds are slow, as noted, the journey from Pittsburgh to New Orleans taking 8 days and 18 hours for 1,852 miles downstream (9 miles per hour) and 14 days upstream (5 miles per hour).

In summary, the place of water transport in the total transport market may be said to be characterized by low cost-large volume movements. Water transport is slow and basically suitable for long distances, and in fact is commercially restricted to longer route mileages than for the other methods of transportation.

ROAD TRANSPORTATION

Road transportation is now a very important part of the domestic transportation system of Western Europe and North America. Now a part of nearly all shipments in those areas go by truck, and in some industries, more than a part. It is a relatively recent phenomenon, and only with the provision of improved highways in the last 30 to 40 years has it been technically able to expand.

Road transportation is particularly adapted to moving *light* loads *short* distances in *short* time; on short hauls, trucks can cost less than the railroads. In most countries, governments build and maintain roads so that many shippers may find it cheaper to send longer distance shipments by trucks. In the United States the ton mileage of intercity freight has grown from 53 billion ton miles in 1939 to 331.9 billion in 1966, more than a 500 percent increase, to take 27 percent of intercity freight ton miles, and 47.6 percent by actual weight. There are three principal reasons for this marked trend:

1 The economy and reliability of road transportation have increased rapidly with improved roads and improved vehicle performance.

2 On many routes with light traffic, this may be the only feasible method of mechanized transport.

3 As the economy develops, there may be greater concern with improved *service* and less concern with transport costs.

The concern of a shipper is not just with the costs of movement, but also with total production and distribution costs; various modes of transport can have significant effects on these total costs. Thus the economy of rail transport may be lessened by slow deliveries. For a wide range of shipments, including both perishable and high valued manufactures, time is important, and to carry large inventories of goods to overcome time lags in delivery may be very costly and tie up needed capital. An advantage of road transport is the wide, flexible areal coverage offered by the highway network (compared with the railroad network), which can be upgraded in stages, beginning with, say, a gravel road for light traffic, but upgraded as traffic increases. Other media, especially rail, water, and pipeline, are designed for substantial capacity from the beginning. The fact that trucks are able to offer a complete door-to-door service is a distinct asset; it avoids transshipment and allows flexibility of scheduling. Truck transportation can be more readily integrated into the total production process, especially if an industry operates its own trucking line, with consequent reduction of inventories and elimination of storage.

Thus diversions to road transport can occur even when the competing mode is cheaper, in order to minimize the total costs of distribution. However, the benefits are most marked for short hauls. In a survey of the movement of fresh fruits and vegetables in the United States, it was found that for all shipments destined for points less than 100 miles away, 88 percent moved by road and only 6 percent by rail; on trips of 1,000 miles and more, railroads carried 66 percent, and at over 2,000 miles, 93 percent went by rail.

A number of cost factors are interesting. Motor carriers operate on very small margins; 96 percent of all revenue may be operating expenses. The required investment is small, however, and though highly competitive, it is relatively easy to enter the trucking business. There are only very limited scale economies, however, and large firms do not have decisive cost advantages over small firms. A more unusual characteristic is the rapid wearing out of vehicles, particularly where they are used intensively; four years are the average life of a truck. Because of this, about 1 million new trucks enter the U.S. highways each year, and about 500,000 are scrapped, thus diffusing technical innovations quickly and limiting excess capacity. Rates charged usually take their lead from railroad prices and compete by offering better service, door-to-door speed, and overnight delivery.

In summary, road transport is inadequate for moving heavy volumes of bulk materials and is costly for long hauls, but offers greater flexibility, better service, and low costs for short hauls. The average length of haul for trucks is 267 miles in the United States compared to 464 miles for railroads. In the United States it has been most successful in the confectionery, beverage, tobacco, clothing, and meat/dairy product industries. Trucks do move a substantial proportion of iron and steel products, though principally these fall into the category of goods that travel less than 400 miles.

Motor transportation, unlike most of the other modes, also has a substantial importance as a passenger carrier, some of the consequences of which are considered in Part Six (*b*). The accompanying table compares the costs of the modes: railroads can provide passenger services on heavily trafficked main routes at 1.9 cents per mile, but the low load factor increases the cost to the passenger to 6.9 cents per mile, higher than that of the popular overseas airlines. Buses provide the cheapest transport and automobiles the next cheapest, though they carry 91 percent of U.S. intercity passenger traffic. The advantages of automobiles are convenience, flexibility, and a concern with factors other than costs. Quite frequently the owner-driver does not perceive all the costs involved, and in evaluating alternative modes he is more concerned with relative levels of service or time than with cost. Surveys have shown that most automobile drivers do not estimate their costs of driving, a factor which is consistent with the relatively inelasticity of response to changes in fares of public transit systems.

AIR TRANSPORTATION

One of the newest of the modes, it has expanded very rapidly since 1950. Airlines are the specialists in transport, being principally passenger carriers,

U.S. Passenger Transportation: Comparative Costs (cents)

	Cost/seat mile	Cost/passenger mile
Railroad	1.90	6.93
Bus	1.29	2.73
Automobile	2.15	4.50
Airline (overseas)	3.81	6.20
Airline (local)	5.45	12.30

Source: Lansing (1966).

and by efficient operation they have captured a high proportion of the "for hire" passenger market. A small but important freight market exists for goods with such characteristics as high value, light weight, need for speedy delivery, and/or perishability. In the following selection, P. W. Brooks sketches the slow development of civilian air transport from 1919 to 1950 and its more rapid expansion since 1950 into a major world transportation mode.

Selection 16

The Development of Air Transport

P. W. Brooks

During the sixty years since the first practical airplane flew in 1905, aviation has developed almost entirely as a result of large-scale government defense expenditure in every industrialized country of the world. Defense budgets have paid for practically all air development, because the great bulk of aviation activity has been in the military field, in which spending by governments has historically always been on a lavish scale. Nevertheless, from the end of the First World War an important by-product of military aviation began to evolve. This was civil air transport, which, after a slow start up to the Second World War, has since progressively emerged as the most important form of long-distance passenger transport, gradually taking over from existing methods by sea and rail. At the same time, it is now beginning to penetrate, to a significant extent, the medium and even short-haul scheduled passenger travel market and is increasingly carrying certain classes of (particularly high-value) freight over similar stage lengths. A large part of the world's mail also is now carried by air. As a result of these developments, the airlines have become a major world industry, and their total turnover, already exceeding $6\frac{1}{2}$ billion per annum, continues to increase by about ten per cent every year. Some 200 companies (of which about half operate internationally) fly the world's scheduled air routes.

Perhaps the most remarkable feature of this development has been that it has resulted from an undiscriminating, and indeed almost naive, belief among a relatively small band of enthusiasts in the possibilities of the new form of transport. In its early years, unlike other forms of transport in their pioneering stages, air transport was completely uneconomic and appeared to offer no prospects of carrying either passengers or freight at rates competitive with existing forms of transport. Even mail could be carried profitably only at much above surface rates, although, in this case, there seemed at first some prospect of justifying the higher costs by substantial time savings. In the event, however, mail proved incapable by itself of supporting a viable development of air transport paid for at rates which could be covered by acceptable postal charges. Mail has been important to air transport development, but only as an adjunct to passenger traffic. Other forms of transport

Journal of Transport Economics and Policy, vol. 1, 1967, pp. 164–183. Reprinted by permission of the author and the editor.

have drawn most of their revenue from freight, but passengers soon became, and have remained, the chief source of airline revenue.

THE FIRST DECADE (1919–30)

During the first ten years after the start of practical air transport in 1919, technical knowledge held out no possibility of even distant prospect of economic, safe and reliable large-scale scheduled operations. Efficient operators during the first part of that period could cover only between ten and twenty percent of their costs at revenue rates which would attract an expanding share of the travel market from existing surface carriers. At the time, aircraft were so unsafe and unreliable and were so limited in their operations by unfavorable weather that they were incapable of competing with surface transport, except in a few special cases which were nothing like numerous enough to support the commercial growth of a new industry. During this period many of the first promoters of the industry, and even some of its economists, prophesied profitable and adequately safe operations in the then not-too-distant future. We can see now, however, that these claims were unjustified at the time with the equipment and techniques available during that first decade or, indeed, even with those then known to be in prospect for the future. Only an overweening enthusiasm and almost instinctive faith on the part of its protagonists provided the incentive to persevere. Governments made available the essential financial support, partly for defense and prestige reasons and to earn foreign exchange and partly because they were persuaded by the claims of the enthusiasts of the prospects of eventual profitability.

The equipment used during the first decade of air transport was adapted from the military aircraft of the First World War, which themselves had evolved directly from the first airplanes of the pioneer era. The tail-first wood/wire/fabric Wright biplane of 1903–05, which first demonstrated practical flight, survived as a never-popular configuration only until about 1910. From 1907–08 the pusher tailed-biplane and then more especially, the tractor monoplane and tractor biplane, still employing the Wrights' type of wood/wire/fabric construction, emerged as the standard airplane types which were to be used throughout the First World War.

The majority of the pioneer airplanes were small, single-engine, one- or two-seat vehicles weighing 750–1,500 lb., loaded and powered with crude piston engines (initially adapted from motor-car practice) developing between 25 and 100 horse power. At first, operating speeds were of the order of 40 m.p.h. and maximum flight endurance two to three hours. By 1914 maximum power had increased to 150/200 h.p. and operating speeds to 55/70 m.p.h. By the end of the war the airplanes in use, although the majority were still basically similar in design to the pioneer types, had much higher performance, load-carrying ability and reliability, mainly because of better engines (now of up to about 400 h.p.) and because large-scale production and operation had provided a broad foundation of experience on which to base more efficient design and manufacture. Cruising speeds had reached 80/100 m.p.h. To enable greater loads to be carried there had, by then, also been substantial increases in size in some types, with multiple power units often providing the higher total power required for these larger machines. However, even the largest aircraft still had configurations and structures similar to those of their smaller predecessors.

The larger military airplanes available in 1919 were, not unnaturally, those best adaptable to civil transport purposes. The first airliners were military, in most cases, single or twin-engine bombers crudely modified to accommodate additional passenger seats. In due course new civil designs were produced to replace the first military adaptations, but these were all straightforward extrapolations employing the same basic design techniques. The pattern of adhering closely in all civil aircraft design to lines of development already paid for by military expenditure was established at this time and has been maintained ever since. The reasons are clear. Since the overwhelming bulk of aeronautical research and development was undertaken either directly or indirectly for military purposes any other course was, and has continued to be, economically out of the question.

Although the majority of airliners in the 1920s were wood/wire/fabric biplanes, a few—particularly towards the end of the period—had metal framework structures of a type first used on a limited scale during the First World War. Some also were externally-braced monoplanes employing this form of structure. A few others incorporated wooden monocoque[1] fuselages of a type which had been employed quite extensively, particularly by the Germans, during the war. However, the most important exceptions to the still predominant "stick-and-string" biplanes during this period were the corrugated-skin light-alloy low-wing cantilever monplanes of Junkers, and the Fokker high-wing monoplanes with plywood-skinned wings and fabric-covered welded steel tube fuselages. The Junkers and Fokker configurations and types of structure had been first used for military aircraft in Germany during the war. The Ford Tri-Motor high-wing monoplane, which employed a Junkers-type structure of Fokker configuration, played an important part in airline development in the United States in the later 1920s.

Although most of the first airliners were single-engined, some had two engines, even though they lacked any real advantage in safety or reliability because they were all incapable of continued sustained flight after failure of one engine. This was then a not infrequent occurrence because of the still poor reliability of engines. Indeed, the increased chance of engine failure with the twin-engine types probably more than counterbalanced their greater chances of pulling off save forced landings.

Three important developments during the mid 1920s were:

1 The general consolidation—mainly in Europe and as a result of government intervention as a condition of subsidy—of the first small operations into larger units with more substantial resources and greater stability of organization. At the same time, the various practical problems of airline operation were gradually explored and the first effective techniques established for dealing with them.

2 The progressive adoption of three-engine aircraft capable of sustained flight after failure of an engine. This was coupled with the development, particularly in Britain and the United States, of air-cooled radial engines of greatly improved reliability and durability and their general adoption by the airlines. Largely as a result of this, engine overhaul lives were increased from 150–200 hours or even less in the early days to 400–500 hours by the early 1930s.

3 The introduction of radio communication (both W/T and R/T) and its use, in primitive direction-finding form, as a navigational aid. Europe was well ahead of the United States in these developments. However, almost all airline flying during this period continued to be confined to contact-flying conditions in daylight. Although crude blind flying instruments had been developed during the First World War, their proper use was outside the experience of the average airline pilot. Map-reading remained the primary method of finding the way. In the United States, where a government-run Post Office air mail service had been started in 1918 and continued to be by far the most important scheduled flying for the next nine years, more progress was made in bad-weather flying than elsewhere. Night flying also started to be adopted there from 1924, many years ahead of other countries: elsewhere carriage of passengers was nearly always the main pre-occupation and tended to delay such developments.

During the first decade of air transport the main area of development was in Europe: Britain, France and Germany each had several small airlines as early as 1919. These small pioneer companies, and others formed subsequently, were to be progressively amalgamated during the 1920s until they formed national flag carriers: Imperial Airways (in 1924), Lufthansa (in 1926) and Air France (in 1933). In the early 1920s most other European countries also formed their own airlines, until by the end of the decade the continent was covered with a comprehensive network of government-subsidized air services.

The next most significant area of development was the United States. This was in spite of the fact that, after pioneering the first practical airplanes in the early years of the century, the Americans remained largely outside the main stream of aeronautical development until the late 1920s. Initial air transport operations in America, however, followed a quite different pattern from that in Europe. The Post Office air mail service, started in 1918, concentrated on a transcontinental mail-only service, using converted military single-engine biplanes—British-designed D.H.4s. This operation was maintained until 1927, but from 1926 subsidized private contractors were brought in to extend and then take over the original network. From an early stage these private contractors carried passengers as well as the heavily subsidized mail; but a major part of the passenger traffic was carried initially, at a heavy loss, by carriers without mail contracts. This traffic soon began to grow rapidly so that, from having no significant scheduled passenger air traffic in 1926, in 1929 the American airlines were carrying a third more passengers than the next busiest air transport nation (Germany). By 1930 the U.S. airlines were carrying as many passengers as the rest of the world taken together—and approximately that ratio was maintained up to the outbreak of the Second World War.

Outside Europe and the United States, air transport development in the 1920s occurred chiefly in:

1 Central and South America, as a result of the extension of the American Pan American Airways network into these areas and of similar operations by the French and Germans. Locally organized airlines were also formed in several of these regions, often sponsored by German or French interests.

2 The Middle East, Africa and southern Asia, mainly because of the progressive extension of European overseas routes into and through these areas. A notable early regional operation in Africa was started by the Belgians in the Congo in 1920. Similarly, the Germans started operations in Persia in 1925.

3 Australia and New Guinea. Three separate government-subsidized airlines had opened networks in Australia by 1925. In New Guinea in 1927 a remarkable unsubsidized airline was formed which operated successfully for many years, carrying mainly freight to the mining areas in the inaccessible interior.

4 Canada, where seasonal scheduled operations into the North-lands supplemented the bush fliers who, on a charter basis, played the major part in opening up these undeveloped territories.

5 The Far East. In Japan airline operations developed after 1922. In the Dutch East Indies (now Indonesia) the Dutch built up a highly efficient regional network from 1928, which was linked to Holland by the KLM Far East service in 1931.

By the end of its first decade, thanks to almost universal government subsidies, air transport was firmly established over most of the great land masses of the world. Russian growth had so far been confined mainly to Europe, but by the late 1920s the U.S.S.R. also was beginning to establish the elements of an extensive network in Asia. China had, as yet, seen only tentative services. By 1930 the airlines in Europe were on average covering about 25 per cent of their costs from revenue; in the United States the figure was probably somewhat higher, at about 30 per cent. A few of the commercially more successful airlines in America and Europe were, however, by this date covering as much as 50 to 60 per cent of their costs. This was probably close to the best which could be achieved with the primitive equipment and operating techniques then available.

THE FIRST "MODERN-TYPE" MONOPLANES (1930–40)

Work in Germany during the First World War, notably by Rohrbach, had pioneered the first stressed-skin cantilever airplanes in light alloy. This development was carried forward during the 1920s, notably by the Short brothers in Britain—on monococque and semi-monocoque light alloy fuselages, flying boat hulls and seaplane floats—and by Rohrbach, Dornier and Messerschmitt in Germany and Wibault in France—on aerodynamically clean, smooth-skinned, all-metal monoplanes. Much of the aerodynamic refinement achieved by the latter, which found expression in cantilever light alloy monoplanes with stressed-skin wings tapered in chord[2] and thickness, resulted from parallel German progress in sailplane design. None of these European monoplanes, however, provided a significant advance in efficiency over contemporary biplanes, then still used by the majority of airlines, because engine powers were insufficient to enable their designers to go to high enough wing loadings.[3]

Towards the end of the 1920s, these structural and aerodynamic developments in Germany stimulated one of the first really fundamental advances in aeronautics to be made in the United States since the Wright brothers. Lockheed and Northrop developed clean cantilever monoplanes with higher wing loadings made possible by the high-power radial engines which were by then becoming available. By the beginning of the 1930s these aircraft had evolved into Boeing and Douglas all-metal, twin-engine cantilever monoplanes, which incorporated such further refinements as retractable undercarriages, flaps, wing-mounted, fully-cowled radial engines, and variable-pitch propellers. They were the first twin-engined aircraft with a reasonable single-engine performance—particularly after feathering propellers were introduced in 1937. They proved to be the progenitors of the twin and four-engine monoplanes which were to carry the bulk of the world's air traffic for the next 25 years.

For the first time, cruising speeds rose significantly above the 100 m.p.h. or less which had seriously limited the useful range and regularity of earlier transport aircraft, and particularly their punctuality in winds of varying strength.[4] The new monoplanes cruised at between 150 and 200 m.p.h., but they also had higher stalling speeds (in the region of 60 to 70 m.p.h.), which meant that they required larger aerodromes with runs of up to perhaps 1,200 yards, as against the 600 to 800 yards which had been adequate previously.

The low level of American expenditure on military aviation in the 1920s and early 1930s resulted in a higher proportion (probably as much as 60 per cent) of the business of the American aircraft industry during this period being in the civil field—more than either before or since and, indeed, more than at any time elsewhere. For this reason, the crucial development of the early American "modern-type" monoplanes owes more to the influences of the civil market than any comparable development in the history of air transport. Even so, the fact that the design of these aircraft was still largely inspired by military requirements and paid for by defense expenditure is illustrated by the B-9 bomber origins of the historic Boeing 247, the first of the new airliners.

The Boeing 247 appeared in 1933, and was followed by the Douglas DC-2 in 1934 and the larger DC-3 in 1935. These were the vehicles with which air transport was at last to be properly established. Their appearance coincided with the widespread adoption of instrument flying and the introduction of effective de-icing equipment. Radio navigational aids, notably the M/F range (Medium Frequency beacon used to define the airways), came into general use at this time, and were soon followed by the appearance of runways and of improved airport lighting. The better equipment and new techniques first became established in the United States, but they spread gradually to the rest of the world. By the later 1930s the new monoplanes were generally accepted everywhere as the dominant equipment, and the pioneering era of the biplane was over. In Europe and America, automatic pilots and instrument approach equipment were being introduced in the later 1930s and early 1940s. These soon provided new standards of regularity and safety in the long struggle against adverse weather conditions.

Overall, however, the 1930s were dominated by the remarkable progress of the airlines in the United States. They were already, at the start of the decade, carrying as many passengers as those in the rest of the world taken together. This ascendancy was maintained throughout the 1930s, during which the "Big Four"—American, Eastern, T.W.A. and United—established themselves astride a booming domestic airline system, while the "chosen instrument," Pan American Airways, expanded overseas, first throughout Latin America and then across the Pacific and Atlantic. Even more significant was the American technical leadership, both in aircraft and ground equipment and in improved techniques of operation. Rapid progress was made towards higher utilizations of aircraft and other facilities; engine and airframe overhaul lives were greatly extended and safety, regularity and punctuality were all much improved. During the ten years between 1929 and 1939 the moving ten-year average number of passenger fatalities per 100 million passenger miles on the U.S. domestic routes fell from 50 to five—a tenfold improvement in safety in ten years.

Although the emphasis shifted from Europe to America during the second decade of air transport, expansion continued to be rapid in the Old World also. The consolidation of most of the French operators into the partly government-owned Air France in 1933 has already been recorded. The French maintained an extensive European network during the 1930s, although there was little development of domestic services inside France, except for a special night postal service from

Paris to provincial centers. Started as Air Bleu in 1935, the service has been maintained ever since—interrupted only by the war years—as a unique example of this kind of operation.

The opening up of domestic air routes within the United Kingdom by a whole string of small private operators was a feature of British air transport during the 1930s. Most of these routes were only seasonal and the majority lost money, but their existence inspired the development of a series of inexpensive British feeder-line aircraft, notably by de Havilland, which played a significant part in the setting up of similar operations in other parts of the world. A few of the early U.K. domestic routes survived through the war and formed the basis on which B.E.A. greatly expanded internal air transport during the following 20 years. In the larger transport aircraft categories Britain lagged seriously behind the U.S., concentrating unduly on flying boats, which, although they eased the problems of providing ground facilities on the "Empire routes," proved less efficient than equivalent landplanes.

During the 1930s all the European nations which had started overseas routes in the 1920s greatly extended and improved their networks, until there were several lines serving Africa, the Middle and Far East, South America and Australia. Experimental services across the Atlantic to North America were just starting at the end of the decade.

In Canada, the 1930s saw a considerable growth in the operations of the many small airlines operating North-South services into the undeveloped areas of the North. Most of these services were to become integrated into Canadian Pacific Airlines under the aegis of the C.P.R. in 1942. Meanwhile, in 1937, Canada belatedly formed T.C.A. as a State-owned transcontinental airline. Steady growth also took place in Australia, where A.N.A. emerged as the dominant domestic operator in 1936. In South Africa, South African Airways was formed as a government department in 1934.

In Central and South America the U.S. carrier, Pan American, was a major force in opening up widespread services in the 1930s, but it was by no means the only outside interest so engaged. The French and particularly the Germans greatly extended activities started in the 1920s, and numerous local interests were active. Similarly, in the Far East, German and American operators centered in China were leaders of airline development during this period, although locally organized companies were also formed. K.N.I.L.M., in what is now Indonesia, continued during the 1930s an impressive growth which carried it outside its home islands and was finally ended only by the Japanese invasion of 1941. Japan and most other Middle and Far Eastern, and several African, countries saw airlines established during this period. Inside the Soviet Union Aeroflot was formed in 1932 and by 1935 had extended a trunk route across the continent to the distant Pacific.

Technical development of transport aircraft in all aircraft manufacturing countries followed the American lead to metal monoplanes during the latter half of the 1930s, but preparations for war in Europe and actual war in the Far East, plus an unjustified conservatism in many places, retarded progress. There was, in fact, no serious competition for the U.S. types in those countries—and they were numerous—which imported the quite unmatched Douglas monoplanes. The greatly improved standards of air transport which they made possible did much to complete the process of bringing the industry out of the pioneering, and almost experimental, atmosphere which in many parts of the world had survived into the 1930s from the 'twenties.

But the most important effect of the technical developments of the 1930s was in the economic field. In the 1920s profitable operation was quite impossible, except in a few specially favorable circumstances, and there did not even seem to be prospects of any fundamental change in this position. The metal monoplanes of the 1930s, however, combined with the new techniques of operation which they made possible, at last put the airlines within reach of profitability, even while they continued to lower fares so as to expand the market at a steadily accelerating pace. Thus, air fares in the United States were reduced by 27 per cent (in constant money values) between 1930 and 1940, and traffic on the U.S. domestic routes increased elevenfold. At the same time, the American domestic airlines improved their economic position from one where they were covering about 30 per cent of their costs from revenue in 1930 to one where they were covering over 80 per cent by 1940. Progress in Europe was slower—traffic increased eightfold between 1930 and 1939—and was inevitably affected, in the later 1930s, by the approaching shadows of war. But even in Europe, from a position where 25 per cent of costs were covered by revenue in 1930, a point had been reached by the mid-1930s where the more efficient carriers were already recovering over 80 per cent of their costs. These advances were made possible by an approximate halving in the direct operating costs per seat-mile, comparing the DC-3 with a representative type of the mid-1920s, the Fokker F.VII/3m. This improvement was mainly due to increased size, higher speed and the lower maintenance and overhaul costs of the all-metal airframe.

THE COMING OF LONG-RANGE AIR TRANSPORT (1940–50)

The first half of air transport's third decade was completely overshadowed by war. It was a time of spectacular technical and operational advance, which would have taken place even if there had been no war, although probably at a rather slower pace. Indeed, although air transport found many new purely military applications between 1939 and 1945, the most important effects of the war on the growth of the industry itself were the added impetus which it gave to the opening up of long-haul intercontinental routes and to the development of new radio, radar and navigational aids and night-and-bad-weather flying facilities, and the very extensive building of runway aerodromes throughout the world.

The most significant transport aircraft developments of the 1940s sprang from design work which had been initiated before the war. New large four-engined monoplanes came into service, notably the American Douglas DC-4 (1942) and Lockheed Constellation (1943), which were straightforward developments of the twin-engine monoplanes of the 1930s. Apart from being larger, and therefore with greater payload/range capabilities, these aircraft had higher wing loadings, made possible by the use of improved flaps and radial engines of greatly increased power and by the use of nose-wheel undercarriages and runways providing much longer runs (of up to perhaps 2,000 yards) than had been available at most pre-war airports. Cruising speeds were in the 200/260 m.p.h. bracket.

The most important feature of the new aircraft was their much greater range with a worthwhile payload. Intercontinental flying on a regular basis became practical for the first time, and all long-distance flying was easier because sector lengths could be greatly increased. At the same time, payload could be larger (40 to 60 passengers compared with the 20 to 30 passenger capacity of the DC-3). The initial versions of the new airplanes could not, however, carry the larger loads on the longer overwater stages. Operating costs per seat-mile of the four-engine monoplanes showed little improvement over those of the earlier twins. But similar cost levels could be maintained over much longer ranges, and the quality of the product offered to the customer was greatly improved by the higher speeds and greater regularity and by the pressurization incorporated in the Constellation and later developments of the DC-4, which came into service after the war.

During the war years the new four-engine monoplanes were used by the Western Allies for long-range strategic transport, in which role they were supplemented by transport adaptations of long-range bombers. Grossly overloaded versions of the prewar twin-engine types were also widely operated over much longer ranges and with much greater loads than their designers had ever intended. When peace returned the airlines, which had greatly curtailed their normal operations during the war, were soon spreading their networks again across the continents. They also added services, on a rapidly expanding scale, across the major oceans, which had only been tentatively bridged before the war. These developments were accelerated by the fact that several of the highly competent U.S. domestic airlines, which had undertaken a great deal of long-range flying for the services during the war, were now permitted to expand overseas in parallel to Pan American.

The U.S. domestic airlines had continued to operate within the United States throughout the war, using Douglas twin-engine airliners almost exclusively. The aircraft and crews available to them, however, were severely limited, so that they continued to expand after 1943 (traffic declined in 1942 and 1943) only by the most intensive use of their resources. Aircraft utilizations of more than ten hours per day, and a completely uncommercial average load factor of almost 90 per cent, were achieved in 1944. This intensity of operation has rarely been rivalled since, and was probably beyond economic limits, because specific costs were not significantly reduced during this period. However, the U.S. airlines did achieve their first profits without subsidy throughout the war years. This was because of the high load factors, which resulted from government control of the sale of seats in the interests of the war effort. By 1945 traffic on the U.S. domestic airlines had increased to 60 per cent of the world total. With the recovery of other airlines after the war, this ratio fell to 43 per cent by 1950.

Elsewhere, except in South America, the airline industry was disrupted even more than in the United States. Those countries which were defeated or overrun early in the war mostly suffered complete eclipse of their airline industries until peace returned. Most of the other major combatant nations on both sides retained rudimentary airline networks throughout the war. But these lost much of their civilian character and were inevitably integrated with their countries' military war efforts. Europe's civil air traffic during the war years fell to between a third and a half of its pre-war volume, but expanded again very rapidly as soon as peace returned. By 1950, it had grown to more than ten times that of 1939.

Britain decided to join its two largest airlines together just before the war, thus creating the State-owned B.O.A.C., which handled all British overseas civil air transport throughout the war. After the war, B.O.A.C. was the pattern for two similar airline corporations—B.E.A., to handle European and domestic traffic, and the short-lived B.S.A.A., for the routes to South America, which was, however, soon absorbed into B.O.A.C. The biggest airline achievement of the British during the war was the leading part they played in establishing round-the-year transatlantic services with landplanes.

Airline development in South America was less affected by the war than elsewhere. Traffic increased fivefold from 1940 to 1945, when it almost equalled Europe's total, although Europe soon drew away again, reaching a level three times higher by 1950. The 1940s saw the gradual elimination of the influence of the European countries and the further consolidation of American influence through Pan American Airways. Brazil emerged as the leading air transport nation in its part of the world.

The broad picture of air transport development during the first half of the 1940s was one of the Western Allies, and particularly the Americans, going ahead with a spectacular expansion of quasi-civil operations under war conditions—with particular emphasis on long-haul routes with the new four-engined aircraft—while the rest of the world held on with existing or improvised equipment until peace returned.

The second half of the decade saw an explosive growth of the airlines of all the victorious and neutral nations. This catered for the pent-up demand for increased travel which had built up during the war years and provided full scope for the new large American airliners. Britain, and to a lesser extent France, attempted to compete with new aircraft of their own but had only limited success, and this only with short-haul types and small feeder liners.

In Australia the immediate post-war period saw the formation of a new State-owned airline, T.A.A., which expanded rapidly on domestic routes in fierce competition with the established privately-owned A.N.A. Qantas (originally formed in 1920) was nationalised in 1947 and continued to grow as Australia's international flag carrier. B.C.P.A. was created in 1946 as a British Commonwealth consortium to operate across the Pacific.

Generally speaking, however, the world picture was dominated at this time by the U.S. airlines—a number in addition to Pan American had acquired long-haul experience working for the services during the war, and they made full use of it. At the same time, U.S. airliners firmly established themselves as standard equipment throughout the world, except in the Soviet bloc. Even there, the DC-3 built under license handled much of the short-haul traffic.

The system of bilaterally negotiated traffic rights between nations, which had applied generally before the war, was reaffirmed by the 1944 Chicago Convention (which set up I.C.A.O. as the United Nations organization controlling air transport) and by the Bermuda Agreement (1946) between Britain and the U.S.A., which set the pattern for most other traffic rights agreements. Under this system, traffic on international routes tends to divide 50-50 between the two nations involved. Mainly for this reason, the American ascendancy on most international routes was held in check in the later 1940s as the airlines of other nations grew stronger. By 1950, traffic carried by American airlines had declined to 55 per cent of the world total from 68 per cent in 1945. But the American share of international traffic was maintained throughout the 1940s and early fifties. It began to decline only in the later 1950s. American aircraft continued to be used by the majority of the world's carriers, and the Douglas DC-6, Lockheed Constellation and Boeing Stratocruiser were carrying almost all the world's long-haul traffic, now at cruising speeds of 270/290 m.p.h.

The universal acceptance, outside the Soviet bloc, of the American four-engined monoplanes as trunk route equipment contributed to a steady further improvement in the profitability of the industry. This is illustrated by the progress of the U.S. domestic airlines, which, from a position where they were covering 80 per cent of costs in 1940, were on average covering all their costs and making a small profit by 1950. This was achieved in spite of a 37 per cent reduction in fares (in constant money values), which, itself, was a major reason for a more than sevenfold increase in traffic. Other factors were greatly improved regularity and comfort and a more than threefold improvement in safety: a moving ten-year average of about five passenger fatalities per 100 million passenger-miles in 1940 reduced to about 1.5 in 1950.

The airlines of other nations lagged behind America to a varying extent, but their progress was relatively at least as significant, so that the industry as a whole had been transformed by the end of the decade. The airlines generally were, in fact, getting near the point where their operations would become an integral part of modern society and profitable operation would be potentially within reach of all, although few were to achieve it consistently.

AIR TRANSPORT COMES INTO ITS OWN (1950-60)

The industry's fourth decade was to see the airlines establishing themselves as the most important method of long-distance passenger transport. At the same time, they were increasingly penetrating the medium and even short-haul passenger market and were building up a still relatively small but nonetheless significant freight traffic in higher-value goods.

In 1955 the U.S. domestic airlines for the first time carried more inter-city passengers than the buses, and in 1957 they also exceeded the number going by rail. By the end of the decade the airlines were carrying almost as many inter-city passengers as the buses and trains together. By 1957, over the North Atlantic, as many passengers were flying as travelled by sea. The pattern of growth elsewhere was similar, although acceptance of the new medium continued to lag behind U.S. progress. However, the competition offered to the American carriers by the airlines of other countries grew steadily throughout the decade. Whereas in 1950 over 60 per cent of Atlantic air passengers still flew American, by 1960 the position had been almost exactly reversed. In 1959 B.O.A.C. became the second most important airline over the Atlantic, still eclipsed only by the ever-dominant Pan American Airways. In Europe, Australia and South America, by the later 1950s the airlines had become the most important method of passenger travel on many of the busiest routes.

The aircraft which made all these developments possible showed little fundamental technical advance over those of the later 1940s. The DC-4 series, in its stretched DC-6 and DC-7 forms, and similar developments of the Constellation provided the backbone of almost all long-haul activity until nearly the end of the decade. By accepting the 50 to 60 per cent increase in runway length required, and by using progressively more developed engines, these stretched types roughly doubled the payload and range capabilities of their predecessors, while offering smaller but still significant increases in speed and reductions in direct operating cost. They were, in fact, striking evidence of the advantages of progressive development of established designs—a process now being repeated in the jet era. Cruising speeds went up to 300/330 m.p.h. but, at the same time, stalling speeds rose to 100 m.p.h. and required runway lengths to 2,500 yards.

On shorter-haul routes the twin-engine Convair series, which had first appeared in the late 1940s, remained the most important type, although from 1953 the turbo-prop British Vickers Viscount appeared as the first non-American airliner to seriously challenge the ever-dominant U.S. types. This acroplane was, by four years, the first of a series of turbo-prop designs which entered service in the later 1950s alongside the established piston-engine types.

Apart from their power plants, these aircraft were closely similar in performance and other characteristics to their piston-engine equivalents—although generally somewhat faster. Some larger medium and long-haul turbo-prop transports—the British Bristol Britannia, the American Lockheed Electra and the Russian Ilyushin Il-18—also came into use. For short range work the Dutch Fokker Friendship established itself in some numbers, although the veteran DC-3 continued to the end of the decade to be by far the most numerous type in use—by now mainly on second-line routes. The newer piston-engine types, however, remained the most important in service across the whole range of the world's airlines until almost the end of the decade.

In addition to the turbo-prop incursion, which now seems in historical perspective to have been but an interim and almost supplementary phase to the piston-engine era, there was the courageous British attempt in 1952 with the de Havilland Comet I to establish scheduled jet services. This venture—after demonstrating the competitive advantages of jet transport on a limited scale over the following two years—unfortunately failed, mainly it now seems because of insufficient British experience during the previous stage of transport aircraft development. In attempting to "leapfrog" the American ascendancy and to exploit their own leadership in gas turbines, the British were perhaps too ambitious—as well as unlucky.

After this episode, the airline industry continued with piston engines, supplemented by turbo-props, until the start of the "jet revolution" proper in 1958.

By 1950 the United States domestic airlines had completely established themselves as an integral part of the nation's economy. Intercity rail and road public carrier passenger traffic reached its peak in 1951 and thereafter declined as air traffic continued to expand. The trunk airlines were by now fully profitable and continued to grow in a fiercely competitive environment, which was, however, government-regulated to prevent competition from becoming uneconomic and to ensure the best service to the customer. At the same time the local service carriers, which had progressively established themselves in the years following the end of the war, had built up a feeder network which by 1960 served by scheduled air services no less than 600 cities within the United States. These carriers required government subsidies throughout the 1950s—and, indeed, continue to receive them to this day—but they play an essential part in feeding traffic into the trunk route network, as well as in the expansion of the economy as a whole.

A much smaller development, but perhaps no less significant for the future, was the gradual evolution of helicopter scheduled services in a number of urban areas. These held promise of eventually bringing air transport into the suburban field, which it had previously been quite unable to serve. Helicopter services in the 1950s were flown with small single-piston engine types. Only at the beginning of the 1960s came the first twin-turbine types capable of carrying 20 to 25 passengers. These pioneer operations were, of course, heavily subsidised.

But, while U.S. domestic growth continued on a massive scale, the example set by the American airlines was perhaps their most significant contribution to worldwide progress of the industry throughout the 1950s. This example was important in leading towards higher operating standards, towards new types of service—coach class, tourist (from 1952), economy (from 1958) and group fares, and "air shuttle" services, all owed much to

American initiative—and in stimulating the American transport aircraft manufacturers on the west coast to produce ever more effective vehicles which became, in due course, the standard equipment of the world's airlines.

Significant developments in British Commonwealth countries during the decade included, in Canada, the emergence of Canadian Pacific Airlines as a second, privately owned, flag carrier alongside the State-owned T.C.A., first on international and then on domestic trunk routes. There was also a steady growth of stronger Canadian regional carriers. In Australia, the struggle continued between the State-owned T.A.A. and the privately owned A.N.A., which amalgamated with Ansett Airways in 1957. A number of smaller regional carriers also played an important part in the phenomenal progress of Australian air transport. Qantas, The Australian international airline, continued its worldwide expansion, including absorption of the trans-Pacific B.C.P.A. in 1954. New Zealand's N.A.C. (formed in 1945) expanded its domestic routes, while Tasman Empire Airways became an Australian-New Zealand company in 1954 and New Zealand's own overseas airline in 1961. Other achievements included the fine reputation and world network built up by Air India International, which was nationalized in 1953 at the same time as the Indian domestic airlines were amalgamated into the State-owned I.A.C. Pakistan's airline interests were taken over by P.I.A., which, like South African Airways in 1934, became a government department in 1951. Even the little colony of Hong Kong was the base of two active airlines through the 1950s until they were amalgamated as Cathay Pacific Airlines in 1959. Finally, many of the new Commonwealth countries took over existing regional airlines and started to expand them as their own flag carriers—because national airlines have come to be recognized as one of the essential trappings of independence, whatever the economic consequences.

Europe regained its pre-war position as the center of the world's international air transport in the 1950s. By 1952 there were no less than twelve carriers flying between Europe and North America, seven to Central America, eight to South America, fourteen to Africa and thirteen to the Far East. This already extensive coverage had increased by more than 50 per cent by the end of the decade. The only inter-continental route of comparable importance which did not radiate from Europe was that between the Americas.

At the same time, air transport within Europe grew at a phenomenal pace. The expansion of the European airlines during the decade was more than 50 per cent greater than that of the American. In contrast to the position before the war, the United Kingdom—mainly thanks to the dynamism of B.E.A.—now had a leading role in this growth. Amongst the European leaders were the nationalised Air France and several privately owned French airlines, the Scandinavian consortium airline, S.A.S., and the historic Dutch and Belgian airlines, K.L.M. and Sabena—which particularly suffered, however, on their long-haul routes from the penalties of loss of traffic rights which the break-up of empires brings. Germany, which before the war had been the most important air transport nation in Europe, was excluded from the airline business for nine years after its defeat. However, Lufthansa was re-formed in West Germany in 1954 (and a similarly-named, but separate, organization in East Germany in the same year) and has since consistently shown a more rapid rate of growth than any of its competitors, so that it seems likely to re-establish soon something of its former ascendancy. All the pre-war European air transport nations, including notably Switzerland, Italy and Spain, have played their part since the war in the expansion of the industry. This development has, moreover, taken place on both sides of the Iron Curtain.

An interesting feature of European progress, despite the dependence on U.S. equipment of most of the airlines most of the time, has been the lead which the continent has been able to give in the introduction of entirely new types of equipment. Thus, the world's first turbo-prop network was established in Europe (with the Viscount from 1953), the first long-haul jet network (with the Comet from 1952) and the first short-haul jet network (with the Caravelle from 1959). A lead had also been given, particularly by the United Kingdom, in other technical fields such as airworthiness requirements, approach lighting, navigational aids, air traffic control techniques and automatic landing.

The Soviet Union started to participate in Western Europe's air transport from the mid-1950s, while its own domestic air traffic increased more than fivefold during the decade. A feature of the Russian growth was the emphasis on freight, which had continued as only a small proportion (about ten per cent) of the airlines' business in the western world. Modernization of Russian equipment started with the introduction of turbine types from 1956.

Airline development in Latin America during the 1950s followed the pattern set in the 1940s. But a spate of amalgamations of smaller airlines into larger units in the early 1950s improved standards of service and the stability and financial success of the survivors. Brazil, in particular, made rapid progress and maintained its position as the leading South American air transport nation, carrying about half the continent's total traffic.

Japan re-emerged as an air transport nation, and a number of other Far Eastern countries built up domestic and overseas airlines. Communist China started its own airline operation, initially with Soviet help and equipment. Garuda Indonesian Airways, formed out of K.N.I.L.M. in 1949, was helped by K.L.M. until 1956 and after that date operated on its own, with increasing links with the communist world.

To sum up the 1950s, this was a period when profitable operation became possible and was, in fact, achieved much of the time by all the American trunk carriers and by the more efficient larger airlines elsewhere. However, a policy of continuing fare reductions (in constant money values), to expand traffic as rapidly as possible, meant that profit margins remained small and, indeed, often nonexistent for all but the most efficient airlines. The International Air Transport Association fare-fixing machinery (working always subject to the approval of governments, who themselves negotiate bilaterally all traffic rights between them) in practice enabled the most powerful airlines—usually the big American carriers—to have an important influence on fares, which they can naturally afford to pitch lower than most of their smaller competitors, who have nonetheless to accept them once they have been internationally agreed.

Contrary to what is often averred, this ensures that the travelling public has the lowest practical fares, but it equally has the effect of holding all but the most efficient carriers just below the level of profitability. As a result, the majority of airlines outside the U.S.A., which are often state-owned and invariably state-regulated, are dependent on direct or indirect government subsidies—even though the margins of unprofitability are often small and certainly proportionately much less than they ever were during the development period of the 1930s and 1940s.

A measure of progress by the industry as a whole is again most conveniently given in figures for U.S. domestic air transport, which continued to set the pace and to be roughly equal in size to that in the rest of the western world. Fares were reduced between 1950 and 1960 by 12 per cent (in constant money values), and this contributed to a 3.8-fold growth in traffic—which was, however, significantly less than the 4.4-fold growth elsewhere where fare reductions were greater. Safety improved nearly fourfold, from a moving ten-year average of 1.5 passenger fatalities per 100 million passenger miles in 1949 to 0.4 in 1959, before the jets affected the picture.

The vehicles which made this possible were, as has been seen, straightforward developments of the original piston-engine monoplanes of the 1930s. Their capabilities had been greatly increased by progressive development, but there had been only modest reductions in basic operating costs, and such reductions as there were seem to have been mainly the result of increased size of vehicles. Most of the other improvements in economy came from greater efficiency of the airlines, improved operating techniques and better engineering reliability and durability (engine overhaul lives rose to 1,500 hours or more), holding in check the adverse effects of ever-growing complexity. By the middle of the decade, when the effects of piston-engine airliner development were at their peak, the U.S. domestic trunks were achieving, on average, a margin of revenue over expenditure of something like 25 per cent.

THE JET REVOLUTION (THE 1960s)

The Comet I episode of the early 1950s had clearly shown the passenger appeal of the jet. It had also come near to giving the British a serious chance of breaking the American near-monopoly in Western world transport aircraft. After the eclipse of the Comet I, it was only a matter of time before the American industry took the plunge to jets. The process was started by Pan American Airways placing orders for Boeing and Douglas jets in 1955. The first and, as time was to show, most important U.S. jet airliner was the Boeing 707, the first production models of which went into service in 1958, at about the same time as the British revived the Comet in enlarged and improved form.

Meanwhile, however, the Russians had for the first time appeared on the airline scene with a development of world-wide significance. In 1956 they put into service their Tupolev Tu-104 jet airliner. This was a straightforward development of the Tu-16 medium bomber, which had already been in service for some years. The Tu-104 exploited for the first time in airline service advances in high subsonic speed aerodynamics which had been discovered mainly in Germany just before and during the Second World War. In particular the use of swept surfaces, due to Busemann, delayed the drag-rise at high subsonic speeds and raised economic cruising speeds to the 500/550 m.p.h. level. Stalling speeds rose at this time to 120/125 m.p.h. and required runway lengths to 3,000/3,500 yards.

The Russians had, until now, lagged behind the west in their air transport development by a gap of many years. Not only had they been quite out of touch with the economic and technical possibilities of the medium, particularly as developed in America, but the level of their aircraft development bore no comparison. They had put a couple of inefficient short-haul piston-engined designs into service since the war and had used a licence-built version of the DC-3, but that was all.

With the appearance of the Tu-104 the position began to change. Although the Russians appear to have been confused, perhaps even more than their Western colleagues, about the role of the turbo-prop in the airline equipment picture—they, like the west, put a number of large and small turbo-prop transports into service in the late 1950s and early 1960s—yet the signs are clear that the Russians are now learning fast both about equipment and about efficient operating techniques. It may be, indeed, that only the Russians, as in other fields, have any real chance of offering a serious challenge to the American domination of air transport. However, at the present rate of progress, it will be some years yet before they are in a position to do this.

By the start of air transport's fifth decade, the "big jets" were fast taking over the world's long-haul air routes. By far the most important of these were the Boeing 707 and the Douglas DC-8, but they were soon supplemented by the medium-range Boeing 720 (a straightforward variant of the 707) and, in smaller numbers, by the Convair CV-880 and 990. In 1964 these types were joined by a few of the long-range British Vickers V.C.10 series, and the Russians will shortly also enter the field with their Ilyushin Il-62 of a similar configuration. In addition, from 1959, the French Sud-Aviation Caravelle was repeating the success of the Viscount in challenging American domination in the short-haul field, this time with a jet. The Caravelle was, however, little in advance of the Comet aerodynamically, and, like the latter and the early versions of the American big jets, was handicapped by the fact that it was fitted with first-generation jet engines of the same basic design as had been used in military aircraft for the first 15 years of the jet era. The latest versions of the Caravelle and of the American long-range jets are now fitted with dual-flow jet engines of greatly reduced fuel consumption and improved economy. Such engines are also used in the whole range of still newer short-haul jets which are now in production in the U.S.A., the Soviet Union and Britain—Boeing 727 and 737, Douglas DC-9, Tupolev Tu-134, Hawker Siddeley Trident and B.A.C. One Eleven. A few belated turbo-prop airliners (Vickers Vanguard, Handley Page Herald, Hawker Siddeley 748, Tupolev Tu-114 and Antonov An-24) have also entered service during the 1960s.

Both Britain and Russia now each have, for the first time, a complete range of modern airliners able to offer effective competition to the Americans' ever-dominant position in the manufacture of transport aircraft. There is little doubt that the Russian airliners will, in due course, be universally adopted in the Communist world. But the chance of British or other European manufacturers achieving a significant penetration of the Western world's airliner market is still in doubt. The British have been far less successful than the Americans in obtaining operator/manufacturer cooperation in the development of transport aircraft. As a result, British airliner exports have often suffered from insufficient support by home operators. The British have also failed to bargain, as they might have done, with other European countries, like the French, Germans, Italians and Dutch, who might well be prepared to buy British if the British in return avoided producing designs directly competitive with other European aircraft and always bought European-produced aircraft as their part of the bargain.

The swing to jets has been the most significant feature in the development of air transport during the first half of the 1960s. However, the first years of the jets unfortunately coincided with one of the periodic pauses which occur from time to time in the otherwise still headlong expansion of air traffic, as a result of a short-term slowing down in the rate of increase in demand. The jets are very much larger than their predecessors, the finally-stretched-out versions of the piston and turbo-prop airliners of the previous generation. When the airlines were re-equipped with the new airplanes, the dictates of adequate frequency and the need to maintain viable fleet sizes meant, in most cases, that capacities offered on many routes were increased more rapidly than usual. These increases, combined with the disappointing traffic trends, gave a sharp fall in load factors and resulted in a serious deterioration in the airlines' financial results for a couple of years.

Some, who had forecast that jet airplanes would be uneconomic, hailed these results as justification for their forebodings. However, the difficult phase passed and the jets have since proved themselves in full. They have now taken over almost all long and medium-haul routes and are rapidly doing the same in the short-haul market also. The reason is that propeller-driven airliners have proved incapable of maintaining economic load factors in the face of jet competition at similar fares. Fare differentials in favor of the older types have not been acceptable to the larger and stronger airlines, which have made large investments in new jet equipment; and they, as has already been pointed out, have the biggest say in the determination of fares. Such differentials are not in any case justifiable on grounds of cost, because the jets have proved substantially more economic than their predecessors. Thus the average specific costs of the world's airlines during the past five years have been reduced about twice as fast as during the last five years of the propeller era. This has been primarily due to increasing vehicle size and to further advances in engineering reliability and durability (engine overhaul lives have risen to 5,000/10,000 hours). Direct operating costs of the jets are, in fact, showing reductions on those of the previous piston-engine types of the order of 50 per cent—much greater than those achieved by the metal monoplanes of the 1930s over the pioneering biplanes which preceded them. Further "stretching" of the existing subsonic jets and the introduction of the scaled-up "jumbo jets"—starting with the Boeing 747, which is due to enter service at the end of the decade—should give continuing reductions in specific costs.

The impact of the jets has already been decisive in its effects on the viability of the industry. Their effect on quality of service has been no less far-reaching, and there has been a sharp upswing in traffic on many routes, apparently mainly stimulated by the greater appeal of quicker and more comfortable journeys. On the world's most important air route, across the North Atlantic, four times as many passengers now fly as cross by sea. Indications are that most of the yardsticks of efficiency—safety, regularity and punctuality—are continuing their favourable trends of past decades, despite the radically new equipment.

The U.S. airlines continue their leadership of the industry, although airlines on all continents are now reaching comparable levels of maturity. However, partly because of the ever larger, more expensive and more technically sophisticated vehicles, there are growing pressures towards further consolidations of the airlines into fewer and stronger companies. Two American lines, United Air Lines and Capitol, were amalgamated in 1961, forming the world's largest operator after Aeroflot, the Soviet airline monopoly. Another important amalgamation in the same year was between Varig and Real in Brazil; this created the largest airline in South America.

In Britain the government induced the smaller private airlines, which had been operating in a minor role alongside B.E.A. and B.O.A.C. through the 1950s, to amalgamate into two stronger groups in 1959. In 1960 the Air Transport Licensing Board was created with a mandate to give the private sector of the industry a larger share of the scheduled business. An important landmark in U.K. air transport was passed in 1961, when, for the first time, more people flew between Britain and the Continent than went by sea. The motorcar air ferries, however, which had been an important development across the English Channel during the 1950s—one, incidentally, unparallelled elsewhere—suffered some recession in the 1960s as more surface ferries became available. An attempt was therefore made to shift the emphasis of the air ferry operations to longer routes to points within the Continent. But the results of this change have also been disappointing.

The Soviet Union has continued its rapid progress during the 1960s. Aeroflot is now carrying nearly 40 million passengers a year (18 per cent of the world total). During 1964 more than three quarters of Aeroflot's capacity was provided by its new turbine aircraft.

Everywhere the jets have provided a stimulus to progress. Indeed, their effect on the financial state of the industry during the remainder of this decade may be sufficient to increase the over-all economy of the industry to a point where it is for the first time completely viable. Although, according to I.C.A.O. statistics, the world's airlines taken together have shown small operating profits (of up to about 5 per cent) every year since 1961, the costs reported to I.C.A.O. are probably incomplete from at least some of the reporting nations. Even allowing for this, it is probable that the industry has just about paid its way during these years, if one ignores the fact that the charges imposed on the airlines for ground facilities (airports, air traffic control, navigational aids, etc.) which they use probably cover only some 55 to 60 per cent of the cost of providing them. There are difficulties in assessing the proportion of the cost of these facilities which should be legitimately charged to the airlines because they are, of course, provided for all air users. Nevertheless, the airline industry overall appears to be currently covering from revenue very nearly all the costs of providing air transport. There are now, at last, prospects that the airlines will achieve complete and sustained profitability with their present jet equipment. To do this, however, a difficult equilibrium will have to be maintained between continued sharp reductions in fares, at something like the average of 3 per cent per annum (in constant money values), which have been made during the past 40 years to maintain essential growth, and some lower rate of reduction which will avoid the knife-edge economic/uneconomic situation of the past.

Aircraft are now probably the cheapest public transport method of carrying passengers over long distances (this is, of course, still very far from being true for freight). The cost advantage of the air narrows and finally disappears over shorter ranges, but it remains competitive in cost for passengers down to quite short inter-city distances. The biggest traffic potentials, moreover, lie on these shorter ranges. Air transport has made remarkable progress during the past 45 years; yet its greatest challenge, in this short-haul field, still lies in the future.

For the good of both the airlines and their customers, the industry must have time to exploit fully the great potentials of the subsonic jets, so as to overcome its economic difficulties. It must also have time to tackle the short-haul market on a far bigger scale than heretofore and to bring in such further operational refinements as automatic landing—for full all-weather capability—before it can go forward with confidence to its next great challenge: the supersonic airliner.

NOTES

1 Monocoque: a rounded shell form of construction in which the outer skin is an essential part of the structure.

2 Chord: width of wing, measured in a fore-and-aft direction.

3 Increased efficiency required the reduced drag (air resistance) and weight of smaller wings to carry a given load. This was not possible, with an acceptable performance, without higher engine power.

4 Regularity and punctuality are important not only to passengers but also to better scheduling and service integration, which contribute much to higher utilization of aircraft and crews and lower operating costs.

SELECTED BIBLIOGRAPHY

Holt Thomas, G.: *Commercial Aeronautics.* Royal Aeronautical Society Reprint No. 5, 1918.

Bonomo, O.: *L'Aviation Commerciale.* Librarie des Sciences Aeronautiques, Paris, 1926.

Bouché, H.: *Economics of Air Transport in Europe.* Organisation for Communications and Transit, League of Nations, Geneva, 1935.

Warner, E. P.: *The Early History of Air Transportation.* James Jackson Cabot Lecture, Norwich University, Vermont, U.S.A., 1937.

Warner, E. P.: *The Modern Development of Air Transport.* James Jackson Cabot Lecture, Norwich University, Vermont, 1938.

Warner, E. P.: *Technical Development and its Effects on Air Transportation.* James Jackson Cabot Lecture, Norwich University, Vermont, 1938.

Lissitzyn, O. J.: *International Air Transport and National Policy.* Council on Foreign Relations, New York, 1942.

Warner, E. P.: "Post-War Transport Aircraft." Thirty-first Wilbur Wright Memorial Lecture. *Journal of the Royal Aeronautical Society,* July 1943.

Masefield, P. G.: "Some Economic Factors of Civil Aviation." Fourth British Commonwealth and Empire Lecture, *J.R.Ae.S.,* October 1948.

Longhurst, J.: *Nationalisation in Practice.* Temple Press Ltd., 1950.

Masefield, P. G.: "Some Economic Factors in Air Transport Operation." Ninth Brancker Memorial Lecture, *Journal of the Institute of Transport,* March 1951.

Brooks, P. W.: "Problems of Short-Haul Air Transport." *J.R.Ae.S.,* June 1952.

Speas, R. Dixon: *Technical Aspects of Air Transport Management.* McGraw-Hill, New York, 1955.

Wheatcroft, S. F.: *The Economics of European Air Transport.* Manchester University Press, 1956.

Douglas of Kirtleside, Lord: "The Economics of Speed." Fourteenth Brancker Memorial Lecture, *Journal of the Institute of Transport,* May 1957.

Birkhead, E.: "The Daimler Airway." *The Journal of Transport History,* Leicester, 1958.

Higham, R.: *Britain's Imperial Air Routes, 1918–1939.* G. T. Foulis & Co. Ltd., 1960.

Brooks, P. W.: *The Modern Airliner.* Putnam, 1961.

Davies, R. E. G.: *History of World Air Transport.* Oxford University Press, 1964.

Air transport can play a different role according to the development characteristics of a region. K. R. Sealy recognizes three stages from pioneer to sophisticated aviation as settlement frontiers are pushed back:*

1 A *pioneer phase* in which aircraft are used for various topographical, forest, or mineral surveys. In some cases, where potential resource exploitation seems to warrant it, aircraft are used to establish the first camps and to aid in the construction of surface links.

2 With the establishment of primary land routes and exploitation on a greater scale, aircraft begin *specialization* in passengers and freight.

3 In the *final phase,* the growth of industry and settlement may sometimes follow, in which case surface modes rise to dominance. Air transport now assumes its more "normal" role, concentrating on passengers, mail, and specialized freight carriage.

*K. R. Sealy, *The Geography of Air Transport* (rev. ed.), London: Hutchinson, 1966.

The "demand" side of air transport is complex and therefore difficult to evaluate. In short-haul conditions, other modes offer services that are close substitutes, but in the long-haul passenger market airlines offer distinct advantages. The long-haul market is constrained, of course, by the ability to pay for travel, and only an adult with an annual income of more than $7,500 has more than a 10 percent likelihood of making an air trip in any one year. There is little variation in the rates charged among airlines, though various promotional fares exist, and competition usually takes the form of ownership of the most technically advanced aircraft.

Fixed costs are small or absent; operating costs are approximately 27 percent for flying operations, 20 percent for maintenance, 43 percent for services, and 10 percent for depreciation. Economies of scale among airlines are small, but there are economies among aircraft types. Factors other than seating capacity influence costs, but there is a strong tendency for operating costs per seat mile to be lower when the aircraft is large (see "Jet Aircraft: Operating Costs"). The important factor is the percentage of seat miles flown in a scheduled service which are *sold.* The cost of operating an aircraft between two points depends only to a limited extent on whether the aircraft is full or empty; the same terminal costs, crew costs, and fuel costs are incurred, so that the load factor is important. For example, on the Boeing 707B, 52 passenger seats must be sold to break even, the remaining 88 being profitmaking passengers; notably the same ratio for the 747B is 101 and 304! The utilization rate of the aircraft is important, since each represents a substantial capital outlay; other factors, such as route density, route structure, and stage length, are also important. Length of the stages flown is important since the costs per aircraft mile are not constant; costs fall as distance increases, since the costs of taxiing, takeoff, climbing, and landing are spread over more miles; cruising costs are much lower. There is, however, a point at which the additional fuel needed to fly longer distances becomes high in cost terms.

Air freight charges are many times higher than those of competitive modes. Average freight revenues per ton mile were about 22.7 cents in 1950, though they have declined with technical improvements to between 10 and 16 cents per ton mile today. The reason that air freight is used at all is the minimization of *total costs* that can be achieved, and users range along a continuum from

Jet Aircraft: Operating Costs

Jet type	Average seats/ mile	Cost/seat mile (cents)
Caravelle	64	3.1
Boeing 720	111	1.5
DC-8	123	1.4
Boeing 707	124	1.4
Boeing 707B	140	1.2
DC-8	127	1.7
Boeing 747A	374	0.9
Boeing 747B	405	0.8

those who use it as an emergency to those who use it regularly. Thus in an emergency a company might fly out replacement parts for a ship rather than have the ship held up for weeks. Commodities that do move regularly by air are perishables such as flowers, fruit, information (e.g., newspapers), and there are instances in which there may be no alternative transport, e.g., flying construction machinery to Alaska or the Canadian north.

Developments in the future may see the emergence of air transport as a substitute for other modes rather than as a complement. Although it is conventional to think of surface transport as the norm, this approach may change as technical innovations increase. Already there is some evidence of changing attitudes. The World Bank recommended that Libya make use of aircraft to service remote communities rather than build roads. (Libya chose to ignore this advice.) In Venezuela meat is flown out of points in the *llanos* which are otherwise inaccessible.

PIPELINES

This too is a relatively new mode, a very specialized carrier at low rates and slow speeds (roughly, walking pace). Basically pipelines carry liquids, with some potential for moving solids. Their increasing role in commodity movements has been made possible by various technical advances—large-scale production of inexpensive pipe, use of electric welding, and improved and more economic ways of laying pipes. There are certain disadvantages to pipelines, such as their inflexibility once laid and a fairly fixed capacity, which can only be marginally improved by the installation of extra pumping equipment. Their advantages lie in their ability to cross most terrain, practically unaffected by climate, although there may be environmental feedback in some sensitive areas, such as the permafrost zones to be traversed by the Alaskan lines from the North Slope. In total, they carry petroleum and natural gas at very low unit costs. Where volumes and market demands are sufficiently great and steady, pipelines are more economic than other forms of transport. Land costs are often minimized by burying a pipeline, and 70 to 75 percent of the costs of installing an average pipeline are the costs of the pipe itself. Pumping stations are installed at 30- to 150-mile intervals, and they can be largely automatic. Annual operating costs run about 3 to 10 percent of the original costs. The actual costs very with the size of pipe, efficiency of use, cost of capital, nature of terrain, and the *viscosity* of the fluid being transmitted.† The average costs of a 1,000-mile-long, 10-inch pipeline in North America is $37,000 per mile, excluding right of way. A comparable length of 20-inch pipeline, carrying 3½ times as much liquid, is about $66,000 per mile, with operating costs about a third as much.

Large volumes of any liquid can be moved at costs similar to those of waterways (except when very large quantities are moved, at about 15 to 25 percent the cost of rail, and at 15 to 18 percent the cost of trucks. Something like 70 percent of U.S. energy resources move through a million-mile net-

†The more viscous the oil, the greater the costs of pumping. It is estimated that the cost of pumping residual fuel oil through a pipe is four to five times the cost of pumping crude oil through a pipe of similar diameter.

work. The total movements of oil, particularly crude, are very large, and pipelines account for about 17 percent of U.S. intercity freight ton mileage. The larger share of the crude petroleum market revealed by the table is due to the special suitability of pipelines for very large movements; for example, flows from oil fields have this character. Refined products distributed to individual points of consumption, often dispersed, are in much smaller quantities. Natural gas is another major product carried, and there are twice as many miles of gas pipeline in the United States as there are miles of rail track.

One of the most important determinants of costs in pipeline transportation, then, is economies of scale, which are especially associated with the pipe diameter, through economies of pipe price or pumping. A 1,000-mile-long pipeline with a diameter of 18 inches and a throughput of 100,000 barrels a day would average about 16 cents per barrel, but with a 32-inch diameter it could throughput 400,000 barrels at a cost 8 cents per barrel. Obviously, in this case it would be wasteful for, say, four competing refineries in a consuming area, taking crude oil from the same area, to use four pipelines, since from the above example they would double the costs of moving the oil. It follows, then, that the costs for moving oil on a route equipped with a large-diameter pipeline will be lower than on another route not thus equipped, so that there will be external economies in the same area.

Whereas pipelines have expanded greatly in route miles in North America, Western Europe has until recently not undergone this growth phrase. In spite of the growth of Western Europe's oil market, there were few individual markets large or regular enough to warrant pipeline installation, which were not already well served by water transport. The diagram below illustrates why the availability of cheap water transport and smaller markets held back pipeline growth in Europe. However, in recent years the growth

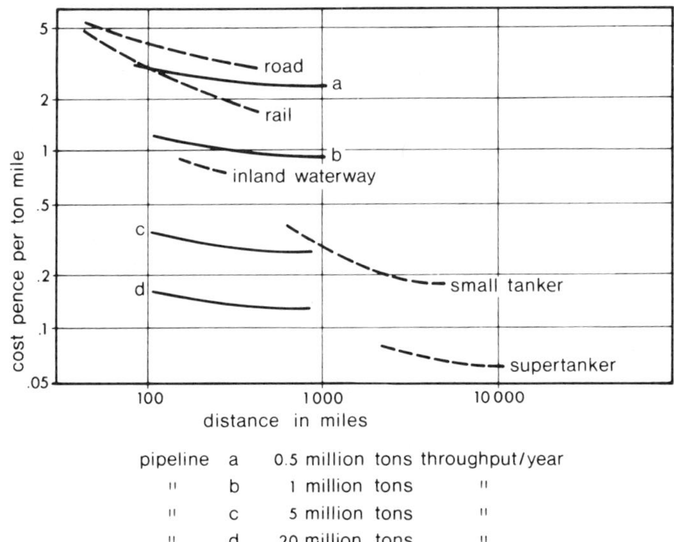

Alternative costs of transporting oil in Europe (c. 1960). (*Source: Manners, 1962, p. 157.*)

of large inland markets for oil at Cologne, Vienna, etc., has justified the construction of a considerable mileage of crude oil pipelines. The most recent change has been the growth in products pipelines, brought about by increasing demand inland and demand for lighter, less viscous products. The development of supertankers is underlining this change, as refining capacity is concentrated at fewer coastal points. So new economic trends are now weighing in favor of product pipelines, though the choice is less than clear-cut when railroads (notably in West Germany) are prepared to quote special rates for the bulk transport of products.

There has been much interest in the use of pipelines in moving solids, accomplished by the use of a carrying fluid, or in the form of capsules. The test example was a 108-mile pipeline constructed in Ohio to move coal to a power plant near Cleveland. The $10\frac{1}{2}$-inch pipeline, including land, cost $125,000 per mile, with a capacity of 1.2 million tons of coal per year. The coal was ground to a consistency of coarse sand and mixed with an equal amount of water to give *slurry,* which was pushed by three pumping stations over the 108-mile route in 30 hours. In fact, the introduction of unit trains over the same stretch running at new rates has caused the closure of the pipeline. More ambitious schemes have been proposed to move Canadian wheat to the Great Lakes, or coal from the British Columbia interior to a bulk loading deepwater port on the coast for export to Japan but their economic feasibility remains to be demonstrated. (See the map of British Columbia's proposed solids pipeline.)

OTHER MODES

We are in a period when new transport developments are in the offing. For example, there are *hovercraft,* operating on cushions of air, which can utilize areas of unstable ground and operate over water in areas with no fixed routes. They are limited only by the steepness of terrain. Costs of operation are not certain, though they have ranged as high as 70 cents per ton mile under experimental conditions. *VTOL* craft, strictly including heli-

BRITISH COLUMBIA Proposed Solids Pipeline

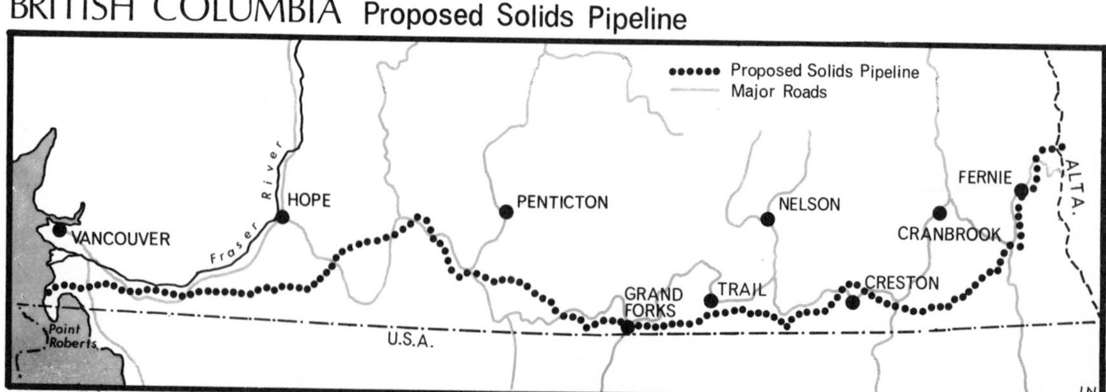

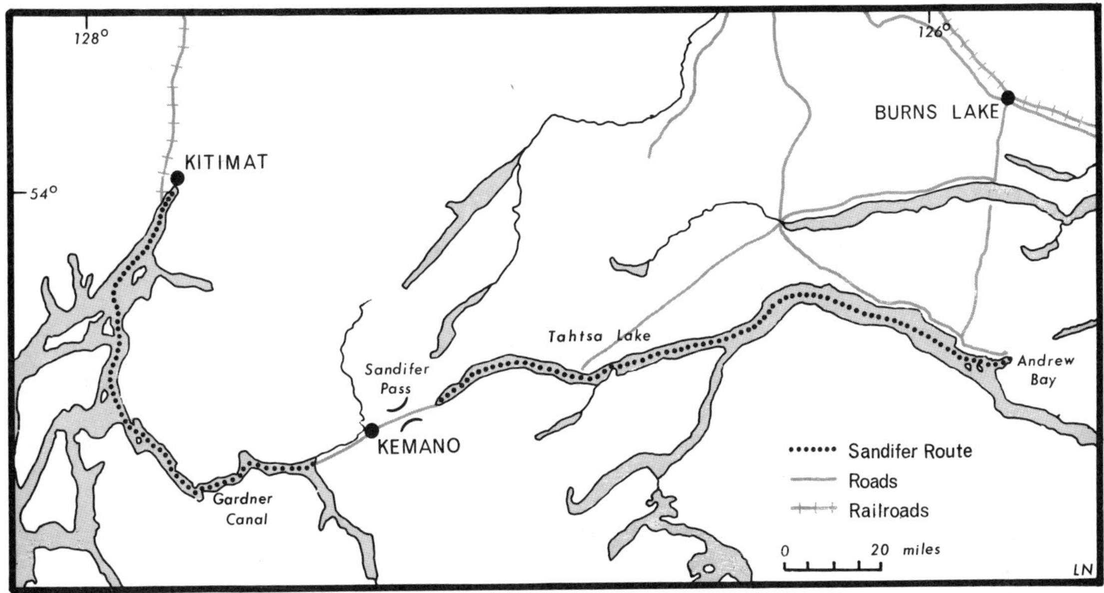

copters, could reduce terminal costs and the problem of access to airports, but they are relatively costly to operate. Helicopters can carry freight short distances for about 16 cents per ton mile with a 75 percent load factor, but they are essentially short-haul operators, and for hauls over 50 miles some combination of fixed-wing and VTOL would be necessary for economic operation. The *hydrofoil* is yet another development for river and coastal services, capable of speeds of 45 to 100 knots and of carrying 5,000 to 20,000 tons of freight. Besides these actual vehicular changes, there may be technical developments to produce efficient and cheap fuel cells, gas turbine engines, and nuclear engines, which may again alter the balance between the modes discussed above.

CONCLUSION

These modal systems have been treated in an isolated manner. In reality, the railway system and its traffic are influenced both by the presence and absence of other modes of transport, their relative efficiencies, and their locations with respect to the particular network studied. The map of the Sandifer transfer route shows just one such interrelationship which may come into play. It is an interlocking system of trucking and waterway to supply the new Eurocan sawmill and pulpmill at Kitimat, B.C. Logs felled at Andrews Bay on Ootsa Lake are moved four times by crane, three times by truck, and are towed twice in the water before they reach the processing plant at the coast. There are many other comparable examples also, thus as was evident in Selection 15 the table "Modal Systems: Comparative Characteristics" (pp. 190–191) must not be looked at in isolation. Equally, although some of the comments above may have treated the modal systems in an isolated manner, others have shown directly or indirectly that in reality each transport system is influenced by the presence and absence of other modes of transport, their relative efficiencies, images, and aptness for technical change. This aspect of the relationship between all transport modes will be pursued further in Part Five.

FURTHER READINGS TO PART FOUR

Many, many articles have been written by geographers and others on the various modes. The rather lengthy list below represents but a small fraction of the coverage in the English language:

General topics are covered by:

A. W. Currie, *Canadian Transportation Economics,* Toronto: University of Toronto Press, 1967.

M. T. Farris and P. T. McElhiney, *Modern Transportation: Selected Readings.* Boston: Houghton Mifflin, 1967, Part 1, Sections A, B, C, and D, pp. 3–208.

J. B. Lansing, *Transportation and Economic Policy,* New York: The Free Press, 1966.

J. R. Meyer, "A Comparison of the Advantages and Disadvantages of the Various Modes of Transport" in R. S. Nelson and E. M. Johnson (eds.), *Technological Change and the Future of the Railways,* Evanston, Ill.: The Transportation Center, 1961, pp. 1–14.

J. R. Meyer et al., *The Economics of Competition in the Transportation Industries,* Cambridge, Mass.: Harvard University Press, 1959.

National Academy of Sciences, National Research Council, *United States Transportation: Resources, Performance and Problems,* Washington, D.C.: National Academy of Sciences, Pub. No. 841-S, 1961.

Railroads:

J. H. Appleton, "Some Geographical Aspects of the Modernisation of British Railways," *Geography,* vol. 52, 1967, pp. 357–373.

A. S. Chapman, "Transportation European Express: Overall Travel Time in Competition for Passengers," *Economic Geography,* vol. 44, 1968, pp. 283–295.

D. W. Meinig, "A Comparative Historical Geography of Two Railnets: Columbia Basin and Southern Australia," *Annals* of the Association of American Geographers, vol. 52, 1962, pp. 394–413.

A. C. O'Dell, *Railways and Geography,* London: Hutchinson University Library, 1956.

F. H. Thomas, "Some Relationships between a Railroad Route and Its Region," *Tijdschrift voor Economische en Sociale Geografie,* vol. 53, 1962, pp. 155–161.

W. R. Siddall, "Railroad Gauges and Spatial Interaction," *Geographical Review,* vol. 59, 1969, pp. 29–57.

W. H. Wallace, "Railroad Traffic Densities and Patterns," *Annals* of the Association of American Geographers, vol. 48, 1958, pp. 352–374.

W. H. Wallace, "Some Freight Traffic Functions of Anglo-American Railroads," *Annals* of the Association of American Geographers, vol. 53, 1963, pp. 312–331.

W. H. Wallace, "The Bridge Line: A Distinctive Type of Anglo-American Railroad," *Economic Geography,* vol. 41, 1965, pp. 1–38.

H. P. White, "London's Rail Terminals and Their Suburban Traffic: A Geographic Appraisal of the Commuter Problem," *Geographical Review,* vol. 54, 1964, pp. 347–365.

Water transportation:

G. Beishlag, "The Container Revolution in Ocean Shipping," *The Pennsylvania Geographer,* 1968, pp. 1–5.

D. K. Fleming, "The Independent Transport Courier in Ocean Tramp Trades," *Economic Geography,* vol. 44, 1968, pp. 21–36.

W. G. Hardwick, "Log Towing Rates in Coastal British Columbia," *Professional Geographer,* vol. 13, no. 5, 1961, pp. 1–5.

M. B. Mazanova, "The Role of Maritime Transportation in the Economic Ties Between the Economic-geographic Regions of the U.S.S.R.," *Soviet Geography,* vol. 1, no. 4, 1960, pp. 59–62.

M. B. Mazanova, "Marine Transport as a National Specialized Activity of a Major Economic Region," *Soviet Geography,* vol. 4, no. 5, 1963, pp. 3–9.

A. A. Michel, "The Canalisation of the Moselle and West European Integration," *Geographical Review,* vol. 52, 1962, pp. 475–491.

K. W. Muckleston and F. Dohrs, "The Relative Importance of Transport on the Volga, Before and After the Communist Revolution," *Professional Geographer,* vol. 17, no. 2, 1965, pp. 22–25.

D. Patton, "The Traffic Pattern on American Inland Waterways," *Economic Geography,* vol. 32, 1956, pp. 29–37.

P. J. Rimmer, "A Resurgence in New Zealand's Coastal Trade," *Geography,* vol. 51, 1966, pp. 248–251.

The subfield of ports is introduced in:

J. Bird, *Seaports and Seaport Terminals,* London: Hutchinson, 1971, which in addition to an extensive bibliography deals with not only port evolution but also hinterland interrelationships, the maritime economy, etc.

Road transportation:

M. L. Burstein et al., *The Cost of Trucking: An Econometric Analysis,* Dubuque, Iowa: Wm. C. Brown, Co., 1965.

W. L. Garrison et al., *Studies of Highway Development and Geographic Change,* Seattle: University of Washington Press, 1959.

T. G. Gibb, "The Carriage of Goods by Road in Europe," *Journal of the Institute of Transport,* vol. 31, 1965, pp. 77–93.

E. H. Holmes, "Highway Transportation" in *United States Transportation: Resources, Performance and Problems,* Washington, D.C.: National Academy of Sciences, Pub. No. 841-S, 1961, pp. 97–105.

R. J. Johnston, "An Index of Accessibility and Its Use in the Study of Bus

Services and Settlement Patterns," *Tijdschrift Voor Economische en Sociale Geografie,* vol. 57, 1966, pp. 33–38.

W. Milkius, "Some Characteristics of Non-regulated For-hire Truck Transportation of Agricultural Commodities," *Land Economics,* vol. 42, 1966, pp. 226–230.

W. Owen, "Road Transportation and Food Production," *Highway Research Record,* no. 125, 1966.

J. P. Pinkney, "Motor Carriage—The Long and Short of It," *Annals* of the Academy of Political and Social Sciences, vol. 345, 1963, pp. 66–72.

D. M. Winch, *The Economics of Highway Planning,* Toronto: University of Toronto Press, 1963.

Pipelines:

M. A. Axelrad, "Petroleum Pipelines in Western Europe," *Professional Geographer,* vol. 16, no. 4, 1964, pp. 1–5.

H. N. Emerson, "Salient Characteristics of Petroleum Pipeline Transportation," *Land Economics,* vol. 26, 1950, pp. 27–39.

E. J. Jensen and H. S. Ellis, "Pipelines," *Scientific American,* vol. 216, no. 1, 1967, pp. 62–72.

G. Manners, "The Pipeline Revolution," *Geography,* vol. 47, 1962, pp. 154–163.

E. G. Parke, "Pipelines and Tankers: Two Complementary Forms of Oil Transportation," *Tijdschrift Voor Vervoerswetenschap,* vol. 4, 1967, pp. 297–312.

G. S. Wolbert, *American Pipelines,* Norman, Okla.: University of Oklahoma Press, 1952.

Air transportation:

P. Coates and G. Nagahima, "Studies of Present Traffic Patterns: Air Transport," *Ekistics,* vol. 22, 1966, pp. 32–35.

J. B. Lansing et al., "An Analysis of Interurban Air Travel," *Quarterly Journal of Economics,* vol. 75, 1961, pp. 87–95.

W. H. Long, "City Characteristics and the Demand for Interurban Air Travel," *Land Economics,* vol. 44, 1968, pp. 197–204.

J. Mecklin, "The $4 Billion Machinery That Reshapes Geography (the SST)," *Fortune,* vol. 75, no. 2, 1967, pp. 112–117, 227–230.

S. R. Richmond, "Interspatial Relationships Affecting Air Travel," *Land Economics,* vol. 33, 1957, pp. 65–73.

B. A. Schriever and W. W. Seifert (eds.), *Air Transportation, 1975 and Beyond: A Systems Approach,* Cambridge: MIT Press, 1968.

K. R. Sealy, *The Geography of Air Transport* (rev. ed.), London: Hutchinson University Library, 1966.

K. R. Sealy, "The Siting and Development of British Airports," *Geographical Journal,* vol. 133, 1967, pp. 148–177.

W. R. Stanley and T. R. Bancom, "Some Spatial Components of Regional Air Service Demands in the Southeast," *Southeastern Geographer,* vol. XII, no. 2, 1972, pp. 145–154.

K. W. Studnicki-Gizbert, *Structure and Growth of Canadian Air Transport Industry,* Ottawa: Canadian Department of Transport, 1960.

E. J. Taaffe, "Trends in Airline Passenger Traffic: A Geographic Case Study," *Annals* of the Association of American Geographers, vol. 49, 1959, pp. 393–408.

E. J. Taaffe, "The Urban Hierarchy: An Air Passenger Definition," *Economic Geography,* vol. 38, 1962, pp. 1–14.

Some other modes, which have not been considered here, are covered by:

L. O. Berthold and H. Pfeiffer, "High Voltage Transmission," *Scientific American,* vol. 210, no. 5, 1964, pp. 38–47.

A. Van Burkalow, "The Geography of New York City's Water Supply: A Study of Interactions," *Geographical Review,* vol. 49, 1959, pp. 369–386.

T. H. Crowley et al., *Modern Communications,* New York: Columbia University Press, 1962.

R. H. Gilman, "Cargo Handling," *Scientific American,* vol. 219, no. 4, 1968, pp. 80–88.

D. J. Innis, "The Geographical Characteristics of Radio," *Canadian Journal of Economics and Political Science,* vol. 20, 1954, pp. 83–87.

O.E.C.D., *Transportation Systems for Major Activity Centres,* Consultative group on Transportation Research, 1970 (includes papers on the *Transdhec, Speedaway, Minirail, Minitube,* and *Telerail* systems).

W.R.D. Sewell, "The Role of Regional Interties in Postwar Energy Resource Development," *Annals* of the Association of American Geographers, vol. 54, 1964, pp. 566–581.

A *reminder* that a very useful source of current publications on modal systems is Northwestern University Transportation Center Library's monthly publication, *Current Literature in Traffic and Transportation.* Categories of publications include air transportation (subdivided into such topics as forwarding, passenger service, commuter service, V/STOL transport, airports, aircraft, etc.), Rail, water, highways, pipelines, freight, industrial distribution, urban transportation, etc.

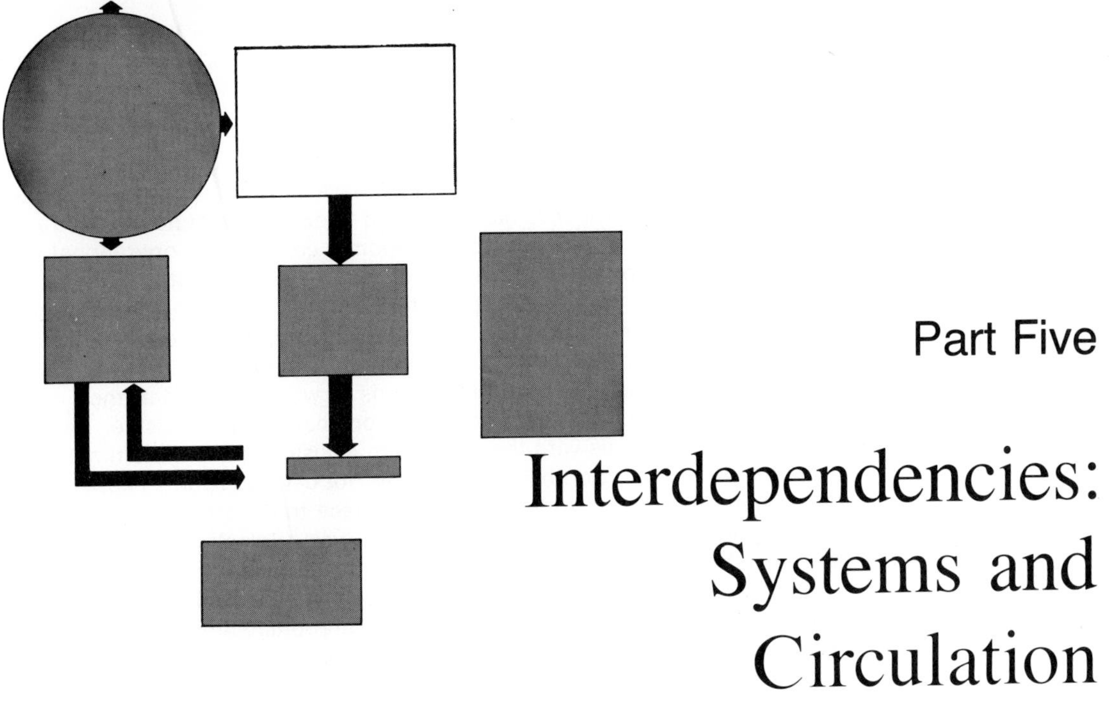

Part Five

Interdependencies: Systems and Circulation

INTRODUCTION

Having reviewed some of the boxes of Fig. 1-2 (p. 8, repeated on p. 289) largely as a disaggregative approach based on the Northwestern University framework, it is time to look at the diagram to fill in the gaps left by the more traditional approaches in geography (see pp. 4–6) and then to treat transport as a holistic concept again. But first we ought to take stock and ask ourselves why these gaps have occurred.

LEVELS OF UNDERSTANDING

The development of transportation geography to date has essentially operated at two levels. At one level, description and data collection have dominated; at the other, statistical "explanation" and the standard of certainty and exactness of the physical sciences have been the overriding guide. Neither of these approaches has attempted to explain and understand transportation geography within a socioeconomic context (the operational and *behavioral* milieu of the decision maker).* Most attempts at understanding have relied on intuition or deceptive theorizing from mathematical or geometric patterns, largely in a sociopolitical vacuum, with one or two exceptions. The few who have broken through to this third level of understanding have bemoaned the lack of information as to what was said at the time of the decision† or have mentioned decision making as an aside. (Siddall, for example, teases us with the committee decisions as to the ultimate railroad gauge width in South Africa but does not develop such an approach.‡) Exceptions would be Wolfe's attempt to place transportation in a political geographic framework,§ and Rimmer's analysis (Selection 17) of the governmental bureaucratic and elitist channels of decision making in shaping Thailand's transportation system, or various behavior studies.‖

Why should transportation be analyzed predominantly in a nineteenth-century framework or be subject to social science flirtations with statistics, mathematical rigor, and "the scientific method"? Part of this inability to take account of the sociopolitical environment stems from the liberal notion of "objectivity"—that to study transport networks we must somehow see them as divorced from the pressure groups, oppressive economic systems, and individualistically exploitative situations in which they so frequently occur. Rimmer notes this in his study of Thailand when he concludes ". . . much of the interagency conflict in Thailand is posturing and shadow boxing as the decision to construct a transport link is in reality the product of highly personalized relations within the Bangkok-concentrated elitist groups; the power group is the military elite which controls the bureaucratic and Chinese business elites." Yet how often are such realities referred to in transportation geography?

The positivistic self-image of the contemporary geographer separates the subject and object of knowledge and takes the statements of science as an observational given. Knowledge is thus conceived of as a picturing of objective fact and overlooks the societal framework within which both the observer and the observed occur. This exemplifies what Husserl has called

*The operational milieu surrounds the individual and overlaps his behavioral environment. The latter is the internalized, rather than the extrinsic, conception of the environment by an individual or group, which is the result of perception, conception, emotion, feeling, learned factors, past experience, and culture. Along with "operational milieu," its importance to transportation geography is obvious, since it is the subjective milieu governing a person's or group's reactions or actions, which may only partly reflect what the observer may see as "objective reality." For more details of this conception see M. E. Eliot Hurst, *A Geography of Economic Behaviour*, North Scituate, Mass.: Duxbury Press, 1972, chap. 4.

†D. W. Meinig, "A Comparative Historical Geography of Two Railnets: Columbia Basin and Southern Australia," *Annals* of the Association of American Geographers, vol. 52, 1962, pp. 394–413.

‡W. R. Siddall, "Regional Gauges and Spatial Interaction," *Geographical Review*, vol. 59, 1969, pp. 29–57.

§R. I. Wolfe, *Transportation and Politics*, Princeton, N.J.: Van Nostrand, 1963.

‖For example, J. Wolpert, "The Transition to Interdependence in Location Decisions," paper presented at the A.A.G. annual meeting, 1968.

the *fallacy of objectivism.*# Hence while the basic approaches in geography and the other social sciences are more and more able to systematize knowledge, they are less and less able to reflect about their own presuppositions or the structuring framework of the society. Such objectivity and value neutrality ". . . amounts in practice to endorsing the status quo, to lending a helping hand to those who are seeking to obstruct any change of the existing order of things. . . ."**

This contention will be spelled out again in Part Seven, but the point must be made here that the tradition of objectivity in transportation geography has made us less able to understand the full relationships of transportation and too frequently causes us to overlook the end results of our fact finding and analyses. Do we know what we perpetrate when we get involved in developing countries or in pushing a freeway through a ghetto? It may seem to some a long jump from an unfocused transportation geography to splitting a neighborhood in two with a concrete swarth, but they are linked by the inattention within the subdiscipline to community organization, regulatory bodies, government legislation, subsidies, lobbying and graft, the legitimization of power and privilege in our economic system, the growth of technocracy, and many other sociopolitical factors.

An argument often enters at this point that to pursue such factors is faddish, and that "relevance" is not for transportation geographers. This is to misunderstand the situation; not all scholarship need become involved in the jungle of contemporary or past socioeconomic struggles. If, however, in our case, in studying transportation we refuse to relate it to the greater socioeconomic reality, including its historical perspective, and if we refuse to refer our analyses back to the fundamental humanist question "Knowledge for what?" we are likely to lapse into the disconnected trivialities, insignificant and even harmful make-work, and alienating mental exercises that distinguish so much contemporary social science.

Where do we go from here? Description, data collection, and statistical analysis must go on, no doubt, but such activities must not be seen as ends in themselves. To interpret this material, to place it in a socioeconomic and political framework, to overcome the obstacles barring the way to the attainment of a better, more humane, more rational social order, to better explain and understand transportation as a factor in the environment should be our ultimate goals in transportation geography.

AN APPROACH TO INTERDEPENDENCE: A HOLISTIC CONCEPTION

As one step toward a more realistic framework for transportation geography, the simplistic systems scheme of Fig. 1-2 is suggested. The use of such a systems framework is not unique,†† though the degree to which the interrelationships are pursued in a societal context may well be.

#E. Husserl, *Phenomenology and the Crisis of Philosophy*, New York: Harper, 1966.

**P. Baran, "The Commitment of the Intellectual," *Monthly Review*, vol. 13, no. 5, 1961, pp. 8–18.

‡‡For example, Manheim, M. L., "Principles of Transport Systems Analysis," *Highway Research Record*, vol. 180, 1967, pp. 11–20.

The initial step is to place the whole approach into its socioeconomic and political setting; this defines the basic operating conditions for the transportation system to be examined (the *operational milieu*). This allows us to take into account such factors as who owns and controls the means of production in a given society, what set of socioeconomic relations are generated around these means, who creates and develops the transportation technologies, and what ends they serve. It is vital to clarify these connections between the socioeconomic structure and transport media from the very beginning, since the later steps of the heuristic device used here (and transportation realities) are defined by such interrelationships. Thus if societal goals are presently defined in these kinds of terms—"investments must be planned in accordance with profit expectations; human needs are satisfied only in relation to 'effective demand' of paying customers"—then the structural form of the various stages of the device are clear. In this context the role of the transportation network in the landscape is explicit: maximize freeways, automobile, and profit-yielding freight links; minimize public transit, rail links to isolated rural communities, and community welfare.

Within this operating environment, the *first stage* in any transportation system is the need or desire for interaction to take place; interaction arises because of the spatial separation of the means of satisfying these needs or desires.‡‡ Interaction, movement, transportation, are not ends to themselves; they are but part of a broader set of utilities influenced by individual and group aspirations, life-styles, political motivations, and socioeconomic relationships. A more realistic thesis seems to be to assume that transportation is governed by the ways in which these influences are structured and utilities assigned. In geographical terms these become translated into the ways in which the dimensions of space are conceptualized; these parameters can be summed up by the term *movement space.*§§

The basic structural components of the transportation system itself are the modes, stocks, and networks (*stage two*). Movement is constrained by the channel of the network, the characteristics of particular modes, and the facilities of the fixed and mobile stocks. The mobile stocks, such as vehicles, provide the interface between the items being transported and the fixed stock of the network, such as the roadway or rail track. With modes, such as pipelines or television, while there are no mobile stocks, there is still some interface between the "goods" and the fixed stocks. The networks consist of nodes and links. Each node or activity site corresponds to the point of demand or supply, each link to specific transportation channels. The links may be tangible and well defined (railroad) or may be relatively diffuse and intangible (radio or face-to-face contacts). Some nodes may be interchange points between links of the same mode (railyards, highway interchanges), while other nodes may be interchange points between links of different

‡‡Obviously there is an immediate feedback to the operational milieu, since the spatial separation of the means of production will be in part determined by the goals of the society; a society with anarcho-syndicalist tendencies, and thus very dispersed means of production, would tend to minimize the need to satisfy spatial interaction (see, for example, M. Bookchin, *Post-Scarcity Anarchism*, Berkeley: Ramparts Press, 1971).

§§M. E. Eliot Hurst, "The Structure of Movement and Household Travel Behaviour," *Urban Studies*, vol. 6, no. 1, 1969, pp. 70–82, and Selection 29.

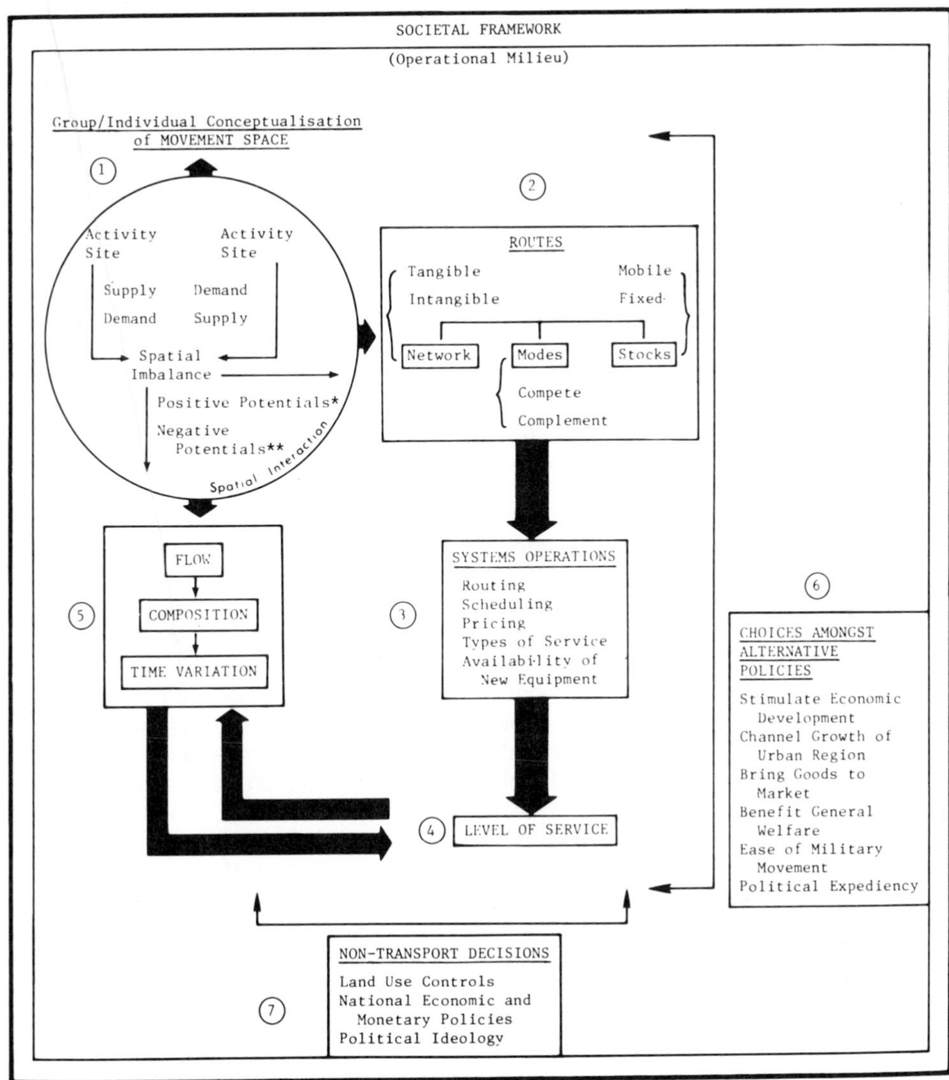

The transport system repeated. Positive potentials refer to complementarity, intervening opportunities, cultural affinity, etc. Negative potentials refer to distance, costs, transferability, political barriers, etc.

modes (the seaport, ferry, rail, or air terminal), where modes are complementary. In capitalist societies, modes frequently compete for traffic over similar link paths.

This second stage establishes the fact that networks exist to channel the movement; that modes and stocks interact over space and time, competing or complementing, but flowing through the channels in a variety of interacting paths. The degree of movement depends on the degree of concentration and specialization in the economy, and the supply of networks and modes and their spatial distribution will vary with the economic ability to invest in transportation or with the societal priorities.||||

Depending on the constraints of the operational milieu, the decision maker has open to him a range and variety of movement options (*stage three*). The individual, whether potential traveler, broadcaster, or shipper, sees the transportation systems as essentially fixed; on the whole, he can only choose his own particular routing and time schedule through the system. The operators and policy makers, however, can establish the routes and schedules, pricing and reliability, and other factors which determine the "level of service" (*stage four*). Such level of service is also constrained by certain societal values and goals, such as profitability and community welfare. In addition, policy makers can govern the types, number, and availability of stocks in the system; add new links and abandon old ones; improve operating characteristics (dredge rivers, widen highways); and at higher levels, where important, regulate competition and assign operating rights and rates. This full set of systems operations is usually open to one agency or organization only in socialist planned economies. In other types of economies many individuals and agencies may be involved, and it becomes essential to study the variety of legislative and regulatory (and sometimes conflicting) constraints that have influenced transportation in its historical, political, and socioeconomic contexts. In all societies, however, the types of options will vary; a specific decision can usually be made rapidly, but network or technological changes may take longer to occur.

Before movement finally occurs, a decision maker considers several characteristics that combine to make up the level of service. Such considerations may include not only cost and travel time but also safety; comfort; reliability; indirect costs (i.e., total transfer costs); and frequency of service, covering a wide range of variables from total trip and schedule times, direct transport charges, and loading and warehousing costs to the various accident probabilities, physical comfort of passengers, their privacy, general amenities, and aesthetic experiences. The level of service at which transportation is provided varies over time and according to economic goals and spatial needs. It is therefore a function of the spatial characteristics of demand and supply, modes, stocks and networks, and the operational milieu.

In response to demand, routes, systems operations and level of service, a flow of persons, goods and ideas, moves through the system (*stage five*). Flows are the volumetric measures of the interaction and the successful interrelationships of the other components. Flows vary in actual composition and in their time-space variations, as for example in the flow of traffic through a city during a weekday. There is a feedback to level of service, operating characteristics, routes, and ultimately to demand itself.

Finally, transport or movement decisions are influenced by a wide variety

||||Ability to invest is brought out in the term *underdevelopment,* albeit an unfortunate one (see, for example, A. G. Frank, "The Sociology of Development and the Under-development of Sociology," *Catalyst,* Summer 1967, pp. 20–73). A marked contrast between the degrees of interaction, modes, and networks will be found between, say, France and Gabon. Certain socialist societies have also chosen to emphasize some modes at the expense of others (rail and, latterly, air in the Soviet Union, for example) or have placed transportation development at a lower priority than we have in the West (China, for example).

of directly related (*stage six*) and indirectly related factors (*stage seven*). The direct factors include general investment decisions to achieve the overall socioeconomic development of an area or region or to increase profitability, either directly from a transport stock or indirectly from the exploitation of a region or nation. In urban areas it might include decisions to plan an integrated multimode system of public transit and freeways which would obviously have feedback effects throughout a region and its transport network. General investment decisions may be made which affect supply and demand, and the general welfare of the people in a region. There may also be military decisions, based on strategic mobility, to best achieve national military objectives through the rapid deployment of forces (e.g., the Interstate and Defense Highways System in the United States). Other transport-oriented developments include the introduction of basically new transport technologies, such as new modes or vehicles; new networks; and new operating systems. All of these options in this sixth stage can shift the workings of the other five.

However, besides direct influences, a number of other external and often operatively nontransport factors must also be taken into account, since they can affect the demands for, and use of, transport systems. National economic policies, or the lack of them, can affect the distribution of demand over space and time, and hence the demand for freight and other services. Shortened work hours, increased leisure time, and the consequent growth of recreational activities, many of which may be movement-oriented, may greatly increase transport demand at certain periods of the year (and increasingly, all year round). Effects resulting from land use controls, the provision of public utilities, industrial logistic systems, the availability of computerized information, differential regional growth policies, and myriad other causes and countercauses will all affect the transportation system. In addition, the impact and the reaction of nonusers of the transport system may have to be taken into account.

The common threads presented in this heuristic device underlie the great variety of interactions that exist in the socioeconomic landscapes of many regions of the world. It is not an exhaustive scheme, but the principles are equally applicable to a study of transport as a whole, communications in general, urban transportation, intercity movements, regional and national interactions, and world trade flows. Hence the approach attempts to take account of the operating realities of a society, as well as to reflect the relations between areas that underlie the geographical concepts mentioned in Part One—spatial interaction and areal differentiation. At the same time, such a systems approach brings together the separate components of a transport system—modes, networks, stocks, and flows—with the reasons for interaction and the operational milieu, showing interactions and operations within a holistic framework.

P. J. Rimmer's study, to which we now turn, is one of those rare works by transportation geographers which does attempt to assess the role of decision making within the operational milieu of one society, Thailand. Rimmer concludes that the decision processes are an amalgam of ad hoc approaches, many laissez-faire as far as the government is concerned, but still far from optimal, even allowing that it is a nation dominated by the capitalist ethos.

Selection 17

Government Influence on Transport Decision-making in Thailand

P. J. Rimmer

INTRODUCTION

The role of the Royal Thai Government in making transport investment decisions is examined here in an analysis of the institutional environment within which transport must operate. Decisions to construct, improve, or maintain transport services are viewed as an integral part of a transportation system model designed to emphasize the inter-relationship between society, the physical environment, and the vehicle network. An omniscient decision-maker would find the prescriptions of the model ideal in planning a system to resolve demands and meet criteria, strategies, and values established by society. In Thailand, however, the decision-making task is divided among several loosely coordinated government agencies, without an optimizing course of conduct for the practitioner in any institution. The spatial expression of inter-departmental conflicts associated with the overlapping of functions is considered after identifying the principal decision-makers and their objectives in transportation planning against the background set by the needs and goals of the society that transcends the system. Plans for resolving inter-departmental conflicts through transport coordination are worth studying because there is evidence that these wrangles, rather than physical or capital constraints, have hampered the Royal Thai Government in realizing its stated aspiration levels for certain goals.

THE TRANSPORTATION SYSTEM MODEL

The transportation system model is derived from research by war-gamers engaged in determining those factors in developing countries, such as Thailand, which allow for economic and social development while ensuring security requirements are met (Lampert, Ramsey, and Walli, 1968). This model has three basic components—man, vehicle, and terrain—which interact on the principal elements of land, sea, or air transportation networks: nodes, links (connections between two nodes), and vehicle capability (Fig. 17-1). The principal features of the model can be summarized as follows:

1 *The society system* (consisting of economic, social, political, and security spheres) which provides:

- **a** Inputs governing the use of vehicle network combinations,[1] namely, supply of resources, demand for resources, priorities in satisfying needs of nodes, time allowed in fulfilling needs, and allowable costs;
- **b** Criteria, strategy, and values used for evaluating the performance of a given vehicle network combination which leads to the modification of response requirements, resource locations or demands, and parameters of vehicle network combination.

2 *The physical environment* which may exert constraints on resource availability, demand and vehicle network combinations.[2]

G. J. R. Linge and P. J. Rimmer (eds.), *Government Influence on the Location of Economic Activities*, chap. 15, pp. 15–1 to 15–34. Department of Human Geography, Publication HG/5 (1971), Research School of Pacific Studies, Australian National University, Canberra.

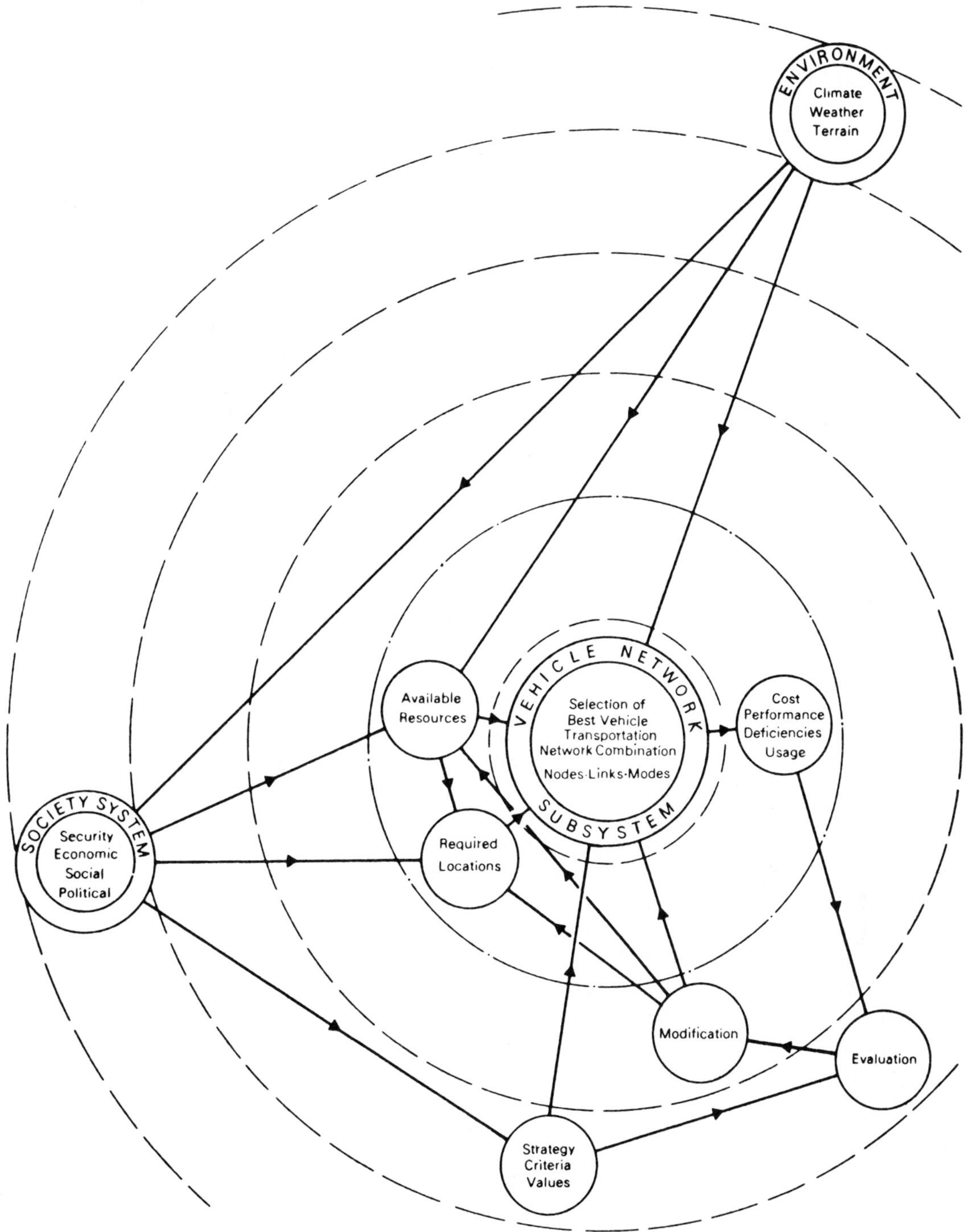

Fig. 17-1 Transportation system model. *(Adapted from Lampert, Ramsey, and Walli, 1968)*

3 *The vehicle network subsystem* which is embedded in the environment of the area under review and is able to:

- **a** Accept inputs provided by the society system;
- **b** Provide outputs to be evaluated against established criteria: performance figures (flows, cost, or deficiencies) for each set of vehicles, use functions, and a given network configuration are assessed in terms of strategies, criteria, and values established, by the society subsystem to determine modifications to either vehicle network combinations or input functions.

This framework for making transport investment is used to examine decisions about the inputs and about the selection criteria operating in Thailand before considering the principal decision-makers and their objectives.

NATIONAL GOALS

The goals of Thai society, expressed through the Royal Thai Government in the Second National Economic and Social Development Plan (1967–71), are the acceleration of the rate of economic growth and an improvement in the standard of living through the maximum use of national, financial, and human resources for the expansion of the economy (National Economic Development Board 1968, pp. 23–5). Once continued and rapid growth in national income is established the problem of initiating and intensifying economic development in spatial terms is concerned with funneling final goods and services from investment in the "major growth poles" through the hierarchy of smaller settlements to consumers in the more remote parts of the country (Friedmann, 1966; Berry, 1969). This trickling down of innovations in Thailand from the single growth pole of Bangkok is weakly articulated with a relationship of 100:4:2 between the three largest population centers—Bangkok, Chiang Mai, and Nakhon Ratchasima (Fig. 17-2). Time-cost constraints stemming from poor and unreliable transport links between separated market areas severely hamper the trickling-down process and accentuate differences in living standards between the center and periphery.[3] If the isolated and self-sufficient peripheral regions in Thailand's dual spatial economy are to make a net contribution to the national product they have to be linked to the mainstream of economic life to permit the expansion of the market area for commodities and factors (labor and capital). In such circumstances new and improved transport services between all levels of the feebly-developed hierarchy of settlements offer the means, through growth center and decentralization strategies, of revamping the role of smaller centers from that of being the articulators of their region's traditional life style to progenitors of rural advancement in their respective hinterlands (Berry, 1969).

Heavy investment in transport since the inception of economic development planning in 1959, accounting for twenty-six per cent of total public expenditure under the First National Economic and Social Development Plan (1961–66) and thirty per cent in the Second Plan (1967–71), is not only designed to stimulate and spread economic development but also to assist social and political cohesiveness. These aims are stressed because there is increasing anxiety in government circles and among allies in the South-East Asia Treaty Organization (SEATO) that the Thai peasant farmer might be susceptible to external subversive influences exploiting his anxiety over economic problems and rising expectations, especially in the more de-

Fig. 17-2 The Express Transport Organization's freight operations.

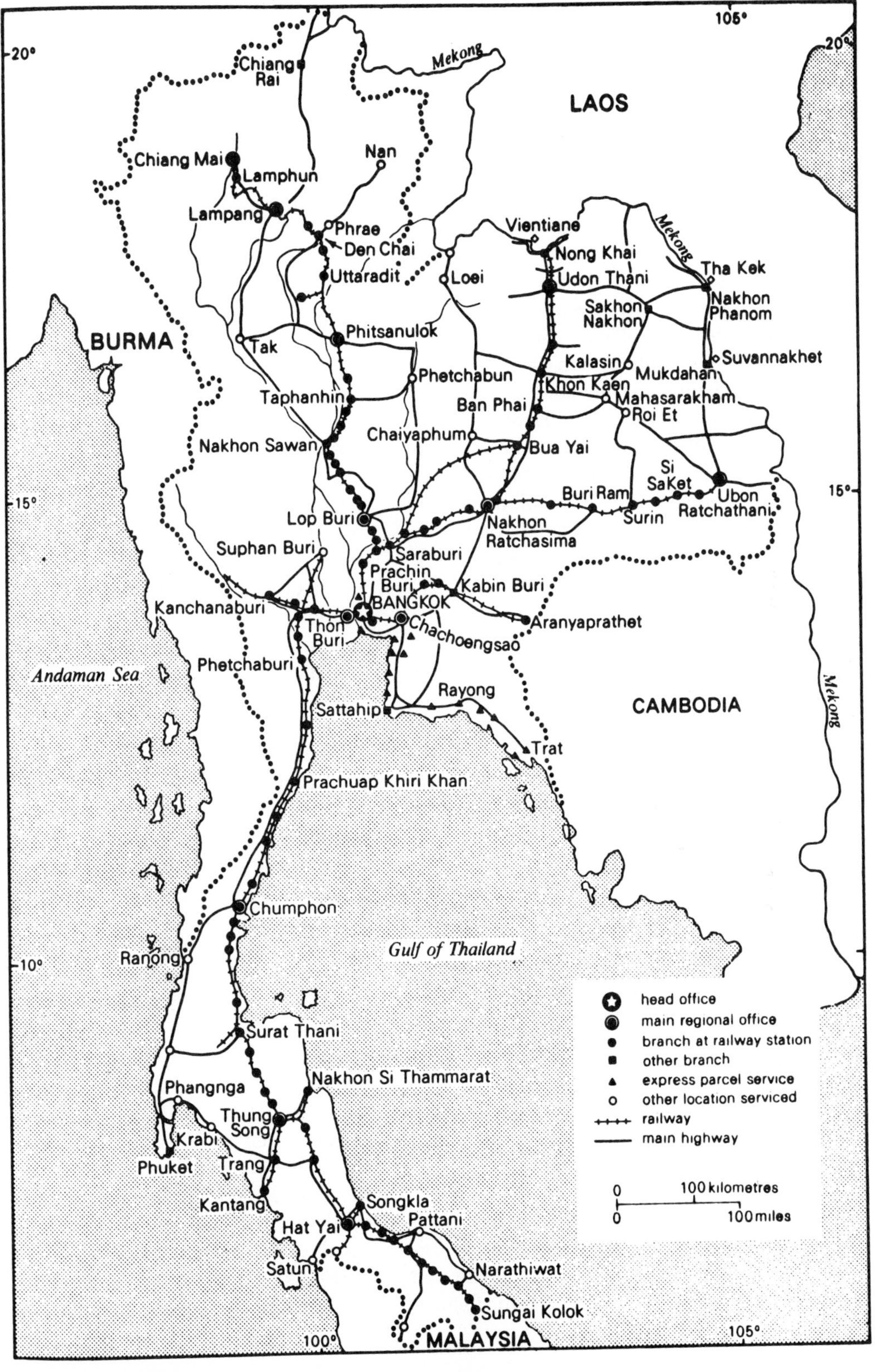

LAOS
BURMA
CAMBODIA
MALAYSIA
Andaman Sea
Gulf of Thailand
Mekong
Chiang Rai
Chiang Mai
Lamphun
Lampang
Nan
Phrae
Den Chai
Uttaradit
Loei
Vientiane
Nong Khai
Udon Thani
Tha Kek
Nakhon Phanom
Sakhon Nakhon
Suvannakhet
Tak
Phitsanulok
Phetchabun
Kalasin
Mukdahan
Khon Kaen
Mahasarakham
Taphanhin
Ban Phai
Roi Et
Chaiyaphum
Bua Yai
Nakhon Sawan
Si SaKet
Ubon Ratchathani
Buri Ram
Surin
Lop Buri
Nakhon Ratchasima
Suphan Buri
Saraburi
Prachin Buri
Kabin Buri
BANGKOK
Kanchanaburi
Thon Buri
Chachoengsao
Aranyaprathet
Phetchaburi
Rayong
Sattahip
Trat
Prachuap Khiri Khan
Chumphon
Ranong
Surat Thani
Nakhon Si Thammarat
Phangnga
Thung Song
Krabi
Phuket
Trang
Kantang
Songkla
Hat Yai
Pattani
Satun
Narathiwat
Sungai Kolok
20°
15°
10°
100°
105°
head office
main regional office
branch at railway station
other branch
express parcel service
other location serviced
railway
main highway
0 100 kilometres
0 100 miles

pressed and neglected areas contiguous to the country's borders (Muscat, 1966, p. 3). An effective transport system would enable the police and the military to respond quickly to recurrent insurgent acts in border areas near Burma, Laos, Cambodia, and Malaysia and, in conjunction with well-conceived investments in irrigation and power, would cement relations with villages long isolated from contact with government officials. With the growing threat of a high-level insurgency phase, transport decisions in Thailand have to accommodate the security requirements of its international allies in addition to inputs from economic, social, and political factors. The shape of the transport network will depend on whether the socio-economic needs or the security requirements have precedence.

DECISION CRITERIA

The transport goals in terms of socio-economic needs in Thailand are to upgrade the efficiency of the existing vehicle network and to design the *best* future vehicle network system in terms of cost effectiveness—a measurement applied to present and future requirements determined by:

1 Rank ordering nodes in terms of population (an inclusive surrogate measure for a node's production and distributive functions, administrative status, socio-cultural-religious importance, and strategic location);

2 Assigning usage values to links between nodes in terms, say, of ton-kilometers of freight per year or average daily traffic to give a priority rating;

3 Selecting appropriate vehicle network combinations to give the chosen rates, frequencies, and qualities of service.

This concept of cost effectiveness, involving the minimization of costs to the user, is imposed on decision-making in Thailand by the need to borrow foreign capital to finance transport improvements. The identification of good projects (that is, those with discounted benefits exceeding discounted costs) is undertaken according to the methods and principles recommended by the main lending authority, the International Bank for Reconstruction and Development. Costs are determined by the construction and maintenance specifications of a project over a set period and benefits (user cost savings) are assessed in terms of the reduced transport costs stemming from the speedier flow of freight, fewer accidents, and lower vehicle maintenance costs.[4] This cost-benefit technique is designed to determine whether projects are justified, but in Thailand benefits in such studies are invariably inflated because of the desire of government agencies to prove that their particular proposal is justified (Burns, 1969, p. 309). Criticism has been leveled at the use of this method of determining the effectiveness of transport routes in Thailand by Sychrava (1968), because the narrow range of benefits employed omits important indirect benefits inherent in a new transport link as an agent of social change. Adler (1969) has countered this criticism by claiming that the invocation of indirect benefits is the last refuge of doubtful projects (see Kolsen and Stokes, 1968, for a discussion of the political implications of cost-benefit analyses).

Whatever the validity of the cost-benefit approach in Thailand—a subject for considerable and continuing dispute (Adler, 1965; Fisher, 1969)—the conventional valuation (costs) scheme has to be able to accommodate security requirements. Relative values can be assigned to security and socio-economic needs based on a subjective judgement and the transport problem can be viewed in terms of cost. This solution may be ineffective for security problems where the critical question involves the placement of men and supplies at particular points within a network. In such circumstances decision-making hinges on the required reaction time (maximum allowable delay), a reflection of the nature of the terrain, the needs (men and machines) for supplying various points of the network, and the nature of the insurgency problem. Where police action is required to pick up propagandists, the transport problem can be couched in terms of the placement of police at the least possible number of points to cope with a single outbreak (the usual maximum allowable delay would be six hours). Under such peacetime or low-level insurgency conditions—a normative condition for Thailand—a simple compromise solution would be to design a transportation network able to handle both military and commercial freight. Where there is a high-level insurgency condition that is non-random in character the compromise solution would be inadequate, and it would be desirable to have a military solution with socio-economic needs added later. The performance of a given system, however, would be evaluated for socio-economic and strategic needs separately before a composite rating is employed as an input to the vehicle network subsystem.

THE NETWORK SELECTION PROCESS

Whichever criteria—choice reaction time or cost effectiveness—take precedence a compatible solution can be derived. Fig. 17-3, devised by Lampert, Ramsey, and Walli (1968), demonstrates the normative situation in Thailand of a system chosen on the basis of cost effectiveness to satisfy specific socio-economic factors which is constrained by security requirements. The stages established by the war-gamers in selecting a cost effective vehicle network combination are:

1 Identify a transport network on the basis of economic, social, or political needs;
2 Determine priority of links that should be constructed, improved, or maintained;
3 Specify for differing weather conditions and vehicle configurations the expected performance and costs involved in existing or projected links;
4 Fix a schedule for allocating funds to the system;
5 Alter the network to improve security capability by calculating allowable reaction times for various insurgency phases (the reaction times are specified independently);
6 Employ feedback to determine the effect of the changed network on the planned social, economic, and political transport system;
7 Continue the iterative process until socio-economic and strategic requirements are reconciled with the "best" cost-effective solution.

Difficulties associated with obtaining appropriate data would hamper the effective implementation of such a selection process on a national or regional basis, but the overriding problem in Thailand in the choice of an appropriate vehicle network combination is the separation of the decision-making process between competing government agencies without any strong control or plan.

> The absence of such a plan has forced those charged with decision-making on government investments . . . to reach a continuing series of *ad hoc* choices which reflect both political pressures and security requirements, and respond to the priority problems and opportunities as best known by those with long experience in the country and those with the most objective and dependable "judgement." In addition the serious lack of adequate data in many areas reduces the reliability of the most sober judgement [Muscat, 1966, p. 4].

THE PRINCIPAL DECISION-MAKERS

There is no single body that controls all forms of transport in Thailand as the Royal Thai Government manages to dissipate its exclusive stranglehold over establishing, improving,

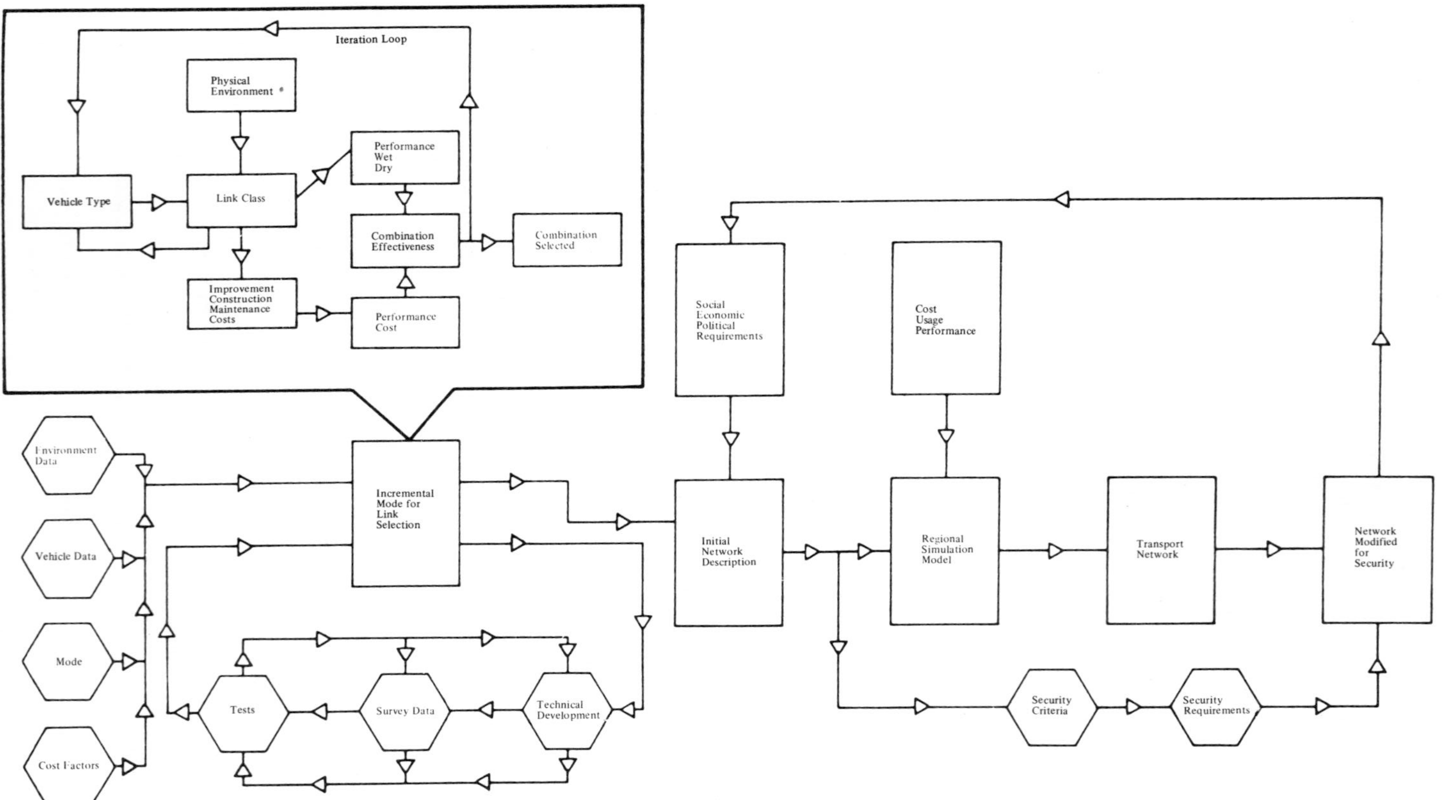

Fig. 17-3 The vehicle network selection process designed to meet socio-economic factors constrained by security requirements. *(Adapted from Lampert, Ramsey, and Walli, 1968)*

or maintaining transport links among its constituent agencies. The Highways Department is under the aegis of the Ministry for National Development; the Thai Navigation Co. Ltd. and its associated Lighterage Company is part of the Ministry for Economic Affairs; while the Ministry of Communications embraces the Harbor Department, the Royal State Railways, the Port Authority of Thailand, the Express Transport Organization, the Thai Airways Co. Ltd., the Transport Co. Ltd., and the Thai Overseas Co. Ltd., in addition to several associated organizations.[5] From such a conglomeration of agencies carrying freight and passengers it is difficult to achieve the overriding objective of transport planning in Thailand that the development of land, water and air transportation should be integrated into an economical and effective system to satisfy the national transport requirement (National Economic Development Board, 1968, p. 128). Such a goal would be difficult to achieve within the organizational coalition under the Minister of Communications because the central secretariat has only supervisory power over its members. Individual agencies enjoy considerable autonomy with power to establish their own operative goals and plans for maintaining, improving, or establishing new links or services. Under such circumstances each member of the coalition handles its own partly-resolved goals and uncertainty by making short-run decisions rather than attempting to anticipate long-run uncertain conditions (Cyert and March, 1963, p. 119). With such a complex organizational decision-making process it is not possible to consider each transport body separately so that only the government agencies and relevant private organizations concerned with the land transport of freight are examined—the Royal State Highways, Express Transport Organization, Highways Department, and private truck operators. For convenience these transport agencies are divided into four classes:

1 Agencies that can establish, improve, or maintain links and operate uni-modal vehicles;
2 Bodies that can establish, improve, or maintain links, but cannot operate vehicles;
3 Bi-modal operators without any capacity to establish, improve, or maintain links;
4 Uni-modal operators without any capacity to establish, improve, or maintain links.

Each class is analyzed in terms of its goals, expectations, and choice (see Cyert and March, 1963, pp. 115–6).

1. The Royal State Railways of Thailand

The objective of the Royal State Railways of Thailand is to improve the existing railway system, except where new construction is an integral part of regional development (National Economic Development Board, 1968, p. 128).[6] Dieselization and track improvement since 1955 have increased track capacity by fifteen to twenty per cent, but the Railways entertain more grandiose ideas of expansion than those outlined in the Second Plan (1967–71). Under the Railways' own ten year plan an expansion of 1,300 km of track is envisaged extending rail services from forty-three to fifty-two provinces. A twenty-five year plan proposes a further 1,450 km of route and connections to a further twelve provinces. With increasing truck (and bus) competition the Railways' problem must become one of survival, not expansion, and the limits of its expectations must be circumscribed within more modest proposals of:

1 Linking the United States naval base at Sattahip and the site of the proposed commercial port at Laem Chabang with the eastern railway line at Chachoengsao (161 km)—estimated cost $US29,500,000 and $US 10,800,000 for rolling stock (Fig. 17-4);

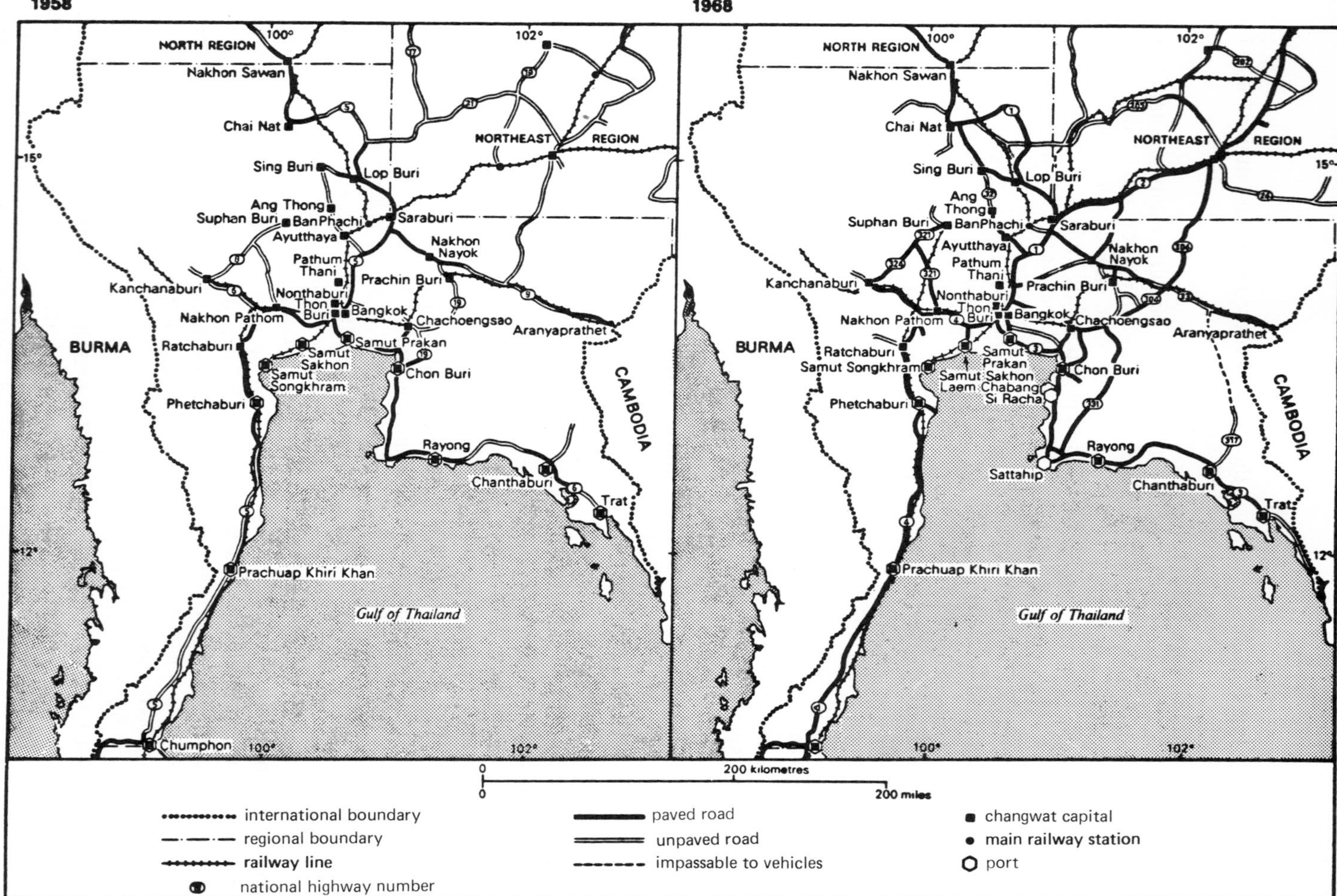

Fig. 17-4 Transportation networks in Central Thailand, 1958 and 1968.

2 Connecting Den Chai on the northern line to Chiang Rai, and important rice growing area (273 km)—estimated cost $US 33,500,000 and $US2,500,000 for rolling stock (Fig. 17-5);

3 Suburban lines in the metropolitan area linking Bangkok, Thon Buri, the Meklong line, and Ratchaburi about which no cost details are available (Fig. 17-4).[7]

With a large share of the nation's planning talent the Railways' feasibility studies are persuasive and well-documented. Under peacetime conditions the implementation of the various proposals depends on approval from the Council of Ministers (given in principle for the Sattahip–Chachoegnsao line) and obtaining the necessary foreign loans—often the more difficult obstacle as overseas lending authorities are not easily convinced of the long-term future of the Railways.

2. The Highways Department and Other Road Building Agencies

The goal of the Highways Department is to "construct a national highway system with linking transport routes to accommodate the increasing number of cargo and passengers and to develop provincial and rural highways to spread benefits into the remote areas (National Economic Development Board, 1968, p. 128). Considerable progress has been made towards the realization of this goal—paved roads increased from 2,000 km in 1956 to 6,000 km in 1966. Current schedules for construction, paving, and bridge replacement, presumably at the request of the country's international allies, show more redirection in aspiration levels as they favor the politically sensitive northeast area (Fig. 17-6). The choices open to the Highways Department are also constrained by its dependence on the Royal Thai Government for half its finance and on overseas loans for the other half. Cost-benefit studies are a prerequisite for such loans, but one lending authority has commented that even though data such as traffic counts, and types and volume of movement on individual roads, are being collected, little systematic use (with certain exceptions) is being made of it (International Bank for Reconstruction and Development, 1966). There is also some evidence that the Highways Department is overstating its capacity to meet its scheduled program and neglecting maintenance (International Bank for Reconstruction and Development, 1966; Wallace, 1969). The maintenance problems of the Highways Department, however, are exacerbated by the persistent overloading of trucks (twelve to fifteen tons on a vehicle designed for a ten-ton payload is not uncommon), but only the police have powers of prosecution. Another difficulty experienced by the Highways Department in its decision-making is that it is susceptible to political interference. For example, all pavement projects in the Second Plan (1967–71) are scheduled for the first three years by cabinet decision (International Bank for Reconstruction and Development, 1966).

The problems of the Highways Department are compounded by uncoordinated road construction by other government departments. Other road construction agencies include the Accelerated Rural Development organization specializing in security roads in fourteen provinces sensitive to insurgency (300 km have been constructed in liaison with the Highways Department but to their own design specifications), the Mobile Development Unit concentrating on economic growth in remote areas of the northeast (250 km have been built) and the Community Development program, under the control of the Ministry of the Interior, which has built roads in development projects (about 150 km). The touted economic, social, and political aims of road building have not been gained as in many cases the

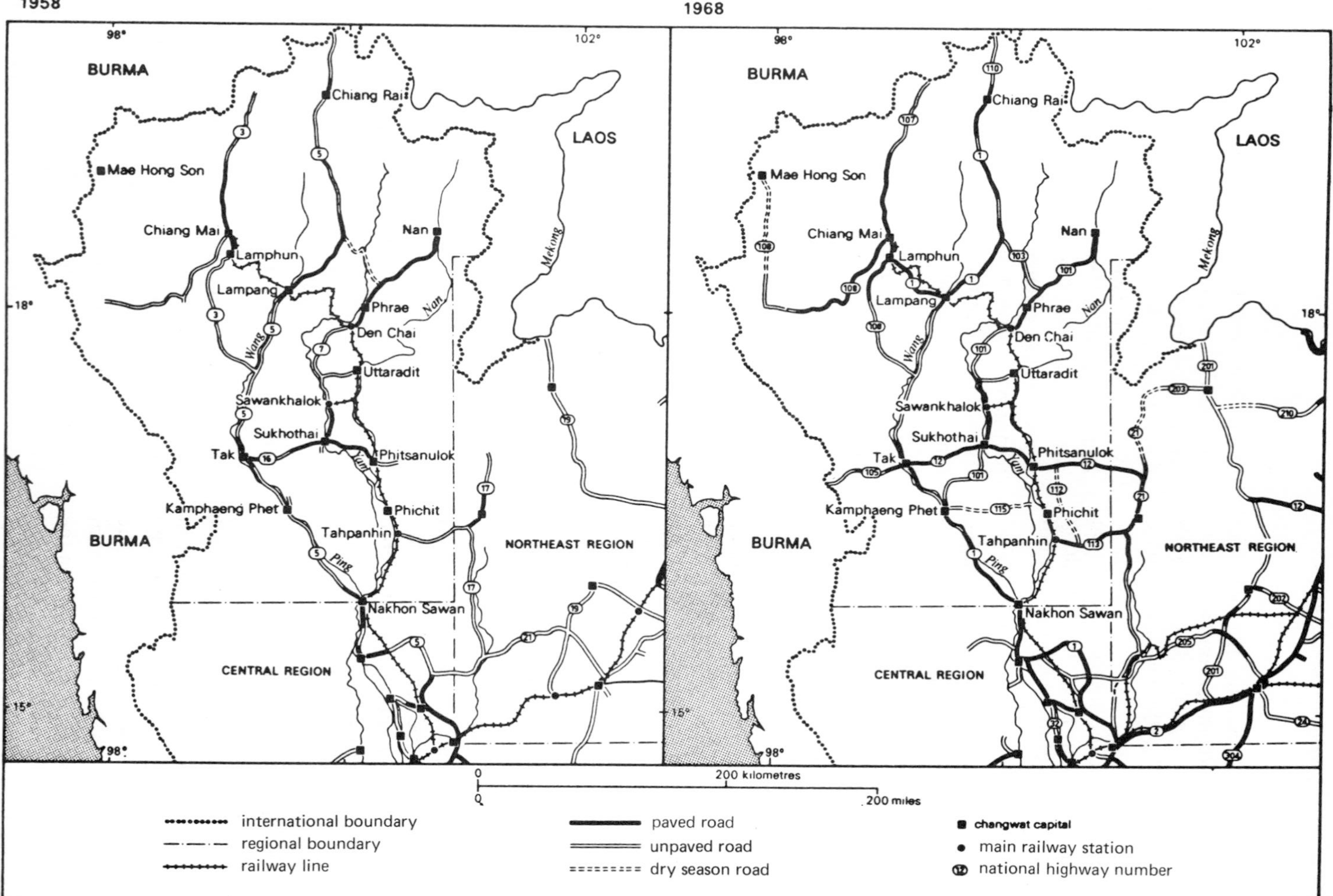

Fig. 17-5 Transportation networks in North Thailand, 1958 and 1968.

net result has been to extend the area of subsistence cultivation (Wallace, 1969).

3. The Express Transport Organization

No goals are specified for the Express Transport Organization in the Second Plan (1967–71) presumably because of the nature of its inception and its multifarious activities. The Organization traces its origins to the government's creation of the Transport Bureau in 1947, which was set up as a separate organization to take over the Railways' handling operations at sixty-three stations that had fallen into the hands of foreigners, thus making it difficult for Thai shippers to obtain railway wagons. The Express Transport Organization, itself, was established within the Ministry of Communications by Royal Decree in 1953 and subsequently expanded its various activities into transport and commerce. Apart from its railway activities, which now include pick-up and delivery services for 109 railway stations,[8] the Express Transport Organization engages in inter-city truck operations in vehicles of five- and ten-ton payloads, express transportation of cargoes, freight forwarding of bulk cargoes, international freight forwarding, city bus operation, inland water transportation, wharf operation, miscellaneous services (operation of service stations, printing house, removals service, packing service, customs brokerage, materials handling, and repair and maintenance service), and automobile trading business and insurance (Fig. 17-2). The Express Transport Organization also has sole rights to the transport of imported cargo from the Port of Bangkok, freight from the Thai Tobacco Monopoly, transit, and re-exported cargo to Laos, and to United States military cargoes.[9] In performing these services the Express Transport Organization makes use of the Railways' carload and less-than-carload services at contract rates, but most of its cargo is handled in its own or in subcontracted trucks. The Express Transport Organization does not have enough of its own trucks (936) to perform these services and hires more than 3,000 private trucks for a twelve per cent fee of the expected income in return for the preparation of documents, payment of taxes, and consolidation of cargo. Apart from its desire to handle all government freight there is little further to be divined about the Express Transport Organization's expectations or decision-making, except that they are made by a board of directors, including a president acting as chief executive, appointed by the government.

4. Private Truck Operators

The aspiration levels of private truck operators are difficult to specify in terms of organizational goals, expectations, and choices because the industry is largely composed of owner-drivers. Theoretically, private truck operations are controlled by the Ministry of Communications (Department of Land Transport) under the *Transport Act B.E. 2497* (1954).[10] Truck companies carrying agricultural products and livestock are obliged to own at least ten trucks and have a minimum capital of $US5,000. Some private companies (largely in the hands of Chinese businessmen) operate under these regulations largely as transport brokers on the basis of a ten per cent commission for loads (two per cent less than the Express Transport Organization), whereas owner-drivers are grouped in cooperatives of at least ten trucks. The freight rates charged by private hauliers are subject to control by the Ministry of Communications under provisions of the Transport Act, but the set charges are scarcely enforced in Bangkok, and along with other provisions of the Act, are almost totally ignored in country areas as freight rates are subject to considerable bargaining.

In Thailand there is within each sub-unit of

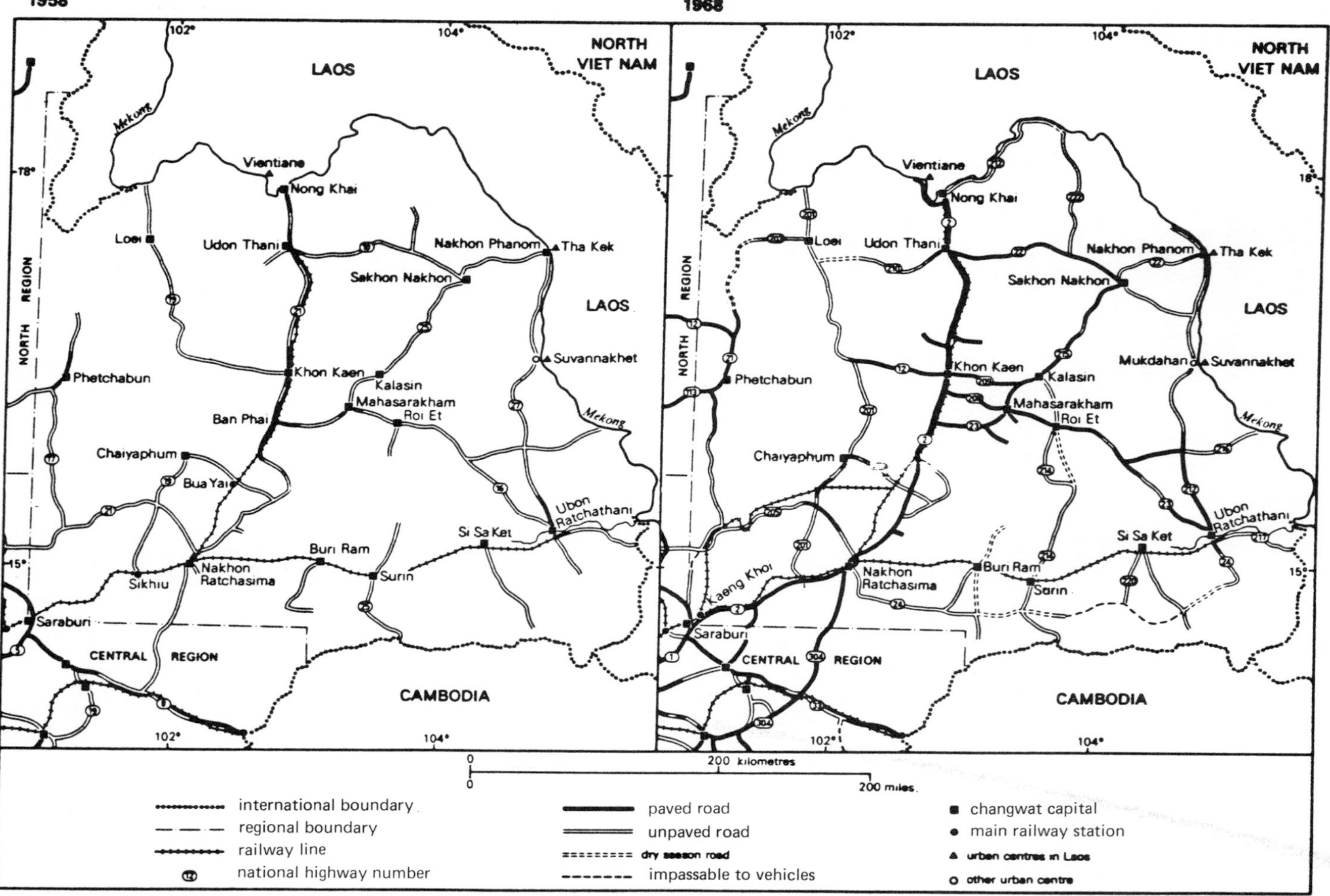

Fig. 17-6 Transportation networks in Northeast Thailand, 1958 and 1968.

the organizational coalition of transport agencies sufficient local rationality to resolve conflicts by adherence to acceptable decision rules (see Cyert and March, 1963, pp. 116–8), but there are few guidelines for resolving differing aims between agencies engaged in the vehicle network selection process. Under such circumstances conflicts over the choice of links and the selection of the appropriate vehicle for the freight task are inevitable.

CONFLICT AMONG THE DECISION-MAKERS

Two types of inter-agency conflict with an overt spatial expression can be recognized in the vehicle network selection process in Thailand.

1 Wrangles over the selection of links involving the Highways Department and the Royal State Railways;
2 Quarrels among vehicle operators:
- **a** The Royal State Railways versus the Express Transport Organization;
- **b** Government versus private transport operators.

1. Highways Versus Railways

The rapid development of all-weather highways, largely at the instigation of United States military advisors, has deprived the Railways of almost monopoly powers over long distance freight either originating or terminating outside the central plain.[11] The Railways has been severely affected by the road construction as instanced by the completion of the Friendship Highway between Saraburi and Nakhon Ratchasima on June 10, 1958—the first of a series of new and upgraded highways—and its extension to Nong Khai on the Laotian border (Fig. 17-5). The reduction in distance by 180 km and journey time by eight hours occasioned by the completion of the Highway deprived the Railways of much freight (Kaeng Khoi section) as did the extension of the road (Nakhon Ratchasima section) (Table 17-1). The possibility of the new all-weather highways being built parallel to existing trunk railway lines resulted in strong pressure from the Railways' Board of Commissioners to pressure the government into forcing the Highways Department to vary the alignment of two trunk roads: the Nakhon Ratchasima–Ubon Ratchathani highway so that it is south of the railway line (Fig. 17-6); the Chumphon–Surat Thani highway which would save vehicles the necessity of traveling on a circuitous route via Ranong (Fig. 17-7). Both roads are incomplete, but the deviations will increase construction costs and will reduce time-cost benefits.

Another problem that will not be settled so readily is the rival schemes for an alternative rail and road route from Bangkok to Ratchaburi (Fig. 17-4). As there is no effective internal means of resolving the wrangle, rival schemes will be submitted to the International Bank for Reconstruction and Development separately. This external decision-making could lead to duplication and a waste of scarce resources because the International Bank for Reconstruction and Development "must assure itself only that the project is justified, but it need not be the highest priority

Table 17-1 Changes in Outward Tonnage and Revenue in Railway Sections Parallel to the Friendship Highway and Its Extension, 1958–1968

		Friendship Highway: Kaeng Khoi main section	Extension to Nong Khai: Nakhon Ratchasima section
Tons (metric)	1958	40,634	364,840
	1968	11,578	37,458
Revenue ($US)			
	1958	113,121	1,392,111
	1968	37,400	122,932

Source: Royal State Railways of Thailand.

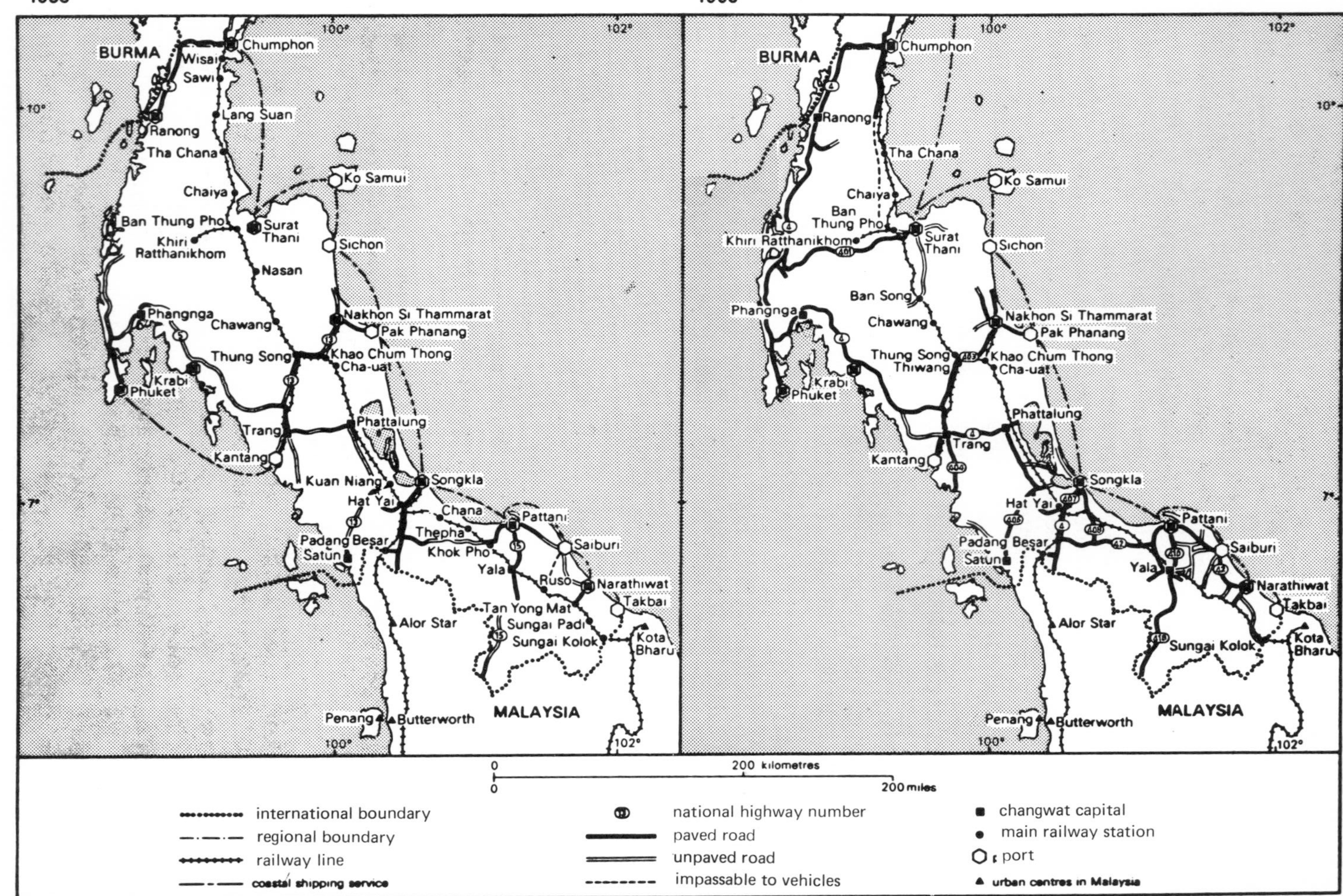

Fig. 17-7 Transportation networks in South Thailand, 1958 and 1968.

project in the country" (Adler, 1969, p. 233). In sifting through the competing claims it is important, as in every other network selection decision, that the losses to rail from highway development are made explicit (and not hidden in induced benefits), because the Royal Thai Government has to determine the future role of the Railways as a freight carrier in a truck-dominated transport system.

2*a*. The Royal State Railways versus the Express Transport Organization

The highway construction program and the associated rise in truck numbers (39,576 in 1961 to 90,057 in 1967) has affected the Railways' rate of return, expressed as a ratio of net operating income over net fixed assets. Between 1958 and 1968 this return has fluctuated between one and three per cent annually —a poor return on the Railways' modernization program and a low interest compared with other parts of the Thai economy. An increase in rates—held steady since 1955—would curb any trend towards over-investment in rail facilities created by an excessive demand for low priced transport space, but any rise by the Railways in isolation would endanger its competitive position vis-à-vis other media. Before rate increases are contemplated the Railways would prefer to see changes in the regulations governing pick-up and delivery services which hamper its attempts to solicit traffic. An aggressive commercial attitude has captured the trade of large volume shippers on a siding to siding basis, but further advances are hamstrung by the Express Transport Organization's monopoly of pick-up and delivery services at 109 railway stations. Only in exceptional cases can consignors and consignees transport their own cargo to and from railway stations in their own trucks and then only with the permission of a committee composed of the Express Transport Organization, the Royal State Railways, and the Ministry of Communications. No railway freight can, therefore, move in or out of specified stations without the intermediary of the Express Transport Organization which also has priority on the ordering of goods wagons irrespective of any commitments to other shippers. In effect, the Express Transport Organization controls a large part of railway freight and can exercise a stranglehold on the Railways' ability to compete against the company's own trucks. At many stations the pick-up and delivery service is subcontracted to private trucks under license. The Express Transport Organization's rates are fifty to one hundred per cent more than those charged by private truckers for comparable loads of non-railway freight. These rates discourage railway users as instanced in comparative Express Transport Organization rates for rail and road cargoes between Bangkok and Ubon Ratchathani, Udon Thani, and Nakhon Ratchasima in the northeast (Table 17-2; Fig. 17-6). Many previous users of rail have chosen to operate their own trucks or employ private operators to avoid the inconvenience and high cost of using the inclusive door to door rail service.[12]

2*b*. Government versus Private Transport Operators

Competition from the private truck operator is felt by both the Express Transport Organization and the Royal State Railways. There is no restriction of entry into the private industry and competition for freight is keen. Freight rates are low, particularly in comparison with the Express Transport Organization (Table 17-3). The higher charges by the Express Transport Organization are attributed by the company to its greater reliability and insurance cover. Private truckers are able to compensate for their lower freight rates by overloading, "padding" cargoes to deceive the hirers of the true weight, and

Table 17-2 Comparative Road and Rail Rates Charged by the Express Transport Organization and the Royal State Railways Ex-Bangkok in 1969

Destination	Road		Rail		
	Distance, km	Ten wheel truck $US	Distance, km	Terminal to terminal $US	Door to door $US
Ubon Ratchathani	760	115	575	66	149
Udon Thani	604	145	569	65	148
Nakhon Ratchasima	256	60	264	39	128

Source: The Express Transport Organization.

evading taxes that are obligatory for government organizations. Overloading by private operators is deemed necessary as part of their perquisites of office. The practice of "tipping" has not deterred the private haulier and its impact on the operations of the Express Transport Organization and the Royal State Railways has been severe. Indeed, the Express Transport Organization has reacted to this challenge by requesting a monopoly of all highway freight. This claim, made in 1964, was later recast in terms of all government freight, but it was refused. Fortunately, the buildup of military cargoes, accounting for one-fifth of the 3,300,000 tons handled by the Express Transport Organization in 1967–68, mitigated direct competition from private operators. The Railways was not so fortunate and the effects of truck competition have increased in severity. An International Bank for Reconstruction and Development (1966) report infers from a series of rough indicators—growth in number of trucks, changes in the location of the trucking fleet, and the expansion of roads—that the interprovincial road freight had increased fivefold between 1955 and 1964 whereas the Railways' freight traffic in terms of ton-kilometers has only doubled.

The conflict between the principal decision-makers in the vehicle network selection process is symptomatic of the lack of direction in the allocation of the freight traffic task to satisfy cost-effective goals. It is widely believed, though it cannot be proved, that a misallocation of resources is occurring, because road transport is under-priced and probably returns less than the three to four per cent made by the Railways on adjusted fixed assets (unprofitable hotels and land holdings are excluded). International Bank for Reconstruction and Development economists estimate that the probable cost of maintaining the national highway system is $US55,000,000, but truck operators pay only $US30,000,000 (International Bank for Reconstruction and Development, 1966). The effect of such a distorted pricing system is to

Table 17-3 A Comparison Between Express Transport Organization (ETO) and Private Trucking Rates for Parcel Freight Ex-Bangkok in 1969

	Distance, km	E.T.O.[a,b] ¢US	Private[c] ¢US
Chiang Ma	809	1.25	0.90–1.25
Ubon Ratchathani	760	1.80	0.50–0.90
Udon Thani	604	1.80	0.75
Nakhon Ratchasima	256	0.90	0.50

a. Rate for cheapest class of freight.
b. These rates vary plus or minus twenty per cent depending on circumstances.
c. Vary according to season, competition, and demand.

Source: Personal interviews.

create an excessive demand for road transport at the expense of other modes and an over-investment in the transport sector as a whole to the detriment of other segments of the economy.

This preoccupation with road construction up-country (little thought has been given to traffic congestion in Bangkok) needs careful scrutiny if the economy is to obtain the fullest return from investments in competing media and the transport sector as a whole, which received over twenty-nine per cent of the budget allocation in the Second Plan. In the past the highway system has been conceived independently of other transport media because of the widespread belief among government agencies that the catalytic effect of any and all highways would realize worthwhile economic benefits. There is little doubt that the road construction program suited the needs and mood of the expanding Thai economy, but without investment planning covering the whole spectrum of benefits and the needs of all competing media there is a danger that new highway capacity is being created at considerable cost to meet an apparent demand for road transport services. Unless the situation is examined, the railways, inland waterways, and coastal shipping could regress into the role of residual carriers by operating below their effective economic capacity. With scarce capital resources Thailand can ill-afford to waste investment on duplicate facilities to meet the needs of pressure groups and opportunities for personal profit. There is, therefore, a pressing need for a plan coordinating individual transport media and allocating traffic among differing modes of transport as a basis for investment decision-making.

TRANSPORT COORDINATION

The need for "integrated planning and the development of all transport facilities to provide and maintain a comprehensive transport system at least possible cost" (Transportation Consultants, Inc., 1959) has been recognized by a succession of advisers. These advisers have proposed similar basic solutions to the problem of coordination.

1. Improved Organization

As no government agency provides effective coordination over the vehicle network selection process, Transportation Consultants, Inc. proposed in 1959 that a Royal Transport Board of Thailand be given the central responsibility of deciding the expansion or curtailment of all transport links and services. It was intended that the Board would be aided in its judgments by a Transport Advisory Committee with a watching brief over transport matters. The Ministry of Communications has taken up the second suggestion and proposes an Institute of Transport and Communications which would advise the government on transport coordination and make policy recommendations. Without an executive body it is difficult to see the Institute providing the necessary coherence for dealing with Thailand's pressing transport problems (International Bank for Reconstruction and Development, 1966; Transportation Consultants, Inc., 1959).

2. Effective Pricing Policies

Competition among the various modes (or vehicle network combinations) can be used in allocating freight traffic and determining investment priorities (see Soberman, 1966), but to be efficient the competition has to be based on prices which reflect the relative cost of providing the service—a method ensuring that the transport needs of the economy are met with a minimum expenditure of scarce resources (Meyer, *et al.*, 1959, p. 242). "In a regulation free model road and rail freight services would be supplied only if users showed by the prices they are willing to pay that each service utilized is better than any available alternative, including storage, alternative location, or even cessation of production" (Kolsen, 1968, p. 173). If this pricing system is to be employed in Thailand higher road charges would be necessary if it could be proved that trucks are charging uneconomically low rates. Such a decision assumes that the vehicle network selection is made on economic and not security grounds.

Developed countries—the United States, the United Kingdom, and Australia—have not solved the problem of allocating freight efficiently between competing media (Kolsen, 1968). In the absence of robust statistics it is unlikely that the transplantation of Western ideas such as a Royal Transport Board or effective pricing policies (licensing, set freight rates, or user taxes) will minimize transport costs or produce the rational planning and coordination of transport. These recommendations fail to appreciate that the real goals and strategy are dictated through the role of elites in the structure of Thai government and authority, and by prebendalism—the derivation of non-salaried income formally or informally derived from the powers of office (Wallace, 1969).

THE "SOFT STATE"

Much of the inter-agency conflict in Thailand is posturing and shadow boxing as the decision to construct a transport link is in reality the product of highly personalized relationships within the Bangkok-concentrated elitist groups; the power group is the military elite which controls the bureaucratic and Chinese business elites (the traditional elites of the King and princes and the Buddhist order of Monks, the *Sangkha,* have little direct economic power [Evers and Silcock, 1967]). The formal system of government operated by the Prime Minister and Council of Ministers, consisting of a majority of generals, is, in essence, an imported Western model grafted onto a Thai organization of patronage and mutual obligation in the bureaucracy, which serves as the informal base of power. This informal system "is necessarily secret, difficult to detect and still more difficult to document" (Evers and Silcock, 1967, p. 96).

Even though the bureaucracy has had massive injections of Western-trained graduates—with skills often inappropriate to the country's needs—personal obligations to the minister subvert attempts at more efficient administration. Indeed, the importance of prebendalism stifles, to some extent, the prosecution of national goals and strategies. It is perhaps an exaggeration to suggest that unofficial sources of income—generous meeting allowances and directors' bonuses for sitting on committees—involve corruption as the Thai system allows and expects its Civil Service to engage in this type of activity. There is, however, evidence that corruption is widespread among the power elite and the upper echelons in the bureaucracy and, together with prebendalism, this must be seen as a corrosive factor alienating the population and destroying loyalty to the central government. Collectively, these activities preserve what has been termed the "soft state"—a condition ripe for insurgency (Myrdal, 1968, II, 937–58).

The full impact and extent of corruption and prebendalism on transport decision-making is difficult to ascertain, but the adherence to other non-national interests and allegiances are sufficiently strong to prevent the government achieving its stated aspiration levels on particular goals and strategies. For example, where government officials have to supplement meager salaries from their powers of office, it follows that only transport projects with a high prebendal income are

Table 17-4 Estimated Changes in the Interprovincial Traffic Task Performed by Road and Rail, 1955 to 1964

Year	Road million ton km	Rail million ton km
1955	900	870
1964	4,500	1,500

Source: International Bank for Reconstruction and Development, 1966.

vigorously prosecuted. In road construction, for instance, there is an under-use and misuse of building equipment which has resulted in inputs capable of producing five kilometers of highway realizing only one kilometer (Wallace, 1969). As road building is a prime source of non-salaried income the overloading of trucks is actively encouraged in some quarters because it is a source of revenue to police at road blocks and on patrol and ultimately will lead to more road construction to repair the damage. The maintenance of roads—a poor source of "tea money"—is studiously neglected.

Under such conditions it is difficult to engender spontaneous change in the bureaucracy to cope with new transport problems. Additional committees have been established to deal with the interrelationship of transport and other economic activities in particular regions. These extra organizations have not been notably successful because disputes from the village level upwards in the administrative hierarchy have to be resolved by the Prime Minister—there are almost one hundred government departments, seventy-one provinces (*changwats*), 509 sub-districts (*amphoes*), 4,926 towns (*tambons*) and 41,360 villages (*mubans*) all endeavoring to get their difficulties solved. In such circumstances the real decisions are made within the informal system. As rational planning would whittle away the informal power base of the bureaucracy it is covertly avoided because it strikes at the roots of the prebendal system. If the efficient use of new and existing resource inputs to transport (and other sectors of the economy) is to be a conscious goal of the society system, non-salaried income would have to be replaced if strategies capable of achieving the stated aims are to be adopted. Until sweeping reforms occur the effective use of the vehicle network selection process will be hampered.

In reality, therefore, transport decision-making in Thailand is a mixture of *ad hoc* approaches, the spatial expression of which is difficult to decipher. There are signs that the decision-making process is being increasingly influenced by professional considerations and less by private interests. As yet, however, there has been no consideration of the optimal array in space of transport decision-making authority and its proper hierarchical structure, which could assist in delimiting the division of power among central, state, and provincial governments. Such a consideration awaits an analytical framework that includes behavioral and cultural factors because, unlike Western countries where the social matrix is permissive of economic development, attitudes and institutions in Thailand provide major obstacles.

NOTES

1 Such combinations can include air, water, and land transport, which can be further subdivided in terms of a vehicle's ability to negotiate different types of terrain. For example, land transport could be further subdivided into all-weather highways, four wheel drive roads, and motorcycle tracks.

2 The reciprocal impact of different vehicle network combinations on the environment is not considered in this study and is not shown on the transport system model (Fig. 17-1).

3 The gross domestic product in Thailand ranged

from $US200 per capita in the central region (encompassing Bangkok), through $US130 in the southern region, $US80 in the northern region to $US60 in the northeast region (Organization for Economic Co-operation and Development, 1966).

4 Where the main purpose of a new transport facility is to open up land for cultivation, the benefits from the additional production made possible should be assessed (Adler, 1969, p. 234).

5 This situation is not unusual in developed countries. For example, eight Commonwealth ministers have some power over transport decision-making in Australia (Rimmer, 1970, p. 153).

6 The Royal State Railways is the public enterprise responsible for the commercial operation of the state-owned railway system and one private line (the Meklong line). It was established in 1890 and became an autonomous organization on July 1, 1951, by the *State Railway of Thailand Act B.E. 2494 (1951)*. The formulation of policies and supervision of the Railways' general affairs are entrusted to a politically influential Board of Commissioners. Only if fares or freight rates are to be reduced below fifty per cent or increased more than twenty-five per cent is the authority of the Council of Ministers necessary.

7 The only other links with potential are from Khiri Rattanikhom on the southern line to Phuket if the latter became a deep-sea port (Fig. 17-7) and a link from Bua Yai Junction in the northeast to Mukdahan as there is the possibility of carrying timber from Laos (see Fig. 17-6).

8 This concession was granted in 1960 to compensate the Express Transport Organization for having to give its terminal operations back to the Royal State Railways.

9 The Express Transport Organization has closed its hotels, and ceased its tourist service, and inter-city bus operations.

10 The Cabinet has presented to Parliament a draft bill covering road transportation companies which will abrogate, if passed, the *Transport Act B.E. 2497* [1954]: *The Investor,* 2 (1970), p. 361.

11 Of the $US855,000,000 allocated to the transport sector in the Second Plan (1967–71) $US460,000,000 are devoted to the completion of the trunk and feeder road program and $US124,000,000 to the Royal State Railways (National Economic Development Board, 1966).

12 Shippers on the Nakhon Ratchasima–Nong Khai line offloaded and loaded their goods at small stations not under the Express Transport Organization's control. The tonnage handled by these stations is anomalous in terms of the size of their captive hinterlands.

REFERENCES

Adler, H. A., "Economic Evaluation of Transport Projects," Chapter 9, pp. 170–94 in G. Fromm (ed.), *Transport Investment and Economic Development,* Washington, 1965.

Adler, H. A., "Some Thoughts on Feasibility Studies," *Journal of Transport Economics and Policy,* 3 (1969), pp. 231–6.

Berry, B. J. L., "Relationships between Urban Economic Development and the Urban System: The Case of Chile," *Tijdschrift voor Economische en Sociale Geografie,* 60 (1969), pp. 283–307.

Burns, R. E., "Transport Planning: Selection of Analytical Techniques," *Journal of Transport Economics and Policy,* 3 (1969), pp. 306–21.

Cyert, R. M., and March, J. G., *A Behavioral Theory of the Firm,* Englewood Cliffs, N.J., 1963.

Evers, H. D., and Silcock, T. H., "Elites and Selection," Chapter 4, pp. 84–104, in T. H. Silcock (ed.), *Thailand: Social and Economic Studies in Development,* Canberra, 1967.

Fisher, N. W. F., "An Introduction to Cost-Benefit Analysis of Road Projects," unpublished paper given to Commonwealth Public Service Board Seminar, Canberra, December 1–4, 1969.

Friedmann, J., *Regional Development Policy: A Case Study of Venezuela,* Cambridge, Mass., 1966.

Kolsen, H. M., *The Economics and Control of Road-Rail Competition,* Sydney, 1968.

Kolsen, H. M., and Stokes, N. C., "The Economics

of Inter-City Highways: The Uses and Abuses of Benefit-Cost Analysis," Chapter 2, pp. 19–46, in *The Economics of Roads and Road Transport,* Commonwealth Bureau of Roads Occasional Paper No. 1, Melbourne, 1968.

International Bank for Reconstruction and Development, *Transportation Sector Report* No. FE-53b, September 2, 1966 (mimeographed report), unpublished paper in the Ministry of Communications, Bangkok (restricted circulation).

Lampert, S., Ramsey, W., and Walli, C., *Developing Area Transportation Study Program Formulation,* Longbeach, Calif., 1968 (restricted circulation).

Meyer, J. R., Peck, M. J., Stenason, J., and Zweck, C., *The Economics of Competition in the Transport Industries,* Cambridge, Mass., 1959.

Muscat, R. J., *Development Strategy in Thailand: A Study of Economic Growth,* New York, 1966.

Myrdal, G., *Asian Drama: An Inquiry into the Poverty of Nations,* 3 vols., London, 1968.

National Economic Development Board, *Government of Thailand: The Second National Economic and Social Development Plan (1967–71),* Government Printer, Bangkok, 1968.

Organization for Economic Cooperation and Development, *A Survey of Technical Assistance to Southern Thailand,* Paris, 1966.

Rimmer, P. J., *Freight Forwarding in Australia,* Department of Human Geography Publication HG/4, Research School of Pacific Studies, Australian National University, Canberra, 1970.

Soberman, R. M., *Transport Technology for Developing Regions,* Cambridge, Mass., 1966.

Sychrava, L., "Some Thoughts on Feasibility Studies Occasioned by the Appraisal of Road Projects in Thailand," *Journal of Transport Economics and Policy,* 2 (1968), pp. 332–48.

Transportation Consultants, Inc., *A Comprehensive Evaluation of Thailand's Transportation System Requirements,* (3 vols.), Washington, 1959.

Wallace, W. M., "Transport Sectoral Goals and Strategy: A Reappraisal," unpublished paper of the NEED Planning Advisory Group, Bangkok.

Not all decision making that we are concerned with in transportation geography is at the entrepreunerial and governmental level. We all make decisions as to what route we take and what mode we use; that we travel at all is an amalgam of voluntary and involuntary factors. Not all the travel we make is "essential" in terms of goods flowing to industries or in terms of people traveling to work. This is a theme to which we will return in Selection 29, but it has its place at this point too. In the following selection R. E. Borgstrom takes a nontraditional look at airline travel (though his approach could be applied to any other mode or combination of modes), examining the concepts of physical, temporal, economic, and sociocultural distance as related to the marketability of a particular route—that between the mainland United States and Hawaii. It becomes very clear in this selection, as it did in Selection 15, that choices of mode and route depend on a wide range of human choices and decisions, including manipulation by various marketing or advertising agencies. It might well be subtitled "Voluntary and Involuntary Decision-making Influences on Nonessential Travel."

Selection 18

Air Travel: Toward a Behavioral Geography of Discretionary Travel

R. E. Borgstrom

Definitions of Transportation

The geography of passenger transportation has long been biased by the exclusive presumption that a functional relationship exists between measurable distances and the interaction of objects with other places. The idea that transportation research is merely the explication of strategic routes and sites of logistical support recurs throughout the literature from the initial works of von Thünen (1826) and Christaller (1935) through numerous normative studies of which Taaffe's work (e.g., 1959, 1962 and 1963) and Garrison's paper on connectivity (1960) are examples.

Thomas suggests that the physical route, the carriers, and the objects being transported are all elements of the transportation system and as such are worthy of study (1956, 2). However, it is important to realize that there are additional and perhaps more relevant approaches to the understanding of travel for discretionary—non-business and non-military—purposes.

In this context, it may be forgotten that transportation refers not to a network of conduits through which inanimate objects stochastically flow, but rather to the aggregate of personal decisions to move from place to place. Such decisions being the result of individually and group conceived life styles, aspirations, and levels of satisfaction, it appears a more realistic thesis to assume that the parameters of movement space—the perceived part of the environment wherein movement occurs—are a function of the perceived intervening physical, temporal, economic and socio-cultural distance. (See Eliot Hurst, 1969, 161, 783, and 938–44; also Deutsch and Isard, 1961, 308–11.)

Herein the spatial implications of perceived distance will be considered by an examination of the passenger air transportation system connecting the mainland United States with Hawaii. Instead of a description of the carrier or an accounting of various distance factors alone, attention will be drawn to an examination of principles by which the development of passenger transportation systems may be understood. Implicit in such a behavioral examination is the question of whether the motivations of passengers traveling on the route were influenced for the generation of traffic and coincidental economic or neo-colonialistic advantage? Or whether the network of routes developed simply to meet the demand for transportation between spatial entities? The overriding consideration is, therefore, a re-evaluation of the traditional ways by which geographers have considered the evolution and spatial relevance of transportation systems.

Characteristics of the Route

In 1968, 910,690 people traveled from North America to stay overnight or longer in Hawaii. Of that population, 76.48 per cent traveled for "pleasure," and 96.48 per cent traveled

This is an original selection prepared especially for this text.

by air. (Hawaii Visitors Bureau—hereafter, H.V.B.—1969, 1, 4, and 21.)

Passenger air service between North America and Hawaii was inaugurated by Pan American World Airways in August 1935, with the weekly operation of the *China Clipper* between Alameda, California, and Honolulu Harbor. The flight took approximately 22 hours and was offered at a round trip fare of $648.00. Because of the weight of the fuel required for this necessarily non-stop flight, usually no more than six passengers were accommodated in addition to the regular seven man crew.

By the summer of 1970, eight airlines operated 322 flights each week from thirteen cities on the mainland United States to Honolulu with an additional thirty-eight weekly flights to Hilo (Table 18-1). A typical flight from California to Hawaii now requires approximately 5 hours aboard a 365-passenger Boeing 747 jet at round trip fares ranging from $170.00 to $330.00 depending upon class of service and day of the week used for travel.

PARAMETERS OF INTERACTION

The Motivation for Travel

Underscoring research in transportation is the spatially grounded notion of complementarity. (See Ullman, 1956, 871.) Extending complementarity to discretionary travel and personal decision making, it can be generalized that people travel to other places to achieve there that which is *perceived* to be necessary or desirable but locally unavailable. It is, therefore, not the mere existence of a particular climate that attracts northern visitors to the beaches of Waikiki, Miami, Ocho Rios or Puerto Vallarta for winter vacations. It is,

Table 18-1 Number of Non-stop Passenger Flights Per Week from Mainland United States Cities to Honolulu and Hilo: 1953, 1963, 1970

	1953		1963		1970	
From:	To: HNL	ITO	HNL	ITO	HNL	ITO
Anchorage					1	
Baltimore-Washington					7	
Chicago					27	3
Dallas-Fort Worth					17	
Detroit					7	
Los Angeles	13		44		128	21
New York					14	
Oakland					7	
Portland, Oregon	9		12		14	2
Saint Louis					7	
San Diego					14	
San Francisco	13		31		61	10
Seattle			2		19	2
All mainland cities	35	0	89	0	322	38

HNL. Honolulu ITO. Hilo

Source: Schedules of American Airlines, Braniff International, Continental Airlines, Northwest Orient Airlines, Pan American World Airways, Trans World Airlines, United Air Lines and Western Airlines.

instead, the encultured value of those people that to visit Hawaii, Florida, Jamaica or Mexico is to achieve at a satisfactory destination those necessary or desirable goods and services which are unattainable in the local environment.

If that same group believed that those places were too many miles away, that to travel there would require too much time, that exposure to the sun induced skin cancer, or that they could not identify with the people at those resorts, the destinations, while retaining all of their physical attributes, move beyond the perimeter of that group's movement space—i.e., beyond the perimeter of that group's range of possible destinations.

The real objective of the traveler is neither the destination nor its attributes, but his own aspirations. Locations and the goods and services offered there are only the means by which those aspirations can be satisfied. A visitor's goal—his aspiration—may be to act out a life style for which the attributes of a warm climate, a tropical setting and the availability of water sports may be valued. The physical situation of Hawaii may, in that case, be a highly satisfactory destination. If, however, the vacationer perceives prohibitive distance barriers between himself and Hawaii, he may elect either to visit a more local place or not to travel at all and, thereby, achieve satisfaction of his aspirations at another level.

In surveying the objectives of travelers to Hawaii, Evelyn Richardson, H.V.B. director of research, concluded that a "change of environment," "rest and relaxation," the "adventure" of new experiences, the opportunity of meeting others, and an "escape from business or family pressures" were principal motivations (Richardson, 1967, 88). Because each of these highly qualitative motives appear as generalized aspirations, there is little to indicate that the satisfaction of each is found only in attributes unique to the Hawaiian Islands. One must, therefore, assume that Hawaii is but one of many potential destinations for the generalized traveler and that traffic is, indeed, governed by the ways in which travelers and groups of travelers perceive Hawaii to be accessible.

The Spatial Continuum

Olsson's bibliography (1965) identifies a literature in which physical distance is a widely used index of accessibility and a determinant of human interaction. The concept assumes that the whole of man's experience can be evaluated on a linear scale of finite and readily perceptible units. From this the inference is made that traffic along a given route is a normative function of the physical distance separating the two points being measured. The implications of this notion seem to be exemplified by a critique of the film "Zabriskie Point," where the reviewer suggested, "Michaelangelo Antonioni's . . . movies seem to deteriorate in direct proportion to the distance they are made from home" (*Time*, February 23, 1970, 76).

Suggested as a departure from that premise of Newtonian analog geography is the idea that travel from place to place is neither a function of locations nor of spatial relationships, but the suspension of experience en route between spatial entities. (See McLuhan, 1964, 94–5.) The notion of perceiving travel as the progression of objects along a tangible route over distinct features of physical geography is anachronistic at best. It implies travel in an era of non-mobility when the intermediate destinations of a heterogeneous physical geography were significant barriers to movement.

Now, and until the electrical process of transporting information achieves such a level of proficiency as to preclude the necessity for physical interaction between places, to travel is to board the dining room or the cocktail lounge and be suspended aloft while the geographic spaces of origins and destinations are rearranged below. It is analogous to the changing scenes during an intermission. The passengers, like an audience, wait in the auditorium for a curtain to open and another set of scenery and props to be made visible. In the airplane, as before the closed proscenium, the processes of changing the scenery or the places are discontinuous and, therefore, imperceptible.

For over 4 hours on the overwater crossing from California to Honolulu, passengers perceive no spatial location in their preoccupation with the destination at Honolulu and the distractions of en route service or inconvenience. It is only when the plane rounds Diamond Head that passengers lose their passive detachment from spatial environments and become cognizant of the realm of sites and geographical destinations. Yet even those who profess the ability to sit at the plane's window and perceive the regionalizing characteristics of a dynamic spatial pattern below can scarcely argue that they are able to translate their cool visual impressions of the passing landscape into the hot currency of measurable, linear distance.

Miles and kilometers, it must be remembered, are semantic conventions by which spatial positioning may be made uniform. It generalizes a relationship between places and as such man learns to communicate that A and B are n miles apart. Yet the spatial relationship actually being perceived is far more complex than such a simple quantitative declaration. One may speak of—and consciously believe—that it is too great a number of linear units separating his home in Chicago from a vacation in Honolulu. But it is important for the researcher to consider that the subject may speak of mileage while actually conceiving of a distance measured in dollars, hours, or socio-cultural variables.

The Temporal Arrangement

Evaluating spatial relationships by the use of minutes, hours or days offers to a temporally oriented culture a more personal definition of spatial arrangements than does the enigmatic idea of mileage. The statement, "I'm ten miles from home," although geographically uniform in its implication, is probably meaningless to most recipients of that information. The statement, "I'll be home in an hour," suggests, however, a more relevant relationship by which Western man can order his activities and his perceptions of distance.

In 1968, the Behavior Science Corporation inquired of people who could afford the economic cost of flying what they believed were the advantages of air travel. Eighty-seven per cent of those surveyed cited "time saved en route" as a great advantage (Schleier, 1968). Similarly, an executive of a major North American airline (remaining anonymous at his request), in correspondence with the author, cites "time saved versus other modes" as the principal factor influencing the decision to travel by air for non-business purposes.

But en route time cannot, for research purposes, be considered a function of physical distance. For example, the 419-mile-flight from Las Vegas, Nevada, to Grand Junction, Colorado, requires 64 minutes flying time by jet aircraft. The fastest non-stop flight between Las Vegas and New York City is 4 hours 45 minutes. Obviously the difference in en route time is a function of the difference in physical distance. Yet in July 1970, only one flight per day was offered on the route to Colorado, whereas three non-stop and two one-stop, through flights were available to New York. Consequently, one may have to wait for up to 24 hours for a plane to Grand Junction while the mean waiting time for a New York flight is only 4 hours 48 minutes. When the mean waiting time is added to the mean en route time—64 minutes to Grand

Junction and 5 hours 12 minutes to New York—it may be said that Las Vegas is effectively 25 hours 4 minutes from Grand Junction and only 10 hours from New York City (*Official Airline Guide*, July 1970).

This situation is similar to Taaffe's idea of a "traffic shadow" (1962) and it exemplifies what may be perceived as a significant barrier but not the sole determinant of travel for the citizens of the communities involved.

When the introduction of jet aircraft virtually halved travel time from New York City to Honolulu, it could be said that those people who were economically and socio-culturally predisposed to travel could, with the faster service, make the crossing to Hawaii with greater ease or frequency. The trip that once consumed 24 hours—or two vacation days if a stop were made en route in California—could now be made within the daylight hours of a single day (Table 18-2).

Thus the traveler predisposed toward visiting Hawaii could now do so during shorter but more frequent vacation periods. Time, for him, is no longer a barrier for travel to that place. But it cannot be extended that others, unable or unwilling to pay the economic cost of the trip, or socio-culturally alienated from such travel, will suddenly take vacations in Hawaii because temporal distance was reduced.

Similarly, if the introduction of supersonic aircraft reduces the temporal distance between New York and Hawaii to four or five

Table 18-2 The Evolution of Temporal Distance Between New York City and Honolulu: 1953–1970

Examples of Expedited Passenger Air Service From New York to Honolulu in 1953, 1958, 1963 and 1970

Year	Local time	Enroute stops	Airline and equipment	
1953	0020 EST	Lv. New York	American	DC-6
	0240 CST	Ar. Chicago		
	0310 CST	Lv. Chicago		
	0835 PST	Ar. Los Angeles		
	1030 PST	Lv. Los Angeles	United	B-377
	1900 HST	Ar. Honolulu		
		23 hrs. 40 min. en route		
1958	0030 EDT	Lv. New York	United	DC-7
	0605 PDT	Ar. Los Angeles		
	0930 PDT	Lv. Los Angeles	Pan American	DC-7
	1535 HST	Ar. Honolulu		
		21 hrs. 5 min. en route		
1963	0945 EST	Lv. New York	American	B-707
	1215 PST	Ar. Los Angeles		
	1330 PST	Lv. Los Angeles	Pan American	B-707
	1650 HST	Ar. Honolulu		
		12 hrs. 5 min. en route		
1970	0920 EDT	Lv. New York	American	B-707
	1357 HST	Ar. Honolulu		
		10 hrs. 37 min. en route		

Source: Schedules of American Airlines, Pan American World Airways and United Air Lines.

hours, there will be some New Yorkers spending the afternoon on the beach at Waikiki just as today some affluent and spatially diverse Californians spend the evening at a theater on Broadway. There will be those who will wait until their retirement to spend the temporal cost of a trip to far distant Hawaii. And there will be those for whom the trip to Hawaii, regardless of the temporal distance, will remain beyond the range of their perceptions.

The Economic Barrier

Economic distance is a measure of spatial separation in terms of transport costs. As such, fares and the perception thereof can seriously restrict man's movement space. But while the notion of measuring distance in dollars and promisory notes—e.g., credit cards—is important, it is an overemphasized parameter to interaction.

Von Thünen derived land rent by calculating transport costs as a positive function with physical distance. Christaller defined hexagonal trading areas on the assumption that people would minimize travel cost. In both schemes, it was assumed that people were omniscient and that their actions would reflect perfect economic rationality. It should be noted that Berry modifies this classical simplicity with the notion that actions are probabilistic (1967, 41–2) and, therefore, individual and group actions may be generalized through the use of stochoastic variates.

This discussion of discretionary travel must diverge from such classical concepts. If man's sole motivation were the maximization of economic profit, the ultimate parsimony would be not to travel at all for non-business or non-military purposes. Vacation travelers buy the intangible and presumably nonessential pleasure of being at a distant place rather than at home.

Because economic distance is perceived in relationship to the value of the destination goal, it may be irrelevant to think of transport costs either as a linear function with distance or as a determinant of interaction. If the traveler believes that the satisfaction of traveling to or being at place B justifies the expenditure of n dollars, specific complementarity such as Ullman speaks of it (1956, 867) is achieved. If, however, the potential traveler believes that n dollars could be spent in another and more satisfactory way, he may move destination B beyond the perimeter of his movement space. The consideration is not totally that of an individual's ability to pay for transportation, but rather a reflection of his life style and propensity to travel

Changes in fare structures affect the magnitude and the frequency of discretionary travel but not the motives for that type of interaction. By lowering the tariff, people predisposed to travel may find their desired destinations more accessible, but there is little to suggest that the act of reducing fares will create new aspirations to visit particular places.

It is assumed that there are groups and individuals who have long since found travel to be temporally and socio-culturally compatible with their life style. If those people perceive that the economic distance between themselves and their destination goal are no longer prohibitive, they may be motivated to make a particular journey. But the fallacy of economic determinism is, in part, that for the person without aspiration to travel, the economic distance was never prohibitive. If it was perceived at all, it was irrelevant.

In considering those for whom economic distance is relevant, it is important to remember that transport costs are neither linear functions of physical distance nor are they correctly perceived. One does not necessarily pay more to travel a greater physical distance. Indeed, air fares from the mainland United States to the resort areas of Hawaii and

Puerto Rico are significantly lower than fares for trips within the contiguous states. The adult, one-way "Y" class fare between Los Angeles and Honolulu is, for example, equal to approximately sixty-one per cent of the fare for the same class on service on the shorter flight from Los Angeles to New York City (Table 18-3).

Furthermore, different people riding in the same compartment on the same flight between the same two cities can pay markedly different fares. American Airlines reported that, in 1966, the undiscounted "Y" class fare from New York to Los Angeles was $153.36. Yet because of the number of passengers using various promotional fares—e.g., excursion, military, youth stand-by, family plan, etc.—the average fare paid by passengers using "Y" class services on that route was $115.00 (Civil Aeronautics Board, 1968, 150).

In addition to the complex structure of transport rates, there is a perceived fare by which groups and individuals measure the distance between two places. Contrary to the notion of economic omniscience, the perceived fare only coincidentally resembles the actual transport costs. A survey by the Behavior Science Corporation revealed that sixty per cent of their sample, within a population of those who presumably could afford the economic cost of flying, overestimated the actual cost of air travel by as much as 250 per cent. This 1968 survey concluded that "the tendency to mentally inflate the price of air travel makes many families reluctant to in-

Table 18-3 Examples of the Relationship Between Economic and Temporal Distance

City pairs	Mileage	One way fares	Cost per mile
		U.S. $	U.S. $
Examples of first class air fares:			
Los Angeles–Miami	2,330	195	.084
Boston–Los Angeles	2,600	200	.077
Honolulu–San Diego	2,612	165	.063
New York–Rome	4,275	469	.110
Honolulu–New York	4,987	369	.072
Examples of economy ("Y") class air fares:			
Chicago–New York	721	56	.078
Los Angeles–New York	2,451	154	.063
Honolulu–Los Angeles	2,556	94	.037
Examples of thrift class or commuter class ("K") air fares:			
Las Vegas–Los Angeles	235	22	.093
Los Angeles–San Francisco	340	16	.047
New York–San Juan	1,622	57	.035
Chicago–Los Angeles	1,746	100	.057
Honolulu–Seattle	2,736	85	.031

Source: The author's calculations, based upon the published fares of American Airlines, Pan American World Airways and Western Airlines.

vestigate the true costs at the time the decision is to be made" (Schleier, 1968).

It can be summarized that transport costs are a complex function of linear distance and, as such, are probably imperceptible to the consumer of transportation services. Furthermore, because individual and group perceptions of economic distance are relative to the perceived importance of the destination goal, transport costs are probably of minor consequence as determinants of interaction. It may, therefore, be valuable for researchers to diverge from the analysis of transport costs and fare structures and to turn their attention toward an analysis of the motives for achieving the destination goal.

Socio-Cultural Distance

Attention is now turned from the semantic conventions of miles, hours, and dollars to the more significant concept of a perceived socio-cultural distance separating spatial entities and governing the propensity to travel.

Man does not travel to unfamiliar environments. McLuhan says that "the world is like a museum of objects that have been encountered in some other medium" (1964, 178). Consequently, man, influenced by the attitudes and values of his social community, selects a destination from the alternatives within his movement space and purchases transportation for the purpose of visiting either spatially distant members of his social community or places where he perceives he can act out his aspired life style.

In the late nineteenth and early twentieth centuries, the "inevitable trip to Europe" was far more than the sale of transportation to reasonably affluent individuals. The *grand tour* was, for some, the highest satisfaction of an aspiration to social achievement, acceptance and the attainment of upward social mobility. It was a rigidly standardized group activity and, for many of those involved, the differences of being at Paris or Saratoga Springs was probably as imperceptible as it was inconsequential.

For some groups, the perceived comforts of home away from the spatial location of home may be the most significant element of socio-cultural distance as a determinant of discretionary travel. Highly successful in reducing this type of distance for a particular group of American travelers is the archetype Hilton International. An exemplary comment from an American staying at the Royal Tehran Hilton is cited in *Business Week:* ". . . the place could just as easily have been Phoenix as Iran" (July 1, 1967, 50). While capitalizing on socio-cultural distance suggests the value laden concept of neo-colonialism, the term is presented here without bias to suggest that it may be relevant to the understanding of non-spatial interaction to remember that for a significant population, socio-cultural distance is synonymous with accessibility to broiled steak, bourbon and running hot water.

Groups may also identify modal choice with specific groups and life styles. In 1936, when American Airlines introduced the Douglas DC-3 equipped with berths and a private "skyroom" for overnight flying, *Newsweek* suggested that "Hollywood-to-Broadway movie stars can loll in all the privacy they could ask for" (July 4, 1936, 25). Similarly, the notion of a "*jet* set" implies an elite group of cosmopolites using a particular mode of travel to act out a spatially diverse life style.

The point of all the memorabilia is a straightforward concept for transportation research and the relevance of spatial separation: If individuals and groups are socio-culturally alienated from travel, distances of miles or hours or dollars are totally inconsequential. When it was noted earlier that people tend mentally to inflate the price of air travel and that their perceived misconception of economic distance prevents them from investigating true costs (Schleier, 1968), the syllogism could be presented: The wealthy and the celebrated travel. I am neither wealthy nor celebrated. Therefore, my life style does not include traveling.

This notion suggests a reason for the decline in ocean travel between North America and Hawaii (Table 18-4). Although the fares for the crossing by sea are higher than the air fares—$230.00–$715.00 vs. $85.00–$165.00 from California to Honolulu—and although the journey by sea requires more time—5 days vs. 5 hours—the ocean voyage came to be regarded as more than just a means of transportation. Billed as a week-long stay in a fashionable resort, the dinner-jacketed life style of the luxury cruise to Hawaii may well be too socio-culturally distant for many potential travelers. The faster and less expensive crossing by air provides, for those people, not only a way to span physical, temporal and economic distance but also a means of avoiding any foreign, socio-cultural obligations which that group associates with the experience of an ocean crossing.

Table 18-4 Use of Surface Carriers for Passenger Travel from North America to Hawaii, 1953–1968

Year	Passengers via sea	Percentage of all passengers
1953	31,092	24.58
1954	33,171	23.44
1955	37,469	21.36
1956	36,463	17.92
1957	60,068	22.98
1958	60,156	22.85
1959	56,393	16.77
1960	56,882	14.22
1961	54,849	12.22
1962	56,576	11.38
1963	54,183	9.42
1964	48,497	7.11
1965	47,124	5.78
1966	46,736	4.79
1967	48,849	4.01
1968	48,857	3.52

Source: After Hawaii Visitors Bureau, 1969, 4.

Presumably some Americans perceive similar socio-cultural barriers prohibiting travel to Communist bloc nations, just as for some, discretionary travel itself is socio-culturally distant and incompatible with their life style. Distinguishing two antipodal perceptions of socio-cultural distance, Webber contrasts the highly territorial localite with the spatially diverse cosmopolite in an exemplary summary of essential value for even the most rudimentary consideration of transportation systems: "There are the notorious Brooklynites who, except for contacts through television, movies and other mass media, have never crossed the East River. But there are others who are at home throughout the world (Webber, 1964, 112).

The Packaged Perception

Discretionary air travel is a marketable consumer item. The propensity to travel from *A* to *B* may, therefore, be as artificially induced as the propensity to buy a particular brand of toothpaste or to shop at a particular store. Nicosia suggests a model of decision making whereby the consumer moves from passive predispositions through generalized attitudes toward active motivations to act in specific ways or to purchase particular products (Nicosia, 1966; summarized by Eliot Hurst, 1969, 652).

In a *ceteris parabus* situation with neutral predispositions toward travel, economic, temporal, and socio-cultural distance, transportation lines market a packaged perception of the environment at particular destinations. They seek first to create the aspiration to achieve a destination goal. They then present the spatial destination as a level of satisfaction for that aspiration. And they finally suggest their line's total travel-related services as the means by which that satisfaction can be achieved.

Airlines, like the steamship lines, railroads, stage lines and canal barges before them, have diversified their corporate interests into a variety of related areas. Of greatest relevance to the Hawaiian market is the relationship between airlines and hotels. Stuart G. Tipton, president of the Air Transport Association of America, speaks of hotels as a "logical extension of airline service" and suggests that "without comfortable accommodations that travelers can depend upon, the airlines would have only the slimmest traffic to many points all over the globe" (Tipton, 1968, 2 and 4).

American, Continental, Eastern, Trans World and United Air Lines all have interests in Hawaiian hotels, and the economic advantage of such airline-hotel liaisons should immediately be apparent. In 1968, 95.7 per cent of those arriving in Hawaii from North America stayed overnight or longer. Of those people, eighty-three per cent stayed at hotels or apartment-hotels. The average party size was 1.47 persons and the median length of stay was 11.1 days (H.V.B., 1969, 9, 16 and 22). Using these values to estimate the demand for hotel rooms (Equation 1), it is suggested that the arrival of 365 passengers on one fully loaded Boeing 747 jet has the potential of generating occupants for over nine per cent of the 22,801 hotel and apartment-hotel rooms in the state of Hawaii (Equation 2).

1 $(M\ N\ D\ H)\ (S\ A)^{-1} = P$

- N = Number of arriving passengers
- D = Percentage of N disembarking for a stay of overnight or longer
- H = Percentage of ND using hotel accommodations
- S = Average party size
- M = Median length of stay
- A = Number of hotel rooms available
- P = Percentage of A expected to be occupied as a result of the arrival of N passengers

Table 18-5 Average Daily Expenditures of 1967 Visitors in Hawaii

	U.S.$
Lodging	12.28
Food	10.23
Clothing	4.67
Nightclub expenses	3.35
Liquor	2.74
Gifts and souvenirs	2.33
Ground transportation	2.09
Entertainment (other than nightclubs)	1.15
Photographic supplies	.45
Beauty parlor/barber shop	.37
All other expenses	1.27
Total daily expenditures	40.93

Source: The author, after Richardson, 1967, 87.

2 $\{(11.1)\ (365)\ (.957)\ (.83)\}$
$\{(1.47)\ (22{,}801)\}^{-1} = .09601$

Furthermore, if each passenger behaved economically according to values derived for visitor expenses in 1967 (Table 18-5), 365 passengers would, over an eleven-day stay, add $119,123.95 to the Hawaiian economy of which $35,735.19 would be spent for hotel accommodations alone (after Richardson, 1967, 87).

The other effect of a packaged perception is the notion of neo-colonialism introduced earlier. It may be inappropriate to speak of this concept in Hawaii for Hawaii's status as a state and formerly as a territory makes non-political subordination to the United States impossible by definition. But it is hard to imagine that the parade of sightseeing busses from Laie to the Nuuanu Pali and the MacDonald's on Kalakaua Avenue are extensions of a Pacific or island culture. For some, the destination goal is an amalgam of areal differentiation in terms of physical and cultural settings along with the comforts and conveniences [of] a more localized life style.

Yet it is remarkable that there are those who fly to Hawaii surrounded by over three hundred travelers on the same plane, select the hour of their departure from among dozens of daily alternatives, and choose accommodations from over one hundred hotels on Waikiki alone, yet still expect a Pacific metropolis to exist as it did in the eleventh century when the Marquesans first came ashore on Kauai. Such naïvté suggests an excellent first time sale of a particular packaged perception of Hawaii that may not be an accurate representation of the place at all.

It should be noted, however, that the experience of a trip to Hawaii is, for most visitors, a highly satisfactory one. Of 4,293 visitors interviewed in 1969, only 9.9 per cent noted their experiences in Hawaii to be disappointing to some degree with regard to their expectations. Despite the stereotyped image of a huckstered, prepaid tour, forty per cent of those interviewed said that they were on a prepaid tour for at least part of their trip and 51.4 per cent of those respondents evaluated such tours to Hawaii's "neighbor" islands—Kauai, Lanai, Maui and Molokai—as "excellent" (H.V.B., 1970). These responses indicate that, for this group of travelers, the packaged perception was an inducement to travel that fairly represented their attitudes and aspirations.

In either case it can be concluded that the understanding of a route rests not upon the number of travelers stochastically processed between two points but upon the motivations of those travelers. The marketing implication of that conclusion is that such motivations may be in response to a façade of the environment contrived for economic or neo-colonialistic profit.

EXTENSIONS

If geographers believe that spatial variation implies the differentiation of attributes by quantity and quality at diverse physical locations, it follows that a geography of discretionary travel could imply a study of the reasons why people believe it desirable to interact with other places and avail themselves of those spatially diverse phenomena.

It is presumed that geographers believe a numerical value can be derived to represent the physical, temporal or economic distance between any two points and that this value is inherently a barrier to interaction. While it is acknowledged that there exists a friction of distance which serves to inhibit travel and which constitutes parameters to movement space, miles, dollars and hours are semantically imposed conventions, not determinants of interaction. Such values should more pertinently be evaluated as a function of the propensity to travel and relative to the traveler's affinity for the destination goal. The spatial significance is the presumption that for purposes of understanding discretionary travel, locations are not separated by semantic conventions but by a complex of behavior patterns that differentiate group life styles and travel patterns.

Webber suggests the construction of an indicator of cosmopolitanism and localism as a means of fusing together these concepts of behavioral analysis with the more traditional, spatially oriented geography. His suggestion is based upon the notion that associated with each role is a propensity to perform in a particular way. Thus the executive who travels frequently in the line of his professional duties but who vacations at home with his family performs as a cosmopolite in the role of executive and as a localite in the role of husband and father. By measuring the number and type of social interactions—e.g., trips taken, messages sent, etc.—per role person, Webber believes researchers could obtain valid correlations between social ranking and travel distance (Webber, 1963, 66–7). Indeed, by this method, one could attempt quantitative expressions for the perception of movement space.

This notion is a valid focal point for future geographic research and especially for what is suggested here as a behavioral geography of discretionary travel. Currently, geography has only the route map and the fragile assumption that transport lines exist in response to a demand for transportation to connect spatial entities. But those tools are inappropriate for considering the myriad behavioral motivations, divorced from locational analysis, creating the perceived necessity for interaction.

Considering those motivations as the basis for future research, the overriding theme for future work in this area is that man's attitudes superimpose man over geography as it is traditionally considered. The precursor to understanding discretionary travel, as well as any form of human interaction, is, therefore, the understanding of those attitudes, predispositions and perceptions.

BIBLIOGRAPHY

Berry, Brian J. L. *Geography of Market Centers and Retail Distribution.* Englewood Cliffs, New Jersey: Prentice-Hall, Inc., 1967.

Christaller, Walter. *Die Zentralen Orte in Süddeutschland.* Jena: G. Fischer Verlag, 1935.

Civil Aeronautics Board. *A Study of the Domestic Passenger Air Fare Structure.* Washington, D.C.: Civil Aeronautics Board, 1968.

Deutsch, Karl W., and Isard, Walter. "A Note on a Generalized Concept of Effective Distance," *Behavioral Science,* Vol. 6 No. 4 (1961), 308–11.

Eliot Hurst, Michael E. *A Geography of Economic Behavior: A Behavioral Systems Analytic Approach.* Belmont, California: Wadsworth Publishing Company, Inc., preliminary edition, 1969.

Garrison, William L. "Connectivity of the Interstate Highway System," *Papers and Proceedings of the Regional Science Association,* Vol. 6 (1960), 121–37.

Hawaii Visitors Bureau. *1968 Annual Research Report.* Honolulu: Hawaii Visitors Bureau, 1969.

———. *Visitor Reaction Survey: 1969.* Honolulu: Research Department, Hawaii Visitors Bureau, 1970.

McLuhan, Herbert Marshall. *Understanding Media: The Extensions of Man.* New York: McGraw-Hill, Inc., 1964.

Nicosia, F. M. *Consumer Decision Processes.* Englewood Cliffs, New Jersey: Prentice-Hall, Inc., 1966.

Olsson, Gunnar. *Distance and Human Interaction: A Review and Bibliography.* Philadelphia: Regional Science Research Institute, 1965.

Richardson, Evelyn K. "Research Activities of the Hawaii Visitors Bureau," *Report of Proceedings, Pacific Area Travel Association Travel Research Seminar: Hawaii 1967,* 85–9.

Schleier, Curt. "Possible Cures for 'Never-Shows'," *Air Travel,* November 1968, 12ff.

Taaffe, Edward J. "Trends in Airline Passenger Traffic: A Geographic Case Study," *Annals of the Association of American Geographers,* Vol. 49 (1959), 393–408.

———. "The Urban Hierarchy: An Air Passenger Definition," *Economic Geography,* Vol. 38 (1962), 1–14.

———, Garner, Barry J., and Yeates, Maurice H. *The Peripheral Journey to Work: A Geographic Consideration.* Evanston, Illinois: Northwestern University Press, 1963.

Thomas, Benjamin E. "Methods and Objectives in Transportation Geography," *Professional Geographer,* Vol. 8 (1956).

Tipton, Stuart G. "Travel in the Seventies—Will There Be Room?" Unpublished remarks before the Hotel Sales Management Association, March 14, 1968.

Ullman, Edward L. "The Role of Transportation and the Basis for Interaction" in William L.

Thomas, ed., *Man's Role in Changing the Face of the Earth.* Chicago: University of Chicago Press, 1956, 862–80.
von Thünen, Johann H. *Der isolierte Staat in Beziehung auf Landwirtschaft and Nationalökonomie.* Hamburg: 1826.
Webber, Melvin M. "Culture, Territoriality, and the Elastic Mile," *Papers and Proceedings of the Regional Science Association,* Vol. 9 (1963), 59–69.
———. "The Urban Place and the Nonplace Realm" in Webber et al., *Explorations into Urban Structure.* Philadelphia: University of Pennsylvania Press, 1964, 79–153.

Whether we come down to the level of the individual traveler or deal with the interaction between larger decision-making units such as corporate bodies, public institutions, government agencies, or for that matter, governments themselves, we assume the existence of ideas, news, and information diffusing over the landscape—Cooley's psychic flow. Transportation geographers have ignored this issue until very recently. But as was stressed at the opening of this part, we cannot ignore the existence of such flows. In building up our holistic interdependent conception, we cannot ignore communications, or a return to the French geographers' conception of *circulation.* In the next two selections we look at circulation on two levels. First, R. F. Abler reviews the mechanical layer of the communications system, including the networks of telephone intercommunications. He does carry this toward the behavioral level by considering the effects of information flow, including reference to that basic geographic concept of spatial interaction. But it is the second selection, by Gunnar Törnqvist, that firmly grounds Abler's ideas into decision-making processes that overtly and covertly shape the geographic landscape.

There may be those who would argue, like C. H. Cooley, that much in these two works is marginal to transportation geography and that so much space in so short a book devoted to information theory unbalances the whole approach. To those who still think that, I can only suggest that they read through this part from the beginning again, and perhaps refer to the Conclusion (pp. 511–517).

Selection 19

The Geography of Communications

R. F. Abler

If we can map the pathways by which information is communicated between different parts of an organization and by which it is applied to the behavior of the organization in relation to the outside world, we will have gone far toward understanding that organization. This will be true of an organization composed of cells in an organism, or of machines in an automatic communications network, or of human beings in a social organization.

Karl Deutsch

Information pathways and their effects are poorly mapped by geographers because of their limited importance in geographical theory. For several decades, the most dynamic branch of spatial inquiry has been economic geography, and economic geographers tend to consider places in relation to things and people. Analyses devoted to explaining agricultural, industrial, and commercial patterns emphasize media which make movements of things and people possible. Explicitly or implicitly, economic geographical theory portrays man as a creature who makes decisions in an environment in which desirable resources are scarce. Such theory explains spatial behavior (especially in the form of the activity patterns man creates) as the result of attempts to make optimal use of such resources. When flows of goods and people were the life-blood of advanced societies, analysts correctly devoted their attention to such flows and to the media which made them possible.

It is now becoming increasingly obvious, however, that we are entering a new, economic era which will be dominated by quarternary (information) activities, and that spatial theory will have to be modified accordingly. In advanced nations, the economics of scarcity is being replaced by the economics of abundance, and flows of information and ideas are increasingly replacing flows of goods and people as the life-blood of such nations. As societies become larger and more complex, the proportion of the labor force that must be devoted to monitoring and management increases. A homogeneous nation of five million, living in a small national territory, can perhaps afford small government; a nation of two hundred million which occupies a good portion of a continent and which is anything but homogeneous socially, economically, culturally, and physically, cannot. The absolute necessity for continuous feedback and control in complex nations like the United States explains why one out of every five people in its labor force works in some federal, state, or local government enterprise.

The need for expanded information and control activities with increasing scale of organization affects everyone. Families today have to spend more time and effort managing their affairs than ever before; one can no longer "just live." Private organizations face similar problems. An increasing fraction of the employment, time, and space of any organization must be devoted to information

This is an original selection prepared especially for this text.

gathering and processing and to management functions (Gottmann, 1961, pp. 565–630). Even in basic industries like mining, the proportion of production workers is dropping as more and more employees fulfill service and management functions (U.S. Department of Labor, 1969, p. 43).

Origins of Communications Geography

The growing importance of communications was first recognized in the latter half of the nineteenth century. Ratzel conceived of nations as organisms rooted in places. Accordingly, he gave considerable attention to the role of transportation and communications as the circulatory and nervous systems of sociospatial organisms. He argued that *verkehr* (transportation and *information* communication) was critical to the formation of both cities and nations (Ratzel, 1921, Chapter 13). *Verkehr* (circulation), for Ratzel, is the "master of space" (*raumbewältiger*), and in political terms, "the most important of the significant accomplishments of circulation is the transmission of information" (Ratzel, 1929, p. 319; Hückel, 1907). Little attention was given to communications thereafter until 1937, when Eugene Van Cleef devoted four chapters of his book *Trade Centers and Trade Routes* to the importance of mass and interpersonal media in trade and transportation, emphasizing the ways modern economic organization depends on efficient intercommunication systems. Cavaillès (1940) summarized a number of earlier studies of transportation and information transmission. Sorre (1948) discussed idea movements but his comments occupy only a small portion of the 200 pages he devoted to "The Conquest of Space."

Cognizance of the importance of communications in human affairs has historically been associated with organic theories of society. Herbert Spencer (1910, Part 2, Volume 1), whose thesis was that society *is* an organism, treated communications in detail. He argued that social systems are composed of three kinds of interdependent organs, which perform alimentary, vascular, and neural functions, respectively. These subsystems are analogous socially to groups engaged in manual production, trade, and control (p. 496). To coordinate the actions of an aggregate, individual or social, there must be not only a governing center, but there must also be a medium of communication through which this center may affect other parts [p. 533]. Spencer felt the efficiency of the electric telegraph gave social organisms of his day a superior coordinating capacity. Many current ideas about communications are similar to Spencer's. Parts of his sociology can be reviewed with profit, since we now think about society in organic terms, although we prefer the term "systems theory" to "organicism." Spencer's notion of the social organism and his ideas about transportation and communication had important (if indirect) influence on Ratzel and thereby on current geography.

Charles H. Cooley (1894), although he quarreled with some of Spencer's ideas, was very much influenced by them, and he gave considerable attention to both transportation and communications. He distinguished two "mechanisms of communication," one for material communication (transportation) and one for psychical communication. Moving physical masses is the essence of transportation, whereas material movements do not take place in communications, or if they do (as in postal communication), such movements are incidental to the essence of the process.

Harold A. Innis, the great Canadian economic historian, published two remarkable books on communications. *Empire and Communications* (1950), in a manner reminiscent of Ratzel, describes the dependence of large-scale political organization on reliable communications media. *The Bias of Communica-*

tion (1964) explores the effects of media on society and culture. Innis originated the *media* interpretation of history and society (Innis, H. A., 1944), and more than any other individual provided the stimulus for modern communication research.

Marshall McLuhan, one of Innis's students, followed in his mentor's footsteps (albeit in a much more flamboyant fashion), and transformed the communications theory of history into a general theory of culture. In *The Gutenberg Galaxy* (1962), and *Understanding Media: The Extensions of Man* (1966), McLuhan argues that communications media are extensions of men's senses, and that their effects—as media—are more important than whatever information they carry. Despite his perverse obscurantism, McLuhan is perceptive, and his ideas, like Innis's are always spatially relevant.

Detailed analyses of the locations of media facilities and information activities are still scarce, as are studies of media operations and flows through communications networks. Early work by geographers was superficial. When non-geographers examined communications, spatial considerations were always peripheral, and thus the spatially-oriented literature on communications produced up to 1960 was limited.

New Theoretical Frameworks

Several bodies of theory—spatial and non-spatial—are now being developed which deal precisely with matters of information and control. Scholars in a number of disciplines have developed new models of human behavior in which information is a dominant explanatory variable. Many theoreticians now argue that the quantity and quality of information that people receive are the major determinants of the decisions they make. We live in a communications era, a period in which phenomena at such polar scales as international relations and the growth processes of cells in the human body are analyzed and explained with reference to communications processes (Deutsch, 1966; Lowenstein, 1970).

Individuals or groups can receive information from outside themselves only through personal experience or via information-transmitting media (Fig. 19-1). Existing ideas (theories and models) about the environment are filters, which pass some information to the receiver in unaltered or modified form and block other information. Similarly, existing notions partially determine the information received; most people read columnists and subscribe to periodicals which share their views rather than seeking viewpoints in conflict with their preconceived notions. The be-

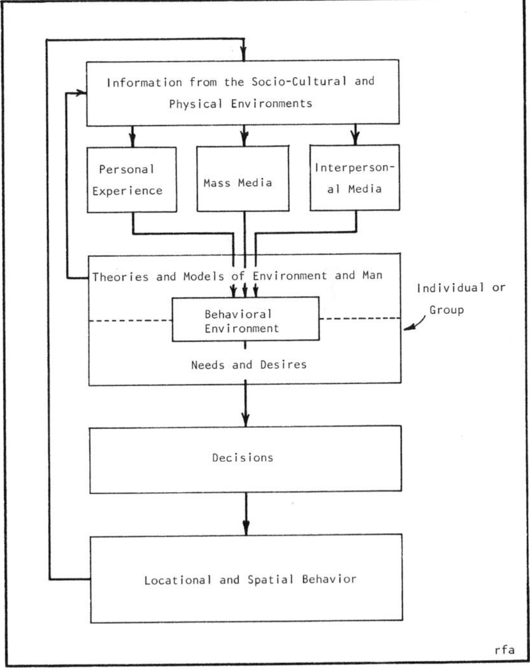

Fig. 19-1 Communication model of human spatial behavior.

havioral environment is composed of filtered information, and in conjunction with needs and desires it produces decisions and behavior which also affect the receipt of information.

Personal experience brings us only a part of our information about the world. A large input is received through other channels which can conveniently be divided into mass and interpersonal media, each of which can be further divided into informal and formal categories (Fig. 19-2). Formal media require prepared channels and are essentially one-way information delivery systems. Very few people can act as senders; most people can only receive the information the few transmit. Formal mass media require a special setting, such as a theater or a cinema, or special equipment such as television or radio transmitters and printing presses. Till recently, informal (no interposed channel) mass media have been almost non-existent. Progress in facsimile technology, however, now permits everyone to be his own publisher (God help us!). The success of underground theater and cinema in the last decade indicates that similar trends toward democratizating communications are underway in those media. Similar democratizing developments will evolve in radio and television in coming decades. New techniques will help overcome existing bandwidth restrictions and reduce costs of entry in such media (Miller, 1966, p. 27).

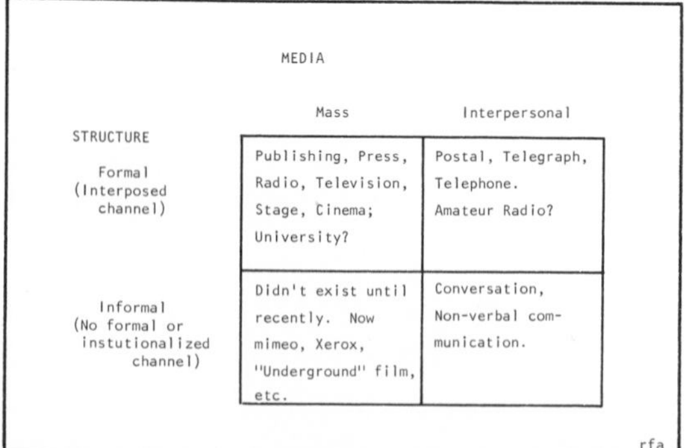

Fig. 19-2 Cross-classification of communications media.

Interpersonal media allow *two-way* information transmission. The average person can act as both sender and receiver, even though the bulk (70–80 percent) of the traffic in the formal interpersonal media is business information. The informal interpersonal media are the most ubiquitous of all. At the same time, they are the most difficult media to map precisely because they are informal.

Communications media are inherently spatial phenomena; they are most useful when they serve extensive regions of the earth's surface. Communications media and the information flows they carry are elements of current affairs which are eminently suitable for geographic analysis. Communications media offer geographers a fertile field wherein they can apply their expertise. Moreover, analyzing communications systems can tell us much about the earth's geography and about geography as a discipline.

Like political organizations, communications networks are inherently space *filling* phenomena, and the problems encountered in designing networks to serve national and larger areas are exceedingly complex. There exists a considerable geographical literature on the analysis and design of transportation networks, but there is no comparable literature on communications media. Sometimes the techniques used to analyze and design optimal transportation systems such as graph theory and matrix algebra can be applied to communications media. On the other hand, communications media usually operate in a different temporal context than transportation systems. When flows are very rapid or instantaneous, some problems with intriguing spatial implications arise which are somewhat unique to communications networks.

Geographers have devoted some attention to flows of information through space. Quite often, geographers have been interested in information flows as indices of other kinds of spatial relationships. Diffusion studies, for example, might be classified under communications geography because they focus on information flows through space. Information movements through informal channels have been most frequently analyzed to date, but some kinds of information flows through formal media also have important effects on innovation diffusion processes.

Communications media will continue to affect peoples' spatial behavior and general spatial organization. Like any other space-adjusting technology, communications media offer people certain behavioral and locational options. Investigations of the spatial effects of information flows and communications media exist but geographers have barely scratched the communications surface of the world they study so intensively from other viewpoints.

It seems to me that contemporary human geography is a science concerned with human spatial and locational behavior (Abler, Adams, and Gould, 1971). Our fundamental concern is what people do in terrestrial space and why they do it. Information is a powerful explanatory variable in this kind of geography. Whether we consider decisions about residential location, recreational travel, or plant and store locations, information (and the media through which it moves) are critical. During the last decade, a geography concerned with the location of communications activities, with information flows, and with the behavioral effects of communications has begun to emerge in recognition of this important variable.

LOCATIONAL ANALYSIS OF COMMUNICATIONS MEDIA AND ACTIVITIES

Mass and interpersonal media are organized industries, and they can be examined in the same way that geographers might analyze the location of the steel industry or some other activity. There exists, however, another category of information and control activities of great interest. Corporate headquarters and other quaternary activities such as banking and insurance are important functions whose spatial distribution is an important element of human geography.

The Mass Media

None of the mass media have been subjected to detailed locational analysis to date. The most extensive discussion of the printing and publishing industry is Gustafson's study (1959), which documents the steady agglomeration of that industry into the New York Metropolitan Area. Publishing had earlier been well-represented in Boston and Philadelphia, but after 1900 New York assumed the commanding position in the industry. Aside from Gustafson's work, we have few insights into the locational behavior of the printing, publishing, and newspaper industries.

Electronic mass media have fared only slightly better. Donald Q. Innis, H. A. Innis's son, explored problems caused by the space-filling nature of broadcast media (1953; 1960). Where settlements with thresholds to support a radio or television station are closely spaced, "crowding" occurs. The average size of cities with broadcast stations is smaller in sparsely settled areas than in densely settled regions because of the interference problems encountered when the broadcast bands are filled to capacity. Thus people in sparsely populated areas sometimes have more radio stations to listen to than people in densely populated areas.

When radio and television diffused across the nation, larger cities tended to accept both radio and television first, with smaller centers starting stations only some years after the larger cities (Bell, 1965). A secondary tendency was for such innovations to be adopted first in the northeast and on the West Coast, whence they diffused into the interior of the nation. A later analysis by Berry (1970) confirmed Bell's conclusion that television diffused down the nation's urban hierarchy. In Sweden the diffusion of television receivers followed a hierarchical course, but with important neighborhood effects (Törnqvist, 1967).

Some very interesting tensions exist between the need to establish national and international networks for ease and rapidity of information flow, and the simultaneous need for regional coverage of local affairs. In the electronic media, this tension results in national networks with local affiliates. National network activities are overwhelmingly concentrated in New York City, with a few outliers in Washington and Los Angeles. Local affiliates purvey national programs to their audiences along with local information.

Similar spatial tensions affect newspaper industry structure. Wire services like United Press International and Associated Press transmit news of national and international interest to all papers, and local editors decide how much of the network material they will use and how much local news they will disseminate. Thus newspapers and broadcasting stations are both receivers and transmitters. If a local event has national or international interest, they will relay the story to the rest of the world via their network and wire service connections.

Interpersonal Media

Formal interpersonal media (telegraph, telephone, and postal communications) are spatial systems, *par excellence,* and we have overlooked a fascinating and functionally critical element of human spatial behavior by not examining them more closely. In advanced and many developing nations, these services are virtually ubiquitous. And while their ubiquity may explain why we have overlooked

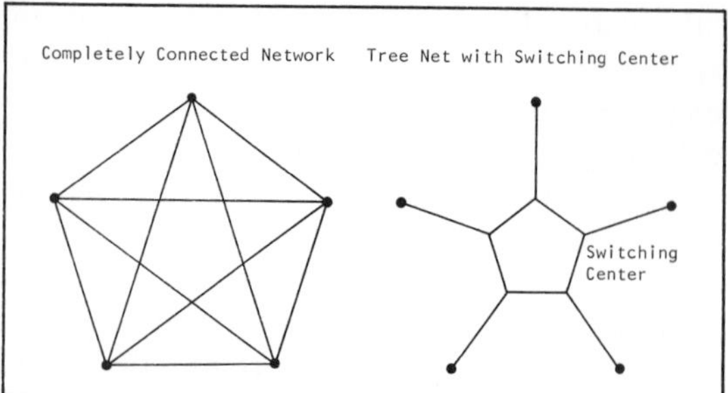

Fig. 19-3 Network design alternatives.

their importance, *because* postal and telecommunications services must be ubiquitous to be effective, and because their managers must also minimize network costs, the problems involved in organizing national postal and telephone networks are complex, even in small nations (Langley, 1963). When continental networks like that in North America are considered, network structure becomes extremely complicated and extremely interesting.

Tensions exist in all networks between complete connectivity, which is expensive in terms of routes and economizes switching, and a more parsimonious switched network which economizes links but involves greater switching costs (Fig. 19-3). Communications and transportation networks are usually compromises between the two polar extremes, and are sensitive to technology. If switching becomes cheap, a hierarchical, treelike structure is favored. When links are cheap, a more connected network results. Postal network structure has become more treelike since World War II because routes have gotten relatively expensive (Smith, 1967; Abler, 1968). For a time between 1920 and 1950, the telephone network grew more treelike. After 1950, two telephone networks developed. A control net of "final" links required by switches with automatic alternate routing capacity remained a tree, while the bulk transmission network grew more and more dense and more connected (Figs. 19-4 and 19-5).

The locational principles which govern the structures of intercommunications networks are somewhat unusual. In the final analysis, the network itself is the best explanation of its spatial structure. A completely connected network uses many links; $\frac{N(n-1)}{2}$ (where N equals the number of points to be connected) but eliminates switching costs. A completely switched network minimizes the number of links to $N - 1$, but would be very expensive in terms of switching costs. All communications and transportation network structures are the result of tradeoffs between link costs and switching costs, and they are usually combinations of local treelike networks and regional, national, and international nets which are more nearly completely connected. The great networks which provide intercommunications on national and international scales have a logic and order all their own; technology and internal requirements are the best explanations of their spatial organization. This principle has important implications given the evolution of giant conglomerates and huge international corporations. Such megaorganizations also possess internal organizing principles and requirements which could easily become the criteria used to choose locations for their components.

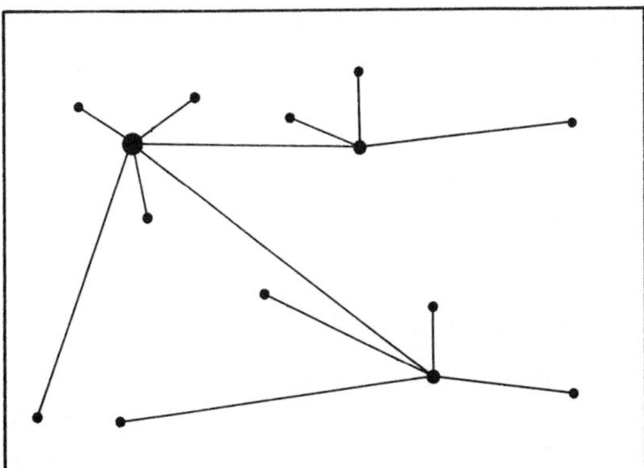

Fig. 19-4 Tree network of final trunk groups (control circuits).

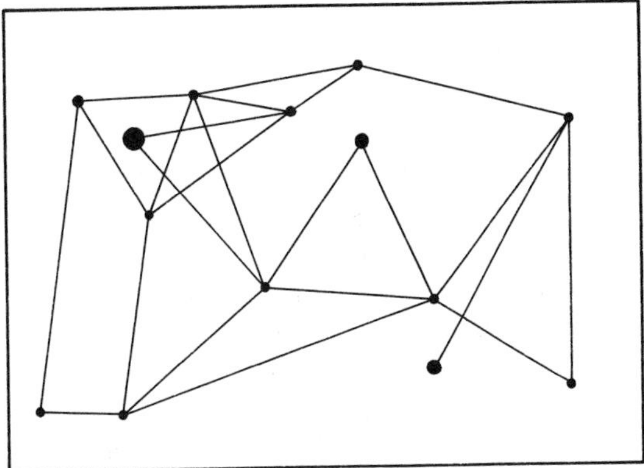

Fig. 19-5 Complex network of volume-based trunk groups.

Quarternary (Information) Activities

There exists a growing literature on the location of information processing and management activities. Government is an important, highly visible quaternary activity, but many other activities which at first glance do not appear to be information handling and management activities are important also. Stockbrokers, real estate agents, insurance companies, and banks all engage in acquiring, processing, storing, and disseminating information of one kind or another, and we need more information than we have about their locational behavior.

One quaternary activity of particular interest is corporate headship. Each year, *Fortune* magazine compiles a list of the 500 largest domestic industrial corporations and five additional lists of the top 50 banks, insurance companies, retail trade firms, transportation companies, and utilities. In 1968, 194 of these 750 concerns (25.9 percent) had their headquarters offices in the New York City area. The Chicago region was the location of 72 (9.6 percent), and Los Angeles of 32 (4.3 percent) headquarters offices. Together, the 30 largest metropolitan areas in the nation contained the headquarters of 563 (75 percent) of the 750 enterprises on *Fortune's* 1968 lists (*Fortune,* May, 1969, pp. 168–199).

Quaternary activities are heavily concentrated in the Megalopolitan complex, especially in New York City (Gottmann, 1961, 1966; Vernon, 1963). An increasing proportion of our urban labor force is engaged in quaternary occupations, whatever the products of the firms for which people work. Our metropolitan areas, and especially their central cores, are turning into information processing machines. Office functions are now a critically important element of urban geography (Cowan, and others, 1969). Cities have become communications media; their *raison d'être* is to enable people to communicate (Meier, 1962; Hall, 1966).

A tendency for controlling and directing centers of large organizations to agglomerate in the upper ranks of the urban hierarchy is also evident in Sweden (Wärneryd, 1968). In contrast to those who argue that modern communications will enable information activities to abandon the cities (e.g., Webber and Webber, 1967), Törnqvist thinks cybernation and other information based techniques will keep such activities concentrated in cities. Whereas programmed or programmable decision making can be dispersed to almost any location, managing organizations also requires many non-programmable decisions. In making such decisions, face-to-face communication is still vitally important (Törnqvist, 1968, pp. 106ff).

The locational behavior of quaternary activities is important. Labor forces in advanced nations are becoming more quaternary oriented, and if we can forecast the location of quaternary activities we can also forecast where people will live over the next several decades. At the moment, the situation is unclear. Some information activities are potentially quite footloose, and others seem to be firmly rooted in central metropolitan locations. We need several detailed studies of the locational behavior of information activities to clarify whatever trends may be in progress.

INFORMATION FLOWS THROUGH COMMUNICATIONS MEDIA

When information flows are considered, we enter the realm of spatial process. Spatial process and spatial structure are duals, and the distinction between them is ultimately artificial (Blaut, 1961). For a long time, geographers studied static distributions and often neglected the processes that produced them. Accurate knowledge of process is just as important as accurate knowledge of pattern, and recently geographers have devoted greater attention to process in studies of spatial interaction and spatial diffusion.

Spatial Interaction Analysis

Crowe's argument that human geography must be based on circulation, on "men and things moving," provided the conceptual foundation for postwar interaction studies (Crowe, 1938, p. 14). Crowe and others thought about spatial interaction largely in terms of commodity and people movements. Even though Ullman's comprehensive statement (1956) urged the inclusion of information flows in spatial interaction studies, substantive work concentrated almost exclusively on transportation and commodity flows.

Despite this bias toward things and people, communications gradually assumed greater theoretical importance. Some analysts, like Zipf (1946; 1949), sought to discover principles which govern spatial flows of information. Zipf, Stewart (1947), and Warntz (1957) worked in the context of the gravity model and its variations. More recently, Seneca and Cicchetti (1969) analyzed spatial variations in telegraph message volume in a gravity model context. Mackay (1958), used the same model to measure the effect of a cultural boundary on information flows. A somewhat different approach was taken by Nystuen and Dacey (1961), who used telephone message flows to derive hierarchical relationships among central places.

Whereas Crowe's conception of a spatial interaction geography did not exclude such considerations, he was primarily interested in using place-to-place movements to delimit human regions. Recent work has been more congruent with this original intention. A common technique in such investigations has been to factor-analyze flow matrices of movements among a set of origins and destinations. The extracted factors are interpreted as regional centers and their respective influence zones. Illeris and Pedersen (1968) used telephone calls to delimit ten influence regions in Denmark in this way. Such studies require accurate origin-destination data, and such information is often scarce. The U.S. Post Office Department for example, began to conduct origin destination surveys only recently, and data on point-to-point mail flows is still fragmentary. Telephone message flow data exist, but are often difficult to obtain. In some nations such problems do not exist, and place-to-place interpersonal message volumes are a valuable data source for spatial interaction studies (Johnsson, 1968).

Geographers are often interested in information flows which do not move through formal interpersonal media. In such cases, they must use indirect or surrogate measures. Since many urban taxi trips are made for purposes of interpersonal intercommunication, Goddard (1970) was able to derive functional information regions by analyzing taxi flow patterns. But as Goddard notes (p. 179), the high costs of taxis as opposed to low postal and telephone costs could make functional information regions appear more compact than they actually are. Research now in progress on formal interpersonal flows in Central London will enable Goddard to check the accuracy of the surrogate measure.

Whereas some analysts use information flows to derive functional economic regions, others map information regions because of their usefulness as explanatory variables. Hägerstrand was the original stimulus for such work. According to Morrill and Pitts (1967, p. 418), Hägerstrand asked Swedish farmers how many farms they could name, starting outward from their own, as a means of delimiting the region from which they would most likely receive information. Marble and Nystuen (1962) developed more direct means of estimating the sizes and shapes of the regions from which groups were likely to receive messages. Morrill and Pitts (1967) proposed that we distinguish among individual, local, regional, and long distance information fields and suggested possible measures by which such fields could be delimited (pp. 418–420). Cox, who describes the individual voter as a "node in a communication network along which flows information relevant for the voting decision," finds information regions very important determinants of voting behavior (Cox, 1969A, p. 43; 1969B).

Information flows can also be useful in explaining production patterns and locational behavior. Farmers in central Sweden, for example, do not produce as much as *homo economicus* would. Their failure to match normative models is attributable to satisficing (rather than optimizing) behavior, and to imperfect information. Spatial biases in information circulation are partially responsible for spatial productivity variations (Wolpert, 1964). Similarly, it appears that the quality and quantity of information available to an entrepreneur and his ability to use it effectively determine his success or failure (Pred,

1967). Information regions are powerful explanatory variables. Individuals are nodes in communications fields (Murphey, 1961), and fields and their information contents are major determinants of behavior. Mapping information regions can be useful in several ways, but communications regions achieve their greatest theoretical importance as explanations of human behavior.

Diffusion Theory

The "diffusion of innovation is by definition a function of communication," and there are two basic elements in the study of diffusion process: "the study of links and the study of nodes" (Hägerstand, 1966, p. 27). Nodes are individuals, and links are routes by which information moves from node to node. Geographers have examined interpersonal informal links most often, on the hypothesis that information resulting in innovation acceptance moves through this medium (Morrill, 1970, p. 259). Excellent summaries of the spatial diffusion literature are readily available (Hägerstrand, 1967; Brown, 1968A, 1968B; Gould, 1969) and no review is necessary here. There exists, however, a bias in diffusion work toward interpersonal informal media, and it is important to note some effects different media have in diffusion processes.

Information movements through informal, interpersonal channels produce contagious (wavelike) adoption patterns which emanate from innovation centers. Generally, the friction of distance is high for interpersonal media and roughly similar in all directions around an information source. Distance friction is, of course, an important determinant (among others) of the pattern of diffusion from a source. Formal media adjust spatial relationships among places and radically change some frictions of distance (Abler, 1971). The diffusion patterns which result when information moves through formal interpersonal media—or when nodes move about from place to place, transmitting information as they go—are often *hierarchical* rather than contagious. Innovations move down or up the central place *hierarchy*. Both contagious and hierarchical diffusion operate at the same time, the former locally and the latter at macroscale (Hudson, 1969). We can well imagine, for example, a rumor that a New York brokerage house is going to fail starting on Wall Street and diffusing down the urban hierarchy to Chicago, Los Angeles, and other cities via the telephone network, while it is simultaneously spreading up Manhattan Island and out to Stamford via word of mouth and local telephone conversations. Hägerstrand (1966) described hierarchical diffusion, but most of his theory and substantive work dealt with contagious diffusion.

An example of a phenomenon which evidently diffuses through space in a hierarchical manner is the complex of innovations called "modernization" (Gould, 1970a; Riddell, 1970). Cities and the transportation links which connect them constitute a powerful "formal" communications medium, and the frontier of economic development in modernizing nations is very much an urban frontier. Geographic development analysis may be contrasted to the less spatial viewpoint of those interested in mass communications (Lerner and Schramm, 1965; Rao, 1966; Rogers, 1969). Those interested in formal mass media argue that stimulating economic development is basically a propaganda problem. Formal interpersonal media are rarely mentioned, let alone considered to be of much importance. On the other hand, considerable importance is attached to information movements through informal interpersonal media.

Those concerned with mass communications may be correct in giving highest priority to making mass media available in developing nations. Education and literacy do seem to be fundamental keys to economic development. On the other hand, feedback and reciprocal intercommunications are critical also (U.P.U., 1970). One-way communication may make people receptive to new ideas, but economic development also requires two-way intercommunications. Questions must be heard and answered, doubts must be assuaged, and development agencies must have rapid and accurate feedback on the progress of their programs.

Ultimately, it is *inter*communications which knit areas into functional economic or political units.

> Transactions [information communications] between areas can be viewed as indicators of the flow and concentration of information within a network of human relations in space, and consequently of mutual awareness and at least potentially integrative behavior. Charting the pattern and measuring the direction, intensity, and persistence of transaction flows in space thus offers an insightful window on the process of territorial integration [Soja, 1969].

At some level of interaction, a threshold is crossed and interacting places become firmly linked together. An integrated community is held together by *salient* information flows, and we can measure the territorial integration of a region or nation by determining the extent to which such salient links exist. An analysis of telephone calls in East Africa demonstrates significant national clustering, with Uganda somewhat separated from the rest of an integrated East African network (Soja, 1969).

We need more accurate knowledge of how information, as information, diffuses through formal media. Geographers have concentrated on the spread of artifacts or practices whose adoption implies information diffusion. Analyzing the spread of information as information has been left to journalists and those interested in opinion research (Funkhouser, 1968). Information is power, and tremendous amounts of social power move through space via formal interpersonal and via mass media in ways which have yet to be mapped, analyzed, and explained.

Mass media are particularly important in this respect. Network radio and television, for example, eliminate both cost and time friction. A population homogeneous in its willingness to accept an idea once it has heard it would, if the idea were transmitted over mass media, accept simultaneously and produce "instantaneous" diffusion. Within minutes, for example, news of the assassination of President John Kennedy diffused to virtually the entire population of the United States (Greenberg, 1965).

Studies of information flow, whatever the scale and whatever the media involved, give us more power to govern these processes and the spatial patterns they produce. As long as we were content to describe static patterns, we could not go much beyond genetic explanation of what existed. The emphasis on process inherent in the spatial interaction approach will enable us to understand and explain better the systems which produce patterns of belief and behavior.

EFFECTS OF COMMUNICATIONS AND INFORMATION ON HUMAN SPATIAL BEHAVIOR

Diffusion and spatial interaction studies, in their concern with process, might be characterized as the spatial "syntactics" of communications geography. Important as they are, it is ultimately pragmatics, or the effects of information patterns and flows, which are most important to us.

Perception of the Environment and Space

In information theoretic terms, individuals or groups are selective filters through which information from the environment must pass (Kirk, 1951, 1963). The "filters" are models and theories of the world (Fig. 19-1). They make some experiences meaningful and others irrelevant and unperceived. Every individual has his own unique filter, but we can group individuals into classes of greater or lesser generality on the basis of the characteristics of their filters (Lowenthal, 1961). The basic perceptual model of human behavior places people in information streams, with both the nature of their filters and the differing content of the message streams influencing behavior.

Agricultural land use, for example, has been explained as a product of perceptions of the environment which vary in response to indigenous ideas about land use and "imported" information concerning prices for various crops (Gould, 1965; Brookfield, 1968). Individual decision makers respond to messages from the physical environment and information from the socio-economic environment. What the individual farmer decides to do is a function of these two message streams plus his own motivations and goals. Similarly, different people have different perceptual definitions of what constitutes wilderness in the Minnesota Boundary Water Canoe Area (Lucas, 1964), and people respond in different ways to threatening messages from the environment. The more frequent the message from the environment (e.g., a flood), the more likely people are to take some defensive action to prevent damage (Kates, 1962). Informal interpersonal media seem to be quite important in shaping perceptions of natural hazards (Saarinen, 1966).

Differing perceptions of the physical environment are certainly important elements of human geography, but socio-cultural characteristics of places also attract and repel people. People get information about places from personal experience, from correspondence and telephone conversations with residents, from films, plays, novels, and music ("I Left My Heart in San Francisco"), from television and radio, and through personal conversation with people who have visited them. By asking people to rank-order states or cities in terms of their residential desirability, data can be obtained which yield desirability surfaces representing the mental maps of the groups surveyed (Gould, 1966, 1967). Such maps summarize the total information set people have received from all sources and media. Desirability surfaces are the results of information flows and group values, and are good predictors of future spatial behavior, especially migration.

Information and Migration

Gravity model approaches to migration have now given way to an information-oriented approach. Migrants are sometimes characterized as nodes with finite action spaces, within which information is more abundant close to the node that at a distance (Wolpert, 1965). Migration is more frequent over short distances because of the potential migrant's greater stock of information about close destinations. Information feedback from destinations is critical in migration, especially in rural to urban migration in developing nations. When migrants send back glowing reports of city life, more people are likely to emigrate. If migrants send or bring back negative reports about a place, potential migrants will stay home or go elsewhere (Mabogunje, 1968). Reports from early migrants create a biased action space which affects migration patterns.

Similar principles apply within cities. Residents of American Midwestern cities make residential moves only within a given sector of the metropolis (Adams, 1969). A family from a city's southwestern sector, for example, rarely moves to the northeastern sector. Urban residents possess *awareness spaces* based on information gathered in the course of movements within their action spaces (Clark, 1969). The journey to work, shopping expeditions, and recreational trips enable individuals to garner information about some parts of a city and not others. The mean information fields produced by movements to obtain various commodities and actual household moves are closely correlated (Clark, 1969). When people have more information about the city sector in which they live than about others, they are unlikely to move to an unknown area.

The ways information governs migration suggest the possibility of an information theoretical reformulation of the gravity model of migration. Traditionally, size has been equated with mass. If we could measure the amount of information about place *A* available to people at place *B*, and vice-versa, these two information stocks could be used as the mass terms. Migration should be a function of the product of the information stocks, divided by some power of the distance between them. Such an information-based gravity model might provide powerful explanations of migration at several scales. Moreover, if we could measure spatial variations in information stocks, we could construct information potential maps analogous to population potential maps (Warntz, 1964).

Understanding the uses people make of the information they receive from all sources is vitally important. We desperately wish to diffuse several kinds of information (birth control, education, economic development, etc.) and until we fully understand information flows among nodes which receive, process, and transmit information *selectively,* we will have great difficulty spreading such ideas.

General Cultural Effects of Communications Media

In the same way that closed gene pools produce distinct racial groups, closed information pools eventually produce distinct cultures and subcultures. Conversely, open information pools produce cultural homogeneity just as open gene pools produce racial homogenization. Thus any technology which promotes spatial interaction should blur boundaries and homogenize, and the general modern trend has been toward reduced racial and cultural isolation and greater racial and cultural homogeneity.

Because the mass media dominate our thinking and because mass media are homogenizing forces, we tend to think that cultural diversity will soon disappear. We hear reports, for example, of local and regional dialects disappearing under the impact of national radio and television ("Talking Like a Native," 1970). We must realize, however, that the mass media dominance characteristic of the period between 1920 and 1970 is a very unusual and transitory development. Throughout history, almost all people received almost all their information via interpersonal media. Books and newspapers changed this situation somewhat, and radio and television changed it even more. But the mass media have probably already peaked in general importance in advanced nations, and during the next several decades the important innovations will be in formal interpersonal communications systems and in do-it-yourself (informal) mass media.

Interpersonal media and informal mass media tend to make people more heterogeneous. Because our time is limited, we normally communicate with people with similar interests or jobs. We form distinct intercommunications groups with the messages flowing among members of one group being quite different from the messages flowing among members of another. Interpersonal media tend to divide people into groups, as do informal mass media, which usually channel messages among small numbers of like-minded people. Because technological innovations will continue to make interpersonal and small group media more sophisticated and less expensive than they are now, diversity will be promoted.

Evidence of increased diversity already exists. Youth culture, with its rural and urban communes and distinctive life style, suggests renewed interest in small group homogeneity (Roszak, 1968). Black power, brown power, and resurgent ethnic consciousness are further examples. The production of regional editions of "national" magazines (Twedt, 1968) further vitiates the homogenizing power of mass printed media. Postal area coding and computerized mailing lists make it possible to vary both advertising and editorial content to suit regional tastes (Abler, 1970).

Similar developments are evident in radio and television. New transmission techniques portend point-to-point communications capacity which appears almost unlimited by today's standards. There appears to be no long-run technological obstacle to widespread use of audio, visual, facsimile, and even three-dimensional holographic communications media by the public at large. Moreover, CATV (Community Antenna Television Systems) open an additional 60 television channels for local or regional use. CATV has been diffusing up the urban hierarchy since 1947 (Darby, 1973), and by the late 1960's and early 1970's the innovation was penetrating the largest metropolitan areas. Thus we can look forward to local television programming analogous to the regional editions of magazines that are now circulating. Twenty years hence, the diverse metropolitan area could have one or more black-oriented television channels, perhaps a Puerto Rican or Chicano channel, and distinct neighborhoods in the city could have their own T.V. channels. CATV lowers the threshold needed to support a T.V. channel and in doing so it makes it easier for small groups of like people to interact and thus reinforce their common similarities and their collective difference from other groups (de Sola Pool, 1968).

Interpersonal and mass media are being scrambled into revolutionary combinations, and the new hybrids will sharply reverse the generally homogenizing trend of the last several centuries. Specialized journals now enable those who are inclined to do so to learn more and more about less and less. Hybrids of interpersonal and mass media will enable small groups to isolate themselves and communicate only with kindred spirits.

Because information affects places as much as places affect information, the spatial corollary seems clear. Places should become more differentiated. Californians may become more Californian, Southerners more Southern, and New York City residents more parochial than ever. Implicit in current and future trends is a renaissance of regionalism and a strong sense of local community, both of which have been on the wane for some decades. The new media could produce a cultural landscape which will make future geographers yearn nostalgically for the uncomplicated spatial organization of the mid-twentieth century.

But differentiation is not guaranteed, any more than homogenization is. In the past, regional homogeneity and differences among regions were based on a circularly causal process: areas became different because they were isolated from each other; and because they were isolated from one another, they became even more different. Today, while new media are making local information circulation easier, they are simultaneously doing peculiar things to distance. Throughout human history, interaction costs have always increased with distance. Costs of movement still increase with distance, but the nature of such functions changes constantly. Generally, terminal costs are rising and line-haul costs are dropping, which means that distance, as such, has a decreasing effect on cost. Many postal services have been available at flat-rate prices for over a century, and flat-rate pricing is increasingly important in telecommunications. When satellite facilities are used, for example, there are no differences in transmission and terminal costs whether the call moves eight or eight thousand kilometers. Utilizing the third dimension completely eliminates distance-cost relationships in two-dimensional terrestrial space. In communications the historic trend has clearly been towards decreased friction of distance (Abler, 1968, pp. 270–277). Electronic media will soon give us the power to create a communications world without distance, and in such a world, it will no longer be necessary to agglomerate together in small areas to communicate with like people.

What a frictionless communications space, in conjunction with the shift to a quaternary-oriented society, portends for general spatial organization is unclear. Current evidence is contradictory. We encounter accounts of migration from central cities by quaternary functions whose managers are using new communications technologies to become footloose in their locational behavior ("The Flight from the Cities," 1970). Within the same month, reports (emanating from the same news organization) tell us that skyscrapers will continue to thrive and multiply in metropolitan centers because of almost insatiable demands for central metropolitan space by quaternary activities (Engels, 1970). What does seem clear is that in the future people who can communicate via formal, interpersonal media will no longer have to be close to one another to do so.

Community no longer requires propinquity and the urban realm of the United States is really a non-place realm (Webber, 1963, 1964). Mass media transmit urbanity to the entire nation. In the future, even more than now, the new hybrid media will permit *inter*communication without respect to the locations of communicators.

The new media will be powerful *necessary* conditions of human behavior. They will make it possible for members of small "systematic" interest groups to scatter over the face of the earth. Alternatively, advanced communication technology will make it possible for special interest groups to gather together in distinct places and intensify human and landscape differences, while at the same time maintaining whatever contacts they must or wish to have with other specialized groups via telecommunications. Which trend will ultimately predominate or which compromise between the two extremes will eventually evolve is an open question. The development of hybrid media and the true shift to quaternary organization are just beginning, and it is genuinely difficult to say which trend will be favored.

Whichever is the case, it does seem evident that general spatial organization in advanced nations is becoming a matter of choice. Many economic constraints on locational behavior are being relaxed. If we choose to create small, intimate, place-based communities, electronic communications will allow us to retain the advantages of limited participation with other peoples at distant places. Alternatively, if we choose to scatter indiscriminately to satisfy idiosyncratic locational criteria, electronic communications keep us in close contact with other members of our non-place based communities. Frictionless communications space is a necessary condition for either alternative, but it is *sufficient* for neither. The sufficient conditions of general spatial organization in the century ahead rest in society's poorly articulated spatial goals and desires.

GENERAL RESEARCH PROBLEMS IN COMMUNICATIONS GEOGRAPHY

Communications media could easily have as much effect on the behavior and general spatial organization of humanity in the next fifty years as automobile and air transportation have had in the last fifty. As social scientists concerned with explaining human spatial behavior, we must describe and analyze information flows and the media through which they move if we wish to understand what people are doing now, modify or govern what they will do in the years ahead, and predict future spatial organization.

Accordingly, several general questions and the numerous specific questions they imply should be answered more completely than they have been.

1. Where are communications activities located? Geographers have produced an abundant literature on the locations of everything from avocado plantations to zinc smelters, but virtually no analyses of the locations of corporate headquarters, government agencies, and communications media. For all our methodological and quantitative sophistication, basic locational descriptions and maps showing where important things are remain the bedrock foundation of geographical analysis. For the most part we simply don't know where communications activities are.

2. How does information circulate in space? We have no maps which identify the places where information is dense and those where it is sparse. Most communications media are black boxes. We address a letter and drop it in a mailbox or dial a sequence of digits into a telephone, and little know (and care less) by what spatial magic these messages arrive at their intended destinations. Similarly, most of us have no idea whatsoever of how the evening news which cascades from our radio and television receivers is gathered from around the world and around the block, evaluated, filtered, summarized, and presented. Geographers know as much and probably more than anyone else about how information diffuses through informal media, but that knowledge is of increasingly limited value because it is not matched by equally detailed knowledge of information flows through mass and formal interpersonal media.

3. How does information affect human spatial behavior? "Man is a goal directed information filter" (Gould, 1970b). The behavioral consequences of a given bit or block of information depend upon peoples' goals and upon the nature of their information filtering processes. To answer the spatial riddles posed by the current, contradictory trends in spatial behavior, we need much better knowledge of both. Further progress in geography depends upon more powerful and quantifiable theories of communications-based behavior in space, and on the substantive investigations which will enable us to empirically verify our theories.

REFERENCES

Abler, Ronald. (1968). "The Geography of Intercommunications Systems: The Postal and Telephone Systems in the United States." Unpublished Ph.D. Dissertation, University of Minnesota.

———. (1970). "ZIP-Code Areas as Statistical Regions," *Professional Geographer,* 22, 5, pp. 270–274.

———. (1971). "Distance, Intercommunications, and Geography," *Proceedings of the Association of American Geographers*, 3, pp. 1–4.

———, John S. Adams, and Peter Gould. (1971). *Spatial Organization: The Geographer's View of the World.* Englewood Cliffs, N.J.: Prentice-Hall.

Adams, John S. (1969). "Directional Bias in Intraurban Migration," *Economic Geography,* 45, 4, (October, 1969), pp. 302–323.

Bell, William H. (1965). "The Diffusion of Radio and Television Broadcasting in the United States." Unpublished M.S. Thesis, Pennsylvania State University, Department of Geography.

Berry, Brian J. L. (1970). "The Geography of the

United States in the Year 2000," *Ekistics*, 29, 174, pp. 339–351.

Blaut, James. (1961). "Space and Process," *Professional Geographer*, 13, 4 (July, 1961), pp. 1–7.

Brookfield, Harold C. (1968). "The Money that Grows on Trees: The Consequences of an Innovation within a Man-environment System," *Australian Geographical Studies*, 6, pp. 97–119.

———. (1969). "On the Environment as Perceived," *Progress in Geography*, Vol. 1. Edited by Christopher Board and others. London: Edward Arnold. pp. 51–80.

Brown, Lawrence, (1968a). *Diffusion Dynamics*. Lund: Gleerup. Lund Studies in Geography. Series B. Human Geography. No. 29.

———. (1968b). *Diffusion Processes and Location: A Conceptual Framework and Bibliography*. Philadelphia: Regional Science Research Institute.

Cavaillès, Henri. (1940). "Introduction a une geographie de la circulation," *Annales de Géographie*, 49, pp. 170–182.

Clark, W. A. V. (1969). "Information Flows and Intra-Urban Migration: An Empirical Analysis," *Proceedings of the Association of American Geographers*, 1, pp. 38–41.

Cooley, Charles H. (1894). "The Theory of Transportation," *Proceedings of the American Economic Association*, 9, 3 (May, 1894). Reprinted in *Sociological Theory and Social Research*. New York: Holt, 1930, a collection of Cooley's works. Page references in this article refer to the reprinting.

Cowan, Peter, and others. (1969). *The Office: A Facet of Urban Growth*. London: Heinemann Educational Books.

Cox, Kevin R. (1969a). "The Voting Decision in Intra-Urban Space," *Proceedings of the Association of American Geographers*, 1 pp. 43–46.

———. (1969b). "The Voting Decision in a Spatial Context," in *Progress in Geography*, Vol. 1. Edited by Christopher Board and others. London: Edward Arnold, pp. 81–117.

Crowe, P. R. (1938). "On Progress in Geography," *Scottish Geographical Magazine*, 54, pp. 1–19.

Darby, David. (1973). "Cable Television: Some Questions and Answers." Unpublished R. D. Hesis, Pennsylvania State University, Department of Geography.

Deutsch, Karl W. (1966). *The Nerves of Government*. N.Y.: The Free Press.

Engels, J. A. (1970). "Skyscrapers: No Refuge in Superlatives," *Washington Post*, November 21.

"The Flight from the Cities." (1970). *Newsweek*, November 30, pp. 58–61. *Fortune* magazine. (1968). May, pp. 168–199.

Funkhouser, G. Ray. (1968). *A General Mathematical Model of Information Diffusion*. Stanford: Stanford University Institute for Communication Research.

Goddard, J. B. (1970). "Functional Regions Within the City Centre: A Study by Factor Analysis of Taxi Flows in Central London," *Transactions of the Institute of British Geographers*, 49, pp. 161–182.

Gottmann, Jean. (1961). *Megalopolis*. Cambridge, Mass.: M.I.T. Press.

———. (1966). "Why the Skyscraper?" *Geographical Review*, 56, 2, pp. 190–212.

Gould, Peter R. (1965) "Wheat on Kilimanjaro: The Perception of Choice within Game and Learning Model Framework," *General Systems Yearbook*, 10, pp. 157–166.

———. (1966). *On Mental Maps*. Ann Arbor: Michigan Inter-University Community of Mathematical Geographers. Discussion Paper No. 9.

———. (1967). "Structuring Information on Spatio-temporal Preferences," *Journal of Regional Science*, 7, 2, (Supplement), pp. 259–274.

———. (1969). *Spatial Diffusion*. Washington; Association of American Geographers. Commission on College Geography Resource Paper No. 4.

———. (1970a) "The Modernization of Tanzania in a Spatial Setting," *World Politics*, 22, 2, pp. 149–170.

———. (1970b). Personal conversation.

Greenberg, Bradley S. (1965). "Diffusion of News About the Kennedy Assassination," in *The Kennedy Assassination and the American Public: Social Communication in Crisis*. ed. by Bradley S. Greenberg and Edwin B. Parker.

Stanford: Stanford University Press, pp. 89–98.

Gustafson, W. Eric. (1959). "Printing and Publishing," in *Made in New York,* ed. by Max Hall. Cambridge, Mass.: Harvard University Press. pp. 135–239.

Hägerstrand, Torsten. (1966). "Aspects of the Spatial Structure of Social Communication and the Diffusion of Information," *Papers of the Regional Science Association,* 16, pp. 27–42.

———. (1967). *Innovation Diffusion as A Spatial Process.* Chicago: University of Chicago Press.

Hall, Peter. (1966). *The World Cities.* London: World University Library.

Hückel, G. A. (1906–7). "La géographie de la circulation selon Friedrich Ratzel," *Annales de Géographie,* 15, pp. 401–418; 16, pp. 1–14.

Hudson, John C. (1969). "Diffusion in a Central Place System," *Geographical Analysis,* 1, 1, pp. 45–58.

Illeris, Sven, and Paul O. Pedersen. (1968). *Central Places and Functional Regions in Denmark: Factor Analysis of Telephone Traffic.* Lund: Gleerup. Lund Studies in Geography, Series B. Human Geography, No. 31.

Innis, Donald Q. (1953). "The Geography of Radio in Canada," *The Canadian Geographer,* 3, pp. 89–97.

———. (1960). "Radio and Television in the United States," *Focus,* January.

Innis, Harold A. (1944). "On the Economic Significance of Culture," *Journal of Economic History, Supplement, the Tasks of Economic History,* 4, pp. 80–97.

———. (1950). *Empire and Communications.* Oxford: The Clarendon Press.

———. (1964). *The Bias of Communication.* Toronto: University of Toronto Press.

Johnsson, Bruno. (1968). "Utilizing Telegrams for Describing Contact Patterns and Spatial Interaction," *Geografiska Annaler,* Series B. Vol. 50, 1, pp. 48–51.

Kates, Robert W. (1962). *Hazard and Choice Perception in Flood Plain Management.* Chicago: Department of Geography, University of Chicago. Department of Geography Research Paper No. 78.

Kirk, William. (1951). "Historical Geography and the Concept of the Behavioral Environment," *Indian Geographical Journal,* 26, pp. 152–160.

———. (1963). "Problems in Geography," *Geography,* 48, pp. 357–371.

Langley, G. A. (1963). "Telecommunications in Malaya," *Journal of Tropical Geography,* 17, pp. 79–91.

Lerner, Daniel, and Wilbur Schramm, eds. (1965). *Communication and Change in the Developing Countries.* Honolulu: East-West Center Press.

Lowenstein, Werner R. (1970). "Intercellular Communication," *Scientific American,* 222, 5, pp. 78–86.

Lowenthal, David. (1961). "Geography, Experience, and Imagination: Towards a Geographical Epistemology," *Annals of the Association of American Geographers,* 51, pp. 241–260.

Lucas, Robert C. (1964). "Wilderness Perception and Use: The Example of the Boundary Waters Canoe Area," *Natural Resources Journal,* 3, 3, pp. 394–411.

Mabogunje, Akin. (1968). *Urbanization in Nigeria.* London: University of London Press.

Mackay, J. R. (1958). "The Interactance Hypothesis and Boundaries in Canada," *Canadian Geographer,* 11, pp. 1–8.

Marble, Duane F., and John D. Nystuen. (1962). "An Approach to the Direct Measurement of Community Mean Information Fields," *Papers and Proceedings of the Regional Science Association,* 11, pp. 99–109.

McLuhan, Marshall. (1962). *The Gutenberg Galaxy.* Toronto: University of Toronto Press.

———. (1966). *Understanding Media: The Extensions of Man.* New York: McGraw-Hill.

Meier, Richard L. (1962). *A Communication Theory of Urban Growth.* Cambridge, Mass.: M.I.T. Press.

Miller, Stewart E. (1966). "Communication by Laser," *Scientific American,* 214, 1, pp. 19–27.

Morrill, Richard L. (1970). "The Shape of Diffusion in Space and Time," *Economic Geography,* 46, 2 (Supplement), pp. 259–268.

———, and Forrest L. Pitts. (1967). "Marriage, Migration, and the Mean Information Field: A Study in Uniqueness and Generality," *Annals of the Association of American Geographers,* 57, 2, pp. 401–422.

Murphey, Gardner. (1961). "Toward a Field

Theory of Communication," *Journal of Communication,* 11, 4, pp. 196–201.

Nystuen, John D., and Michael F. Dacey. (1961). "A Graph Theory Interpretation of Nodal Regions," *Papers and Proceedings of the Regional Science Association,* 7, pp. 29–42.

de Sola Pool, Ithiel. (1968). "Social Trends," *Science and Technology,* April, pp. 87–101.

Pred, Allan. (1967). *Behavior and Location.* Lund: Gleerup. Lund Studies in Geography, Series B, Human Geography, No. 27.

Rao, Y. V. Lakshamana. (1966). *Communications and Development.* Minneapolis: University of Minnesota Press.

Ratzel, Friedrich. (1921). *Anthropogeographie.* Third Edition. Stuttgart: Engelhorns.

———. (1929). *Politische Geographie.* Third edition. Munich: Oldenbourg.

Riddell, Barry. (1970). *The Spatial Development of the Transportation Infrastructure of Sierra Leone: Economic Development and National Cohesion.* Evanston, Illinois: Northwestern University Press.

Rogers, Everett M. (1969). *Modernization Among Peasants: The Impact of Communication.* New York: Holt, Rinehart, and Winston.

Roszak, Theodore. (1966). *The Making of a Counter Culture.* Garden City, New York: Doubleday.

Saarinen, Thomas F. (1966). *Perception of Drought Hazard on the Great Plains.* Chicago: Department of Geography, University of Chicago. Department of Geography Research Paper No. 106.

Seneca, Joseph J., and Charles J. Cicchetti. (1969). "A Gravity Model Analysis of the Demand for Public Communication," *Journal of Regional Science,* 9, 3, pp. 459–470.

Smith, Gregory L. (1967). "The Functional Basis of the ZIP Code and Sectional Center System," *Yearbook of the Association of Pacific Coast Geographers,* 29, pp. 97–109.

Soja, Edward W. (1969). "Telephone Communications and Territorial Integration in East Africa: An Introduction to Transaction Flow Analysis," *Ekistics,* 28, 168, pp. 356–359. Reprinted from *The East Lakes Geographer,* 4 (1968), pp. 39–57.

———. (1970). "Talking Like A Native," *Newsweek,* March 9, 1970.

Sorre, Max. (1948). *Les Fondements de la Géographie Humaine. Tome II. Les Fondements Techniques.* Paris: Armand Colin.

Spencer, Herbert. (1910). *Principles of Sociology,* Vol. 1. Third edition. New York: Appleton.

Stewart, John Q. (1947). "Empirical Mathematical Rules Concerning the Distribution and Equilibrium of Population," *Geographical Review,* 37, pp. 461–485.

Törnqvist, Gunnar. (1967). *TV-ägandets utveckling i Sverige 1956–65 (Growth of TV Ownership in Sweden, 1956–65).* Stockholm: Alqvist and Wiksell. English Summary.

———. (1968). *Flows of Information and the Location of Economic Activity.* Lund: Gleerup. Lund Studies in Geography, Series B. Human Geography, No. 30.

Twedt, Dik Warren. (1968). "Toward a Single System of Standard Geographical Units," *Journal of Marketing,* 32, pp. 71–73.

Ullman, Edward L. (1956). "The Role of Transportation and the Bases for Interaction," *Man's Role in Chaging the Face of the Earth.* William L. Thomas, Jr., Ed. Chicago: University of Chicago Press, pp. 862–882.

Universal Postal Union. (1970). "Memorandum on the Role of the Post as a Factor in Economic and Social Development," *Union Postale,* September, 1970, pp. 132A–147A.

U.S. Department of Labor, Bureau of Labor Statistics. (1969). *Tomorrow's Manpower Needs.* Vol. IV, *The National Industry-Occupational Matrix and Other Manpower Data.* Washington, U.S.G.P.O. Bulletin No. 1606.

Van Cleef, Eugene. (1937). *Trade Centers and Trade Routes.* New York: D. Appleton-Century.

Vernon, Raymond. (1963). *Metropolis, 1985.* Garden City, N. Y.: Doubleday.

Wärneryd, Olof. (1968). *Interdependence in Urban Systems.* Göteborg: Regiondonsult Aktiebolag.

Warntz, William. (1957). "Contributions Toward a Macro-economic Geography: A Review," *Geographical Review,* 47, pp. 420–424.

———. (1964). "A New Map of the Surface of Population Potential for the United States,

1960," *Geographical Review*, 54, pp. 170–184.

Webber, Melvin. (1963). "Order in Diversity, Community Without Propinquity," in *Cities and Space: The Future Use of Urban Land*, ed. by Lowden Wingo. Baltimore: Johns Hopkins University Press.

———. (1964). "The Urban Place and the Non-place Urban Realm," in *Explorations into Urban Structure*, ed. by Melvin Webber and others. Philadelphia: University of Philadelphia Press.

———, and Carolyn Webber. (1967). "Culture, Territoriality, and the Elastic Mile," in *Taming Megalopolis*, Vol. 1, ed. by H. Wentworth Eldredge. Garden City, N. Y.: Doubleday.

Wolpert, Julian. (1964). "The Decision Process in Spatial Context," *Annals of the Association of American Geographers*, 54, 4, pp. 537–558.

———. (1965). "Behavioral Aspects of the Decision to Migrate," *Papers of the Regional Science Association*, 15, pp. 159–169.

Zipf, George Kingsley. (1946). "Some Determinants of the Circulation of Information," *American Journal of Sociology*, 59, pp. 401–421.

———. (1949). *Human Behavior and the Principle of Least Effort*. Cambridge, Mass.: Addison-Wesley.

Selection 20

Flows of Information and the Location of Economic Activities

G. Törnqvist

INTRODUCTION

On the occasion of the installation of professors at the University of Lund on 9th December 1967, two inaugural lectures were given under the common title of "The process of urbanization in the perspective of organizational theory." The first of these lectures contained a synoptic presentation of some of the ideas on which are based research projects now in progress on the subject of economic geography at Lund. The present article is a translation of this lecture with the subtitle "Flows of information and the location of economic activities."

In the second lecture, Eric Rhenman, professor of business administration, spoke on the subject of "Company environment and administration systems." Some of the opinions expressed in the latter lecture will be presented briefly at the end of this article.

The subjects of the two lectures were chosen so that they would show important points of contact between matters of particular topical interest in the sphere of (*a*) economic geography, and (*b*) the organizational theory that has been developed and the research concerning administration systems that is being carried on within the field of business administration.

It should thus be borne in mind that the presentation in this article has been written in order to give a purely oral report within definite time-limits. The descriptions of the research in progress are therefore of a highly summarized nature. Maps, reports on experimental models that have been constructed, and compilations of quantitative data, have been omitted. Detailed accounts of theories, methodology, material collections and results will be presented in several separate research-reports during 1968 and 1969.

Geografiska Annaler, vol. 50B, 1968, pp. 99–107. Reprinted by permission of the author and editor.

SWEDISH URBANIZATION—SOME DATA[1]

Like many other countries, Sweden has undergone during the present century a thorough transformation from an agrarian to an urbanized society. The occupational structure of the Swedish economy has radically changed. At the turn of the century, more than half of the country's economically active population was still engaged in agriculture and its ancillary industries; by 1965 the figure had dropped to a mere 12 percent. In their stead, the "urban" sectors of the economy—manufacturing industry, transport, storage and communications, trade and services—have increased their proportions and now employ nearly 90 percent of the economically active population.

During recent years, important changes have taken place among the urban sectors of the economy. The increase in the numbers of employees engaged in manufacturing industry, transport and communications has declined. The employment figures for trade have continued to increase, but it is primarily the sector of the economy called "services etc." in the official statistics that has shown the largest relative increase.

The changes in employment between different sectors of the economy, and between subsectors in them, have been successively accompanied by an adaptation to them of the location of workplaces and homes, and thus by a change in the geographical distribution of the population in the country as a whole. About a hundred years ago, probably hardly more than 10 percent of the population of Sweden lived in what are called "densely populated places or localities"[2] in today's official statistics. At the turn of the century, 36 percent lived in such localities, and in 1965 approximately 77 percent. It is expected that by 1980 the proportion of the population living in densely populated places will be 80–85 percent.

However, the present definition of a "densely populated place" is not suitable for a satisfactory evaluation of the extent of the present and future process of urbanization. As a result of the increase in car ownership, for example, many people may have their homes outside the densely populated places but their place of work in such places. Perhaps I may conclude this introductory survey with a few words about development in some of the country's densely populated regions and urban regions. These regions can be regarded as functional units which may consist of a densely populated place and its trade, service or commutation environment areas. The major urban regions are often multinucleate, i.e., they consist of several large and small closely-adjoining centers with interrelationships of such a kind that the regions should be regarded as units in future planning.

Without entering in detail into any questions of demarcation, it should be mentioned that the 12 largest urban regions in 1965 accommodated more than 4 million people, or about 55 percent of the country's population. Of these, Greater Stockholm, Greater Gothenburg, and the Malmö–Lund–Landskrona–Helsingborg region contained a total of 3 million. Present forecasts indicate a continued heavy concentration of economic activities and of population in the large urban regions. A much-discussed forecast expects, for example, that about half of Sweden's population will be living in the three big-city regions by the year 2000 (Kristensson, 1967, and Skiss till regionplan för Stockholmstrakten "Draft regional plan for the Stockholm region," 1967).

THE RESEARCH PROGRAM ON THE URBANIZATION PROCESS

The process of transformation I have outlined, its causes, and its consequences for the community, for different sectors of the economy and for the individual, is occupying and will continue to occupy researchers working within a wide range of disciplines—medical students, technologists, scientists, sociologists and economists. For those engaged on national, regional and local planning, the production of reliable forecasts of future development is a matter of fundamental importance. At the same time it is essential to know something about the means by which it may be possible for development to be affected, bearing in mind the already existing potential for the society of the future.

During the next few years, Sweden's departments of social and economic geography will devote thorough study to questions concerned with the process of urbanization. Within a total of about twenty research projects, different aspects of the urbanization process—its causes and effects—will be dealt with. Several of these projects will be conducted in close collaboration with the departments of political economy, business administration and sociology at various universities.

Within the field of economic geography, we regard it as an essential task to study the process of urbanization from the points of view of the national economy and of individual firms. I shall content myself here with giving a brief account of the investigations that have been started on this subject at the Lund department of geography.

FROM THE STUDY OF FLOWS OF GOODS TO THE STUDY OF FLOWS OF INFORMATION

It has been said that:

> Ultimately, urbanization is one aspect of the specialization of technique, and of the horizontal linkage between activities that is thereby rendered necessary. Specialists can arrive at finished wholes only through collaboration. The aggregation of enterprises and people has shown itself in the course of time to be a beneficial framework of organization—at least from the point of view of production—for this necessary teamwork.
>
> The principle of horizontal linkage, and thus urbanization itself, is based on the art of moving materials, people and information. (Translated from Hägerstrand, 1964.)

Difficulties in effecting these removals affect the location of different economic activities. Great attention has been devoted, for example in the theories concerning the location of industry, to the cost of transporting goods. (For a more detailed presentation, see e.g., Lösch, 1944, Ponsard, 1955 and 1958, Greenhut, 1956, and Isard, 1956.) The flows of goods and payments between different sectors of our national economy have been surveyed by "input-output" analysis and by other means. (Höglund & Werin, 1964.) In known location-theories, however, relatively little attention has been paid to what I should like to call flows of information in the community, and to the ways in which these may conceivably in certain circumstances affect the location of the activities concerned. But a start has been made in this direction in the discussion that has been carried on regarding "external economies." (Bohm, 1964, and Thorngren, 1967.)

The investigations carried out show that for many firms the cost of the transportation of goods is no longer a factor of essential importance that is taken into account when they have to make a decision on location. (Törnqvist, 1963.) There are of course still heavy basic manufacturing industries that are strongly tied to their sources of raw materials. There are also industries that are tied to regionally restricted marked-areas because of transport costs. However, there has been a manifest tendency among these two groups of industries for the advantages of large-scale operation to weigh more and more heavily in the scales while at the same time the cost of transportation has diminished in relative importance. In Sweden, as elsewhere, this has had the result that we have obtained increasingly large yet fewer and fewer production-units or plants of this type. At the same time, in many cases the production processes have been very strongly rationalized, so that employment in these units has stopped growing despite a great increase in production.

Manufacturing industries in Sweden employing increasingly large numbers of workers are of another type. Many of them can be described as assembly plants. The raw material consists of semi-manufactured goods and finished parts. The finished products have a high commercial value in relation to their weight. The industrial units form components in mighty systems of assembly plants with subsuppliers in many stages of production, dispersed over a great many different places throughout Sweden. This growing group of industries employs today approximately between one-half and two-thirds of all the employees in manufacturing industries in Sweden. For production units in this sector, the cost of transportation is a matter of secondary importance as far as their expansion and their choice of a location are concerned. Other factors are of greater importance.

If it is desired to explain the growth of the big-city regions in particular, we have thought it necessary to divert attention from flows and handling of goods towards flows of information, and the contacts that are needed for these between firms, organizations and public administration. In other words, interest has been focused on a study of the transportation of information instead of on a study of the transportation of goods.

PERSONAL CONTACTS AND LOCATION OF ECONOMIC ACTIVITIES

The following assumption is the basis of the investigations I shall now present:

An essential motive force in the process of urbanization—and in this case primarily the concentration of certain activities in large urban regions—is the need for contacts and for the exchange of information between increasingly specialized operational functions in the community.

Many of these contacts are of such a routine nature that they can be maintained by means of telecommunications and correspondence. These flows of information are of interest if it is desired to survey contact-patterns between different activities. But they are probably scarcely capable of affecting the location of the activities. However, there is much evidence to support the view that the most important contacts cannot be maintained with adequate efficiency by letters and telecommunications but demand *direct personal contacts* between personnel, and thus passenger transportation. That these contacts demand the personal attendance of often highly expert personnel is probably bound up with the fact that the contacts in many cases involve considerable elements of what we might call problem-solving, planning, keeping an eye on the course of events, pulse-feeling and reconnaissance. The contacts often take the form of talks and discussions in which personal effort is of great importance. Time studies show that business leaders and high-ranking executives spend a great deal of their working time on this kind of activity. (Höglund, 1953, Carlson, 1964, Stewart, 1967.)

> Executives spend a large fraction of their time surveying the economic, technical, political, and social environment to identify new conditions that call for new actions. They probably spend an ever larger fraction of their time, individually or with their associates, seeking to invent, design, and develop possible courses of action for handling situations where a decision is needed. They spend a small fraction of their time in choosing among alternative actions already de-

veloped to meet an identified problem and already analysed for their consequensis. The three fractions, added together, account for most of what executives do [Simon, 1965].

The importance of personal effort can hardly be measured. But we know from research in the psychology of economics, in sociology and in the innovation theory that has been developed in social geography, for example, as well as from other sources, that the information and impulses that are of importance for human behavior and action are diffused mostly by means of personal face-to-face contacts between individuals. The diffusion of information via mass media has its greatest influence on leaders of public opinion in the community, and these in their turn affect their environment through personal contacts. The diffusion models that have been developed are very similar to those used for describing the spread of epidemics. (For a general scientific survey, see Törnqvist, 1967.)

As regards flows of information by means of personal contacts between firms, organizations and public administration, we believe that these follow a quite well-developed contact-pattern. It appears to be an essential task to approach and survey these.

So far, there exists only one special investigation referring to personal contacts through a special communications-network—namely, all the internal airlines in Sweden. 75 to 80 percent of the flights made on these are business trips. During a certain period, those traveling on business have been filling in a questionnaire. Among the information they have given on this form is their function or position in their company, the organization or government department concerned, and the function or functions they are visiting in other companies, organizations etc. (the purpose of their journey). For indicating the "functions" in question, lists are used containing 60 positions designated in accordance with the nomenclature for positions that is used by the Swedish Employers Confederation and other organizations, with some additions. Incidentally it may be mentioned that these positions in their turn are divided into position levels.

By systematizing and analyzing this comprehensive material it is possible to show, in a highly aggregated form, part of the mutual dependence on contacts by personal approaches between different functions in the community. The frequency of contacts between different operational functions varies greatly.[3] The data show distinct contact-blocks containing functions with high mutual contact-frequencies. Other groups of functions appear to be remarkably isolated. Investigations are at present being made referring to personal contacts made by the use of other means of communication and over short distances, for example *within* our big-city regions. As these investigations have not been concluded, the following must be regarded as preliminary and indefinite information.

If, for example, we take the considerable part of the data that concerns persons employed in manufacturing industries, the investigations made so far show that the functions or positions having active personal contacts with one another are to be found inside what in organization theory are called the firm's *administrative units* (*information units or decision units*). It may be said that a distinctive feature of these is that they receive, process, and give information. (A in Fig. 20-1) The personal contacts between the information units in different firms show high rates of frequency. There is also a lively flow of information between these information units in the firms and, for example, certain functions in government administration, banks and research outside industry.

The isolated functions with few personal

contacts are found primarily in the firms' *operating units* (*production units or manufacturing units*), i.e., the units that primarily receive, process and issue materials and goods. (P in Fig. 20-1) Personal contacts between these operating units, and between them and the previously-mentioned information units, seem to be very limited.

Other investigations indicate that the contacts referring to the operating units are routinized, often take the form of the giving of orders, and can be dealt with by telecommunications and correspondence. (Thorngren, 1967.)

It would take up too much time here to enter in detail into the available possibilities of using experimental models to quantify the importance of these personal contacts as a location factor. Moreover, hitherto it has been necessary to restrict these experimental models to apply to the cost of personal transportation and the time that is needed for maintaining these contacts in the cases of different location-alternatives. Let me merely mention that the experiments made indicate that a regional agglomeration of the firms' information units bring about considerable savings in expenses for the firms. I do not believe, however, that the costs side is the most important one in this connection.

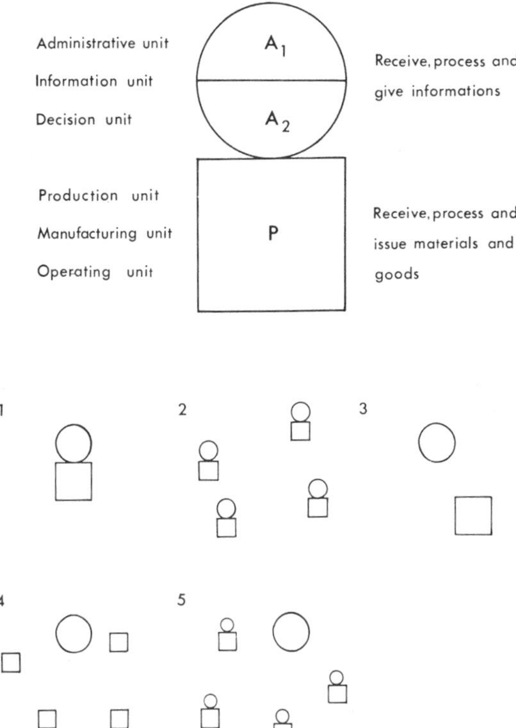

Fig. 20-1 Top: Theoretical division of a firm into functional units or layers. Bottom: Five possible location-alternatives or combinations of these units.

FUNCTIONAL CLASSIFICATION OF THE SWEDISH ECONOMY

In the perspective of what I have said, I shall conclude my presentation by drawing attention to some regional development-tendencies in the Swedish economy.

For the regional descriptions of employment development in the Swedish economy that have been made hitherto, the starting point has been the sector concept that has long been used in our and in other nations' official statistics. This standard industrial classification is mainly based on a product- or commodity-classification of different economic activities. If we continue to take manufacturing industry as an example, this means that all the employees in an industrial plant or firm—regardless of the function they perform or the position they hold in the firm—are assigned to a particular sector, according to the products that are manufactured in the firm's operating units. The sector designations state which raw material or production process predominates in the actual operation or production. (Törnqvist, 1964.)

As I have mentioned, in the location analysis that have now been started, attention has passed from studies of product flows to studies of information flows. This being the case, classifications of the Swedish economy according to sectors and products seem hardly suitable for a description of regional employment development.

In order to get at what we believe to be the essential features of regional development, it appears necessary to make a more functional analysis of our economy—an analysis that is based on organizational or informational classifications of different economic activities. For this analysis, use is made of the nomenclature for positions that I have mentioned previously, by which personnel are gathered in groups according to their operational function. Also used is the occupational code found in the 1960 census, according to which individuals with similar duties are gathered in occupational spheres, occupational groups and occupational families irrespective of the sectors in which they work. The source materials used are the primary data for the payroll statistics of different organizations, and the domiciliary registration data upon which the censuses are partly based.

These investigations of regional employment development have not yet been concluded. However, from a sample inquiry that merely covers manufacturing industry during the period 1957–65, it is possible to discern the following development tendencies.

Employment expansion in the Swedish community has moved up to the administrative level. The functions that, according to the investigations made, account for the exchange and processing of information are employing more and more people, while the handling and manufacture of goods no longer show any perceptible increase in employment figures.

The contact-accentuated functions in enterprises, i.e. the *information units* (A in Fig. 20-1), tend to conglomerate in the big-city regions. The number of employees in the most heavily contact-accentuated functions (A_1) have more than doubled their numbers during the nine years to which the test investigation refers. The expansion in the Stockholm region is especially remarkable.

Other development tendencies apply to what I have previously called the *operating units* (P in Fig. 20-1). Chiefly in the Stockholm region, but in the Malmö region as well, employment in these units has been stagnant. The increased employment that has occurred in Sweden on the production side has taken place primarily in small and medium-sized urban regions.

There seems to be an obvious tendency for the informational and operating functions specially in larger firms to diverge as far as location is concerned. The operational units show a relatively scattered location, while information units in enterprises and organizations are concentrated in one or a few decision-making centers on a national level, and in ten or so on a regional level.

To judge by the investigations hitherto carried out, it seems reasonable to assume that the need for contacts, and primarily for direct personal contacts between specialized functions in the national economy and public administration, is an important driving force in the process of urbanization. In a society that is undergoing rapid structural and technical changes, it appears to be essential to have close contacts with the flows of information that are particularly intensive in the large urban regions.

Those who are immediately in charge of this exchange of information (A_1) establish connections with personnel for the filing and processing of information and impulses (A_2 in Fig. 20-1). In the neighborhood of these information units there develop what we may call "administrative subsuppliers" of the consulting-firm type.

As the result of the accumulation of people with high incomes and advanced education, the multiplier factor with respect to employment becomes substantial. Purchasing power attracts more and more specialized service and trade. There is a growing demand for a diversified life as far as cultural interests and amusements are concerned. Freedom of choice on the labor market is enlarged in the biggest agglomerations. The individual in today's society finds that the more advanced his education is, and the greater the degree to which specialization has been carried, the narrower is his choice of possible places of residence.

FUTURE DEVELOPMENT

However, it is not self-evident that the course of evolution described will continue in the long run. Olof Johannesson, *alias* the physicist Hannes Alfvén, describes in his vision of the future, *Sagan om den stora datamaskinen* ("The Tale of the Big Computer") an evolutionary process in which the "datas"—the great data-processing computer installations—will first of all make it possible for routine manufacturing to be completely automated. The next step will be automation of the work of lower-ranking salaried personnel. The purchasing and sales departments will then be rationalized by entrusting the "datas" with the task of precalculating the economic consequences of various alternatives for firms.

In time, the making of certain decisions can be delegated to the "datas." But according to this fantasy of what is to come, it will be a long time before the "datas" can liberate high-ranking salaried personnel, called top management, from the troublesome task of undertaking business trips for maintaining the personal contacts that are essential for business. But little by little these too will become unnecessary thanks to an invention called "teletotal," a combination of automatic telephone, radio and television. It will give a three-dimensional colored picture, with stereophonic sound, which will provide a vivid impression that the person one is talking to is actually in the same room. "Datas" will be built that will be capable of producing "synthetic" conferences without those involved being present in the room. The most difficult thing, no doubt, will be to obtain via teletotal a satisfactory substitute for the convivial atmosphere prevailing at conference lunches.

When teletotal makes its final breakthrough, for increasingly large numbers of people it will become unnecessary to live in big cities at all. The big cities will therefore begin to wither away. (Johannesson, 1966.)

Thus according to this prophetic vision, the rapid development of informational technology that is now in progress will change the administration of enterprises and with it their location-requirements. Over the long run this would make it possible to change the physical shape of society and its regional structure completely. Physical distances would lack significance even for such "face-to-face" personal contacts as those described above.

However, in the inaugural lecture mentioned in the introduction, Eric Rhenman expressed his doubts—on the basis of the experience he had gained of development in different companies—about the reliability of this vision of the future. (The further presentation forms a summary of Rhenman's argument. See Törnqvist, Rhenman, 1967.)

At present [1968] there are about 450 computers in Sweden. Many companies use some of these for their most important administrative routines—for example payroll calculation, invoicing, inventory control, personnel accounting, order treatment, statistics, bookkeeping and costs accounting. On the other hand, progress in the development of methods for production planning and the control of processes has proceeded more slowly than had been expected. In several quarters, however, successful efforts have been made to combine routines into complete systems of control. This means that most of the routine work and a good deal of the decision-making for day-to-day management and control in medium-sized and large firms are being taken over by computers.

This seems to be a development of the kind described in Alfvén-Johannesson's vision of the future, and one that justifies the assumption that the big cities in future will lose their attractive power for business and population. However, there are development tendencies which contradict such an assumption.

It has been mentioned above that employment expansion in Sweden has moved up to the administrative level. Similar observations have been made in other inquiries. Between 1960 and 1965, the number of salaried employees increased by 54,000. According to current forecasts, office work in Sweden will cost in 1970 a sum equivalent to 85 percent of operatives' wages in the same year. In 1960 the corresponding figure was 45 percent. (*IVA-meddelande*, 1966.)

One of the reasons for this development may be that computers are not primarily used as aids to rationalization, but mainly as instruments for obtaining better administration. Moreover, we have so far been experiencing a stage of development during which large numbers of personnel have been required for the development work itself and for attending to the difficulties that have arisen in connection with the automated routines.

Eric Rhenman (*op.cit.*) draws attention, however, to another circumstance which can explain the expansion of employment on the administrative level despite the increased automation of different routines.

Firms live and work today in an environment that is constantly changing. Changes in the economic trend, and seasonal variations, interfere with the demand for goods. Customers disappear and new ones arrive. Conditions change with regard to competition. Changes in fashion become a veritable pest, not merely in traditional fashion-sectors but also for manufacturers of durables, for instance. New products make their appearance, old ones vanish from the market. Production costs change, and so do the laws governing the activities of firms. Trade barriers are torn down, others are set up.

The systems of control existing in enterprises and which are now being mechanized are aids intended to counteract interferences from variations such as those which Rhenman calls *"random or stochastic changes."* But they are of no use at all in coping with *structural changes in the environment.* With the help of a well-developed system for controlling materials, for instance, a company is in a better position to deal with seasonal variations, but it has no advantages when its problem is how to meet market changes which render its products outdated. It is more likely to be the case that the better developed and the more highly mechanized the administrative instruments of control are, the more difficult it will be for the firm to deal efficiently with such structural changes as, for example, rising wage costs and the resultant necessity for rationalization, or technical progress with its demand for product development etc.

This is probably the chief reason why mechanization and automation of the administration of firms and of public administration does *not* lead to a reduced need for administrative personnel. For at the same time as these possibilities of automation are utilized, administrative problems grow in consequence of faster structural changes in the environment. Greater numbers of expert personnel are needed to solve these problems.

This development is reflected in the composition of the salariat. The number of employees occupied with "clerical" work falls, but groups engaged in development work and planning greatly increase. Even in the biggest and technically most advanced companies in the U.S., the computers are used practically exclusively as aids for the personnel at work in the "intermediate" level of administration. Higher executives have obtained little or no help in their work through the introduction of automatic data-processing. (Brady, 1967.)

In his book *The Shape of Automation for Men and Management* Herbert A. Simon distinguishes two polar types of decisions—*programmed decisions* and *nonprogrammed decisions*, respectively.

> Decisions are programmed to the extent that they are repetitive and routine, to the extent that a definite procedure has been worked out for handling them so that they don't have to be treated *de novo* each time they occur. The obvious reason why programmed decisions tend to be repetitive, and vice versa, is that if a particular problem recurs often enough, a routine procedure will usually be worked out for solving it.
>
> Decisions are nonprogrammed to the extent that they are novel, unstructured, and consequential. There is no cut-and-dried method for handling the problem because it hasn't arisen before, or because its precise nature and structure are elusive or complex, or because it is so important that it deserves a custom-tailored treatment.

Administrative automation concerned with structural changes in the environment can only occur in the distant future. It is probable that it will never be put into effect, because of the constantly increasing complexity of these changes. As a result of the fact that different parts of the economy and of the community are becoming more and more closely interwoven, it is becoming practically impossible to prophesy the effect of technical development, for example:

In order to be able to adapt themselves rapidly to changes in the environment, in order to be able to plan and perhaps to influence the course of development, company managements seek cooperation with governments, the various organs of public administration and with universities and research institutes. Contacts and collaboration are also frequently sought with competitors and with firms in other sectors of industry. Moreover, is it not only firms that seek contact and cooperation with governments, public administration and universities. Efforts to establish such contacts are at least as great in the opposite direction. The previously-mentioned importance of personal contacts between different functions in the community accordingly enters the picture at this point.

The *conclusion* to be drawn from this line of reasoning must be that in studying the location-behavior of firms a distinction must be made not only between administrative units and operating units; administration units or information units must also be divided into two types. One of these types aims at counteracting difficulties caused by variations and random changes (*programmed decisions*). This type of administration (A_2 in Fig. 20-1) can be automated. The other type of administration has to be able to deal with the enterprise's problems in an environment whose structure is changing (*nonprogrammed decisions*). The latter is about to become the most important type of administration. The possibilities of mechanizing this growing part of the administration of firms (A_1 in Fig. 20-1) seem to become less and less as time goes on.

It is possible that the production or operating units in oases of the rural or less urbanized areas will keep company with computer centers. But this simply adds a new dimension to the process of urbanization, i.e., reinforces the tendency for work concerned with planning and development for the future to be concentrated in the big urban regions, around administrative centers and universities. On the other hand, day-to-day production and handling of goods, and even the direct management of it, can be located in the periphery.

NOTES

1 For reasons of time, this introductory survey was very brief in the oral statement. For a more detailed description, refer for example to Godlund, S.: *Den svenska urbaniseringen* ("Swedish urbanization"), *IVA-meddelande nr 139* (Report No. 139 of the Royal Swedish Academy of Engineering Sciences). Stockholm 1964, and to Hägerstrand, T.: *Regionala utvecklingstendenser och problem. Urbaniseringen, Appendix 3 i SOU 1966: 1* ("Regional development tendencies and problems. Urbanization," Appendix 3 in Swedish Government Official Reports, 1966:1). See also Official Statistics of Sweden: Censuses 1960 and 1965.

2 In Swedish statistics called "tätorter," i.e. densely populated places with a population in excess of 200.

3 The flows of information between different functions have been surveyed in big *input-output flow tables*. The calculations were made in a computer with the aid of a standard program made on other purposes.

REFERENCES

Administrativ rationalisering—behov av ökad samordning ("Administrative rationalization—needs for increased coordination"), *IVA-meddelande nr 145* (Report No. 145 of the Royal Swedish Academy of Engineering Sciences). Stockholm 1966.

Bohm, P., *External economies in production*. Uppsala 1964.

Brady, R. H., Computers in top-level decision making, *Harvard Business Review*, vol. 45, No. 4, 1967.

Carlson, S., *Företagsledare i arbete* ("Managers at work"). Solna 1964.

Godlund, S., Den svenska urbaniseringen ("Swedish urbanization"), *IVA-meddelande nr 139*. Stockholm 1964.

Greenhut, M. L., *Plant location in theory and practice*. Chapel Hill 1956.

Hägerstrand, T., Urbaniseringen som världsproblem. Från vertikal till horisontell länkning ("Urbanization—a world problem. From vertical to horizontal linkage"), *IVA-meddelande nr 139*. Stockholm 1964.

Hägerstrand, T., Regionala utvecklingstendenser och problem. Urbaniseringen ("Regional development-tendencies and problems. Urbanization"), Appendix 3, *SOU* 1966: 1 (Swedish Government Official Reports, 1966: 1).

Höglund, B., & Werin, L., *The production system of the Swedish economy. An input-output study*. Uppsala 1964.

Höglund, R., *Företaget i samhället* ("The firm in the community"). Stockholm 1953.

Isard, W., *Location and space-economy*. New York 1956.

Johannesson, O., *Sagan om den stora datamaskinen* ("The Tale of the Big Computer"). Stockholm 1966.

Kristensson, F., *Människor, företag och regioner* ("People, firms and regions"). Stockholm 1967.

Lösch, A., *Die räumliche Ordnung der Wirtschaft*. Jena 1944.

Ponsard, C., *Economie et espace*. Paris 1955.

Ponsard, C., *Histoire des théories économiques spatiales*. Paris 1958.

Simon, H., *The shape of automation for men and management*. New York 1965.

Skiss 1966 till regionplan för stockholmstrakten ("Draft regional plan for Stockholm"). Stockholmstraktens regionplanekontor (Stockholm Region Planning Office). Stockholm 1967.

Stewart, R., *Managers and their jobs*. London 1967.

Thorngren, B., *Regionala "external economies"* ("Regional 'external economies'"). EFI (Economic Research Institute, Stockholm School of Economics). Stockholm 1967.

Törnqvist, G., *Studier i industrilokalisering* ("Studies in plant location"). Stockholm 1963.

Törnqvist, G., *Lokaliseringsförändringar inom svensk industri* ("Location changes in Swedish manufacturing industry"). Uppsala 1964.

Törnqvist, G., *TV-ägandets utveckling i Sverige 1956—65. En empirisk-teoretisk studie* (With summary: Growth of TV ownership in Sweden, 1956—65. An empirical-theoretical study). Uppsala 1967.

Törnqvist, G., Rhenman, E., *Urbaniseringsprocessen mot organisations-teoretisk bakgrund—Två installations-föreläsningar* ("The urbanization process from the viewpoint of organizational theory—two inaugural lectures"). Swedish Institute for Administrative Research, SIAR—S—12, 1967.

Folkräkningen den 1 november 1960, vol. 1—11. Statistiska Centralbyrån (The census of 1st November 1960, vols. 1—11. Central Bureau of Statistics). *SOS:* (Official Statistics of Sweden) Folkmängden och dess förändringar ("Population and its changes").

Folk- och bostadsräkningen den 1 november 1965, vol. 1—4. Statistiska Centralbyrån (The population and housing census of 1st November 1965, vols. 1—4. Central Bureau of Statistics). *SOS:* Official Statistics of Sweden, Folkmängden och dess förändringar ("Population and its changes").

Törnqvist brings us a full circle to the geographic landscape again, one of the centerpins of the geographer's discipline. He also underlines the holistic approach called for earlier. The relationship between spatial organization, the temporal evolution of the transportation system, and landscape can now be dealt with. D. G. Janelle, in the final selection in this part, looks at the landscape in a holistic way. He examines the role of transportation technologies in the spatial organization of human activities, how the spatial pattern changes over time, and why differences occur between areas on the earth's surface. By emphasizing changes in transportation technology he zeroes in again on the concept of *accessibility* introduced earlier in this book. The weaknesses of his approach center on his assumption of "rational" behavior, even though he acknowledges this point in the conclusion, and his marginal consideration of the political-regulatory milieu stressed by P. J. Rimmer earlier. However, despite these drawbacks this selection does summarize some of the interrelationships introduced in this book.

Selection 21

Spatial Reorganization: A Model and Concept

D. G. Janelle

Abstract: Travel-time connectivity is a key factor in defining a process of the spatial reorganization of man's functional establishments. A case study relating highway development with the growth in wholesale activity for selected cities in the upper midwest of the United States indicates that, aside from being a good surrogate of transport efficiency, travel-time connectivity is also a good measure of the relative advantage of a given place in attracting to itself the centralization and specialization of human activity.

A functional framework which includes a measure of the friction of distance, such as time or cost of travel, seems essential in a study of central place development. Furthermore, as Blaut noted, structure (the areal arrangement of earth-space phenomena) and process (the rearrangement of these phenomena over time) are one and the same thing—that is: ". . . structures of the real world are simply slow processes of long duration."[1] Inherent in Blaut's view is the implicit existence of a temporal pattern in each and every spatial pattern.[2] Thus, these two factors, the friction of distance (measured in travel-time) and historical development, have been incorporated into the following statement of a model of spatial reorganization.[3]

A MODEL OF SPATIAL REORGANIZATION

In this study, the concept of spatial reorganization identifies a process by which places adapt both the locational structure and the characteristics of their social, economic, and political activities to changes in time-space connectivity (the time required to travel between desired origins and destinations). As an example of such areal reorganization, Fox noted how, for the food retailing industry, spatial adaptations to advances in transportation have tended towards fewer, larger, and more distantly spaced establishments—an abandonment of the corner grocery store in favor of the supermarket.[4]

A model has been designed to depict a normative process of such areal development. Later this model (the basic model) will be expanded so as to present a more comprehensive view. Although these models are intended to be applicable to urban-exchange economies typical of the United States and Western Europe, the writer believes that they may have some predictive value in forecasting the areal development of areas which have only recently begun progressing through the industrial-commercial revolution. Before describing the models, a concept which is central to the overall process of reorganization needs to be considered—this is the notion of *locational utility.*

Locational Utility

Very simply, utility is a measure of value. However, the term locational utility used in

Annals of the Association of American Geographers, vol. 59, no. 2, 1969, pp. 348–364. Reprinted by permission of the author and the editor.

this study should be distinguished from *place utility* as defined by Wolpert.[5] Wolpert recognized in his discussion on the decision to migrate that utility is inherently individualistic. Thus, place utility is an individual's subjective measure of the degree to which the opportunities at a particular place permit his perceived or actual achievement level to be in as close as possible accordance with his aspiration level. By integrating this individualistic concept with information on the life cycles, life styles, and life spaces of specific socioeconomic groups, Wolpert developed an aggregate measure of the utility of specific places relative to the mover-stayer decision.

In contrast to place utility, locational utility is defined in a context which, in part, overlooks the individualistic and subjective connotation of value. It is a measure of the utility of specific places or areas, which in this case is defined by the aggregate time-expenditure (cost or effort) in transport required for that place or area to satisfy its operational needs.[6] Operational need refers to those natural and human resource requirements which permit the place or area to fulfill its functional roles in the larger spatial system of places and areas. The alternative possibilities of a place, either to decrease, maintain, or increase its existing competitive status within the bounds of either its present spatial system of socioeconomic activities or in an expanded sphere of influence, are here considered to be functions of its locational utility. Thus, as shown in Fig. 21-1, the locational utility or value of places and areas increases as travel-time expenditure per unit of operational success (profit or some other form of amenity benefit) decreases. Whereas a first degree linear function is used to express this relationship, it is likely that a second, third, or higher degree function would be more appropriate.

In reality, the spatial variance in the locational utility for a system of places may be

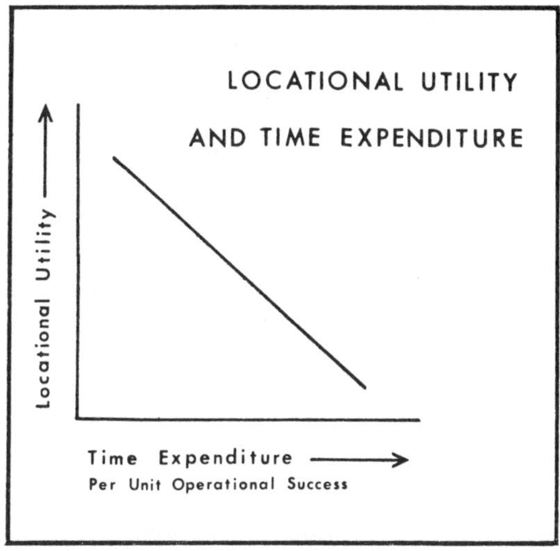

Fig. 21-1 Locational utility and time expenditure per unit operational success. Some curvilinear function might express the reality of this relationship better than the linear function represented in this graph.

characterized by surfaces of utility. In a given spatial system there exists one surface for each of the many possible functional roles to be performed. Theoretically, with possible loss of much information, it might be feasible to treat these surfaces in an additive sense and to arrive at a surface of composite locational utility for the system.

Once the surface of utility has been described, one can then focus attention on a more significant problem—the dynamics of surface change. For example, the depletion or the discovery of a resource which is an operational need for the success of a given economic activity would alter the utility surface for that activity, and could necessitate the selection of a new production site.

In that locational utility is defined as a function of time-expenditure, it is evident that innovations which speed transportation will also lead to changes in the utility surface. Thus, for a given place, the increase in locational utility from time t_1 to time t_2 that is derived from a transport innovation at time t_2 is indicated in Fig. 21-2. Such changes pose many questions of practical relevance. For example, are these innovations and certain distributive forces leading towards greater equilibrium in the utility surface and, thus, possibly towards a more homogeneous distribution of man's socioeconomic activities? Or, do transport improvements and certain agglomerative forces lead to increasing spatial variance in locational utility and, thus, towards greater place-concentration of human enterprise?

These questions, along with the process of spatial reorganization will be clarified as the concepts integrated into the model in Fig. 21-3 are defined. These concepts include:

1 Demand for accessibility;
2 transport innovations;
3 time-space convergence;
4 spatial adaptations—centralization and specialization; and
5 spatial interaction.

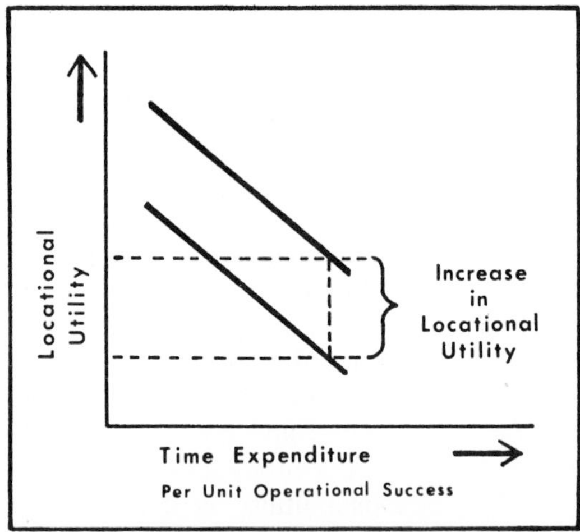

Fig. 21-2 The increase in locational utility for time period t_1 through t_2 resulting from the introduction of a transport innovation in time t_2.

Demand for Accessibility

Accessibility is a measure of the ease (time, cost, or effort) in which transfer occurs between the places and areas of a system. The demand for accessibility, then, is really a quest to decrease the transport effort expended per unit of operational success or, very simply, to augment locational utility. A useful and more objective measure of accessibility (not used in this study) is provided by the graph theoretic approaches employed by Garrison, Kansky, and others.[7]

Transport Innovations

In this study, transport innovations are any technologies or methods which serve to increase accessibility between places or which permit an increase in the quantity of goods or the number of passengers that can be moved between these places per unit of time. Thus, a transport innovation may be a new and faster type of carrier, improved traffic routing procedures, better gasoline, improved lighting for night travel, the straightening of angular routes, and so forth. All such introductions are likely to result in what the author describes as time-space convergence (step 4 of the model).

Time-space Convergence

By time-space convergence, the writer is implying that, as a result of transport innovations, places approach each other in time-space; that is, the travel-time required between places decreases and distance declines in significance.[8] An example of this phenomenon is illustrated in Fig. 21-4 for travel between Detroit and Lansing, Michigan. As a consequence of such convergence, man has found that it is possible and practical to adapt the spatial organization of his activities to their evolving time-space framework (step 5 of the model).

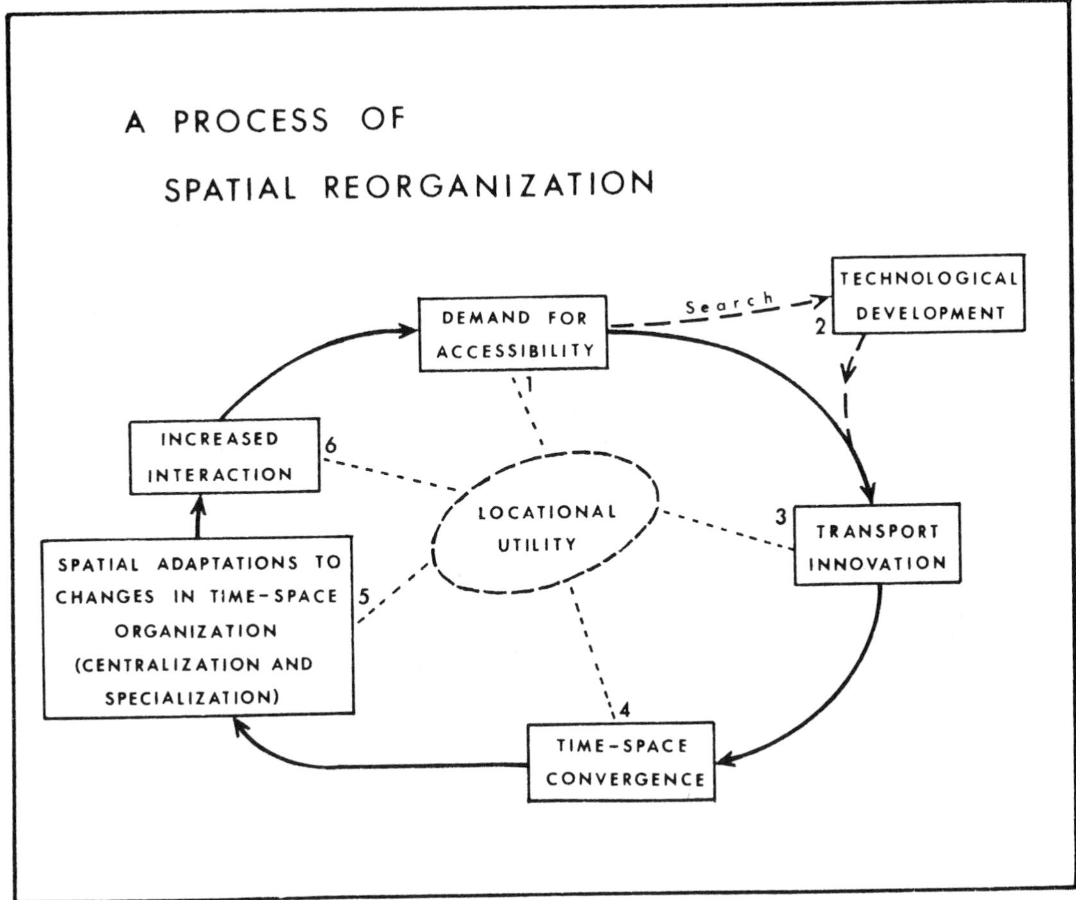

Fig. 21-3.

SPATIAL ADAPTATIONS TO CHANGES IN TIME-SPACE ORGANIZATION

In the basic model under consideration, the spatial adaptations of man's activities to their changing time-space framework will lead to the centralization and specialization of secondary and tertiary economic activities in specific places and, as is frequently the case, to the specialization of primary economic activities in the resource-oriented hinterlands of these places. Centralization (of which urbanization is a form) refers to the increasing focus of human activity upon a particular place; it results in the growth of an economically, culturally and, sometimes, politically integrated area over which this particular place is dominant (its hinterland). The economies that result when the scale of an economic, political, or cultural endeavor is increased at a particular place or in a particular area are generally considered to be the motivating forces behind centralization. As a rule, increased scale permits lower per-unit production or opera-

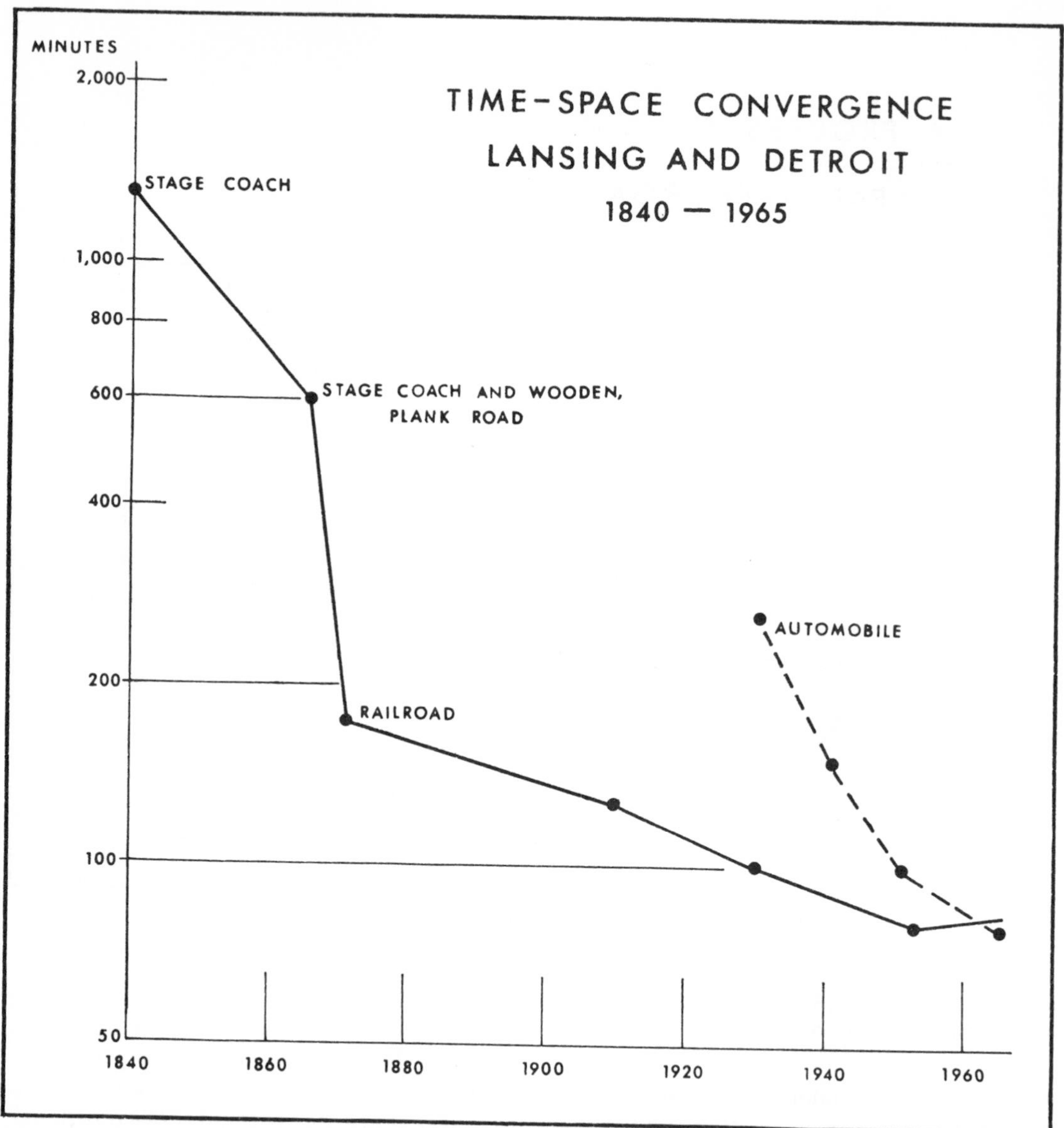

Fig. 21-4.

tion costs—unless diminishing returns set in.

Specialization (of which industrialization is a form) develops when places or areas concentrate their efforts on particular activities at the expense of others. Many regional economists and economic geographers note that the most intense concentration of any given economic activity will (or at least should) be in a locale having a comparative advantage relative to other places and areas. On the other hand, a less favored place should choose to specialize in that activity for which it has (relative to the rest of the system) a least comparative disadvantage.[9] For the mechanistic model in question, the surfaces of locational utility dictate the specialties of places and areas.

The greater the centralization and specialization of man's activities, the greater is the need for efficient transport and increased locational utility (steps 1–4 of the basic model). As man speeds up his means of movement, it becomes possible for him to travel further in a given time, to increase his access to a larger surrounding area and, possibly, to more and better resources. This idea is in line with Ullman's concept of transferability.[10] Likewise, secondary and tertiary functions can serve more people; and the perishable agricultural products and other primary products can be profitably marketed over a larger area. In essence these changes are manifestations of an increasing degree of locational utility (greater operational success can be derived per unit of time-expenditure from a given place) that permits the increasing centralization and specialization of human endeavors. Thus, these scale economies are, in part, both forms of spatial adaptation to an evolving time-space framework.

Unlike centralization and specialization, suburbanization (a form of spatial decentralization) represents an alternative response to time-space convergence which is not treated in this basic model. Improvements in individual mobility have made it possible for some families and for some firms to trade off central accessibility for the amenities associated with suburban life and industrial parks. These adaptations are considered in the expanded model of spatial reorganization (Fig. 21-5).

Interaction

Step 6 of the basic model indicates that an increase in interaction results between places and areas that experience increasing centralization and specialization.[11] As secondary and tertiary activities centralize within given places, it is necessary for those places to interact in the forms of products, service, and

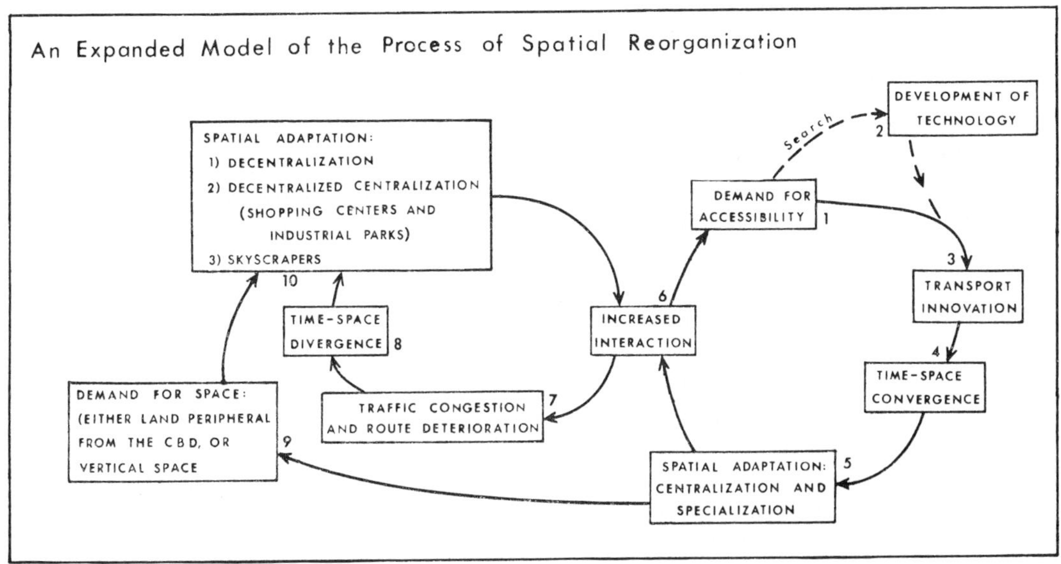

Fig. 21-5.

information exchange with their resource-oriented hinterlands. These hinterlands provide the necessities of primary production and they demand the products and services of secondary and tertiary establishments. Similarly, if central places concentrate on a given type of economic activity or, if resource-oriented areas specialize in a specific form of primary activity (e.g., wheat or iron ore), it is necessary for them to trade and exchange with one another so that they can attain those needs or desirable items that they themselves do not produce.

The increasing intercourse that results from the concentration of human activities at particular places is likely to lead to an overextension of man's transport facilities and result in their deterioration from overuse and in the development of traffic congestion. It is, therefore, likely that the operational success of these places can only be continued through increased costs. Consequently, the increasing interaction that results from centralization and specialization leads to further demands for increased accessibility, greater degrees of locational utility, and transport innovations (steps 6, 1–3 in basic model). Thus, the spatial reorganization of human activities is perpetuated in what, theoretically, is a never ending and accelerating cycle. This notion of a multiplier effect or positive feedback[12] implies that the state of a system (that is, the degree of convergence between interacting settlements, their demands for accessibility, and so forth) at a given time is determined completely from within the system and by the previous state of the system.[13] Thus, the positive feedback system, as indicated by the completed circuit in the basic model, is self-perpetuating.

Support for the notion that a transport improvement, in itself, encourages increased interaction is also available. Studies by Coverdale and Colpitts show that improvements in highway facilities result in traffic volumes greater than the number accounted for by the diverted traffic.[14] That is, many new facilities (i.e., bridges and freeways) will attract considerably more traffic than would be expected had the previous facilities continued to operate alone. This increase is frequently termed induced traffic. The volumes of induced traffic encouraged by bridges replacing ferries have ranged, in many instances, from sixty-five percent to seventy-five percent of that before the improvement. For the Philadelphia-Camden Bridge it was seventy-eight percent, and for the San Francisco-Oakland Bay Bridge it was about sixty-four percent. This finding lends additional support for the inclusion of a positive feedback system in the basic model of spatial reorganization.

AN EVALUATION OF THE BASIC MODEL

Changes in the time-spatial and spatial organization of human endeavors present places and areas with possibilities for greater scale economies and with problems of developing more efficient means of transport. It is man's awareness or perception of these possibilities and problems that enables him to take advantage of the changes in the time-space structure of his activities. In reality, however, the process that has been described is not so simple—not all men will perceive the changes described in the model nor will they see the implications of these changes in the same way. Furthermore, some of the assumptions of the model lack complete accord with reality.

Varying Conceptions of Utility and Time

Whereas the basic model is based on an objective measure of locational utility (time-expenditure), it was indicated earlier that utility is inherently individualistic; that is, it is perceived according to one's values, goals, and technical and institutional means of living. At the level of places and areas it is likely that the criteria for utility are based on factors other than just the expenditure of time.

It is also apparent that man's perceived value of a given unit of time has increased as the tempo of his activities has increased. A component to represent this change is not included in the model. Yet, by sole reason of the tremendously greater commodity, passenger, and information flows today as compared with past periods, man is motivated to seek greater utility for his expenditure of time. Imagine the magnitude of storage that would be necessary if New York City had to store food for its population to meet their needs over the winter months. With faster transport, the city can rely on more distant sources. Food can be moved to the city when it is needed, thus reducing its storage costs and increasing its operational success.

There is the additional likelihood that a person's perception of the utility of time will differ for various travel purposes. For example, an individual may be willing to spend an hour in travel to receive the medicinal services of an eye specialist; but, he may only grudgingly give up ten minutes to purchase a loaf of bread. No model of the process of spatial reorganization could account for all of the multitudinous goals and criteria of all persons, places, and areas, and the changing value of time for each. Therefore, in the development of the model, a standard pattern of human place-behavior has been assumed.

A Basic Assumption: Rationality in Human Place-Behavior

The principal assumption upon which the spatial process model is based is that man is rational. This concept of a rational man or the economic man has been well developed elsewhere and only the implications relevant to this discussion are presented.[15] These include the following:

1 Man has perfect knowledge. Thus, in an aggregate sense, places and areas show complete awareness of all factors operative in the areal reformation of their activities; they are aware of all their operational needs and of all the possibilities for fulfilling these needs.

2 Man has no uncertainty—he has perfect predictability. Thus, the rational place foresees the time-space convergence that will result from any transport innovation; it foresees the degree of increased interaction that will be derived from greater centralization and specialization of its activities.

3 Man is interested solely in maximizing the utility of time at a given place. This permits the necessary spatial reorganization to augment the operational success of places. Net social benefits, inclusive of all possible benefits—whether economic, political, or cultural—could be substituted for operational success.

Limitations and Omissions of the Model

Although the inclusion of the rational place concept may limit the correspondence of the basic model with reality, it does permit one to consider the process of reorganization under controlled circumstances with a minimum of conflicting factors (i.e., changing criteria and varying degrees of rationality that have to be accounted for). Other factors which are, in part, attributable to a lack of perfect rationality may be summed up as perceptive, responsive, and technological lags. Spatial change is not necessarily characterized by a smooth flow through the six-step process identified in the basic model.

There may be lags or delays in the process resulting from man's inefficient behavior—his slowness in adapting the spatial organization of human activity to its changing time-space framework, or his slowness in introducing more efficient forms of transportation. It is also possible that improvements in transfer technology will lag behind the need for such development. It will be noted from Fig. 21-3 that the development of technology, although intimately related, is considered exogenous to the system depicting the process of spatial change. Such development may take place independently of any need present within the system—innovations developed for an entirely different purpose may be readily applicable to transportation.

AN EXPANDED MODEL OF SPATIAL REORGANIZATION

If the restraints of rationality, as defined above, are relaxed, and, if another factor, the demand for land, is introduced, then the mechanism of the basic model breaks down. In reality, places and areas do not always seek to maximize their degree of locational utility and, in many cases, they find it impossible to do so. Thus, if there is no demand for increased accessibility in response to increases in interaction or if there is no technology available for meeting demands for greater accessibility, then it is likely that either traffic congestion, route deterioration, or both will occur. This, in turn, would lead to time-space divergence (places getting further apart in time-space). This is indicated by steps 7 and 8 of the expanded model depicted in Fig. 21-5.

The demand for land or space (step 9) is a form of decentralization which is a direct consequence of the centralization and specialization associated with time-space convergence. Factories, warehouses and so forth, which seek to augment scale economies, find land scarce and expensive in the central areas of cities and, thus, move to the peripheries of the built-up areas where it is available and comparatively cheap. Jobs created by this expansion may increase the population attraction power of places and lead to further demands for land. Additional factors accounting for a demand for land peripheral to the built-up areas include the population holding power of the urban area itself and the amenity goal to gain more elbow room—to get out of the noisy, crowded city. This demand to leave the central city results as interaction accelerates beyond a tolerable threshold. It seems likely that this demand for land coupled with time-space divergence will lead to a completely different form of areal adaptation than was the case with convergence.

Spatial Adaptation: Decentralized Centralization and the Expansion of the City

Because the land available for expansion is generally peripheral to that portion of the city area which is already developed, the new and relocated establishments (residents, retail and service firms, and so forth) find themselves at a time-disadvantage in attaining goods and services that are only offered in the central core of the city. To obviate this problem these families and firms can either demand greater transport access (steps 1–3), or they can encourage the location of new establishments in the city's peripheral area to serve and to employ them (step 10). Frequently, the demand for new commercial, industrial, and cultural establishments is met prior to any substantial improvements in transport access. The pattern of such development is typified by shopping centers carrying on many retail and service functions and by the nucleation of secondary activities in planned industrial parks.

The decentralized nucleation of man's activities in planned shopping centers and in industrial parks may owe to the desire to reduce the number of trips or the distance of movement needed to attain a given quantity of goods and services.[16] This is made possible by grouping many functions at one center. Such nucleation of activities within given subregions of the urban area may lead to increased interaction within the subregion and, eventually, to an even greater demand for accessibility (step 1). Thus, in this manner, the subregion finds itself in a new stage of areal rearrangement—it is operative within the basic model of spatial reorganization and will develop greater centralization and specialization (steps 1–5).

With the continuance of this process, it is easily seen how subnucleated secondary and tertiary activities can eventually become a part of the very core of the urban area—the increasing concentration of activities within the urban core and within the subnucleated secondary and tertiary centers leads to further demands for land (step 9). It is possible that they will engulf each other in their expansion and become fused into one highly integrated unit. Without some form of control or planning, this process could lead to one vast urban-society—a megalopolis.[17]

In the absence of planning, it is evident that decentralization is merely an intermediate or lag-stage in the general process (described by the basic model) leading towards an expanded area of centralization and specialization. This model highlights only the basic components of spatial reorganization and clearly expresses the cyclical tendency towards the increasing centralization and specialization of human activity.

An Evaluation of the Expanded Model

Unlike the basic model of spatial reorganization, the expanded model accounts for what happens when the degree of rationality, as defined for the basic model, is lessened or when the criteria of rationality change. This model permits consideration of the spatial consequences to the alternative demands of either accessibility or space (land and air).

In concluding the discussion on the development and evaluation of the model, one further observation is necessary. Spatial reorganization is not operative everywhere to the same degree and it does not occur simultaneously at all points in earth space. Therefore, it is essential to determine why this process is so selective and why some places undergo a more rapid areal reorganization than others.[18]

THE PROCESS OF SPATIAL REORGANIZATION AND THE CONCEPT OF RELATIVE ADVANTAGE

The concept of relative advantage states that the process of spatial reorganization in the form of centralization and specialization will accelerate most rapidly at those places which stand to benefit most from increasing accessibility.[19] In other words, transport innovations are most likely between those places which will benefit most from a lessening in the expenditure of time (cost or effort) to attain needed and desirable goods and services. Relative advantage is defined in terms of the benefits of operational success (inclusive of all economic, political, and cultural benefits) that can be derived from a particular place with a given expenditure of time. The concept is based on the same assumptions of rationality as were the process models.

Since locational decentralization, as defined in the expanded model, is simply an intermediate or lag-stage in the overall trend towards centralization (given the continuance of the process and the assumption that a point of diminishing returns does not set in), it is possible to confine the evaluation of the relative advantage concept to the basic model of spatial reorganization. The question is, where will this process be likely to accelerate most rapidly? Or, where is man most likely to introduce a transport improvement? In seeking answers to these questions, the concepts of relative advantage and spatial reorganization will be applied to a selected set of cities in the northern, midwest of the United States.

Relative Advantage and Spatial Reorganization in the Upper Midwest

Because of their significance as times of automobile and highway innovation, the periods of 1900 to 1925, and 1940 to 1965, were selected for evaluating the real world applicability of the concepts proposed in this study. In the early twentieth century, prior to about 1930, railways and electric interurban lines not only dominated intercity travel in the United States, they also had a definite speed advantage over the automobile. For example, although in 1930 a typical forty-five mile auto trip from Dexter, Michigan, to Detroit took three hours, interurban lines averaging anywhere from forty to sixty miles per hour connected most of the nation's major cities.[20] Nonetheless, people increasingly sought the personal convenience and versatility of the automobile and demanded better roads.[21] The tangible results of this demand are illustrated in Fig. 21-6 by a series of five highway status maps for southern Michigan.

Relative Advantage for Transport Improvement in Southern Michigan

In Fig. 21-7*a* a closed system of seven major Michigan cities and eleven highway links has been selected to evaluate the concept of relative advantage. The immediate objective is to predict highway status for 1925 on the basis of information for 1900 and similarly, to project the status of highways in 1965 from information known in 1940. For the initial years of each period, 1900 and 1940, the principal highway trunklines were nearly homogeneous in quality—mostly unimproved clay and sand roads in 1900 and, as shown in Fig. 21-6, mostly two-lane paved roads in 1940.[22] Thus, the calculation of travel-times between cities for these two years assumes standard speeds of ten miles per hour for 1900 and forty miles per hour for 1940. For the years 1925 and 1965, travel-times are based on the following criteria:

1925—unimproved roads (10 miles per hour)
—gravel roads (25 miles per hour)
—brick roads (35 miles per hour)
—paved two-lane roads (40 miles per hour)

1965—where possible, actual travel-time data from the Michigan State Highway Department are used.[23]
Otherwise:
—paved two-lane roads (45 miles per hour)
—divided highways (55 miles per hour)
—limited access roads (60 miles per hour)

Through application of the above criteria in calculating travel-times, a convergence measure of actual route improvement—minutes saved per route mile—is derived for the two periods in question. This convergence measure will be used to evaluate the success of the predictive variable—relative advantage. The hypothesis under investigation is as follows: the degree of innovation will increase as relative advantage increases. The surrogate used to represent relative advantage is an index of link-demand derived from the simple gravity model

$$\frac{P_i P_j}{d_{ij}^2}$$

where $p_i p_j$ is the product of the populations of the two places joined by the link, and d_{ij}^2 is the square of the route mileage between them.[24]

The above procedure is complicated somewhat when a system has several places demanding travel over the same link. For example, the demand for travel over link 9 in Fig. 21-7*b* is not only a function of travel-demand between Battle Creek and Jackson,

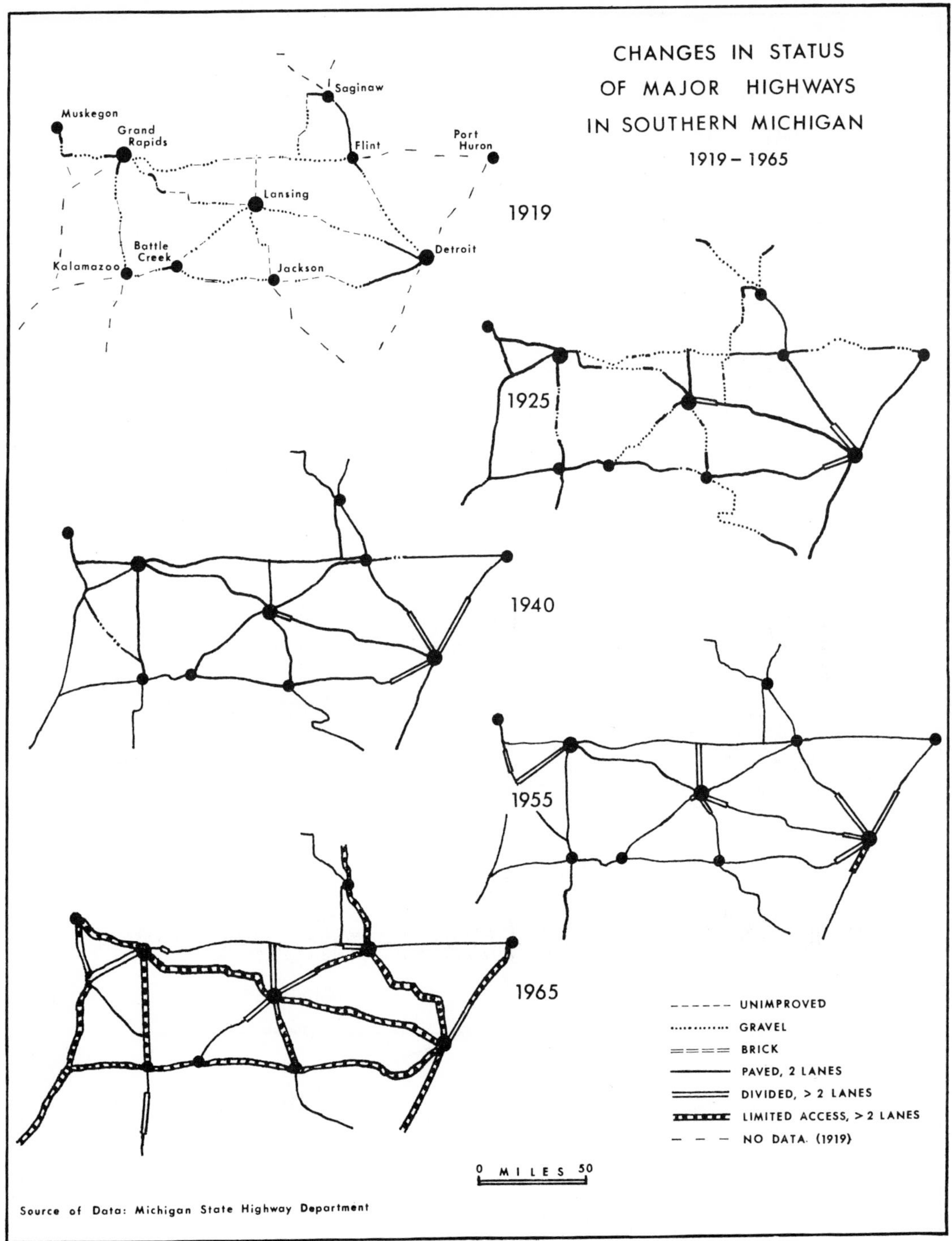
CHANGES IN STATUS
OF MAJOR HIGHWAYS
IN SOUTHERN MICHIGAN
1919 – 1965
Saginaw
Muskegon
Grand Rapids
Flint
Port Huron
Lansing
1919
Battle Creek
Detroit
Kalamazoo
Jackson
1925
1940
1955
1965
UNIMPROVED
GRAVEL
BRICK
PAVED, 2 LANES
DIVIDED, > 2 LANES
LIMITED ACCESS, > 2 LANES
NO DATA (1919)
0 MILES 50
Source of Data: Michigan State Highway Department

Fig. 21-6.

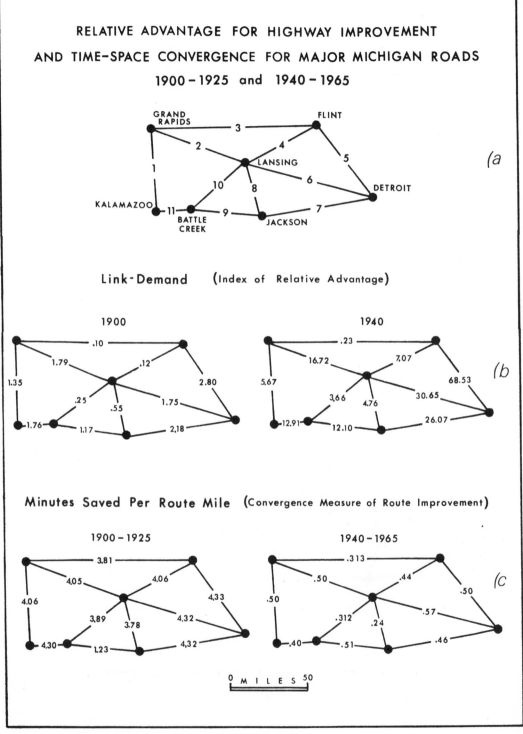

RELATIVE ADVANTAGE FOR HIGHWAY IMPROVEMENT AND TIME-SPACE CONVERGENCE FOR MAJOR MICHIGAN ROADS 1900-1925 and 1940-1965

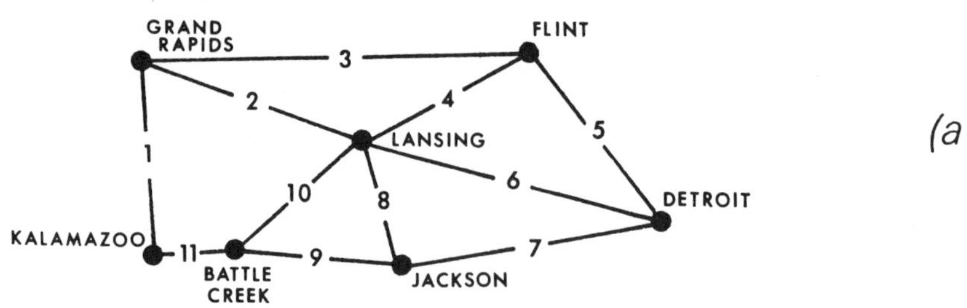

Link-Demand (Index of Relative Advantage)

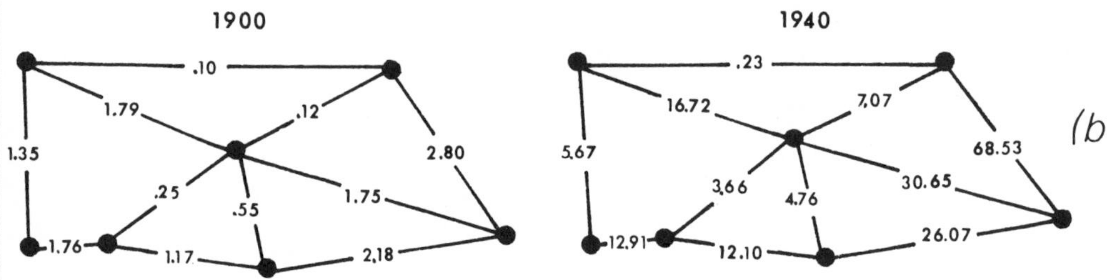

Minutes Saved Per Route Mile (Convergence Measure of Route Improvement)

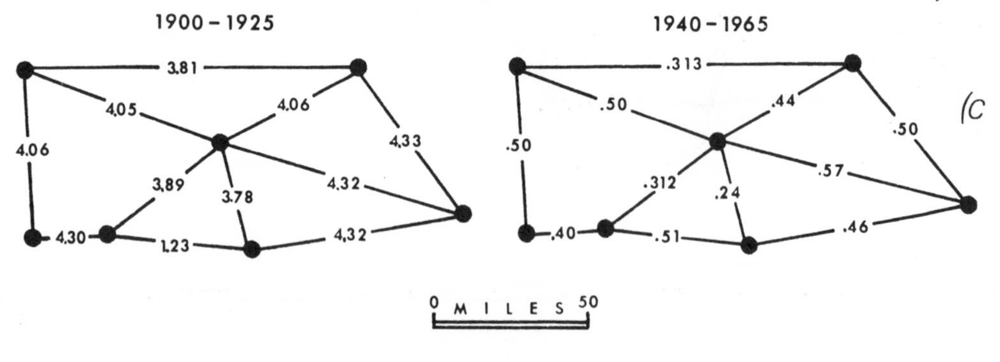

Fig. 21-7.

but it is also a function of the demands for travel between Detroit and Battle Creek, Detroit and Kalamazoo, and Kalamazoo and Jackson. Thus, as illustrated in Fig. 21-8, the link-demand for a highway improvement between Battle Creek and Jackson represents the sum of the gravity model indices for each pair of places whose interconnections requires use of link 9. The demand values for the other ten links were determined in similar fashion and are shown in Fig. 21-7*b* for the years 1900 and 1940. Shown in Fig. 21-7*c* are the convergence values of actual route improvement for the periods 1900 to 1925 and 1940 to 1965. Data pertinent to these calculations are included in Tables 21-1 and 21-2.

Spearman's rank correlation technique was used to measure the statistical association of the rankings of the demand and improvement variables. This technique yielded *R* values (significant at the ninety-five percent level) of .74 for the 1900–1925 period and .69 for the 1940–1965 period.[25] The results, though not conclusive, are encouraging. It is evident that the inclusion of places outside the chosen system of seven cities such as Chicago, Toledo, Saginaw, and others might have greatly altered both the rankings of the link-demand and the results. Furthermore, the gravity model used here may be a comparatively crude measure of the relative advantage for transport improvement.

Although a comparison of the rankings of the link-demands for 1900 and for 1940 show a high degree of stability (*R* equals .87 at the ninety-nine percent level of significance), a similar comparison of the convergence rankings for the two periods reveals some signs of significant change in the time-space con-

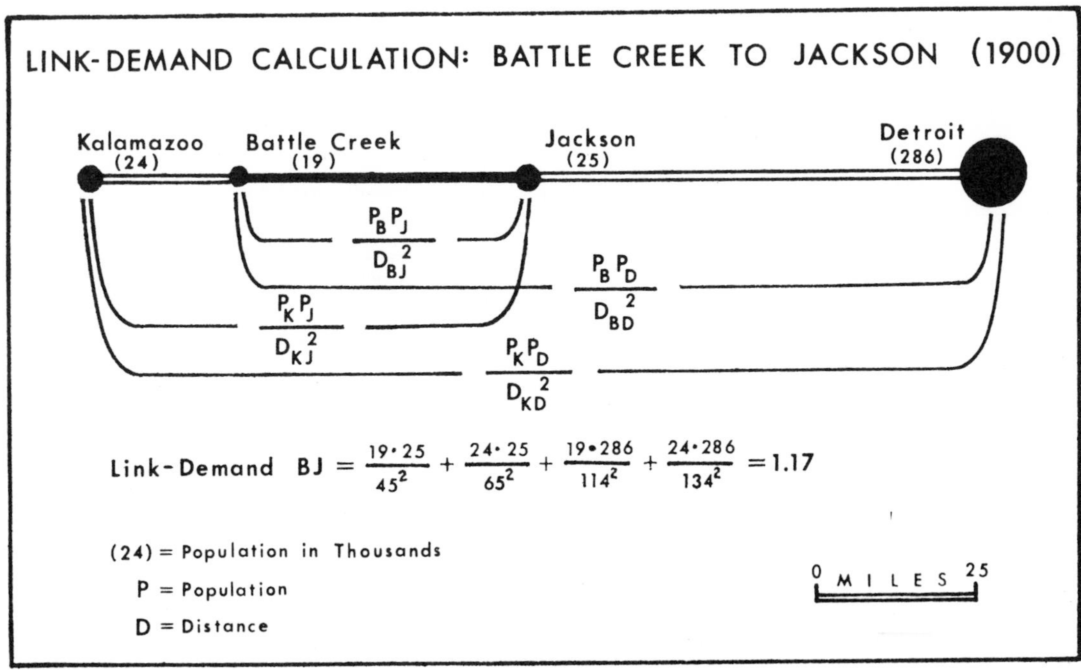

Fig. 21-8.

nectivity of Michigan's transport network. For example, link 2 from Grand Rapids to Lansing moved from eighth in the convergence ranking for 1900–1925 to fourth during the 1940–1965 period. On the whole, however, the changes for 1940–1965 were consistent with those of the 1900–1925 period of route improvement (*R* equals .67 at the ninety-five percent level of significance).

In general, this evaluation suggests that highway development in Michigan has varied with the changes in relative advantage. And, owing to the pronounced stability in the rankings of the link-demands, it is evident that transport innovations helped to confirm and to augment the existing advantages in time-space connectivity for dominant places. For example, during both periods, Detroit ranked first among the seven cities in the average number of minutes saved per route mile along each of its radiating links. In essense, Detroit has been favored by a greater increase in locational utility than any of the other six places in the system. Thus, in accordance with the norm of spatial reorganization as outlined in the basic model (Fig. 21-3), Detroit should also be favored by the greatest increase among the seven cities in the centralization and specialization of human activity. This concept will be tested against the background of wholesale enterprise in thirteen upper midwestern United States cities.

Spatial Reorganization: Wholesale Activity in the Upper Midwest

Wholesale activity is a form of economic specialization which, according to Philbrick, shows dominant centralization in places of third order and above.[26] It seems reasonable to assume that wholesale firms would fare best if they located at those places which are most accessible to their customers. If this is so, then places offering high degrees of locational utility relative to other places should be dominant wholesale centers. However, as indicated for the highway network of southern Michigan, the time-space surface of locational utility is in a state of sporadic flux—differential transportation development induces variations in the relative rates with which places improve their time-space connectivity with one another. Thus, this factor of non-

Table 21-1 Link-demands for 1900 and Time-space Convergence for 1900–1925

Linkages (see Fig. 7)	Calculations of link-demand*	Link-demand value (LDV)	Rank (LDV)	Travel-time over link** (minutes) 1900	1925	Route miles	Minutes saved per route mile 1900–1925	Rank (Minutes saved)
1 (KG)	KG + BG	1.35	6	288	93	48	4.06	6.5
2 (GL)	GL + GD + GJ	1.79	3	378	123	63	4.05	8
3 (GF)	GF	.10	11	630	230	105	3.81	10
4 (LF)	LF + BF + KF + JF	.12	10	360	116	60	4.06	6.5
5 (FD)	FD	2.80	1	360	100	60	4.33	1
6 (LD)	LD + GD	1.75	5	510	143	85	4.32	2.5
7 (JD)	JD + BD + KD	2.18	2	432	121	72	4.32	2.5
8 (JL)	JL + FJ + GJ	.55	8	222	82	37	3.78	11
9 (BJ)	BJ + KJ + KD + BD	1.17	7	270	84	44	4.23	5
10 (BL)	BL + KL + BF + FK	.25	9	288	101	48	3.89	9
11 (KB)	KB + KJ + KD + KL + KF	1.76	4	120	34	20	4.30	4

* Link-demands for 1900 were calculated as indicated in text and are based on the following city limit populations (in thousands): Battle Creek (B), 19; Detroit (D), 286; Flint (F), 13; Grand Rapids (G), 88; Jackson (J), 25; Kalamazoo (K), 24; and Lansing (L), 16. Source: U.S. Bureau of Census, *Twelfth Census of the United States: 1900, Population, Number and Distribution of Inhabitants*, Vol. I.

** Based on criteria established by author (see text). Source: Compiled and calculated by author.

Table 21-2 Link-demands for 1940 and Time-space Convergence for 1940–1965

Linkages (see Fig. 7)	Calculations of link-demand*	Link-demand value (LDV)	Rank (LDV)	Travel-time over link** (minutes) 1940	1965	Route miles	Minutes saved per route mile 1900–1925	Rank (minutes saved)
1 (KG)	KG + BG	5.67	8	72	48	48	.50	4
2 (GL)	GL + GD + GJ	16.72	4	93	62	62	.50	4
3 (GF)	GF	.23	11	158	125	105	.313	9
4 (LF)	LF + BF + KF + JF	7.07	7	75	53	50	.44	7
5 (FD)	FD	68.53	1	90	60	60	.50	4
6 (LD)	LD + GD	30.65	2	126	78	84	.57	1
7 (JD)	JD + BD + KD	26.07	3	108	70	72	.46	6
8 (JL)	JL + JF + JG	4.76	9	56	40	37	.24	11
9 (BJ)	BJ + KJ +KD + BD	12.10	6	68	45	45	.51	2
10 (BL)	BL + KL + BF + KF	3.66	10	72	57	48	.312	10
11 (KB)	KB + KJ + KD + KL + KF	12.91	5	30	22	20	.41	8

* Link-demands for 1940 were calculated as indicated in text and are based on the following city limit populations (in thousands): Battle Creek (B), 43; Detroit (D), 1,623; Flint (F), 152; Grand Rapids (G), 164; Jackson (J), 50; Kalamazoo (K), 54; and Lansing (L), 79. Source: U.S. Bureau of Census, *Sixteenth Census of the United States: 1940. Population, Number of Inhabitants by States*, Vol. I.

** Based on criteria established by author (see text). Source: Compiled and calculated by author.

homogeneous transport change is incorporated in the general hypothesis that the wholesale activity in a place will increase as the time-expenditure per unit of operational success decreases. In other words, that place which experiences the greatest degree of time-space convergence, compared to all other places in the system, will be expected to show the greatest absolute growth in wholesale activity.

A system of thirteen metropolitan areas in the Upper Midwest has been selected to test this hypothesis. Indicated in Table 21-3 are the travel-times for 1940 and 1965 and the time saved per route mile between each city and the other twelve places in the system. In Table 21-4 the average convergence of each place to all other places in the system between 1940 and 1965 is included along with various indicators of wholesale growth during roughly the same period—1939 to 1963. These cities were ranked from one to thirteen on the convergence and wholesale variables, and Spearman's rank correlation was used to measure the statistical association of the rankings of time-space convergence with each of the indicators of wholesale growth. The three wholesale measures showed close association with the convergence factor; *R* values, significant at the ninety-nine percent level, equaled .76 for the increase in dollar sales, .81 for the increase in the number of wholesale establishments, and .77 for the increase in the number of paid wholesale employees. These findings lend cautious support for the notion that, at least for the wholesale function, time-space convergence is a useful surrogate for estimating the centralization and specialization possible at given places.

In this example, convergence was least effective in suggesting the rank changes resulting from the growth in wholesale activities for Kalamazoo, Flint, and Toledo. Among the thirteen cities, Kalamazoo stood four positions lower in wholesale growth than it did in convergence. In contrast, Flint and Toledo each ranked four positions higher in change of wholesale activity than they did in the ranking of time-space convergence. Thus, relative to the locational utility of other places in the system, it is possible that Kalamazoo has

Table 21-3 Travel-time and Time-space Convergence (1940–65) Between Selected Cities in the Northern Midwest

	D	F	GR	J	K	L	M	PH	S	SB	T	Chicago
BATTLE CREEK	170 105 .58	147 114 .34	93 60 .53	68 45 .51	30 22 .40	72 57 .31	146 101 .46	248 230 .11	179 150 .24	131 91 .46	168 135 .29	234 157 .49
DETROIT		90 60 .50	219 140 .54	108 70 .53	200 135 .49	126 78 .57	276 182 .51	86 64 .39	137 91 .51	272 188 .46	86 53 .58	402 268 .50
FLINT			158 125 .31	131 98 .38	177 135 .36	75 53 .44	215 165 .35	100 80 .30	47 31 .52	278 225 .29	162 115 .44	381 265 .46
GRAND RAPIDS				146 100 .47	72 48 .50	93 62 .50	57 40 .44	258 200 .34	173 145 .24	168 118 .44	246 195 .31	254 180 .44
JACKSON					98 67 .46	56 40 .43	203 150 .39	193 149 .34	162 125 .34	174 135 .34	100 85 .18	291 200 .46
KALAMAZOO						102 81 .32	123 82 .50	278 208 .34	209 165 .32	100 70 .45	198 150 .36	204 136 .50
LANSING							150 100 .50	176 140 .31	107 80 .38	203 150 .39	156 130 .25	306 215 .45
MUSKEGON								315 252 .30	192 180 .09	177 158 .16	303 240 .31	263 180 .47
PORT HURON									147 120 .28	357 260 .41	171 120 .45	488 333 .48
SAGINAW										309 234 .36	209 140 .50	413 300 .41
SOUTH BEND											219 135 .58	131 80 .59
TOLEDO												349 215 .58

Key: 170 — 1940, 105 — 1965: Travel-time in minutes; .58 — Minutes saved per route mile (1940–65)

Source: Based on criteria established by author (see text).

increased, and Flint and Toledo have declined, in status as potential sites for wholesale activity. Interestingly, dollar sales by wholesale firms in the Kalamazoo metropolitan area increased 8.9 times between 1939 and 1963 in contrast to increases of 5.1 and 8.0 for the Flint and Toledo metropolitan areas. The average growth factor for the thirteen areas was 7.5. It appears, therefore, that even in those cases where convergence showed comparatively little rank association with wholesale growth, wholesale activity did gradually shift in association with changes in the surface of locational utility. As indicated in the evaluation of the basic model, there is an inherent inefficiency in human place-behavior and, therefore, such lags in spatial reorganization are to be expected.

CONCLUSION

The objective of this study has been threefold:

1 To conceptualize the role of transport technology as a key factor in the spatial reorganization of man's activities;
2 to outline the "steps" in the process of spatial reorganization; and
3 to propose a conceptual framework that accounts for the differential operation of this process at various places.

The premise upon which the study was based was that man adapts the areal structure of his activities in response to changes in transport technology which enable him to travel faster and to have access to larger areas and to more resources.

Given the assumptions of rationality as developed earlier in this study, the proposed theses seem tenable: 1) that time-space convergence is a significant factor leading towards spatial adaptation, and that 2) spatial reorganization will accelerate most rapidly at those places which stand to benefit most from increasing accessibility. However, in light of the limitations posed by the assumption of rationality, it is evident that the concept of relative advantage, as applied to the process of spatial reorganization, is not in complete accord with reality. The relative advantage concept seeks to explain man's decisions on the basis of motivation (i.e., desire for net social benefits, locational utility, operational success, and the like). The decisions of man,

Table 21-4 Time-space Convergence (1940–1965) and Wholesale Growth (1939–1963) for Selected Metropolitan Areas in the Northern Midwest

Place	Avg. TSC* 1940–1965 (minutes saved per route mile)	Indices of wholesale growth (1939–1963)**									Rankings of Change			
		Wholesale sales (millions of dollars)			No. establishments			No. paid employees (thousands)						
		1939	1963	Change	1939	1963	Change	1939	1963	Change	TSC	Sales	Estab.	Employ.
Battle Creek	.393	18	117	99	107	180	73	.6	1.5	.9	9	12	11	10
Detroit	.513	1,392	9,952	8,560	3,100	5,640	2,540	29.7	65.0	35.3	1	2	2	2
Flint	.391	76	386	310	181	420	239	2.1	7.6	5.5	10	7	6	5
Grand Rapids	.422	91	1,008	917	500	1,000	500	3.6	10.3	6.7	3	4	3	3
Jackson	.403	16	147	131	109	200	91	.9	1.6	.7	7.5	10	10	12
Kalamazoo	.416	23	205	182	134	290	156	1.1	2.6	1.5	4	9	8	8
Lansing	.404	45	411	366	260	440	180	1.7	4.0	2.3	6	6	7	7
Muskegon	.373	16	123	107	113	180	67	.6	1.6	1.0	11	11	12	9
Port Huron	.338	18	62	44	76	130	54	1.3	.7	–.6	13	13	13	13
Saginaw	.349	42	240	198	190	290	100	1.9	2.7	.8	12	8	9	11
South Bend	.411	50	512	462	190	460	270	1.7	4.8	3.1	5	5	5	6
Toledo	.403	137	1,096	959	530	1,000	470	5.7	11.5	5.8	7.5	3	4	4
Chicago	.486	4,150	23,682	19,532	8,200	12,210	4,010	98.3	171.0	72.7	2	1	1	1

* This is the average convergence of each place to the other twelve places in the system. Calculated by author from data in Table 3.

** The values of wholesale indices are for the SMSA's as defined for the 1960 U.S. Census. County data are used for Battle Creek and Port Huron.

Source: U.S. Bureau of Census, *Sixteenth Census of the United States: 1940. Census of Business 1939, Wholesale Trade,* Vol. II; and *1963 Census of Business, Wholesale Trade Area Statistics,* Vol. V.

however, are often conditioned by his lack of information, or non-maxima goals.

In that much of man's areal development is presently directed by various government agencies (at the city, region, state, and nation levels) rather than by the demand for locational utility, it seems that complete understanding of the process of spatial reorganization may rest upon one's knowledge of the decision-making processes of these agencies.[27] Upon what information are their decisions made? By what goals are they motivated? Answers to these questions were beyond the scope of this study. Nonetheless, until answers to such questions are found, the understanding of spatial reorganization will be limited to mechanistic concepts similar to those outlined herein. It is believed that a more refined understanding of spatial reorganization must await efforts to account for lags in the process and to evaluate the significance of both spatially and temporally variant goals. Dynamic programming techniques may hold some promise for the solution of these problems.[28]

NOTES

1 J. M. Blaut, "Space and Process," *The Professional Geographer,* Vol. 13 (July, 1961), p. 4.

2 This notion, first recognized by the physicists and physical philosophers, has been adknowledged by many geographers and other social scientists, including W. J. Cahnman, "Outline of a Theory of Area Studies," *Annals,* Association of American Geographers, Vol. 38 (1948), pp. 233–43; A. H. Hawley, *Human Ecology: A Theory of Community Structure* (New York The Ronald Press, 1950), p. 288; W. Isard, *Location and Space-Economy* (Cambridge, Mass.: The Massachusetts Institute of Technology Press, 1956), p. 11; F. Lukermann, "The Role of Theory in Geographical Inquiry,"

The Professional Geographer, Vol. 13 (March, 1961), p. 1; and R. L. Morrill, "The Development of Spatial Distributions of Towns in Sweden: A Historical-Predictive Approach," *Annals,* Association of American Geographers, Vol. 53 (1963), pp. 2–3.

3 The term "spatial reorganization" is not new. It has been used by W. L. Garrison. See "Notes on Benefits of Highway Improvements," in W. L. Garrison, B. J. L. Berry, D. F. Marble, J. D. Nystuen, R. L. Morrill, *Studies of Highway Development and Geographic Change* (Seattle: University of Washington Press, 1959), p. 23. This and other impact studies of the post-1956 period suggests that although the term has not seen wide use, the concept is one of immediate concern.

4 K. A. Fox, "The Study of Interactions Between Agriculture and the Nonfarm Economy: Local, Regional and National," *Journal of Farm Economics,* Vol. 44 (February, 1962), pp. 1–34.

5 J. Wolpert, "Behavioral Aspects of the Decision to Migrate," *Papers, Regional Science Association,* Vol. 15 (1965), pp. 159–69.

6 The terms place and area are used as designators of areal scale. In this study they are used interchangeably.

7 W. L. Garrison, "Connectivity of the Interstate Highway System," *Papers and Proceedings of the Regional Science Association,* Vol. 6 (1960), pp. 121–37; K. J. Kansky, *Structure of Transportation Networks* (Chicago: Department of Geography Research Paper No. 84, University of Chicago Press, 1963).

8 For a more thorough discussion of time-space convergence, see D. G. Janelle, "Central Place Development in a Time-space Framework," *The Professional Geographer,* Vol. 20 (1968), pp. 5–10.

9 For a discussion on the law of comparative advantage, see P. A. Samuelson, "The Gains from International Trade," *Canadian Journal of Economics and Political Science,* Vol. 5 (May 1939).

10 E. L. Ullman, "The Role of Transportation and the Bases of Interaction," in W. L. Thomas, Jr. (Ed.), *Man's Role in Changing the Face of the Earth* (Chicago: University of Chicago Press, 1956), pp. 862–80.

11 For a more complete treatment of this notion, see Ullman, *op. cit.*

12 The application of the feedback concept in this context was suggested to the author by James H. Stine, Department of Geology and Geography, Oklahoma State University.

13 An excellent discussion on both positive and negative feedback systems is provided by M. Maruyama, "The Second Cybernetics: Deviation-Amplifying Mutual Causal Processes," *American Scientist,* Vol. 51 (1963), pp. 164–79; also, see L. von Bertalanffy, "General System Theory," *General Systems,* Vol. 1 (1956), pp. 1–10.

14 Coverdale and Colpitts, Consultant Engineers, *Report on Traffic and Revenues, Proposed Mackinac Straits Bridge* (New York: Coverdale and Colpitts, January 22, 1952), p. 18.

15 R. M. Cyert and J. G. March, *A Behavioral Theory of the Firm* (Englewood Cliffs, N. J.: Prentice-Hall, Inc., 1963); J. H. Henderson and R. E. Quandt, *Micro-Economic Theory, A Mathematical Approach* (New York: McGraw-Hill Book Co., Inc., 1958); H. A. Simon, "Some Strategic Considerations in the Construction of Social Science Models," in P. F. Lazarsfeld (Ed.), *Mathematical Thinking in the Social Sciences,* (Glencoe, Ill.: The Free Press, 1954), pp. 388–415.

16 For information on the multiple nuclei concept of urban growth, see C. D. Harris and E. L. Ullman, "The Nature of Cities," *Annals of the American Academy of Political and Social Science,* Vol. 242 (November, 1945), pp. 7–17; E. L. Ullman, "The Nature of Cities Reconsidered," *Papers and Proceedings of the Regional Science Association,* Vol. 9 (1962), pp. 7–23.

17 J. Gottman, "Megalopolis, Or the Urbanization of the Northeastern Seaboard," *Economic Geography,* Vol. 33 (1957), pp. 189–200.

18 The skyscraper is an alternative choice in attaining more space while still retaining central access. The skyscraper, however, is a form of centralization which fosters greater interaction and additional demand for accessibility. Thus, this spatial adaptation also helps to perpetuate the trend towards greater centralization.

19 Interesting statements on a concept of relative

advantage similar to that proposed here are provided by Z. Griliches, "Hybrid Corn and the Economics of Innovation," *Science,* Vol. 132 (July 29, 1960), pp. 275–80, and "Hybrid Corn: An Exploration in the Economics of Technological Change," *Econometrica, Vol. 25 (1957), pp. 501–22.*

20 G. W. Hilton and J. F. Due, *The Electric Interurban Railways in America* (Stanford, Calif.: Stanford University Press, 1960).

21 The number of automobiles in Michigan increased from 2,700 in 1905 to more than 60,000 by 1913. See Michigan State Highway Department, *History of Michigan Highways and the Michigan State Highway Department* (Lansing, Mich.: Michigan State Highway Department, 1965), pp. 6–7.

22 Of the 68,000 miles of roads in Michigan in 1905, only 7,700 miles were graveled and only 245 miles were stone or macadam. See Michigan State Highway Department, *op. cit.,* footnote 22, p. 6.

23 Michigan State Highway Department, *Highways Connecting Pertinent Cities with O'Hare Field (Chicago) or Metropolitan Airport (Detroit)* (Lansing, Mich.: Michigan State Highway Department, 1963).

24 For a good review and appraisal of the gravity model, see G. Olson, *Distance and Human Interaction* (Philadelphia: Regional Science Research Institute, 1965).

25 The test of the significance of R values was based on the use of Student's t as suggested by M. J. Moroney, *Facts from Figures* (Baltimore: Penguin Books, 1956), pp. 331–36. In this study, findings based on Spearman's rank correlation technique are to be regarded as tentative rather than conclusive.

26 A. K. Philbrick, "Principles of Areal Functional Organization in Regional Human Geography," *Economic Geography,* Vol. 33 (1957), pp. 299–336.

27 For an excellent review of studies on decision theory and their applicability in planning, see J. W. Dyckman, "Planning and Decision Theory," *Journal of the American Institute of Planners,* Vol. 27 (1961), pp. 335–45.

28 A brief review of dynamic programming is provided by R. Bellman, "Dynamic Programming," *Science,* Vol. 153 (July 1, 1966), pp. 34–37.

FURTHER READINGS TO PART FIVE

There are a number of alternative approaches to the one suggested in this part. The principal alternative is to approach the interdependency of spatial structure (the landscape) and spatial behavior (in part, transportation) within a *positivistic* framework, as in Selection 21. Behavior is seen as rational and capable of simulation by rigorous statistical/quantitative techniques. (See, for example, B. J. L. Berry, "Interdependency of Spatial Structure and Spatial Behavior: A General Field Theory Formation," *Papers,* Regional Science Association, Vol. 21, 1968, pp. 205–227.) In this article the structure of the Indian landscape is approached through a multivariate study of flows; the resulting maps are intriguing but do not particularly help us to understand the landscape or behavior. Similar approaches in seeking a geometrical or abstract representation of the interdependency between landscape and transportation are:

W. L. Garrison, "The Spatial Structure of the Economy," *Annals* of the Association of American Geographers, Part 2, vol. 49, 1959, pp. 471–482; Part 3, vol. 50, 1960, pp. 357–373.

W. L. Garrison, "The Estimates of the Parameters of Spatial Interaction," *Papers and Proceedings,* Regional Science Association, vol. 2, 1966, pp. 280–288.

W. Isard, "Distance Inputs and the Space Economy," *Quarterly Journal of Economics,* vol. 65, 1951, pp. 181–198, pp. 373–399.

W. Isard, *Location and Space Economy,* Cambridge, Mass.: MIT Press, 1956.

W. Isard, *Methods of Regional Analysis,* Cambridge, Mass.: MIT Press, 1960.

W. Isard, *General Theory: Social, Political, Economic, and Regional,* Cambridge, Mass.: MIT Press, 1969.

G. Ollson and S. Gale, "Spatial Theory and Human Behaviour," *Papers and Proceedings,* Regional Science Association, vol. 21, 1969, pp. 229–242.

G. Ollson, "Trends in Spatial Model Building: An Overview," *Geographical Analysis,* vol. 1, no. 3, 1969, pp. 219–224.

E. Orr, "A Synthesis of Theories of Location, of Transport Rates, and of Spatial Price Equilibrium," *Papers and Proceedings,* Regional Science Association, vol. 3, 1957, pp. 61–73.

E. von Boventer, "Towards a Unified Theory of Spatial-economic Structure," *Papers and Proceedings*, Regional Science Association, vol. 10, 1963, pp. 163–187.

W. Warntz, "Geography of Prices and Spatial Interaction," *Papers and Proceedings,* Regional Science Association, vol. 3, 1957, pp. 118–129.

W. Warntz, "The Topology of a Socio-economic Terrain and Spatial Flows," *Papers and Proceedings,* Regional Science Association, vol. 17, 1966, pp. 47–64.

Similar, but in some ways more approachable, viewpoints are taken in:

E. M. Hoover, *The Location of Economic Activity,* New York: McGraw-Hill, 1948.

J. Labasse, *L'organisation de l'espace: elements de geographie volontaire,* Paris: Hermann, 1966.

A. Losch, *The Economics of Location,* trans. by W. Woglom and W. Stolper, New Haven: Yale University Press, 1954.

A. Philbrick, "Principles of Areal Functional Organization in Regional Human Geography," *Economic Geography,* vol. 33, 1957, pp. 299–336.

A. Pred, *The Spatial Dynamics of U.S. Urban-industrial Growth, 1840–1900,* Cambridge, Mass.: MIT Press, 1966.

The areas of communications and spatial behavior are only just opening up to geographic attention. The latter area will be covered in Part Six (*b*) but readings in the former could include geographical works such as:

R. Abler, "Distance, Communications, and Geography," *Proceedings of the Association of American Geographers*, vol. 3, 1971, pp. 1–4.

R. Abler, J. S. Adams, and P. Gould, *Spatial Organization*, Englewood Cliffs, N.J.: Prentice-Hall, 1971, especially chap. 12, 13, and 14.

K. R. Cox, *Man, Location and Behavior: An Introduction to Human Geography*, New York: Wiley, 1972, chap. 5.

G. Murphey, "Toward a Field Theory of Communication," *Journal of Communication,* vol. 11, no. 4, 1961, pp. 196–201.

A. Pred, *Behaviour and Location,* vol. 1, Lund Studies in Geography, Series B, No. 27, 1967.
F. Redlich, "Ideas–Their Migration in Space and Transmittal Over Time," *Kyklos,* vol. 6, 1954, pp. 301–322.
S. J. Seneca and C. J. Cicchetti, "A Gravity Model Analysis of the Demand for Public Communication," *Journal of Regional Science,* vol. 9, no. 3, 1969, pp. 459–470.
E. W. Soja, "Telephone Communications and Territorial Integration in East Africa: An Introduction to Transaction Flow Analysis," *East Lakes Geographer,* vol. 4, 1968, pp. 39–57.
P. L. Wagner, "Cultural Landscapes and Regions: Aspects of Communication," in B. F. Perkins (ed.), *Geoscience and Man,* vol. V, Baton Rouge, La.: Louisiana State University Press, 1972.
J. Wolpert, "The Decision Process in Spatial Context," *Annals* of the Association of American Geographers, vol. 54, 1964, pp. 537–558.

The works cited here are very variable, from the purely mechanistic approach of Soja to the behavioral approach of Pred and Wolpert and the cultural approach of Wagner. Just as variable are the works of wider concern with communication:

C. Cherry, *On Human Communication* (2d. ed.), Cambridge, Mass.: MIT Press, 1966.
H. A. Innis, *The Bias of Communication,* Toronto: University of Toronto Press, 1964.
M. McLuhan, *Understanding Media: The Extensions of Man,* New York: McGraw-Hill, 1964.
M. McLuhan and Q. Fiore, *The Medium Is the Message: An Inventory of Effects,* New York: Bantam, 1967.
R. L. Meier, *A Communication Theory of Urban Growth,* Cambridge, Mass.: MIT Press, 1962.
R. T. Oliver, *Culture and Communication,* Springfield, Ill.: Charles C. Thomas, 1962.
L. W. Pye, *Communications and Political Development,* Princeton, N.J.: Princeton University Press, 1963.
E. M. Rogers, *Diffusion of Innovations,* New York: The Free Press, 1962.
P. Rossi, *Why Families Move: A Study in the Serial Psychology of Urban Residential Mobility,* New York: The Free Press, 1955.
C. E. Shannon and W. Weaver, *The Mathematical Theory of Communication,* Urbana, Ill.: University of Illinois Press.
P. L. Wagner, *Environments and People,* Englewood Cliffs, N.J.: Prentice-Hall, 1971.

And there are many many more; two recent bibliographies which will introduce you to yet wider horizons in this field are:

R. C. Harkness, *Communication Innovations, Urban Form and Travel Demand,* Council of Planning Librarians, Exchange Bibliography 285, 1972.
B. Wellman and M. Whitaker, *Community-Network-Communication: An*

Annotated Bibliography, Council of Planning Libraries, Exchange Bibliography 282/3, 1972.

The inclusion of a reference to diffusion (the work of E. M. Rogers) opens up yet another area in which geographers have been concerned—spatial diffusion and migration. With a few exceptions this field has been rather sterile, but for those interested the following sample of references are included:

J. S. Adams, "Directional Bias in Intraurban Migration," *Economic Geography,* vol. 45, no. 4, 1969, pp. 302–323.

L. Brown, *Diffusion Processes and Location: A Conceptual Framework and Bibliography,* Philadelphia: Regional Science Research Institute, 1968.

W. A. V. Clark, "Information Flows and Intra-urban Migration: An Empirical Analysis," *Proceedings* of the Association of American Geographers, vol. 1, 1969, pp. 38–41.

P. R. Gould, "Spatial Diffusion," Association of American Geographers *Resource Paper* No. 4, Commission on College Geography, 1969.

T. Hagerstrand, *Innovation Diffusion and a Spatial Process,* trans. by A. Pred, Chicago: University of Chicago Press, 1967.

R. Lycan, "Interprovincial Migration in Canada: The Role of Spatial and Economic Factors," *The Canadian Geographer,* vol. 13, no. 3, 1969, pp. 237–254.

J. Wolpert, "Behavioural Aspects of the Decision to Migrate," *Papers,* Regional Science Association, vol. 15, 1965, pp. 159–169.

The total milieu within which transportation and communication are treated is covered by Pred, Wagner, and:

M. E. Eliot Hurst, *A Geography of Economic Behaviour: An Introduction,* North Scituate, Mass.: Duxbury Press, 1972.

Government regulation, which is a critical governing factor in such an area as transportation, has not received attention from geographers. Transportation is so highly constrained by all levels of government that such an omission may seem, at first sight, strange. However, as was pointed out in the section "Levels of Understanding" (pp. 285) such a study might disturb the status quo a little too much. Recommendations about such studies are made in Part Seven.

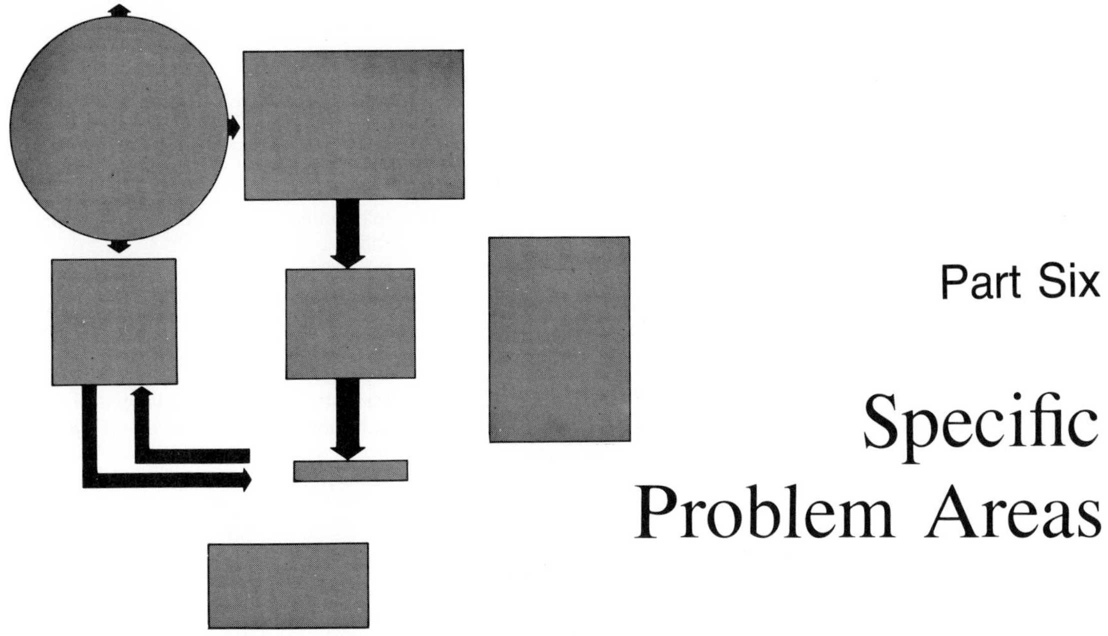

Part Six

Specific Problem Areas

INTRODUCTION

The threads we have drawn together so far in this book underline the great variety of interactions present in the landscapes around us. Obviously the approach has not been exhaustive simply because the work carried out and the literature published are extremely diverse. We began by disaggregating the transportation conception by vertical cross sections of flows, networks, and modes, and then reaggregating them and stressing the spatial, behavioral, cultural, and political interrelationships. It is also possible, however, to view transportation horizontally, as set out in the table "A Horizontal Analysis of Transportation," by looking at specific amalgams of transportation routes, stocks, modes, networks, and flows. Of these horizontal sections, some represent particular settings, such as the city or recreational areas, while others represent particular situations, such as the impact of new transportation structures or the role of transportation in developing economies.

It is not possible to examine here all of these horizontal cross sections. Accordingly, just two are examined below: developing areas and urban

A Horizontal Analysis of Transportation

	Inventory	Network	Flow	Mode	Relationship
Human communication	Words, sounds, symbols, smells, taste	Fields of personal, public and visual contacts; distribution channels, radio-TV networks	Flows of ideas, facts	Face-to-face, telephone, radio, television, printed word	Social communication
Urban transport	Cars, trucks, buses, trains; miles of street, freeway, subway	Streets, sidewalks, tracks, freeways	Flows of ideas, money, goods, people	Pedestrian, automobile, truck, bus, rapid transit	Balanced urban transport system
Developing areas	Cars, trucks, freight cars, etc.; miles of road, track, etc.	Road, rail, water, air networks	Flows of goods, equipment, machinery, people, ideas	Railroad, truck, automobile, water transport, airplane, hovercraft	Transport as a neutral factor; concomitant with growth, sometimes a catalyst
Highway impact	New and projected highway miles, expected traffic units	New freeway, roadway networks	Volume of diverted, generated, non-diverted traffic	Automobile, truck, bus	Impact on region —growth and change of tertiary activities, and other economic activities
Recreation	Cars, buses, planes, ski lifts, etc.; highways, airline miles	Road, rail, air networks	Flows of people, money	Automobile, bus, plane, skidoo, etc.	Increased leisure time, regional impact, growth of tertiary activities

transportation. The other sections in the table are just as crucial, however, to the transportation geographer, and the reader may well wish to pursue those fields on his own.

A. TRANSPORT AND DEVELOPMENT

Holland Hunter has posed the question: Is ample transport capacity a prerequisite for economic development?* As he points out, the conventional Western attitude tends to view transport as playing such a role, although the

*H. Hunter, "Transport in Soviet and Chinese Development," *Economic Development and Cultural Change*, vol. 14, 1965, pp. 71–84.

attitude of centrally planned economies has tended to place transportation in a more secondary position. One of the factors which Hunter stresses in his examination of Soviet and Chinese transportation development is that transport improves in any economy as a concomitant of economic development, not a precondition for it. He draws on evidence from outside those two countries, such as the role of railroad development in the nineteenth-century United States,† to show that "massive expansion of transport capacity is not a prior condition for economic progress."

We know that the functioning of an economy requires the use of transport, and that, as economies develop, specialized production increases and relatively more transport is required. It might be possible, therefore, to analyze economies with varying structures and levels of development, see how transport is used, and discover how the variations in its use relate to other determinants of spatial variations. This would be a complex undertaking because of the many ways in which transport is used in an economy. One could list all the outputs of an economy—beef, steel, aluminum, automobiles, and so on—and calculate for each the amount of transport required for each unit of output. Thus a summary of transportation intensity in a country would consist of a list of numbers showing the input of transport per unit of output for every economic activity.

However, the role of transport is not completely unambiguous. Rather than being autonomous, it is always a part of something else. Without resources to be utilized, access has no meaning. Investment in transport may be contingent upon the fact that it is already being provided, but as Heymann has pointed out, there is no assurance that this fact will necessarily call forth investment.‡ It thus becomes essential to consider transport within a matrix of potential demand. Otherwise, it may become an underutilized facility within its region. Frequently one reads such remarks as: "Lack of adequate transport can be one of the greatest obstacles to economic progress . . . the difficulty comes when the choice has to be made between the various types of transport . . .".§ What is rarely mentioned is the choice within the socioeconomic context, which may dictate not so much *which* mode of transport is used but *how much* (or *little*) investment in transport is needed at all.

In some senses, then, transport may be a neutral factor. It needs to be related to what it is going to be used for, and to who is going to use it, before any development and investment can take place. Transportation is rarely desired for itself; it is really a means to serve other objectives. Both K. J. Storey and G. W. Wilson, in pursuing this point, have come up with three causal possibilities.‖ Using Storey's categories, these are:

†Noted by, among others, P. Cootner, in "The Role of Railroads in U.S. Economic Growth," *Journal of Economic History,* vol. 23, 1963, pp. 477–521; R. W. Fogel, *Railroads and American Economic Growth,* Johns Hopkins University Press, 1964.

‡H. Heymann, "The Objectives of Transportation," in *Transport Investment and Economic Development,* G. Fromm (ed.), Washington, D.C.: Brookings Institution, 1965.

§C. H. Dale, "What Kind of Transport for Developing Countries?" *International Railway Journal,* April 1966, pp. 35–38, 40, 48.

‖K. J. Storey, "Transport and Economic Development," unpublished M. A. Thesis, Simon Fraser University, 1969; G. W. Wilson in the introduction to *The Impact of Highway Investment on Development,* Washington, D.C.: Brookings Institution, 1966.

1 A *positive effect* (+) wherein new, directly productive activities are the direct result of providing transportation facilities.

2 A *neutral effect* (o) wherein transportation facilities do not themselves call forth directly productive activities and subsequent increases in the level of economic growth.

3 A *negative effect* (–) wherein the presence of transportation facilities eliminates directly productive activity and effectively reduces the level of economic growth, as, for example, where a newly developing country's overambitious and prestigious efforts to create a national airline may well divert investment from areas where it could have led to economic growth.

Wilson categorizes these as (1) a positive stimulus to further development; (2) a middle case, where there may be a declaration of growth accompanying new transport investment; and (3) a negative case, where absolute declines in the level of per capita income in a country are recorded. The two latter categories are clear cases of Storey's negative category, based on the seriousness or degree of the decline of economic growth (middle) or absolute decrease (negative case). Wilson does remind us that in all cases involving transportation there is a large element of *contingency;* neither Storey's nor Wilson's alleged "factors" are inevitable; they *may* exist, but then again they may not. This is where we return to the points I made at the beginning of this section. Evidence has accumulated that frequently transport has followed rather than preceded growth. Storey goes on to add temporal components to the three causal factors:

1 The provision of transportation facilities *predates* economic growth in temporal terms (PRE).

2 Provision of transportation is *concomitant* with economic growth (CON).

3 The provision of transportation *postdates* economic growth (POST).

These components are set out in the table "Transportation and Development: A Possibility Matrix of Causal and Temporal Factors." The letter *X* in the matrix indicates a common view of transport as a precondition or prerequisite of development, implying both causal and temporal precedence. Evidence seems to suggest that place *Y* in the matrix may well be a more reasonable representation of reality. That is, transport may play a neutral role, developing concomitantly with the expansion of productive activity and economic growth. As Wilson concludes after examining a series of empirical case studies, it suggests that ". . . there are, in fact, few magical properties in transport investments that warrant the excessive attention frequently paid them . . . transport investment is like any other [investment] . . . the role of transport investment in economic growth is similarly not unique. Transport investment is no more an initiator of growth than any other form of investment or deliberate policy."#

Bearing in mind the framework suggested by Storey and Wilson's warning of "contingency" and lack of magical properties, we can examine transport's

#Wilson, *op. cit.*, p. 218

Transportation and Development:
A Possibility Matrix of Causal and Temporal Factors

Causal factors

Temporal factors	Positive +	Neutral o	Negative —
PRE condition	X		
CON comitant		Y	
POST dates			

***Source:* Storey (1969).**

role, or assumed role, in developing areas. Selection 22 by Taaffe, Morrill, and Gould is a spinoff of the research carried out at Northwestern University; it attempts to place the growth of transport stocks, networks, and flows in an evolutionary framework. Based largely on data collected in West Africa, the model is nevertheless a reasonable facsimile of the kinds of transportation spatial changes occurring as the economic landscape develops and changes in many parts of the world. Their warning as to accepting at face value any "stage" model should be heeded.

No matter what role one ascribes to transportation in the development process as a whole, it is obvious that the kind of sequence development for transport itself, noted in Selection 22, should not be allowed to occur haphazardly. B. V. Martin and C. B. Warden, in Selection 23, suggest in fact a holistic systems rationale for the planned development of the network. Their initial statements may not seem to accord with those of Storey and Wilson, but at no time has it been suggested that transport plays no role at all. As D. J. Janelle showed earlier (Selection 21), improvements in transportation may well alter the relative "accessibility" of the spatial landscape, which may later open the way to landscape change.

Having dealt so much with the abstract, we must come down, as Wilson urged, to the empirical level. Selections 24 and 25 are representative of this approach. W. R. Stanley deals with what we would more conventionally think of as a developing area (Selection 24), but J. M. Munro reminds us (Selection 25) that there are areas in so-called developed nations that have been singled out as depressed regions. In his case study of Appalachia he again draws our attention to how easy it is to choose transportation as a prime ingredient of a development program, but how little attention is paid to the *actual* role of transportation in such a process.

Selection 22

Transport Expansion in Underdeveloped Countries: A Comparative Analysis

E. J. Taaffe, R. L. Morrill, and P. R. Gould

In the economic growth of underdeveloped countries a critical factor has been the improvement of internal accessibility through the expansion of a transportation network. This expansion is from its beginning at once a continuous process of spatial diffusion and an irregular or sporadic process influenced by many specific economic, social, or political forces. In the present [work] both processes are examined as they have been evident in the growth of modern transportation facilities in several underdeveloped areas. Certain broad regularities underlying the spatial diffusion process are brought to light, which permit a descriptive generalization of an ideal-typical sequence of transportation development. The relationship between transportation and population is discussed and is used as the basis for examination of such additional factors as the physical environment, rail competition, intermediate location, and commercialization. Throughout the study, Ghana and Nigeria are used as examples.[1]

SEQUENCE OF TRANSPORTATION DEVELOPMENT

Fig. 22-1 presents the authors' interpretation of an ideal-typical sequence of transport development. The first phase (A) consists of a scattering of small ports and trading posts along the seacoast. There is little lateral interconnection except for small indigenous fishing craft and irregularly scheduled trading vessels, and each port has an extremely limited hinterland. With the emergence of major lines of penetration (B), hinterland transportation costs are reduced for certain ports. Markets expand both at the port and at the interior center. Port concentration then begins, as illustrated by the circles P_1 and P_2. Feeder routes begin to focus on the major ports and interior centers (C). These feeder routes give rise to a sort of hinterland piracy that permits the major port to enlarge its hinterland at the expense of adjacent smaller ports. Small nodes begin to develop along the main lines of penetration, and as feeder development continues (D), certain of the nodes, exemplified by N_1 and N_2, become focal points for feeder networks of their own. Interior concentration then begins, and N_1 and N_2 pirate the hinterlands of the smaller nodes on each side. As the feeder networks continue to develop around the ports, interior centers, and main on-line nodes, certain of the larger feeders begin to link up (E). Lateral interconnection should theoretically continue until all the ports, interior centers, and main nodes are linked. It is postulated that once this level is reached, or even before, the next phase consists of the development of national trunk-line routes or "main streets" (F). In a sense, this is the process of concentration repeated, but at a higher level. Since certain centers will grow at the expense of the others, the result will be a set of high-priority linkages among the largest. For example, in the diagram the best rail schedules, the widest paved roads, and the densest air traffic would be over the P_1-I_2 and P_1-P_2 routes.

It is probably most realistic to think of the

Geographical Review, vol. 53, 1963, pp. 503–529. Reprinted by permission of the authors and editor.

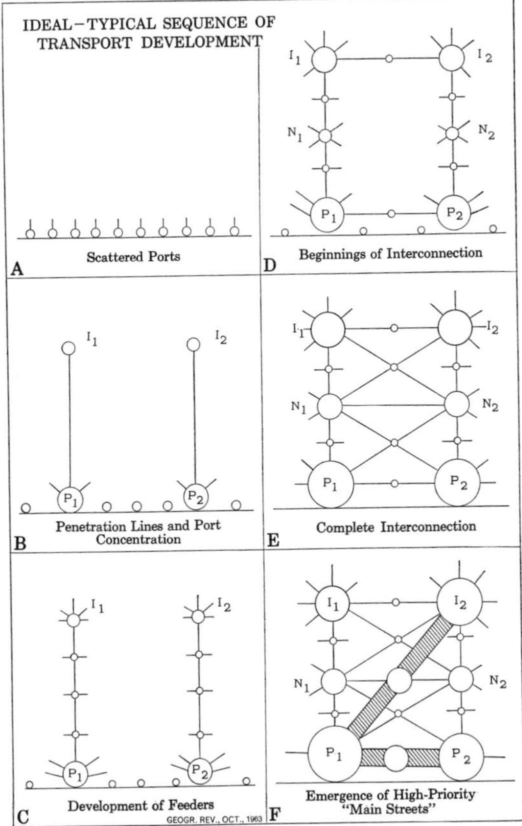

Fig. 22-1.

entire sequence as a process rather than as a series of discrete historical stages.[2] Thus at a given point in time a country's total transport pattern may show evidence of all the phases. Lateral interconnection may be going on in one region at the same time that new penetration lines are developing in another.

THE FIRST PHASE: SCATTERED PORTS

In both Ghana and Nigeria[3] an early period of numerous small, scattered ports and coastal settlements with trading functions may be easily identified (Figs. 22-3 and 22-4). These settlements, most of which existed or came into being between the end of the fifteenth century and the end of the nineteenth, were populated by the indigenous people around a European trading station or fort. Many of the people engaged in trade with the Europeans and served as middlemen for trade with the interior, a function jealously guarded for centuries against European encroachment. Penetration lines to the interior were weakly developed, but networks of circuitous bush trails connected the small centers to their restricted hinterlands. River mouths were important, particularly in the Niger delta, but with a few exceptions during the early periods of European encroachment the rivers did not develop as the main lines of thrust when pene-

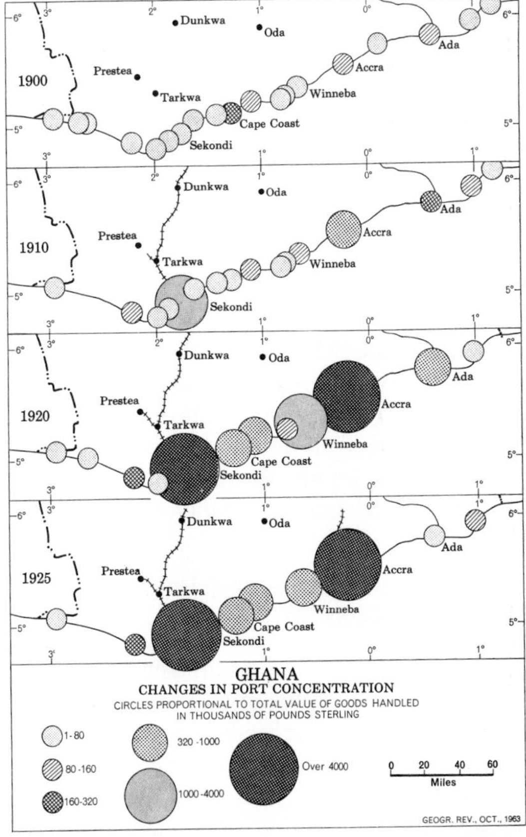

Fig. 22-2 Changes in port concentration, Ghana, 1900–1925. (Redrawn from map in Gould, *The Development of the Transportation Pattern in Ghana*, p. 45)

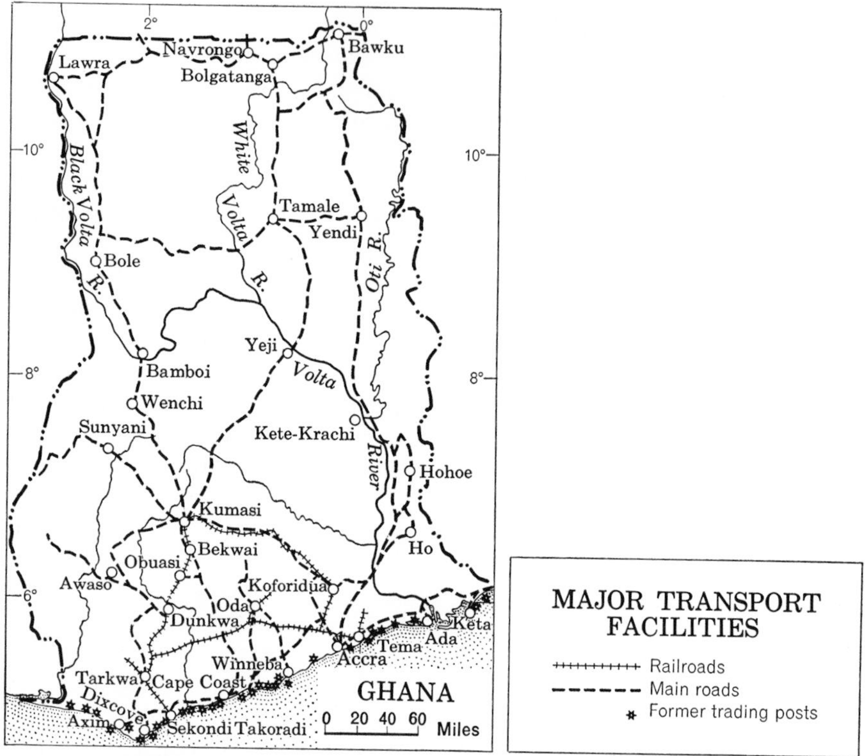

Fig. 22-3 Major transport facilities, Ghana, (Generalized from several maps in Gould, *The Development of the Transportation Pattern in Ghana*)

tration began. Most of these early trading centers have long since disappeared, destroyed by the growth of the main ports, or else they linger on as relict ports, with visits of occasional tramp steamers to remind them of their former trading heyday.

THE SECOND PHASE: PENETRATION LINES AND PORT CONCENTRATION

Perhaps the most important single phase in the transportation history of an underdeveloped country is the emergence of the first major penetration line from the seacoast to the interior. Later phases typically evolve around the penetration lines, and ultimately there is a strong tendency for them to serve as the trunk-line routes for more highly developed transportation networks. Three principal motives for building lines of penetration have been active in the past: (1) the desire to connect an administrative center on the seacoast with an interior area for political and military control; (2) the desire to reach areas of mineral exploitation; (3) the desire to reach areas of potential agricultural export production. In the cases examined, the political motive has been the strongest. Political and military control dominated official thinking of the day in Africa, often as a direct result of extra-African rivalries. The second motive, mineral exploitation, is typically associated with rail penetration. It is today probably the principal motive for the building of railways in Africa, and then only after careful surveys and international agreements have virtually guaranteed the steady haul of a bulk commodity to amortize the loans required for construction.[4]

The development of a penetration line sets in motion a series of spatial processes and readjustments as the comparative locational advantages of all centers shift. Concentration of port activity is particularly important, and the ports at the termini of the earliest penetration lines are usually the ones that thrive at the expense of their neighbors (Fig. 22-2). Typically, one or two ports in a country dominate both import and export traffic, and often the smaller ports have lost their functions in external commerce.

In Ghana several interesting variations on the penetration theme appear (Fig. 22-3). The desire to reach Kumasi, capital of a then aggressive Ashanti, formed the essentially military-political motive for the first penetration road, which followed an old bush track, sporadically cleared whenever the local people were goaded into activity. The road was built from Cape Coast, and although it is still important as one of Ghana's main north-south links, the port function of Cape Coast declined as Sekondi increased in importance. Sekondi's great impetus came with the building of the rail penetration line to Kumasi at the turn of the century, after which adjacent ports such as Axim, Dixcove, Adjua, Shama, Komena, and Elmina suffered a rapid decline in traffic. The Pra and Ankobra Rivers, east and west of Sekondi, which were formerly of some significance as avenues of penetration, also experienced marked traffic decreases. The initial motive for the western railroad was primarily mineral production (the goldfield at Tarkwa), and secondarily provision of a rapid connection for administration between the seacoast and a troublesome internal center of population.

The eastern railroad penetration line was slower in developing, partly as a result of the interruption of the First World War and of smallpox outbreaks in the railroad camps. The link between Kumasi and Accra was not completed until 1923, twenty years after the Sekondi-Kumasi link. Connection with the rapidly expanding cocoa areas north of Accra was the immediate reason for this line, underlain by the political desire to connect the leading city, Accra, with Kumasi, the main population and distribution center in the interior. As in the case of Sekondi-Takoradi, Accra's importance increased steadily at the expense of adjacent ports as the railroad penetrated inland.

The two penetration lines forming the sides of the rail triangle were now complete, and a considerable amount of subsequent transportation development of the country was based on these two trunk lines. Penetration north of Kumasi was entirely by road, despite grand railroad plans at one time. There were no minerals to provide an economic incentive for railroads, and the barren middle zone, which separated the rail-triangle area from the densely settled north, acted as a deterrent to the continuation of the railroad in short stages.

The Great North Road is the chief line of penetration north of Kumasi, built with a strong political-administrative motive to Tamale, a town deliberately laid out as the capital of the Northern Territories in the early years of this century. Early feeder development focusing on Tamale helped to fix the position of this trunk line and its extension to the northern markets of Bolgatanga, Navrongo, and Bawku. The Western Trunk Road was built with similar motives and grew out of the extensive Kumasi feeder network to link that city with a moderately populated area north of the barren middle zone. In the building of the Eastern Trunk Road political and economic motives were mixed. This road through former British Togoland was originally extended from the Hohoe cocoa area to Yendi for transport of yams to the rapidly growing urban centers of the south, but its extention to the northern border hinged in large part on political motives that were very strong immediately before the United Nations plebiscite and Togo's resultant political affiliation with Ghana. The original road links from the rail triangle and Accra to the Hohoe cocoa area were associated with a political desire to forge a link with British Togoland, and with an economic desire to prevent the diversion of this area's cocoa traffic to the port of Lomé in then-French Togoland.

The process of penetration and port concentration in Nigeria (Fig. 22-4) was markedly similar to that in Ghana; the main difference lay in the greater emphasis on long-haul rail development and the subsequent higher level of economic development in the north. Again the initial motives were somewhat more political than economic; for even the early penetration to the north via the Niger River by the Royal Niger Company had imperialistic as well as economic motives. In a sense, Kano might be regarded as analogous to Kumasi. Both are important interior centers which predate European settlement and which were later connected to the main ports by rail penetration lines. The chief differences, of course, are the vastly greater distance between Kano and the coast and the greater width of Nigeria's relatively barren middle zone. Mineral exploitation was also a major motive for the

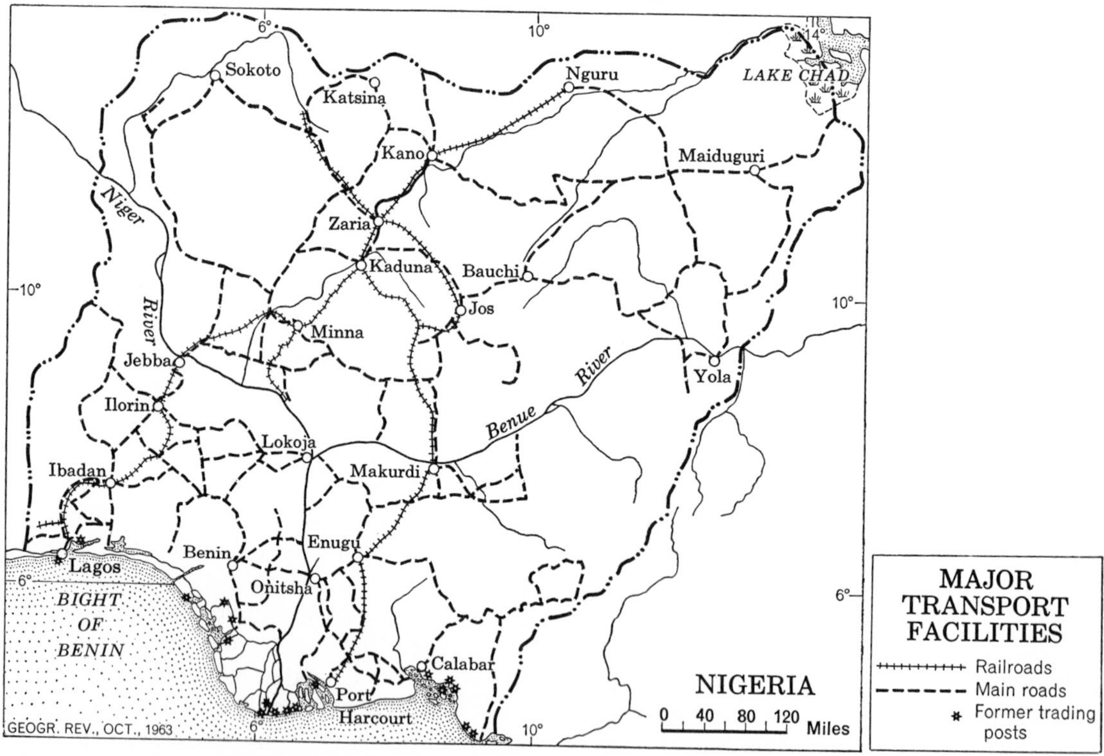

Fig. 22-4 Major transport facilities, Nigeria. (Adapted from Map 1 in "The Economic Development of Nigeria")

building of rail penetration lines in Nigeria, particularly the eastern railroad. The line from Port Harcourt was started in 1913 and was connected with the important Enugu coalfields three years later. This port serves also as the principal outlet for the tin output of the Jos Plateau. The connecting of agricultural regions to the coast, though not a strong initial penetration motive, was apparently associated with the actual linking of the northern and southern lines.

As in Ghana, the rail penetration lines form the basis for the entire transportation network. The only area of extensive road penetration is in the northeast, from the railroad at Jos and Nguru to Maiduguri. The main motive for establishing tarred roads and large-scale trucking services was the attraction of the Lake Chad region to the northeast. However, the Maiduguri region is now being connected by rail to the main network, despite the recommendation of a mission of the International Bank for Reconstruction and Development, which felt that roads could more efficiently accommodate the expected increase in traffic. In the southeast there is no effective road or rail penetration line.

Port concentration has been marked. The decline of the delta ports began with the building of the rail penetration line from Lagos and was accentuated by the building of the eastern line and the concomitant growth of Port Harcourt. In 1958 these two major ports accounted for more than three-quarters of Nigeria's export and import trade.

THE THIRD PHASE: FEEDERS AND LATERAL INTERCONNECTIONS

Penetration is followed by lateral interconnection as feeder lines begin to move out both from the ports and from the nodes along the penetration lines. The process of concentration among the nodes is analogous to the process of port concentration; it results when the feeder networks of certain centers reach out and tap the hinterlands of their neighbors. As feeder networks become stronger at the interior centers and intermediate nodes some of them link and thereby interconnect the original penetration lines.[5]

Figs. 22-5, 22-6, and 22-7 present a sequence of road development in Ghana from 1922 to 1958. The shading represents road-mileage density as recorded in a series of grid cells of 283 square miles superimposed on a highway map. In 1922 Ghana had just entered the phase of lateral interconnection, with east–west linkages both in the south, along the coast, and among the centers of the north, and with an extensive feeder network steadily drawing more and more of the smaller population centers into the orbit of Kumasi. Development in the southwest was weak, owing to railroad competition and to a deliberate policy of maintaining an economic road gap between Sekondi-Takoradi and Kumasi. This gap was finally filled in 1958, and only now is the southwest beginning to realize its great potential in cocoa and timber. By 1937 lateral interconnection had become more marked. The connections east and west of Tamale provide a good example of links between intermediate nodes. The 1–20-mile shading, for example, now reaches west from the Tamale node on the Great North Road to the node at Bole, which was just developing on the Western Trunk Road in 1922; Yendi on the Eastern Trunk has been similarly linked. Lateral interconnection has become intensified in the north, and the 21–40-mile shading now covers the entire zone between Bawku and Lawra. In the Kumasi area feeder development has continued, and the 21–40-mile shading blankets the Wenchi–Sunyani area to provide a fairly good network of interconnections between the Western Trunk and the Great North Road in the zone where both

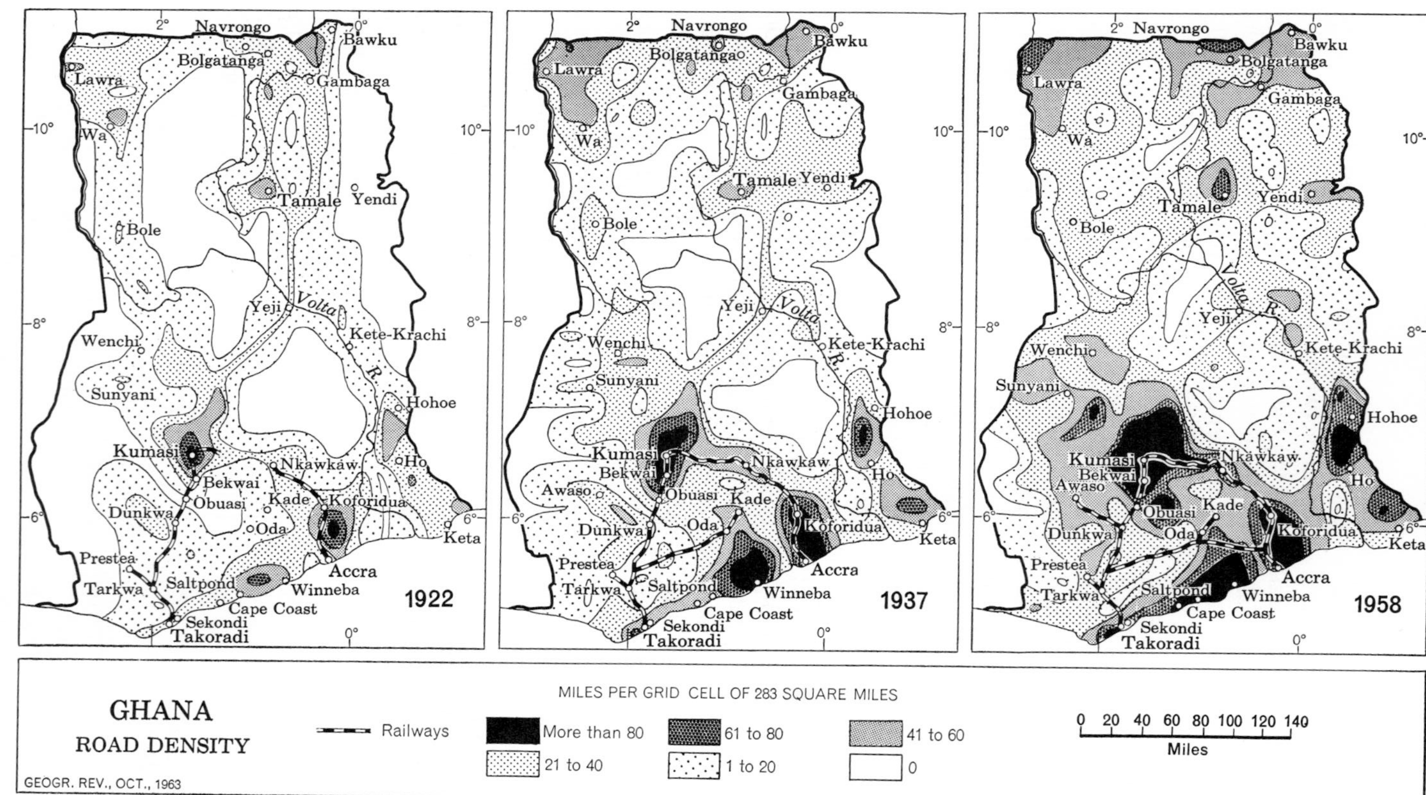

Figs. 22-5–22-7 Road density in Ghana, 1922, 1937, and 1958. (Redrawn from maps in Gould, *The Development of the Transportation Pattern in Ghana*, pp. 104, 107, and 109)

converge on Kumasi. Urban geographers will note the strong analogy to the process of interstitial filling between major radial roads converging on a central business district.

In 1958 the lateral interconnection process is fairly well developed. Only a few areas are still without road links, formerly inaccessible areas having been tapped by the expanding road network. A new series of high-density nodes have developed since 1937 and already are reaching out toward one another. Marked examples occur in the north between Tamale, Yendi, and other northern population centers, and in the south in the developing and extending nodes around Kumasi and east of the Volta River.

It is clear from the regularity of the progression of the highway-density patterns that extrapolation of the density maps to some future date would be reasonable. In a sense the map sequence is a crude predictive device. For instance, the probability of an increase in road miles for any area between two nodes is greater than that for a comparable area elsewhere.

In Nigeria a basically similar pattern had developed by 1953 (Fig. 22-8), with many of the earlier nodes of high accessibility in the south linking laterally to form an almost continuous high-density strip, broken only by the Niger River near Onitsha. Lines of penetration linking the north and south across the barren middle zone, a feature clearly brought out by the map, are relatively weakly developed, and the degree of lateral linkage is well below that of northern Ghana. Only the Kano and Zaria nodes, in areas of high agricultural production and at the center of strong administrative webs, and the Jos node, at the center of the tin and columbium mineral complex, stand out as exceptions. Heavy rail competition, which resulted in severe restraints on long-haul trucking for many years, has clearly weakened the western road penetration lines, and the similarity to southwestern Ghana is strong. Areas totally inaccessible by road are still numerous, particularly in the barren middle zone and along the periphery of the country. To the political geographer the general weakness of the linkages between the Eastern, Western, and Northern Regions will be of particular interest. There is, in fact, a clear visual impression that the general pattern of accessibility by road in Nigeria in 1953 is similar to that of Ghana in 1937—hardly surprising in view of the much larger size of Nigeria, the longer distances, and the lower per capita tax base from which the greater part of road development funds must come.

THE FOURTH PHASE: HIGH-PRIORITY LINKAGES

The phase following the development of a fairly complete and coherent network is difficult to identify, and a variety of labels might be applied to it. Certainly the most marked characteristic of the most recent phase in the cases studied is the dominance of road over railroad. A common theme throughout the evolution of the transportation system in Ghana and Nigeria, and also in the other examples studied, has been the steady rise in the importance of road traffic, which first complements the railroad, then competes with it, and finally overwhelms it. However, the evidence available seems to indicate that this occurs irrespective of the stage of transport development, and it is possible that a greater number of road penetration lines are now being built in areas which would have required rail penetration lines in the past.

The idea of a phase of high-priority linkages is based, somewhat weakly, on a logical extrapolation of the concentration processes noted in the earlier stages of transport development in Ghana and Nigeria, and is supported in part by highly generalized evidence

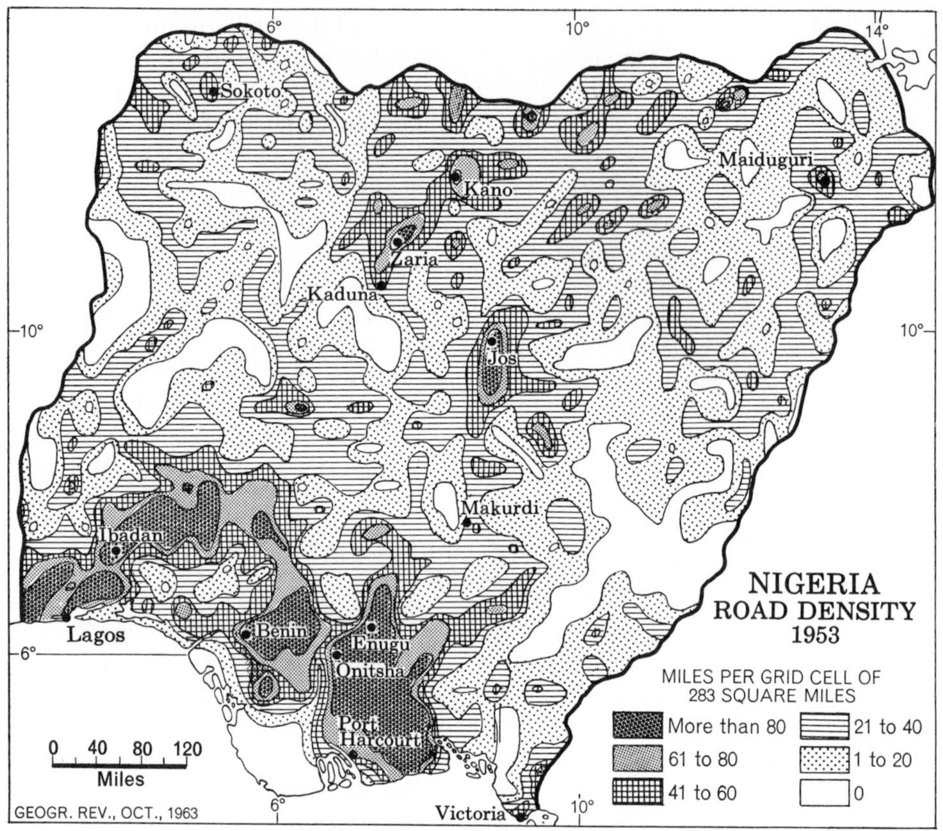

Fig. 22-8 Road density in Nigeria, 1953. (Compiled from sheets of the 1:250,000 map series published by the Federal Survey Department, Lagos)

from areas with well-developed transportation systems.

Interior centers, intermediate nodes, and ports do not develop at precisely the same rate. As some of these centers grow more rapidly than others, their feeder networks become intensified and reach into the hinterlands of nearby centers. Ultimately certain interior centers and ports assert a geographic dominance over the entire country. This creates a disproportionately large demand for transportation between them, and since some transport facilities already exist, the new demand may take such forms as the widening of roads or the introduction of jet aircraft. In general, transport innovations are first applied to these trunk routes. For example, in the United States the best passenger rates, schedules, and equipment are usually initiated over high-density routes such as New York–Chicago. In underdeveloped countries high-priority linkages would seem to be less likely to develop along an export trunk line than along a route connecting two centers concerned in internal exchange. There is some weak evidence that high-priority links may be developing in the two study countries. High-density, short-haul traffic in the vicinity of Lagos may be the forerunner of a "main street" between cities of the western part of the rail bifurcation. In Ghana the heavy traffic flows focusing on Accra (flows that have tripled every five years since the war) have virtually forced the authorities to bring the basic road triangle up to first-class standards of alignment and surface.

RELATIONSHIPS BETWEEN ROAD MILEAGES AND SELECTED PHENOMENA

The lateral-interconnection phase of the ideal-typical sequence is the one that best depicts the current extent of transportation development in most underdeveloped countries. This phase has been accompanied by a steady increase in the importance of motor vehicles, so that at present the dominant transport characteristic of most underdeveloped countries is the expansion of the road network. Closer examination of the road networks of Ghana and Nigeria affords deeper insight into the factors that affect the spatial diffusion of roads at a time when interconnection is a prominent motive for transport development. For example, how close a relation is there between roads and population? Do such additional factors as environment, competitive transportation, and income have an effect on the distribution of roads over and above the population effect? Attempts to answer these questions are in the form of a basic regression model supplemented by cartographic analysis. In the basic regression model, road mileage within subregional units is treated as a dependent variable, population and area as the independent variables.[6]

The results of the regression analysis indicate a close relationship between the internal distribution of road mileage and total population as corrected for the differing areas of reporting units. Briefly, it has been found that in a given unit road mileage is in general proportional to the square root (approximately) of the population times the square root (approximately) of the area. Three-quarters of the internal spatial variation in road mileage is associated with these two factors alone.[7] Thus to achieve a fair first approximation of the internal distribution of road mileage at a given point in time, we look first to the population distribution. Effects of difficult terrain, unequal distribution of resources, rail competition, and the like on the distribution of roads may be regarded as being partly subsumed by the population and area variables. Much of the impact of these factors on the transportation system is expressed through their relationship to the population pattern.

As expected, total population accounts for more of the variation in total road mileage than area accounts for; in both Ghana and Nigeria it accounts for about 50 per cent. The addition of area as an independent variable accounts for 20 per cent more. Obviously, there is a greater need for transportation for a given population in a large unit than in a small one. Although the demand for roads generally reflects the distribution of the population, a large, sparsely settled unit will require a large per capita road investment to be served at all. Thus the relative weights of the two independent variables, and the closeness of the correlation, are seen to be significantly affected by variations in the size of the reporting units; hence the use of simple population densities would have been deceptive in that an understatement of road-mileage expectations for large, sparsely settled units would have resulted.

On the other hand, it is not clear that meaning may be ascribed to the area variable as a separate factor. The problem of modifiable areal reporting units is, in general, a difficult one.[8] Internal variations in size of reporting units affect the degree of apparent correlation between variables. Even if the sizes of reporting units were uniform, different correlations and different regression equations would be obtained for different levels of areal aggregation (a grid cell of 10 square miles as opposed to 100 square miles, for instance). In this case, it is best to regard the use of an area variable as a means of including the effects of any internal variations in size of reporting units on road mileage along with any effects of variations in population. Thus it can be said that three-quarters of the variation in road mileage among the areal subunits in Ghana and Nigeria is statistically associated with their combined variations in population and size. However, if the average size of the subunits were to be significantly increased or decreased, the amount of statistically "explained" variation would be affected.

This relatively simple regression analysis may now be tied directly to the maps in an attempt to uncover further possible factors that seem to be particularly relevant to the development of road transportation. In what parts of Ghana and Nigeria does there seem to be a great deal of residual variation? Where, in other words, does the population-area equation seem to give significant overestimates or underestimates of road mileage?[9] Examination of the residuals maps for Ghana and Nigeria suggests five additional factors: hostile environment; rail competition; intermediate location; income or degree of commercialization; and relationship to the ideal-typical sequence. Precise quantification of these factors did not seem to be warranted by the data. Therefore, a subjective examination was made of the relationship between each of the five factors and the distribution of regression residuals. In many instances the lack of data resulted in highly generalized and arbitrary quantifications.

HOSTILE ENVIRONMENT

Consideration of the effects of the physical environment on highway mileage gives rise to some interesting speculations. The first finding is negative: namely, that the inclusion of difficult terrain in the analysis does not add greatly to one's ability to predict the road mileage in a given unit once population and area have been considered. Although visual comparison of road maps and topographic maps might suggest such a relationship, the effects of sloping land seem already to have been discounted in individual units by the fact that they are thinly populated. Comparison of slope percentages with regression residuals indicated no significant relationship. Thus there is no consistent evidence that a unit with a high percentage of sloping land has less road mileage than would be expected from its population and area as expressed in the basic equation. It should be noted, however, that this statement too is conditioned by the size of the reporting units. At the scale of observation implied by the reporting units there was little evidence of a separate effect of sloping land. But if reporting units were to become smaller, it is obvious that, at some scale, slope would have a marked effect on the selection of specific routes irrespective of population. More refined slope measures might also have produced different results at different scales.

Examination of the residuals maps (Fig. 22-9*a* and *b*)[10] does indicate that, at the scale of observation employed, two specific environmental conditions seem to be related to the tendency for road mileage to be less than would be expected from a unit's population and area.[11] These are a very steep and consistent slope, such as an escarpment, the trend of which is in general at right angles to the country's alignment of traffic, and the presence of extremely swampy land. Circles on the residuals maps have been shaded according to the amount of "hostile" land in a particular unit, and since the presence of swamps or escarpments should reduce the road mileage associated with a given population and area, we should expect to find most of the shaded circles on the negative residuals map. This proves to be the case. In Ghana fourteen of the twenty districts with more than 5 per cent of their land classified as hostile, and all six of the districts with more than 10 per cent, are on the negative residuals map. Low road-mileage figures are most closely associated with the swampy lands in the Keta, Ada, and Volta River districts. In Mpraeso North and Kibi there is strong evidence of the deterrent effect of steep slopes where the prominent Mampong escarpment has sharply curtailed the development of feeder routes.

In Nigeria low residuals are associated with swampy land in the Colony and, in the Niger Delta, Delta and Rivers districts. An important difference, however, between the swampy lands of Nigeria and Ghana is that in Nigeria the low residuals are associated not only with an environment unfavorable to road building but also with effective and long-established competitive water transportation. Waterway competition is also reflected in the low residuals in Lowland, Wukari, Lafia, Tiv, and Idoma. These districts are located along the middle and lower Benue, where waterway traffic is important in view of the absence of other effective connections to the zone of maximum economic activity. In Nigeria the only consistent relationship between slope and low road density appears where there is a steep slope over a fairly large area, such as an escarpment lying across the transport grain, or where there is a large number of steep volcanic ranges (the Cameroons districts of Kumba-Victoria, Mamfe, Bamenda, and Adamawa). In the latter example, climate may also have played an important role.

RAILROAD COMPETITION

Logically, railroad competition could affect road mileage either way. It could reduce the need for roads by providing an alternative form of transportation; it could increase the need for roads by promoting commercial production for interregional export. In the latter, or complementary, case one might expect a proliferation of feeder roads from nodes on rail penetration lines. Although there is some evidence of the validity of both possibilities, the stronger evidence seems to be on the side of the positive effect. It is perhaps more accurate to say that units with railroad mileage have more road mileage than would be expected from their areas and populations. Either the railroad itself promotes feeder development, or both rail and road are transport manifestations of a high level of income, urbanization, or commercialization. There are instances where low road-mileage figures are associated with the presence of railroads, but this seems to be where a deliberate government policy of protecting the railroad from competition has been in effect. It is for the last reason that the residuals maps of Ghana (Fig. 22-10*a*) are difficult to interpret: railroad competition has had sharply different effects in different parts of the country. Tarkwa's large negative residual seems to be associated with the "economic gap" policy under which the building of important through roads parallel to the western line was forbidden so as to preserve the railroad from competition.[12] In Kumasi, on the other hand, and to a smaller extent along the eastern line, the building of feeder networks to the railroad appears to have had a positive effect on the residuals.

In Nigeria (Fig. 22-10*b*) there is clearly no map evidence that rail competition reduces road mileage below the level expected from population and area. The concentration of high rail-mileage figures on the positive residuals map indicates that the complementary aspect of the relationship is much more evident. In Nigeria, however, it is difficult to separate the effects because of the more consistent distribution of the residuals in the zone of maximum economic activity, where such

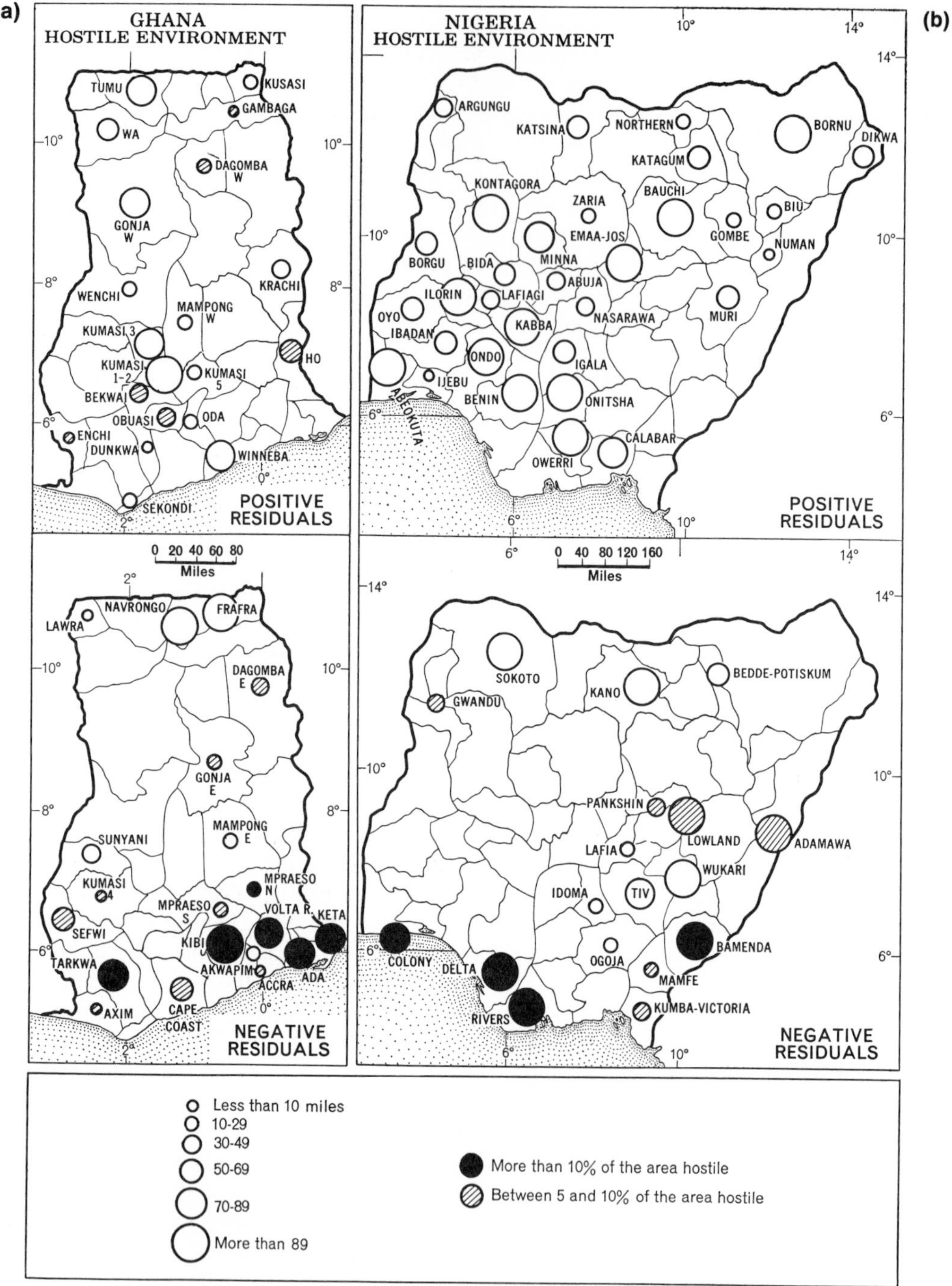
(a)
GHANA
HOSTILE ENVIRONMENT
POSITIVE RESIDUALS
TUMU
KUSASI
GAMBAGA
WA
DAGOMBA W
GONJA W
KRACHI
WENCHI
MAMPONG W
KUMASI 3
HO
KUMASI 1-2
KUMASI 5
BEKWAI
OBUASI
ODA
ENCHI
DUNKWA
WINNEBA
SEKONDI
NEGATIVE RESIDUALS
0 20 40 60 80
Miles
NAVRONGO
FRAFRA
LAWRA
DAGOMBA E
GONJA E
SUNYANI
MAMPONG E
KUMASI 4
MPRAESO N
MPRAESO S
VOLTA R.
KETA
SEFWI
KIBI
TARKWA
AKWAPIM
ACCRA
ADA
AXIM
CAPE COAST
(b)
NIGERIA
HOSTILE ENVIRONMENT
POSITIVE RESIDUALS
ARGUNGU
KATSINA
NORTHERN
BORNU
DIKWA
KATAGUM
KONTAGORA
ZARIA
BAUCHI
BIU
GOMBE
EMAA-JOS
NUMAN
BORGU
BIDA
MINNA
ABUJA
ILORIN
LAFIAGI
MURI
OYO
NASARAWA
IBADAN
KABBA
ONDO
IGALA
IJEBU
ABEOKUTA
BENIN
ONITSHA
CALABAR
OWERRI
NEGATIVE RESIDUALS
0 40 80 120 160
Miles
SOKOTO
BEDDE-POTISKUM
KANO
GWANDU
PANKSHIN
LOWLAND
ADAMAWA
LAFIA
WUKARI
IDOMA
TIV
COLONY
BAMENDA
DELTA
OGOJA
MAMFE
KUMBA-VICTORIA
RIVERS
Less than 10 miles
10-29
30-49
50-69
70-89
More than 89
More than 10% of the area hostile
Between 5 and 10% of the area hostile

measures as railroad mileage, commercial production, income, and degree of urganization would also be expected to be high.[13]

INTERMEDIATE LOCATION

In addition to the factors already discussed, the location of a reporting unit with respect to other distributions may have considerable bearing on its road mileage. For example, a unit with a low population density located between two large cities would tend to have more road mileage than one with the same density and area surrounded by units of correspondingly low densities. To some extent the importance of the area variable in the basic equation is attributable to its inclusion of this effect. A large unit is more likely to include centers between which highways are needed. It is also more likely to include some territory that owes its road mileage to its position between two centers outside the unit itself.

The first attempt to treat this effect systematically was in the form of a potential map. This consisted in computing for all reporting units an index of the aggregate proximity of the rest of the country's population according to a gravity-model formulation in which the potential between any two units was regarded as being directly proportional to the product of their populations and inversely proportional to the distance between them.[14] Thus a unit between two centers would register a higher potential than an outlying unit. This should have given a better estimate of road mileage than the population and area figures. Such was not the case, however. The use of potential figures in a regression analysis gave a poorer correlation than either population and area or population alone. Nor did it aid in the explanation of variation of highway mileage when modified and treated as an additional independent variable designed to isolate the effects of intermediate location.

Examination of the residuals maps indicates that the failure of this apparently logical index to provide a better explanation than the straight population-area equation was associated with the fact that the intermediate-location effect was not widespread but seemed evident only where major interregional roads traversed a unit. In other instances the area variable had apparently transmitted much of the effect. It should be noted, however, that need for explicit treatment of this effect becomes progressively greater as the scale of observation becomes closer. The smaller the reporting unit, the more likely it is that road mileage will be influenced by external distributions.

On the residuals maps of Ghana (Fig. 22-11*a*) the shaded residuals represent the districts traversed by the two large interregional roads. These districts should have more mileage (from feeders as well as from the trunk roads themselves) than would be expected from their populations and areas. The maps provide reasonably good visual evidence of the positive effects of these interregional roads. The string of positive residuals along the Western Trunk Road from Kumasi to Tumu is particularly striking. The association of positive residuals with the Great North

Fig. 22-9*a* Hostile environment, Ghana. Estimates were made of the area within a district which would be classified as swampy or noticeably dissected. Maps used were at the scale of 1:250,000. Circles are graded in size according to the differences between actual road mileages and road mileages estimated from the equation "Road mileage equals (1.482) (Population)$^{(0.6285)}$ times (Area)$^{(0.4139)}$.

Fig. 22-9*b* Hostile environment, Nigeria. Estimates were made of the area within a district which could be classified as swampy, noticeably dissected or containing high mountains. Circles are graded in size according to the differences between actual road mileages and road mileages estimated from the equation "Road mileage $= \frac{(\text{Population})^{(0.4458)} \text{ times } (\text{Area})^{(0.4823)}}{(2.799)}$."

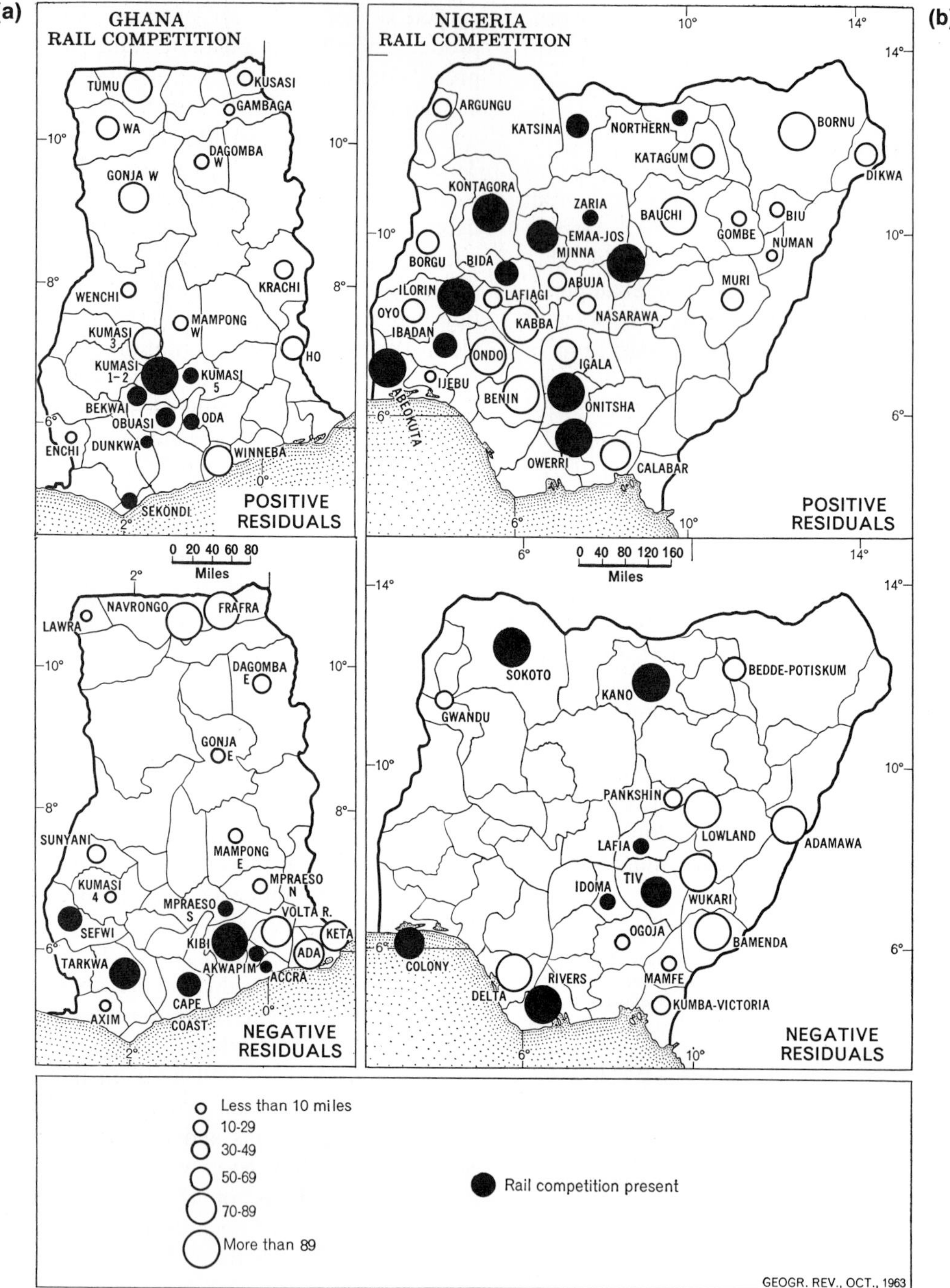

Figs. 22-10*a* and *b* Rail competition, (*a*) Ghana and (*b*) Nigeria.

Road is less spectacular. There is one contradictory district (Gonja East), and none of the residuals are more than half a standard error above or below the regression estimate. The contrast among the northern districts in this respect is interesting. Tumu has a very high residual; Navrongo and Frafra have low residuals. The explanation seems to lie in the population densities rather than in the road mileages. Road mileage does not differ greatly among the three districts, but Navrongo and Frafra are much more densely populated than Tumu. Thus the negative residuals for Navrongo and Frafra may be associated with a generally lower level of feeder-road development in the north than in districts of corresponding population density in the south.

In Nigeria (Fig. 22-11*b*) major interregional roads are in general parallel to the railroads. There are, however, two areas without railroad mileage where the positive residuals seem to be associated with the presence of important interregional roads. In both the use of the interregional designation may be legitimately questioned. One road, through the northeastern districts of Bauchi, Gombe, Biu, Bornu, and Dikwa, is an extension from the zone of maximum rail and economic activity to Maiduguri and the Lake Chad area outside Nigeria. The traffic density on this road is relatively high, and it represents one of the few cases where long-haul trucking is of major importance in Nigeria. In the south two roads serve as lateral interconnections between the two parts of Nigeria's bifurcated rail pattern. They are classed as interregional roads because they carry heavy long-haul traffic and serve to link the Eastern and Western Regions of a federated Nigeria.

COMMERCIALIZATION AND RELATION TO THE IDEAL-TYPICAL SEQUENCE

It can be assumed that unusually productive units have relatively high incomes and therefore have more road mileage than is called for in the population-area equation. Although the resulting relationships are somewhat ambiguous and difficult to isolate from other factors, there is a general tendency for the more productive units to have more road mileage than expected. Units focused on export agriculture appear to be more important with respect to highways than units focused on mineral production. The maps are visually inconclusive, owing chiefly to difficulties in obtaining data that realistically measured commercial production in the individual units, and in separating commercial production from population that had already been considered in the regression equation. For example, in Ghana (Fig. 22-12*a*) it is probable that the highs around Kumasi and in Ho and Krachi are associated with export agricultural production. On the other hand, Tarkwa appears on the negative residuals map despite its large production for export, because much of the production consists of mineral ores (manganese and bauxite) hauled almost exclusively by rail. Thus, despite its relatively high commercialization, this district has less road mileage than would be expected from its population and area. There seems also to be an interesting time element in the relation between the cocoa districts and road transportation. Although the districts cited above show high residuals, the very new cocoa districts (Sunyani, Sefwi, and Kumasi 4) show negative residuals. This may represent a tendency for transportation development to lag behind population in rapidly growing districts.

In Nigeria (Fig. 22-12*b*), as expected, the districts with a large commercial production add little to the correspondence with the positive residuals already noted on the railroad and interregional-road maps. However, the commercialization maps do point up the persistent anomaly of the two important northern districts of Kano and Sokoto. These districts

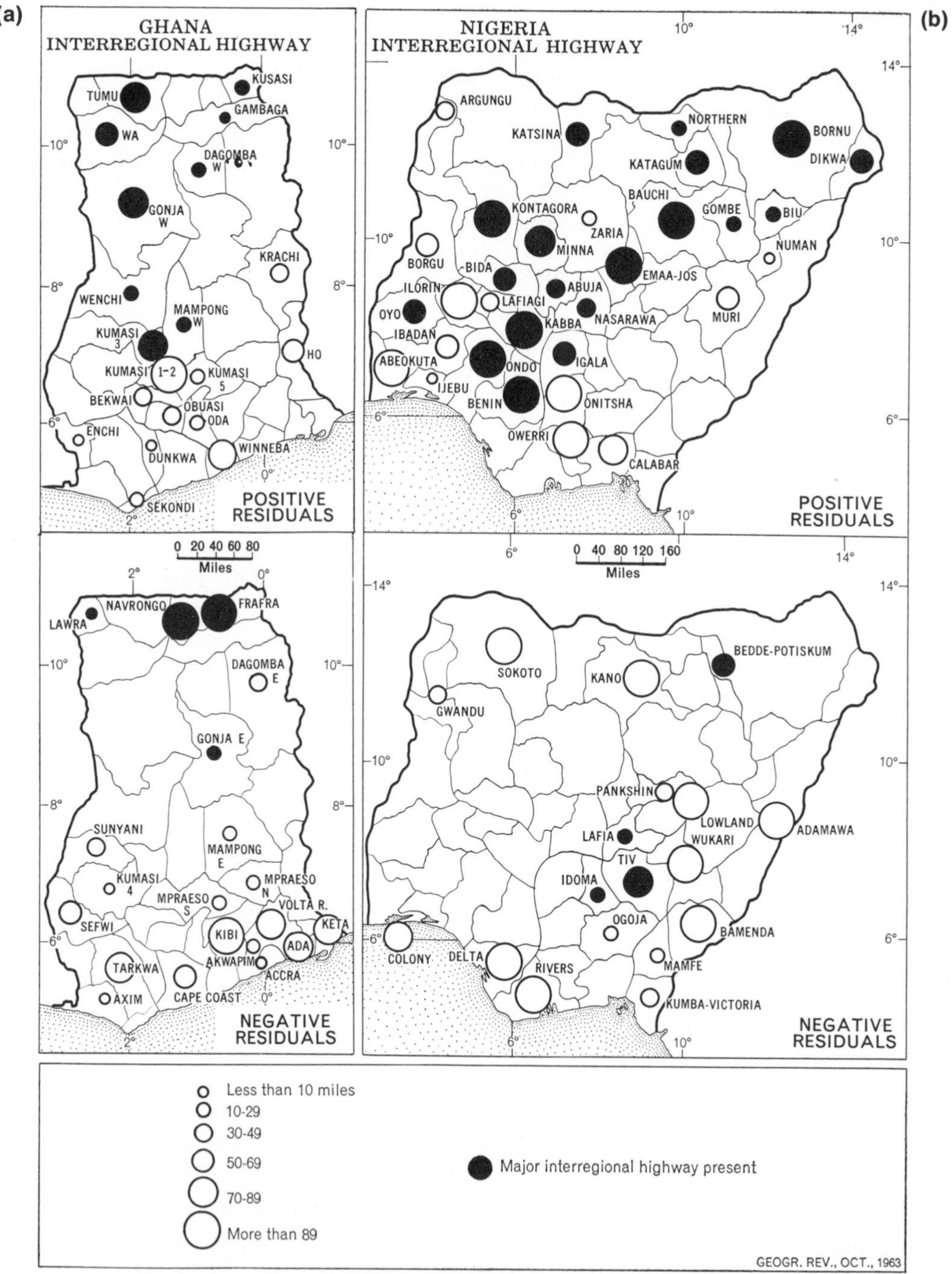

Figs. 22-11*a* and *b* Interregional highways, (*a*) Ghana and (*b*) Nigeria.

register negative residuals despite a high degree of commercialization and the presence both of railroads and of interregional roads. There is an interesting analogy here to the new cocoa districts of Ghana, because Kano is also an area of rapid and recent economic expansion, and it, too, may well show a lag-and-lead pattern.

The tendency for commercialization to be intercorrelated with population and road mileage, and to occur within the general frame of the transport network, leads to a consideration of the relation between the residuals maps and the ideal-typical sequence. As a rule, high residuals, representing large road mileage, are found in units that also have large populations, a high degree of commercialization, and large railroad mileages. These units are usually in a zone of maximum activity, which includes the early penetration lines, the "main streets," and the majority of the interconnections. Outside this zone, toward the borders of the country, transportation development seems weaker, as is evidenced by negative residuals.

In Ghana the zone of maximum activity comprises the railroad triangle and some parts of the northern penetration lines. Districts peripheral to this zone that exhibit weaker road development are the new cocoa districts, the northern districts of Navrongo and Frafra, and the southeast. Ho and Krachi are conspicuous exceptions, though this may be associated with the political factors mentioned earlier.

In Nigeria there is a similarly striking concentration of positive residuals within the zone of maximum transport activity, as would be expected from the ideal-typical sequence. Most of the districts in this zone also rate high in commercialization as well as in either rail mileage or interregional roads. Conversely, the tendency for the peripheral areas to have less road mileage than would be expected from the population-area equation is even more marked than in Ghana. The only major exception is the northeast, in the districts traversed by the trunk-road connection to Maiduguri and the Lake Chad region. A combination of factors is also responsible for the negative residuals in the south, southeast, and north. All these areas are peripheral (with the possible exception of some in the south), but hostile environment and waterway competition also effectively reduce road mileages. In Kano the large negative residual may be associated both with peripheral position and with the lag-and-lead pattern in which newly developing areas may have less transportation than their populations would seem to warrant.

THE ANALYSIS IN PERSPECTIVE

As population increases in an area, the demand for transportation is intensified; as new transport lines are built into the area, a greater population increase is encouraged, which, in turn, calls for still more transportation. In a sense, the models artificially separated these two effects: the ideal-typical sequence considered transportation expansion as though it were independent of population distribution; the regressions treated transportation as though it were caused by population. However, the residuals maps provided intuitive evidence of the lag-and-lead nature of transport development, as was cited in cases of Northern Nigeria and the new cocoa districts in Ghana. One might postulate a tendency through time for these alternate overexpansions and deficits of the transport system to become gradually smaller until a temporary equilibrium is reached. A transport innovation or a sudden demand for a new penetration line, such as that occasioned by a mineral discovery, could then reactivate the process. This suggests that a possible avenue of future investigation of transport expansion in underdeveloped countries might be the application

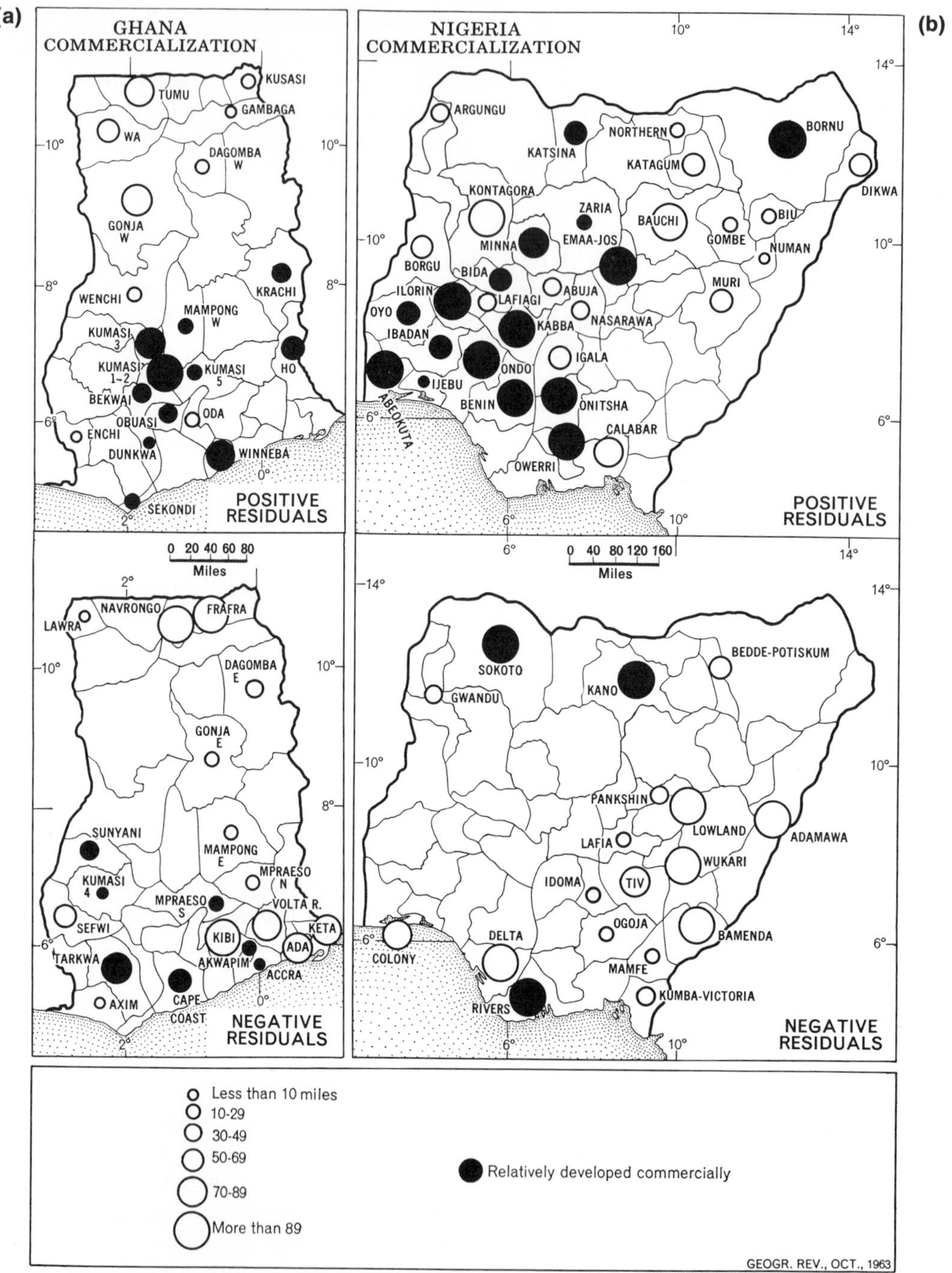

Figs. 22-12*a* and *b* Commercialization, (*a*) Ghana and (*b*) Nigeria. Circles have been shaded in those districts which have been subjectively classified as being relatively urbanized or as containing a relatively large amount of commercial agriculture.

of a simulation model such as the Monte Carlo technique applied by Torsten Hägerstrand in his migration studies.[15] The spatial evolution of a transport and population pattern might be simulated through time by using for each stage in the process a set of probabilities dependent on the transport and population pattern of the preceding stage, thus bringing the essentially stochastic nature of transportation development into the model. The direction of the extension of a transport line from a given point might be based on probabilities derived from factors similar to those noted in the discussion of penetration lines and the Ghana highway-density maps.

Finally, it should be noted that the generalizations in this study are designed to provide an initial perspective on the expansion of transportation in underdeveloped countries. At the moment, it is probable that the variations from the typical sequence and the regressions are of more interest than their explicit application.[16] It is to be hoped that future studies will bring about fundamental changes in the perspective presented here, at the same or a higher level of generalization. This may be accomplished by field investigations, by the development of more useful transportation parameters, and by the application of increasingly rigorous methods of analysis and model verification.

NOTES

1 Other areas examined in some detail, though from secondary sources, are Brazil, Kenya, Tanganyika, and Malaya.

2 It is interesting to note a few analogies to some of W. W. Rostow's stages of economic development. The scattered, weakly connected ports might be considered evidences of the isolation of Rostow's traditional society; the development of a penetration line might be viewed as a sort of spatial "takeoff"; the lateral-interconnection phase might be a spatial symptom of the internal diffusion of technology; and the impact of the auto on the latter phases of the sequence might be an expression of the emergence of certain aspects of an era of higher mass consumption in underdeveloped countries.

3 For Ghana, the examples are based on the field data and primary statistical source material gathered by Peter R. Gould. For Nigeria, primary statistical sources are indicated where necessary. Secondary sources include Kenneth O. Dike: *Trade and Politics in the Niger Delta, 1830–1885* (Oxford Studies in African Affairs; London, 1956); Gilbert Walker: Traffic and Transport in Nigeria: The Example of an Underdeveloped Tropical Territory, *Colonial Research Studies No. 27,* Colonial Office, London, 1959; "The Economic Development of Nigeria" (International Bank for Reconstruction and Development, Baltimore, 1955). The authors are also indebted to Dr. Akin Mabogunje, of University College, Ibadan, for his comments.

4 For example, the extension of the Uganda railway to Kasese to haul copper ore; the long northward extension of the Cameroon railway from Yaoundé to Garoua to haul manganese; and the new railway from Port-Étienne to Fort Gouraud in Mauritania to haul iron ore.

5 The degree of interconnectedness of a transport network could be precisely evaluated by the use of such new measures as those presented in William L. Garrison: Connectivity of the Interstate Highway System, *Papers and Proc. Regional Science Assn.,* Vol. 6 (6th Annual Meeting), 1960 (Philadelphia, 1961), pp. 121–137.

6 Sources for population figures were "Population Census of Nigeria, 1952–1953" (Lagos, 1954), and "The Gold Coast Census of Population, 1948: Report and Tables" (London and Accra, 1950); for road mileages, "Mobil Road Map of Nigeria," 1:750,000 and 1:500,000 (Federal Survey Department, Lagos, 1957), and "Road Map of the Gold Coast," 1:500,000 (Department of Surveys, Accra, 1950). Only first- and second-class roads were included. No weighting system was applied.

7 For Ghana the regression equation was $\log Y_c = 0.1709 + 0.6285 \log X_1 + 0.4139 \log X_2$ or

$Y_c = 1.482\, X_1^{0.6285}\, X_2^{0.4139}$, with Y_c the estimated highway mileage, X_1 the district population in thousands, and X_2 the district area. The r^2 or explained variation was 0.75 or 75 per cent. For Nigeria the regression equation was $\log Y_c = -0.44771 + 0.4458 \log X_1 + 0.4823 \log X_2$ or $Y_c = (X_1^{0.4458}\, X_2^{0.4823})/2.799$. The explained variation in this case was 81 per cent. In both cases the particular form of the equation was the result of normalizing the data by means of log transformations.

8 Some aspects of the problem are discussed in Arthur H. Robinson: The Necessity of Weighting Values in Correlation Analysis of Areal Data, *Annals Assn. of Amer. Geogrs.*, Vol. 46, 1956, pp. 233–236, and Otis Dudley Duncan, Ray P. Cuzzort, and Beverly Duncan: *Statistical Geography: Problems in Analyzing Areal Data* (Glencoe, Ill., 1961).

9 The use of residuals maps has been discussed by Edwin N. Thomas: Maps of Residuals from Regression: Their Characteristics and Uses in Geographic Research, *State Univ. of Iowa, Dept. of Geogr.,* [*Publ.*] *No. 2,* Iowa City [1960]. Examples of the use of residuals maps are Edward J. Taaffe: A Map Analysis of Airline Competition, Part 2, *Journ. of Air Law and Commerce,* Vol. 25, 1958, pp. 402–427, and Peter R. Gould and Robert H. T. Smith: Method in Commodity Flow Studies, *Australian Geographer,* Vol. 8, 1960–1962, pp. 73–77.

10 On all the residuals maps circles are proportional to the residual deviation from the regression formula. For example, on the positive residuals maps the large circles for Tumu, Ghana, and Abeokuta, Nigeria, indicate that they had considerably *more* highway mileage than would be expected from the regression formula, which takes into account population and area. Similarly, on the negative residuals maps the large circles for Kibi, Ghana, and Delta, Nigeria, indicate that they had considerably *less* highway mileage than expected. In effect, then, these units show the distribution of the variation in highway mileage attributable to factors other than population and area.

11 For a consideration of other specific environmental features see Benjamin E. Thomas: *Transportation and Physical Geography in West Africa* (Prepared for the Human Environments in Central Africa Project, National Academy of Sciences—National Research Council, Division of Anthropology and Psychology [Department of Geography, University of California, Los Angeles, 1960]). For example, Thomas documents the marked effect of seasonality on the utilization of roads in West Africa.

12 Gould, *op. cit.,* pp. 44, 71, 102, 106, and 110.

13 A multiple regression was also run using four independent variables (in logarithms): population, area, railway mileage, and waterway mileage. The results did not add significantly to the amount of variation in road mileage statistically "explained" by population and area. The regression coefficients for both railway and waterway mileage tested as statistically insignificant.

14 See John Q. Stewart and William Warntz: Macrogeography and Social Science, *Geogr. Rev.,* Vol. 48, 1958, pp. 167–184.

15 Torsten Hägerstrand: Innovationsförloppet ur korologisk synpunkt, *Meddellanden från Lunds Univ. Geogr. Anstn., Avhandl.* 25, 1953.

16 Cursory examination of the Brazilian pattern, for instance, indicates a continued viability of some of the scattered ports in coastal commerce, due in part to weak lateral interconnection by land along the coast. Preliminary results from field investigations carried on in the state of São Paulo by Howard L. Gauthier, Jr., indicate a stronger emphasis on expansion of secondary roads toward the interior from railhead than on lateral interconnection during the period following the development of penetration lines. In former British East Africa the political boundary between Kenya and Tanganyika has apparently restricted lateral interconnection between two widely separated rail penetration lines. Population-area regressions run on road mileages for selected South American countries by Lawrence A. Brown, [then] graduate student at Northwestern University, also resulted in explained variations of about 80 per cent. The population exponent, however, ranged from 0.41 to 0.85 and the area exponent from 0.22 to 0.37.

Selection 23

Transportation Planning in Developing Countries

B. V. Martin and C. B. Warden

National planners in aspiring backward countries look longingly toward transportation investment as the catalyst of economic development, because in the past transportation has usually played a big role in the development of land and natural resources. The era of canals and railroads in the nineteenth century is, of course, the classic example to support this belief. The relationship between transportation and economic development has been well expressed by Charles Kindleberger, who noted:

> . . . markets grow because of improvements in transportation and communication. The market is originally local and small. Demand is restricted by the cost of getting goods out of the village and ignorance of how much they can be bought for outside. In these circumstances, markets grow through increases in transport and communication. The expansion becomes cumulative. Increased outlets in turn raise the demand for other products. As new supplies of these come on the market, in turn, incomes grow further. The linkage of markets by an improvement in transportation, or by the improvement in a product that makes it lighter and more readily transported, becomes part of the developmental process.[1]

Transportation improvements alone cannot produce economic growth, though in a suitable environment they can be the missing agent. Furthermore, overcommitment of scarce resources to transportation can strangle development hopes as quickly as will insufficient transportation facilities. So there is a balancing act of discovering how much and what sort of transportation investment is required. Historically this has been the exclusive domain of the transportation engineer, partly because of professional parochialism and partly because the broader backdrop of general economic planning did not exist. Now economic development planning is becoming more sophisticated, and the more complex role of combining economics with transportation engineering is emerging for the transportation planner.

Unfortunately, the tides of time and history have not endowed many of the developing regions with the conditions for development that existed in Europe or the United States. Lacking the experienced advisers required to begin significant progress, the problems of these countries created the now celebrated "foreign adviser" to guide them along an efficient path of economic development. But this was a new role for professionals of the western world, whose experiences extended principally from developed countries, where concern had been confined to projects rather than broad programs. The emerging nations desired immediate development, instantaneous transportation and unlimited growth, while at the same time governments providing the foreign aid and loans required short term results to substantiate their ventures and satisfy domestic politicians. In these circumstances, projects were judged on superficial values rather than within the broader context of a development plan, disciplined by a body of theoretical understanding.

In retrospect this may well have been an expedient procedure for, in fact, some de-

Traffic Quarterly, vol. 19, no. 1, 1965, pp. 59–75. Reprinted by permission of the authors, editor, and the Eno Foundation.

velopment has occurred, and foreign aid is gradually being accepted as a responsibility by the western world. On the other hand, partial project analysis has also caused serious misallocation of scarce resources. Computer technology and more sophisticated analytical techniques have now made it feasible for systems analysis to overcome the deficiencies inherent in partial project evaluation, so it is possible to consider integrating the analysis and evaluation of an entire transportation system into the broader economic development plan.

THE NEED FOR COMPREHENSIVE PLANNING AND ANALYSIS

A more integrated and comprehensive approach to transportation planning and analysis is aimed at three principal deficiencies in the present project approach:

1 Total system effects are not considered in the evaluation of single projects.
2 The transportation plan is not related to the over-all economic plan.
3 Different effects of alternative pricing policies are not considered in conjunction with investment decisions.

The Systems Approach

A system can be described as a number of parts making a complex whole, and systems analysis means consideration of the complex whole as opposed to project analysis that considers the individual parts separately. Systems analysis is not an invention of academicians to add a false sense of sophistication to an otherwise simple problem. Rather it is the realization that, although each part of a system may play an individual role in the operation of that system, no part is entirely independent of the others, and that a change in the operation of one part will have significant effects on the operation of other parts. A transportation program (or plan) is just such a system.

In the past, transportation programs in developing countries have been evaluated on a single project basis, and both intermodal and intramodal effects have been overlooked. Railroad projects, for example, were analyzed without reference to existing or planned highways and waterways. Individual links of highway or railroad were considered in isolation from the rest of the highway or railroad, and terminal facilities have not been related to feeder services.

The experiences in Colombia during the last fifteen years serve to illustrate the difficulties which arise in the absence of a systems approach. Since 1950, the Colombian government has been expanding all modes of transport including highways, railroads, waterways and their related terminal facilities. Investments were in the order of 10 billion pesos (approximately U.S. $2.7 billion) between 1950 and 1960. Each transport mode was planned independently and, because some of the funds were obtained from international lending organizations, the project evaluations were often reviewed by lenders without concern for the nature of alternatives, or complementary transport activities. For highways, a loan of sixteen million dollars was obtained in 1950, followed in 1953, 1956 and 1961 by loans of fourteen million, sixteen million, and thirty-nine million dollars, respectively. At the same time, as the highways were being improved, large investments were being made in railroads: to improve their competitive position and to provide key links in the system. The railroad improvements were also partly financed with international loans in 1952, 1955, and 1960 amounting to twenty million, sixteen million, and five million dollars, respectively.

Most of this money was used to construct the Atlantico Railroad in order to provide access from the interior to the Atlantic ports via connections through an improved inland waterway project. Because of independent planning of modes, many sections of the improved highway paralleled existing railroad facilities as well as parts of the new Atlantico Railroad under construction.[2] Subsequently, a decision was made to extend the Atlantico Railroad directly to the coast to another port, avoiding the final waterway connection, but the inland waterway improvement still went ahead. As a result, the terminal connection of the Atlantico Railroad did not have adequate port facilities, while adjacent ports had surplus capacity and equipment. Furthermore, the Atlantico Project was anticipated to be much more efficient than the existing lines, due to more modern equipment, bigger freight cars, etc. But the fact that the Atlantico Railroad itself relied on many sections of the older system for feeder service had been overlooked. And with increased traffic on the older parts of the system, the total railroad system operated at a greater net loss after the Atlantico Railroad was opened than before.

It is not the intention of this illustration to wag a condemning finger at the people behind these investments, for no more exemplary evaluations accompanied the Friendship Highway in Thailand, the new port in Guayaquil, the Venezuelan highway from Caracas to the coast, or the improvements in the Mexican highway systems. Rather, it is to demonstrate that a systems analysis of all mode and link effects should be considered in order to generate more rational decisions.

Comprehensive Planning

The second deficiency in present techniques is the absence of integration between the general economic plan and the transportation plan. Transportation is not an end in itself but is a means toward achieving the general economic goals of the country which, therefore, must be known to the transportation planner. The separation of general economic planning and transport planning is largely due to the division of professional responsibilities between economists and engineers. Generally, the transportation plan's only link with the general development plan devised by economists has been sequential. That is, the engineers work from general information on the expected volume and location of commodity flows forecast by the economist. Engineers derive actual facility designs to determine final capacities and transportation costs, but there is no feedback to determine how the transportation costs and final pattern of facilities will interact with the general conditions of the economic plan.

In some cases, the transportation program is the country's only planning operation, because international lending agencies seem more willing to provide funds for transport than other sectors of the economy. Developing countries naturally tend to use the available loans and, therefore, there is a tendency toward over-investment in transportation at the expense of other less frequently articulated needs, such as housing, health or education.

Pricing Policies

The third major deficiency in current transportation planning practices is that pricing policy has been ignored by transportation planners and left to a government regulating agency which normally operates independently of the planning agency. As a result, the supply of and demand for transportation is not correlated in preparing investment plans. Demand has been predicted by straight-line extrapolation, quite independently of any transportation analysis; and supply is determined partly as a result of the prespecified demands and partly as a result of engineering feasibility and cost. Little effort is made to match supply and demand relationships through a pricing mechanism. Though the planner should not be obliged to set prices, these prices must be considered in the planning process, and the consequences of alternative policies explored.

Pricing policies show up as rate schedules, and ultimately affect both the spatial development of industry and the extent of particular transport mode utilization. For example, some countries have subsidized rail transport of bulk commodities in the belief that they are basic to economic development, and that railroads should be encouraged because they are efficient and have inherent scale economies. But such a policy also encourages industrial processing plants to locate at the consumer end of the market (to minimize transport costs on the final product) and to ship raw materials such as coal, iron ore and timber on the subsidized railroads. Therefore, railroads become congested with these "induced demands," and real system costs are increased. The issue is simply that pricing is an integral part of the transport decision-making process and that pricing policies, established without reference to the broader transport and economic planning process, are likely to be wrong.

By way of summary, the following list of recommended improvements in planning practices is proposed:

1 There should be a more direct link between the analysis of transportation plans and the general economic development plan. In particular, alternative uses of investment funds should be considered to determine the relative attractiveness of transportation investments.

2 All modes of transportation should be considered together as one interacting system, and all phases of each transportation mode's operation should be included in evaluating new projects.

3 Procedures must be developed for determining the effects of transportation plans on other sectors of the economy, whether or not they are direct benefits (or costs) of a transport project.

4 There should be a basis for evaluating different transport pricing policies within the context of the broader economic development plan.

5 An effort should be made to investigate the effects of variances in the estimates of key independent variables, like population growth, foreign trade, or weather.

6 Engineers and economists should collaborate to relate the transportation plan to the economic plan.

A MODEL FOR THE EVALUATION OF TRANSPORT ALTERNATIVES

In an attempt to improve the basis for the evaluation of transportation plans in developing countries, the Harvard Transportation and Economic Development Program[3] is currently working on the formulation of a model embodying some of the principles laid out in the previous section.

The purpose of the model is to evaluate, for particular combinations of economic and geographic conditions (i.e., a country), alternative transportation plans and the associated long-term investment requirements. The transportation plan will include all modes of transport and will specify the locational characteristics, the particular technology (e.g., type of highway pavement), the time schedule of investments and expenditures, as well as availability dates for additions to the transport network. The study is restricted to freight movements between major resource, production and consumption centers. Transport movements within urban areas and passenger transport are not explicitly considered, though they are reflected as part of general consumer demand.

The scheme may be thought of at three levels. One, the more detailed, is the transportation model (or sub-model) which determines interregional flows, the actual level of transport facility usage, real (social) costs of providing the transport service, as well as the realized total cost to the users of the transport system. The second, called the general economic model, interrelates general economic variables like prices, incomes, consumption, savings, investments and profits, and specifies the appropriate regional or industry location. All activities, including resource extraction, intermediate goods processing, and the production of final goods are included in this general model. This is broader than restricting the accounting to final goods and services as is ordinarily done in the familiar national income and product accounts like Gross National Product (GNP) and Disposable Income. Some of the variables (e.g., regional income distribution and industry profits) are determined endogenously from the interplay with the other variables; the remaining variables, particularly ones with stable long-term growth paths, are exogenously prespecified though they are permitted to vary modestly as the remainder of the model is simulated in time. The third level of concern involves the pertinent policy variables on which the planner or public official may operate. These include, for example, pricing policy, public investments, exchange rates and related foreign trade variables, and the general monetary and fiscal policy variables.

The transportation sector interacts with the remainder of the model in a number of direct and indirect ways. For example, the transport charges are derived jointly from the transport pricing policy and from the costs of providing transport service.[4]

Transport charges and congestion costs (e.g., inventory costs to overcome time delays or interest charges on loans to cover goods in transit) are reflected in the industry production costs and in the price of final goods. Changes in these transport charges and congestion costs are ultimately reflected in changes in profit levels and in the prices of final and intermediate goods. Also, investment in the transportation sector requires specific goods such as steel rails, cement, road graders, and electronic equipment. These become demands on domestic industries and sometimes affect the balance of payments by being imported. Because capital is scarce, such investments in transportation improvements divert capital from other sectors. As a final example, the availability of transport facilities in one region and not in another, or the existence of regional differences in transport costs, can make one region more competitive than another in particular markets, thus leading to regional differences in growth.

Fig. 23-1 is a schematic diagram showing the major phases of the model operation and the manner in which they are related. The model will be aged by time periods of one year to produce time profiles of the economic and transport variables.

There are four reasons for introducing the time period concept into the model:

1 To permit the introduction of independently specified control variables over time; these might be key variables of a long-range economic plan.

2 To permit the introduction of time lags and feedbacks in the cause and effect of investment decisions.

3 To provide a convenient means for obtaining the time profiles for variables.

4 To avoid the computational difficulties implied by having to solve the system in a simultaneous fashion.

For the purposes of the model analysis, the country is divided into a number of geographical regions of activity.[5] The transportation

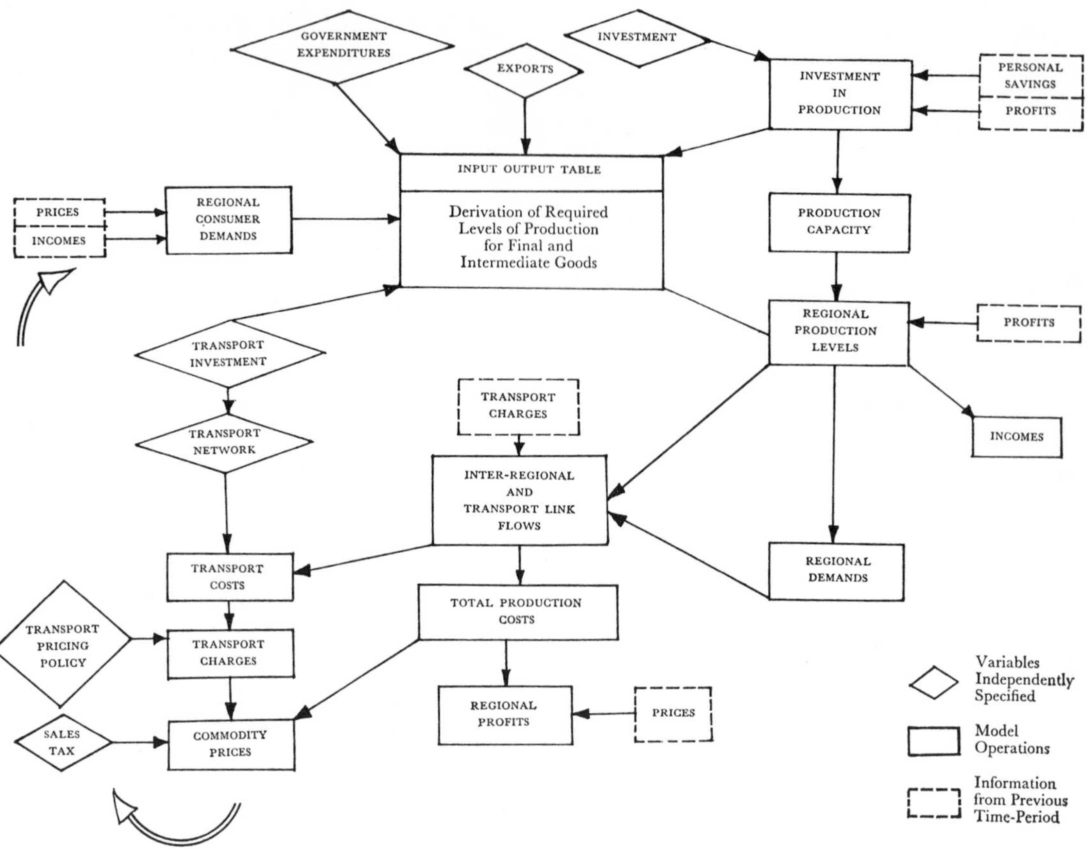

Fig. 23-1 Major phases of model operation.

network is represented as a series of links and nodes between the regions.

The economy will be described in terms of industries representing the major classes of production, consumer goods, and major resources. Each region will have one supply and/or demand function for any commodity, and this will be considered representative of the whole zone. Generally, the regions will represent specific production areas: large consuming areas such as cities, sites of natural resources, and other key areas such as ports.

Regional Consumption, Incomes and Prices

Regional consumer demands for final goods are a function of the regional income and the price of a commodity in that region. The precise form of the demand function is to be established by empirical analysis. Incomes and prices are obtained from the previous time period, when incomes are generated by production, and prices are based on production and transport costs. Prices remain fixed during a time period, but may change between periods to reflect changes in production or transport costs.

Aggregate Demand, Production and Growth

Total national demand is equivalent to the sum of all regional consumer demand for final goods and services, plus investment demands to replace worn-out plant and equipment or to increase capacity, plus government and export demand. This is virtually equivalent to the familiar concept of Gross National Product. As would be expected, national income (i.e. the sum of wages, profits, etc.) is equated with total national production by appropriate adjustments in inventories and savings. Production levels by industry are determined by the input-output relationships which link the production activity at all stages to the level and composition of final demand. The year-to-year levels of GNP are generally constrained by an independently specified growth rate, but are actually related immediately to changes in capacity coming from previous investments. The growth rate, of course, is one of the policy goals to which the model is made to conform.

Input-Output Relationships

An input-output table indicates the flow of goods from one industry to another. The source of all direct and indirect inputs is shown, and distribution of each industry's output is specified. Input-output analysis assumes that there is a known relationship between the level and composition of inputs and the ultimate output. These relationships are expressed in technological coefficients because they depend upon the particular technology being employed. Given the list of final demands and the technological coefficients, all production levels can be determined. Furthermore, reverberations of changes in final demand can be traced through the matrix of these relationships, and the impact on the level of production in supporting industries can be observed.

The input-output analysis is performed on a country-wide basis, primarily because regional technological coefficients are beyond our present ability to calculate. The total amount of each industry's production is then apportioned to regions according to the relative capacity and profitability of the regions. It should be noted that the level of regional industrial activity reflects more than the bundle of goods which make up final demand. It includes all of the intermediate goods, like steel and wool thread, which are eventually processed into either final consumer goods, like razor blades and wool mittens, or investment goods, like lathes.

Investment and Capacity

The investment function leads to increases in the production capacity of each industry. The total investment for a time period is derived from an exogenous term and an internally derived term based on savings and profit levels. The exogenous term includes foreign grants, loans, and also more complicated phenomena like changes in capital flight and hoarding practices. From the total investment available for a time period, the transport investment is subtracted, because the level of investment in transportation is precisely one of the postulated conditions of the model which we are expecting to evaluate. The remaining investment is distributed among the industries in each region according to relative levels of sales and profits. Increases in production capacity are related to investment in the previous time periods, and a lag is introduced to account for the time required to increase capacity, i.e., put plant in place. Because investment is distributed to regions according to relative regional profitability, the eventual location of industrial capacity should conform to an approximation of social efficiency.

Transportation Sector

We now have the information to define the transportation problem. Regional production or supply levels have been calculated as are regional demands, and the transportation system is specified. Transport charges—price schedules for the current time period—are known, having been derived at the end of the previous time period. However, in choosing a mode, the shipper will also consider other additional costs which may be caused through congestion delays in transit, delays in loading and unloading, or through unreliability. These costs depend on system utilization which, of course, is not known at the beginning of a time period. (Also an estimate is made from previous time-period experiences and checked later.) To the user, the transport cost will be the sum of the transport charge and the other realized congestion costs. These will vary according to the mode and to the commodity, when differences in commodity characteristics warrant that distinction.

We are now faced with a familiar transport problem, given points of supply and demand for goods, and network costs determining interregional flows. There are several ways of determining the final transport link flows, including a number of gravity model procedures and various linear programming techniques for minimizing (or maximizing) different combinations of key variables. The technique most applicable to any situation is determined by the amount of knowledge the analyst assumes the shipper to have, and to the extent of control any public authority has over the shipper to enforce system optimization, say, to minimize total system transport costs. In our model it has been assumed that control will be exercised through the use of transport prices and that within this framework each shipper will maximize his own objectives, which may or may not be exclusively related to cost minimization.

One over-all constraint on the problem that arises from the solution of the input-output table is that all demands must be met, while supply sources are limited to given quantities. In effect, there is no slack in the system, a characteristic of a mathematical model requiring equilibrium for solution. Our initial approach, therefore, has been to use a gravity model in which flows between regions are assumed directly proportional to the relative outputs and demands in each region, and inversely proportional to the transport and production costs. The use of a model of this type has a certain intuitive appeal. If a production center is very large it will serve many markets. Conversely, large markets are likely to receive products from several production centers. Modifying these tendencies by relative production and transport costs insures a natural tendency for production centers to serve their most profitable markets.

Against these advantages must be weighed some disadvantages of the gravity model approach. The first is that the above conditions tend to be distorted by adjustment techniques required to obtain a numerical equilibrium of the supply and demand centers. Second, if blindly followed, the model will derive flows between every possible pair of regions. In some cases this would produce small and unrealistic flows. This latter problem can probably be avoided by modifying the adjustment procedure.

The transport cost used in the gravity model is the minimum cost to move the commodity between the regions. The computation of this cost implies a particular mode or combination of modes (making allowance for transfer costs in the latter case), and this path will be used directly to assign the inter-regional flows.[6] A more sophisticated assignment procedure does not seem worthwhile, bearing in mind the relatively simple networks (as compared with urban areas) and often relatively small number of trips relative to capacity.

Once the transport flows have been computed, the shipping costs for each region are known and the current time period's production costs can be established. The total revenues can also be established from the quantity of goods delivered to a region and prices in the region. The regional profits or losses by industry can then be computed for use in the following time period. It may also be noted that regional production levels permit wage costs to be derived, and hence indicate the income available for consumption and savings in a region.

The cost of providing the transportation service is considered in more detail in a transport costing routine. For this it is necessary to describe the network in terms of the mode on each link, the technology employed, the type of service being offered, speed, frequency, etc., as well as the cost functions for fixed maintenance and operating costs. Those costs that are a function of volume are computed, and the remaining costs are given to the model independently.

Transport charges are considered at the end of the time period for possible adjustment before the following period. Charges depend upon the pricing policy used, which could be any of the following:

1 Prices constructed to cover only the system's real costs, like maintenance, operating costs, and debt.

2 Intermodal subsidies to encourage full-capacity utilization of some mode (say railroads) having significant economies of scale.

3 Prices intended to equalize direct line ton/mile charges regardless of mode or actual route linkage.

4 Demand pricing designed to maximize revenues of the system.

5 Profit maximizing prices.

6 Prices related to the value of the goods being shipped rather than the costs of shipping the goods.

Each pricing policy requires a different transport charge routine, and some will require individual techniques, such as procedures to allocate joint costs.

At the end of a time period, congestion costs for the next time period are estimated so that total transport user costs can be anticipated. Transport costs are used in the price adjustment routine to adjust regional commodity prices in the direction of long-run production costs (including transport charges) of the cheapest supplier to the region. The price adjustment routine also reacts to scarcity, so prices are increased to reflect an excess of demands over production capacity. Included in the prices of goods are any sales taxes imposed by the government to collect revenue or control consumption.

Between time periods the current values of economic variables, such as gross sales, GNP, etc., and of transport variables, such as link flows, modal profits or loss, returns on investment, etc., can be output by the model so that the analyst can review, over time, the performance of the transport plan under evaluation.

This description of the model has been brief, and many of the finer points have been ignored in order to add to the over-all clarity. Our main intent has been to describe the model in terms engineers will more readily comprehend.

REVIEW OF MODEL CHARACTERISTICS

In reviewing the model, we should like to emphasize the manner in which the transport sector interacts with the remainder of the model. Transport charges are reflected in the prices of goods, these prices affect the amounts demanded by consumers and, hence, production levels, that in turn affect transport demands. Thus, from one time period to another, the supply characteristics of the transportation system and the pricing policy directly affect transport demands. Furthermore, it will be noted that transport charges affect profits, both in magnitude and in regional distribution. Profits, in turn, are used in the investment functions and in determining regional allocations in production. Thus, over the long run, transport costs influence the rise or decline of industries on a regional basis.

One of the dangers that has confronted us in developing the model has been the overemphasis of the transportation sector and its influence on general economic growth. Clearly, to bias the model (intentionally or unintentionally) toward over or underemphasizing transportation would, in fact, defeat the purpose of the whole project. It is partly for these reasons that certain areas of the economy, such as parts of investment exports and government expenditures, have been independently specified. This provides the analyst not only a tool to specify the features of known economic plans, but also a device for correcting any inherent imbalances in the model structure.

MODEL APPLICATIONS

One objective in constructing a model of this type is to set it up on a parametric basis, so that the particular conditions of individual countries can be reflected in the various functions. Initially our experiments with the model will be restricted to two hypothetical countries, constructed from data obtained in developing countries in South America and Asia.[7] Two examples have been chosen so that different population distributions, geographical and climatical conditions can be used.

Experiments with the model in these two hypothetical situations can take various forms; for example, the effects of transportation plans emphasizing different transport technologies could be investigated. The technologies need not necessarily be the same as those used in the more developed countries, but could include such things as ground effect machines and overland trains made up of vehicles with large low-pressure tires. Highways with low capital costs but high operating costs might be compared with more expensive highways having lower operating costs. Investigations can also be made on the effects of different transport pricing schemes, and on the location patterns resulting from particular transport plans. By doing the study for two different geographic and economic conditions, an initial insight can be obtained for the changes that occur from one country to another.

Clearly, there are numerous other experiments and studies that can be conducted once some experience has been obtained with the operation of the model and the required supporting data. In the short run, we hope that our efforts contribute in a small way to furthering knowledge on transport policy in developing countries. In the long run, we hope to apply our research directly to the conditions of particular countries.

There are not very many works directed toward transportation planning in developing countries. However, there are two books which will certainly interest any readers who have a desire to learn more about these challenging problems. They are: Wilfred Owen, *Strategy for Mobility,* The Brookings Institution, July 1964, and *Transport and Economic Development: Introductory Theory*, edited by Gary Fromm, The Brookings Institution, January 1965.

NOTES

1 Charles P. Kindleberger, *Economic Development.* New York: McGraw Book Co., 1958. p. 95.

2 In one case, two independent engineering studies used the same future freight demands to justify the respective highway and railroad projects.

3 The Harvard Transportation and Economic Development Program is a seminar and research project directed by Professor John R. Meyer, Harvard University, and financed by a research

grant from The Brookings Institution, Washington, D.C.

4 Note that the transport charges in any particular mode do not necessarily equal the costs of operating that mode. Transport pricing policies in developing countries are often designed to deliberately bias the use of one mode or another.

5 The external world is represented as one region for the purposes of handling imports and exports.

6 This is the point at which a consistency check for congestion costs may be made.

7 For initial experiments with the model, it is not worthwhile to choose a particular country, because of the problems of obtaining the required data conveniently and inexpensively.

Selection 24

Evaluating Construction Priorities of Farm-to-Market Roads in Developing Countries: A Case Study

W. R. Stanley

That the improvement of transportation is a critical factor in the developmental process of countries can hardly be overemphasized.[1] In developing areas in particular, transportation is claiming a substantial percentage of the local tax dollar, as well as of funds provided for economic development by international lending agencies and individual states.[2] Concomitant with the increasing need for transport facilities is the ever present dilemma: For which element of the transport sector should the available funds be used first? Roads and road development are increasingly making first claim on national budget allotments for transportation, for road transport, because of its versatility and flexibility, represents a uniquely useful instrument for economic and social progress.[3]

Several recent case studies have focused upon the social, political, and economic impact of new road construction in lesser developed areas.[4] While the specifics differ among these studies, and while many variables are involved, one must conclude that the total effect of new roads in developing countries is indeed profound.[5] Accepting the premise that there is a justifiable need for new road construction, and realizing that funds are limited, the question often becomes: Where should one road be built in an area which could use several new roads? Resolution of this problem goes beyond the realm of the highway planner and is of vital concern to other agencies of government. Establishment of final priorities often is a difficult task. Should national defense rank first in determining road need, or should economic and social considerations head the list? A regional or national highway obviously would have strategic significance in addition to other considerations, whereas a farm-to-market road which follows the contour of the land would have its greatest impact in the economic and social sectors. Invariably, the question regarding priorities of particular routes remains.

Farm-to-market roads have often received less emphasis in developing countries than one might think should be the case considering the widespread need for agricultural develop-

Journal of Developing Areas, vol. 5, no. 3, 1971, pp. 371–400. Reprinted by permission of the author and editor.

ment. That this type of road has not been stressed in some areas can be attributed to a variety of reasons. First, there is the greater "official" attention given to construction of regional and national-unity roads. It is axiomatic that the machinery of governmental administration is thought by most governments to be more important than improvements in the agricultural sector. Whereas subsistence agriculture can offer a living to farmers without roads, a government must have at least minimal road access throughout its domain.[6] An equally important and perhaps more basic cause for the post-World War II emphasis on primary road construction rather than farm-to-market roads has been (and to some extent still is) the elaborate cost/benefit ratios demanded by international lending institutions and foreign aid organizations in developed countries. Varieties of cost/benefit ratios are applied in the more technically advanced countries, and thus it seems only appropriate (to the lending agencies) to require similar justification for road projects in developing states.

DeBeer suggests that present methods of assessing the economic value of roads, expressed as cost/benefit ratios, have been derived essentially from the conditions of road congestion in industrialized countries—in which roads generally carry traffic flows close to or greater than their economic capacity.[7] Most roads in developing countries, however, are not operating at capacity and few seem destined to attain this distinction in the near future. Admittedly, roads near large urban areas are sometimes congested, but this is not representative of the entire route networks. Industrial development which might be stimulated by new roads, while desirable and important, simply is not forthcoming in many developing states. Even where there is noticeable industrial development (Ghana and Nigeria in Africa come immediately to mind), it is agriculture which, for the foreseeable future, must continue to provide the principal employment for the population if not the chief means of obtaining foreign exchange.

Road construction projects of all types constitute but a portion of the total investment schemes in developing countries and must compete for whatever developmental capital is available. Thus it seems all the more necessary for farm-to-market road proposals to stress the indirect benefits accruing both to the local economy and to the whole country if construction of these roads is to be favored by lending institutions. Farm-to-market roads do not often lend themselves neatly to traditional benefits-over-cost analyses.

This study deals with the development and application of a model for field evaluation of rural road construction priorities in Liberia.[8] Some or all of the suggested criteria for rating these priorities may also be useful in rural road evaluation studies in other developing countries. Universal applicability of this model is not claimed, but in lesser developed portions of the world where there often is a dearth of reliable social and economic statistics, a premium has to be placed upon fieldwork. In such areas, the final selection of a farm-to-market route often has a critical bearing on regional development; therefore, there seems to be a need for simple, practical guidelines for field evaluation of farm-to-market route construction priorities. Lastly, the reader should not infer that each and every one of the following evaluation criteria is suited for speedy application and analysis in the field—this most certainly is not the case. What the model does provide is a means of applying several evaluation criteria with minimal reliance upon published statistics or maps. The model also necessitates observing firsthand those areas through which rural road construction has been proposed.

THE MODEL

The model suggested for evaluating construction priorities of farm-to-market roads consists of 9 weighted rating items (Table 24-1). These items (or evaluation criteria) represent both direct and indirect benefits which might accrue to the local economy in the proposed road construction area, as well as those which should help to develop the whole country. These criteria also permit the investigator to isolate proposed roads which would afford maximum accessibility for the most people as well as those which would supplement

Table 24-1 Road Priority Rating Model

Priority Classification Item and Weight Percentage	Rating Variable	Rating Percentage	Relative Rating Score of Road								
			1	2	3	4	5	6	7	8	9
1. Population served by proposed road—15	For road serving highest estimated population...	100	5.85	15.00	9.90	12.30	11.55	3.90	2.25	3.30	0.00
2. Future rice production—10	Surplus................	100	.....	.....	.....	.....	.....	.....	.....	.....	.....
	Deficient...............	75	.....	7.50	7.50	.....	.....	.....	.....	.....	7.50
	Self-sufficient...........	0	0.00	.....	.....	0.00	0.00	0.00	0.00	0.00	.....
3. Future agricultural production of export items (coffee, cacao, and palm kernels)—10	High..................	100	.....	.....	10.00	10.00	.....	.....	.....	.....	.....
	Average................	50	5.00	5.00	.....	.....	5.00	5.00	5.00	5.00	5.00
	None..................	0	.....	.....	.....	.....	.....	.....	.....	.....	.....
4. Perishable food production—5	Surplus................	100	.....	5.00	5.00	.....	.....	5.00	.....	5.00	.....
	Deficient...............	75	.....	.....	.....	.....	.....	.....	.....	.....	3.75
	Self-sufficient...........	0	0.00	.....	.....	0.00	0.00	.....	0.00	.....	.....
5. Availability of other means of transportation—15	None..................	100	15.00	15.00	15.00	.....	.....	15.00	15.00	15.00	.....
	Railway or waterway....	50	.....	.....	.....	7.50	7.50	.....	.....	.....	.....
	Railway and waterway (arterial or parallel)....	0	.....	.....	.....	.....	.....	.....	.....	.....	0.00
6. Cost of construction per mile of road including ferries and/or bridges—15	Low..................	100	.....	15.00	.....	.....	.....	.....	.....	.....	.....
	Average (by country's standards)...........	50	7.50	.....	7.50	.....	.....	7.50	.....	.....	7.50
	High (major stream crossing with bridge or ferry necessary).....	0	.....	.....	.....	0.00	0.00	.....	0.00	0.00	.....
7. Potential for small- to medium-scale forest industries—5	For country's consumption and export.......	100	.....	.....	.....	.....	.....	.....	.....	.....	.....
	For country's consumption only............	75	.....	.....	.....	.....	.....	.....	.....	.....	.....
	For local consumption....	0	0.00	0.00	0.00	0.00	0.00	0.00	0.00	0.00	0.00
8. Connectivity value—15	Connecting two elements of national road system (high connectivity factor)..............	100	.....	.....	.....	.....	15.00	.....	.....	.....	.....
	Connecting two elements of national road system (low connectivity factor)..............	75	.....	11.25	.....	.....	.....	.....	.....	11.25	.....
	Connection to national road system..........	50	7.50	.....	7.50	7.50	.....	7.50	7.50	.....	7.50
9. Administrative factor—county or other administrative center at origin, termination, or along proposed road—10	Two or more...........	100	10.00	.....	.....	10.00	.....	10.00	.....	.....	.....
	One....................	50	.....	5.00	5.00	.....	5.00	.....	.....	.....	.....
	None..................	0	.....	.....	.....	.....	.....	.....	0.00	0.00	0.00
	Total rating score.......		50.85	78.75	67.40	47.30	44.05	53.90	29.75	39.55	31.25

Notes: The numbers under roads 1–9 are derived by multiplying the weight of the classification item by the rating. In classification item 1, the 100 rating was assigned to the proposed road which would serve the most people; values for the other roads were prorated by the number of inhabitants to be served.

The proposed roads are:

1. Bopolu to Belle Yella
2. Gbahn to Kahnple
3. Kolahun to Kailahun
4. Plebo to Kru Coast
5. Tapeta to Yila
6. Tchien to Zia Town
7. Kahnple to Ivory Coast
8. Senje to Lofa River
9. Todee District to Mt. Coffee area

already existing communications, so that duplication of transport facilities may be avoided as much as possible. Use of several differently weighted items permits a meaningful final score to be tabulated; thus an area (to be served by a road) ranking low in some items might still rank high in construction priority because of other items. Much, of course, will depend upon the weights assigned to each classification item.

The 9 classification items used do not preclude the use of others which might also have significance. It is suggested, however, that those selected cover a wide range of activities associated with rural road expansion in developing areas and that their values, direct or indirect, relate to the entire country in measurable terms. For instance, measurements of agricultural development relating to the local population (classification items 2, 3, and 4) consitute 25 percent of the total weight of the model; if population to be served by the proposed road is included, local benefits become 40 percent of the total priority weight. When the less obvious yet important benefits to the entire country's economy are considered (classification items 8 and 9), another 25 percent of the total priority weight is added. Other evaluation criteria might have been employed for the present model, as well as for other countries or regions, but the following questions must be foremost in the investigator's mind while establishing the model: Will construction of this particular road help to develop the agricultural potential of the immediate area and, in the process, help to develop the economic infrastructure of the entire country? Will the government be using its rural road development funds to build roads where construction costs are lowest, other factors being equal? Will construction needlessly overlap other means of transport even though a road would be desirable? Which roads will best help to develop the existing route network? Lastly, which roads will best assist the government in its ability to govern and, just as important, to minister to the social needs of people presently lacking many benefits?

WEIGHTS AND RATINGS

For 8 of the 9 classification items used, there were 3 subvariables. (Item 1 was computed with one subvariable, prorated values being assigned to each road.) Each of the 3 subvariables was rated either 100, 75, 50, or 0 percent of the weighted value of the classification item. For instance, road 1 was rated 50 in classification item 6 (cost of construction). This meant that road 1 was valued at only 50 percent of the weight of item 6 (15 percent) and was scored at 7.50 rather than a possible 15.00. This road could also have been rated 0, in which case there would have been no score for this item.

Using 3 subvariables in each of 8 classification items allows a range of choice which, while substantially subjective, seems both desirable and necessary. This is not to suggest that 3 subvariables with 4 numerical ratings cover every possibility, but rather that a sufficiently broad range of selection is available. Ratings of 100, 75, 50, and 0 not only offer ease of computation but, equally important, satisfy the requirements of scaling: variables should represent meaningful choice in deciding the extent of road-associated economic and social development; they should be weighted realistically; and highest ratings should be associated with greatest need for roads. Ratings assigned in Table 24-1 can be considered a ratio scale in that the values are additive and zero is defined operationally rather than arbitrarily.[9] Substituting 75 for 50 in the ratings for items 2, 4, 7, and 8 was done to narrow the arithmetic difference between 100 and 50 in order to raise the final score if the 100 rating were not selected. It will become evident that such substitution will have little effect upon the final relative order of priorities derived from the model. Classification item weights of 5, 10, and 15 percent were arrived at in much the same manner as ratings were selected and substituted. What the weights and ratings do not permit, however, is precise interpretation of the final rating score of each road; rather, the scores must be considered in relative terms. This caution is necessary because of the subjective establishment of weights and ratings; it is obvious that different values would lead to an altered final score. This limitation of the model should not be overemphasized, however, since the evaluator seeks relative position rather than arithmetic scores in deciding the construction "worthiness" of proposed roads. In this respect the present evaluation model is similar to most cost/benefit analyses in that the evaluation is designed primarily for the comparison and ranking of alternative projects rather than for testing their absolute desirability.[10]

Population to be served by the road (item 1), availability of other means of transport (item 5), cost of construction (item 6), and connectivity value to the total road system (item 8) were judged to be more significant than those assigned lower weights. While there are undoubtedly a multitude of indexes by which one can analyze indirect benefits derived from farm-to-market road construction, most require adequate statistics—the lack of which is the rationale for much of this study.

The percentages of the total rating score contributed by classification items grouped according to weight are presented in Table 24-2. It can be deduced from these scores that the combination of items weighted 5 percent and the combination weighted 10 percent contribute less to the final score on a percentage basis, than the combination of items weighted 15 percent. The share of each category in the total score is less than maximum for 7 of the 9 roads with respect to items weighted 5 percent, for 6 of 9 roads in the 10 percent weightings, and for only 3 of 9 roads in the 15 percent weightings. Put another way, the 4 classification items weighted 15 percent constitute a greater proportion of the final scores of 6 of 9 roads than the maximum value (60 percent) of these items to the model. This suggests an imbalance which is not necessarily desirable. A major cause of the distorted relationship between maximum model weight and actual contribution to the final score of the 2 items weighted 5 percent is due in large part to the fact that item 7 (potential for small-scale forest industries) furnished no scores whatsoever. This item had no significance in the model, and its very inclusion might be questioned. It should be noted, however, that the incidence of item ratings could only be determined after the study was completed—not before.[11]

The model was then tested for possible distortion by (1) varying the weighting of classification items within a 5 to 15 percent range and (2) alternating the ratings of 50 and 75. Item weights were equalized in 4 of the 5 variant models, while in 3 models no 75 ratings were used. Scores for these (Table 24-3) indicate that the relative priority rank-

Table 24-2 Percentage Distribution of Road Ratings by Priority Classification Categories

Road	Total Rating Score Out of Possible 100	Classification Category		
		Items Weighted 5 Percent (2)	Items Weighted 10 Percent (3)	Items Weighted 15 Percent (4)
1	50.85	0.00	29.50	70.50
2	78.75	6.35	22.22	71.43
3	67.40	7.42	33.38	59.20
4	47.30	0.00	42.28	57.72
5	44.05	0.00	22.70	77.30
6	53.90	9.28	27.83	62.89
7	29.75	0.00	16.81	83.19
8	39.55	12.64	12.64	74.72
9	31.25	12.00	40.00	48.00

Table 24-3 Variant Road Priority Rating Models Based on Alternative Weights and Ratings

Road Priority Rank	Original Model	Variant Model				
	Road—Rating Score	1 Road—Rating Score	2 Road—Rating Score	3 Road—Rating Score	4 Road—Rating Score	5 Road—Rating Score
1.	2—78.75	2—75.00	2—72.22	2—72.50	2—70.00	2—66.68
2.	3—67.40	3—64.00	3—60.01	3—57.40	3—56.50	3—51.68
3.	6—53.90	6—57.20	6—52.45	6—46.40	6—52.20	6—46.89
4.	1—50.85	1—48.90	1—43.23	5—44.05	1—43.90	1—37.67
5.	4—47.30	4—46.60	4—40.67	1—43.35	5—43.20	5—36.90
6.	5—44.05	8—45.10	8—39.00	4—39.80	8—42.60	8—36.23
7.	8—39.55	5—43.20	5—36.90	8—35.80	4—41.60	4—35.11
8.	9—31.25	9—40.00	9—33.34	7—22.25	7—32.70	7—25.22
9.	7—29.75	7—37.70	7—30.78	9—20.00	9—30.00	9—22.24

NOTES: Original model: weights and ratings as in table 24-1.
Variant model 1: all items weighted 10 percent; ratings as in table 24-1; 10 points added to each rating score.
Variant model 2: all items weighted 11.1 percent; ratings as in table 24-1.
Variant model 3: weights as in table 24-1; ratings as in table 24-1, except 50 substituted for 75 ratings.
Variant model 4: all items weighted 10 percent; ratings as in Table 24-1, except 50 substituted for 75 ratings; 10 points added to each rating score.
Variant model 5: all items weighted 11.1 percent; ratings as in Table 24-1, except 50 substituted for 75 ratings.

ings of the roads have been generally maintained in each model. Some change in rank is apparent, but where this occurs differences in scores are small. As suggested earlier, choice between roads with nearly similar scores should not be inferred from the model. These additional models suggest that the bias associated with applying varied weights and rankings is less important than it might appear at first. The variant models also indicate groupings of roads by rating scores.

The mean and the interpolated median scores of the point differences between roads of consecutive rank in decreasing priority order for all 6 models are: 13.03/12.8 (for roads in ranks 1 and 2); 7.99/7.18 (2 and 3); 6.74/8.30 (3 and 4); 1.76/1.54 (4 and 5); 1.87/1.59 (5 and 6); 2.44/2.00 (6 and 7); 7.90/8.60 (7 and 8); and 2.38/2.43 (8 and 9). These scores clearly indicate the high relative priorities of roads in ranks 1–3, not only from each other, but equally important, from roads in lower priority rankings. Indeed, the models suggest 3 relative priority groupings: Roads in ranks 1, 2, and 3 in first priority; roads in ranks 4, 5, 6, and 7 in second priority; and roads in ranks 8 and 9 in third and last priority. It is also possible for the evaluator to differentiate within each group, especially the first group.

Another method of differentiating the relative ranking of roads in the 6 models is to assign scores for each rank. For instance, one can allocate 9 points in rank 1; 8 points to roads in rank 2; and so on until 1 point is allocated to roads in rank 9. Combining these points for the 6 models suggests the following matrix:

Road 1: 6 6 6 6 6 5 = 35
Road 2: 9 9 9 9 9 9 = 54
Road 3: 8 8 8 8 8 8 = 48
Road 4: 5 5 5 4 3 3 = 25
Road 5: 6 5 5 4 3 3 = 26
Road 6: 7 7 7 7 7 7 = 42
Road 7: 2 2 2 1 1 1 = 9
Road 8: 4 4 4 4 3 3 = 22
Road 9: 2 2 2 1 1 1 = 9

These rating scores indicate a road construction priority of the following order: roads 2, 3, 6, 5, 4, 8, and a tie between 7 and 9. Comparing the priorities of this composite of all 6 models to those indicated in the original model (Table 24-1) reveals a reversal in rank between roads 4 and 5, and 7 and 9. For the most part, however, the roads with high priority are the same and stand out in both ranking approaches.

STUDY AREA

Most observers would agree that there is a need for the construction of all types of roads in Liberia. For the most part, the existing road network has been organized on a national basis, with unification objectives ranking foremost in construction priorities. Those living any distance from principal roads are forced to rely primarily upon human porterage to move their goods to and from market, especially since there is no practical alternative water route system.

Liberia's physical conditions present problems to the development and improvement of modern road transportation. The tropical, rainy climate supports a lush vegetation which adds to the cost of road clearing and maintenance; there are some 11,000 square miles of virgin evergreen forest in a country of 43,000 square miles. During the rainy season (April–October), coastal areas record upwards of 200 inches of precipitation, and rivers already difficult to cross become major barriers to bridging and ferry operations, particularly near the coast. Where roads do exist, they tend to parallel major water courses and cross them in their upstream portions. Road maintenance is a problem of the first order, and it is not unusual for sections of the principal highway between Monrovia (the capital) and the interior to be washed out for several days or to be so churned up that passage is restricted to vehicles having 4-wheel drive.

Sites and approximate distances of proposed rural-access or farm-to-market roads analyzed and ranked in this study (see Fig. 24-1) are as follows: Bopolu to Belle Yella (67 mi.), Gbahn to Kahnple (35 mi.), Kahnple to Ivory Coast (12 mi.), Kolahun to Kailahun (25 mi.), Plebo to Kru Coast (60 mi.), Senje to Lofa River (28 mi.), Tapeta to Yila (32 mi.), and Tchien to Zia Town (35 mi.). The ninth proposed road, Todee District to Mt. Coffee area (6 mi.) is located north of Monrovia in Montserrado County; because of its length, it could not adequately be depicted on Fig. 24-1. These routes are widely distributed throughout the country and vary greatly in length. In all instances, they tie into the principal road network and in 3 cases unite 2 segments of it. Furthermore, in each instance it was understood that there was local desire, as well as administrative encouragement, for the proposed route.[12] Local interest in farm-to-market roads should not be underrated. Owen notes that "the provision of good transportation is not capable by itself of promoting economic growth. It is only where there are resources to be developed and people capable of developing them that transport becomes the catalyst that transforms land and other resources into the things that people need."[13]

It has already been suggested that new roads of all types are needed in this country. The historical dichotomy of development between the coastal and interior areas can be partially attributed to difficulty of communication and transportation. Because of post-World War II construction, it is now possible in most instances to travel more cheaply from the coast to the interior than it is to travel along the coastal roads (Fig. 24-2). At the same time, there is a lag between the improving communications between regions and the spreading of socioeconomic opportunities still available primarily in the coastal region. Such a lag is evident from Schulze's 1965 study of the student body at the University of Liberia in which he noted that a total of 80.1 percent of the Liberian students are born within a 30-mile belt along the coast.[14] A great deal more needs to be done to increase social and economic opportunity for all of Liberia's people.

Do the final relative priority ranks for these farm-to-market roads relate to a scale of road and population densities for the counties? To answer this question, the proposed roads were ranked by comparing (1) road miles per square

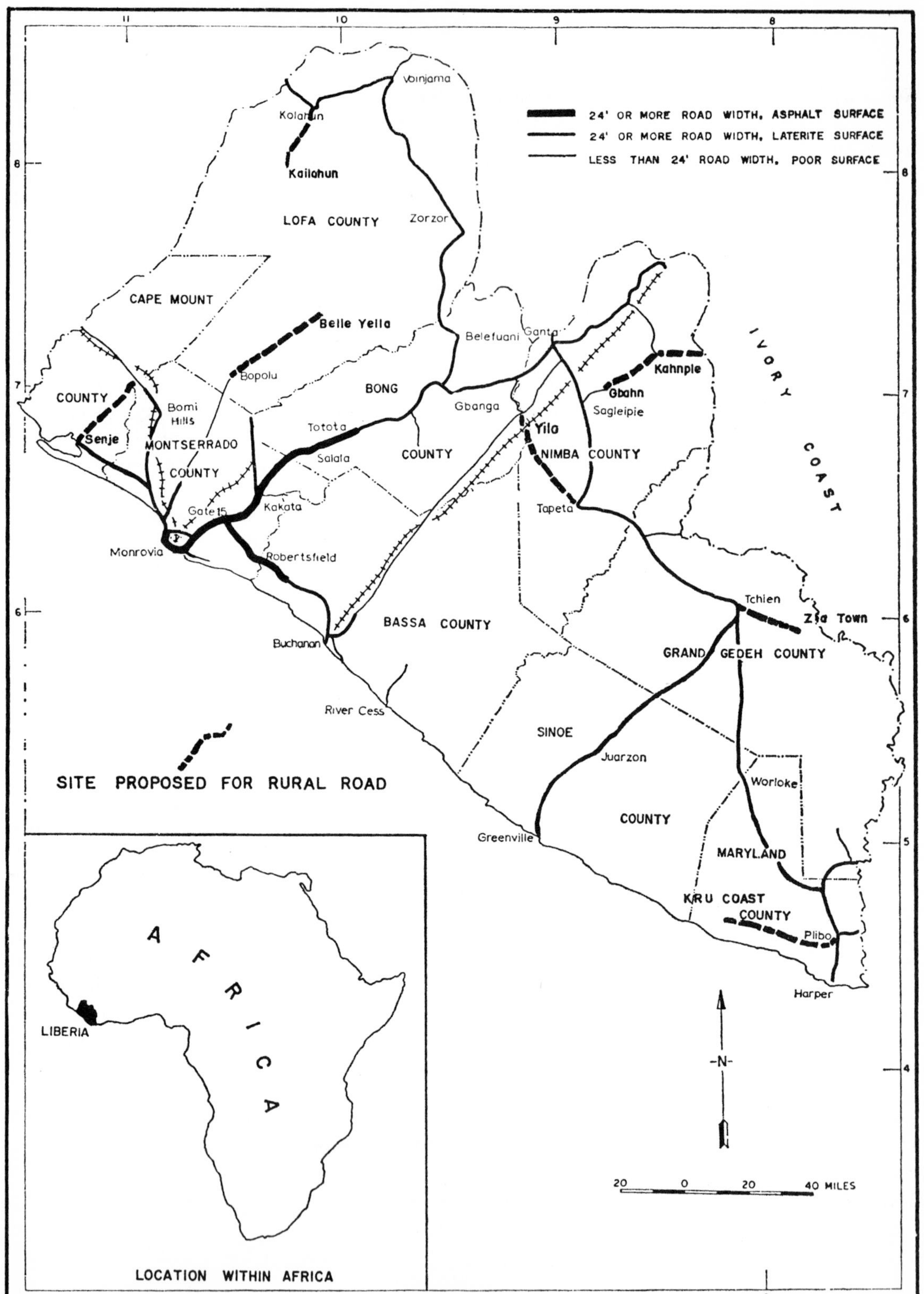

24' OR MORE ROAD WIDTH, ASPHALT SURFACE
24' OR MORE ROAD WIDTH, LATERITE SURFACE
LESS THAN 24' ROAD WIDTH, POOR SURFACE
Voinjama
Kolahun
Kailahun
LOFA COUNTY
Zorzor
CAPE MOUNT
Belle Yella
Bopolu
COUNTY
Bomi Hills
Senje
MONTSERRADO
COUNTY
BONG
COUNTY
Totota
Salala
Kakata
Gate 15
Monrovia
Robertsfield
Belefuani
Ganta
Gbanga
Yila
NIMBA COUNTY
Gbahn
Kahnple
Sagleipie
Tapeta
IVORY COAST
BASSA COUNTY
Buchanan
River Cess
Tchien
Zia Town
GRAND GEDEH COUNTY
SINOE
Juarzon
COUNTY
Greenville
Worloke
MARYLAND
KRU COAST
COUNTY
Plibo
Harper
SITE PROPOSED FOR RURAL ROAD
-N-
20 0 20 40 MILES
AFRICA
LIBERIA
LOCATION WITHIN AFRICA

Fig. 24-1.

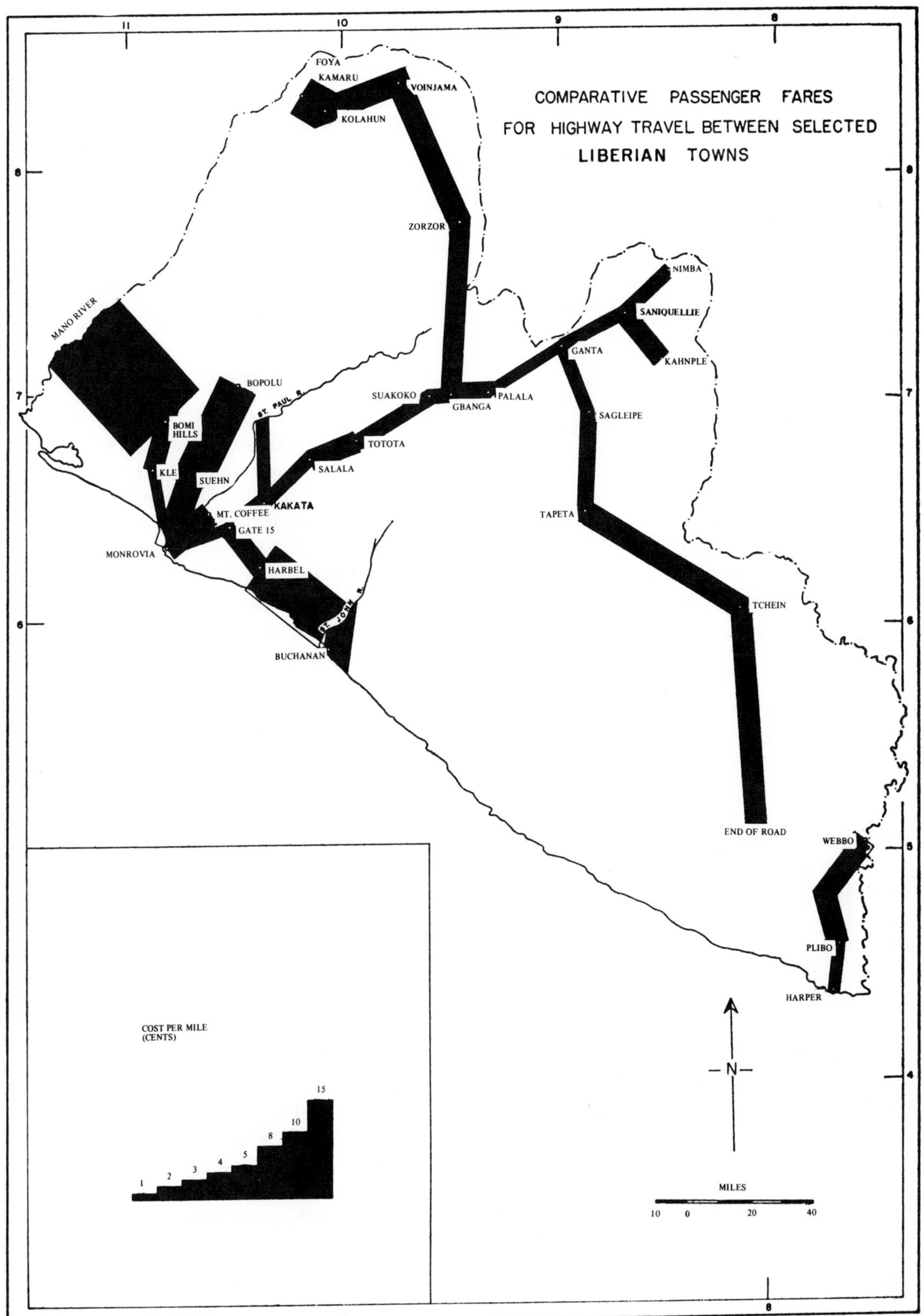
COMPARATIVE PASSENGER FARES
FOR HIGHWAY TRAVEL BETWEEN SELECTED
LIBERIAN TOWNS
FOYA
KAMARU
VOINJAMA
KOLAHUN
ZORZOR
NIMBA
SANIQUELLIE
GANTA
KAHNPLE
MANO RIVER
BOPOLU
SUAKOKO
GBANGA
PALALA
SAGLEIPE
BOMI HILLS
ST. PAUL R.
TOTOTA
KLE
SUEHN
SALALA
KAKATA
MT. COFFEE
TAPETA
GATE 15
MONROVIA
HARBEL
ST. JOHN R.
TCHEIN
BUCHANAN
END OF ROAD
WEBBO
PLIBO
HARPER
COST PER MILE
(CENTS)
1
2
3
4
5
8
10
15
N
MILES
10
0
20
40
11
10
9
8
7
6
5
4

Fig. 24-2.

Table 24-4 Road Mileage and Population Factors as Related to Counties

County	Road Reference and Number	Population per Square Mile (1)	Road Miles per Square Mile (2)	Population per Mile of Road (1÷2)
Montserrado.......	Bopolu-Belle Yella (1) Todee District (9)	95	0.116	819
Nimba............	Kahnple-Ivory Coast (7) Gbahn-Kahnple (2) Tapeta-Yila (5)	32	0.042	762
Bong..............	Tapeta-Yila (5)	34	0.057	596
Maryland..........	Plebo-Kru Coast (4)	32	0.039	821
Grand Bassa.......		24	0.025	960
Lofa..............	Kolahun-Kailahun (3) Bopolu-Belle Yella (1)	16	0.024	667
Grand Gedeh......	Tchien-Zia Town (6)	9	0.016	562
Sinoe..............	Plebo-Kru Coast (4)	12	0.015	800
Grand Cape Mount.	Senje-Lofa River (8)	13	0.025	520

NOTE: Population data based on 1962 estimates.

mile and (2) population per mile of road for counties through which proposed roads would pass (Table 24-4). The ideal would be for roads with highest relative priority rankings to be located in counties with a combination of fewest miles of road per square mile and highest population per mile of road. In this way, the completed road would not only help to reduce the population-road mile ratio, but would also increase Liberia's road density. Both of these indexes suggest need for additional road mileage, and increases in one or both ratios should ultimately expand the range where agricultural produce is marketed and make it easier for rural people to enter into the exchange economy.

Although there are some significant positive correlations between the relative rank of a proposed road and the road density and population indexes, no clear pattern emerges. For instance, the Bopolu to Belle Yella and the Todee District roads will be completely or partially in Montserrado County, which has the highest road density, but also the greatest population per road mile. The low priority ranking of these 2 routes seems valid because of the high ratio of road miles to area, but is rendered less so by the amount of population per mile of road. The proposed Senje-Lofa River road in Grand Cape Mount County would relate poorly to both indexes. For the most part, there is a closer relationship between a road's relative priority rank and higher population per road mile than there is with miles of road per square mile.

APPLICATION OF THE MODEL TO THE STUDY AREA

The next step is to apply the 9 classification items to the study area. The relationship of each item to Liberia will be analyzed, as well as the reasons for its particular rating.

Item 1: Population. The derivation of scores for this classification item involves simple computation rather than a choice between rating variables. First, a "zone of influence" was established for each of the proposed roads. Steiner defines the zone of influence of a social road in Mexico as "that area whose boundaries are set as the maximum distance from the road that a person can travel during one day in any direction using any available method of transportation."[15] Hawkins, on the other hand, suggests that "if transport routes are to stimulate trade they must reach as large a proportion of the total area of the country as possible. Any part of the country more than one mile from a road is virtually without transport facilities as far as most low-value, bulky articles are concerned."[16] For this study, zone of influence is defined as the area containing the population within one day's walk of the site of a proposed road—approximately 20 miles in either direction. Population statistics for 8 of 9 zones of influence are provided in Table 24.5.[17] Fig. 24-3, based on air photos taken in 1953, provides the reader with a measure of Liberia's population distribution and density.

Computation of scores for each of 8 proposed roads was as follows: Road 2 (Gbahn-Kahnple) will serve a zone of influence containing the largest calculated population per mile of any proposed road, hence it became the base for further computations. Populations per mile within zones of influence for the other proposed roads were then expressed as percentages of road 2's population number. These percentages were: road 1 (38.9), 2 (100), 3 (15.3), 4 (66.3), 5 (81.6), 6 (21.5), 7 (76.6), and 8 (26.2). Scores for each proposed road were then found by multiplying a 15.00 score (15 percent item weight times 100 rating) by the road's population percentage; for example, 5.85 for road 1 equals 38.9 percent of 15.00.

Item 2: Future Rice Production. Rice is the staple of the Liberian's diet. Internal production deficiencies are made up by increasing imports of rice—to the detriment of the country's foreign exchange holdings. Importing rice is a relatively new experience, for until World War II Liberia was usually able to meet its rice requirements from domestic production. After the war, increased mobility for the population as a result of new road construction and the rise in employment opportunities at large-scale rubber plantations and iron ore mines encouraged workers in ever greater numbers to leave subsistence farming. Any increase in domestic production or improvement in the distribution of existing local surpluses should be considered favorably (100 rating) when assigning construction priorities. More efficient distribution of surplus rice is important since the cost of moving it to rice-deficient areas might be so high as to preclude shipment.[18] The lower priority (75 rating) allocated to a rice-deficient area presumes that there is no famine there; if this should be the case, the government would be morally obligated to open the area to adequate food distribution with little thought to expense. If the zone of influence is self-sufficient in rice production, road construction funds are better allocated elsewhere.

Item 3: Future Agricultural Production of Export Items. Liberia has a long history of exporting agricultural products.[19] Although the importance of coffee, palm kernels, and cacao in the country's exports has declined following the growth of rubber production, the government has professed encouragement of export-oriented agriculture wherever possible. Unfortunately, little information is avail-

Table 24-5 Estimated Population to Receive Maximum Social and Economic Benefits from New Road Construction

Proposed Road	Minimum Estimated Mileage of New Construction[a]	Number of Inhabitants Residing Within the Road's Zone of Influence[b]	Number of Inhabitants to be Served by One Mile of New Road Construction[a]	Minimum Estimated Mileage of New Construction[c]	Number of Inhabitants to be Served by One Mile of New Road Construction[c]
1. Bopolu-Belle Yella.....	67.0	17,000	254	60.0	283
2. Gbahn-Kahnple........	35.2	23,000	653	20.0	1,150
3. Kolahun-Kailahun......	25.4	11,000	433	10.0	1,100
4. Plebo-Kru Coast.......	60.0	32,000	533	35.0	914
5. Tapeta-Yila...........	32.0	16,000	500	26.6	601
6. Tchien-Zia Town.......	35.0	6,000	171	35.0	171
7. Kahnple-Ivory Coast...	12.0	1,200	100	8.0	150
8. Senje-Lofa River.......	28.4	4,000	141	12.0	333

[a] Including refurbishing of existing mileage for road or "brushed" trail.
[b] Figures rounded to the nearest thousand.
[c] Excluding any refurbishing of existing mileage.

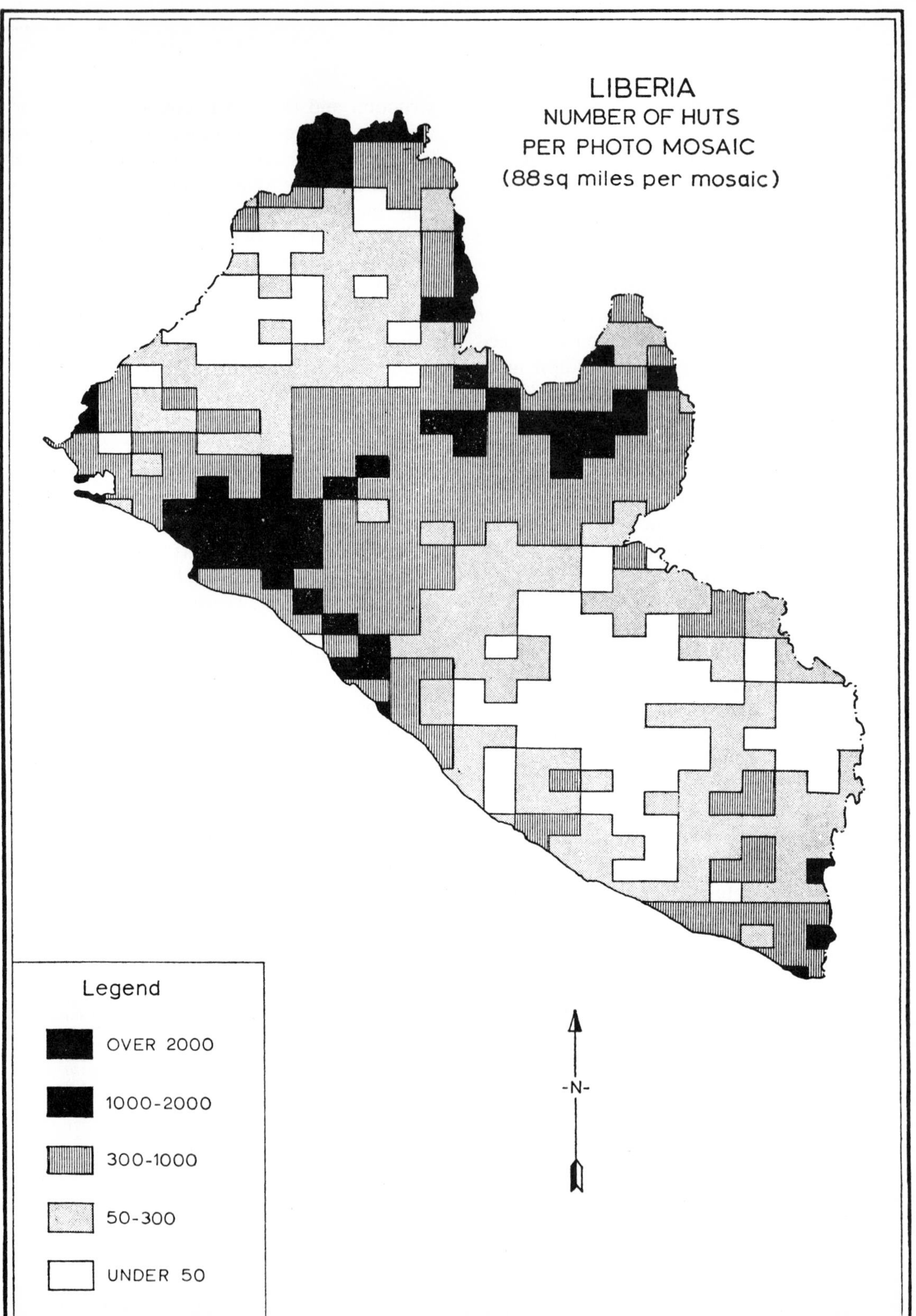
LIBERIA
NUMBER OF HUTS
PER PHOTO MOSAIC
(88sq miles per mosaic)
Legend
OVER 2000
1000-2000
300-1000
50-300
UNDER 50
-N-

Fig. 24-3

able concerning the locations in the interior where export agricultural commodities are grown and collected; reliable statistics are available only for port of export. To help detect future production patterns of agricultural exports within zones of influence of the proposed 9 roads, use was made of data collected in 1964 on the volume of palm kernels and coffee sold and bartered at Lebanese stores—the principal and often only marketing mechanism in the interior for export-oriented agricultural products. The degree of Lebanese involvement in Liberian agriculture (and export agriculture throughout West Africa) cannot be overstated. Their influence has increased despite the fact that the Liberia Produce Marketing Corporation, a government-sanctioned marketing board, was founded in 1963 for the purpose of increasing agricultural production through the establishment of more equitable prices and improved marketing procedures. Nonetheless, Lebanese merchants continue to dominate both retail and wholesale aspects of agricultural marketing.

Figs. 24-4 and 24-5 relate area and population to coffee and palm kernel collections recorded by Lebanese merchants. Fig. 24-6 depicts a partial distribution of their stores.[20] Palm kernel collection data are more meaningful than those for coffee since a large proportion of the coffee marketed in northwest Liberia is known to have come from adjacent areas in Guinea.

Field investigation substantiated the general patterns of production and collection depicted in Figs. 24-4 and 24-5. As it turned out, 2 proposed routes were assigned highest priority (100 rating) in this classification item—one in the coffee producing region in the northwest and one in the southeast where much cacao cultivation was observed. In both areas farmers were encountering serious marketing difficulties—so much so that in some instances production was either not being marketed or was being left to rot on the tree or bush.

Item 4: Perishable Food Production. Commodities included in this category are vegetables and fruit, some of which traditionally have been consumed on the farm. Increasing amounts, however, are being grown for sale in nearby towns and cities. Because fresh vegetables and fruit spoil rapidly, if they are to reach outside markets, some form of improved transport beyond human porterage is necessary (refrigeration facilities are rare in the producing areas and can be acquired only by the largest shippers). As in the case of coffee, cacao, and palm kernels, sale of perishable produce adds to the farmer's purchasing power and increases the overall monetization level in agricultural areas. The amount of produce consumed on the farms in relation to that grown for export and domestic markets testifies to the low monetization levels of large portions of the Liberian economy. Yudelman suggests that the organization of production in tropical Africa passes through 4 stages: (1) production for direct consumption; (2) production primarily for direct consumption with some for market; (3) production mostly for market with some for direct consumption; and (4) specialized production for market.[21] Since stages 1 and 4 represent extreme situations, neither of which properly describe changing Africa, the immediate development problem is to encourage movement from 2 to 3 and in a few isolated areas from 3 to 4.

Several of the European-owned retail food stores in the more populous coastal cities have found it desirable to contract for fresh vegetables from a few large-scale Liberian vegetable growers who have farms near principal highways. Previous reliance upon haphazard deliveries by small-scale farmers from less accessible areas was generally unsatisfactory to both parties. For the farmer, ex-

COFFEE AND PALM KERNEL COLLECTIONS 1964

PRE 1963 POLITICAL SUBDIVISIONS AS THE RECORDING UNIT; 1962 CENSUS OF POPULATION

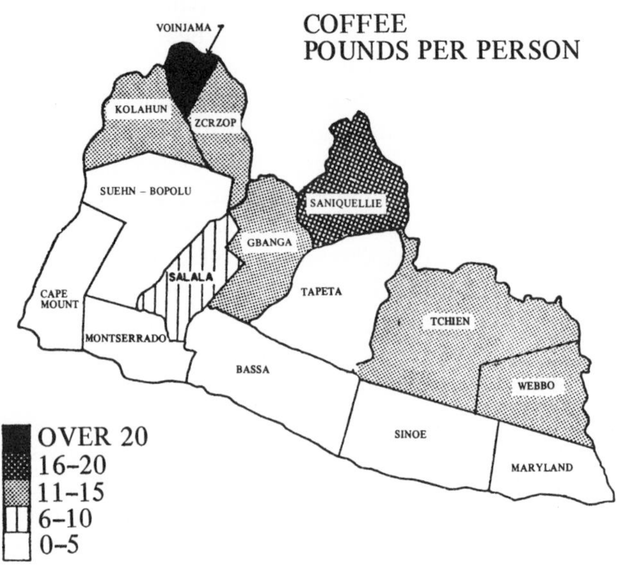

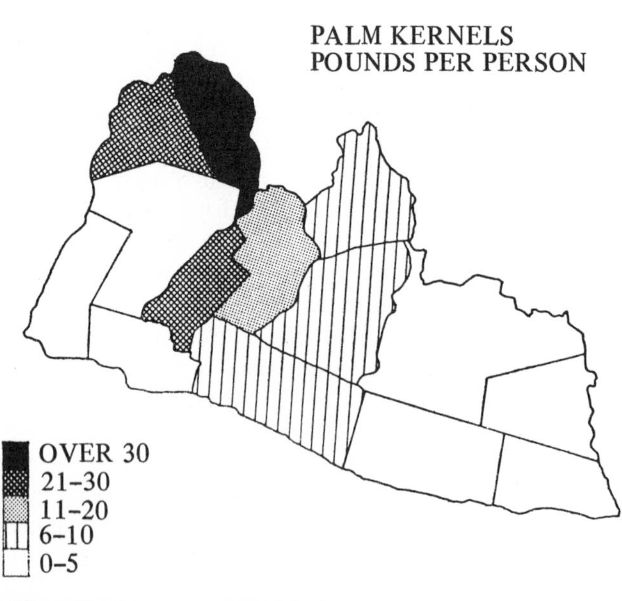

Fig. 24-4.

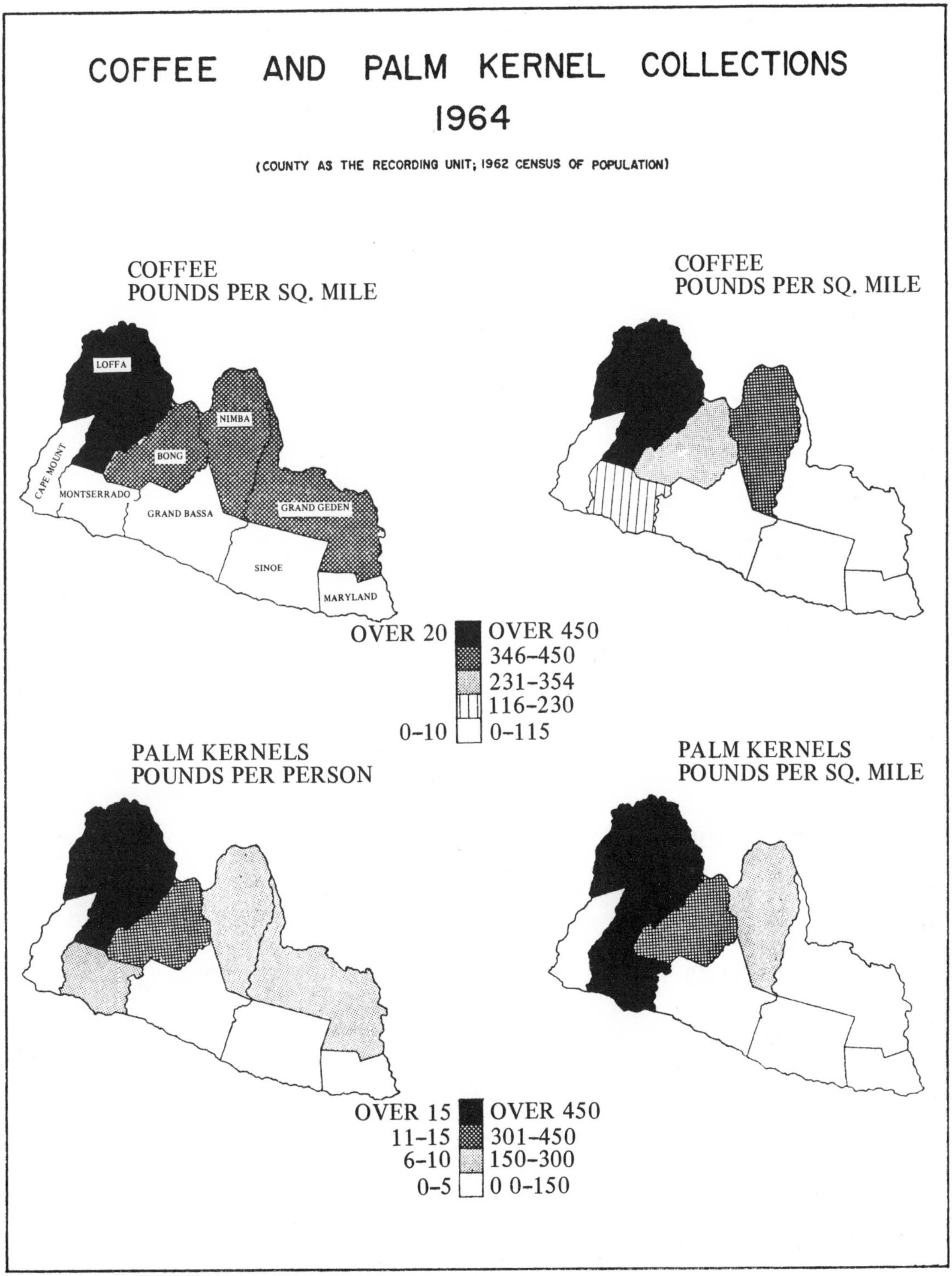

COFFEE AND PALM KERNEL COLLECTIONS 1964

(COUNTY AS THE RECORDING UNIT; 1962 CENSUS OF POPULATION)

COFFEE
POUNDS PER SQ. MILE

LOFFA
NIMBA
BONG
CAPE MOUNT
MONTSERRADO
GRAND BASSA
GRAND GEDEN
SINOE
MARYLAND

COFFEE
POUNDS PER SQ. MILE

OVER 20	■	OVER 450
		346–450
		231–354
		116–230
0–10	□	0–115

PALM KERNELS
POUNDS PER PERSON

PALM KERNELS
POUNDS PER SQ. MILE

OVER 15	■	OVER 450
11–15		301–450
6–10		150–300
0–5	□	0 0–150

Fig. 24-5.

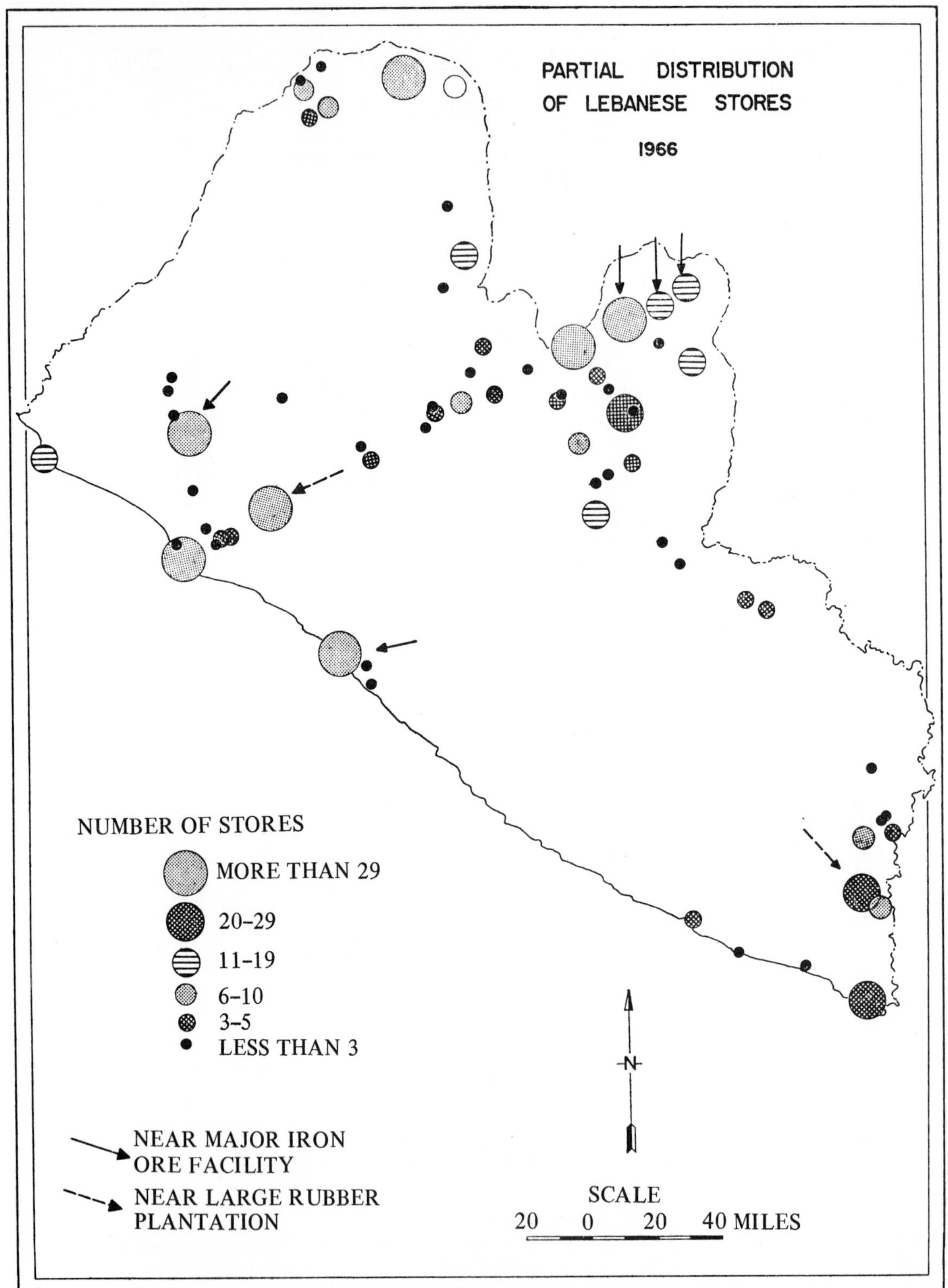
PARTIAL DISTRIBUTION
OF LEBANESE STORES
1966
NUMBER OF STORES
MORE THAN 29
20–29
11–19
6–10
3–5
LESS THAN 3
NEAR MAJOR IRON
ORE FACILITY
NEAR LARGE RUBBER
PLANTATION
N
SCALE
20 0 20 40 MILES

Fig. 24-6.

treme price fluctuations were a major problem. If prices were often too low, he might either abandon future shipments and pay less attention to his fields or, if a large village were nearby, he might concentrate his marketing efforts there and accept the lower local prices. Improved distribution of perishable farm produce would expand the market hinterlands of larger cities and partially stabilize the flow of commodities at any particular time, thus benefiting urban citizens and farmers alike.

Item 5: Availability of Other Means of Transportation. While there are railroads in Liberia, rail as an alternative to road transport presents a special problem because, to date, railroads are owned and operated by concession holders and are not general freight and passenger carriers. There has been increasing interest, however, in utilizing one or more of the iron ore hauling railways for shipping timber and possibly agricultural products to the ports of Monrovia and Buchanan.[22] It is interesting to compare this effort by the Liberian government to expand the role of iron ore hauling lines with those of other African states to protect state railways from increasingly effective competition by road carriers. In Sierra Leone competition from road transport has become so effective that the first of several recommendations made by a private consulting firm concerning the government railway was "to stop operations as soon as road transport is in a position to take over the passengers and goods; that the railway be removed and all parts having any value be disposed of."[23] Railroad protection is manifested in freight rate differentials, restricting vehicle size on roads where road and rail are competitive, and minimizing repair and maintenance facilities on roads to market areas served by railroads. For instance, in Dahomey the principal north-south highway which parallels the Benin-Niger Railway between Abomey and Parakou is laterite surfaced and often in poor repair, whereas north of Parakou, the railhead town, this road is asphalt covered as far as the Niger River. Liberia has not yet been faced with this type of road/rail competition which, in spite of its duplication of services and demands on scarce capital resources, does have the advantages of providing broader and, in some instances, better transport facilities. Perhaps Liberia's efforts to expand the services of some of the iron ore hauling lines can be attributed to the fact that, as privately owned and operated lines, they are not competing with roads for development funds.

Inclusion of railroads as an alternative means of transport is predicated upon (1) the possible expansion of rail service to commodities other than iron ore and (2) the significance, if any, of these new services upon prevailing transport patterns in each zone of influence. Proposed rural access roads in areas having no alternative means of transport should receive highest priority (100 rating) in this classification item. Areas with existing rail *or* water facilities would have reasonably adequate transport even without a road (50 rating), while areas with rail *and* water transport, whether arterial or parallel, would receive the lowest priority.

Item 6: Cost of Construction. As suggested earlier, road construction and maintenance in the tropics is exceptionally costly because of the frequency of watercourses and generally heavy precipitation. Proposals to build rural roads through areas with many and sometimes large watercourses must therefore consider bridging and ferry costs. To a large extent, need for bridges has been circumvented by the use of small 1-or-2-vehicle pulley-operated ferries which utilize stream currents to help propel them across the water while attached to cables. Such ferries can be installed for as little as $15,000 each.[24] Unlike bridges, which entail large capital expenditures but few recurring costs, even small ferries require provision for operating costs, particularly the ferry operator's salary. Charging tolls for small ferries should be discouraged, for even without tolls, ferries are generally less costly than bridges.

Upon observing the route terrain for each proposed road, it became apparent that only the broadest cost evaluations and comparisons were possible. It would be difficult indeed to provide precise figures for the eventual construction costs of any of the roads. In addition to physical factors, the decision to use local labor exclusively or a combination of local labor and modern equipment influences construction costs. In most labor-intensive societies there is a tendency to use much manual labor and relatively little equipment on the grounds that labor is cheap and usually available in surplus. Baranson considers this rationale valid only if the combined wage of this labor is less than equipment rental costs.[25]

In general, farm-to-market road construction should approximate the cost of logging roads since both are essentially of the contour type. While a logging road is likely to have a poor surface, bridges and culverts would be at least as strong as those in a rural access road because of the weights to which they would be subjected. The highest estimate given by any of the logging companies in Liberia was $5,000 per mile, while the median cost was about $3,500 per mile. These costs have been substantiated by O'Connor who suggests a minimal construction cost of $4,200 a mile for local earth roads in "easy" country in Uganda.[26]

Item 7: Potential for Small- to Medium-scale Forest Industries. None of the proposed roads would penetrate areas where logging operations are in progress or where timber surveys have been made (Fig. 24-7), and none enter areas which are under consideration for timber surveys. Furthermore, no large-scale logging operations were observed during field traverses. As a result, the only rating used in this classification item was that for "local consumption." In some cases, however, a slight modification of the proposed route would have brought a road into marketable stands of timber and would have resulted in an altered priority rank.

Item 8: Connectivity Value. Would the road, if constructed, increase the accessibility to and connectivity of the existing route network? It is necessary to ask this question even though the primary purpose of the rural road is to open up farming areas hitherto inaccessible from roads. Many developing countries have so few miles of road and so great a need for additional mileage that overall national improvement in road accessibility has to be considered, even in localized projects.

Accessibility and connectivity can be measured more objectively than was possible in 6 of the preceding 7 priority evaluation criteria (item 1 excepted). To be calculated is a numerical factor which is then related, on a subjective basis, to alternative rating variables. The initial step is to apply graph topology to transport systems and then analyze the systems by means of matrix algebra. Properties which characterize ordinary graphs (and thus transport systems so treated) are: (1) a network has a finite number of places, (2) each route is a set consisting of 2 places, (3) each route joins 2 different places, (4) at most, only 1 route may join 2 places, and (5) no distinctions are made between the routes' initial and terminal places, in other words, routes are 2-way.[27]

Each of the proposed roads, singly or in combination, can be evaluated in terms of the increased accessibility which its construction will afford to places on the road network. Stated another way, they can be evaluated as to the degree to which their construction reduces overall dispersion within the network. Fig. 24-8 represents the central section of the Liberian road system, drawn to the same scale

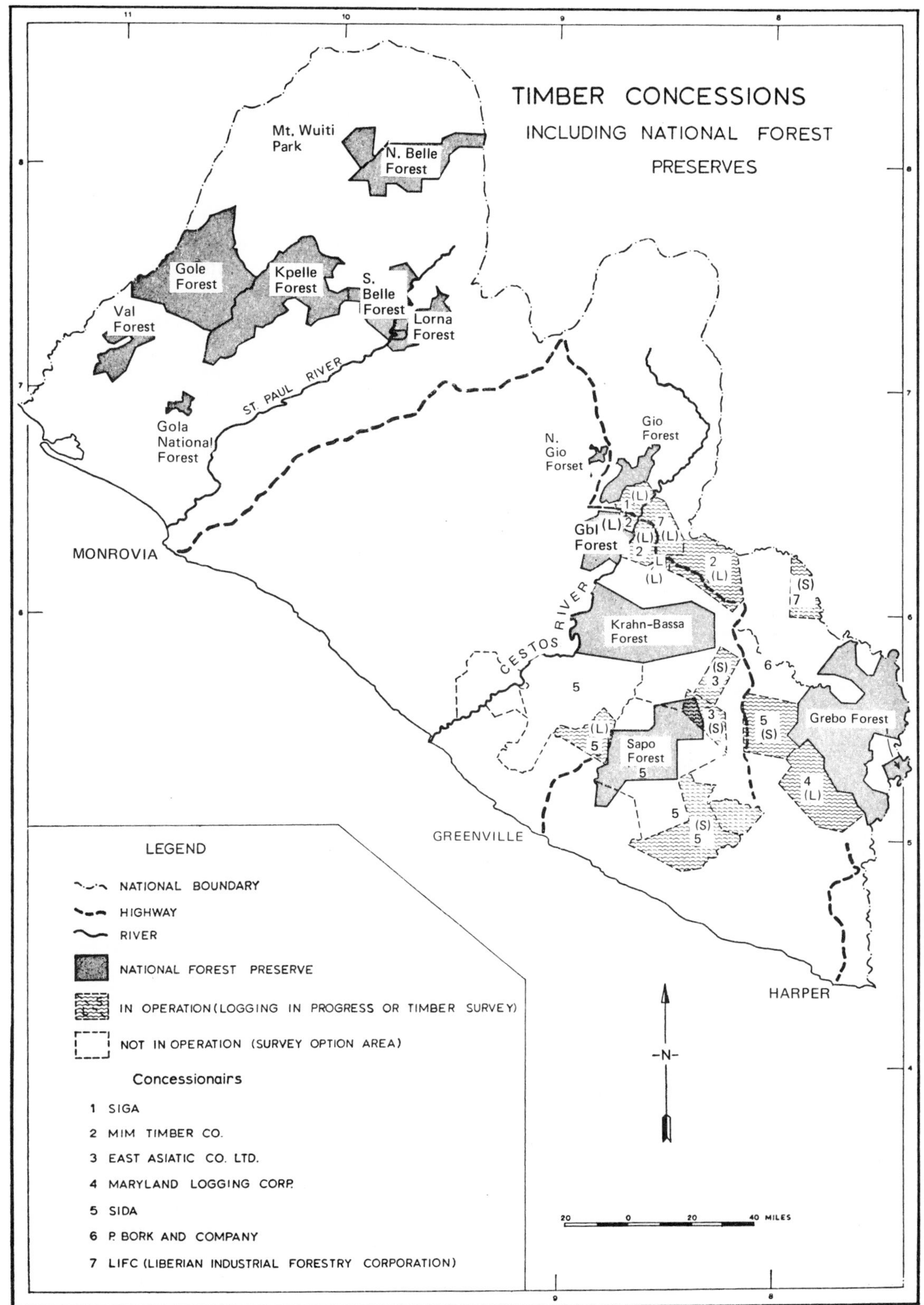

TIMBER CONCESSIONS
INCLUDING NATIONAL FOREST PRESERVES
Mt. Wuiti Park
N. Belle Forest
Gole Forest
Kpelle Forest
S. Belle Forest
Lorna Forest
Val Forest
Gola National Forest
ST. PAUL RIVER
MONROVIA
N. Gio Forset
Gio Forest
Gbl Forest
CESTOS RIVER
Krahn-Bassa Forest
Sapo Forest
Grebo Forest
GREENVILLE
HARPER
LEGEND
NATIONAL BOUNDARY
HIGHWAY
RIVER
NATIONAL FOREST PRESERVE
IN OPERATION (LOGGING IN PROGRESS OR TIMBER SURVEY)
NOT IN OPERATION (SURVEY OPTION AREA)
Concessionairs
1 SIGA
2 MIM TIMBER CO.
3 EAST ASIATIC CO. LTD.
4 MARYLAND LOGGING CORP.
5 SIDA
6 P. BORK AND COMPANY
7 LIFC (LIBERIAN INDUSTRIAL FORESTRY CORPORATION)
-N-
20 0 20 40 MILES

Fig. 24-7.

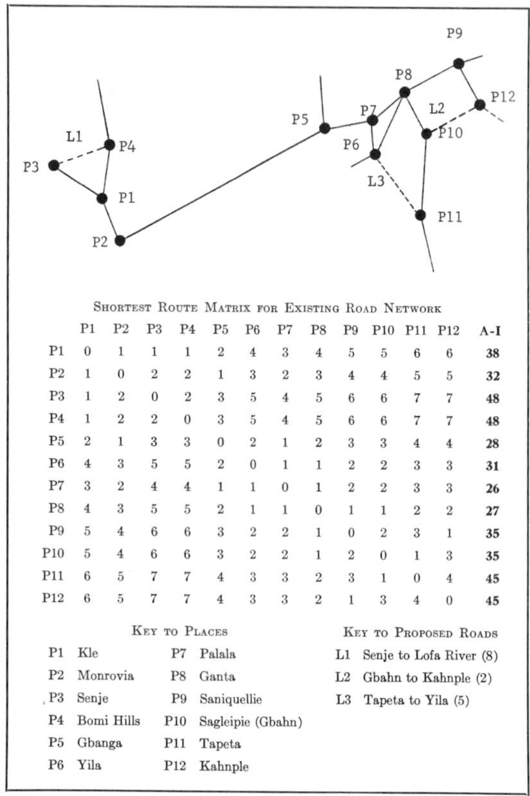

SHORTEST ROUTE MATRIX FOR EXISTING ROAD NETWORK

	P1	P2	P3	P4	P5	P6	P7	P8	P9	P10	P11	P12	A-I
P1	0	1	1	1	2	4	3	4	5	5	6	6	**38**
P2	1	0	2	2	1	3	2	3	4	4	5	5	**32**
P3	1	2	0	2	3	5	4	5	6	6	7	7	**48**
P4	1	2	2	0	3	5	4	5	6	6	7	7	**48**
P5	2	1	3	3	0	2	1	2	3	3	4	4	**28**
P6	4	3	5	5	2	0	1	1	2	2	3	3	**31**
P7	3	2	4	4	1	1	0	1	2	2	3	3	**26**
P8	4	3	5	5	2	1	1	0	1	1	2	2	**27**
P9	5	4	6	6	3	2	2	1	0	2	3	1	**35**
P10	5	4	6	6	3	2	2	1	2	0	1	3	**35**
P11	6	5	7	7	4	3	3	2	3	1	0	4	**45**
P12	6	5	7	7	4	3	3	2	1	3	4	0	**45**

KEY TO PLACES

P1	Kle	P7	Palala
P2	Monrovia	P8	Ganta
P3	Senje	P9	Saniquellie
P4	Bomi Hills	P10	Sagleipie (Gbahn)
P5	Gbanga	P11	Tapeta
P6	Yila	P12	Kahnple

KEY TO PROPOSED ROADS

L1	Senje to Lofa River (8)
L2	Gbahn to Kahnple (2)
L3	Tapeta to Yila (5)

Fig. 24-8.

as Fig. 24-1, with the roads (links) represented as straight lines. Each of 12 towns (places) is specified, and each link in the existing or proposed system may be identified by places which it connects. In addition, proposed roads 8, 2, and 5 are also designated as L1, L2, and L3 respectively. These are the only ones which will connect 2 elements of the existing road network, hence the only ones which can alter the existing connectivity and accessibility of the system. Thus, these 3 proposed roads could be rated 100 or 75 in item 8; the 6 other roads will each be assigned a 50 rating.

Connectivity values for each place in the road network matrix are equal to the highest number of links required to reach each of the other places in the network by the shortest route.[28] The shortest route from P1 to P6 thus requires 4 links. The connectivity value for P3, P4, P11, and P12 is 7, while that for P5 and P7 is 4. Thus, P5 and P7 are tied for being most accessible (or most central) to other places in the network.

Prihar suggests another method for determining the degree of connectivity of an existing road network.[29] The maximum number of links in a network L, with m places, may be calculated from $L = m(m - 1)/2$. Thus, for the network in Fig. 24-8, the maximum connectivity would be 66; the minimum connectivity, $L/(m - 1)$, would be 6; the degree of connectivity, L divided by the actual number of links, would be 5.5 for the existing 12 places. By this analysis, the addition of any of the 3 proposed roads will improve the degree of connectivity by 0.42 (5.5 minus 5.08).

Accessibility can also be stated as an index which is the sum of the links from a given place to all other places in the network by the shortest routes. By this definition, P7 is the most accessible place in the network with an index of 26, while P3 and P4 are least accessible with indexes of 48. The sum of all accessibility indexes (the dispersion of the network) is 438. Use of the accessibility index permits a more specific ranking of places than was possible with the connectivity values.

Of particular interest to road construction priority analysis are the changes in the dispersion of the network when the proposed links (roads) are added, singly or in combination. These changes are presented in Table 24-6. Quite clearly, the construction of road 5 (Tapeta to Yila) offers the greatest reduction in dispersion (16) of any of the 3 proposed roads, indeed it offers a reduction in dispersion greater than roads 2 and 8 combined.[30] Each of the proposed links can be ranked in order of its net effect upon accessibility (Table 24-7). Road 5 clearly warrants the highest priority (100 rating) in item 8. Roads 2 and 8,

Table 24-6 Changes in Accessibility Indexes Resulting from the Addition of 1–3 New Roads

Original Road Network (N) by Place and Accessibility Index		Projected Road Networks by Accessibility Index (I) and Accessibility Index Differential (D)													
		N + L1		N + L2		N + L3		N + L1, L2		N + L1, L3		N + L2, L3		N + L1, L2, L3	
		I	D	I	D	I	D	I	D	I	D	I	D	I	D
P1	38	38	0	38	0	37	1	38	0	37	1	37	1	37	1
P2	32	32	0	32	0	31	1	32	0	31	1	31	1	31	1
P3	48	47	1	48	0	47	1	47	1	46	2	47	1	46	2
P4	48	47	1	48	0	47	1	47	1	46	2	47	1	46	2
P5	28	28	0	28	0	27	1	28	0	27	1	27	1	27	1
P6	31	31	0	31	0	29	2	31	0	29	2	29	2	29	2
P7	26	26	0	26	0	25	1	26	0	25	1	25	1	25	1
P8	27	27	0	27	0	27	0	27	0	27	0	27	0	27	0
P9	35	35	0	35	0	35	0	35	0	35	0	35	0	35	0
P10	35	35	0	33	2	35	0	35	0	35	0	33	2	33	2
P11	45	45	0	43	2	37	8	43	2	37	8	35	10	35	10
P12	45	45	0	41	4	45	0	41	4	45	0	41	4	41	4
Reduction in dispersion of projected networks			2		8		16		8		18		24		26

Note: See figure 24–8 for keys to places and proposed roads.

with reduction in dispersion factors of 8 and 2 respectively, were assigned lesser priorities (75 rating), even though road 2 provides a greater reduction in dispersion. (Another evaluator might relate reduction in dispersion differently to each rating.)

Item 9: Administrative Factor. A road connecting an administrative center to rural villages should bring the people living within its zone of influence any benefits resulting from the government's increased capacity to reach them. Such benefits might include improvements in school, health, and agricultural (extension) services. Such a road is also more likely to be well maintained than one not serving an administrative center. Priority in this classification item is based upon the number of administrative centers the road will connect: a zero rating is given for no centers linked, a 50 rating for 1, and a 100 rating for 2 or more. This method does not distinguish between size and/or type of administrative center. Such differentiation was not necessary in Liberia, but might be elsewhere. In another area, a scaling of administrative centers by hierarchy and size should not be difficult and quite likely could be fitted into rating values utilized here.

FINAL COMMENT

Seldom are road evaluation models suited for universal application. Universality is attained at the expense of specificity and while both the universal and the specific approaches have their proponents, few would deny the merits of the other. In the rural road construction-priorities evaluation model presented above, simplicity was emphasized. Essentially, the model is subjective; and while some classification items are approached less subjectively than others, it remains what it is. Nevertheless, the model encompasses many, if not most, of the prominent factors associated with rural road expansion in developing areas. It should be noted that, while cost/benefit analyses in the traditional sense are

Table 24-7 New Roads Ranked by Accessibility Indexes

New Road or Roads	Reduction in Dispersion	Gain per Road	Rank
L1	2	2.00	7
L2	8	8.00	4
L3	16	16.00	1
L1, L2	8	4.00	6
L1, L3	18	9.00	3
L2, L3	24	12.00	2
L1, L2, L3	26	8.66	5

Note: See figure 24–8 for key to proposed roads.

deemphasized, the fundamental concept of costs and benefits, particularly the latter, is stressed throughout the model.

NOTES

1 See Wilfred Owen, *Distance and Development: Transport and Communications in India* (Washington, D.C.: Brookings Institution, 1968), especially "Effects of Transport Improvement," pp. 59–60; E. H. Holmes, "The Impact of the Highway on Economic Development: Highway Planning" (Washington, D.C.: U.S. Department of Transportation, Bureau of Public Roads, 1967), pp. 18–19, mimeographed; and David C. Fulton, "A Road to the West," *Finance and Development* 6 (September 1969): 2–8. Fulton describes the change brought about by the construction of a single road in a hitherto isolated region in Honduras. Lastly, see M. Alexander Ketter, *Proposed Road Construction Program: Five Year National Development Plan* (Monrovia: Department of Public Works and Utilities, July 1964), p. 2, in which the secretary states: "Public health and education programs cannot be effective in inaccessible areas with a population density that does not permit the financial support of the basic institutions of a modern economy in the fields of health, education, and communication. At present, the isolated farmer contributes very little to the national economy; he is merely self-supporting. The creation of accessible centers of population along roads will provide an opportunity for the native element to participate actively in the nation's economy."

2 For detailed statistics on 15 countries, see Wilfred Owen, *Strategy for Mobility* (Washington, D.C.: Brookings Institution, 1964), table 3-1. Percentages of total public expenditures planned for transport and communications in the 2 African states noted were 46.5 percent for Nigeria (1955–59) and 18.7 percent for Senegal (1961–64). Martin Meyerson suggests that most countries with economic plans allocate one-fifth or more of their public investment to transportation; see his "Strategy Planning for Transportation and Economic Development," in *Transportaton,* vol. 5 of *United States Papers Prepared for the United Nations Conference on the Application of Science and Technology for the Benefit of the Less Developed Areas* (Washington, D.C.: Government Printing Office, 1963), p. 5, hereafter cited as *Transportation-5.*

3 Choice between rail and road is often difficult. At the Conference on the Application of Science and Technology for the Benefit of the Less Developed Areas, Geneva, 1963, the biggest transport problem raised (and left unresolved) was, "What factors should influence the choice between one form of transport and another?" See *Science and Technology for Development,* vol. 1, *World of Opportunity* (New York: United Nations, 1963), p. 137. An imprecise yet meaningful measure of relative national budgetary support for road and rail in underdeveloped areas is presented in R. J. Harrison Church, *West Africa,* 5th ed. (London: Longmans, 1966), p. 158. The following data provide national averages for population per kilometer of track and population per kilometer of road in 7 West African countries: Guinea—4,380 vs. 276; Sierra Leone—4,383 vs. 343; Ivory Coast—5,850 vs. 131; Ghana—6,985 vs. 779; Togo—3,535 vs. 538; Dahomey—3,800 vs. 374; and Nigeria—15,328 vs. 756. Concerning road transport's versatility, see *Science and Technology for Development,* vol. 4, *Industry* (New York: United Nations, 1963), p. 144. See also Kent T. Healy, "General Social, Political, and Economic Factors in Relation to Transport for Less Developed Areas," in *Transportation-5,* p. 2.

4 George W. Wilson et al., *The Impact of Highway Investment on Development* (Washington, D.C.: Brookings Institution, 1966); International Bank for Reconstruction and Development, *Appraisal of a Road Project for Liberia,* Report of Technical Information TO-375 (Washington, June 6 1963); and Katherine D. Warden, "Selected Bibliography: Transportation and Economic Development," in *Trans-*

port Investment and Economic Development, ed. Gary Fromm (Washington, D.C.: Brookings Institution, 1965), pp. 277–305.

5 Measuring the economic benefits of transport projects is usually much more difficult than measuring their economic costs. See Hans A. Adler, "Economic Evaluation of Transport Projects," in *Transport Investment,* p. 179.

6 Escott Reid suggests that "leaders of underdeveloped countries are being constantly tempted, by their own desires for prestige, by the pressures of local special interests and of special interests in aid-giving countries, to give a high priority to projects which have a high prestige value but a low real economic yield." Another reason for possible neglect of needed farm-to-market roads can be inferred from their lowly prestige status in overall communications development. See *The Future of the World Bank* (Washington, D.C.: I.B.R.D., 1965), p. 26.

7 Alan R. DeBeer, "The Economic Justification of Roads in Developing Countries," *Road International* (April 1963), p. 32. A mathematical model for evaluating both direct and indirect effects of road projects has been suggested by Jan Tinbergen, "The Appraisal of Road Construction: Two Calculation Schemes," *Review of Economics and Statistics* 39 (August 1957): 241–49. Tinbergen's model is of doubtful utility in developing areas since it demands adequate and reliable data—both of which are generally lacking outside of the industrialized countries.

8 Fieldwork was undertaken in December 1966 and January 1967 to evaluate sites of proposed rural access roads for the purpose of establishing construction priorities.

9 See Gerald Hodge, "Use and Mis-Use of Measurement Scales in City Planning," *Journal of the American Institute of Planners* 29 (May 1963): 115–18.

10 See Morris Hill, "A Goals-Achievement Matrix for Evaluating Alternative Plans," *Journal of the American Institute of Planners* 34 (January 1968): 19–29.

11 This does not mean that certain broad assessments cannot be made prior to undertaking fieldwork. Much, of course, depends upon the familiarity of the investigator with the study area.

12 See Liberia, *Supplement to Application for Development Loan: Construction of Rural Access Roads, Equipment Repair Shops, and Procurement of Heavy Equipment for Road Construction and Maintenance,* under Title I, U.S. Public Law 87–195, submitted to the U.S. Agency for International Development, May 31 1966.

13 Wilfred Owen, "Transport and Economic Development," *American Economic Review* 49 (May 1959): 186.

14 Willi Schulze, "Geographical Data on the Student Body of the University of Liberia," *University of Liberia Journal 5* (January 1965): 24.

15 Henry M. Steiner, "Mexican Social Roads," *International Development Review,* vol. 8, no. 3 (1966), p. 23.

16 Edward K. Hawkins, *Road Transport in Nigeria* (London: Oxford University Press, 1958), pp. 15–16.

17 The short Todee District road was proposed for an area already within zones of influence of other roads. Population data were derived from *Republic of Liberia 1962 Census of Population: Area Reports and Summary Report* (Monrovia: Office of National Planning, Bureau of Statistics, 1964). Inasmuch as this census does not define clan and other ethnic boundaries on a map, population within each zone of influence was rounded to the nearest thousand inhabitants.

18 See William R. Stanley, "The Cost of Road Transport in Liberia: A Case Study of the Independent Rubber Farmers," *Journal of Developing Areas* 2 (July 1968): 495–510, for a partial analysis of road-induced freight rates.

19 An early description of the volume and variety of Liberia's agricultural exports may be found in Gerald Ralston, "On the Republic of Liberia, Its Products and Resources," *Journal of the Royal Society of Arts,* vol. 10, no. 496 (1862), pp. 433–38.

20 The difference in time between the data in Figs. 24-4 and 24-5 and that in Fig. 24-6 should not seriously affect any comparisons. Marketing statistics for palm kernels and coffee were furnished by (1) Middle East Trading Company (METCO), (2) Rasamny Brothers Corporation, and (3) Liberia Produce Marketing Corporation (LPMC). These 3 organizations account for practically all of the agricultural produce purchased for export. METCO and Rasamny Brothers, the 2 largest Lebanese-controlled businesses, have commercial ties with practically all of the Lebanese stores in the interior and with a significant percentage of those in the coastal towns.

21 Montague Yudelman, "Some Aspects of African Agricultural Development," in *Economic Development for Africa South of the Sahara,* ed. E. A. G. Robinson (New York: St. Martin's Press, 1964), pp. 554–55.

22 *Using the LAMCO Railway for Timber Exports* (Monrovia: Office of National Planning, Bureau of Economic Research, July 1965).

23 Transportation Consultants, Inc., *Transportation Survey of Sierra Leone* (Washington, D.C., March 1963), p. 97.

24 This figure was used in estimating construction costs in *Buchanan-Kabli Road: Reconnaissance for Possible Improvement* (Monrovia: Department of Public Works and Utilities, May 20 1964), typescript. The difficulty in bridging watercourses can be demonstrated by Nigeria's road transport system. In 1953 Nigeria had a road system of nearly 29,000 miles, yet had only one bridge over the Niger and one over the Benue. Ferries constituted an important element in linking this road mileage. See International Bank for Reconstruction and Development, *The Economic Development of Nigeria* (Baltimore, Md.: Johns Hopkins Press, 1955), p. 490.

25 Jack Baranson, "The Challenge of Underdevelopment," in *Technology in Western Civilization,* ed. Melvin Kranzberg and Carroll W. Pursell, Jr. (New York: Oxford University Press, 1967), 2: 519–20.

26 Anthony M. O'Connor, *Railways and Development in Uganda* (New York: Oxford University Press for the East African Institute of Social Research, 1965), p. 132.

27 William L. Garrison, "Connectivity of the Interstate Highway System," in *Spatial Analysis,* ed. B. J. L. Berry and D. F. Marble (Englewood Cliffs, N.J.: Prentice-Hall, 1968), pp. 242–43.

28 Ibid., p. 243. For an informative, detailed, and easy to follow analysis of graph theory applied to a transport system, see Ian Burton, "Accessibility in Northern Ontario: An Application of Graph Theory to a Regional Highway Network" (Toronto: University of Toronto, Department of Geography, December 1962), typescript.

29 Zvi Prihar, "Topological Properties of Telecommunication Networks," *Proceedings of the Institute of Radio Engineers* 44 (July 1956): 927–33.

30 A weakness in the accessibility index is that all existing or proposed links are assigned the same value when, in reality, perhaps some should be of greater value to the network, if only because of location. For instance, link P1-P2 in Fig. 24-8 is more valuable than either links P1-P3 or P1-P4, since both P3 and P4 need the P1-P2 link for connection to the network. To indicate this, diminishing values (scalars) are assigned to links which are farther away. An arbitrary value (e.g., 0.3) is assigned to single-link paths (connectivity value of 1), its square (0.09) to 2-link paths (connectivity value of 2), and so on. For instance, P1's scalar value would be determined as follows: 1-link connections ($3 \times 0.3 = 0.9$); 2-link connections ($1 \times 0.09 = 0.09$; 3-link connections ($1 \times 0.027 = 0.027$); 4-link connections ($2 \times 0.0081 = 0.0162$); 5-link connections ($2 \times 0.00243 = 0.00486$); and 6-link connections ($2 \times 0.000729 = 0.001458$)—a total of 1.039518. Scalar values for all places in each network are then added, and calculations for reduction in dispersion similar to that in tables 6 and 7 can be made. Use of the scalar 0.3 in analyzing the existing network not only indicated less difference in reduction in dispersion between road 5 and roads 2 and 8 combined, but it revealed only a small difference between roads 2 and 8. See Alfonso Shimbel, "Structural Parameters of Communication Networks," *Bulletin of Mathematical Biophysics* 15 (1953): 501–7.

Selection 25

Depressed Regions and Transportation Investment

J. M. Munro

Transportation is a favorite sector to receive assistance in the course of programs of regional development. In many European countries, notably France and Italy, programs to stimulate regional economic growth by expenditures on transportation are fairly common. The United States has also engaged in regional subsidization through spending on transport. In Canada we are all familiar with such regionally-oriented federal programs as operating subsidies for coastal shipping, the Maritime Freight Rates Act, and the Crow's Nest rates on grain. Such programs seem quite popular in most quarters. For example, the report of the MacPherson Commission stated that:

> We are able to suggest that it is not unwise to use transportation, properly applied, as an instrument for the pursuit of National Policy objectives, particularly in a setting where great distances are a limiting factor to balanced national growth. It may be that, in the future, National Policy for development of resources, industries, or regions will go even further than at present in taking upon the shoulders of the nation a share of the burdensome costs of distance.[1]

The purpose of this [work] is to discuss some considerations that should influence government investment in transportation facilities in depressed regions. The development highway system in the Appalachian region of the United States authorized by the Appalachian Redevelopment Act of 1965 will provide examples of the motivation and planning for programs of this type.

[We] will begin by considering at some length the causes of regional depression with a view towards revealing suitable policy measures to eliminate this condition. The next section will carry this discussion further by exploring the question: Should a government help depressed regions? It will be seen that the justification for such assistance varies in terms of the government's expressed goals and the actual conditions of the depressed region. Then [we] will consider the use of transportation investment as a form of aid to depressed regions, paying particular attention to the often-heard contention that the "inadequacy" of transportation facilities and services is a cause of regional depression. Finally, the planning and impact of the Appalachian development highway system will be examined.

I

All depressed regions share the unhappy characteristics of levels of per capita income and other measures of the standard of living that are "low," according to generally-accepted criteria. The selection of the cut-off point between poor regions and rich regions must of necessity be rather arbitrary. For a depressed region—one which is markedly poorer than some other regions in the country in which it is located—the standard of regional poverty is based on inter-regional comparisons within that country.

The basic causes of regional depression are typically similar in all cases. Almost all depressed regions exhibit resource immobility

Transportation Research Forum, 1966, pp. 391–401. Reprinted by permission of the author and editor.

—the failure of resources to seek their most profitable employment. For labor this involves the unwillingness or inability of workers to migrate to areas where higher real wages may be earned. For capital, immobility occurs when investment in one area with low rates of return is preferred to those with higher rates of return in another area or areas. Resource immobility is essentially irrational economically, but it is a very real fact of economic life and should be expected to continue distorting the optimal interregional allocation of resources as long as such factors as ignorance of opportunities, unemployable labor, and regional emotionalism are present. In other words, some degree of resource immobility is more or less permanent.

The most promising adjustment towards prosperity for both underdeveloped and depressed regions is for labor to move out and/or capital to move in.[2] For depressed regions, given the existence of a prospering national economy, the out-migration of labor seems to offer the best hope of regional economic improvement. An influx of capital in quest of highly profitable investment opportunities is not to be expected. Recognizing that out-migration of labor is not always a possible or acceptable policy for governments to embrace, we will next examine the conditions under which government aid to depressed regions can follow the other route to regional development—increasing the stock of capital in the region. Even though private capital is unlikely to flow into depressed regions, can the public sector provide capital and duplicate the effects that would be achieved through an inflow of private capital?

II

It would seem that the national government probably can do this, although in nonsocialist economy the inflow of public capital (presumably restricted to such things as transportation, education, health and welfare, electric power, and water resource development) may not be as flexible or produce the same results as would an inflow of private capital into the private sector. Investment by the public sector, however, often calls forth additional investment by the private sector, and vice versa. But acceptance of the fact that the government can influence the growth of depressed regions by means of specially-directed investment does not relieve us of the responsibility of considering whether it should. To explore this question further we will consider how we might classify the motives for government aid to depressed regions.

First, there are the purely economic motives—those which support the implementation of regional assistance programs because of their contribution to the economic welfare of the whole nation. There are three of these:[3]

1 The existence of unexploited opportunities for investment in social overhead capital because of the fiscal weakness of regional governments. For example, a region's government(s) may be unable to construct a highway that is justified in that its estimated benefits exceed its costs.

2 The avoidance of the social costs associated with economic decline and outmigration in a region. These costs could arise either out of the financial arrangements for capital already in place or out of the inability of the reduced population to support certain business and public services of high quality. An example of the first situation would be a bridge financed by tolls. If traffic declined by 50 per cent, tolls would have to be doubled to maintain the same level of total revenue (assuming perfectly inelastic demand). The second situation could be exemplified by an area with a declining population being unable to support a good secondary school system, a resident physician, or a wide range of retail outlets. The alternatives would all impose higher costs, in various forms, on the remaining population.

3 The avoidance of social costs in the regions, usually urban, that receive people that leave depressed regions. These costs arise out of the low educational attainment of many migrants, their all-too-common lack of marketable labor skills, and the pressure they place on urban facilities. Programs justified by this reason may involve improving the education and vocational training of potential migrants from depressed regions.

The last two of these three reasons for programs of regional aid both rest on the existence of benefits that are external to the project being evaluated. They should be adopted with caution. The second may have economic relevance only in the short run. When the time comes to replace the region's capital stock it should, where possible, be reduced in size. This will solve at least part of the over-capacity problem. The problem with the third reason is that it may serve to justify programs designed solely to discourage population migration from depressed regions. The argument here would be that since migrants impose extra welfare, education, and other costs on the regions to which they move, a more desirable alternative would be to keep them at home. In fact, immigration has historically been both a sign and a source of regional prosperity and development (once the initial problems of adjustment have been overcome) and efforts to fix the existing distribution of population can only cut back on economic development in the prospering regions and in the country as a whole.

Two further points need to be made concerning these economic justifications for programs of regional aid. First, such programs should be evaluated with reference to other possible uses for federal funds. This means that the benefits and costs of regional development programs need to be measured from a "national" point of view[4] and the programs carried out only if they bring a greater return than alternative programs. If $10 million spent on highways in depressed region "M" will retain discounted benefits of $12 million while the same amount spent on aid to university education in prosperous region "O" will produce discounted benefits of $15 million, the government's decision is clear. If efficiency considerations are to be paramount, the funds should be devoted to university education in region "O," prosperous though it may already be.

This is an appropriate place to raise the second qualification of economically-justified programs of regional aid. As we all know, governments are rarely motivated solely by economic considerations. Other factors play roles of varying importance in government decisions and are equally defensible as goals of national policy. Two such factors, or goals, are the achievement of income equality between regions and the elimination of poverty. This first objective is area-oriented. It presumes that the inequalities of regional depression are an offense against the nation's collective conscience and that their partial or total elimination is needed. This goal is often expressed in terms of the belief that "if only" a given depressed region could get some help from outside it could take its rightful place among the nation's community of prosperous, productive regions. The second goal, the elimination of poverty, is people-oriented rather than area-oriented. Here it is not the general equality of regional averages that is sought but rather the alleviation of the effects of regional depression on those who live in depressed regions.

III

Regional requests for assistance in the form of transportation investment typically revolve around complaints that the existing transport system is "inadequate" or that costs of transportation are "too high." These complaints usually include, sometimes implicitly, comparisons with more prosperous regions which are believed to be favored as far as transportation is concerned. The first comment that we can make here is that investment in right-of-way and structures is not the only way in which transport costs can be lowered. Improvements in vehicle design and technology, elimination of inefficient transport operating practices, and adoption of better logistics practices by regional shippers can all be very effective in lowering the level of transportation costs in a region.

A second comment may be directed at the assumption, implicit in the above approach, that the existence of interregional inequalities in average transportation costs indicates a need for elimination of these differences. Even assuming that inefficiencies in transportation operations have been corrected, that vehicle design is the most advanced that is practicable, and that logistics practices minimize total transport costs to shippers, there is still nothing that can be said concerning the desirability of investing in improved transport right-of-way in order to achieve more equal transportation costs for all regions. The equalization of transport costs in different regions as an express and unqualified goal of government policy is basically no more logical than a policy of equalizing the space-heating costs incurred in different regions. Vancouver has about 5,100 degree days (using a 65 degree base) per year while Winnipeg has some 10,400.[5] Yet no one argues for a program of subsidies to Winnipeg residents and businesses to help them keep warm; the higher cost of heating is accepted as an inherent feature of the environment. So, too, in many situations, should higher costs of transportation be viewed.

We would contend that a region's transport system is only inadequate, given the assumptions in the preceding paragraph, if there exist unexploited, socially profitable opportunities for investment in transport facilities. The term "socially profitable" implies that the benefits and costs of prospective transport investments will be evaluated with reference to their effect on all segments of society and that those projects for which benefits exceed costs by the greatest amount will be constructed first. The crucial point here is that costs should be incurred commensurate with the benefits that can be obtained from specific programs and projects.

For those modes of transportation for which facilities are provided by the private sector (railroads[6] and pipelines) this means that the desirability of an investment should be evaluated in a rather broader and more socially-oriented context than the pursuit of private profit would indicate. The existence of unexploited investment opportunities in these two privately-supplied modes could only be explained by:

1 No consideration of spillover-type benefits that accrue to society as a whole but are not reflected in the transport firm's profits.
2 The transport firm's lack of awareness of good investment opportunities.
3 Pursuing of monopolistic policies and practices by the transport firm.

For the transport modes for which facilities are supplied by the public sector (highways, waterways, airways) investment evaluation with reference to social profitability means that careful attention must be paid to cost and benefit spillovers; it is not enough just to calculate the direct costs and benefits or proposed projects or programs and use these estimates in benefit-cost analysis. Transport inadequacy in the public-sector modes could then arise in one or both of two ways:

1 Failure to evaluate correctly the direct and indirect costs and benefits of transport investment projects. This is particularly likely to happen with respect to benefits since services are not "sold" directly (in the way, for example, railway services are sold) and

since indirect benefits are often widely diffused throughout an entire regional economy.

2 Fiscal weakness of governments responsible for providing transport facilities. Governments may be unable, for example, to build needed roads because they do not have sufficient tax and other revenues. "Needed" here means that benefits, correctly evaluated, exceed costs similarly correctly evaluated.

Both these situations undoubtedly exist now in some regions and have existed in the past, but this should not lead us to conclude that they are universal. Indirect benefits are by no means always of importance in transport investment nor do poor governments always have *necessary* investment projects that their poverty precludes them from pursuing.

We may identify four important conclusions that were developed in this section.

1 Total unit transportation costs do not consist mainly of costs associated with right-of-way facilities. Vehicles, operating practices, and logistics policies of shippers also determine the pattern of a region's transportation costs.

2 There is no particular reason to expect interregional equality in transportation costs and the existence of inequality does not constitute a *prima facie* case for programs to change this.

3 Interregional inequality with respect to transport costs may very well be inevitable unless provision is made for extensive subsidization of transportation in disadvantaged regions.

4 Transport "inadequacy" only exists, in the economic sense, when one or more of several rather restrictive conditions are present. The declaration that transport costs are "too high" is insufficient to prove inadequacy.

IV

The development highway system authorized by the Appalachian Redevelopment Act of 1965 provides interesting illustrations of several of the points developed in previous sections . . . .[7]

Appalachia, as defined in this Act, includes 373 counties in 12 states that reach from just north of Montgomery, Alabama to just south of Syracuse, New York. Their 1960 population was 17.2 million. The westernmost point of the region is the Alabama-Mississippi boundary and the easternmost point (in northeastern Pennsylvania) is within 60 miles of New York City. This is an extremely diverse area in terms of economic and social conditions and the topographical orientation of the region's original definition provides little foundation for generalizations about Appalachia's society and economy. About all that we can say with any certainty is that large parts of this Appalachian region are more or less unique in their combination of low per capita incomes, high rates of unemployment, and low rates of participation in the labor force. The persistence and extent of these shortfalls from national U.S. averages justify Appalachia, or at least parts of it, being titled a depressed region.[8]

Upwards of 2 million people left Appalachia in just the 1950–1960 decade, but this exodus was insufficient to bring about the economic readjustment required to move the region out of the depressed category. Nor is outmigration likely to be a total solution for Applalachian depression in the future. Not only do state and local government officials in the region resist any overt federal policy designed to stimulate migration to more prosperous regions[9] but the Appalachian people themselves are reluctant to leave the region. Moreover, their generally poor education and lack of desirable employment skills and attitudes tend to reduce the usefulness of Appalachian migrants, even in regions experiencing labor shortages.

This suggests that if the goal of government policy is to be the rejuvenation of the Appalachian economy and the improvement of the lot of the region's residents, an inflow of capital will be required. Given the lack of attractive opportunities for private profit in Appalachia, additions to the region's stock of capital will have to come from, or be stimulated by, investment by the public sector.

This may be identified as the economic purpose of the Appalachian development highway system.[10] It also appears to have interesting political purposes, using the term "political" in the narrowest of its meanings, but there is not time to consider them here. The development highway system represents an effort to stimulate the economic development of the Appalachian region by adding to the region's stock of social overhead capital in the form of highways. It has been alleged that the region's highway system is inadequate and that as a result Appalachia is being "strangled by (its) isolation from the mainstream of American life."[11] To overcome this, 2,350 miles of high-type primary highways and 1,000 miles of lower quality access roads are to be built in 11 of the 12 Appalachian states (all except New York, which will probably receive a supplementary program). The cost of the program, to run through July, 1971, was set at $1.2 billion,[12] with 70 per cent to be provided by the federal government and 30 per cent by each of the affected states.

Several criticisms may be made of the assumptions and process of the planning of the development highway system. First, and most important, no convincing evidence was presented to prove the case that the existing Appalachian highway system is inadequate. On the contrary, available data from the Bureau of Public Roads and the 1963 Census of Transportation indicates that the extent and financing of Appalachian highways compares favorably with national U.S. averages, that operators of trucks registered in the Appalachian states use their vehicles more efficiently than the national average, and that Appalachian shippers make rather greater use of highway transportation than do shippers in the rest of the United States. Perhaps because of the absence of proof of inadequacy, no attempt was made to measure or even identify (beyond the level of superficial platitudes) the actual benefits of this program. This omission is partly explained, although not excused, by the equally glaring absence of any comprehensive plan of development for the Appalachian region.

The direct costs of the development highway system were only vaguely estimated and varied considerably at different stages of the program. The final authorization of $840 million in federal funds appears to fall short by at least $125 million for the development highway system and $35 million for the access road system, even with the latter's size reduced by one-half to 500 miles. Inflationary increases in construction costs could further enlarge this deficiency.

A third criticism involves the selection of the routes of the development highway system. The system's purpose has been described as: ". . . to create traffic and open up areas where commerce and communication of people with people have been sorely inhibited by lack of ready access."[13] But the Appalachian system's "corridors" generally coincide, in fact, with the most-travelled highways in the region, with the exception of those highways which are part of the Interstate System. Furthermore, the basis for selection of the corridor segments that require reconstruction (i.e., on which the $1.2 billion is to be spent) is an adequacy rating based on *current* traffic levels.[14] This is a strange sort of criterion to use for a highway system that is supposed to generate traffic in the *future* by stimulating economic development. Finally, the Appalachian Regional Commission, the federal-state body which is responsible for the program, has stated that the "prime objective" in designing the development highways shall be the provision of a 50 mile per hour average travel speed between major termini.[15] The relevance of the goal to the promotion of the economic development of Appalachia is at best highly indirect.

We may develop two conclusions from this brief discussion of the Appalachian development highway system. First, the region, or at least large parts of it, are characterized by long-lasting depression. Therefore, if a greater measure of interregional equality is deemed to be an important goal of government policy and if the more automatic economic devices for achieving this equality—outflow of population and inflow of private capital—are inadequate, then government investment can be justified. But the government investment should be directed to sectors where it will be most effective in stimulating regional economic development and the details of investment programs must be carefully planned and correlated with other related and unrelated changes expected in the region's economic environment. For our second conclusion we would contend that the Appalachian development highway system satisfies niether of these criteria.

V

This [work] suggests three conclusions that have some relevance to the Canadian situation. First, government programs designed to benefit one region, or a group of regions, may very well result in a reduction in the rate of national economic progress. Exceptions to this statement do exist, as discussed in section II, but they are not required to justify regional development programs. It may be deemed necessary to have a greater measure of regional economic equality, even at the price of a lower national income and we can accept this regional subsidy if it is the will of the nation as expressed through the political process. However, the subsidy should be the most efficient possible. If the goal of the subsidy is to promote the economic development of the nation's lagging regions, then it would make sense to allocate the subsidy to those sectors of the regions' economies that can contribute the most to this end. Section III . . . impels the second general conclusion; namely, that the transportation sector is apt to be an ineffective vehicle for achieving greater interregional economic equality. Depressed regions have, almost by definition, little of the unexploited natural resources or, especially, the economic dynamism that have been found to be necessary for successful transportation investment.[16] Other directions for growth-stimulating investments would appear to be more effective in producing a significant change in the fortunes of a depressed region. Finally, section IV's discussion of the Appalachian development highway program points out how apparently easy it is to choose transportation as a prime ingredient of programs of regional development. The ease with which this choice is made was, in this case at least, not at all inhibited by the economic realities of the Appalachian region. Whether by ignorance or intention, little consideration was given to the actual effects of or need for this program.

This omission illustrates once more that we need better information and more research concerning the process and determinants of regional economic development and transport's role in that process. Had better knowledge been available it is unlikely, for example, that the last Royal Commission on Transportation would have recommended the elimination of most of the intra-select territory subsidy authorized by the Maritime Freight Rates Act.[17] Whatever the actual merits of this particular regional transportation subsidy (a question that, to my knowledge, has never received careful analysis in terms of the Act's role in stimulating the development of the Atlantic Provinces), this modification will probably harm the region that is supposed to be helped. This change should result in an increase in the region's imports. Higher imports will reduce regional income, thus increasing the inequality between the Atlantic Region and other Canadian regions. If we are to offer effective aid to chronically depressed areas, we must become better informed about the causes of depression, the process of regional economic development, and the comparative effectiveness of various types of development programs.

Transportation is a favorite sector to receive assistance in the course of programs of regional development. This [work] discusses some considerations that should influence government investment in transportation facilities in depressed regions. The development highway system under construction in the Appalachian region of the United States provides examples of the motivation and planning for programs of this type.

Three conclusions are developed that have some relevance to the Canadian situation. First, government programs designed to benefit one region may well result in a reduction in the rate of national economic progress, unless certain conditions are met. These conditions, which involve divergences between social and private costs and benefits in the region and the nation, are not, however, necessary to justify regional development programs. It may be deemed necessary to have a greater measure of regional economic equality, even at the price of a lower national income, and we can accept this regional subsidy if it is the will of the nation as expressed through the political process. However, the subsidy should surely be the most efficient possible. If the goal of the subsidy is to promote the economic development of a lagging region, then it would make sense to allocate the subsidy to those sectors of the region's economy that can contribute the most to this end.

The second conclusion is that the transportation sector is likely to be an ineffective vehicle for achieving greater interregional economic equality. Depressed regions have, almost by definition, little of the unexploited natural resources, or especially, the economic dynamism that have been found to be necessary for successful transportation investment. Other directions for growth-stimulating investment would appear to be more effective in producing a significant change in the fortunes of a depressed region.

Finally, the Appalachian development highway program provides an illustration of how easy it is to choose transportation as a prime ingredient of programs of regional development. The ease with which this choice is made was, in this case at least, not at all inhibited by the economic realities of the Appalachian region. Whether by ignorance or intention, little consideration was given to the actual effects of or need for this program. This omission provides additional evidence that we need better information and more research concerning the process and determinants of regional economic development generally and transport's role in that process.

NOTES

1 Canada, Royal Commission on Transportation, *Report,* Vol. II (Ottawa: Queen's Printer, 1961), pp. 5–6.

2 This is the desired end result. The means by which the government may achieve or induce the export of labor and/or the import of capital are quite varied and may involve expenditures on a wide range of projects. But the purpose of the expenditures should always be kept in mind. The spending of government funds on projects which serve neither of the ultimate ends of moving labor out and capital in will not

make a lasting and substantial contribution to regional economic progress.

3 These points are taken, in part, from George H. Borts, "Criteria for the Evaluation of Regional Development Programs," paper presented to the Third Conference on Regional Accounts, Committee on Regional Accounts and Resources for the Future, Miami Beach, Fla., November 19–21, 1964, pp. 1–8.

4 This means, for example, that program benefits in the depressed region must be measured net of any disbenefits in other regions. Also, program costs supplied by the federal government must be included. To the region they may be manna from Heaven but the national government, which should perform the benefit-cost analysis itself, can hardly so regard them.

5 Author's rough calculation based on Department of Transport information. The degree day is a unit which measures the nominal heating load. On a 65-degree base, a degree day may be defined as follows: for any one day there exist as many degree days as there are positive degrees of temperature difference between 65 degrees and the average temperature for the day.

6 Canadian National Railways is here included with the private sector although in fact as a Crown corporation it rather straddles both public and private sectors.

7 The material in this section is a necessarily brief summary of parts of [Munro's] doctoral dissertation, *"Transportation Investment and Depressed Regions: The Case of Appalachia."* (Unpublished D.B.A. dissertation, Graduate School of Business, Indiana University, 1966.)

8 Appalachia is not the poorest region, in terms of median family income, in the United States. Only 13 of the 50 poorest U.S. counties in 1959 were located in the region. Most of the poorest counties are found in the cotton belt of Mississippi, Alabama, Georgia, and Arkansas.

9 Their viewpoint has been very well expressed by former Governor Combs of Kentucky. "If these people want to live there [in the Appalachian region], I think they are entitled to do so, and they should be provided a way to make a decent, honorable, honest living. And I think it is incumbent on those of us who have some position of leadership to make every possible effort to find the means by which those people can make an honest living in this area." Mary Jean Bowman and W. Warren Haynes, *Resources and People in East Kentucky: Problems and Potentials of a Lagging Economy* (Baltimore: Johns Hopkins, 1963), p. 253.

10 The other programs authorized by the Appalachian Redevelopment Act of 1965 include the following: construction and operation of demonstration health facilities; land improvement, pasture development, and erosion control; improvement of timber resource management and utilization; restoration of mining areas and study of strip mining practices; development and utilization of water resources; vocational school construction; construction of sewage treatment works; and supplements to other federal grant-in-aid programs. See Public Law 89-4.

11 The quotation is from Congressional testimony by Franklin D. Roosevelt, Jr., Chairman of the President's Appalachian Regional Development, *Hearings, Appalachian Redevelopment Act of 1964,* 88th Cong., 2nd Sess., 1964, p. 19. This Commission developed the program incorporated in the Appalachian Redevelopment Act of 1965.

12 Exact comparison of this part of the Appalachian program with other parts is impossible because of differing authorization periods. However, over the first two years it appears that highways will receive 63 per cent of total federal and state expenditures and all other programs (see footnote 10) the remaining 37 per cent.

13 President's Appalachian Regional Commission, *Appalachia* (Washington: U.S. Government Printing Office, 1964), p. 33.

14 U.S. Department of Commerce, Bureau of Public Roads, *Instruction Manual for Preparation and Submission of the 1966 Estimate of Cost of Improving Inadequate Segments of the Appalachian Development Highway System* (Washington: U.S. Department of Commerce, 1965), p. 10.

15 Appalachian Regional Commission, *Resolution No. 10,* May 12, 1965.

16 For a discussion of these prerequisites see

George W. Wilson, "Transportation Investment and Economic Development in Underdeveloped Countries," Canadian Transportation Research Forum, *Papers, First Annual Meeting,* pp. 425–433. Other skeptical views of the strength and generality of the causal relationship between transportation investment and economic development are contained in two recent studies of the railroads' role in U.S. economic growth. These volumes are Albert Fishlow, *American Railroads and the Transformation of the Ante-Bellum Economy* (Cambridge, Mass.: Harvard University Press, 1965) and Robert W. Fogel, *Railroads and American Economic Growth: Essays in Econometric History* (Baltimore: Johns Hopkins, 1964).

17 Canada, Royal Commission on Transportation, *op. cit.,* pp. 212–213.

FURTHER READINGS TO PART SIX (a)

Again a wide range of literature exists. The following may be helpful:

M. Abramovitz, "The Economic Characteristics of Railroads and the Problem of Economic Development," *Far Eastern Quarterly,* vol. 14, 1955, pp. 169–178.

H. A. Adler, "Sector and Project Planning in Transportation," *World Bank Staff Occasional Papers* no. 4, Baltimore, Md.: Johns Hopkins University Press, 1967.

D. Alagoma, "Transport in Africa in Relation to Economic Development," *Journal of the Institute of Transport,* vol. 31, 1965, pp. 53–56.

R. T. Brown, *Transport and the Economic Integration of South America,* Washington, D.C.: The Brookings Institution, 1966.

P. H. Cootner, "The Role of the Railroad in U.S. Economic Growth," *Journal of Economic History,* vol. 23, 1963, pp. 477–521.

M. E. Eliot Hurst and A. P. L. Horsman, "The Role of Transport in the Developing Canadian North," *B.C. Occasional Papers in Geography,* no. 8, 1967, pp. 31–38.

A. Fishlow, *American Railroads and the Transformation of the Antebellum Economy,* Cambridge, Mass.: Harvard University Press, 1965.

R. W. Fogel, *Railroads and American Economic Growth,* Baltimore, Md.: Johns Hopkins University Press, 1964.

G. Fromm (ed.), *Transport Investment and Economic Development,* Washington, D.C.: The Brookings Institution, 1965.

E. T. Haefle and E. B. Steinberg, *Government Controls on Transportation: An African Case,* Washington, D.C.: The Brookings Institution, 1965.

H. Hunter, "Transport in Soviet and Chinese Development," *Economic Development and Cultural Change,* vol. 14, 1965, pp. 71–84.

D. Marble, "Some Cultural and Social Aspects of Transport Impact in Underdeveloped Areas," in F. Pitts (ed.), *Urban Systems and Economic Development,* Eugene, Ore.: University of Oregon, School of Business Administration, 1962, pp. 39–43.

P. D. McClelland, "Railroads, American Growth, and the New Economic History: A Critique," *Journal of Economic History,* vol. 28, 1968, pp. 102–123.

J. R. Meyer, "Transport Technologies for Developing Countries," *American Economic Review,* vol. 56, 1966, pp. 83–90.

B. R. Mitchell, "The Coming of the Railway and United Kingdom Economic Growth," *Journal of Economic History,* September 1964, pp. 315–336.

A. M. O'Connor, "New Railway Construction and the Pattern of Economic Development in East Africa," *Transactions* of the Institute of British Geographers, no. 36, 1965, pp. 21–30.

W. Owen, *Distance and Development: Transportation and Communication in India,* Washington, D.C.: The Brookings Institution, 1968.

W. Owen, "Transportation and Economic Development," *American Economic Review,* vol. 49, 1959, pp. 179–187.

W. Owen, *Strategy for Mobility: Transportation for the Developing Countries,* Washington, D.C.: The Brookings Institution, 1964.

P. O. Roberts, "Multi-viewpoint Evaluation of Transportation Projects and Systems," *Transportation Research Forum,* seventh meeting, 1966, pp. 169–183.

A. Scaperlanda, "The Role of Transportation in the Economic Integration of Underdeveloped Areas," *Land Economics,* vol. 42, 1966, pp. 205–309.

W. R. Siddall, "The Yukon Waterway in the Development of Interior Alaska," *Pacific Historical Review,* vol. 28, 1959, pp. 361–376.

R. H. T. Smith and A. M. Hay, "A Theory of the Spatial Structure of Internal Trade in Underdeveloped Countries," *Geographical Analysis,* vol. 1, no. 2, 1969, pp. 121–136.

C. J. Stokes, *Transport and Economic Development in Latin America,* New York, Praeger, 1968.

L. I. Vasilevskiy, "Basic Research Problems in the Geography of Transportation of Capitalist and Underdeveloped Countries," *Soviet Geography,* vol. 4, no. 7, 1963, pp. 36–58.

G. W. Wilson, "Transportation Investment and Economic Development in Underdeveloped Countries," *Canadian Transportation Research Forum,* first annual meeting, pp. 425–433.

V. V. Yegorova, "The Economic Effectiveness of the Construction of Pioneering Railroads in Newly Developed Areas (as illustrated by the Lena Railroad)" *Soviet Geography,* vol. 5, no. 4, 1964, pp. 46–55.

B. URBAN TRANSPORTATION

Here we return to much more familiar ground, since it is a sector of reality to which most of us are subjected daily. It is a vast topic with a substantial literature of its own. Suffice to say here that two distinctive patterns exist today in urban transport: pre- and postmotorized. The time and space flexibility of the truck and automobile, coinciding with a period of urban population growth, smaller family size, change in life-style, and greater spatial mobility, have led to an extensive utilization of urban space. The premotorized city, on the other hand, was characterized by patterns of more intensive land use. Urban interaction in both types of city is a function of land use patterns, as will be seen in Selection 26, and differences in the distribution and dispersion of urban land usages lead to a spatial imbalance of supply and demand. In the postmotorized city, increasing use of the car and the resulting spatial dispersion of land uses have led almost inevitably to a decline in the use of public transport. Nevertheless, as long as the downtown core dominates urban travel patterns, public transit remains the most efficient and least costly means of reaching it. Contributing to the decline in public transit facilities have been the flexibility and convenience of the automobile, public ignorance of actual car commuting costs, lack of investment in efficient transit systems, and a powerful freeway lobby. These and other factors have given rise to the myth that public transit systems are necessarily slow, rundown, and inefficient. Despite this myth, public transport is making a comeback, though so far more as an idea than an actuality.

The approach of transportation geographers to urban transport has been quite routine, and the intent of the following articles is simply to survey the principal approach taken. Selections 26, 27 and 28 examine the spatial implications of land use and traffic movements in the city. They are examples of the *macroscopic* approach to urban movement patterns; here the trip makers' responses to the transportation system are frozen as habit patterns. Basically the empirical data on which these analyses are based consist of only a small number of behavior-affecting functions, such as car ownership, family size, and occasionally travel time and costs. Thus Selection 26 by D. F. Marble, although written in the late 1950s, is still an excellent example of this approach. The emphasis here is on the urban residential site leading to the examination of overall travel movements, a description of what movement occurs; we could add at which time, at certain volumes, and between particular traffic zones. Selection 27 zeros in on one particular type of urban movement: the use of automobiles in the daily journey to work. D. F. Marble's and R. Aagneenbrug's selections represent the uses of two main propositions in this approach:

1 The establishment for the present time of travel patterns and certain socioeconomic variables. Concern is also with the elimination of congestion, or the provision of capacity for travel at certain levels of congestion, often arbitrarily selected without reference to individual choice situations.

2 The projection of certain of these criteria to some future date. Most of the studies in North America and Western Europe by planners and engineers, as well as by geographers, have been reports of these kinds, usually carried out in an individual city. Most of the analyses use gravity models or correlation techniques, the former to assign flows between areas in the city at the present and some future date, and the latter to find relationships between origin-destination data and socioeconomic characteristics.* One of the frequently used correlations is that of trips from the home and the car-ownership level, which merely seems to produce as many regression equations as there are investigators! The logical step from this point is to try to produce generalizations and hopefully to base some conceptualization of urban movements upon them. This is what Selection 28 attempts to do, beginning with an empirical case study and (based on it) a model of urban movements.

*See, for example, a transportation planning textbook which carries on this tradition—R. L. Creighton, *Urban Transportation Planning*, Urbana, Ill.: University of Illinois Press, 1970.

Selection 26

Transport Inputs at Urban Residential Sites

D. F. Marble

General location theory indicates that a relationship exists between the quantity of transport inputs consumed by a household and the value of the residential site which the household occupies. However, empirical studies which have attempted to associate variations in the level of household transport inputs with variations in the level of site rentals have not been noticeably successful. It is felt that some of the reasons for the low level of attainment of these studies may be found in the current inadequate level of information regarding transport inputs to households.[1] The study reported upon here represents an attempt to raise this level through an empirical examination of the transport inputs to a number of households in a medium-sized American city.

PROBLEMS IN MODEL FORMULATION

Before attempting to undertake this study, several basic problems had to be solved. The first, and perhaps the most obvious, was to determine what set of factors influence the level of transport inputs to a given household. Secondly, before attempting to measure items such as transport inputs, reasonable operational definitions of these factors had to be formulated. These and similar problems had to be solved prior to the start of actual analysis.

Factors Influencing the Level of Transport Inputs

In attempting to delimit the factors which influence the level of transport inputs, it is necessary to proceed from a careful consideration of previous theoretical and empirical studies. While it is obviously impractical to enter upon a detailed review of all relevant work at this time, it will be interesting to examine the structures suggested by several workers in order to illustrate current thinking on this topic.

Theoretical Structures Turning to general location theory, as exemplified by the works of Isard, Lefeber, and others, we find that only a small amount of attention has been given to the spatial problems of the individual consumer. Most of the attention of workers in this field has been directed toward problems of a broader scale than those encountered by the individual moving in space. Lefeber's recent analysis, for instance, does not discuss optimality conditions for consumers, and Isard admits in his study that current concepts in location theory are unable to account for variations in transport inputs from household to household.[2]

Isard does, however, provide some indication that spatial relationships may not be the only factor of importance when he introduces the concept of the consumer's space preference (which is defined as a measure of the individual's desired level of social contact). For instance, different individuals placed in the same spatial situation with identical levels of information may exhibit different patterns of spatial behavior, and it is postulated that these differences in behavior arise out of the differences in the space preferences of the individuals involved. These space preferences are

Proceedings, Regional Science Association, vol. 5, 1959, pp. 253–266. Reprinted by permission of the author and editor.

determined by social and psychological forces which are exogenous to the general spatial system. One simple measure of an individual's space preference might be a set of desired trip frequencies. Under this definition, trip frequencies would not vary with changes in the individual's position in the spatial system. For instance, a consumer with a given level of space preference, say five trips per time period, would tend to make these trips whether he was one mile or ten miles from the desired destination.

In addition to the work of the location theorists, a little known analysis by Troxel of the demand for the movement of persons provides some additional insights on the decision-making process of the individual consumer.[3] Troxel's analysis is conducted in terms of total elapsed time, and he concludes that for each household or individual consumer there is some total amount of time spent away from home which will maximize the net travel products obtained. This maximum level is related to the individual's own level of wants (somewhat analogous to the concept of space preference discussed above), his position in the spatial system, and the ease with which he is able to move within the system. While some attempt is made to relate the concept of total elapsed time to actual distances moved, only very weak links are established.

A more explicit model is offered by Baumol and Ide who, in their study of optimal variety levels in retailing, present a simple decision model for the individual consumer.[4] They postulate that for a given shopping trip the probability of a successful outcome at any given store is a function of the number of items stocked by the store. This probability is denoted by $p(N)$. Balanced against the probability of a successful outcome are the costs of the shopping trip. These include costs of movement from the place of residence to the store, and of movement within the store itself, as well as certain opportunity costs. The cost function is given by:

$$C_d D + C_n \sqrt{N} + C_i$$

where D is the consumer's distance from the store and N is the number of items stocked. Assumed costs are C_d, the unit cost of movement to the store, C_n, the unit cost of actual shopping, and C_i, the total opportunity cost. The two elements are combined into an equation:

$$f(N, D) = wp(N) - v(C_d D + C_n \sqrt{N} + C_i)$$

where w and v are subjective weights assigned by the consumer. A shopping trip will be undertaken only in those cases where $f(N, D)$ is positive. Berry and Garrison have recently shown that this decision model is entirely compatible with existing central place theory.[5]

Empirical Studies Turning to empirical studies, we encounter only a small number of analytic studies which deal, even remotely, with items which may be considered to be measures of the transport inputs of individual households. Recently studies in Detroit and Washington, D.C., have attempted to relate the number of trips per time period to such factors as the availability of automobile transportation, airline distance of the residence from the central business district, income level, etc.[6] Both these studies contained one spatial referent term, but conflicting results were obtained in estimating its effect. The Detroit study reported a significant, and nonlinear, increase in the number of vehicular trips as the distance from the CBD increased, while the Washington study reported no significant relationship between location and total number of trips.

From the point of view of the present investigation, both the studies suffer from two common failings. First, they dealt entirely with vehicular trips (which while constituting a large proportion of all trips can scarcely be held to be an adequate measure of total transport inputs), and secondly, all household data utilized in the studies was imputed from small area data. The trips per household measure, for instance, was developed by dividing the total number of trips originating in some small area by the total number of households within the area. Other measures, such as the number of automobiles per household, were obtained in a similar fashion.

A few years ago, Garrison conducted a study which examined the relationship of household travel patterns to the value of parcels of rural property in Washington State.[7] During the course of this study it became necessary to examine the associations between road-location and trip frequency of the sample households. Regression techniques were utilized to examine the relationship between trip frequency, length of trip, and road type for eighteen combinations of trip types and study areas. The results failed to show any significant relationship existing between (1) trip frequency and distance to trip termini, and (2) trip frequency and the type of road over which the trip is taken. Garrison concluded that the propensity to travel, at any given time, is distributed among households without any apparent relationship to the type of road service locally available, and that the frequency of shopping is independent of the distance from the shopping center, although the place visited is a function of distance.

Mention was made earlier of the possible effect of factors outside the spatial system upon household travel patterns. Some light is shed on this problem by a study conducted in Virginia which was designed to examine the relationship between certain socio-economic factors and the amount of household travel.[8] The results of this study point toward the existence of non-linear relationships between measures of household socio-economic status and the total number of trips per week. Some relationship also appeared to exist between socio-economic status and the total mileage traveled per week. A recent study on long-distance movements by households lends some support to these results.[9]

On the basis of the studies outlined here and other currently available theoretical and empirical work, it appears that three sets of factors operate so as to influence the level of transport inputs to individual households. These are: (1) the socio-economic structures of the household, (2) the availability of transportation, and (3) the location of the household's residential site relative to other elements of the spatial system.

Operational Definitions

Before proceeding further with the analysis, it is necessary to operationally define measures of these three factors as well as to select some measure of transport inputs.

Perhaps the most difficult of the definitions is posed by the question of selecting a measure of transport inputs. The use of total miles traveled by members of the household during a given time period is immediately suggested from the concepts of general location theory, but it was noted earlier that most empirical studies have made use of the measure "trips per household per time period." The relationship between these two measures is largely an unexplored one. Some workers seem to feel that there is a pronounced diminution of trip frequency with increasing distance.[10] If trip frequency does vary with distance, then the transport inputs of a given household would be characterized by a two element vector (frequency, distance) and a multi-equation model would have to be adopted. The empirical studies which have been conducted do not seem to support this contention, and upon close examination there seems to be little theoretical justification for accepting it.

Since the evidence currently available does not seem to justify the more complex multi-equation approach, the present study does not proceed at that level. Instead, two single equation systems are examined, the first testing the relationship of trip frequencies to the three factors, and the second examining the associations between the three sets of factors and the total distance traveled by the household during the study period.

It is unfortunate that the structure of the data made it impossible to utilize any of the various scales available for the measurement of the socio-economic status of the household. The present study attempted this measurement through the use of a series of factors which included: size of the household, income level, age and educational level of the head of the household, and the presence or absence of school children or employed persons. It is freely admitted that these factors do not present an ideal picture of the socio-economic structure of the household, but they do represent the best that could be constructed with the information available.

Three types of transport: movement on foot, movement by automobile, and movement by public transit were assumed to be available in some degree to each household. While every household has available the ability to make trips on foot, the ability to make trips by automobile and public transit varies from household to household. The ownership of one or more motor vehicles by the household was entered as a dichotomous variable; while the availability of public transit was assumed to be proportional to the distance of the residence from the nearest transit facility.

The measurement of residential location poses a rather difficult problem. The spatial structure of the modern urban region is exceedingly complex, and any attempt to define the relative location of a residence by means of a single simple measure is likely to prove both inadequate and misleading. As an example of the complexity of the urban region, let us examine just one sector: retail business. Recent theoretical and empirical studies have extended the traditional concepts of central place theory to include the structure of intra-urban business, and have shown that a hierarchy of retail business centers exists within the city.[11] Because of the highly interdependent structure of the urban region the household is forced to interact with various members of this retail hierarchy in order to maintain its existence. How then are we to define the location of the household? Interaction takes place with all levels of the hierarchy, and it would seem that, as a minimum, there should be as many reference factors as there are levels in the hierarchy. The same argument holds when our outlook is extended to include the numerous other contacts of the household with other demand points for purposes of work, schooling, recreation, etc.

For the purposes of the present study, the location of the household was related only to the nearest member of each level of the retail hierarchy. It is recognized that other demand points within the urban region may well be of major importance, but it is felt that this measure represented as great a degree of complexity as was necessary at the time.

EMPIRICAL STUDIES IN CEDAR RAPIDS, IOWA

The following empirical studies are based upon travel information collected by the Traffic Audit Bureau, Inc., and made available to the University of Washington through the generous cooperation of that organization and the Outdoor Advertising Association of America. The information was collected in 1949 as part of a larger project designed to measure the impact of outdoor poster advertising.[12] The sample consisted of 256 households in Linn Co., Iowa, about 77 percent of which were within the city of Cedar Rapids. At the time of the study, Cedar Rapids was a city of about 75,000 persons, with a moderately concentrated commercial structure (see Fig. 26-1). Each person ten years of age or older in the sample households kept a detailed travel diary for a thirty day period. The following information was entered for each trip made: (1) the time of departure from the home, and the time of return, (2) a block-by-block description of the route followed, (3) the address and purpose of each stop, and (4) the mode of travel utilized on each leg of the trip.

Because of time limitations data reduction was possible for only one-half of the urban households the locations of which are shown in Fig. 26-2. For each of these 100 households, all trips made during a two-week period were examined in detail and trip lengths obtained. Studies elsewhere have indicated that the structure of retail business in Cedar Rapids forms a four-level hierarchy (see Fig. 26-3), and the location of the sample residences was therefore defined by four over-the-road distance measurements—one to the nearest member of each level of the retail hierarchy.[13]

Form of the Model

A linear regression model having the general form:

$$Y = \alpha + \sum_i \beta_i x_i + u \qquad (i = 1, 2, \ldots, 14)$$

was utilized. Two separate studies were undertaken, with trip frequency as the dependent variable in the first study, and the total distance traveled as the dependent variable in the second study. The independent variables were as described above, and estimates of α and the β's were, in each case, developed from the sample data.

The Trip Frequency Study

In the calculation of total trip frequency for each household, movements purely for the purpose of pleasure driving or visiting friends were omitted. With these omissions the average household made just under 36 trips during the two week study period. In this study a trip is defined as a movement which has its ultimate origin and destination at the place of residence. This definition differs considerably from the one used in most movement studies. For instance, a person who goes from home to work, and from work to home and who stops for gas en route is—in most movement studies—considered as having made three trips. In the present study, this movement pattern is viewed as a whole, and the individual is counted as having made only one trip.

Application of the linear regression model described above produced an estimating equation which was able to explain about half of the observed variation in trip frequency. The only variables which showed a high degree of statistical significance fell in the socio-economic group. Only one of the spatial variables, road distance to the nearest low order retail center, appeared to have any significance at all, and this was of a very low order.

Thus it appears that trip frequency is not significantly affected by the location of the residence relative to the retail structure of the city. This offers some evidence to support Isard's theoretical contention that space preferences (which we may assume to be roughly equivalent to trip frequencies) are determined by social and psychological factors exogenous to the spatial system.

The Total Distance Study

Since trip frequency does not seem to be significantly related to residential location, we would then expect total miles traveled to be quite sensitive to variations in residential location. However, application of the linear re-

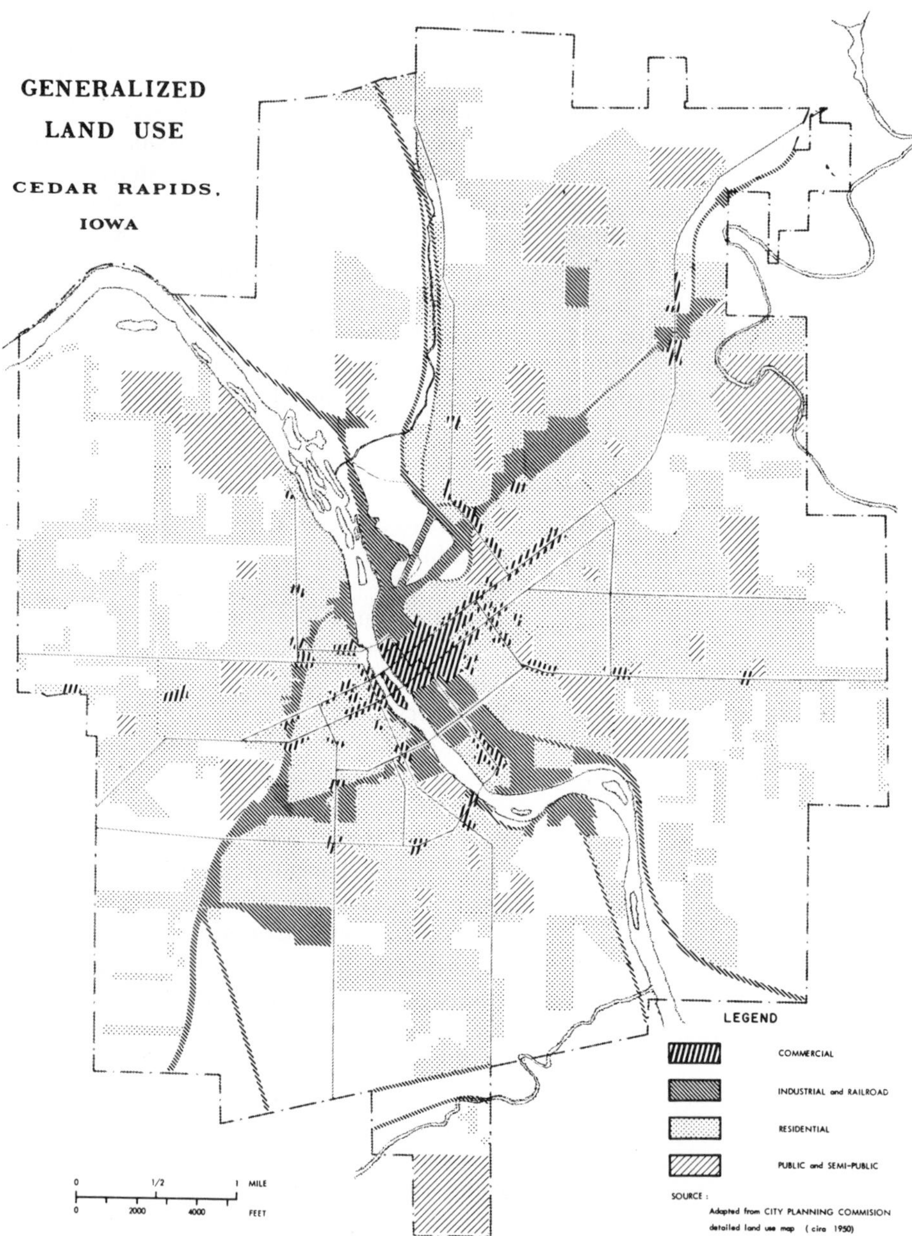

Fig. 26-1 Generalized land use, Cedar Rapids, Iowa.

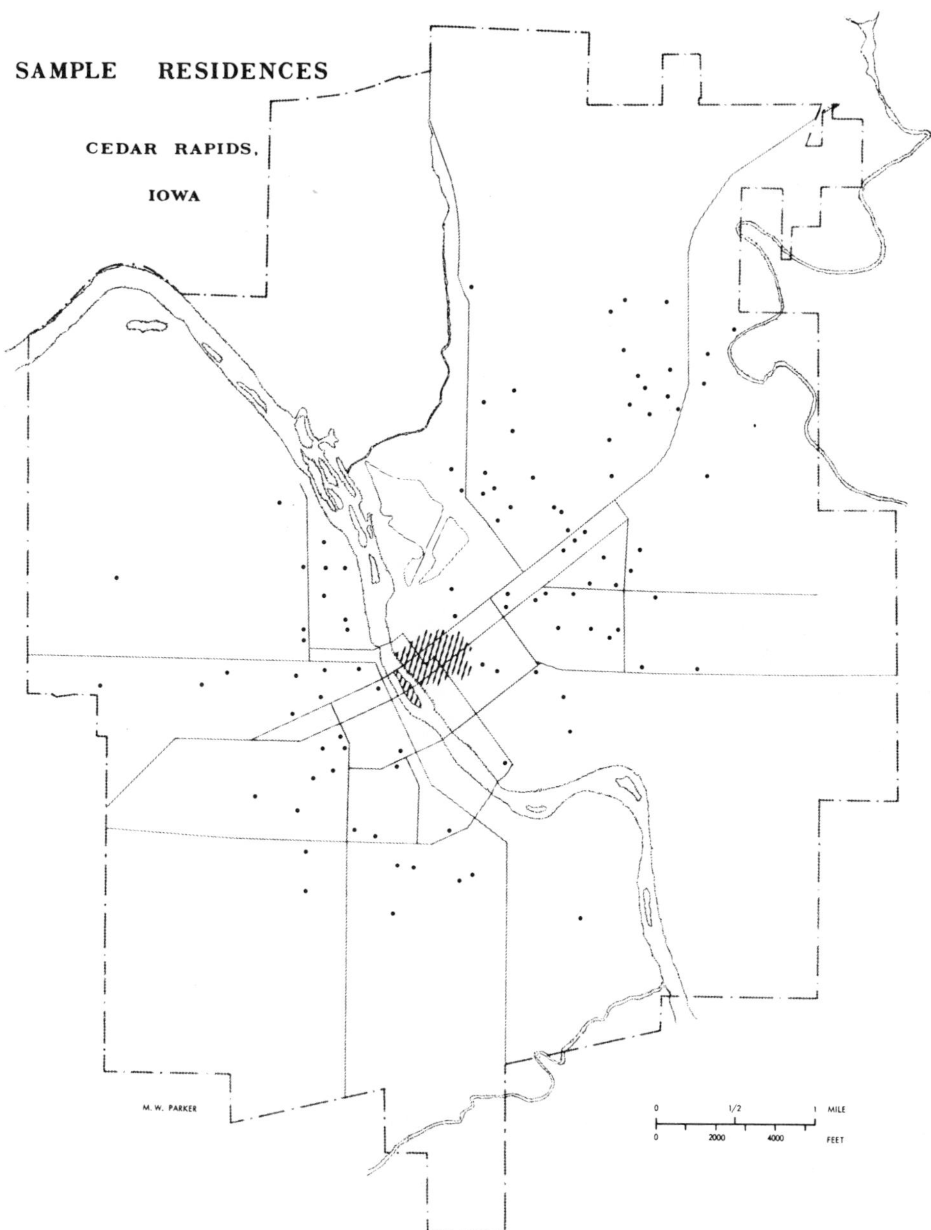

Fig. 26-2 Sample residences, Cedar Rapids, Iowa.

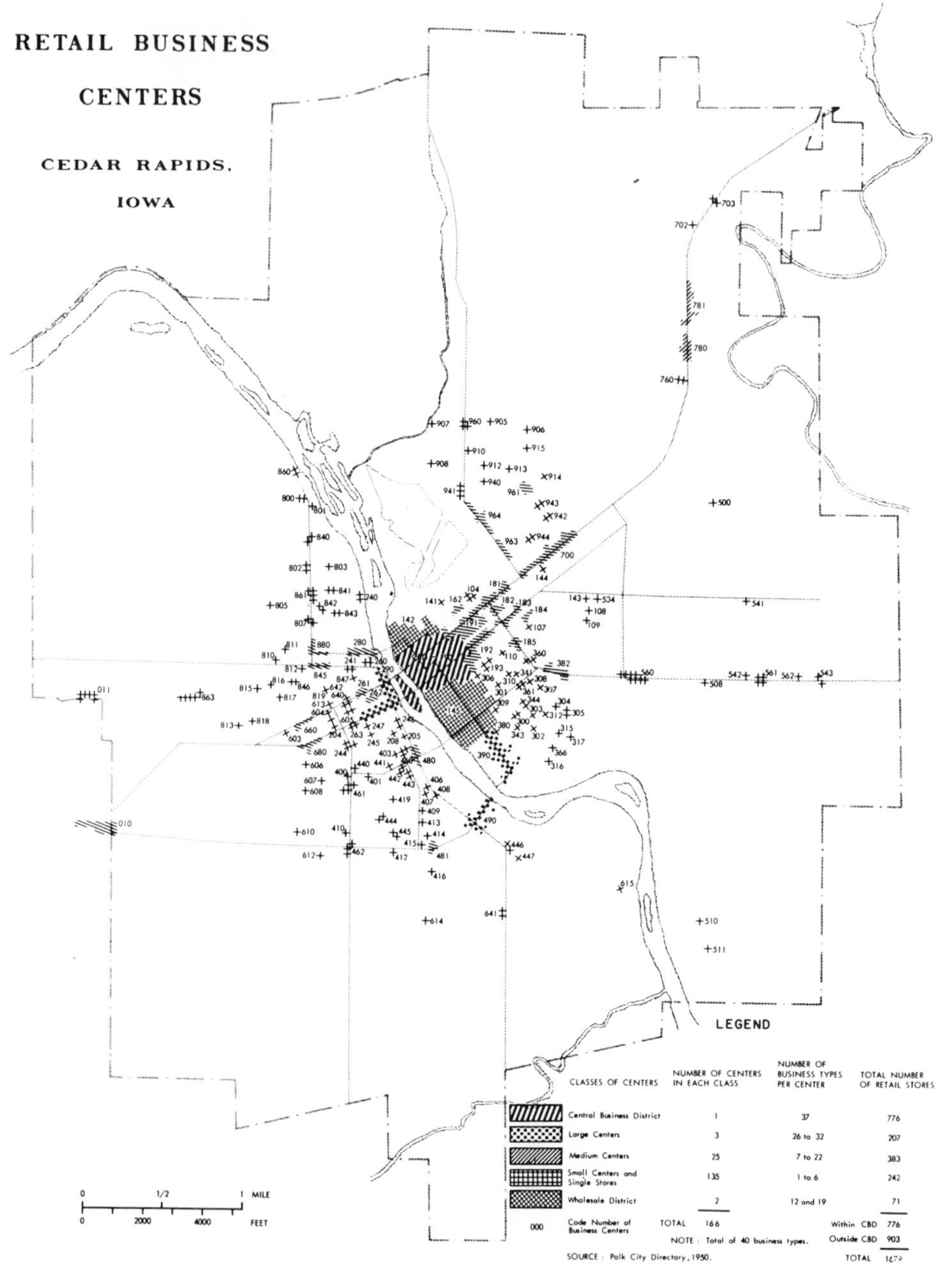

Fig. 26-3 Retail business centers, Cedar Rapids, Iowa.

gression model resulted in explanation of only 14 percent of the observed variation in total distance traveled. Only three variables were statistically significant, even at relatively low confidence levels. There were: (1) distance to the nearest transit line, (2) distance to the nearest high order retail center, and (3) distance to the nearest low order retail center.

Although locational variables were the only ones to show any degree of significance, the low degree of confidence which must be attached to them together with the overall poor performance of the model in this case, leaves much to be desired. Application of a nonlinear model of the general form:

$$\log Y = \log \alpha + \Sigma\, \beta_i \log x_i$$

resulted in only a small increase in the level of explanation. The independent variables in this case were: (1) distance to the CBD, (2) distance to the nearest medium order retail center, (3) distance to the nearest low order retail center, and (4) distance to the place of work of the head of the household.

From the above we conclude, in agreement with Isard, that current concepts of location theory—even when expressed in a relatively complex manner (as the measure of residential location)—are unable to account for the variations in the level of transport inputs to households. It would appear then that a new framework must be sought which will provide a better structure for the analysis of this problem.

A PROPOSED DECISION MODEL

The individual consumer appears to operate with incomplete information regarding the extent and characteristics of the spatial system. The problem which he faces would then appear to be one of individual decision making under conditions of uncertainty, with the movements of the individual in space as physical analogs of his movements among the branches of a game tree.[14] The game is one played against "nature," and has the general form set forth in the following table.

States of Nature

Trips		s_1	s_2	. . . s_j	. . . s_n
	t_1	u_{11}	u_{12}	. . . u_{1j}	. . . u_{1n}
	t_2	u_{21}	u_{22}	. . . u_{2j}	. . . u_{2n}
	.	.	.	.	.
	.	.	.	.	.
	.	.	.	.	.
	t_i	u_{i1}	u_{i2}	. . . u_{ij}	. . . u_{in}
	.	.	.	.	.
	.	.	.	.	.
	.	.	.	.	.
	t_m	u_{m1}	u_{m2}	. . . u_{mj}	. . . u_{mn}

The individual must choose from among a set of trips whose relative desirability depends upon which "state of nature" prevails. The u_{ij} in the table represent utilities or outcomes of given pairs of trips and states of nature. The individual's problem is to select a trip or set of trips which is in some sense optimal. Four possible cases, defined on the individual's level of knowledge regarding the possible states of nature, may exist. These are (1) certainty, where it is known exactly which state of nature will prevail under any set of conditions, (2) risk, where an a priori knowledge of the probability of occurrence of each state of nature exists, (3) complete ignorance, where the individual has no idea of the probability of occurrence of any state of nature, and (4) partial ignorance, representing a combination of states (2) and (3). The results of certain "shopping games" conducted by Wroe Alderson, as well as recent work by Berry, seem to indicate that consumers placed in a new spatial situation act in such a manner as to approach state (2) as closely as possible.[15]

The game appears to be a stochastic one. That is, the player's strategies control not only the payoff but also the transition probabilities which govern the game to be played at the next stage. What are the stages of this game? They appear to be equivalent to the purposeful stops on the trip. The individual selects his first destination as a result of the outcome of the first stage. Upon arrival at this destination, the second stage commences and the next destination is selected. The process continues until at some stage the residence becomes the next destination, and the game terminates.[16]

NOTES

1 A more detailed discussion of this point is contained in: William L. Garrison, Brian J. L. Berry, Duane F. Marble, John D. Nystuen, and Richard L. Morrill, *Studies of Highway Development and Geographic Change* (Seattle: University of Washington Press, 1959).

2 Louis Lefeber, *Allocation in Space* (Amsterdam: North-Holland Publishing Co., 1958), Walter Isard, *Location and Space-economy,* (New York: John Wiley and Sons, 1956).

3 Emery Troxel, *Economics of Transport* (New York: Rinehart, 1955).

4 William J. Baumol and Edward A. Ide, "Variety in Retailing," *Management Science,* Vol. 3 (October 1956), pp. 93–101.

5 Brian J. L. Berry and William L. Garrison, "Recent Developments of Central Place Theory," *Papers and Proceedings of the Regional Science Association,* Vol. 4 (1958), pp. 107–120.

6 John R. Hamburg, "Some Social and Economic Factors Related to Intra-City Movement," Unpublished Master's Thesis, Wayne State University, 1957. William L. Mertz and Lemelle B. Hamner, "A Study of Factors Related to Urban Travel," *Public Roads,* Vol. 29 (1957), pp. 170–174.

7 William L. Garrison, *The Benefits of Rural Roads to Rural Property* (Seattle: Washington State Council for Highway Research, 1956).

8 University of Virginia, Bureau of Population and Economic Research, *The Impact of a New Manufacturing Plant upon the Socio-economic Characteristics and Travel Habits of the People in Charlotte County, Virginia.* (Preliminary mimeographed edition dated 1951)

9 Richard E. O'Brien, *Socio-economic Forces and Family Pleasure Travel* (Jefferson City: Missouri Division of Resources and Development, 1958).

10 See for instance: Fred C. Ikle, "Sociological Relationship of Traffic to Population and Distance," *Traffic Quarterly,* Vol. 8, (1954), pp. 123–136.

11 William L. Garrison et al., *op. cit.*

12 Traffic Audit Bureau, Inc., *Coverage, Repetition and Impact Provided by Poster Showings* (New York: Traffic Audit Bureau, 1950).

13 William L. Garrison et al., *op. cit.*

14 For a discussion of these terms see: R. Duncan Luce and Howard Raiffa, *Games and Decisions* (New York: John Wiley and Sons, 1957).

15 Alderson and Sessions, *Basic Research Report on Consumer Behavior,* (mimeographed) April, 1957. Brian J. L. Berry, *Pre-equilibrium Consumer Connections and the Spatial Structure of Retail Business,* unpublished paper, Department of Geography, University of Washington.

16 Further research and associated empirical problems are reported in D. Marble, "A Heoretical Exploration of Individual Travel Behavior," in W. Garison and D. Marble (eds.), *Quantitative Geography*, Part 1, Evanston, Ill.: Northwestern University Press, 1967, pp. 33–53; and in a useful bibliography by W. R. Black and F. E. Horton. *A Bibliography of Selected Research on Networks and Urban Transportation Relevant to Current Transportation Geography Research*, Northwestern University, Department of Geography. Research Report No. 28., n.d.

Selection 27

Automobile Commuting in Large Suburbs: A Comparative Analysis of Private Car Use in the Daily Journey to Work

R. T. Aangeenbrug

INTRODUCTION

The object of this [work] is to account for the spatial variations in relative automobile use in the journey to work among large United States suburban areas. The order of analysis will be: (1) measurement of automobile commuting, (2) identification of the spatial variation of the phenomenon, and (3) accounting for the existence of the spatial variation.

Automobile commuting in the selected metropolitan rings is measured as the percentage of the total employed labor force in each ring that uses a private car in the journey to work. The 1960 Census of Population[1] is used for a cross-sectional comparative analysis of the phenomenon among large United States metropolitan rings and for relating such data to socioeconomic characteristics of these urban peripheries. The percentage of workers employed in each ring using the automobile in the daily work trip is the dependent variable in the analysis.

A simplified model of an urban area in its spatial aspects is used to classify journey-to-work flows.[2] The classification is in terms of three categories, each of which is one spatial segment of the metropolitan areas. The three are identified as follows: (1) central cities, (2) rings, and (3) extra-metropolitan areas (Fig. 27-1). Nine streams of workers within and between these areas can be delimited (Fig. 27-2). This was done for the fifty largest SMSA's.

Each flow is identified by its area of origin, the first initial, and its area of destination, the second letter. In most SMSA's, the three largest flows are the intra-city (CC), the peripheral (RR), and the centripetal (RC) streams.[3]

Nearly thirty percent of the total work force employed in the SMSA's live and work in the ring of the sample SMSA's. Nearly three-fourths of these workers use a private car in their journey to work. The mean for the dependent variable among the peripheral streams is 71.9. The standard deviation around this mean in 10.1 percent. The range of relative automobile use in the RR flows is from thirty

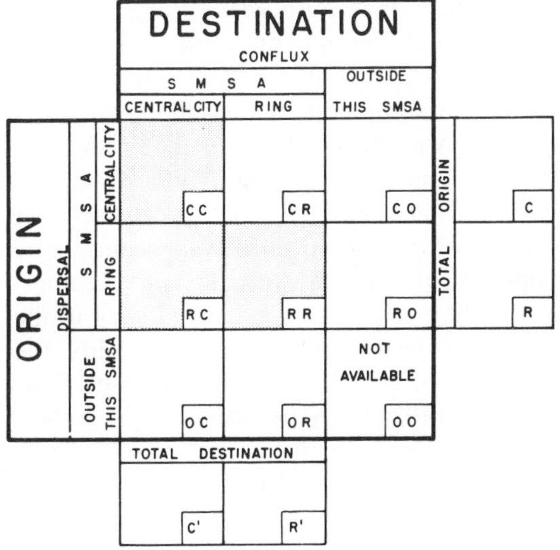

Fig. 27-1.

Northwestern University: *Studies in Geography,* No. 16, 1968, pp. 1–19. Reprinted by permission of the author and editor.

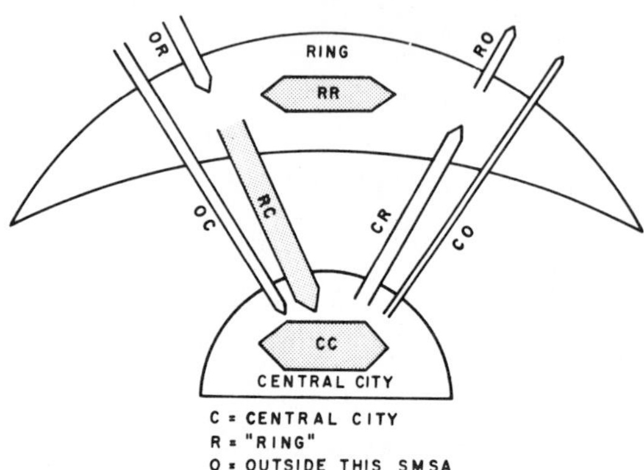

Fig. 27-2 (After Hoover and Vernon).

to eighty-four percent, but the vast majority of large metropolitan areas in the United States have a labor force dependent upon automobile use (Fig. 27-3). All but three of the sample SMSA's indicate automobile dominance (more than 50 percent using the automobile) in the peripheral work journey, and in all but eight sample SMSA's the relative use of the automobile among the work force exceeds two-thirds. The anomalous SMSA's (San Antonio, Jersey City, and Memphis) deviate from the general distribution because of fairly obvious conditions in their peripheral employment. In San Antonio and Memphis the relative importance of the military in the peripheral labor force heavily weights the measures of peripheral transport use. Few, if any, of the military personnel in these rings need to travel a significant distance. The ring of Jersey City is for all intents and purposes a part of the central core of the New York metropolitan region[4] and in this heavily industrialized "suburb," many persons are employed near their place of work.

The spatial distribution of peripheral commuting indicates a generally higher trend toward automobile use in the rings of the cities south and west of the Eastern Seaboard, but we find that for the country as a whole, including the Northeast, most rings are dominated by automobile commuting.

HYPOTHESIZED INDICATORS

Previous studies[5] indicated that such factors as population density, city age, and availability of public transportation are clearly relevant to an understanding of the degree of automobile use among large metropolitan areas of the United States. The question which then arises is whether the same factors provide a necessary and sufficient explanation of the degree of automobile use in the peripheral metropolitan traffic flows. Three independent variables are suggested as hypothesized indicators that will test this hypothesis: population density, the age of the SMSA (the number of decades since the central city reached 50,000—"age" of SMSA), and availability of public transportation (measured as the percent of workers utilizing public transportation).

The three suggested indicators used to account for the variation of the dependent variable for total SMSA work trips were correlated with the dependent variable for RR streams and each indicated a weak negative association with the dependent variable. (See Table 27-2.) Only the public transport variable indicated a significant association with relative automobile use. The failure of these indicators to account for the variation of relative automobile commuting is not unexpected. The density of the rings is not expected to be a good indicator of relative automobile use. It is generally quite low and reveals little of the high density concentrations clustered along major transport arteries. Also, in many of the peripheral areas, particu-

PER CENT OF EMPLOYED LABOR FORCE USING AUTOMOBILE IN JOURNEY TO WORK - SUBURBAN FLOWS

(a)

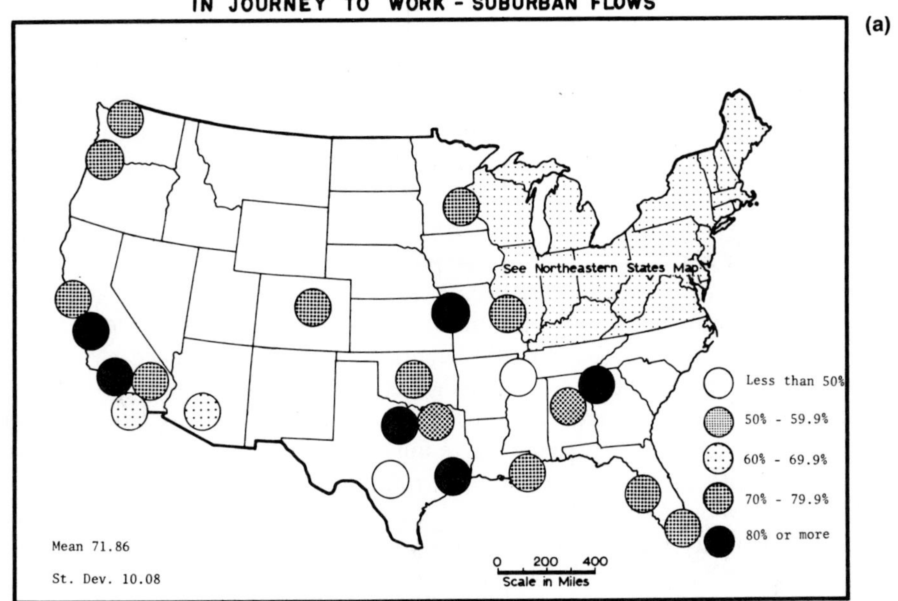

PER CENT OF EMPLOYED LABOR FORCE USING AUTOMOBILE IN JOURNEY TO WORK - SUBURBAN FLOWS

(b)

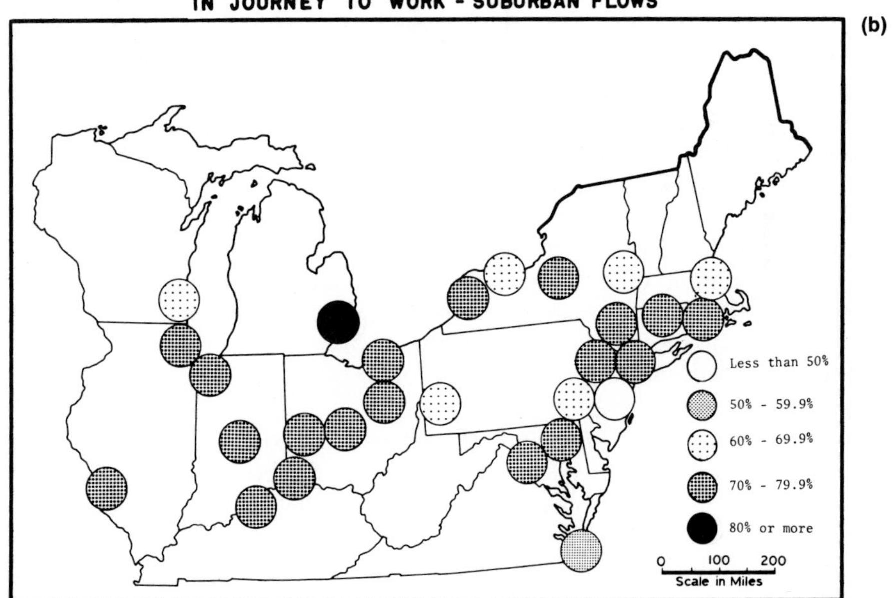

Figs. 27-3*a* and *b*.

larly those with low densities, the relative use of the automobile would tend to decrease with a relative increase of agricultural workers in the total labor force.

Public transport use in peripheral work journeys is generally fairly unimportant in total work trips. Even in the peripheral traffic of the seaboard SMSA's such as New York, Boston, and Philadelphia, less than ten percent of the employed labor force use public transport facilities in their work trip. As has been noted before, the orientation of the public transit facilities toward the central business district and the low densities generate little demand for extensive public transit in the rings.[6] SMSA's whose rings have fairly low automobile use usually contain a relatively large agricultural labor force.

Obviously, the independent variables do not adequately account for the variation of automobile use in the peripheral work trip. Additional socioeconomic variables probably account for this "unexplained" variation.

Hypotheses for seven groups of measures of the socioeconomic structure of the sample streams are proposed. In addition, several measures of the total structure of the SMSA are included, such as population density and the age of the SMSA. Age, sex, race, family, industries, occupation, and income composition of the aggregate of workers in each journey-to-work flow are hypothesized to reflect the relation of this structure to the choice of mode of transport and to account for the variation of the dependent variable. In addition, modal choice variables are also included. (See Table 27-2.)

A reasonably simple prediction model is expected to produce a set of significant indicators which will aid us in our understanding of peripheral journey-to-work flows. In most of the urban transport studies, time and limited funds restrict an exhaustive study of the specific association of the dependent variable with a number of indicators. The general literature is still incomplete in its description and evaluation of the choice of the automobile in the journey to work.[7] Even though cost and time variables have been ignored in the census studies, recent transport studies have not been able to confirm these as completely satisfactory and/or useful indicators of automobile use.

The composition of the labor force is postulated to explain variations in the dependent variable. The decreased competition for residential space has allowed workers to live near their place of work.[8] It has been noted that those employees not able to use the automobile in the peripheral work trip are generally female, young, or poor.[9] Where the age structure of the labor force in the suburbs is dominated by older age groups, more typical in developed suburbs, you would expect to find more automobile use. In suburbs where the labor force is composed of many young persons, in agricultural areas, and near military establishments automobile use is expected to be less important.

In suburbs with a high degree of skilled industrial employees, one would expect to find high relative automobile use,[10] but in industrial suburbs with a relatively large number of semi-skilled industrial employees, typical of older establishments, one would expect less automobile use. Such groups of workers tend to cluster around their place of employment.

THE REGRESSION MODEL

A correlation analysis measures the observed direction and degree of association between the variables. Among this large number of hypothesized indicators we find numerous significant correlations (Table 27-3). In every variable group we can find a significant indicator. The stepwise regression method[11] is

Table 27-1 The Stepwise Regression Equation: Summary Table—RR Flows

Step number	Variable entered		Multiple		Increase in RSQ
	Code	#	R	RSQ	
1	PMMIDL	11	.7880	.6209	.6209
2	PWWALK	8	.8710	.7587	.1337
3	PWOLD	3	.9317	.8681	.1095
4	PHWFHD	18	.9484	.8996	.0314
5	PNMALE	16	.9638	.9289	.0294
6	PICRIC	36	.9689	.9387	.0098
7	PNOLD	15	.9768	.9541	.0154
8	PICRAF	29	.9796	.9596	.0055

$$Y_c = -40.45 + .63X_3 - 1.21X_8 + 1.19X_{11} + .18X_{15} + .21X_{16} + 1.28X_{18} + .49X_{29} - .81X_{36} + E$$

used to select the variables which reduce the "unexplained" variation of the dependent variable.

The equation estimated for the fifty RR flows is summarized in . . . (Table 27-1). The hypotheses relating variations of the dependent variable to the age and sex structure of the labor force are strongly supported. With the interrelated effects of other variables removed, the coefficient for variable eleven (the percent of middle-aged males in the male labor force), declined from .788 (the simple coefficient, R_{y11}) to .713 (the partial coefficient, $R_{y11.1,2..57}$).

In step two the relative number of persons who walked to work (variable X_8), enters as the next most closely related variable. It is also complementary but of limited significance in other flows.

The regression equation indicates, empirically for the sample SMSA's, the significant association of the composition of the labor force to the variation of automobile use. The variables entered confirm the hypotheses at the beginning of this paper. A surprising entry among these indicators is variable X_{18} (the percent of working wives in households). Taaffe[12] had reported a tendency for females employed in the peripheral labor force to be employed near their place of residence and consequently to be less dependent upon the automobile for their journey to work. The preemption of the family automobile, particularly in the suburbs, for the use of the head of the household, is normally expected. It is rather surprising to see that an increase in the number of working wives in the labor force suggests increased automobile use. Perhaps the incidence of two-car families increases where both husband and wife are employed. Of, if they remain a one-car family, car pools are probably necessary due to the general absence of public transport. Husbands who are employed in suburban industries may be more amenable to sharing rides with fellow employees, particularly if their wives work part-time and need the family car to get to work and later pick up the children or go shopping. Or the data suggests that in suburban families where the wife participates in the labor force, she needs the car due to central city employment.

The effectiveness of the regression equation in accounting for the variation of the de-

Table 27-2 Independent Variables Used in the Analysis of the Relative Use of the Automobile in the Journey to Work

Variable Number	Variable Code	Description
1	PWYOUN	Percent of the total employed labor force, 14 to 24 years.
2	PWMIDL	Percent of the total employed labor force, 25 to 44 years.
3	PWOLD	Percent of the total employed labor force, 45 years and over.
4	PWMALE	Percent of the total employed labor force, male.
5	PWNONW	Percent of the total employed labor force, non-white.
6	PWGRPQ	Percent of the total employed labor force, in group quarters.
8	PWWALK	Percent of the total employed labor force, who walk to work.
10	PMYOUN	Percent of the total male employed labor force, 14 to 24 years.
11	PMMIDL	Percent of the total male employed labor force, 25 to 44 years.
12	PMOLD	Percent of the total male employed labor force, 45 years and over.
13	PNYOUN	Percent of the total nonwhite employed labor force, 14 to 24 years.
14	PNMIDL	Percent of the total nonwhite employed labor force, 24 to 44 years.
15	PNOLD	Percent of the total nonwhite employed labor force, 45 years and over.
16	PNMALE	Percent of the total nonwhite employed labor force, male.
17	PHHEAD	Percent of labor force in household, head of household.
18	PHWFHD	Percent of labor force in household, wife of head.
19	PHWOTH	Percent of labor force in household, other member of household.
20	PHWYOU	Percent of labor force in husband-wife family, head under 45 years old.
21	PHWMID	Percent of labor force in husband-wife family, head 45 to 64 years old.
22	PHWOLD	Percent of labor force in husband-wife family, head 65 and over.

Table 27-2 (continued)

Variable Number	Variable Code	Description
23	PYHKID	Percent of variable 20, with own children under 18.
24	PNHKID	Percent of variable 21, with own children under 18.
25	POPROF	Percent in major occupation group, professional, technical and kindred workers.
26	POMNGR	Percent in major occupation group, managers, officials, and proprietors, incl. farm.
27	POSALE	Percent in major occupation group, salesworkers.
28	POCLER	Percent in major occupation group, clerical and kindred workers.
29	POCRAF	Percent in major occupation group, craftsmen, foremen, and kindred workers.
30	POPERA	Percent in major occupation group, operatives and kindred workers.
31	POPRIV	Percent in major occupation group, private household workers.
32	POSERV	Percent in major occupation group, service workers, except pvt. household.
33	POLABO	Percent in major occupation group, laborers, except mine.
34	PICONS	Percent in major industry group, construction.
35	PIMANF	Percent in major industry group, manufacturing.
36	PICIRC	Percent in major industry group, transportation, communications, etc.
37	PITRAD	Percent in major industry group, wholesale and retail trade.
38	PIFINA	Percent in major industry group, finance, insurance, and real estate.
39	PIBURP	Percent in major industry group, business and repair services.
40	PIPERS	Percent in major industry group, personal services.
41	PIENTR	Percent in major industry group, entertainment and recreation services.
42	PIPROF	Percent in major industry group, professional and related services.
43	PIPUBA	Percent in major industry group, public administration.
44	PIPOOR	Percent of workers with earnings in 1959, less than $4,000.

Table 27-2 (continued)

Variable Number	Variable Code	Description
45	PIRICH	Percent of workers with earnings in 1959, $10,000 and over.
47	WHCOLR	Percent of total employed labor force, in white-collar occupations.
48	WHBLUE	Percent of total employed labor force, in blue-collar occupations.
49	CTYAGE	Number of census decades since central city reached 50,000 population—"age" of SMSA.
50	LGDNSM	The logarithm of the population density of the SMSA.
51	LGDNCY	The logarithm of the population density of the central city.
52	LGDNRG	The logarithm of the population density of the ring.
54	MILITP	Percent of the total employed labor force, military personnel.
55	MDINCC	Mean earnings of workers with earnings in 1959, in flow CC.
56	MDINRC	Mean earnings of workers with earnings in 1959, in flow RC.
57	MDINRR	Mean earnings of workers with earnings in 1959, in flow RR.

Source: U.S. Bureau of the Census, *U.S. Census of Population: 1960, Detailed Characteristics, United States Summary.* Final Report PC(1); U.S. Bureau of the Census, *U.S. Census of Population: Subject Reports. Journey to Work,* Final Report PC(2)-6B.

pendent variable can be established from a comparison of the standard deviation of the dependent variable with the standard error of the estimate. It is rather evident that the large reduction of the variation around the mean indicates an effective model. The total explained variation increased to 96 percent and can also be considered quite effective.

CONCLUSION

The final model strongly suggests that the socioeconomic characteristics of the labor force account for the characteristic of automobile use in peripheral flows. The final composition of the labor force in peripheral work trips reflects the expected pattern of automobile use. More intensive use of the automobile is found in rings with a relatively old labor force employed in skilled trades and in which family-oriented, middle-aged males and an older, predominantly male nonwhite labor force are dominant. In other words, the nonwhite labor flow in suburbia, at least on the aggregate level, seems to reflect conformity to the general pattern of the dominant white labor force.

The presence of working wives in the labor force apparently contributes to increased automobile use. That may indicate a temporary entry of females in the labor force to pay for the move into suburbia, probably leaving both husband and wife dependent on the automobile for work trip transportation.

The other significant variables entered: the percentage of older workers, the relative number of craftsmen, the percentage of males and older persons among the nonwhite labor force, the relative number of workers in the transport and communication industries, and the relative share of workers who walked to work, confirmed our previous hypotheses. The residual pattern (Fig. 27-3) indicates no extreme variations in the prediction of the estimation of the dependent variable.

An examination of the patterns reveals in rings where the relative automobile use was overestimated. Either a densely settled satellite type suburb exists employing a relatively large number of industrial employees (New-

Table 27-3 Coefficients of Correlation between the Dependent Variable and the Hypothesized Indicators in Suburban Flows

Variable Number	Variable Code″	RR	Variable Number	Variable Code″	RR
1	PWYOUN	−.696*	29	POCRAF	.532*
2	PWMIDL	.764*	30	POPERA	.064
3	PWOLD	.341	31	POPRIV	−.336†
4	PWMALE	−.443*	32	POSERV	.123
5	PWNONW	−.211	33	POLABO	−.300†
6	PWGRPQ	−.743*	34	PICONS	.099
8	PWWALK	−.399*	35	PIMANF	.280†
9	PWPUBL	−.311†	36	PICIRC	−.037
10	PMYOUN	−.684*	37	PITRAD	.104
11	PMMIDL	.788*	38	PIFINA	−.004
12	PMOLD	.364*	39	PIBURP	.141
13	PNYOUN	−.566*	40	PIPERS	−.219
14	PNMIDL	.389*	41	PIENTR	.194
15	PNOLD	.313†	42	PIPROF	.100
16	PNMALE	−.239	43	PIPUBA	−.393*
17	PHHEAD	−.075	44	PTPOOR	−.584*
18	PHWFHD	.341†	45	PTRICH	.428*
19	PHWOTH	−.188	47	WHCOLR	.052
20	PHWYOU	.144	48	WHBLUE	−.017
21	PHWMID	−.052	49	CTYAGE	−.033
22	PHWOLD	−.388*	50	LGDNSM	−.163
23	PYHKID	.154	51	LGDNCY	−.071
24	PMHKID	−.159	52	LGDNRC	−.042
25	POPROF	.265	54	MILITP	−.539*
26	POMNGR	−.342†	55	MDINCC	...
27	POSALE	.200	56	MDINRC	...
28	POCLER	.173	57	MDINRR	.550*

* Significant at the 99% level.

† Significant at the 95% level.

″ See Table 27-2.

‡ Variable 7—percent of the total employed labor force in each flow, using a private automobile or car pool as means of transportation to work.

ACCURACY OF ESTIMATE, RR FLOWS $\frac{Y_c - Y}{Sy_c}$

(a)

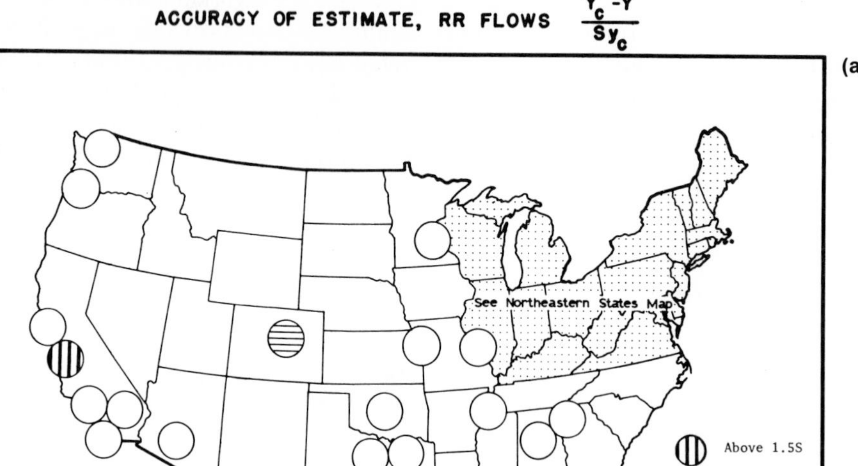

ACCURACY OF ESTIMATE, RR FLOWS $\frac{Y_c - Y}{Sy_c}$

(b)

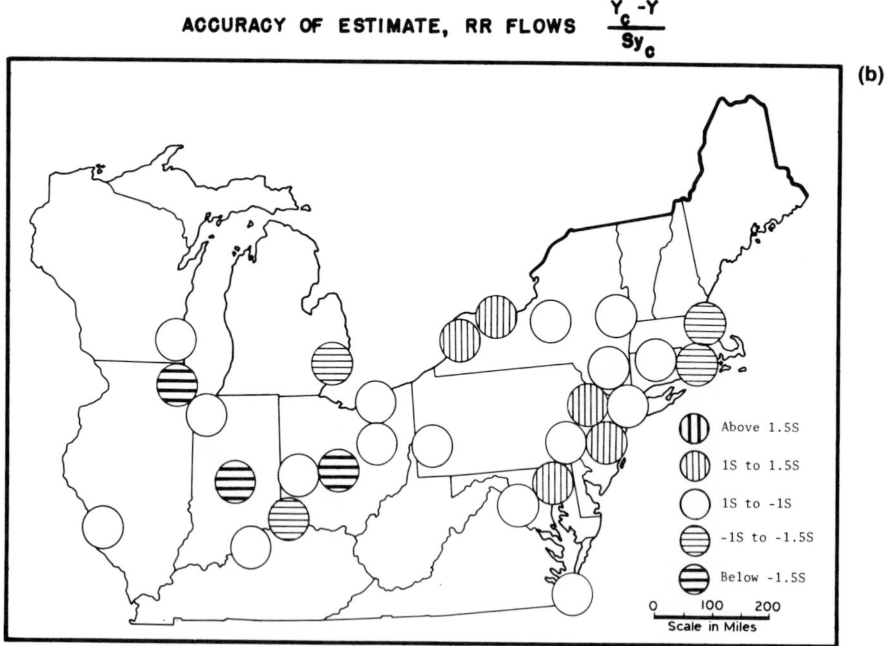

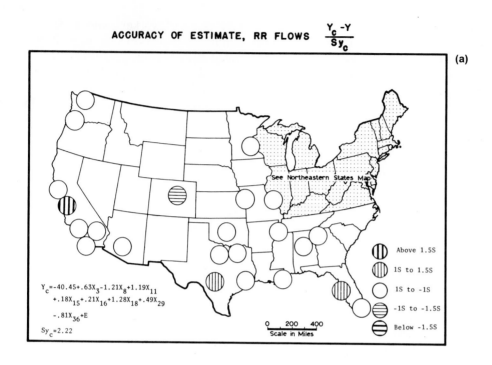

Figs. 27-4*a* and *b*.

ark, Jersey City, Buffalo and Baltimore), or a suburb with excessive military employment.

The rings in which automobile use was higher than predicted by the model are those with considerable important new industrial concentrations in the suburbs where the skilled workers live in sprawling residential sectors.[13] The model confirms the notion that socioeconomic variables are useful in estimating relative automobile use. It seems that the general nature of the peripheral labor force needs further examination in order to reveal the relationship between these and modal choice.

REFERENCES

1 U.S. Bureau of the Census, *U.S. Census of Population: 1960, Detailed Characteristics, United States Summary*. Final Report PC (1); U.S. Bureau of the Census. *U.S. Census of Population: Subject Reports. Journey to Work*, Final Report PC (2)-6B, Table 27-2.

2 R. T. Aangeenbrug, "Automobile Commuting: A Geographic Analysis of Private Car Use in the Daily Journey to Work in Large Cities," (unpublished Ph.D dissertation, Department of Geography, University of Wisconsin, 1965).

3 *Ibid.*, pp. 20–25.

4 E. M. Hoover and Raymond Vernon, *Anatomy of a Metropolis* (Garden City, New York: Doubleday and Company, 1962), pp. 6–15.

5 L. P. Adams and T. Mackesey. *Commuting Patterns of Industrial Workers* (Ithaca, New York: Cornell University Housing Research Center, 1955), p. 180; B. Duncan. "Factors in Work-Residence Separation, Chicago, 1951," *American Sociological Review*, 21, (February 1956), pp. 48–56; L. G. Reeder, "Social Differentials in Mode of Travel, Time and Cost in the Journey to Work," *American Sociological Review*, 21 (February 1956), pp. 56–63; J. Smith, *Some Social Aspects of Mass Transit in Selected American Cities* (East Lansing, Michigan: Institute for Community Development and Services, 1959).

6 W. Goldner. "Spatial and Locational Aspects of Metropolitan Labor Markets," *American Economic Review*, XLV (March 1955), pp. 113–128; L. F. Schnore, "The Separation of Home and Work. A Problem for Human Ecology." *Social Forces*. 32 (May, 1954), p. 336.

7 Aangeenbrug, *op. cit.*, pp. 1–7.

8 *Ibid.*

9 *Ibid.* pp. 37–53.

10 E. J. Burt, Jr. *Labor Supply Characteristics of Route 128 Firms*, Research Report No. 1 (Boston: Federal Reserve Bank of Boston, 1958) and *Changing Labor Supply Characteristics Along Route 128*, Research Report No. 17, (Boston: Federal Reserve Bank of Boston, 1961).

11 M. A. Efroymson, "Multiple Regression Analysis," pp. 191–203 in A. Ralston and H. S. Wilf, *Mathematical Methods for Digital Computers*, (New York: J. Wiley, 1960).

12 E. J. Taaffe, B. J. Garner and M. Yeates. *The Peripheral Journey to Work: A Geographic Consideration* (Evanston, Illinois: Northwestern University Press, 1963).

13 Burt, *op. cit.*

Selection 28

Land Use/Travel Movement Relationships

M. E. Eliot Hurst

In a recent study in Perth, Scotland, an attempt was made to examine the spatial implications of land use/travel movement relationships.[1] Movement patterns were studied at the macroscopic level, the level of reference commonly used by engineers and planners.[2]

Until fairly recently the "buildings" (the urban fabric) and "traffic" (the human response) were from the engineers' and planners' points of view quite separate.[3] The purpose of this [work] is to try to establish a conceptual framework for the relationship, to test the frame by simple models based on its components, utilizing the traffic movements measured in the Perth study, and thus to show that land use and traffic are but two facets of the same general problem, or but two components in a general system of urban structure.

Land-use patterns—residential and nonresidential uses—and the spatial structuring of those patterns help to initiate movement. With activity specialization, origin and destination, desires and fulfillments, or demand and supply, have become separated. Movement has become the means of correcting any spatial imbalance[4] resulting from the bringing together of spatially separated demands and supply through the various journey purposes. Few trips are made for the sake of movement itself. Most trips are for the purpose of doing something which cannot be fulfilled at the place of origin. That movement is limited, directed, and channeled by a composite network system, a conglomerate of several modes and elements acting in unison of competition in what can be termed a "communications" network. Thus movement becomes a function of the nature of demands and supplies (desires and fulfillments) and of the character of the available transport systems. The amount of a flow (the quantity of traffic) is a function of the character of the available transport systems and their environments.[5]

This concept can be shown by a simple diagram (Fig. 28-1). People function at different points in space, and in order to do so and to communicate with one another they must pass through a communications system. In practice the relationship is not really as simple as this. For example, feedback effects occur. As the transportation network influences the development of land use and population distribution, it is influenced in turn by such developments. So rather than consider a simple causal representation the diagram should try to represent a system varying between times of balance and imbalance (Fig. 28-2). People in a particular functional relationship have particular travel needs as they pass through a network or system which in turn influences and is influenced by those relationships. These can be termed *positive potentials*. But also implicit in this functional relationship (the spatial imbalance of the desire and the fulfillment) are *negative potentials* which operate in opposition to the aforementioned desires and fulfillments, and *changing potentials* (the dynamic aspect) which, with advancing technology, would alter the concepts of accessibility and alter both the positive and negative potentials.

It is possible from an examination of previous work to identify a number of negative potentials:

1 *Household size:* Many travel surveys

Traffic Quarterly, vol. 23, 1969, pp. 263–274. Reprinted by permission of the Eno Foundation and the editor.

have identified a household economy-of-scale effect whereby trips fall off relatively with increasing family size, a variable of age composition, etc.[6]

2 *Income or socioeconomic status:* A measure of the ability to pay for travel, particularly the ability to own and operate a car; as car ownership rises the number of trips per person increases and vice versa.[7]

3 *Location and distance (with the corollary of density):* A location near the central area, with a higher density of population and the easier satisfaction of any spatial imbalance, leads to fewer person trips. A more sparsely developed area, distant from the central area where spatial imbalance is greater, generates more trips per person.[8]

4 *The potential surface:* Induced by each land-use type, this varies with various needs and satisfaction. That is, the degree of satisfaction varies among the means of fulfillment (measured, say, by land uses) and therefore the spatial imbalance created is modified. Retail desires, especially convenience shopping, must be satisfied more frequently, for instance, than medical desires.

What has been postulated is a simple system of movement, described in terms of the correlation of parameters to represent population and of parameters to represent land use, and in terms of individual elements as well as a functioning whole. Literally this shows that the amount of movement (number of trips) induced by a particular imbalance is greatest for a small multi-car-owning family, distant from the Central Business District (CBD), which finds satisfaction in a great variety of retail and recreational pursuits.

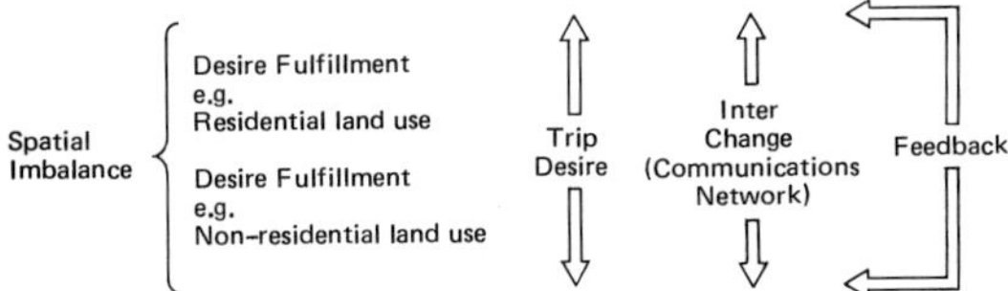

Fig. 28-1 A simple land-use–traffic movement conceptualization.

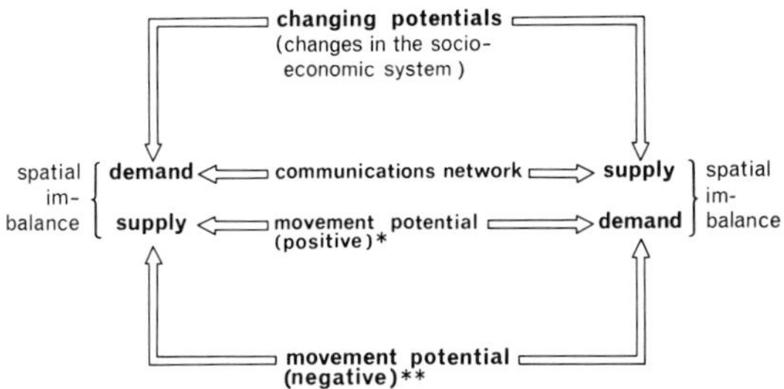

Fig. 28-2 A movement system.

THE MODELS

An attempt was then made, using these general principles, to establish some kind of mathematical summary of total travel. The development of total movement linkages, however, is not easy to analyze. When it is decided to make a trip, a search is made for the land-use destinations to best fulfill the desire and a choice is made among the alternatives, with the limitations imposed by imperfect knowledge, a "bounded rationality," and the particular perceived environment of the individual.[9] When these decision-making processes of many individuals are amalgamated, however, the movement linkages appear regular and orderly. There are demonstrable time and space patterns of travel, subject to recognizable rules like repetitiveness, directional symmetry, and balance between origins and destinations.

A number of techniques exist to estimate aggregate travel behavior and travel linkages in a spatial context. The techniques used to estimate these patterns of movement are mainly distinguished by the methods they employ to identify the frictional effect of the distances between origin and destination—the growth factor method;[10] the gravity method;[11] and the probability method.[12] The present state of knowledge does not allow all of the relevant factors to be quantified or related, hence the models available oversimplify the situation. In most cases considerable skill is required to interpret real situations into the language of models and, similarly, skill is required in translating back from models to real situations. All three techniques are lacking in some respect.[13] In their main usage to predict future interzonal travel patterns and traffic studies models are chosen not so much because of their adequacy, but rather because of their lack of inadequacies. In this particular situation the matter is not prediction but rather the representation of simple concepts, i.e., not just simulation without theoretical substance but an explanation. For this, alternatives to the above methods exist,[14] including the much neglected multivariate model, which can treat traffic interchanges individually and explicitly and can represent the concepts set out above.[15]

Earlier workers have reported a general relationship for a given system of movement. Lapin and Godlund, for example, used the form:

$$y = c + b \cdot x^a \tag{1}$$

where a is a negative exponent and c and b are the values for the given movement system.[16]

This expression is derived by considering the proportion of the movement to a particular desired destination, at each destination category from the destination. y is a measure of such originating movement to the given destination, x is the distance measure, b is an ultimate but unattainable frequency of movement or trips which may be measured at one unit of distance from the destination. This expression has the desirable characteristic that a line representing it becomes asymptotic to the distance axis with increasing values of x. Thus this mathematical format has a major characteristic compatible with the real situation.[17] This compares with the gravity model situation of $y = b \cdot x^a$. Having established in part an approximation to a "real" situation as identified in Fig. 28-2, Equation 1 can be included in a multiple regression model:

$$y = Co + Y \cdot (1 + x)^a \tag{2}$$

where Y is a multiplier calculated for a particular movement interchange volume between two specific points. This may be restated in the form:

$$y = Co + (c_1b_1 + c_2b_2 + c_3b_3 + c_4b_4) \cdot (1 + x)^a \tag{3a}$$

Or in the alternative form:

$$Tij = Co + (c_1Pj + c_2Ej + \dots) \cdot (1 + Dij)^a \tag{3b}$$

In Equation 3b, Tij equals movement between points i and j, Pj, Ej, etc. represent the multiplier Y of Equation 2, by certain attraction indices, such as population and employment, in the destination zone j. In the form of Equation 3a, generation from the origin zone i is expressed in the values of the coefficients Co, c_1, c_2, etc., which would be unique to each urban area tested; the b values of this same equation represent particular zonal or cordon point/zone characteristics. No distinctions are made in this particular formulation for different modes, purposes, or directions, though some of these variations could be encompassed.

Returning to Fig. 28-2, and in particular to the negative potential detailed, this multivariate model (Equation 3b) can be substantiated since:

1 Earlier analyses[18] have shown that location is important, and that the movement volumes between one origin and each of the possible destination points will tend to decrease as distance increases, although the number of journeys per person increases. This is essentially Equation 1.

2 Income, socioeconomic status, car ownership, and household size, which may be measured in various ways, affect positively or negatively the number of journeys generated.[19] So some parameter must be established in the model to represent them.

3 The attractiveness of the destination may be represented by various parameters of land use, etc.[20] The selection of the factors best suited for use in regression depends primarily on two features: can the factor reasonably be measured, and secondly, will it logically and consistently contribute to a reduction of errors of estimation?

Table 28-1 sets out a possible selection of models of the general form of Equation 3 above; model *a* is the same as Osofsky's Modesto model, *b* to his Vallejo model Form I, and *d* to his Vallejo model Form II.[21] Some of these models (Table 28-2) were then used to calculate theoretical vehicle movements as compared to actual movements (Table 28-3). Table 28-2 sets out some of the results from the regression computations, noting the constant, regression coefficient, standard error of estimate, the *t* test, and the multiple coefficient of determination. One result from each model run is shown, except for the more successful models *a* and *d*, illustrating a high degree of success. Table 28-3 examines for model *a* the variation from Perth traffic zone 2 to all other zones as set out, between observed and calculated values. The form of the basic test was, then, to take movement measured as trips or journeys from one traffic zone in the Perth survey to twenty-four other zones. Model *a* in the example shown has a

Table 28-1 Simple Land Use/Movement Models

Basic model	$y = Co + (c_1b_1 + c_2b_2 + c_3b_3 + c_4b_4) \cdot (1 + x)^a$
Model *a*	$y = Co + \frac{P}{(1+D)^2} + \frac{E^2}{(1+D)^2} + \frac{V}{(1+D)^2} + \frac{L.U.I.}{(1+D)^2}$
Model *b*	$y = Co + \frac{P^2}{(1+D)^2} + \frac{E^2}{(1+D)^2} + \frac{V}{(1+D)^2} + \frac{L.U.I.}{(1+D)^2}$
Model *c*	$y = Co + \frac{P}{(1+D)^3} + \frac{E^2}{(1+D)^3} + \frac{V}{(1+D)^3} + \frac{L.U.I.}{(1+D)^3}$
Model *d*	$y = Co + \frac{P.V}{(1+D)^2} + \frac{E^2}{(1+D)^2} + \frac{CFS}{(1+D)^2} + \frac{IFS}{(1+D)^2}$
Model *e*	$y = Co + \frac{P.V}{(1+D)^3} + \frac{E^3}{(1+D)^3} + \frac{CFS}{(1+D)^3} + \frac{IFS}{(1+D)^3}$
Model *f*	$y = Co + P + E^2 + V + L.U.I. + D^2$

Explanation of symbols, models *a* to *f*

y = trips between points of origin and destination.
D = distance between origin and destination.
P = population at each point.
E = employment at each point.
V = car ownership at each point.
L.U.I. = a land-use index for each point.
CFS = commercial floor space for each point.
IFS = industrial floor space for each point.

Table 28-2 Some Results of Applying Models *A* to *E* to Selected Zones in Perth

Model	Constant	Coef. 1	Coef. 2	Coef. 3	Coef. 4	R^2
a		−0.0000495	0.00000269	0.05810	1.0750	
Origin,	38.57	0.0000140	0.00000055	0.01875	0.4028 (SE)	0.98
Zone 2.		3.53	4.92	3.09	2.67 (*t*)	
a		0.02513	0.0002213	0.007375	−6.0060	
Origin,	95.82	0.00285	0.0000212	0.001585	2.1781 (SE)	0.93
Zone 15.		8.77	10.45	4.10	2.84 (*t*)	
b		0.00000061	0.00000262	0.02980	−0.6090	
Origin,	32.16	0.00000024	0.00000045	0.00813	0.2035 (SE)	0.89
Zone 2.		2.47	5.83	2.83	2.93 (*t*)	
c		−0.002555	0.00000026	0.06022	−0.1481	
Origin,	38.97	0.000816	0.00000007	0.02363	0.0554 (SE)	0.79
Zone 2.		3.11	3.56	2.55	2.67 (*t*)	
d		0.017890	0.00000779	−0.000106	−0.000014	
Origin,	40.15	0.004536	0.00000181	0.000032	0.000005 (SE)	0.87
Zone 2.		3.94	4.31	3.37	3.13 (*t*)	
d		0.08556	0.0002188	0.0000274	−0.0000336	
Origin,	84.20	0.01080	0.0000451	0.0000074	0.0000120 (SE)	0.93
Zone 15.		7.92	4.85	3.69	2.79 (*t*)	
d		0.03865	0.0004199	0.000112	−0.000519	
Origin,	149.50	0.00596	0.0000872	0.000023	0.000137 (SE)	0.81
Zone 21.		6.48	4.81	4.80	7.36 (*t*)	
c		0.005495	0.00000087	−0.0000081	0.0000167	
Origin,	51.30	0.001741	0.00000033	0.0000018	0.0000059 (SE)	0.72
Zone 2.		3.15	2.64	4.64	2.79 (*t*)	

fairly high overall position, although there is a great deal of variation. In fact, model *b*, despite its lower coefficient of determination, had a better standard error of estimate, 33.52. It was notable that the same destination points caused problems with both these models. These points were in fact characterized by large industrial employment and large industrial capacity, and were better predicted by model *d* though at some expense to the other destination points. The general fit of the equations was good with no excessive differences between the observations and calculated values. (None were greater than 2.00 from the calculation $(ycn—yc)/Syc$ [22] and the standard errors of estimate were no greater than 40.00.) It is interesting to compare these results with those of Osofsky. In both Osofsky tests and with the Perth models good overall fit was found using employees, commercial and industrial floor space, airline distances between zones, and the product of population and vehicles. It is notable also that in both cases zones of abnormally high employee numbers and industrial averages presented prediction problems. The Perth test definitely substantiates Osofsky's optimism about the use of the multiple regression method.

Like the other methods mentioned earlier, this multiple regression technique has its limitations, and some of the theoretical assumptions may be questioned. The net regression effect of the variables is not always completely understood, for instance, and the variables may be highly correlated or not truly descriptive of an area, that is, they may not be "explanatory" but merely summaries of data. The characteristics of b to b_n and the form of x require to be chosen arbitrarily, so that they vary from one application of the model to another, though a comparison of the Perth, Modesto, and other results is not of any particular advantage because of this. Again it is thought by some that a separate linear multiple regression calculation for each zone of origin is a laborious procedure, but with the use of library programs and computers this is hardly a valid criticism.[23] Full survey data are required for every zone and a measurement of every interzonal travel movement is needed to calibrate the data, although this is also true of most other descriptive and predictive methods. However, it is not possible to use the multiple regression technique with much confidence to estimate the number of travel movements from a zone

Table 28-3 Comparison of Calculated and Real Values: Model "A" Zone 2

$$y = 38.57 - 0.0000495b_1 + 0.00000269b_2 + 0.05810b_3 + 1.075b_4$$

Destination	Observed	Calculated	(ycn-yn)/Syc *
1	315.00	324.05	−0.24
2	343.00	328.43	0.39
3	50.00	47.94	0.06
4	5.00	31.83	−0.72
5	6.00	16.67	−0.28
6	41.00	80.96	−1.07
7	63.00	20.53	1.14
8	41.00	51.81	−0.29
9	29.00	3.39	0.87
10	57.00	110.68	−1.44
11	211.00	134.79	2.04
12	70.00	107.09	−0.99
13	18.00	44.58	−0.71
14	117.00	43.41	1.97
15	97.00	63.42	0.90
16	58.00	58.44	−0.01
17	59.00	76.49	−0.47
18	23.00	35.50	−0.33
19	30.00	24.97	0.14
20	35.00	44.89	−0.27
21	100.00	65.16	0.94
22	34.00	40.84	−0.18
23	8.00	39.61	−0.85
24	23.00	43.79	−0.55

Standard error of estimate 37.19.
*yc = observed value.

which was not included in the original calibration. Since, in fact, strong theoretical, conceptual, and practical reasons can be produced to back the form of the model, these criticisms of the technique can be overcome to a large extent.

The factors used in these models, and postulated in the conceptual diagrams set out at the beginning, were substantiated in earlier findings. Number of employees, the product of the multiplication of population and car ownership, or value of population and car ownership separately, distance, and land-use indices and floor space represent proven factors influencing the movement of people or mass.[24] The success of combining these factors in the models in nearly paralleling the real-life situation seems to indicate that the conceptual relationship set out earlier has some basis in reality. Of course it need not be the only way of representing total movement, but it does seem to have some degree of substantiation as a holistic and descriptive conceptualization and model.

While these equations and models are not necessarily transferable from urban area to urban area, since the constants and coefficients of the equations will vary between study areas, a start has been made, a general model form erected, and a technique provisionally elucidated, that can be the basis for further investigation. Future empirical and theoretical work will contribute to continuing refinements and improvements, for example, to encompass the dynamic aspects (changing potentials) not considered by these simple models. This will lead to the creation of new and more efficient models, through linear programming or other methods, which can more easily analyze and manipulate the myriad variables operating to produce movement patterns. In particular the probability methods, though to date far from perfect, would also seem to offer great potentiality.[25] These methods loosen the distance control in a realistic way and assume a nonmetric distribution of destinations with distance.

It is evident both from the conceptualization and from the models that the study of land use and traffic can no longer be thought of as separate, but related, fields of study. The study of land use and traffic is not a dual one; it is axiomatic that there is an interaction between the two activities, between the desire and the fulfillment, the demand and the supply. They are mutually dependent, and it suffices to say that land can only be effectively utilized when it is accessible. Urban travel is therefore spatially, as well as activity, orientated and the definition and physical location of the activities are an essential part of any analysis. Mere measurement of traffic volumes by themselves, produced by a given generator or set of generators without a consideration of function, links, competitors, and tributary areas, will not provide the necessary understanding of urban travel.

NOTES

1 M. E. Eliot Hurst, "Land Use and Traffic Generation in Urban Area, with Particular Reference to Perth," University of Durham, unpublished Ph.D. thesis, 1966.

2 M. E. Eliot Hurst, "The Structure of Movement and Household Travel Behaviour," *Urban Studies,* February 1969, points out the disadvantages of continuing to ignore other than macroscopic patterns of movement.

3 See for example "Traffic in Towns," H.M.S.O., London, 1963 (the Buchanan Report).

4 Spatial imbalance is implicit in the concepts of "complementarity," "intervening opportunity," and "transferability." See E. L. Ullman, "The Role of Transportation and the Bases for Interaction," in W. L. Thomas (ed.), *Man's Role in Changing the Face of the Earth,* Chicago, 1956, pp. 862–877. It is also implicit in J. D. Carroll and H. W. Bevis, "Predicting Local

Travel in Urban Regions," *Papers and Procs. of the Regional Science Association,* Vol. 3, 1957, pp. 183–197; and in W. J. Garrison, "Estimates of the Parameters of Spatial Interaction," *Papers and Procs. of the Regional Science Association,* Vol. 2, 1956, pp. 280–288.

5 M. E. Eliot Hurst, *A Geography of Economic Behaviour*, North Scituate, Mass.: Duxbury Press, 1972, Chaps. 12 and 13.

6 Eliot Hurst, "Land Use . . . ," *op. cit.;* Carroll and Bevis, *op. cit.;* and W. Y. Oi and P. W. Schuldiner, *An Analysis of Urban Travel Demands,* Northwestern University Press, Evanston, 1962.

7 *Ibid.*

8 *Ibid.*

9 Eliot Hurst, "The Structure . . . ," *op. cit.*

10 The "average factor," Detroit, Fratar, Furness, and "Time function iteration" method, are all growth factor methods. See for example T. J. Fratar, "Vehicular Trip Distribution by Successive Approximations," *Traffic Quarterly,* January 1954, Vol. 8, pp. 53–65, or Detroit Metropolitan Area Traffic Study, Vols. 1 and 2, Detroit, 1955–56.

11 A. M. Voorhees, "Forecasting Peak Hours of Travel," Highway Research Board, *Bulletin 203,* 1958, or Tanner, "Factors affecting the Amount of Travel," Road Research Technical Paper No. 51, H.M.S.O., London, 1961.

12 Carroll and Bevis, *op. cit.;* M. Schneider, "Gravity Models and Trip Distribution Theory," *Papers and Procs. of the Regional Science Association,* Vol. 5, 1959, pp. 51–56; and the Chicago Area Transportation Study, Vol. 2, Chicago, 1959.

13 See for example the panel discussion on "Inter-area Travel Formulas," Highway Research Board, *Bulletin 253,* 1960, pp. 128–138.

14 Among others are Howe's "electrostatic field" theory of trip attraction, R. T. Howe, "A Theoretical Prediction of Work-trip Patterns," Highway Research Board, *Bulletin 253,* 1960, pp. 155–165; and Osofsky's use of linear regression, S. Osofsky, "The Multiple Regression Method of Forecasting Traffic Volumes," *Traffic Quarterly,* Vol. 13, 1959, pp. 423–445.

15 Osofsky, *op. cit.*

16 H. S. Lapin, "Structuring the Journey to Work," Philadelphia, University of Pennsylvania Press, 1964; and Sven Godlund, "The Function and Growth of Bus Traffic within the Sphere of Urban Influence," Lund Series in Human Geography, No. 18, 1956.

17 Eliot Hurst, "Land Use . . . ,"; Lapin; Godlund, *op. cit.*

18 Postulate *three,* earlier section.

19 Postulate *one* and *two,* earlier section.

20 Postulate *four,* earlier section.

21 Osofsky, *op. cit.,* p. 440.

22 See E. N. Thomas, "Maps of Residuals from Regression: Their Characteristics and Uses in Geographic Research," Paper No. 2, Department of Geography, State University of Iowa, Iowa City, 1960, espec. pp. 21–24.

23 Osofsky, *op. cit.,* pp. 442–443 *et al.,* discussed the laboriousness of this technique compared to the gravity model.

24 Eliot Hurst, "Land Use . . . ," Oi and Shuldiner, *op. cit.;* or almost any transportation survey.

25 For example, the Chicago Area and Penn-Jersey Transportation Studies used different forms of a probability technique.

The treatment of urban transportation on the levels of Selections 26, 27, and 28, which are representative of a whole substudy within transportation geography, presupposes that we know more about the factors of actual travel motivation and behavior than we actually do. Apart from using such explicit factors as family size or car ownership, a great many other attributes, varying according to group and individual values and goals, are of significant importance for most people. What we now need to investigate are the ways in which individuals themselves view the "choice" situations in which they make travel decisions, rather than simply assuming that those "choice" situations are explicable in economically rational terms or can be understood via the gravity model or regression analysis. The particulars of those "choice" situations are at least of equal importance to the less personal characteristics normally used in travel analyses. Equally the subjective, cultural, and political values present about an individual are at least as important as the more stringent types of economic or rational control.

The final selection in this book examines travel decisions at the more personal level and without the constraints of the more usual level of analysis. It is representative of a small but growing area of transportation geography, that also spills over to the more general area of behavioral geography.

Selection 29

Micromovement and the Urban Dweller

M. E. Eliot Hurst

Conventional urban transportation studies take a macroscopic view of traffic patterns. Despite the larger number of such studies in both North America and Western Europe, surprisingly little is known or understood about the basic underlying human urban activities, functions, and attitudes. Currently there is no reliable information on the *causes* underlying travel demand or on the level of satisfaction with the urban transportation system and its elements.

Existing macroscopic studies have generally been based on a random sample of households for one day's travel by vehicular modes only. In addition, a limited amount of income, occupation, and other household socioeconomic information has been collected, usually by means of a home interview survey. This type of survey has provided the basis for most of the socioeconomic–urban transportation relationships which are known. These procedures have tended to *freeze* the trip maker's response to the system and to make the assumption that *habit patterns* will reliably describe demands in the future, whether 25 or 50 years away.[1] In addition, these studies have used methods such as the "gravity model" to *represent* such habitual movements, without any reference to underlying causes and explanation, since such physical analogies are limited to superficial interrelationships.[2]

There are many shortcomings in these macroscopic surveys. The data currently collected and projected to some future data are essentially habits magnified to a gross level. No attempt is made to measure the individual trip maker's satisfaction with and use of the urban transportation system; one day's response magnified to a zonal trip pattern can be quite misleading. Some investigators have found relatively little temporal stability or repetitive behavior at the microlevel, despite the implicit assumptions made to the contrary by traffic engineers and others. With the ex-

This is a considerably revised version of a paper first given at the annual meeting of the Pacific North West Science Association held at Ellensburg, Washington, 1969. Acknowledgement must be given to Don Gale and Jim Miles, who helped me in the field survey, and to Wendy Eliot Hurst and Ed Gibson, who stimulated my interest in the behavioral approach to urban transportation.

ception of trips to "captive" locations (work, school), the pattern of travel in urban areas over both time and space has been reported as predominantly irregular. Yet macrolevel studies seem to find what they want to find—habitual responses to an extremely stable transportation system.

Trip forecasting and distribution, the basis of planning for future transportation systems, in its turn becomes a matter of establishing present habit patterns, correlating these with existing land use and other socioeconomic characteristics, and projecting both of these patterns forward in order to predict some future demands and then some future system. Since, however, neither of these patterns, nor the parameters, are likely to be descriptive of the future, and since much of the work in predicting future land uses is also carried out with little understanding of forces shaping land use, the prediction of transportation demand is obviously subject to considerable doubt.

The "traditional" approach to urban transportation is open to question on the basis of inadequate statistical techniques and mathematical models, questionable conceptual frameworks, and unrealistic assumptions about human behavior (as for example in Selection 28!). Further investigation is obviously needed into the causes of urban movement, beginning at the individual level, but also stepping into the area of land use development and urban form, as links between individual decisions, transportation systems, and urban activities are identified.[3]

It is generally recognized today that urban transportation studies must seek alternative frameworks to those currently used, and that a great deal more knowledge of the individual's perception and conception of the transport alternatives is required. In fact a substantial literature is coming into being, some of which is reviewed elsewhere.[4] To obtain such information, both the *habits* and the *motives* of the urban traveler must be analyzed and understood. Interest in micromovement, individual travel motivations, and patterns has arisen because of the obvious inadequacy of macrolevel postulates to *explain* travel patterns and associated urban land uses.

In order to move toward an understanding of micromovement, a number of related concepts from the broad area of social science must be explored.

SOCIAL SCIENCE CONCEPTS RELATED TO MICROMOVEMENT

The large and complex real urban world must be handled by the urban dweller, despite the human nervous system's limited capacity for information storage, manipulation, and retrieval. The urban resident thus makes certain simplifications and adjustments, in accordance with his needs and experiences, in the conceptualization of the complex built environment surrounding him. That surrounding environment, and its geographic or spatial dimensions, is apprehended (or "perceived") and cognitively organized by each of us into what have been variously called "mental maps,"[5] "cognitive maps,"[6] "activity spaces,"[7] and so on. These mental or psychological maps are not coterminus with geographic space, since they are distorted by each individual's cognitive processes, which in turn are influenced by a whole range of differing needs, motivations, and learning experiences.[8] The magnitude and direction of the distortion vary from person to person; the urban environment, what Stephen Carr calls "the city of the mind,"[9] as perceived by each individual resident and traveler, will also vary.*

*"The environment is a bigger book than we can read. It contains far more potential information at any moment than we have the cognitive capacity to deal with. Because of our limitations, we are by nature selective." S. Carr, "The City of the Mind," in *Environment for Man*, W. R. Ewald (ed.), Bloomington: Indiana University Press, 1967, p. 205. See also M. E. Eliot Hurst, *I Came to the City* . . . Parts 1 and 4, Boston: Houghton Mifflin, 1973.

This does not necessarily mean that there is a "geography in the head" or a recordable imagery, but that individuals behave *as if* such a conceptualization (a "map") existed. However, various researchers have attempted to make individuals describe an imagined interaction with the environment through sketching a map from memory or by directed recall.[10] Another direction is simply to observe an individual's actions in the built environment and to infer the "image" yielding the observed behavior.[11] Whether individuals are observed, sketch maps, or recall an experience, we are assuming a mental representation of space which is different from some basic geographic reality. David Stea has described this ". . . space of which we are speaking" as "bounded; one-, two-, or three-dimensional; as consisting of a large collection of locations, paths, and interposed barriers."[12]

This brief introduction is based on a number of parallel studies by social scientists. Kurt Lewin, for example, has as the central concept of his "field theory" a **life space,**† which he defines as "the person and the psychological environment as it exists for him . . . at any given time."[13]

All human behavior to Lewin, including thinking, wishing, striving, actions, valuations, and achievements, can be thought of in terms of the function of the life space. This he expressed as $B = F(P, E) = F(L.Sp)$, where behavior B is a function F of the person P and his environment E, which in turn is a function of the life space $L.Sp$. Thus in order to understand individual behavior, ". . . the person and his environment have to be considered as one constellation of interdependent factors."[14] Understanding of this field or life space, Lewin believes, aids the prediction of personal behavior. In this regard he identified a "boundary zone" of the life space:

> . . . certain parts of the physical or social world do affect the state of the life space at that time. The process of perception . . . is intimately linked with this boundary zone because what is perceived is partly determined by the physical "stimuli," that is, that part of the physical world which affects the sensory organs at that time. Another process located in the boundary zone is the "execution" of an action.[15]

Julian Wolpert has also used a spatial concept, in this case to aid the understanding of migration.[16] Wolpert's **action space** resembles Lewin's life space in that it involves the individual's perception of his environment. He states that, although theoretically the individual has access to a very extensive environment, in fact only some limited portion of this

> . . . environment is relevant and applicable for his decision behavior. This immediate subjective environment or action space is the set of place utilities which the individual perceives and to which he responds . . . the subjective action space is perceived by the individual through a sampling process whose parameters are determined by the individual's needs, drives, and abilities.[17]

While the individual may not be conscious of this sampling process, it nevertheless does exist and is involved in the individual's acquisition of knowledge about his environment.

A third space or movement conceptualization which backs up the initial identification of a cognitive map is F. Stuart Chapin's **activity space.**[18] Chapin, a planner, emphasizes the links between the built environment, including the "transportation system," and what he calls "activity systems." The latter are defined as:

> . . . behavior patterns of individuals, families, institutions, and firms which occur in spatial patterns that have meaning for land use . . . there

†The space conceptions, printed in boldface, will be found defined in the glossary on page 503.

> are many aspects of movement systems (activity systems) that pose difficult and complex problems for the planner—many of them in the realm of human behavior.[19]

He emphasizes that too many assumptions are made about the behavior of people and their activities, and that not enough research is directed to underlying causes. Planners, such as transportation planners, assume a constant mode of behavior and ignore rapid changes in community and social systems. As a basis for his activity space, an aid toward understanding behavior, Chapin introduces a typology of activity systems to relate activity agents and types to their various activity systems within the city (Table 29-1). The typology suggests a wide variety of possible destinations that any individual may select, as an initiator of movement. The selection of alternative goals rests with the individual decision maker; once selected, these goals would define an activity system.

Another planner, Kevin Lynch, has stated his interests to be ". . . the visual quality of the American city . . . and . . . the mental image of that city which is held by its citizens."[20] He concentrates on one important visual quality: the *legibility* of the city. Legibility is the way in which its parts (edges, nodes, paths, landmarks, and districts) "can be recognized and . . . organized into a coherent pattern . . . to understand this, we must consider not just the city as a thing in itself, but the city being perceived by its inhabitants."[21] To determine that legibility and to build up a picture of the city's perceived spatial dimensions, Lynch particularly relied on citizens to sketch maps from memory so that the relative positions of the parts of the city in "mental" space could be compared to their positions in real space.

Lynch's work is somewhat static and is couched in macro terms, but it has made some contribution to the idea of micromovement. If an individual perceives the city in a legible manner, his movements through it may become much easier.

The work of other social scientists also contains reference and insights into parallel situations to the life, action, and activity spaces just mentioned. In particular, the extent to which affinity for places or communities is shared by groups of people, and conversely, how a social or class group affects an individual's behavior, have both been topics of study.[22]

RECENT WORK IN GEOGRAPHY

Before an attempt is made to draw these threads together in some conceptualization of a *movement space,* the increased interest by geographers themselves in the general area of perception should be noted. Three major approaches can be distinguished, falling within two broad philosophical paradigms. The three approaches reviewed by Roger Downs in his bibliographic survey[23] are, first, the *structural,* concerned with the identity and structure of space perceptions. What is stored in our minds? How is it stored and structured? What is the relationship between the image and the real world?[24] Secondly, there is the *evaluative,* where the concern is to go one step further, focusing on what factors people consider important in their perceived worlds and how these factors affect decision making.[25] A third avenue of research has been that of *preferences;* given a set of spatially differentiated objects, how do people assess their choice between them?[26] In terms of micromovement, these three avenues of investigation by geographers can provide us with some epistemological props concerning the image of the transportation systems and the built environment; what perceived factors affect modal or route choice; and how the final destination

Table 29-1 A Typology of Activity Systems

Activity agents	Activity types	Activity systems
Firms	Productive activities	Goods-producing activities (extraction, processing, communications, distribution) Service activities (to firms, institutions, households, and individuals)
Institutions	General welfare activities	Human development activities (education, religious and recreation) Basic community service activities (police, fire, water, waste disposal, etc.) Activities for welfare of special (groups—labor, social, etc.)
Households and individuals	Residential activities	
	a. Income-producing	On-the-job activity, moonlighting Professional activity (union, professional societies, etc.) Activity to improve income-producing potential (evening school, inventing, writing, etc.)
	b. Child-raising and family activities	Overseeing and participating in play Overseeing children's study (practicing, etc.) Expeditions with children (family outings, picnics, etc.)
	c. Education and intellectual development	Attending school, college, adult classes, etc. Attending meetings for improvement of education (arts, PTA, Art Guild, Music for Children) Participating in drama, orchestra, Great Books, and similar group activities Attending plays, exhibitions, etc.
	d. Spiritual development	Attending and participating in organized social activities Taking part in organizations concerned with human welfare
	e. Social activities	Attending and participating in organized social activities (country club, city club, athletic club, etc.) Engaging in informal forms of socializing (visiting friends, dating, attending parties, etc.)

Table 29-1 (continued)

Activity agents	Activity types	Activity systems
	f. Recreation and relaxation	Attending spectator events (ball games, races, fights, etc.) Participating in recreation activities with others (golf, tennis, bowling, softball, swimming, fishing, etc.) Individual forms of physical and mental relaxation (taking naps, gardening, walking, reading, viewing TV, working on hobby, crafts, etc.)
	g. Club activities	Taking part in special-interest clubs (garden club, stamp club, etc.) Attending luncheon or dinner clubs (Rotary, Altrusa, etc.) Attending meetings of patriotic groups (American Legion, D.A.R., etc.) Attending meetings of fraternal groups (Masons, Elks, Eastern Star, etc.)
	h. Community service and political activities	Attending and/or participating in civic improvement activities (LWV, Civic Association, etc.) Serving on City Council, Planning Board, etc. Political action activities Fund-raising activities and similar volunteer efforts
	i. Activities associated with food, shopping, health and similar needs	Meals at home, restaurants Shopping—convenience, specialty, and consumer goods Visits to doctor, hospital Home and yard maintenance

Source: F. Stuart Chapin, **Urban Land Use Planning Urbana: University of Illinois Press, 1955, pp. 226, 242–243.**

point is chosen from an array of end points.

These three approaches fall within two basic frameworks—the *behaviorist,* which attempts to measure rigorously and evaluate these perceptual dimensions,[27] and the *behavioral,* which attempts to obtain explanation and understanding of both the measurable and unmeasurable dimensions and where the tendency is to consider alternative philosophical frameworks in addition to scientific empiricism.[28] Given this work in geography, attention has been given to micromovement, but largely within the behaviorist framework.

Lawrence Brown and Eric Moore, in a study tangential to our concern with micromovements, focused on intra-urban residence movements,[29] postulated that the search for housing vacancies begins with a household's

awareness space, formed by its **activity space** and its **indirect contact space.** As the search process begins, a **search space** is part of the awareness space, but after initial explorations it expands rapidly. The awareness space is that part of the total urban space familiar to the household through its direct activity space (that part of the urban area known through direct contact as the result of day-to-day activities) and its indirect contact space (that part of the city which the household perceives secondhand through such channels as mass media, advertising, etc.). Brown and Moore attempt to combine the decisions to move, and where to relocate, into a single extended process of adjustment to stress. Passage through the life cycle is seen as creating certain stresses which, together with aspirations, can be overcome by adjusting aspirations downward at the existing location or by movement into a more satisfactory environment.

As will be seen later, this structure, and to some degree the vocabulary, are useful in developing a general heuristic framework for micromovement. The Brown-Moore decision model (Fig. 29-1) begins with a household subjected to *stress* from two sources: (1) internal changes in family structure which make the house or neighborhood unsuitable and (2) external changes in the immediate environment which make the location unsuitable for the particular household. Although both types of stress change through time, they identify the main source as lying within the household. Stress is converted to behaviorist adjustments called *strain,* according to the household's particular reaction to stress. The Brown-Moore model operationally defines stress as the difference between the *need set* (as defined by the household) and the *environment set.* Strain is the resulting alteration of the need set or the environment set which requires either a redefinition of needs and a decision to stay at that site, or, above some threshold of presumably unalterable stress, to initiate a search for an alternative site.

Once the decision to eliminate stress by relocation is made, the need set is made explicit in the form of an **aspiration region**—i.e., an area within the awareness space which could provide a new location. Some of these locations may be aspired to, but not actively sought, since they may be too expensive, too far from the work place or services. Thus aspiration regions and search spaces may not be coterminus. Operationally each alternative site, with attribute vector $\overline{X}_j$, must be within

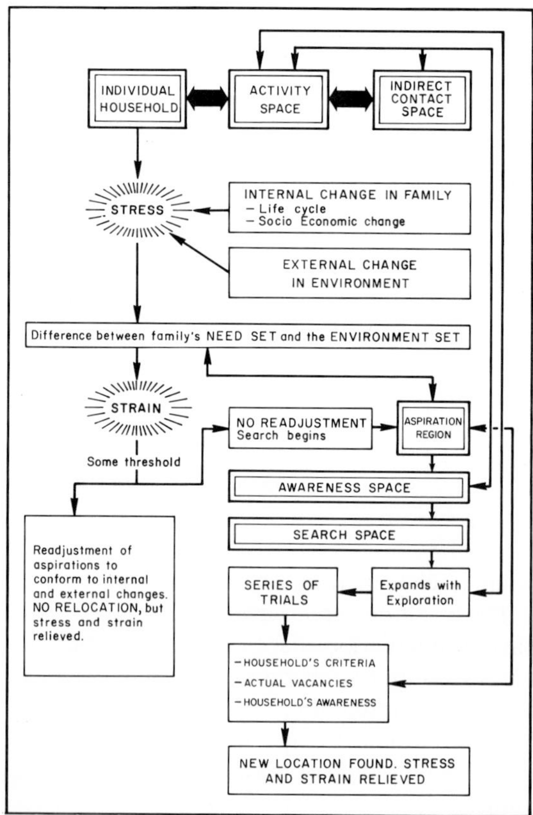

Fig. 29-1 The conceptual framework of the Brown-Moore decision model.

the upper limit vector $\overline{A}_u$ and the lower limit vector $\overline{A}_1$ which define the aspiration region:

$$\overline{A}_1 < \overline{X}_j < \overline{A}_u$$

The model devotes considerable effort to defining the search procedure by which vacancies are discovered and evaluated. Acceptable housing alternatives are defined by the intersection of three sets of factors: $\overline{V}$, the criteria set up by the household; $\overline{K}$, the existence and distribution of housing vacancies; and $\overline{A}$, the awareness of those vacancies by the households concerned. The intersection of $\overline{V}.\overline{K}.\overline{A}$ will indicate available vacancies which are both perceived by and acceptable to the household.‡ In the case of micromovement, in place of "vacancy" one could read "alternative destination." The search begins with an awareness space formed by the activity space and the indirect contact space. As the search begins, the search space is part of the awareness space, but as the search continues it expands rapidly. The initial experiences modify the aspiration region and may change the mode of search because of time pressures; thus early preferences for informal driving around may be replaced by an organized search with a real estate agent. Carl Werthman, in a study of relocation choices, has noted that shopping for a new home is not so much a comparison of alternatives as it is a succession of *trials*.

From the work of Brown, Moore and others, within the context of urban housing relocations, it is only a short step to the framework of an **action space** postulated by Frank Horton and David Reynolds.[30] Based on Wolpert's earlier work in migration decision making, this space is defined as "the collection of all urban locations about which the individual has information and the subjective utility or preference he associates with these locations." Fig. 29-2 describes the conceptual framework lying behind that definitional statement.

Horton and Reynolds begin with the assumption, noted earlier, that only a limited portion of the built environment is relevant to spatial behavior. The degree to which an individual's action space reflects the total environment depends on his abilities to collect and assimilate information, which in turn vary with educational experience, income, social status and class group, etc. Since no two individuals will perceive the built environment from exactly the same point simultaneously, and since each one bases his interpretation of information on past experiences, action spaces will vary from individual to individual. Like Brown and Moore, Horton and Reynolds stress the importance of change and the temporal dimension, and they note among other factors the effect of the learning process itself as well as external changes such as the introduction of the private automobile. The last, with its time/space flexibility of operation, has had profound effects on the extent of an individual's action spaces. In addition, Horton and Reynolds stress an individual's time preferences and time budget. Here they argue, following Richard Meier's work,[31] that time preferences will vary systematically through an individual's life cycle from birth through maturity and old age, and that action space will similarly change. However, concomitant factors—income, education, occupations, etc.—will also change and affect the time/space bounds of the action space. "For example, the low income factory operative, although he might wish to allocate more of his leisure time to certain types of space-consuming activities, is constrained by his

‡The vector product $\overline{V}.\overline{K}.\overline{A}.$, is represented by $\overline{V}$ as the $1 \times n$ row vector of available vacancies; $\overline{K}$ as an $n \times n$ matrix in which the entry in the diagonal equals 1 if the vacancy is known to the householder and 0 if not; and $\overline{A}$ is a matrix like $\overline{K}$, with entries equal to 1 if acceptable (within the aspiration space) and 0 if not. The result is a row vector indicating available vacancies perceived by, and acceptable to, the household.

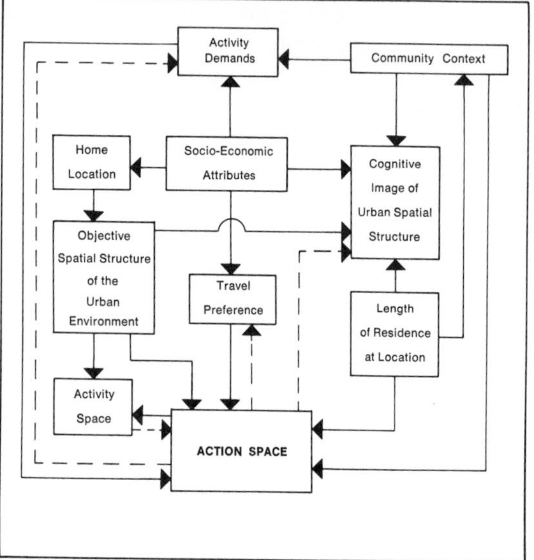

Fig. 29-2 The conceptual framework of the Horton-Reynolds *action space* concept. (F. E. Horton and D. Reynolds, "Action Space Differentials in Cities," in H. McConnell and D. W. Yaseen (eds.), *Perspectives in Geography* Vol. 1., *Models of Spatial Variation,* Dekalb, Illinois: Northern Illinois University Press, 1971, p. 87.)

income and work schedule from doing so."[32]

Thus in Fig. 29-2, assuming that an individual has already selected his residence, action space is postulated as a result of various interlinked components. These include the activity space centered on residence and work place; the cognitive image of the urban area, built upon the individual's visual experience incurred on his way to work and other regular routes, and upon the visual images of his immediate residential areas; his set and level of activity demands; his travel preferences, and his expectations of satisfaction at certain types of destinations such as regional shopping centers, gas stations, or the central business district. In addition to these factors and the objective spatial structure (the actual built environment), a number of socioeconomic factors are included, such as occupation, income, age, marital status, home location, length of occupancy of home, and the community context including social network ties, and membership of community or other groups.[33]

Most of their empirical work has focused on the community context and income differentials, intercommunity differences in action spaces in so far as distance biases arise, and the effect of income and location on an individual's idea of residential quality. In time, their aim is to "quantitatively specify the relationships in the conceptual model of inputs to an action space." Initial results have indicated that income per se is less important than residence location in action space formation, but their work is ongoing and it is too early to speculate on their final results.[34]

The Horton-Reynolds scheme is significant as another input to the microlevel of travel behavior, although by itself, especially at the operational level, their work is behavioristic and so far has not revealed explanatory factors, other than at a statistical level.§

TOWARDS A CONCEPT OF MICROMOVEMENT

In order to understand the nature of individual travel behavior, we need to examine a number of ancillary propositions. H. A. Simon, for example, has put forward the notion of *bounded rationality.* Simon has a parallel concern to ours, that of the ineffectiveness of propositions and notions produced by macrostudies to provide answers to problems at the microlevel.[38] He introduces the idea of the individual as *satisficer* as an alternative to the

§Other work has also been undertaken by geographers, based on the kind of formulations set out above. Thus, Johnston[35] found evidence of a hierarchy of action spaces in his work, and Mercer[36] noted that recreation trips resulted in wedge-shaped mental maps similar to those proposed by Adams.[37]

economist's conception of *economic man.*‖ He does not deny the validity of the latter conception for certain types of problems, but he does argue that as soon as one turns from "very broad economic problems" to those which require more intricate investigation, the number of anomalies becomes more frequent. Simon states his principle of bounded rationality as follows:

> The capacity of the human mind for formulating and solving complex problems is very small compared with the size of the problems whose solutions is required for objectively rational behavior in the real world—or even for a reasonable approximation to such objective rationality.[39]

If this is so, then to attempt to predict individual choice by classical macrotheory without consideration of man's psychological properties which influence such choice is to place such a goal out of reach. For this reason Simon puts forward the idea of man as a "satisficer" rather than an "optimizer."

> The key to the simplification of the choice process in both bases is the replacement of the goal of *maximizing* with the goal of *satisficing,* of finding a course of action that is "good enough" . . . an organism that satisfices has no need of estimates of joint probability distribution, or of complete and consistent preference orderings of all possible alternatives of action.[40]

The concept of the "bounded rational satisficer" allows for the individual's not being cognizant of all the available alternatives, a more real situation than the concept of economic man. However, if such is the true case, it becomes important to define the psychological determinants of satisfaction for the individual and to measure the role they play in the establishment of patterns of movement.

Jean Piaget takes this further when he maintains that the conceptions of space are not an inherent quality, but rather are learned traits. ". . . It is quite obvious that the perception of space involves a gradual construction and certainly does not exist ready made at the outset of mental development."[41]

As a result of his research, Piaget was able to show that images and sense data perform the function of relating what they signify. Because of this, it is obvious that individuals vary in the symbolic meaning which they place on space.

Piaget's work is not confined to space perception. He makes a definite distinction between the perception and conception of space. Thus he states:

> In examining successive stages in the child's development we drew a fundamental distinction between spatial perception and the earliest spatial imagery. Because spatial perception takes place in the presence of the object whereas the image arises only in its absence, perceptual space develops far more rapidly than conceptual space, the former even reaching a projective and quasimetric level while the latter has barely begun. There is therefore an interval of several years between perceptual and conceptual construction, despite their pursuing a similar path of development. And moreover, should the existence of these two distinct levels be overlooked, the illusion arises that the idea of space begins to be worked out on the basis of simple euclidean shapes. The actual study of children's reactions to such shapes between the ages of 2–4 years showed that from the perceptual standpoint these reactions are not innate but developed . . . while at the same time such shapes are not yet conceptualized. . . .[42]

Piaget analyzed children's art to provide an example of concept development as characterized through representation. He suggests

‖This crucial distinction between the optimizer and the satisficer is pursued at length by myself elsewhere.

three distinct stages of development characteristic of children's drawing and notes that such development is not complete until they become eight or nine years old.

Rene Dubos has expressed the implications that can be drawn from both Simon and Piaget as follows:

> Physicians and experimenters interested in the forces which determined the physical and mental processes of man find it useful to differentiate between genetic, historical, and environmental factors, or between conscious and unconscious responses. In reality, however, man is an integrated entity and all these forces operate simultaneously in every event of his life. The body and the mind are the living records of countless influences which have shaped each individual person from the most distant past to the present instant. Man is indeed the product of his history. . . .[43]

Dubos in this statement makes two points which are pertinent to micromovement. First, man must be looked on as an integrated being, with the factors of his environment, history, and biological processes. Second, at any one time man is influenced by these integrated influences at two levels: his past, which produces much of his habitual responses, and his present influences, which are conceptualized within limited bounds that are elastic and change with extended awareness.

An additional dimension has been supplied by the phenomenologist O. F. Bollnow.[44] He takes Minkowski's idea of a "lived space"[45] and develops a conception of an experiential **felt space.** This is space as it appears concretely to an individual in his experience. But that "concreteness" depends strongly on how an individual *feels* at a given moment. In that sense, lived space depends on an individual's present disposition.

> We all know how the distance of remote objects changes with atmospheric conditions. In sunshine they recede into the blue mist and in the clarity preceding a rain again approach within reach. So also they change with the moods of man . . . when fear departs the world spreads out and opens a larger space for action, in which a man can move freely and easily.[46]

To the dimensions of bounded rationality of learned perceptions and conceptions, of physiological factors, we must now also add that of "being." This is not to argue that we can explain why a householder chooses mode *X* over *Y* or route *A* over *B* only in terms of his bad temper that morning at being served the proverbial two-minute egg (which would take the disaggregation of a macromovement to an extreme) but in terms of a whole subset of personal experiences which are explicable only in phenomenological terms. In this vein, psychiatrists

> . . . have analyzed the space experience of the dancer: it is an undirected space in which the movement of the dance back and forth and around a point of origin on a restricted surface can still be executed without a feeling of being hemmed in . . . [there seems to be] . . . a "present" space reposing in the present without a future commitment. In it movement takes place which rests in itself . . . [this] . . . contrasts sharply with the "historical space" of our purposive activity. . . .[47]

A starting point of note to all recreational geographers!

In their attempt to provide an explanatory framework for perception and conception, geographers have particularly turned to psychology, and most notably to gestalt psychology and stimulus-response theory.[48] These frameworks have been criticized for their failure to consider more than just the perception of the stimuli. To this end, Harold and Margaret Sprout have suggested the term *apperception* (i.e., as perceived and reacted to) of the objective environment as the necessary unit of study, since such an apperceptual process involves more than just perception.[49]

Charles Osgood goes one step still further when he states:

> . . . psychologists . . . limit themselves to observing what goes into the organism (stimuli) and what comes out (responses). Between these two lines a *great unknown,* the nervous system . . . psychological theory is made up of hunches about what goes on in this little black box . . . the S-R model may adequately handle rather simple relations between stimulus and response variables, but it says little or nothing about either the integration of sensory events (perception) or the integration of response events (motor skill), and . . . has not had much to contribute to an understanding of symbolic processes.[50]

This suggests that there is a complex of variables involved in encoding and decoding stimuli. As a result the framework within which behavior, including micromovement, is conceptualized, must make allowances for all these variables (Fig. 29-3). Such a framework requires the understanding of the individual's apperception to his environment as related to personal goals of his socio-economic group. Several investigators have concentrated on these latter goals, as, for example, Sonnenfeld, who suggests that "the major determinants of spatial and landscape preference are most obviously culture, society, and economy. Culture is of basic importance."[51]

In anthropology, Evans-Pritchard, in his study of different socio-economic levels, notes differences in the perception of distance:

> A Nuer village may be equidistant from two other villages, but if one of these belongs to another tribe and the other to the same tribe, it may be said to be structurally more distant from the first than from the second. A Nuer tribe which is separated by 40 miles from another Nuer tribe is structurally nearer to it than to a Dinka tribe from which it is separated by only 20 miles.[52]

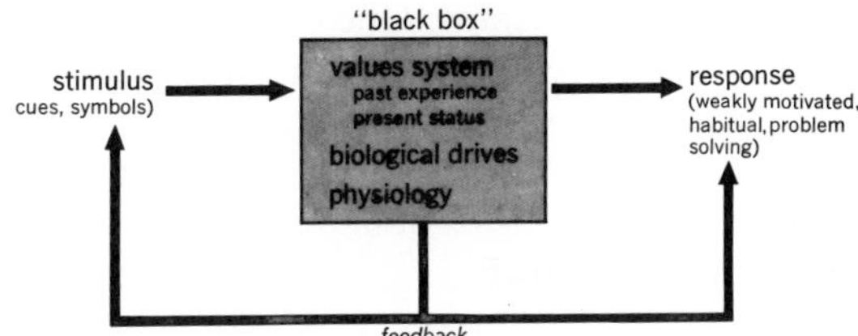

Fig. 29-3 Framework for travel behavior. (M. E. Eliot Hurst, *A Geography of Economic Behaviour,* North Scituate, Mass.: Duxbury Press, 1972, p. 48.)

Such a situation infers a very wide differentiation in distance perception, though it may be that in our own society, the variations would be less. The important point, however, is that group and kinship bonds play a significant role in the perception of distance, which obviously would influence the shape and direction of movement behavior and space.[53]

These three sections involved with trends in geographical and other thought suggest that man should be considered more at the micro-level than past theories and concepts of man's relationship with his environment have done. Man appears to be subjected to differing experiences because of the filtering processes of perception, conception, values, experience and varying socio-economic organization. Thus the apperceived environment is not a place which can be located in physical space, but rather only in the psychic space which is set for him by his needs, desires, abilities, and awareness.

Thus we have reached a point where we can postulate the existence of individual, and perhaps group, psychic spaces which are unique to the persons involved. Such a theme has two major weaknesses. First, there would be a tendency to overemphasize the unique qualities of the individual environment, and second, there would be a tendency toward descriptive analysis rather than a seeking out of causal relationships. One of the basic problems in formulating ideas of micromovement is to seek out explanatory variables.

MOVEMENT SPACE

There now seems little doubt that as an individual moves around an urban area in the course of work trips, shopping, social visits, or finding a new residence location, he perceives, learns, feels, conceives of, and then reinforces a more or less unique spatial pattern, an image of the objective total built environment. Although there is no direct proof of the existence of mental maps, there is little doubt that individuals do react to some cognitive structure which represents only a selected part of the urban area. It follows also that the dimensions and orientation of this map are strongly constrained by the individual's perception of such things as distance and neighborhood quality, and that a change in the place of residence results in the learning of a new cognitive map and thus the ascendancy of a new set of movement responses.

It is at this point that the earlier conceptions of personal space can be distilled, for our purposes in looking at micromovement, to a **movement space**—the perceived, felt, and conceived part of the built environment within which movement occurs.[54] Examination of such a space conception could lead us to a better understanding of urban travel patterns.

This movement space is the specifically restricted space within which the trip maker receives his stimuli and makes his responses. It is a universe of space and time within which the person conceives and feels that he can or might move about in, and is only a limited portion of the actual environment. To the trip maker, the space about him is the more or less immediate subjectively perceived portion of the environment within which sets of positional utilities occur. This movement space is the surface over which the organism moves and on which it depends for its needs, drives, goals, and perceptual apparatus.[55] This subjective environment is filtered through conscious and unconscious brain processes programmed by his needs, desires, and abilities.[56] The limits of the movement space unique to a particular trip maker are set by his finite abilities to perceive and by his learning experiences. It might in fact be possible to identify three types of movement space (Fig. 29-4):

1 A *core,* the frequently traveled space with which the trip maker is most familiar. This is the space within which regular journeys, frequent visits to friends, and shopping trips are made.

2 A *median* area, the occasionally traveled space within which journeys to visit relatives and on holidays would be made by many people.

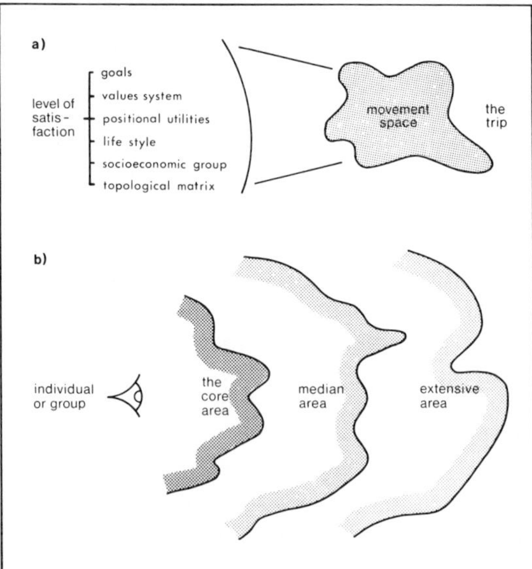

Fig. 29-4 ***a.*** The conception of movement space and the determination of making a journey.

b. The varying intensities of information about movement space. (M. E. Eliot Hurst, *A Geography of Economic Behaviour*, North Scituate, Mass.: Duxbury Press, 1972, p. 300.)

3 An *extensive* movement space, the conceived, concept-learned, or cosmological space.

For some trip makers all three types of movement might be virtually coterminus; for others they might vary considerably. For the purposes of urban transportation studies the first type of movement space is of the greatest importance. Even this movement space varies from the limited realm of a young child to, say, the extensive realm of an international entrepreneur. This space varies with experience and intensity of contact with the environment. The degree of contact could perhaps be measured by knowing the rate or receipt of "hubits," or informational bits.[57]

The trip maker can now be conceived of within a particular space, perceiving, besides his origin, a number of alternative destinations or positional utilities among which he chooses a goal, according to the valence of the intended destination(s). His positional utilities, however conspicuous at any one time, will mainly include a cluster of alternate destinations within close proximity; all positional utilities will be contained within the limits of the trip maker's movement space. The wider his communication with friends and relatives, his contact with mass media and travel, the more comprehensive will be his movement space.

MICROMOVEMENT

It is now necessary to determine what factors are common to the movement space and behavior of all individuals. Based on the earlier review of related work in geography and other social sciences, eight elements can be postulated as holding significance to micromovements. These are the *trip; goals* that influence the initiation of a trip; *positional utilities* that influence the initiation of a trip; the *topological matrix,* or matter of residence location; the *values system* operational for the trip maker; *style of life* of the trip maker; socioeconomic or *cultural determinants,* and the extent of fulfillment or *level of satisfaction* as a result of a trip. These replace the conventional measures of age, income, and household size used by the average urban transportation survey. These eight factors are related conceptually, as is shown in Fig. 29-5.

THE TRIP

Implicit in micromovement is the *trip.* Macrolevel studies have used various definitions, but for present purposes the trip can be defined as "travel from one point to another for a particular purpose by an individual trip maker by any mode or modes."[58] Emphasis should be placed on *purpose,* the objective or goal, as obviously the trip is not terminated until some objective is fulfilled (either satisfactory or otherwise). Thus a trip may be *simple,* as with a work or school journey, an uninterrupted journey from origin (home) to destination (work place), even though several modes of transport are involved. The trip is completed when the objective is fulfilled. Secondly, trips may be *multiple;* if the trip maker combines a single trip to work or school with the purpose of shopping, for example, it may be one-way or a *round* trip. The latter begins and ends at the same origin; obviously multiple trips consist of segments, each segment being a part trip to intervening destinations. The multiple trip is terminated when all purposes are fulfilled. Further inquiry into relationships between movement space and varying trip types could help in the explanation of why movement occurs.

GOALS

The trip must then have a purpose, objective, or *goal,* even though this may not be consciously formulated. The objective is to ac-

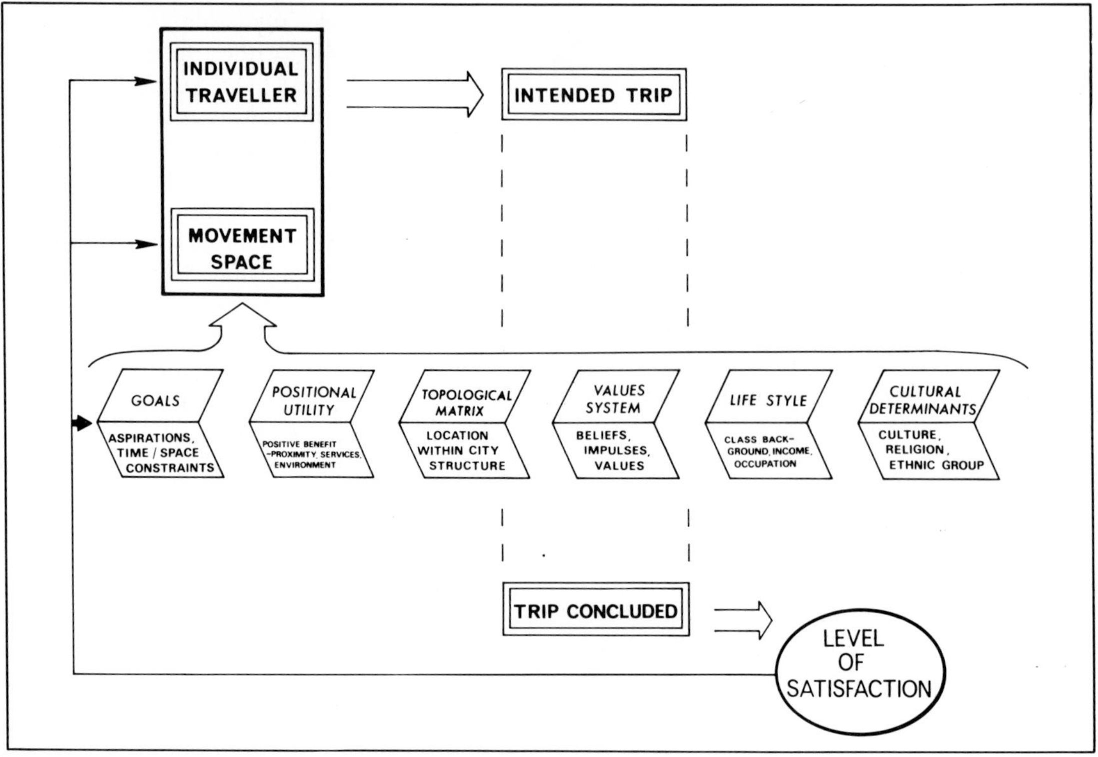

Fig. 29-5 Suggested conceptual framework for movement space.

complish goal events at one or more *intended* destinations, so that the trip decision involves both the identification of an event and a point(s) at which it occurs. To someone making the decision to begin a journey, a goal event is a desired or intended action that is expected to be fulfilled at a particular point in space and time, even though the latter may be indefinite at the time of decision.

Cyert and March use four concepts, though in a different context, which are applicable to the decision-making process involved in goal implementation:

1 Consideration of how goals arise, change over time, and how the individual attends to them.

2 Consideration of expectations of goals and how and when new information or new alternatives are processed.

3 How the choice of alternatives are ordered and the selection is made.

4 Concern with the difference between the choice made and the decision actually implemented.[59]

While only the first of these considers goals per se, the remaining three have considerable bearing on goal achievement. To these elements of alternatives, change, information, selection, and control must be added other variables. Time pressure, for instance, can play a significant role: ". . . the presence of two goals will introduce a consistency requirement—the time consumed in attaining one goal will limit the time available for pursuit of the other."[60] The individual may place other constraints on fulfillment. For example, specific time and distance allocations may be set as maximum constraints. If a goal is not realized within these periods, all alternatives may be rejected despite a high probability of fulfillment.

Goals are also not confined to the individual trip maker but may be set by the joint participation of the household, social group, or subcultural affiliation. Some goals may not be freely selected but instead influenced by internal pressures, as for example, in the use of a particular shop because of friendship with the owner or because this is where people of this particular life style "always shop." Finally, consideration must be given to the role of substitution; at some point or level the trip maker will accept a substitute for the original goal. This level may vary as a function of time or distance, or when a factor such as the values system becomes operational. As with many of these aspects of micromovement, these variables will be difficult to identify.

Distinct from these interactions or goals are actual occurrences, such as a particular transaction. A transaction is any significant event which consciously terminates the trip or sequence, whether it be premeditated or spontaneous. The point at which this occurs becomes the actual destination, which may be a particular establishment or a conglomerate such as a shopping center where a number of transactions will occur. The goal event, the intended destination, and the degree of determinateness all change as the goal is approached.

Having identified the trip and the goal, as well as the intended destination, occurrence, and destination point, we can now examine the initial motivation, the isolation of the desire or tension within a traveler (conscious or not) which he hopes to satisfy in the course of a trip—that is, the translation of a desire into an action-decision.

POSITIONAL UTILITY

Individual movement is an expression of spatial interaction, movement being the means of correcting any spatial imbalance. Thus spatial interaction occurs because people function at different points in space, and because, in order to do so and to communicate with one another, they must pass through a communications system. With activity specialization, origins and destinations, desires and fulfillments have become separated.[61] Thus when the individual has a need which cannot be fulfilled at his origin, he must seek out a destination from the many available which he believes will best fulfill it.

To represent this stage of the travel motivation, we can use the concept of *utility*. This refers to the fulfilling of a need and is separate from "goals," which are at another level of conceptualization. Goals refer to how one is motivated to integrate the fulfillment or a number of separate utilities, and to the degree of utility expected before the initiation of the trip. The utility raised by the need and the goal of the trip are not necessarily of the same intensity.

The idea of utility, man's desire to fulfill his need or needs, begins with the concept of "intendedly rational man" who can differentiate between courses of action by way of their relative utility, even though man has a finite ability to perceive or calculate.[62] The trip maker has a level of aspiration and expected attainment adjusted by experience. This threshold level operates as an evaluative mechanism to distinguish between positive or negative new utilities.[63] Transferring this notion to the travel decision environment and to a spatial context, we can say that a *posi-*

tional utility indicates the net utilities derived from the trip maker's integration at some point in space. The threshold for the trip maker is a function of his experience of previous travel. The positional utility is positive or negative, indicating the trip maker's satisfaction or dissatisfaction with the anticipated move. Just as there are degrees of satisfaction and dissatisfaction, so there are degrees of attraction or repulsion. "The process itself is self-adjusting because aspirations tend to adjust to the attainable. Satisfaction leads to slack which may induce a lower level of attainment. Dissatisfaction acts as a stimulus to search behavior."[64]

Assuming, then, this intendedly rational behavior, the planning of a trip from an origin to a destination is the result of a decision-making process which recognizes differences in utility associated with different places. Table 29-2 suggests an array of variables which might be important.[65] The trip maker moves to a destination whose characteristics he knows to possess or promise a relatively higher utility than other destinations. In this sense movement reflects a subjective positional utility evaluation. The move from origin to destination can be conceived of in this way as proceeding from varyingly perceived stimuli within a satisfaction framework. Some of these processes will be relatively simple, such as the decisions preceding the journey to work or school, for instance, while others, such as the decisions prior to shopping, pleasure trips, or social visits will be more complex.

Movement space thus includes the range of choices defined by the trip maker's evaluatory abilities. Movement space fashioned in this way includes not just the trip maker's origin but also a finite number of alternative destinations presented to him through a combination of search and communication. The movement space becomes a set of destinations, intended or not, toward which the trip maker has a set of utilities. He attaches a utility to his present position (the origin or the trip) and assigns relatively higher or lower utilities to the alternative destinations. The variables are the number of alternative destinations and their spatial arrangement with respect to the origin. The destinations may be neighbors' homes within the same block, homes of friends in another suburb, or relatives in another urban area. Not all of these alternatives may be presented simultaneously, since as mentioned earlier there are other constraints, such as time and cost.

Table 29-2 Variables Found Relevant to Positional Utility

Accessibility or proximity:
CBD, major highways, public transportation, work, shopping, schools, parks, playgrounds

Physical characteristics of neighborhood:
Street and sidewalk conditions (paved?, well lit?), street patterns, privacy, neighborhood beauty, cleanliness, quietness, spaciousness

Services and facilities:
The quality of police protection, fire protection, sewer and water system

Social environment:
Neighborhood friendliness, neighborhood prestige, social-economic-ethnic-racial composition of neighborhood

Individual site and dwelling:
Lot size, topography, trees and landscaping, house size, house design, rent or purchase value, maintenance costs

Source: L. A. Brown and D. B. Longbrake, "Migration Flows in Intra-urban Space: An Operational View of Place Utility," mimeograph, Department of Geography, University of Iowa, 1968, p. 3.

TOPOLOGICAL MATRIX

Location in respect to the total urban structure, literally a topological matrix, has been stressed in all earlier studies of micromovement. It is in part linked to positional utility and to values systems and life styles.

The residence site and situation, and similarly those of the work place, are obvious foci in the daily lives of individuals. John Adams has come to the conclusion that the typical urban resident stylistically views his city as a narrow wedge focused on the central city and running from the outer suburbs through the home neighborhood.[66] Adams argues that areas on either side of the wedge and on the far side of the city are parts of the median and extensive spaces rather than the core movement space. This is not to say that the individual does not hold attitudes and opinions (positional utilities) about points outside that wedge. They may in fact be strongly positive or negative, but since they lie outside the residence/work place-focused trips, they are not part of the clearly defined mental map of the individual. In this case the topological location of the individual's house and work place may be crucial axes in determining his movement space.

VALUES SYSTEM

Recognizing the existence of alternative goals, routes, modes, times, and varying residential location, the trip maker must come to a *decision;* that is, the trip maker becomes a decision maker. Hence a judgment has to be made between various positional utilities, a judgment which cannot be divorced from the trip maker's value system.

> The essential thrust of the argument is that a statement of fact is itself a statement of judgment affected by the whole set of the mind and outlook of the person making the statement. Hence, to distinguish the "is" from the "ought" is both impossible and meaningless. To confine the decision-maker to taking account only of so-called fact would not assume his objectivity or neutrality.[67]

An individual's operative value system has components which are subtly interrelated. Some have identified values with "goal events," whereas others see them as "basic" values equivalent to human "motives" or "needs."[68] The problem becomes one of distinguishing between values as related to basic needs and those that are preference oriented as a result of having to choose between competing goals and desires. Two other related concepts are those of "beliefs" and "impulses." The first of these, though interwoven with the individual's value system, does not constitute the value system or the norms involved but tends to be an internal set of perceptions regarding the individual's role in relation to his world. Impulses, on the other hand, influence actions without regard to value or beliefs and are almost compulsive in nature. The following operational indices of values have been suggested: first, simple declarations of approval and disapproval; secondly, statements of what should or should not be done; and finally, expressions of guilt, shame, or demands for punishment.[69] Again, the identification of these factors and their relationship to movement behavior may be difficult to show empirically.

LIFE STYLE

The fact that different life styles exist within any given community is well documented.[70] The concern here is how the style of life of an individual will affect his movement space. To this end, Boskoff states, "a style of life is a meaningful composite of values, activities, possessions, and motives . . . a distinctive style of life takes years to develop—and years to unlearn—and therefore is an important source of stability in the flux of urban stratification . . . urban studies have identified six, and possibly seven, styles of life."[71] Measurement of life styles has been carried out, and many criteria are laid down by which to do this in Western society. Only by actual field tests could we empirically show that the "social elite" have a more extensive movement space than the "exurban style" (two of Boskoff's categories). In the meantime, we can only hypothesize that this relationship occurs. However, it is unlikely to be a result of this alone, and socioeconomic or cultural factors are no doubt interrelated.

CULTURAL DETERMINANTS

It was stated earlier that culture determines how an individual perceives his environment. The perception differential will play a role in the movement behavior of an individual. Webber suggests that culture plays a major role in establishing the propensity to interact as distance varies.[72] Webber states that the propensity to perceive movement and movement opportunities results from a composite of factors. Historical change brings about increased social mobility; some persons retain life styles of past periods; and there is a mixing of cultural groups with varying cultural determinants. The combination of these factors produces a conflict of perceptions because of the unequal rates of change between the unbounded mobility patterns and the bounded value systems of sociocultural life styles.

LEVEL OF SATISFACTION

As Fig. 29-5 shows, the decision having been made, and the trip carried through, there is an important feedback, i.e., the learning experience expressed as satisfaction or dissatisfaction with the trip. Most research in this area comes from the consumer-tertiary activities area, concerned with repetitive purchases of one product or brand.[73] In the case of route or modal choice, the experience of a choice decision must be registered in some part of the cognitive map (what psychologists call "reinforcement"). The future cycles of the decision process depend on how and where reinforcement occurs. If the trip choice was completely satisfying at each successive decision point, the traveler would "learn" to make the same trip choice with fewer and fewer cognitive activities. That is, memory of the means previously used is increased, goals and positional utilities are more firmly established, and the mental map is increasingly strengthened. In time, where satisfaction was achieved, route or modal choice may become habitual. Evidence shows, however, that the high degree of satisfaction needed to produce such a repetitive pattern is largely confined to journeys to work or school, and that in most other trip making considerable variance occurs. Presumably in these cases lesser rather than greater utility was achieved, and a low level of satisfaction resulted. This learning experience again feeds back to the cognitive structure, but it causes greater search activity rather than habitual responses on future trip choice occasions.

CONCLUSION

The assumptions implicit in this heuristic representation of micromovement are: (1) individuals behave in accordance with mental representations of a physical urban reality and (2) the mental map is influenced by a series of factors, unique in their degree and interplay, such as positional utility, life style, value system, and geographic position in the city. These behavioral factors are said to influence daily travel patterns, choice of mode, and choice of route. Because of individual cognitive variations, those movements when analyzed at the microscale reveal a rather different pattern than the macro surveys of car ownership and distance variables.

Many investigators in urban movement studies, or related studies in the social sciences, have traveled the path laid out here.

The behaviorist at this point urgently tries to find measures, even invents them, in order to provide an orderly way of quantifying his data and postulates. The different qualities suggested here are not concrete facts, such as income or family size, but rather are linked notions like aspiration and arousal levels, feelings, levels of uncertainty and redundancy, ideology, and information. It may not be possible in terms of scientific empiricism to measure, say, the amount of information received or the degree to which the individual trip maker could use that information. Measures would have to account for the relationship of the complexity of different sets, and the types of information which are gathered by the trip maker and how they are filtered, selected, and evaluated. The same consideration would have to be given to the techniques for measurement of the other themes. Some researchers are working on parallel problems: for example, Hebb on arousal levels, Berlyne on the effects of redundancy, and Kate and Wohwill on stimuli and response to the physical environment.[74]

The existence of uniqueness within the system of movement space creates a problem of aggregation. This process is usually accomplished through the selection of only those variables which appear to be meaningful. Meaningful behavior is usually linked with notions of motive and reason. However, some action takes on meaning only as it relates to something else, with the result that meaning is attached to movement solely within the context of how this is viewed by the whole set of interactions, and not only as it is applied to the individual. Thus Aron states ". . . all the subjects of investigation which are attributed to sociology . . . or the relations between social conditions and mental constructions . . . are in fact difficult to isolate, and have the character of total *phenomena* which are connected with society as a whole and with the nature of society."[75] Thus with personal movement space there is a dichotomy of relationships. Movement space focuses on the motivations, information, values, and so on, of the individual, but the expression of such phenomena as operational hypotheses must be done in terms of language, concepts, and theories which belong to the group as a whole, not to the individual. Peter Winch expresses this problem as follows:

> . . . The given is that first there is language (with words having a meaning, statements capable of being true or false), and then, this being given, it comes to enter into human relationships and to be modified by particular human relationships into which it does so enter. What is missed is that those very categories of meaning etc., are *logically* dependant for their sense on social interaction between men.[76]

The meanings of the themes identified earlier will vary with the individual. At the same time, the variance between the response to any question of relevance to the above themes may be meaningless if the respondents remain ignorant of the group concepts within which the questions are asked. Therefore, in order to gain relevant information to establish the influence of such variables, the questions asked must be in a form that is concrete enough to gather information given in similar contexts.

Finally comes the question of the micro-unit itself—the individual. Is the unit of personal movement space too fine a distinction to be of much significance to society as a whole? If the movement of the individual is to be used as a unit, the comparison will require that care be taken to overcome such problems of assimilating the group concepts to provide a common basis for comparison. It may be proper to work first within similar cultural, social, and economic grounds to find the similarities and differentiations within these groups of personal movement. Such a beginning may then provide a more adequate basis for moving to cross-cultural and cross-social comparisons.

Bearing these strictures in mind, two interview tests have been carried out so far, both on a very limited test basis. The first, reported in detail elsewhere was an a posteriori examination of in-depth interviews, conducted originally for a slightly different purpose, so that the results have to be treated with some caution.[77] This survey appeared to show that route choice, for example, varied as a result of habit, experience, tension, and amenity, rather than as simple functions of family size. The role and status of the trip maker influenced attitudes, values, and preferences toward trip making as well as the extent of the movement space. The movement space of the head of the household tended to be more restricted than that of other members of the household at a similar point in the life cycle. The wife in particular had wide spatial limits, limits which increased with the status or life style group, irrespective of car driving. These higher-status groups spent more of their leisure time activities outside the residence. Finally, trip makers could satisfy their preferences, in the sense that those who had strong preferences seemed to choose routes which displayed them, and vice versa.

The most recent test was again exploratory and was mainly carried out to test the value of a questionnaire for future micromovement studies. Actual results from the questionnaire were not conclusive, since no attempt at proper sampling had been made; the aim was evaluatory, not substantive. A question was inserted asking respondents to rank types of trips in the order of significance they would be held when making a residential location choice, for example. From this there did appear to be a difference of evaluation of the importance of trip types, with the journey to work being predominant, although evidence from elsewhere suggests the contrary.# However, a significant proportion chose the "social and related trip" as of major importance. A hierarchy of movement spaces based on differentiation of values placed on trip types, income, education, or social participation was not apparent from the limited sampling carried out by the survey. The greatest differentiation seemed to be the spatial distribution of friends and relatives.

This second pilot study suggested that the questionnaire would perhaps be better directed at the family unit, as the first one was, if measurement is the goal, because of the intricate relationships involved in micromovement.

The conceptions reviewed and developed here are exploratory. To gain an understanding of micromovement, much more work is needed of both the behaviorist and the behavioral nature. Further explanation will occur if we zero in on such factors as: what effect differing degrees of community participation have on the dimensions and intensity of movement space; whether a hierarchy of movement spaces exists which is explicable in terms of class, so that higher class results in a more extensive movement space; whether the dimensions of movement space vary directly with the degree of dominance of an accepted ideology; and to what degree within a given ideology, community, or economic class group the subcultural variations cause variance in the spatial dimentions of movement space.

The literature, theory and concepts re-

#Many workers have assumed that costs incurred in work travel are a major determinant of residential location, and that therefore most workers attempt to minimize the length of the work journey. In fact, considerable doubt is felt by some concerning this statement, and a recent investigation of public housing occupants in Vancouver showed that they did not perceive the work trip expenditure as being a large or significant part of the household budget, and that location in relation to work was not a major factor in the choice of a residential site.

viewed here suggest that both a philosophical and a theoretical foundation exist for a reorientation of movement studies away from a description of habit patterns to an analysis of the causes behind movement behavior. Until transportation studies consider the disciminatory attitudes of the trip maker and the explanation of trip-making behavior, plans for present systems will be based on "facts" made to fit the formulas, further obscuring the possibility of gaining insight into the true conditions governing transportation demands.

GLOSSARY

Action space (Wolpert): ". . . a set of place utilities which the individual perceives and to which he responds . . . the subjective action space is perceived by the individual through a sampling process whose parameters are determined by the individual's needs, drives, and abilities."[17]

Action space (Horton and Reynolds): "The collection of all urban locations about which the individual has information and the subjective utility or preferences he associates with these locations."[30]

Activity space (Chapin): The space identified with a range of human activities.[19]

Activity space (Brown and Moore): That part of the urban area with which direct contact occurs as the result of daily activities.[29]

Aspiration region (Brown and Moore): That part of the urban area which conforms to a household's aspirations (as far as housing relocation goes) and within which alternative residences are both available and perceived.[29]

Awareness space (Brown and Moore): That part of the total urban area about which a household has knowledge, gained through its activity and indirect contact spaces.[29]

Felt space (Bollnow): An extension of Minkowski's "lived space"—space as it appears concretely to an individual in his experiences and feelings.[44]

Indirect contact space (Brown and Moore): That part of the urban area about which the household has perceptions as the result of secondhand contact through such channels as acquaintances, mass media, etc.[29]

Life space (Lewin): "The person and the psychological environment as it exists for him . . . at any given time."[13]

Movement space (Eliot Hurst): The perceived, felt, conceived part of the built environment within which movement occurs, or about which some conception is held.[4]

Search space (Brown and Moore): That part of the urban area which is actively searched for alternative housing locations.[29]

NOTES

1 An examination of any of the reports of the major transportation studies such as those of Chicago, Detroit, Tri-State, etc., will show this; see also W. Y. Oi and P. W. Schuldiner, *An Analysis of Urban Travel Demands,* Evanston: Northwestern University Press, 1962.

2 See, for example, G. A. P. Carrothers, "An Historical Review of the Gravity and Potential Concepts of Human Interaction," *Journal of the American Institute of Planners,* vol. 22, 1956, pp. 94–102; A. M. Voorhees, "Forecasting Peak Hours of Travel," Highway Research Board, *Bulletin* 203, 1958; M. Schneider, "Gravity Models and Trip Distribution Theory," *Papers and Proceedings,* Regional Science Association, vol. 5, 1959, pp. 51–56; R. I. Wolfe, "Discussion of Vacation Homes, Environmental Preferences, and Spatial Behaviour," *Journal of Leisure Research,* vol. 2, no. 1, 1970, pp. 85–87, and R. I. Wolfe, "The Inertia Model," *Journal of Leisure Research,* vol. 4, no. 1, 1972, pp. 73–76.

3 See, for example, J. Kofoed, "Person Movement Research: A Discussion of Concepts," Copenhagen; Department for Road Construction, Traffic Engineering and Town Planning, mimeo 1969; or Damas and Smith Ltd., "Proposal for Research Project Trip Habits and Attitudes in Six Canadian Cities," submitted

to the Canadian Council on Urban and Regional Research, 1963.

4 M. E. Eliot Hurst, "The Structure of Movement and Household Travel Behaviour," *Urban Studies,* vol. 6, no. 1, 1969, pp. 70–82. Reprinted in L. S. Bourne (ed.), *Internal Structure of the City,* New York: Oxford University Press, 1971, pp. 248–255.

5 See, for example, P. Gould, "On Mental Maps," Michigan Inter-University Community of Mathematical Geographers, *Discussion Paper,* No. 9, 1966; T. R. Lee, "Psychology and Living Space," *Transactions of the Bartlett Society,* vol. 2, 1964, pp. 9–36; and R. J. Johnston, "Mental Maps of the City: Suburban Preference Patterns," *Environment and Planning,* vol. 3, 1971, pp. 63–72.

6 See, for example, J. Wolpert "Behavioural Aspects of the Decision to Migrate," *Papers and Proceedings* of the Regional Science Association, vol. 15, 1965, pp. 159–169; F. E. Horton and D. R. Reynolds, "Urban Environmental Perception and Individual Travel Behaviour," Department of Geography, University of Iowa, *Special Publication* no. 2, 1970.

7 For example, E. C. Tolman, "Cognitive Maps in Rats and Man," *Psychological Review,* vol. 55, 1948, pp. 189–208, or W. Bogaras, "Ideas of Space and Time in the Conception of Primitive Religion," *American Anthropologist,* vol. 27, 1925, pp. 212–215. These three conceptions grade into one another, and useful accounts transcending these divisions include W. H. Ittelson, L. Rivilin, and H. M. Proshansky, "The Use of Behavioural Maps in Behavioural Psychology," in H. M. Proshansky, W. H. Ittelson, and L. G. Rivilin (eds.), *Environmental Psychology* (New York: Holt, Rinehart and Winston, 1970); K. R. Cox and G. Zannaras, *Designative Perceptions of Macro Spaces,* Discussion Paper No. 17, Dept. of Geography, Ohio State University, 1970; D. de Jonge, "Images of Urban Areas: Their Structure and Psychological Foundations," *Journal of the American Institute of Planners,* vol. 28, 1962, pp. 266–276; and F. C. Ladd, "Black Youths View Their Environment: Neighbourhood Maps," *Environment and Behaviour,* vol. 2, 1970, pp. 74–99.

8 D. Stea, "On the Measurement of 'Mental Maps'," mimeo, Departments of Psychology and Geography, Clark University, 1968.

9 S. Carr, "The City of the Mind," in *Environment for Man,* ed. by W. R. Ewald, Bloomington: Indiana University Press, 1967, pp. 197–231.

10 Such as the techniques used by Kevin Lynch in *The Image of the City,* Cambridge, Mass: MIT Press, 1960.

11 The "Chicago School" including T. F. Saarinen's *Perception of the Drought Hazard on the Great Plains,* University of Chicago, Department of Geography, Research Paper No. 106, 1966, would fit here.

12 Stea, op. cit., p. 3.

13 K. Lewin, *Principles of Topological Psychology,* New York: McGraw-Hill, 1936; and *Field Theory in Social Science,* New York: Harper & Row, 1951.

14 Lewin, 1951, op. cit., pp. 57 and 240.

15 Ibid, p. 40.

16 Wolpert, 1965, op. cit.

17 Ibid., p. 163.

18 F. Stuart Chapin, *Urban Land Use Planning,* 2d. ed., Urbana: University of Illinois Press, 1965; see also F. S. Chapin and H. C. Hightower, "Household Activity Patterns and Land Use," *Journal of the American Planners,"* vol. 30, no. 3, August 1965, pp. 222–231; and F. S. Chapin and H. C. Hightower, "Household Activity Systems—A Pilot Investigation," *Urban Studies Research Monograph,* 1966, Institute for Research in Social Science, University of North Carolina.

19 F. S. Chapin, op. cit., pp. 224–225.

20 Lynch, op. cit., p. 2.

21 Ibid., p. 3.

22 S. Koch (ed.), *Psychology, a Study of Science,* vol. 6, New York: McGraw-Hill, 1962, and A. H. Rubenstein and C. J. Haberstrol, *Some Theories of Organization,* Homewood, Ill.: R. D. Irwin, Inc.,/Dorsey Press, 1964, illustrate the former; and L. Festinger, S. Schaeter and K. Bach, *Social Pressures in Informal*

Groups, New York: Harper & Row, 1950, and R. K. Merton, *Social Theory and Social Structure,* New York: Free Press, 1957, represent the latter.

23 R. M. Downs, "Geographic Space Perception: Past Approaches and Future Prospects" in *Progress in Geography,* vol. 2, 1970, pp. 65–108.

24 Typical work is represented by Lee, op. cit., Lynch, op. cit., and W. H. Heinemeyer, "The Urban Core as a Centre of Attraction," in *Urban Core and Inner City,* Leiden: W. H. Brill, 1967, pp. 82–99.

25 Most of this work has lain in the area of the perception of natural hazards, such as Saarinen, op. cit., or I. Burton and R. W. Kates, "The Perception of Natural Hazards in Resource Management," *Natural Resources Journal,* vol. 3, 1964, pp. 412–441.

26 Least work has been carried out in this third area; but see Wolpert, op. cit., Gould, op. cit. or P. R. Gould, "Structuring Information on Spatio-temporal Preferences, *"Journal of Regional Science,"* vol. 7, no. 2 (suppl.), 1967, pp. 259–274.

27 Almost all the previous references fall into this category, particularly Gould (1967) op. cit., Horton and Reynolds, op. cit., and F. E. Horton and D. Reynolds, "Action Space Differentials in Cities," in H. McConnell and D. W. Yaseen, *Perspectives in Geography,* vol. 1, *Models of Spatial Variation,* Dekalb, Ill.: Northern Illinois University Press, 1971, pp. 84–102.

28 The best examples here would be D. Lowenthal, "Geography, Experience, and Imagination: Towards a Geographical Epistemology," *Annals of the A.A.G.,* vol. 51, 1961, pp. 241–260; and H. and M. Sprout, *The Ecological Perspective on Human Affairs,* Princeton, N.J.: Princeton University Press, 1965.

29 L. A. Brown and E. G. Moore, "The Intra-urban Migration Process: An Action Oriented Model," mimeo, Department of Geography, Iowa City, Iowa: State University of Iowa, 1968.

30 Horton and Reynolds, 1971, op. cit.

31 Time budgets are discussed in R. Meier, *A Communication Theory of Urban Growth,* Cambridge, Mass: MIT Press, 1962, pp. 48–54.

32 Horton and Reynolds, 1970, op. cit., p. 5.

33 Horton and Reynolds, 1971, op. cit.

34 See also by the same authors, "An Investigation of Individual Action Spaces: A Progress Report," *Proceedings of the A.A.G.,* vol. 1, 1969, pp. 70–75; "Intra Urban Migration and the Perception of Residential Quality," Research Paper No. 13, Department of Geography, Columbus, Ohio: Ohio State University, 1970; and "Effects of Urban Spatial Structure on Individual Behaviour," *Economic Geography,* vol. 47, 1971, pp. 36–48.

35 R. J. Johnston, "Activity Spaces and Residential Preferences: Some Tests of the Hypotheses of Sectoral Mental Maps," *Economic Geography,* vol. 48, no. 2, 1972, pp. 199–211.

36 D. C. Mercer, "Discretionary Travel Behaviour and the Urban Mental Map," *Australian Geographical Studies,* 1971.

37 J. S. Adams, "Directional Bias in Intra-urban Migration," *Economic Geography,* vol. 45, no. 4, 1969, pp. 302–323.

38 H. A. Simon, *Models of Man,* New York: Wiley, 1957, p. 197.

39 Ibid, p. 198.

40 Ibid, pp. 204–205.

41 J. Piaget and B. Inhilder, *The Child's Conception of Space,* London: Routledge & Kegan Paul, 1963, p. 6.

42 Ibid., p. 451.

43 Rene Dubos, *Man Adapting,* New Haven: Yale University Press, 1965, p. 1.

44 O. F. Bollnow, "Lived Space," in N. Lawrence and D. O'Connor (eds.), *Readings in Existential Phenomenology,* Englewood Cliffs, N.J.: Prentice-Hall, 1967, pp. 178–186.

45 E. Minkowski, *Le Temps Vecu,* Paris: 1933.

46 Bollnow, op. cit., p. 185.

47 Ibid., p. 186.

48 See, for example, W. Kirk "The Problems of Geography," *Geography,* vol. XLVII, no. 4, 1963, pp. 357–371; and M. E. Eliot Hurst, *A Geography of Economic Behaviour,* North Scituate, Mass: Duxbury Press, 1972, chap. 4.

49 Sprouts, op. cit., pp. 117–141.

50 C. E. Osgood, "A Behavioristic Analysis of

Perception and Language as Cognitive Phenomena," reprinted in R. Harper et al, *Cognitive Processes* Englewood Cliffs, N.J.: Prentice-Hall, 1964, p. 184, and M. E. Eliot Hurst, 1972, op. cit.

51 J. Sonnenfeld, "Variable Values in Space and Landscape: An Inquiry into the Nature of Environmental Necessity," *Journal of Social Issues,* vol. 22, no. 4, 1966, p. 76.

52 E. Evans-Pritchard, *The Nuer,* Oxford, England: Clarendon Press, 1965, p. 110.

53 A number of other investigators have pursued this theme of culture and space: M. Herskovits et al, *The Influence of Culture on Visual Perception,* New York: Bobbs-Merrill, 1966; R. A. Murdie, "Culture Differences in Consumer Travel," *Economic Geography,* vol. 41, no. 3, 1966, pp. 211–233; A. Pred, *Behaviour and Location,* Lund: C. W. K. Gleerup Ltd., 1967, 1969, *Lund Studies in Geography,* Series B, Parts 1 and 2; M. D. Ray, "Cultural Differences in Consumer Travel Behaviour in Eastern Ontario," *The Canadian Geographer,* vol. XI, no. 3, 1967; R. Sommer, "Man's Proximate Environment," *Journal of Social Issues,* vol. 22, no. 4, 1966; and M. M. Webber, "Culture, Territoriality, and the Elastic Mile," *Papers and Proceedings,* Regional Science Association, vol. 13, 1964, pp. 59–69.

54 Eliot Hurst, 1969, op. cit., and Eliot Hurst, 1972, op. cit., pp. 298–301.

55 H. A. Simon, "Rational Choice and the Structure of the Environment," *Psychological Review,* vol. 63, 1956, pp. 129–138.

56 H. and M. Sprout, op. cit.

57 Meier, op. cit.

58 Compare Oi and Schuldiner, op. cit., p. 200; Lansing and Lilienstein, op. cit., p. 3, or U.S. Bureau of Public Roads, "Manual of Procedures for the Home Interview Traffic Study," 1954, p. 39.

59 R. M. Cyert and J. G. March, *A Behavioural Theory of the Firm,* Englewood Cliffs, N.J.: Prentice-Hall, 1963, p. 21.

60 H. A. Simon, *Models of Man,* New York: Wiley, 1957, p. 266.

61 As noted in Selection 28.

62 H. A. Simon, "Economics and Psychology," in S. Koch (ed.), *Psychology, A Study of a Science,* New York: McGraw-Hill, 1963, chap. 6.

63 Compare J. Wolpert, "Behavioural Aspects of the Decision to Migrate," *Papers and Proceedings,* Regional Science Association, vol. 15, pp. 159–169, especially pp. 161–163.

64 Wolpert, op. cit., footnote 42, p. 162.

65 L. A. Brown and D. B. Longbrake, "Migration Flows in Intra-urban Space: An Operational View of Place Utility," mimeo, Department of Geography, Iowa City, Iowa: State University of Iowa, 1968.

66 Adams, op. cit.

67 K. Deutsch et al., *The Integration of Political Communities,* New York: Lippincott, 1964, p. 240.

68 Ibid., footnote 41, p. 221.

69 Ibid., p. 225.

70 See, for example, Webber, op. cit.; A. Boskoff, *The Sociology of Urban Regions,* New York: Appleton-Century-Crofts, 1962; E. M. Gibson, "Geography Imbalanced: Theory in Human Geography" and M. E. Eliot Hurst, "Future City Forms," both in *The Geographer and the Public Environment,* British Columbia Geographical Series No. 6, 1966, pp. 20–24.

71 Boskoff, op. cit., p. 200. The styles of life are: the social elite, nouveaux riches, exurban, middle class, solid or aspiring lower group, and marginal life style.

72 Webber, op. cit., footnote.

73 See Eliot Hurst, 1972, op. cit., pp. 210–213; J. A. Howard and J. N. Sleth, *The Theory of Buyer Behaviour,* New York: Wiley, 1969; F. M. Nicosia, *Consumer Decision Processes,* Englewood Cliffs, N.J.: Prentice-Hall, 1966.

74 D. O. Hebb, "Drive and the C.N.S. (conceptual nervous system)," in Harper, op. cit., pp. 19–31; D. E. Berlyne, "The Influence of Complexity and Novelty in Visual Figures on Orienting Responses," Harper op. cit., pp. 120–129; R. W. Kates and J. F. Wohlwill (eds.), "Man's Response to the Physical Environment," special issue of *The Journal of Social Issues,* vol. 22, no. 4, October 1966.

75 R. Aron, *German Sociology,* London: Heinemann, 1957, p. 119.

76 P. Winch, *The Idea of a Social Science,* New York: Humanities Press, 1958, p. 44.
77 Eliot Hurst, 1969, op. cit., appendix.

FURTHER SOURCES

Apart from the monthly bibliography *Current Literature in Traffic and Transportation* previously mentioned, some of the Council of Planning Librarians *Exchange Bibliographies*** are worth looking at. They vary in quality from good annotations and commentary to simply alphabetical lists, but the following are particularly pertinent to the subject of micromovement:

**Council of Planning Librarians, *Exchange Bibliographies,* P. O. Box 229, Monticello, Ill. 61856.

D. Appleyard, "The Urban Environment: Selected Bibliography," *Pub. No. 291,* June 1972.

R. C. Harkness, "Communication Innovations, Urban Form and Travel Demand: Some Hypotheses and a Bibliography," *Pub. No. 285,* May 1972.

S. R. Lieber, "A Working Bibliography on Geographic and Psychological Perception and Related Subjects," *Pub. No. 299,* July 1972.

F. B. Stutz, "Research on Intra-urban Social Travel: Introduction and Bibliography," *Pub. No. 173,* February 1971;

B. Wellman and M. Whitaker, "Community-Network-Communication: An Annotated Bibliography," *Pub. No. 282/283,* May 1972.

FURTHER READINGS TO PART SIX(*b*)

The macroscopic approach to urban transportation will be found, among others, in:

D. Berry et al., *The Technology of Urban Transportation,* Evanston, Ill.: Northwestern University Press, 1963.

R. L. Creighton, *Urban Transportation Planning,* Urbana, Ill.: University of Illinois Press, 1970.

M. E. Eliot Hurst, "An Employee Work-journey Survey," *Traffic Engineering and Control,* vol. 10, no. 4, 1968, pp. 164–167.

M. E. Eliot Hurst, "An Approach to the Study of Non-residential Land Use Traffic Generation," *Annals* of the Association of American Geographers, vol. 60, 1970, pp. 153–173.

M. E. Eliot Hurst, "Confluence and the Workplace: An Approach to Urban Work-journey Analyses," *Transportation Research*, vol. 4, 1970, pp. 163–184.

W. Garrison, "Intra- and Inter-urban Networks" in F. Pitts (ed.), *Urban Systems and Economic Development,* Eugene, Ore.: University of Oregon, School of Business Administration, 1962, pp. 28–38.

W. Garrison, "Urban Transportation Planning Models in 1975," *Journal* of the American Institute of Planners, vol. 31, 1965, pp. 156–158.

W. Garrison, "Urban Transportation Studies" in S. Ostry and T. Rymes (eds.), *Papers on Regional Statistical Studies,* Toronto: University of Toronto Press, 1967.

K. J. Kansky, "Travel Patterns of Urban Residents," *Transportation Science*, vol. 1967.

L. Keefer, "Urban Travel Patterns for Airports, Shopping Centers and Industrial Plants," *Highway Research Board,* Report 24, 1966.

J. Lansing and G. Hendricks, "How People Perceive the Cost of the Journey-to-work," *Highway Research Record,* no. 197, 1967, pp. 44–55.

H. S. Lapin, *Structuring the Journey to Work,* Philadelphia: University of Pennsylvania Press, 1964.

N. Leathers, "Residential Location and Mode of Transportation to Work: A Model of Choice," *Transportation Research,* vol. 1, 1967, pp. 129–156.

D. Marble, "A Theoretical Exploration of Individual Travel Behaviour" in W. Garrison and D. Marble (eds.), *Quantitative Geography,* Part 1, Evanston, Ill.: Northwestern University Press, 1967, pp. 33–53.

B. Martin, F. Memmott, and A. Bone, *Principles and Techniques of Predicting Future Demand for Urban Area Transportation,* Cambridge, Mass.: MIT Press, 1965.

H. Meyer, "Urban Geography and Urban Transportation Planning," *Traffic Quarterly,* vol. 17, 1963, pp. 610–631.

J. Meyer, J. Kain, and M. Wohl, *The Urban Transportation Problem,* Cambridge, Mass.: Harvard University Press, 1965.

Ministry of Transport, United Kingdom, *Traffic in Towns,* London: H.M.S.O. 1963 (the *Buchanan* report); also published in shortened form by Penguin Books Ltd., 1964.

R. B. Mitchell and C. Rapkin, *Urban Traffic, a Function of Land Use,* New York: Columbia University Press, 1954.

Lewis Mumford, *The Highway and the City,* New York: Harcourt, Brace and World, 1963.

W. Y. Oi and P. Schuldiner, *An Analysis of Urban Travel Demands,* Evanston, Ill.: Northwestern University Press, 1962.

W. Owen, *The Metropolitan Transportation Problem,* Washington, D.C.: The Brookings Institution, 1959.

P. Schuldiner, *Non-residential Trip Generation Analysis,* Evanston, Ill.: Transportation Center, Northwestern University, Research Report, 1965.

G. M. Smerk, *Readings in Urban Transportation,* Bloomington, Ind.: Indiana University Press, 1968.

D. N. M. Starkie, "Traffic and Industry: A Study of Traffic Generation and Spatial Interaction," *Geographical Papers,* no. 3, London School of Economics, 1967.

E. J. Taaffe, B. J. Garner, and M. Yeates, *The Peripheral Journey to Work: A Geographic Consideration,* Evanston, Ill.: Northwestern University Press, 1963.

Transportation Center, *A Reference Guide to Metropolitan Transportation: An Annotated Bibliography,* Evanston, Ill.: Northwestern University Press, 1964.

A. M. Voorhees, "A General Theory of Traffic Movement," *Papers and Proceedings,* Institute of Traffic Engineers, vol. 26, 1955, pp. 46–56.

A. Voorhees, G. Sharpe, and J. Stegmaier, "Shopping Habits and Travel

Patterns,'' *Special Report,* High Research Board, No. 11B 1955.
J. Wheeler and S. Stutz, ''Urban Social Travel,'' *Annals* of the Association of American Geographers, vol. 61, 1971, pp. 371–386.
T. E. H. Williams, *Urban Survival and Traffic:* London, Spon, 1962.
R. I. Wolfe, ''Effect of Ribbon Development on Traffic Flow,'' *Traffic Quarterly,* vol. 18, 1964, pp. 105–117.

Micromovements have been treated by fewer researchers, but notable publications include:

J. S. Adams, ''Directional Bias in Intra Urban Migration,'' *Economic Geography,* vol. 45, 1969, pp. 302–323.
F. Stuart Chapin and H. C. Hightower, ''Household Activity Patterns and Land Use,'' *Journal* of the American Institute of Planners, August 1965, pp. 222–231.
F. E. Horton and D. R. Reynolds, ''Action Space Differentials in Cities,'' in *Perspectives in Geography,* Vol. 1, *Models of Spatial Variation,* H. McConnel and D. W. Yaseen (eds.), 1971, pp. 83–104.
F. E. Horton and D. R. Reynolds, ''Effects of Urban Spatial Structure on Individual Behaviour,'' *Economic Geography,* vol. 47, 1971, pp. 36–48.
M. E. Eliot Hurst, ''The Structure of Movement and Household Travel Behaviour,'' *Urban Studies,* vol. 6, no. 1, 1969, pp. 70–82; reprinted in L. S. Bourne (ed.), *Internal Structure of the City,* New York: Oxford University Press, 1971, pp. 248–255.
R. J. Johnstone, ''Activity Spaces and Residential Preferences: Some Tests of the Hypothesis of Sectoral Mental Maps,'' *Economic Geography,* vol. 48, 1972, pp. 199–211.
D. C. Mercer, ''Discretionary Travel Behaviour and the Urban Mental Map,'' *Australian Geographical Studies*, 1971.

Public participation in urban transportation conflict situations are dealt with by:

G. J. Fielding, ''Locating Urban Freeways: A Method for Resolving Conflict,'' in *Geographic Studies of Urban Transportation and Network Analysis,* F. E. Horton (ed.), Northwestern University, Studies in Geography, No. 16, pp. 76–101.
D. and N. Nowland, *The Bad Trip: The Untold Story of the Spavina Expressway,* Toronto: New Press, 1970. (An excellent account of the community and corporate pressures to build or not to build a new urban freeway in Toronto.)
J. Wolpert, ''The Transition to Interdependence in Location Decisions,'' paper presented at the Association of American Geographers' annual meeting, 1968.

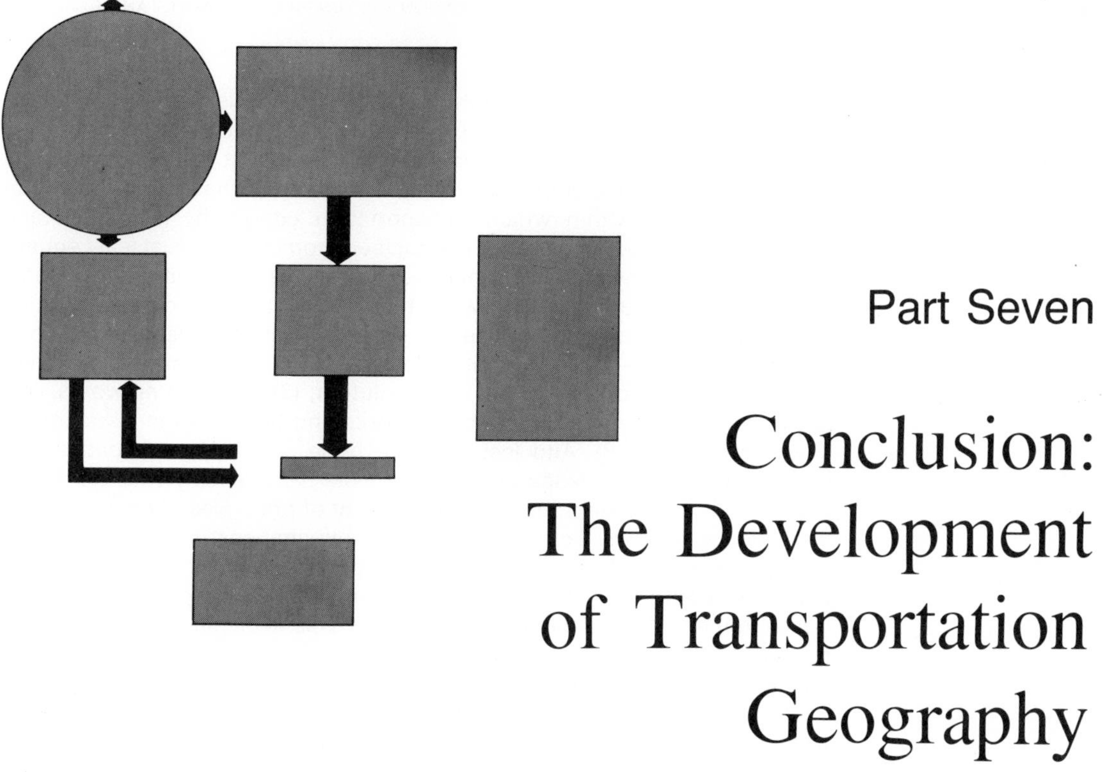

Part Seven

Conclusion: The Development of Transportation Geography

"Transportation is a measure of the relations between areas, and is essentially therefore geographical." Those were the words used to open this book, and few geographers would probably dispute that claim. But how much of transportation geography has taken place within the context of the holistic framework postulated in Part Five, or at least has taken note of the socioeconomic framework or operational milieu within which both the investigator, and the networks and flows he is studying, operate and exist? This is a crucial point, made to some extent by C. H. Cooley as long ago as 1894 and largely ignored by transportation geographers ever since.

What is transportation geography to be? The relatively mechanistic analyses noted in Selection 1 and illustrated throughout much of this book? This is not the point in time to be Luddites and turn on that stockpiling; it must go on. But this is the point at which we must ask, what about the socioeconomic reality within which transportation geography is studied and transportation systems operate? The socioeconomic reality is at least equally important as the mechanistic analyses, and yet very little attention is paid to it. If we read two recent reviews of the "state of the art" in transportation geography, which also emphasize the research frontiers, these kinds of comments are found*—". . . these interrelated research focuses are . . . (1) networks: their location, structure, and evolution; (2) flows on networks; and (3) the significance and impact of networks and flows on the space economy" (Wheeler, p. 8). And lest you find hope of broader socioeconomic horizons in that third research focus, Wheeler very quickly sets the record straight: "These studies seek to develop a set of principles of network interdependence with the economy, showing how changes in accessibility, for example, may result in nodal growth or decline. Basically these studies attempt to establish the role of transportation change on regional specialization within an urban hierarchy" (ibid., p. 10). This work may need to be done for sure, but the examples he gives are Gauthier's study of the highway change in the São Paulo area and Taaffe's work on agricultural changes in Soviet Central Asia with the coming of rail linkages,† neither of which really explains the transportation developments within the framework of the very real exploitation of the Brazilian economy or of the political/ideological struggles within a centrally planned economy. Yet without those socioeconomic frameworks, the developments they describe have little meaning except to notch up one more publication or merit point in the academic promotion/salary system. Useful descriptive work is nullified simply by its inability to take account of the holistic framework presented in Part Five.

Muller begins more realistically in his review by referring to the lack of an organizing framework in transportation geography, but he sweeps away reality in one fell swoop by describing the approach of Abler, Adams, and Gould‡ as laudable; he says their study ". . . stresses: (1) transportation development in relation to Ullman's own three-factor theory of spatial interaction formulated in 1956, (2) types and causes of movement as embodied in migration, trade, and diffusion theory, (3) areal specialization studied through input-output analysis, (4) interaction theory as expressed by gravity and potential models, and (5) analysis of transportation systems using techniques of movement geometry, network analysis, and flow analysis" (Muller,

*J. O. Wheeler, "An Overview of Research in Transportation Geography, *East Lakes Geographer,* vol. 7, 1971, pp. 3–12; P. O. Muller, "Recent Developments in the Spatial Analysis of Transportation," *The Pennsylvania Geographer,* vol. IX, 1971, pp. 14–17.

†H. L. Gauthier, "Transportation and the Growth of the São Paulo Economy," *Journal of Regional Science,* vol. 8 (1968), pp. 77–94, and R. N. Taaffe, "Transportation and Regional Specialization: The Example of Soviet Central Asia," *Annals* of the Association of American Geographers, vol. 52, 1962, pp. 80–98.

‡R. Abler, J. S. Adams, and P. Gould, *Spatial Organization,* Englewood Cliffs, N.J.: Prentice-Hall, 1971.

pp. 14–15). In addition, Muller sees urban transportation analysis as *the* emerging specialty within transportation geography. Just as he sees Abler et al. in their very narrowly conceived positivistic/scientistic statement as the pinnacle of the "theoretical" broad-scale work in transportation, so he sees Frank Horton "as one of the leading practitioners" (ibid., p. 15) in this newly emerging field. Yet Horton's work represents only the macroscopic view of urban transport§ (Part Six *b*), or when he sorties into the field of micromovement, he takes with him scientistic rattomorphism. Neither Abler and his colleagues nor Horton takes account of anything beyond their very narrowly defined reality. Again this is not to denigrate their work as such, but to emphasize that before we can understand the role of transportation in society, and people's reaction to and use of such systems of movement, we must admit the larger socioeconomic framework of which it is but a part. Cooley knew that in 1894!

Why should we come to this apparent impasse? Admittedly, as pointed out in Selection 1, the development of both geography and transportation geography, seen through its literature, has consistently shown its inability to face the realities of its own operating environment. Two factors seem to be useful in explaining this position: one is the role of all social sciences in the Western world to maintain the established socioeconomic system; the other is the rise of what I have been calling *positivism.*

POSITIVISM AND TRANSPORTATION GEOGRAPHY

The dominant mode of thought in transportation geography today is positivism. The basic idea behind the positivist approach is the dichotomy of life and knowledge, knowing and living, that there exists an objective world with knowable laws that can be determined through empirical testing procedures. This leads to the view that knowledge as such is inherently neutral and that the standards and exactness of the positivist approach, particularly as displayed in the work of the physical sciences, constitute the only explanatory model for knowledge. In turn, we find an emphasis on observation, normative laws, and statistical verification; "quality," formal elegance and mathematical rigor, carried to extremes, can count for more than the purposes for which, in our case, transportation geography is employed. The goal is the elevation of the subdiscipline to the level of an objective science: this is the approach of Abler, Adams and Gould, Horton and many others.

The customary explanations of the rise of positivism usually center on

§Muller cites these references: B. J. L. Berry and F. E. Horton, *Geographic Perspectives on Urban Systems,* Englewood Cliffs, N.J.: Prentice-Hall, Inc., 1970; W. R. Black and F. E. Horton, *A Bibliography of Selected Research on Networks and Urban Transportation Relevant to Current Transportation Geography Research,* Dept. of Geography, Northwestern University, Research Report No. 28, 1970; F. E. Horton (ed.), *Geographic Studies of Urban Transportation and Network Analysis,* Evanston, Ill: Department of Geography, Northwestern University, Studies in Geography, No. 16, 1968, 170 pp.

references concerning the pitfalls of doing geography any other way. Thus its practitioners speak of positivism as a reaction to mere description (ideographic geography) or to historicism.‖ Others have offered the jaundiced view that positivistic geography coincides with the general analyticity and pursuit of scientism of the present age.# And then there are those who see in the positivistic stance the best method for obtaining "factual" results independent of ideological or value judgments.**

In response to this *prescriptive scientism,* as we also can call it, geography has become concerned with, among other things, "law" seeking, model building, and the articulation of theory. Few geographers seem to question whether scientism is appropriate to the study of geography's principal focus—people. In fact no "laws" have been produced in geography, or transportation geography, and probably never will be. Scientism can make some descriptions more exact, as in Garrison's analysis of highway connectivity (Selection 6), but it is of no explanatory value, no aid to understanding. In fact, it is now comparatively easy in transportation geography to describe in mathematical terms fairly complex patterns without any understanding of the basic processes involved, as for example when simulating the diffusion of an innovation through space without understanding why some people accept the innovation and others do not. Few transportation geographers have actually gone beyond the first step of *pattern identification.* Patterns of flows or networks are described and can be simulated, but it is usually beyond the competence of geographers using the ideographic or nomothetic approaches to explain them. Rather than *scientific,* perhaps we should call transportation geographers merely *technique-oriented.*

Scientism, as the positivistic self-image of science, also separates the subject and object of knowledge and takes the statements of science as an observational given. Knowledge is thus conceived of as a neutral picturing of fact. In geographical terms this implies that people learn about their environment only through objective study; cognitive processes light the path for human progress. Events that are still mysterious are not yet understood only because they have not been adequately studied in an objective manner.

The positivist tradition has had an extremely high payoff in the physical sciences, and it is not surprising that the methods of these sciences should be seized by social scientists, including transportation geographers, to "advance" their own disciplines. However, it should also be obvious that

‖Among others, Ian Burton makes this clear when he sees ". . . the movement towards quantification as part of the general spread and growth of scientific analysis into a world formerly dominated by a concern with the exceptional and unique," in "The Quantitative Revolution and Theoretical Geography," *Canadian Geographer,* vol. 7, 1963.

#The report of the Ad Hoc Committee on Geography (Division of Earth Sciences) makes this very clear (N.A.S.-N.R.C., 1965).

**The best way to illustrate this is Sellers' prophetic statement: "The literature of establishment geography essentially begins with Ackerman's *Geography as a Fundamental Research Discipline,* is crystallized in the Ad Hoc Committee's *Science of Geography,* and most recently reinforced by Golledge and Amedeo. . . . We can expect it to be perpetuated by David Harvey's forthcoming text *Explanation in Geography.*" Harvey's text (1969) from which he has since admittedly backtracked, did in fact prove to be the pinnacle of the positivistic value-free approach, only since surpassed and pushed to an almost ludicrous extreme by Abler, Adams and Gould's text. J. B. Sellers, "Open Geography and its Enemies," reprinted in M. E. Eliot Hurst, *The Geographer and Society,* North Scituate, Mass.: Duxbury Press, 1974.

there are considerable drawbacks when people become the center of study. At the core of logical empiricism lies the principle of *verifiability*, and it is this principle that determines what questions can be asked. Thus, to have any meaning, a proposition must be such that either it is true by definition or that some possible sense experience would be relevant to the determination of its truth. By such a criterion, propositions such as "I exist" would be meaningless, as would other human emotions such as joy, hate, love or grief. Now I am not advocating a geography of love, although there is no reason why there should not be such an approach,†† but any approach to landscape patterns which involves people as a centrepital figure—as geography must—whether we are studying transportation or not, would in a positivist approach either have to relegate people to "object" or "unit" status or face much legerdemain in trying to cast such an approach in synthetic propositional form. In fact, this is exactly what occurs in quantitative studies and in many of the so-called behavioral studies which have a positivist twist (for example, Morrill, as a treatment of person, the object, or Horton and Reynolds, for rattomorphic man—both in McConnell and Yaseen).‡‡ Unfortunately the same "objective" values and the belief in the neutrality of the observer are rampant throughout the social sciences, including transportation geographers who are taking nonquantitative approaches.

Positivism is of course only *one* of a number of philosophical positions that can be adopted in the social sciences. I would agree with Maslow that a positivistically based social science may help us study people as *objects*, but we also desperately need to study them as *subjects* who *do* exist. Unfortunately the latter approach might be too revealing of the values perpetrated by our own socioeconomic system. As such, most geography is presented in a positivistic vacuum, since is supports the status quo.

ESTABLISHMENT TRANSPORTATION GEOGRAPHY

This last sentence brings us to the other supportive factor leading to a narrowly conceived transportation geography. As a discipline, geography is an integral part of the established socioeconomic system, and, as John Porter has remarked, ". . . a view of intellectuals as a class opposed to the social order is, of course, wrong . . . it is the commitment of most intellectuals to the status quo that gives rise to the term 'establishment' and brings about a link between intellectuals and other institutional leaders."§§ Or as Daniel Foss mentions in his analysis of the Parsonian paradigm in sociology ". . . [Parsons] . . . neutralizes, through theoretical legerdemain, the potentially hostility-provoking aspects of the fact of concentration in minority hands of the control of the dominant economic institutions. The holders

‡‡See, for example, the work of one geographer, K. Buchanan, *The Map of Love*, New York: Pergamon, 1970.

‡‡R. L. Morrill, "On the Arrangement and Concentration of Points in the Plane"; F. E. Horton and D. R. Reynolds, "Action Space Differentials in Cities"; in H. McConnell and D. Yaseen (eds.), *Perspectives in Geography*, Vol. 1, *Models of Spatial Variation*, Northern Illinois University Press, 1971.

§§J. Porter, *The Vertical Mosaic*, Toronto University Press, 1965, p. 492.

of corporate power, it is implied, are merely doing a job on behalf of the 'total system', and would never dream of using their positions solely to advance their own interests."|||| The history of decision making in transportation is full of the self-interest and profiteering of entrepreneurs. The development of that crucial spatial axis in the formation of the Canadian landscape, the Canadian Pacific Railroad, cannot be properly understood without studying the operating environment of Sir John A. MacDonald and his Conservative party in the nineteenth century, the financial chicanery of George Stephen and Donald Smith, and the blustering visions of the myriad other lackeys and small-time businessmen; without that historical perspective one could not understand why today the CPR is, more than a transportation company, an important molder of landscapes, urban and rural, through its varying real estate and mining holdings. Yet no transportation geographer has studied the landscape impact of any of the transportation entrepreneurs.

TRANSPORTATION GEOGRAPHY IN THE FUTURE

In order to overcome existing shortcomings, and drawing on the kind of breakdown suggested in the heuristic device (figure, p. 289), the following areas are suggested for future study in transportation geography:

1 An analysis of the connections between socioeconomic and political structures and transportation, leading to a study of the contribution of transport to the processes of industrialization, economic specialization, and socioeconomic underdevelopment. Specifically a review of the means and social relations of production of transportation (including communication) in North America should be undertaken.

2 A study of the role of legislative and regulatory constraints on the production and distribution of transportation modes, etc., in their historical, political, and socioeconomic contexts. The historical development of institutions, networks, lobbies, monopolies, regulatory agencies and state corporations should also be considered and their roles in the transport system evaluated. Anticipated trends in legislation, and their landscape impact, should also be examined.

3 A historical survey of models, methods and problems in the study of transportation, as an aspect of the development of the social sciences and geography, should be pursued. Alternative contemporary analyses of transportation, communications, and socioeconomic change, including the approach postulated in this part, should be critically reviewed and evaluated.

4 Increasing attention should be given to the newly developing areas of communications. An examination of contemporary trends in communication technology, their spatial impact, and their implication for the socioeconomic structure of societies should be undertaken. Potential contradictions between the technological and socioeconomic possibilities will doubtless be revealed; we should not hesitate to emphasize the best spatial-welfare solution to such contradictions. Pursuant to this area

||||"The World View of Talcott Parsons" in *Sociology on Trial,* Englewood Cliffs, N.J.: Prentice-Hall, 1965, p. 105.

of study, communications media as a means of socioeconomic control or community mobilization, patterns of control of the means of production and distribution of communications (with their socioeconomic and technological prerequisites), and the definition of community goals through the use of communications media would have to be analyzed.

Further data collection and statistical analysis by itself, without understanding the further societal relationships and ramifications of transportation, will not help us to understand and explain the transport system as such. Pursuit of the four suggested areas of study will equally not get us far, if they are not combined with a thorough overhaul of our so-called objective stance. I hope, however, that these four avenues will lead us to many more, and to the ultimate better understanding of transport's role in shaping the geographic landscape.

NAME INDEX

Page references in *italics* indicate Table; in **boldface** indicate Map or Diagram.

SUBJECT INDEX

Page references in *italics* indicate Table; in **boldface** indicate Map or Diagram.